DAVID FELLMAN
Vilas Professor of Political Science
University of Wisconsin
ADVISORY EDITOR TO DODD, MEAD & COMPANY

THE AMERICAN PARTY PROCESS

Readings and Comments

THE AMERICAN PARTY PROCESS

Readings and Comments

NORMAN L. ZUCKER

UNIVERSITY OF RHODE ISLAND

DODD, MEAD & COMPANY

New York   Toronto   1968

For Sara

For Sara

PREFACE

THE rhetoric and bombast of the campaign and the excitement of the election immediately past or immediately forthcoming are too frequently mistaken for the substance of politics. This overriding concern with the present, admittedly important and necessary, obscures the long-term forces and trends within the political process. The substance of political analysis involves both transitory contemporary events and those deeper currents which flow beneath the daily headlines. This book of comments and readings is an attempt to place these two distinct, but correlated, elements of the political process into tandem perspective. Essentially this book is an outgrowth of the editor's teaching and writing experiences, and as such, reflects his belief that an understanding of the political process requires some knowledge of history, political institutions, and political behavior. One cannot possibly understand, for example, the strategy of presidential campaigning without comprehending the electoral college.

The editor's comments, which can be read independently or in sequence, are designed to re-enforce each other and unify the entire book as well as provide the necessary background for the readings. The scholarly footnotes have been deleted from the readings. None of the readings has been truncated so that its meaning would be distorted, or so that it is no longer a complete reading. The placing of the readings within the sections follows the editor's logic; many of the readings could have been placed in different sections. But with both comments and readings the aim is identical: to inform and explain, and, just as importantly, to raise questions and to force thinking.

In writing the comments and securing the readings the editor has been aided by a number of people whom he wishes to acknowledge, though in no way imputing to them responsibility for errors or omissions—which faults will have to be the editor's alone. The editor is indebted to David Smith for his help in tracking down and suggesting readings and for his criticism of the outline and some of the comments. Mrs. Stella Briere struggled with the editor's copy and put it uncomplainingly into typescript. Professor David Fellman made valuable comments on the entire manuscript and nurtured it into publication. At Dodd, Mead & Company William Oman encouraged the project from its inception and Philip Winsor saw it through press. My greatest debt goes to my most honest critic and most helpful co-worker, my wife Naomi, who secured the permissions and with her blue pencil made the comments intelligible. This book is dedicated to Sara, who, because of her age, associates elephants and donkeys only with zoos.

NORMAN L. ZUCKER

CONTENTS

I. POLITICS AND THE AMERICAN PARTY STATE

1. The Party State, Party Systems, and the American Setting

IT would be inconceivable today to try to study the political process of the United States or of most other countries without examining the role of political parties and the nature of the party system. Yet this was not always so. The rise of political parties to their present central position in the modern state has constituted a revolution in the governance of man. Originally considered destructive of good government, parties are now regarded as essential to that end.

Party systems vary from nation to nation and are a product of specific national history. Depending on its cultural base, party government assumes different political styles and performs a variety of functions. In democratic societies, particularly since the advent of universal suffrage, political parties have directed, organized, and registered mass support; this is the electoral function. Parties are the link between the governed and the governors and provide the mechanism for implementing and organizing executive and legislative institutions. (In the United States, for example, state legislatures and the Congress are internally organized by the elected membership according to political party lines.) Furthermore, other institutions such as courts and the bureaucracy, although not directly controlled by the party process, nonetheless are influenced by it. Correlative to their electoral function, political parties act as educational and socializing agents, in that they help to reconcile competing claims on governmental authority (sometimes termed the "brokerage" function), clarify programmatic alternatives, and articulate popular feelings toward public policy.

Just as the functions of political parties are various, so too are their ideological and organizational bases. Ideologically, political parties may be classified as either doctrinal or nondoctrinal. A doctrine-based party (for example, the Communist or a religious party) is one committed to a principle (or set of principles) and is not prepared to compromise except in furtherance of its political goals. On the other hand, the nondoctrinal party avoids ideological rigidities and attempts to make its appeal as broad as possible (the Democratic and Republican parties are examples of nondoctrinaire parties). But the doctrine-nondoctrine classification, while theoretically interesting, runs into practical difficulties. When doctrine-based parties assume political authority, principle often bends to pragmatism; and nondoctrine-based parties may clothe their appeals in ideological garb. Consequently, this classification scheme, like most other classification schemes in the social sciences, is not "pure."

A convenient and much-used offshoot of classification according to ideology is to categorize parties according to their positions left and right of some nebulous political point selected as the center. As a shorthand guide this is useful; in general most people can agree on the stances which define leftness and rightness. For example, on the issue of "What role should the government play in regulating the economy?," the center position would be some regulation. Moving from center to the right, the amount of regulation would attenuate until no regulation would be acceptable; this would be the "pure" right. Conversely, moving from the center to the left, the amount of regulation would increase until regulation was total; and this would be the "pure" left. But since a political party takes positions on many issues, it is problematic that it would line up exactly on the same point of the left-right spectrum on every issue. Moreover, not all issues lend themselves easily and accurately to a left-right analysis.

Other ways to categorize political parties could deal with organizational or structural base and would pose questions such as: Is the party's structure direct or indirect? What are the party's constituent units? How do they mesh? Some parties are built on an indirect structure and utilize other social formations as their basic component units. (The British Labor party, which is based in large part on trade-union affiliation, is an example of this.) In the United States parties are built on a direct structure; that is, individuals associate themselves directly with the party of their choice. The potential for raising typological questions to be used as classification devices is seemingly infinite; but obviously not all questions are of equal relevance or importance. Substantive questions would go to the ethos of the party process, and equally could involve institutional and behavioral analysis. Some substantive questions would be: What is the leader-membership relationship? Is party responsibility enforced?

Allied to the classification of political parties, and sharing the pitfalls of grouping schemes, is the classification of party systems. The most common party system classification is based on the number of parties that seriously compete in elections. Standard systematization uses the terminology single-party, two-party, and multiparty. But caveats are in order here. Single-party systems are associated, in the popular mind, with totalitarian states, but this is a gross oversimplification. Although the classic prototype of totalitarian one-party states is the U.S.S.R., more precise terminology would call this a one-party dictatorship. The crucial distinction here is that in a totalitarian one-party society, only one party is permitted to participate meaningfully in elections. But in a single-party system, although one party regularly wins practically all the offices, there may exist a substantial number of voters who maintain some sort of organized and competitive opposition, even though they rarely win any significant number of electoral offices. Examples of this would be the Congress party in India or the Party of Revolutionary Institutions (P.R.I.) of Mexico. Also associated with single-party typologies are the variety of single-party systems appearing in some of the new Asian and African states, which may have authoritarian characteristics but are not necessarily totalitarian in nature. A fundamental distinction between totalitarian and authoritarian single-party systems is based on the acceptance of opposition, both within and without the dominant party.

At the opposite extreme is the multiparty system in which three or more parties share votes and public offices and in which no single party wins a majority of either. France, under the Third and Fourth Republics, is the outstanding illustration of this type of system. Standing between the multiparty systems of the Western democracies and the tendency toward one-party rule in some of the developing countries, the two-party system occupies a middle ground. Prime examples of this middle ground are the American and British systems.

Although both the United States and Great Britain typologically support a two-party system, to bracket them together is misleading, because the two systems differ significantly. The British system is characterized by ideological distinctions between the two major parties (Labor and Conservative), executive-legislative cohesion based on a responsible parliamentary government, and centralized powers. These factors are not present in the American political universe, which embraces nonideologically oriented major parties, executive-legislative separation, a presidential system operating without party responsibility, and a federal system which creates decentralization and localism.

Given the diversity of regions and interests in the United States, one might reasonably expect to find a multiparty system in operation. But the American experience with multipartyism has been sporadic, extending only occasionally to a national third party. The 1912 four-party race in which the Socialists came in a poor fourth was an aberration. And although a third party may operate regionally (Dixiecrats) or locally (Liberal party in New York City), it operates in relation to the dominant two-party system. But the national two-party system embraces one-party subsystems. This is so because the American federal system disperses power (party conflict occurs at the local level in the states and congressional districts) and provides a basis for regional and state politics. Until recently, serious Republican competition in the Democratic South was considered an idle expenditure of energy and resources, as was serious Democratic competition in the Republican one-party areas in New England and the Middle West. The absence of genuine party competition leads to one-party subsystems. In these subsystems politics occurs, but it is intraparty and takes the form of bi- or multifactionalism.

In the readings which follow, Hugh McD. Clokie describes, in broad historic strokes, party government as the distinctive feature of modern politics and makes insightful generalizations about and comparisons among single-party, two-party, and multiparty systems. In a somewhat different approach, Gordon Smith raises the question "What Is a Party System?" and in answer analyzes interrelated problems. Addressing himself specifically to the American party process, Professor E. E. Schatt-schneider details the factors which channel American politics into a two-party system and also notes some of the secondary political characteristics flowing from this pattern.

THE MODERN PARTY STATE *

Hugh McDowall Clokie

PARTY government is without doubt the distinctive feature of modern politics. The advent of the partisan politician to a dominant role in government constitutes a revolutionary change in the conduct of public affairs. In former

* From Hugh McDowall Clokie, "The Modern Party State," in *Canadian Journal of Economics and Political Science,* Vol. XIV, No. 2 (May, 1949), pp. 140-157. Reprinted by permission of Professor Clokie and the *Canadian Journal of Economics and Political Science.*

ages the right to rule was assumed by or accorded to military adventurers, religious leaders, royal personages, or oligarchic groups variously qualified by birth, wealth, or special political skill. Throughout countless centuries custom, tradition, and necessity have combined to establish force, religion, property, or family as the legitimate foundations for the exercise of political power. But in recent times it is apparent that these ancient claims to authority have been rudely swept aside and superseded by a new one. It has become increasingly fashionable throughout the world to discard the accustomed princes and ruling classes and to entrust government to the leaders of the novel and interesting associations known as political parties.

Thirty years ago it would have been asserted that the current acceptance of government by parties was the necessary concomitant of universal imitation of the parliamentary system of western democracy. Today, however, it will be observed that this modern trend to government by the leaders of organized partisans is not confined to those polities drawing their inspiration and form from the British model or utilizing as she does the rivalry of two or more political parties. The practice of relying upon partisan politicians is now to be found in new types of party-states, states in which only one party is permitted to exist. Frequently, but not always, this latter development has occurred in countries that have hitherto been supposedly untouched by the political influences radiating from the western centres of party government. The appearance of party rule in regions where the standard devices of parliamentary partisanship have not hitherto been practised emphasizes the universality of the revolutionary trend to partisanship as a foundation for the new politics and indicates that the latest form of party state, the one-party type, is not merely a corruption of the western type produced by its too hasty introduction into a "backward" country. . . .

Parties, then, are not the simple elemental things that their adherents allege them to be nor are they the intrinsically pure types for which observers are likely to look. They may not be entirely products of circumstance, though they are evidently influenced and shaped by the social background in which they work—remembering of course that they are also factors in creating this background. It should be expected, therefore, that parties of the same name, profession, and structure may play different roles in the several countries. Such a statement, however, when made with reference to the Communist party will provoke dissent both from those communists who extol the "monolithic" character of the party and from those blinded by fear and hatred of it. Every human association has to fit itself to the system in which it operates. The boy scout movement, for example, has to adapt its purposes to such considerations as the amount of urbanization and industrialization of the countries in which it operates. So likewise with the Roman Catholic Church, which despite its uniformity of religious doctrine and ecclesiastical form conducts itself quite differently when it is a missionary enterprise in an alien culture, when it is one of several competing organizations as in Britain or the United States, and when it is the dominant religious body as in Spain. The spirit and role of any association changes inevitably with its function and role in the society where it is placed. The same Communist party may thus be expected to serve different purposes in the several constitutional systems of the world.

A preliminary view of the new governmental systems indicates that the novelty of the contemporary trend does not lie in the existence of partisan associations of one kind or another, in their possession of principles, nor in the fact that party leaders actually attain dominance in the practice of public business. The distinctive characteristic of the modern political order is the constitutional status of parties, that is, the recognition of their "governing" function in the modern state.

Needless to say, parties must exist before they can assume a constitutional role or undertake the task of guiding the destinies of a people. But the mere existence of parties is not a novelty. Groups of ambitious politicians, surrounded by throngs of followers managed or organized in various ways, have frequently appeared in the past in guise appropriate for the circumstances of their day. Some of these earlier factions may seem to bear striking resemblance to the political parties of the present, and for certain limited purposes comparision may possibly be made between the political divisions in ancient Athens and those of modern democracies, between the stratagems of Julius Caesar and those of recent imitators of caesarism, of between the Green and Blue contestants at Byzantium and the factions in later metropolitan centres. Yet all comparisons of ancient and modern parties immediately reveal a notable and fundamental difference between former ages and the present. The earlier partisan associations were relatively accidental, transient, and transitional bodies, and their existence, with or without principles, never attained the distinction of characterizing a widespread type of government. While they were not always anti-constitutional, they were at least extra-constitutional organs, springing sporadically into being for ephemeral purposes as the result of special local conditions. Modern parties, on the other hand, are regarded as necessary, purposeful, and constitutional. The political parties of the present time are not simply just another series of associations into which men group themselves, like religious sects, labour unions, or sports clubs. Nor are they merely the portions of a community that have political consciousness and possess special views on how public affairs ought to be conducted. Regardless of their possible anti-constitutional origin—a birthmark that still distinguishes some—they are now not simply legitimate associations but are often the only privileged ones. They are in fact fully accepted today as essential organizations for government in the modern state, recognized under varying conditions as entitled to give direction to the course of politics, and endowed either by law or usage with a special status and function in the constitutional systems in which they operate.

The elevation of political party leaders to the rank of legitimate or constitutional rulers is thus not merely revolutionary in practical politics, it amounts to a constitutional revolution and is tantamount to the inauguration of a new state form, the party-state. Whether party-states can be brought within the traditional or Aristotelian classification need not be discussed here. If they can be, it will be evident that this is because of the nature of party structure. At any rate, instead of obvious former types of government by one man, a few, or the many the modern party states seem to fall into three categories—one-party, two-party, and multi-party. And just as Aristotle found that number alone was not the sole feature that distinguished his categories, so it may be perceived that party systems differ not only with respect to number of parties but also in the role these play in the constitutional establishment and in the spirit in which they perform their functions.

In the one-party state, recently demonstrated on a significant scale by Bolshevik Russia, Fascist Italy, and Nazi Germany, a permanence in power by the one party permitted is set as the goal. The party is wedded to, if not identified with, the government, and the struggle for control by persons or factions is conducted within the single party in secretive and underhand fashion, often with fatal consequences for those who fail in the contest.

In the two-party states, such as those of the English-speaking world, alternation in power by the two dominant parties is promoted by competition for office judged by the amount of popular support they receive periodically and the contest is conducted largely in public in accordance with agreed rules. Other organizations may, of course, exist, but generally speaking these smaller factions have little prospect of providing their organizers with the chance of attaining temporary power, which is the goal of partisanship in this type of state. In the two-party system, a minor political association must be content to live as a propagandist body, spurred on by the hope that it may soon be able to displace one of the two major parties; but, failing this, it must be content to acquiesce in the status of a mere "pressure group." As the political contest in these states is thus essentially a struggle between the politicians of the major parties, the electoral and parliamentary proceedings assume a characteristic form that is distinctive ("government" and "opposition," "ins" and "outs"), whether the formal machinery is cabinet and parliamentary or presidential and congressional.

In the multi-party states, of which France, Italy, and Switzerland have long been the outstanding examples, there is less of a struggle for complete power, temporary or permanent, between the parties than of jockeying for influence or for a share of office at the centres of authority. As no party can expect to gain full control with many rivals—a situation that proportional representation may be utilized to perpetuate—each aims at acquiring sufficient popular support to enable it to be eligible for membership in the coalition or bloc of parties required to constitute the government. This necessarily gives a special tone to parliamentary manoeuvres; it also permits theoretical principles to dominate in electoral appeals, though its successful operation requires compromise and conciliation among the diverse partisans who share in the "government."

Partisan leaders, then, are entrusted with permanent power in the one-party state, with temporary power in the two-party state, and with partial or shared power in the multi-party state.

The different roles that party may play in the three types of party-state are evidently accompanied, if not directly caused, by differences between the basic assumptions or principles upon which the party systems rest. The foundation of the one-party system is apparently the quality of absolutism. The party, at least according to its members, is entitled to rule because it alone is qualified by truth, wisdom, intuition, or virtue. The Communist party, for example, is the custodian of "scientific" socialism, the Nazis possessed the correct Germanic Weltanschauung, the Fascists had intuitive knowledge of how to attain Italy's destiny. The leaders of these parties were allegedly gifted with the excellence or virtue that Plato and Aristotle deemed essential for good government. It is from this "fundamentalist" certainty that the characteristic conformity and discipline of the dictatorship party is derived. They are distinctive features of all human relationships in which a cocksure *élite* is introduced. The restriction of political power to one party and the careful indoctrination of its selected members are obvious consequences of the general principle—as Plato elaborated it. Whether it is necessary to impose on the public divine myths of the Platonic variety or to extinguish all critics and opponents is doubtful, though in practice every such one-party *élite* has done so or has sought to do so. These new parties are, in Christendom at least, the spiritual heirs of religious dogmatism; but instead of relying on divine revelation they have elevated racial prejudice, nationalist romanticism, or economic hypothesis to the height of absolute truth, and instead of being guided by an ordained priesthood they are directed by a self-assertive set of partisans.

The two-party state is, on the contrary, distinctively relativist or utilitarian in spirit or quality. The parties govern in alternation, and thus for a temporary period, because each is understood to be only somewhat sound in its policies for the common good, each only moderately efficient in carrying on the government, and each only partially representative of the continuous life of the community. So pragmatic is the system that the choice of which party is to be in power at any given period is accomplished in the somewhat haphazard processes of election or selection that are the despair of mathematically-minded observers; a "minority" party may assume the role otherwise supposed to be reserved for the "majority" party. Even the formal or nominal head of the state may influence the choice; and the leaders of a party "in power" with a representative majority may actually abdicate (or resign) before suffering defeat. The empirical attitude to political affairs is likewise indicated by the admitted continuance of the "opposition" or minority party as critic and spur. The party in office has the power to govern, but is so uncertain of its own rightness that it recognizes the value of its opponent's criticisms and alternative suggestions. The usefulness of the two-party system in preserving the elector's opportunity to choose his rulers is so frequently asserted as to need no further elaboration. Throughout the various aspects of the two-party state runs the underlying assumption that justice and good government are not concentrated in any one part or party of the body politic. The two parties are in fact regarded as complementary and nothing could be worse than the continuance of one of them in power for too long a period. Tolerance is often said to characterize the system, for division of opinion is not only tolerated but is institutionalized—a feature that is often explained on the ground that truth is two-faced, but is sometimes defended with the proposition that political justice arises from pursuing certain processes of arriving at decisions. The primary concern, however, is to get a major party into office, encourage it to rule with self-imposed moderation and restraint, and impose responsibility by temporary or conditional office-holding. Coalitions, bipartisanship, and of course non-partisanship are naturally deplored as diffusing responsibility, side-tracking the party man, and generally undermining the constitutional status of party.

The essential quality of the multi-party state appears to be its representative character. Representation is no doubt usually claimed as the distinguishing feature of the two-party system, but such a view evidently confuses parliamentary institutions with the party system that operates within it. The British Parliament and the American Congress are intended to be representative of the citizenry of the two countries respectively, yet the governments or administrations installed in each are clearly not "representative," the partisanship of British and American administrations is normally that of a single party. By those who recognize the primary requirement of political responsibility in the two-party state, it is now generally deplored when Presidency and Congress are not dominated by the same party, just as in Britain it is deplored when the House of Lords proves a partisan handicap to the ministry of the day. So likewise it will be recalled that the single-party state may employ representative institutions, either soviet or corporative, for purposes that are appropriate for that particular system. In the multi-party states of continental Europe, however, the representative principle is found not only in the legislatures but also in the cabinets. A ministry that is composed exclusively (unless for temporary reasons) of one party's leaders is both rare in practice and improper in theory. The rulers are partisans, of course, but collectively they are not of a single partisan colour. The goal of a head of government is to create a coalition or combination of partisan leaders as a national bloc or popular front for this is the approved combination that carries weight. It is no doubt true that the composite government rarely attains the full representative character; but neither is the government of a one-party state as consistent in its certainty or absolutism as its principle implies (a feature that reversals of policy and practice indicate), nor is the governing party in a two-party state always as self-restrained and tolerant as it ought to be (as appears when such a party professes to have the sole key to justice or sound policy). But though a completely representative character is never fully attained in the multi-party system, the line is rarely if ever sharply drawn between government and opposition. At popular elections the government never faces the voters as a unit and in the legislature it makes its appeal to the several participant parties (or prospective participants) one by one. The kaleidoscopic changes that are so notable in such governments indicate that parties may and do enter or leave the government coalition with but transient effects. The non-participating parties are not ordinarily cut off from office permanently; office-holding is a matter of practical considerations involving how many posts there are to distribute, how many parties are required to secure the "confidence" of the nation's representatives, the extent of personal rivalry and ideological animosity on the one hand and of compromise on the other. For, in the nature of the multi-party system, it has to be noted that the several partisan groups, having no individual responsibility for permanent or temporary rule of the country, are more rigorous in their doctrinal differentiation than the large composite parties in the two-party state and, at their worst, are less flexible in adaptation to necessity than the one party of the single-party state, especially when some of the many parties ape the pretended "monolithic" purity of the latter.

In an era that is extremely conscious of social change and that conceives of development as natural and inevitable, interest in the three types of party state is necessarily directed to the discovery of a progressive or successive relationship between them. Even if one abandons the ancient attempt to devise a cycle or spiral and the more modern and typically Anglo-American idea of ebb and flow (the swing of the pendulum between liberals and conservatives) in order to pursue the latest evolutionary or developmental concept, it still remains important to connect the three varieties of party system in a sequence of origin and development if not of logic and coherence. We need not, perhaps, ask if there is an ideal party system nor if the three forms can be arranged in order of merit. We can observe, however, that they did arise in different times and in different places—the accepted view being apparently that the two-party system comes first (sometime in or before the eighteenth century in England), the multi-party system second (in nineteenth-century France or in related countries), and the one-party system last (in twentieth-century Russia). From this it is likely to be deduced that party rule, being an accompaniment of certain stages in modern social development, will tend to assume the one-party form. But one must ask whether the two-party system tends to turn into the multi-party form and the latter into the one-party type.

The classical mode of approaching the problem of the three types of state and the transition from one to another was to seek the cause of the change in the internal aspects of the systems, and this was usually found in a corruption of principle or in the nature of the deviation from the "good" type. The examination of corruption of principle may possibly still be usefully pursued, but reference to an ideal or "best" form is less likely to be profitable. As the three types of party state are all in existence at one time, two conclusions are likely to be drawn: that no one of them is suitable to all peoples in their various stages of development and that each of them has its defects. The first conclusion is not very helpful in testing the assertion that destiny leads into one form of party state for it leaves unanswered the question whether social development must everywhere follow an identical pattern and thus produce the supposed sequence of party systems. The second conclusion, that each system has intrinsic difficulties and inconsistencies, is, in the nature of human deficiencies, a more useful one on which to work.

So far as change and transition from one type to another is concerned then, one may commence with observing the comparative stability or instability of the several systems. On the face of it the two-party type is most stable, for it has persisted with varying degrees of success for a long period in Britain and the United States, despite foreign civil wars, territorial expansion and contraction, and the economic transformation wrought by the industrial revolution. Moreover, the countries of its first adoption have never permanently given up the system. That it was not introduced into other countries at comparable stages of their social and economic development must be attributed either to foreign ignorance or to its undesirability in their eyes. It is occasionally assumed that the non-adoption of a two-party system is due to cultural differentiation or incompatibilities. Yet this is seemingly refuted by the widespread imitation of the known and formally described institutions (representative assemblies, cabinets, etc.) that have swept around the world. Ignorance no doubt played a fairly decisive role; two-party government and its meaning did not receive acknowledgment in the books on which imitators rely until long after the copying had ceased. Imitators had either to believe that representative institutions ran themselves or to accept what English politicians said of parties (which is like asking businessmen what makes their economic system work). Moreover, those outsiders who did comprehend the system fully found the two-party system undesirable because it appeared illogical and even dangerous. Why entrust even for a few years the nations' welfare to a prejudiced group of partisan leaders simply because they possess a momentary majority? They may put party before country. They may become so filled with their own self-interest, importance, or rightness that they refuse to surrender temporary power to the other party. Few newcomers to politics are sufficiently pragmatic to accept the relativist concepts on which the two-party system rests. Furthermore, in most countries that emerged from a traditional non-party state by violent revolution, the victorious partisans were either imbued with absolutist convictions or with representative ideals. The latter, it must be observed, are the nominal goals of the parliamentary institutions of the two-party system, and it is the representative technicalities that have been universally copied. It is representation that is the elusive attraction in British politics (elections, bicameralism, parliamentary procedure, etc.) rather than its illogical temporary government by one party at a time, even though the latter has become the actual character of the Anglo-American form. Yet it remains true that, though rarely copied, the two-party system has continued to be the most stable of all forms—when it is understood and practised.

The multi-party system has been the commonest form of party government, partly because it is most in keeping with the purpose of the representative institutions that have been introduced everywhere. At the same time it is usually thought to be the most unstable, a defect that has often been attributed to the national character of the countries where it is practised, or to particular aspects of the representative machinery, such as proportional representation or ministerial dependence on the legislature.

There is good reason for ascribing instability in the multi-party system to the particular relations of executive and legislative bodies for it is here that the incongruity of the essential principles is revealed. The object of representation in an assembly is to reproduce on a small scale the political diversity of a country. It is a commonplace that such an assembly itself cannot rule; it is equally true that a smaller and more concentrated body, the composite cabinet, will have exactly the same difficulties in ruling. In practice, it appears that the legislative parties often seek a portion of power in the government, not to create an efficient multi-hued ruling body, but to block opponents or to prevent action being taken when they do not approve of it. Accordingly the conflict of wills in the centre of affairs is so intense that no governing is possible; if, nevertheless, action is determined on, then an uncompromising legislative party may withdraw its ministers and the government falls. In other words, just as in the two-party system neither parliament nor congress can rule because agreement on action between organized opponents is rarely possible, so in the multi-party system a coalition of incompatibles rarely attains unity; each partisan group insists on a veto or withdraws. In Switzerland, it may be observed that the system works well because the party members elected to the executive shed much of their partisanship and definitely cease to be dependent on their parties. A multi-party scheme thus appears at first sight as a most attractive form of party government, but suffers from the fatal defect that unless it moderates or overcomes partisanship at some stage it fails to provide government, encourages irresponsible "splintering" of parties, and fortifies the veto power of intransigents and incompatibles. When successful its manipulators are accused of conciliation and compromise; when unsuccessful they are, of course, incompetent and impotent.

The instability of the multi-party system must not be confused with ministerial instability. It is a matter of indifference how many times ministers are reshuffled, so long as they operate the system. The severest criticism is the frequency with which the system has been overthrown and displaced, temporarily at least, by another—usually the one-party system. These changes have not always, or even characteristically, been the consequence of war and invasion. After 1920 as well as since 1945 the same cause is evident; the rise of one or more parties that did not accept the representative principle of the multi-party system and that held themselves out to be the sole guides to national welfare. Obviously, then, the system often fails to impress on the constituent partisans the merits of compromise and conciliation which are essential to any representative scheme.

The current single-party system is of such recent origin that it might seem too early to speak of its defects. Yet it must be observed that only under external pressure, chiefly conquest, has one-party rule been displaced, and then it has been succeeded by uneasy and often transitional multi-party rule before reverting to one-party form. Nevertheless, its deficiencies are obvious. One may perhaps put aside the logical incoherences when one is faced with rival claims to certainty; one of them, but only one, may be justified in the claim, and the wrong one may actually gain power. But admitting that the one is known and gets to power, it is difficult in this world of human error to believe that the party will always perceive the public good or know how to attain it. A miscalculation of war-potential brought Hitler's party to collapse; lack of foresight humbled Mussolini's party; the Bolsheviks in Russia were only saved by new economic policies in 1922 and 1928; future mistakes may bring them down also. The single-party politicians, too, may be inadequately recruited or improperly indoctrinated. Politics being what it is, policies often have to be adopted that are not within the purview of the original programme, and ultimately, therefore, the partisans may lose their sense of certainty. Secessionist movements may occur and be incapable of extinction. Politics in the one-party state, instead of being the pursuit of a clear-cut policy may become a matter of discussion or one in which differences of opinion may reasonably be held and advocated. Evidently the greatest defect of the one-party system is its pretence of omniscience and omnicompetence. In reality, of course, there is division of opinion in every dynamic system, and discussion, invention, and compromise take place in varying forms. In the one-party system this tends to be concealed from the public or is controlled within the party. Only the novice or new convert believes the absolutist myth; it is mainly an apparatus for deluding the ignorant. In time, criticism must emerge, even if admitted as self-criticism; in time, councils or representative bodies must be utilized in the great territorial states of today, even if disguised as soviets, corporative chambers, or what not. And in time, also, the diversities of interest and opinion that appear in every human society may well explode the absolutist nonsense and split the pretentious "monolithic" party asunder.

A general survey of the contemporary forms of party government appears to indicate that there are no good grounds for believing in a cycle or necessary succession of party-state forms. The two-party system remains entrenched where it originated and has long been practised; the establishment of a multiparty system is a recurrent effort, succeeding where the participant parties approve the principle required, failing when political divisions take on the aspect of concealed or "cold" civil war; the single-party type has swept into countries torn by civil conflict or in chaos after invasion or economic adversity, but it has never been adopted peacefully, voluntarily, or spontaneously by any people who have been accustomed to another form. On this evidence it is, however, too early to conclude that the latest variety of party system is or is not destined to prevail in future. It is possible, however, that some light might be thrown on the matter by some consideration of the nature and role of partisanship, the causes of its rise, and the functions that modern parties serve. . . .

When party government is at last firmly established in the constitutional system, it thus implies the participation of large numbers of men bound together on a novel basis who exercise political influence with varying degrees of tolerance and intolerance, hold office permanently or transiently, and use new processes of recruitment of participants and new devices for connecting the rulers and the public at large.

Political parties are thus the modern type of association by which the age-long struggle for power is waged when an enlarged portion of the community claims or has thrust on it a share in the decision of public affairs. The rise of parties is therefore related to the increasing "democratization" of life. This development, it is needless to say, could concur only in societies of growing wealth, in which the traditional bonds of political relationship have been loosened, and in which there are new classes with time, opportunity, and desire to pursue their interests and express their views on political matters. In the past two or three centuries the astonishingly productive nature of western industrialism has created the material conditions for this development. Successive waves of literary renaissance, religious reformation, and contact with "new worlds" gradually undermined the historic foundations of European political life. And as western civilization has overwhelmed the traditional and often primitive social systems of the rest of the world, it has carried the political as well as the economic and cultural revolution to every corner of the globe, with many of its benefits but with many of its most noticeable deficiencies.

Once entered upon, party government works profound changes in the art and principles of government. Not only does it mean in practice the displacement in various degrees of soldier, priest, prince, and property owner as sole arbiters of law and policy and their supersession by party politicians, but it carries with it the need for a new foundation of political authority. Just as the modern industrial system rests on a prodigious "rationalistic" foundation of calculation—profit and loss, cost and price, etc., which is common to both capitalist enterprise and socialist planning—so the new politics rests on what one might describe as the rationalized mathematics of collectivized individualism. What salesmanship and advertising are to the economy, persuasion and propaganda are to the polity. Under all varieties of party system the endorsement of the public is sought by partisan leadership, agitation, and exhortation. The pretentiously "rational" activities of electoral campaigns, voting for representatives, parliamentary procedures, etc., have comparable utility (though varying efficacy) in the different one-party, two-party and multi-party systems.

But as the economy is never based entirely on "rationalist" calculation, so neither is the polity on a purely rational manipulation of voters. Politicians have to adapt themselves to crosscurrents of apparent anti-rationalism such as prejudices, nationalism, localism, etc., to the same extent that businessmen and planners have been impeded in their pursuit of pure calculated private or public profit in the face of humanitarian and fashionable considerations in economics. The party politician, therefore, has had to devise new modes of winning adherents by devious appeals to emotions of hate, fear, self-interest, and patriotism in addition to making reasoned arguments. Partisan leaders everywhere have to accommodate themselves to vagaries of public opinion, and if unable to control the mass must reconcile themselves to the ebb and flow of party fortune with the best grace possible.

No one should imagine that the functions and problems of government will have changed when party leaders replace former rulers or when "the people" in their serried ranks as partisans become the sovereign in the new political order. It is the methods, processes, and mechanisms of politics that change when new modes of selecting rulers and new bonds of allegiance come into operation. The old debates concerning the end of government, the nature of the good state, and the obligation of the individual will go on for all time. Under party rule, however, a larger proportion of the public are encouraged to think in terms of ends and distant objectives and how to attain them by their own efforts. The parties will no doubt be encouraged to advance their own goals as final ends with the absoluteness of religious fervour, forgetful of the obvious fact that they are but means and that political justice and wisdom are not objective moral or ethical qualities, but are the products of a process of deciding on government.

What the destiny of party government is no one can say—except perhaps that it will not be what is expected. In many places it is probable that the public—especially when material and social conditions fail to improve proportionately to modest expectations—may ultimately weary of the constant excitement of being invited to support one party or another and will take refuge in the security and stability that is supposed to have been offered by tradition; custom will then replace the exhausting process of debating and doubting that "rational" choice in partisanship involves. But in more satisfactory societies, where greater amplitude of pleasant living continues, those systems of party rule that foster the individual's voluntary participation and self-respect will no doubt remain firmly entrenched so long as the public remembers that they are human and therefore limited, and that parties are one of the useful modes of attaining some small degree of popular control over the rulers of society.

WHAT IS A PARTY SYSTEM? *
Gordon Smith

AND what *is* a party system?" . . . The answers to some straight-forward questions in political science reveal how much is taken for granted and how fundamental disagreement is possible even with the most "neutral" political terms. The deceptive simplicity of the hallowed phrase "party system" is a case

* From Gordon Smith, "What Is a Party System?" in *Parliamentary Affairs*, Vol. XIX, No. 3 (Summer, 1966), pp. 351–362. Reprinted by permission of the Hansard Society for Parliamentary Government.

in point, used as it is with conflicting assumptions and an underlying spirit of contention. The lack of agreement on the meaning of the term is an obvious barrier in comparative studies; too often the question is shelved or answered by coolly excluding "systems" that others regard as legitimate.

The answer is certainly more complex than the original question implies. In fact, there are three inter-related problems: to find the essential components of a party system, to agree on a basis of distinguishing between systems, and, finally, to decide whether the "one party state" can properly be included as a form of party system. It is best to tackle the problem of the one party state first, for without agreement on its place neither definition nor adequate classification is possible. Besides, writers are happier to commit themselves to an attitude towards single party systems than they are to give explicit definitions.

The question is whether the existence of a single party is compatible with the concept of the "party state," a state whose present form depends on the activities of political parties, whether, in fact, "le parti unique" is a real political party. An array of experts finds the single party and its system inadmissible. Heckscher says it is "really a negation of the idea of political parties." Sigmund Neumann dismisses the single party on almost dialectical grounds as ". . . a contradiction in itself. Only the co-existence of at least one other competitive group makes a political party real. . . . If one [functioning opposition] does not exist, it must still be assumed. . . ." Max Beloff also holds that it is a contradiction since, "Only with more than one party can one hope to get the continual emergence of new ideas and the continual questioning of old abuses. . . ." Beloff's views, in part, imply functions for the parties which others would consider to be incidental to a political party's quest for power.

These critics, and others, feel that a one party system raises the party to the status of a permanent aspect of the state, but that the essence of a party system is precisely that this guarantee of permanence should not be present. Yet the justification of this view seems to rest mainly on historical developments and ideological assertions rather than on sufficient analytical grounds. To take the historical aspect first: the long-established party systems of the western world arose within the growth of capitalist society, and historically parties have been an expression of conflicting class interests; the party system itself can be described as a phenomenon of capitalism, a political device which helps "to moderate and contain a conflict of class interests. . . . Nothing except a party system can preserve the stability of a capitalist society where there is popular franchise." The nature of party systems is often determined by this common origin, and the colouring remains even where the conflict has apparently become residual. However, the idea and value of a system does not necessarily become inoperative in developed situations where, temporarily or permanently, a capitalist system ceases to provide the determining and normative features of society. In other words, a party can still perform a function in society after the basic conflict has gone, and with no such conflict the need for several parties also disappears.

This can be appreciated in the distinct movements of fascism, twentieth-century nationalism and of communism. In all three cases the prevalent capitalist society has been replaced or transmuted and the nature of the party system has changed accordingly. We have witnessed a "Gleichschaltung" of the parties in many states where the emerging society does not depend, as the capitalist system does, on inter-party competition to resolve competing stresses. Additionally, such has been the imperative claim of movements which have supplanted capitalist modes, that attempts at competition on a party basis have been regarded as denials of that claim. What has not yet appeared is a situation where the norms of capitalist society have been supplanted by a movement which either needs, or at least does not reject inter-party competition. The chances of such a society coming into being, necessarily diffused in its appeal, would largely depend on the future of capitalist society itself. Inter-party competition could also appear as a secondary stage in one party states, but it is difficult to forsee the basis of party cleavage or why it should not be contained within the existing party.

The ideological objection to the one party state is that a democratic system can only be maintained by guaranteeing the right of freely competing parties to determine the actions and form of government, that freedom of association in the fullest sense can alone give a legitimate party system. Apart from sheer dogma, there are two practical objections to democracy in the one party state: that the one party set-up fails to give a proper group representation, and secondly, that in its working it will always fail to preserve intra-party democracy. These objections are largely based on observation, but this does not give them a general validity, and present experience of one party states in Africa does not show a necessary incompatibility between the single party and basic democratic criteria, even if opposition parties have been summarily disposed of. Indeed, part of the problem of African states can be seen as resulting from an initial attempt to incorporate a western-type party system. In reviewing single-party states in West Africa, Ruth Schachter concluded that certain single parties of mass integration did contain within them elements of consent, participation, striving towards social equality and provision for opposition. "At the present state of African social history the mass party organisation makes it possible for people to disagree within it, without necessarily triggering off incidents endangering the rule of the elite and the stability of the state."

Such evidence can only be fragmentary, but it is confirmed by others. Moreover, the very extent and readiness of the peoples concerned to adopt the single party state should not be written off as political immaturity, it shows also the wide consensus of aims, all the more remarkable in the absence of parties based on strict ideology. It is an open-minded one-party approach which may succeed in by-passing the historical dualism.

If one party practice cannot fully substantiate the ideological viewpoint, neither can attempts to invoke Michels to show that intra-party democracy must of necessity be a fiction. The "iron law of oligarchy" is often uncritically accepted, ". . . for no better reason than that no democratic party is run either by one absolute leader or by each individual adherent, and that all are, therefore, presumably oligarchies. While this assumption makes the iron law universal it also robs it of most of its meaning." In western states the nuances, limits, and susceptibilities are well-appreciated, and, whilst the effect of any oligarchy in a one-party state will be greater, nuances still exist, intra-party conflict still smoulders and blazes, leaders are still toppled, and they are not all palace revolutions.

It seems that unless one starts defining the party system in terms of a plurality of parties, there is no valid objection to including one-party states as part of a more general classification. In taking this course one has to exclude "competitiveness" on an extra-party level as an essential characteristic of a political party, and replace it with a more basic criterion.

II

The quest for basic criteria is made easier if one looks first at the problem of classifying party systems. The idea of a "system" gives the impression of precise form and the usual numerical classification tends to reinforce this with a false exactitude. The attempt to describe systems "two and a half" or "one and a half", although giving an indication of the lack of balance in certain states, can hardly be very useful if the terms "one party" and "two party" are themselves suspect and cover a large number of varieties. Use of the decimal point is no way out either!

However, the traditional method can serve as a starting-point for showing an alternative breakdown. The simplest case is that of the two-party system, and even here it is possible to show numerous variations. J. A. Schlesinger distinguishes no less than five categories within the United States alone, based on the degree of inter-party competition: competitive states, cyclically competitive states, one-party cyclical, one-party predominant and one-party states. Even such a detailed analysis fails to tell the whole story. States which are dominated by one party may secure a degree of intra-party democracy by use of the party primary, so that "durable factions" within the dominant party greatly modify its one-party aspect.

In other countries with two parties the possibility of cooperation and coalition between them opens up a new dimension to the party system. Coalition may take place only spasmodically, as in British war coalitions, or it may be on an almost permanent basis. Thus the highly competitive position in Austria operates with a coalition of the Austrian People's Party and the Socialists which has lasted for almost twenty years. Both the distribution of power and the balance of decision-making have been exactly shared on the indispensable "proporz" system, whereby marginal shifts in election results affect power distribution. The whole system is governed by a coalition treaty of a strict and detailed nature. The development in Austria alone plays havoc with the traditional idea of a two-party system. The pendulum has become rusty and there is no alternative government. Instead the "continuous embrace" of coalition makes the sharing of power an everyday reality.

As the number of parties increases, so in theory does the scope for variation in the party system increase rapidly. In practice, this may well not be the case. The three-party system is a case in point with a simpler range of alternatives. It has as its essential feature a combination of two parties against an excluded third (only rarely is the third party able to make an independent bid for power). The balance of this relatively simple system is provided on two levels—tensions between the government parties leading to the recurring threat of defection by one to the excluded third and the very significant shifts in voting support operating within the coalition and between it and the opposition. The combined effect is to give a stable government combination, as in pre-war Belgium and post-war Germany.

Variations in multi-party systems are so great as to make a numerical classification almost useless. There can be a virtual disintegration (polypartism), a disguised one-party domination, an underlying bi-polarity with the minor parties giving a 'cluster-effect' around one or two major parties. Indonesia after independence is often cited as a case of polypartism. At the other end of the scale the UNR in France had an overall majority after the 1962 elections with a total of eight parties in the Assembly. Finland's multi-party system (with eight parties in 1962) shows a marked bi-polarity. The left "cluster" is to be seen in Israel with no less than four left-wing parties, whilst in West Germany the cluster was to be found on the right until the virtual disappearance of the smaller parties.

Besides the number of parties and their relative position on the political spectrum, there are two other variables of importance: the extent of government responsibility to the parties and the range of coalition possibilities. Despite the number of parties in the Weimar Republic after 1930 there was a complete lack of possible coalition combination. Multi-party systems in Scandinavia rarely face such difficulties. Extremes in governmental responsibility are shown in the powerlessness of the Reichstag in Imperial Germany and the frequent "government by assembly" associated with the Third and Fourth French Republics.

Multi-partyism is an unsatisfactory concept when there is provision for permanent party cooperation at government level. Switzerland has the proven form of collegial government, but it is no longer an isolated instance, and there are some interesting variations on this model, particularly in South America. Uruguay's system is only nominally a two-party one, for the two parties of any importance, the "Blancos" and the "Colorados" have a sub-system of organised factions, seven in all, which are really the constituents of the system. These officially-recognised factions present their own lists of candidates for seats in the legislature. The total party vote decides which of the two parties shall have a majority on the executive body, the National Council (as a result of the 1962 elections the Blancos had six seats and the Colorados three—this ratio is always used whatever the voting majority). The intra-party factions share in the party's allocation on the National Council according to their relative strength at the election.

In Colombia there is a similar combination of numerous factions with an overall two-party set-up. There are also some important differences. In Uruguay other parties can compete freely, but Colombia has a restricted system, and all the seats in the legislature are divided equally between the two "parties" (with six factions in all) as are the cabinet posts. The "parity formula" written into the constitution gives the presidency to each party for alternate terms.

The Colombian party system provides an adequate commentary on the numerical classification. There is the underlying multi-partism, an official two-party umbrella (with a built-in pendulum!), and a party-exclusiveness reminiscent of a single-party state. It would be better to stop classifying by numbers—providing that a workable alternative exists.

III

Obviously there are various alternative schemes of classification. Duverger gives one range: ". . . systems with independent parties in balance or with dominant parties; systems with major or with minor parties, with stable or unstable parties; systems in which power moves leftwards (Leftism) or immobile systems and so on." W. Zakrzewski, from a Marxist viewpoint, distinguishes between systems according to the type of state, type of party structure and relationship with social groups. Essentially all classification either allocates according to some ideological premise or by attempting to show differences in the working of systems. A satisfactory scheme should avoid pre-judgement and should show up clearly all the major differences—many of Duverger's suggestions would fail to give an informative picture by themselves.

A fruitful approach is to study the differences in the location of decision-making in party systems. The general importance of studying "decision-making" is well-recognised in comparative government and politics. It is "the most universal function of politics", says Macridis, and he discerns two elements: deliberation and the formulation of decisions. "By deliberation is meant the various forms and procedures in terms of which a political community attempts to meet and solve problems confronting it . . . decisions (are) made by certain official organs with the expectation that they will be obeyed." What is necessary is to apply this "universal function" in a systematic way to its main exponents—the political parties.

Differences in "decision-making" appear to constitute the major distinction between party systems. That this should be so stems from the nature of a political party: a party strives after power and seeks to use it on as exclusive a basis as possible. In studying the "loci" of the decision-making processes one is looking at the net result of many independent efforts of parties or factions to share in power, "the community's stakes of political power". A party which neither sought this power nor a share in the decisions made would really qualify as an "unparty."

An analysis and classification of party systems would require careful procedure and definition. It is clear that only certain types of decisions are relevant. We should leave on one side what can be termed "administrative" decisions and concentrate upon those of a legislative character in the widest sense. It would be necessary at the same time to detail examples of decisions with which party systems are normally associated, regardless of the number of parties or type of government. Comparison of the process of "deliberation," both within and external to the parties, would show the point at which decisions are effectively made. Major obstacles exist in distinguishing between the real and the formal processes of deliberation and decision and in determining the extent to which groups other than the parties participate. Seen as a comparative study, such a task is formidable even if, on a national basis, much of the ground has been covered. Here it is only possible to provide a scaffolding, to show how existing systems might be re-classified.

Three basic system types can be postulated according to the broad location of decision-making and method of deliberation. The first type occurs when all the main decisions are made within a single party (the intra-party type). The second, often a weak or at least a fluid form, is where decisions tend to be made outside the framework of the party system (the extra-party type). The third case is where decisions are more the result of negotiation and compromise between the parties (the inter-party type). From these three, a number of subordinate types emerge based on related criteria.

A study of intra-party decision-making need not be limited to the one-party state, totalitarian or authoritarian. Situations of one-party dominance as in Japan, Mexico and India, as well as in South Africa and many states in the USA show important affinities. Indeed, the ease of transfer that was effected from one-party dominance to a single-party state in Tanganyika and Kenya show the connection. There are differences. The very fact that a dominant party is prepared to tolerate the "flea-bites" of its impotent competitors indicates greater tolerance to dissident factions in its own party. Intra-party "democracy" can be partly gauged by the degree of permanence of its "durable factions." Thus Mexico's PRI contains a surprising number and variety of these factions, stretching from left to right, and as a consequence the pattern of deliberation contrasts strongly with the single party state where internal opposition is accorded the dubious status of being, say, the "anti-party group."

Yet in both cases effective decisions come from within the party; outside groups must work through the party hierarchy. How far a party manages to extend real deliberation to a low or peripheral area will depend on a variety of factors but an extended classification would have to take them into account. Thus legal provision for party primaries or for the direct participation of party factions in elections, provision for consultation with outside organisations, whether the party is of an exclusive cadre type or one of mass integration—all of these provide important sub-divisions. Another distinction is in the position of the party leadership, whether it is in some way controlled by the party, as might be argued in the recent changes of Soviet leadership, or whether, like the relationship of the UNR to de Gaulle it treats the party as a "supporters' club". In the case of the Fifth Republic, the party system has been effectively by-passed, and the use of the referendum has enabled the president to maintain himself by a direct "dialogue with the nation."

In fact, such cases can easily lead to systems based on extra-party decision-making, and the party becomes an appendage. Cassinelli holds that, "The party of the totalitarian state not only does not 'rule', but, unlike other parties, it could be dispensed with as an instrument of political action", that, in effect, "the leading role of the party" (in Communist parlance) is a camouflage: "Its decision-making function could easily be taken over by a unit (or units) of the government, but it is conceivable that the Party is essential as a façade." The Leader gains his strength from his independence of *any* organisation—not merely through his control over the party apparatus. This extra-party structure does not just weaken the party system, it negates it.

Cassinelli's interpretation need not be accepted as a general rule, applying to all totalitarian parties, but it often accords with reality. Additionally, it is applicable to authoritarian states and to "unrestricted" systems with a dominant party. One can also refer to "pseudo" party systems, where the "party game" is played out parallel to the real exercise of power; the classic example was the period of "democracy under licence" in Germany after 1945.

Such systems may have great stability, but the extra-party aspect may be relevant to systems in dissolution, where the parties are rapidly losing control over vital decisions and a new state form is possibly imminent. Those decisions which are made can well be directed against the prevailing system—rule by presidential decree at the close of the Weimar Republic provides an excellent study of a system in dissolution.

In systems with many favoured parties, susceptibility to electoral pressures tends to diminish for the good reason that a loss of voting support does not proportionately weaken a party's chances of sharing in government; decision-making is much more a permanent function of inter-party negotiation. This applies both to government formation and the governing process. An extreme of one kind is the "irresponsibility" of many systems; decisions are normally negative, government precarious, and no power outside the system can immediately break the stalemate. On the other hand multi-party systems can develop a high degree of stability and responsibility. Institutional devices, such as the referendum in Switzerland, may operate as a continual check, as does a federal structure, or a fine balance may exist between the competing groups giving greater sensitivity to changing support. All the same, the very stability of such systems based on inter-party negotiation tends to weaken outside checks. There is an undeniable pressure to insulate the parties from external influences: the coalition committee becomes the vital organ of state. This is most true of collegial government forms, for the electorate virtually has to take what it is given.

To the three basic system types a fourth can be added to take full account of the working of the classic two-party system and related types. Such a system may be geared fully to take account of extra-party response, so that decisions reached only in a limited sense can be said to emanate from the party in power. An evenly-matched party dualism can give intense inter-party compe-

tition and, even if either or both parties are dominated by an entrenched oligarchy, the result often means that basic decisions are referred to the electorate
—at least in the negative sense that party decisions must be made acceptable
to a large number of social groups.

At a more basic level the vote-competition can mean that the parties will
model themselves on supposed preferences of the electorate rather than rely on
a traditional ideology. The metamorphosis of continental socialist parties illustrates this; the post-war transformation of the Austrian Socialist Party and
the SPD in West Germany from Marxism to "people's parties" have been
particularly rapid exercises.

Once the ideologies have been scrapped, the pressure groups move in, and
these too, weaken the governing party's power to reach independent decisions.
These two influences result in an accepted division of power in which
Lipset finds that, "the source and agents of authority (should) be institutionally
and legitimately separated, so that neither major party can aspire to become
the source of authority."

The net result is often an ambivalence: power of effective decision-making
wanders, both from one party to another and from inside the party to the
electorate at large or to points in the whole network of economic and social
relationships. This fluidity provides a balance and an adaptability which other
systems often lack.

IV

The third and final part of the problem is to establish the essential components of a party system. Definitions, by themselves, do not help to give precise
characteristics. Thus Ranney and Kendall say it is "the term which political
scientists customarily apply to the rules of a community's party 'game'." They
also term it "a shorthand expression for the totality of party conflict." Duverger
defines a system as "the forms and modes" of party co-existence in a state. It
can be agreed that definitions must include ideas of "mode of operation" and
"nature of interaction," but this still leaves open the issue whether a particular
state does have a party system, even if "parties" apparently function.

One essential characteristic follows from the suggested method of classifying systems, that of decision-making. In order that a system should exist it is
essential that key decisions should be in the hands of the dominant party or
parties, either directly or by control over key personnel. Once this is no longer
the case, excluding temporary aberrations, then a "party state" ceases to exist:
the parties remain merely as a shell.

A further characteristic, "competitiveness," has already been considered,
and rejected, since it requires inter-party competition. All the same the concept
of competition is useful for it indicates the existence of a variable relationship,
not only between the parties, but also between them and the state. The important point is that a relationship exists and not an identity. Competitive systems
require a shifting relationship to state power which operates mainly external to
the parties. In non-competitive systems there is a fixed relationship of power

between the state and the party as a whole; it is within the party that the shifts take place.

Once there is a fixed relationship in all respects, a disappearance of any fluidity of structure or power within the party, then an identity obtains, and it becomes profitless to distinguish between party and state. Similarly when the party becomes an appendage, a dispensable instrument of political power in the hands of an autocrat, an identity of another kind has been reached in which the party acts purely as an executive agent of decisions already reached. Obviously non-competitive systems are in the greatest danger of losing their identities in one way or another. They operate on a fine balance, and since the real relationships of party to state power will not be formalised, there is a need to distinguish between apparently similar types.

The existence of a bona fide party system depends on these two fundamental requirements: power of the parties over fundamental decision-making and the absence of a "fixed identity" between state and party (effectively, complete subordination of the party to a leadership controlling state coercive power). As long as these conditions are fulfilled, we are not specifically concerned with the number of parties, their nature, or the type of state in which they operate. These are certainly factors which help us to understand the nature of party systems: they are not suitable criteria for deciding whether a system exists.

THE SPECIAL CHARACTER OF AMERICAN
PARTIES *
E. E. Schattschneider

WHAT are the qualities that distinguish American parties from all others? First of all, American politics is dominated and distinguished by *the two-party system*. This is the most conspicuous and perhaps the most important fact about the system. It accounts for a great variety of secondary characteristics of the parties and differentiates the major parties from all minor parties and all varieties of political organizations found in multiparty systems. Second, the *internal processes* of American parties indicate that the distribution of power within these parties, always a significant datum, is so unusual as to require explanation. To say that American parties are decentralized is to open up a world of inquiries. Obviously any account of the parties that does not attempt

* From E. E. Schattschneider, *Party Government* (Holt, Rinehart and Winston, 1942), pp. 66–85.
Copyright 1942 by E. E. Schattschneider. Reprinted by permission of Holt, Rinehart and Winston, Inc., publishers. All rights reserved.

to discover the *locus* of power in the parties or fails to explain this fact is not worth the paper on which it is written. Related to the distribution of power within the parties is the special character of American nominating procedures. *Local party organization* assumes a form and an importance that cannot be easily understood by anyone who has not become familiar with the peculiar political institutions of this country, for the American local party boss is as indigenous as baseball. Intimately related to the boss system is the professionalization of American politics, another distinguishing mark of the system. Finally, *the hypertrophy of a system of pressure politics,* parallel to the system of party politics, challenges inquiry. Nearly all of the distinctive characteristics of the American parties turn about the problem of the locus of power within the parties or some aspect of the internal processes of these parties. Even the two-party system is interesting principally for the light it sheds on the composition and internal structure of the major parties. Only when the special characteristics of the interior operations and the internal relations of the American parties have been described and explained can we pretend to understand the place of the parties in American government.

THE TWO-PARTY SYSTEM

The two-party system is the most conspicuous feature of American political organization. How does it happen that party politics in the United States has been organized on this pattern? In spite of the fact that the two-party system has been explained by saying that it is a mark of the "political maturity" of Anglo-American peoples (while the multiparty systems of prewar France expressed the "national character" of Frenchmen), we are reasonably certain that definite circumstances, easily identified, make this system inevitable in the United States regardless of the personal preferences of individual critics. We could not discard the two-party system and adopt a multiparty system in the United States, exactly as a lady might change her hat, even if we wanted to do so. What we wish for has very little bearing on what we get in the style of parties.

What do we mean by the expression "the two-party system"? Certainly not that there have been only two parties. We have in fact usually had about as *many* parties as the French had in the palmiest days of the Third Republic, though few people have ever heard of most of them. Attempts to break up the two-party system by organizing third party and minor party movements have been made in substantially every presidential election in the last century. What we have in mind when we say that we have a two-party system is an organization of politics in which there are two major parties and a number of minor parties. The major parties monopolize power, while the minor parties use the elections as an occasion for a subsidiary political agitation that does not lead to power. The major parties maintain their position in the face of a continuing effort to undermine it. In view of the assaults made on the major parties by the minor parties, it must be said that the two-party system (the monopoly of votes and power maintained by the major parties) is one of the most firmly established American institutions. The strength of the two-party system is important because the politics of the major parties in a two-party system is fundamentally unlike the politics of a multiparty system. If this is true, the system deserves examination and analysis.

The relation between the major and minor parties is the crucial point in the two-party system. In the United States the minor parties are excluded from power. This is done so effectively that these parties cease to be genuine parties at all and should probably be spoken of simply as educational movements. In a multiparty system the distinction between major and minor parties is not clearly marked, if it exists at all, and all parties may hope to get a fraction of the power to govern, though none hopes to get the whole of the power to govern. In practice the two-party system means that there are only two major parties, one or the other of which usually has the power to govern, though they may share power sometimes, and that no minor party is able to become a third major party permanently. The gap between the second major party and the greatest minor party is enormous and insurmountable; no minor party in American history has ever become a major party, and no major party has ever become a minor party.

The monopoly of power by the major parties is real. It means that ordinarily they will poll not less than 95 per cent of the total popular vote cast in a presidential election. They will usually win every one of the places in the electoral college, all but a handful of the seats in the House and Senate, and all but one or two of the governorships of the states; and, with the exception of two or three states, they will win all or very nearly all of the seats in both houses of the legislatures. Only in municipal elections, where nonpartisan ballots are used more extensively, is the monopoly of the major parties relaxed appreciably, and even this concession is slightly unreal. Attacks on the monopoly of the major parties have produced only the most negligible results. The two-party system is therefore the Rock of Gibraltar of American politics. How does it happen that the two-party system is one of the fixed points of the political universe? There is in fact nothing mysterious about the causes of this condition. The demonstration is mathematical and conclusive.

Causes of the Two-Party System. The American two-party system is the direct consequence of the American election system, or system of representation, which is only another way of saying the same thing. The elective process is used more extensively in the United States than it has ever been used anywhere else in the world. About 800,000 officials in the national, state, and local governments are elected by the people. This is a colossal performance, and *since parties are built around elections* it would be amazing if the form of the party system were not influenced profoundly by the nature of these elections. The bulk of the elective places in the government are of two principal kinds: (1) members of legislative bodies, and (2) executives. It is probably most instructive to examine first the process of electing representatives to legislative bodies, more particularly the election of members of the United States House of Representatives, as a type.

With certain exceptions that need not be considered here, members of the United States House of Representatives are elected from single-member districts, one district for each representative. Consequently, to elect 435 members, separate elections are held in approximately 435 districts, and in each case the candidate receiving the greatest number of votes wins, even if he does not receive a majority of the votes cast. Though this arrangement seems simple, the results from the standpoint of the parties are amazing. As far as the parties are concerned, the *geographical distribution of their electoral strength* becomes, as a consequence of this system, one of the decisive factors in determining the outcome of the election. That is, the result of the election is determined by *two* factors: (1) the size of the vote, and (2) the geographical distribution of the vote; the total vote cast for the candidates of the two parties does not alone decide the issue. The single-member district system complicates all calculations governing the outcome of elections by injecting into them the second factor. Even a very slight change in the geographical distribution of the party vote in an election held under the single-member district system may produce an effect that seems incredible when first observed. If, for example, one were told merely that a given party received a total of 10,000,000 votes in all of the 435 districts taken together, out of a vote of 40,000,000, it would be impossible to guess even approximately the number of seats won by the party until something were known of the distribution of the vote. In an extreme case the party in question might win all of the seats, or it might win none at all merely by virtue of the fact that it received 25 per cent of the total vote. The accident of the geographical distribution of the popular support of a party has therefore been made a factor of great consequence by the special kind of election system used in the United States.

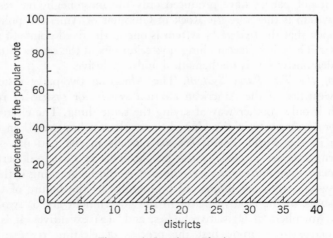

Fig. 1.—*An Imaginary Election*

A party receiving 40% of the total popular vote *distributed uniformly* throughout the electorate (i.e., the party candidates receive 40% of the vote in each district) would win no seats at all.

A precisely proportionate representation of the parties in the House, i.e., proportionate to the popular vote, would result in the single-member district system if all of the electoral strength of all of the parties were concentrated perfectly by congressional districts in each case. That is, if party A received 100 per cent of the vote in some districts and no votes whatever in the others, and party B likewise received all of the votes cast in a number of the districts and none whatever in any other districts, and so on, each would be represented in the House in exact proportion to its popular strength. On the other hand, if the vote of all parties were distributed uniformly throughout the country (so that a party receiving 33 per cent of the total vote would receive 33 per cent of the vote in each of the 435 districts) it follows that the *strongest party would win all of the seats* and the other parties would win none whatever.

Since it is unlikely, however, that party strength will be concentrated perfectly or will be distributed with perfect uniformity throughout the country,

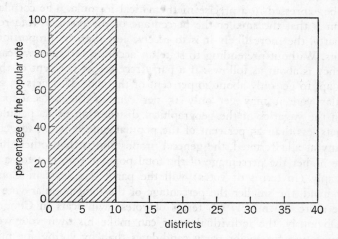

Fig. 2.—*An Imaginary Election*

A party receiving 25% of the vote perfectly concentrated in 10 districts out of 40 (i.e., the party in question receives 100% of the vote in 10 districts and no votes whatever in the remaining 30 districts) would win 25% of the seats. In this kind of election representation would be exactly proportional to the popular vote.

the number of seats likely to be won in an election is highly unpredictable even when the total party vote is known. This is so true that relatively slight adjustments of the system of representation affecting the factor of distribution may produce great consequences. A major change in the system, such as a provision that all representatives be elected at large on a single national ticket, would give the strongest party all of the seats, while the other parties would be reduced to zero, as has been demonstrated in the dictatorships where this device has been used to destroy the opposition parties. Again, an arrangement whereby congressmen are elected on a state-wide basis (i.e., from 48 districts, each state being one district—as presidential electors are now elected) would exaggerate the victory of the winning party even more than the present system does. This can be demonstrated by comparing the vote in the electoral college with the results of the congressional election. On the other hand, a system of proportional representation or vocational representation, by abolishing the geographical factor, would almost certainly destroy the two-party system altogether.

DISTORTION OF RESULTS BY THE SINGLE-MEMBER DISTRICT SYSTEM

We are now in a position to observe the effects on the parties of the single-member-district-system-plus-plurality-elections. First, this system tends to exaggerate the representation of the winning party. Second, the greater the victory the more will it be exaggerated proportionately. Thus a party getting 55 per cent of the vote is likely to win 60 per cent of the seats, let us say. If, however, it gets 65 per cent of the vote it is likely to win 85 per cent of the seats, and so on, though it is not asserted that these proportions are accurate, or that they can be expressed in a precise mathematical formula. The corollary of this proposition is that the smaller the percentage of the popular vote received by a given party, the more likely it is to receive less than its proportionate share of the seats. Without pretending to state an accurate formula, we can say that the tendency is about as follows: if a party receives 45 per cent of the popular vote, it is apt to get only about 40 per cent of the seats. If it gets 35 per cent of the popular vote it may get only 15 per cent of the seats, depending, of course, on the vagaries of the geographical distribution of its popular vote. If a party gets less than 25 per cent of the popular vote it is apt to get very few seats, if any at all. Restated, the general proposition is that, other things being equal, the higher the percentage of the total popular vote cast for a party, the more cheaply (in terms of votes) will the party win seats in Congress. On the other hand, the smaller the percentage of the total popular vote cast for a party, the more expensively (in terms of votes) will seats in Congress be acquired. Obviously, the individual voter can make his own vote weigh more heavily by voting for major party candidates than by voting for minor party candidates.

Although the tendency of the single-member district system described in the preceding paragraph is not stated with the precision of a mathematical formula, it is clear that the operation of the system is to exaggerate the victory of the strongest party and to discriminate radically against lesser parties. The system discriminates *moderately* against the second party but against the third, fourth, and fifth parties the force of this tendency is multiplied to the point of extinguishing their chances of winning seats altogether. The odds against a minor party are especially great because it is certain to be no more than the third party, *unless it has strongly concentrated its strength in one section.* . . .

THE CRUCIAL POSITION OF THE SECOND MAJOR PARTY

The foregoing statement seems to demonstrate sufficiently that minor parties are swamped by the single-member district system, but it raises a question.

Why does this system not crush the second major party also? Why does it fail to produce a one-party system? This question goes to the heart of the subject. There are two answers. First, the second major party, (i.e., the defeated major party) is not easily wiped out completely because it is very likely to have sufficient sectional strength to protect itself against annihilation even in a crushing defeat. Since the defeated party is the first party in some regions, it benefits by the system, to an extent. Thus the Democratic party, operating from a strong sectional base in the Solid South, is certain to win substantial representation in Congress even when all else is lost. In other words, even if disastrously defeated, a major party will still be a major party. The distribution of the popular vote is almost certain to be so irregular that the defeated major party will win *some* seats, sufficient representation to enable it to continue its agitation in the interval between elections and enough to maintain a formidable lead over all other opposition parties, i.e., to be *the* opposition. The sectional base of party alignments is thus likely to enable a defeated major party to outlive electoral disasters. The single-member district system distorts the result in favor of the winner, but it does not annihilate the defeated major party. . . .

The status of the second major party is the critical point in the two-party system. On the one side this party is protected against annihilation by the victorious party. On the other side it is protected against destruction by the minor parties. The same mathematical tendency that exaggerates the representation of the first party as against the second party operates even more drastically in favor of the second party as against the third, fourth, fifth, and sixth parties.

The system does not operate to destroy the defeated major party because the defeated major party is able to retain a *monopoly of the opposition*. The cutting edge of the two-party system is precisely at the point of contact of the second major party and the third party (or the first minor party aspiring to become third major party). What it amounts to is this: the advantage of the second party over the third is overwhelming. It usually wins all seats or very nearly all seats not won by the first party. Among all the opposition parties in the field it has by a very wide margin the best chance of displacing the party in power. Because this is true it is extremely likely that it can assemble about its banner nearly all of the elements in the country seriously opposed to the party in power and seriously interested in an early party overturn. *The monopoly of the opposition* is the most important asset of the second major party. As long as it can monopolize the movement to overthrow the party in power, the second party is important; any party able to monopolize the opposition is certain to come into power sooner or later. The second major party is able to argue, therefore, that people who vote for minor opposition parties dissipate the opposition, that the supporters of the minor parties *waste their votes*. All who oppose the party in power are made to feel a certain need for concentrating their support behind the party most likely to lead a successful opposition. As a consequence the tendency to support minor parties is checked. The tendency of the single-member district system to give the second major party a great advantage over all minor parties is extremely important. In this way it is possible to explain the *longevity* of the major parties and the instability of the minor parties. Thus, while the major parties seem to go on forever, what has become of, and who remembers a long series of Labor, Farmer-Labor, Workers', United Labor, Socialist-Labor, Peoples', Union, and American parties launched since the Civil War?

Why are third parties with highly sectional support unable to survive? In this case, the single-member district system operates in favor of the third party and against one or the other of the major parties within the section. A third party ought therefore to be able to entrench itself in a region and maintain itself permanently. Obviously, the system of representation cannot account for the tendency of sectional third parties to fade away; the explanation must be found elsewhere. As a matter of fact, it is not necessary to go far afield for an explanation. Even more important than congressional elections are presidential elections, which might properly be described as the focus of American politics. American parties are loose leagues of state and local party bosses for the purposes of electing a president, though this statement does not exhaust the truth. In other words, presidential elections probably influence the behavior of parties even more strongly than congressional elections do. Now it is clear that a purely sectional party can never win a presidential election. Presidents can be elected only by combinations of sections, by parties that cross sectional lines. An exclusively sectional party is doomed to a permanent futility, therefore, in the pursuit of the most important single objective of party strategy. Sooner or later exclusively sectional parties are likely to lose even their sectional support in favor of a major party which has a real chance of winning the supreme prize. For this reason narrowly sectional parties cannot displace the traditional type of major party, even though the single-member district system of electing representatives might sometimes give them an advantage. We conclude that the two-party system is firmly established because the second major party is able to defend itself against purely sectional parties as well as against all other varieties of minor parties.

SIGNIFICANCE OF THE TWO-PARTY SYSTEM

Does the fact that we have a two-party system make any difference? Most emphatically, it does! The distinctive characteristics of the major party in a two-party system are strongly marked; the parties in a multiparty system belong to another species entirely. What are the special qualities of American politics that result from the fact that we have a well-established two-party system?

First, *the two-party system produces majorities automatically*. Since there are only two major parties actually in the competition for power and these parties monopolize the vote, it is almost certain that one of them will get a majority. The voters have *no other place to go*. When the alternatives are simplified to this extent, there must be more of one than of the other, i.e., there must be a majority of one or the other. The difficulty of assembling a majority is thus reduced very greatly. Party politicians work hard to assemble a majority, but they do not perform miracles by piecing together a great diversity of groups having an infinity of free choices. On the other hand, because they have only two alternatives, the groups, segments, classes, and occupations have less bargaining power than might be supposed. If this were not the case the difficulties of assembling a majority would be so great that no majorities would ever be produced at all. Party managers perform great labors of negotiation in order that their party, and not the other major party, may get a majority, but one or the other is certain to get it; the value of this fact to the party managers is difficult to exaggerate.

THE MODERATING EFFECT OF THE ATTEMPT TO CREATE A MAJORITY

The second effect of the two-party system is the fact that it produces moderate parties. The basis of the moderating effect of the process of creating a majority has already been described in an earlier chapter dealing with the multiplicity of interests. These influences affect both major parties equally. A large party must be supported by a great variety of interests sufficiently tolerant of each other to collaborate, held together by compromise and concession, and the discovery of certain common interest, and so on, and bearing in mind the fact that a major party has only one competitor and that party managers *need not meet every demand made by every interest*. To make extreme concessions to one interest at the expense of the others is likely to be fatal to the alignment of interests that make up the constituency of a major party. The process moderates the course of party action, though the language of politics is usually immoderate. A homogeneous party might be oppressive, but the tentative aggregates of miscellaneous elements collected within the loose framework of a major party are unthinkable as instruments of tyranny. The major party cannot afford to take an extreme stand, but neither is it condemned to futility. When one stops to consider the amount of thought and energy that has been devoted to the effort to protect people against oppression, it is difficult to imagine anything more important than the tendency of the parties to avoid extreme policies.

2.   The Major Parties

THE contemporary pattern of American party politics assumes full meaning only when examined in relation to past events. The fulsome campaign oratory which extols past party leaders (and implies that the incumbent candidate is blessed with similar, if not superior, virtues) emphasizes the most banal aspect of historic continuity. It would be hard to imagine a Democratic party rally that did not refer to the g-r-e-a-t tradition of Jefferson and Jackson, or a Republican party rally that failed to honor the memory of Abraham Lincoln. But these campaign theatrics neglect the more complex and substantive forces contributing to present-day Democratic-Republican party competition.

When the Founding Fathers gathered in Philadelphia in 1787, they did not envision a party system. Consequently, the Constitution nowhere mentions or alludes to political parties. Nevertheless, with a hospitable constitutional base that granted free speech and freedom of association, as well as related freedoms, political parties arose. The origins of the American party system can in the most general terms be traced to socioeconomic divisions in the colonies, where mercantile, financial, and industrial interests ranged against debtors and independent agrarians. This cleavage carried over into the debates over the ratification of the Constitution; the proponents of a strong central government came to be known as Federalists and their opponents as Anti-Federalists. It was the Federalists who controlled the new government which was organized in the spring of 1789. Under the leadership of Alexander Hamilton, as Secretary of the Treasury, they succeeded in enacting a legislative program designed to ally the propertied class with the new government. It was Hamilton's fiscal program that provoked Thomas Jefferson, in the cabinet, and James Madison, in the House, to take counteraction. In 1791 Jefferson and Madison went on a "botanizing" excursion (recollected by the late President John F. Kennedy in his 1960 campaign) to New York and New England. Out of this journey grew the alliance between the Virginia planters and the New York politicians, among whom was Aaron Burr, leader of the Sons of Tammany. The excursion was politically as well as botanically successful. From Maine to Georgia the back-country grain growers began to combine with the mechanics and small tradesmen of the seaboard towns against the propertied merchants, manufacturers, and security holders. In the presidential election of 1792 the Republican—or as it was also called, the Democratic-Republican—party was beginning to emerge.

When George Washington in his famous Farewell Address solemnly warned "against the baneful effects of the spirit of party," he was only echoing established fear and sentiments. By then, the antiparty advice of Washington and others was of little consequence in braking forces already in motion. Political factions and groupings, as old as politics itself, were being replaced by political parties. By 1796 (the year of Washington's Farewell Address), the Republicans had become a political party; they had a structure, a following, a distinct partisan ideology, and had arranged for nominating and electioneering. In the presidential election of 1796, Federalist political hegemony was seriously challenged, and four years later the Republicans won the presidency, the Senate, and the House.

Following the Republican victory, Jefferson moderated some of his differences with the Federalists and embarked on a successful administration. Republican success was accompanied by Federalist decline; after the elections of 1816 the Federalists ceased to be a factor in national politics. The Federalists did not oppose Monroe's reelection to the presidency, and his second administration, in which party partisanship declined, has come to be known as the "Era of Good Feelings." But political factions and groups were again flourishing. Within the Republican party two factions, the "Old" and the "Young" Republicans, were crystallizing. The "Old" Republicans advocated strict construction along the lines of the Virginia and Kentucky Resolutions and opposed the War of 1812. The "Young" Republicans under the leadership of Henry Clay, John C. Calhoun, and William H. Crawford, in contrast, wanted a neo-Hamiltonian "American System" (protective tariffs, internal improvements at federal expense, perpetuation of the national bank, and a continuing public debt) and favored the War of 1812 and nationalist expansion in Canada and Spanish Florida. Factionalism and party disintegration reached their height in the election of 1824.

That year, in the absence of party competition, four Republicans—Clay, Crawford, John Quincy Adams, and Andrew Jackson—engaged in a bitter contest for the presidency. Their candidacies represented quasi-national factions and sectional interests. Jackson obtained the highest number of popular and electoral votes, but failed to obtain a majority of the electoral college. Following the requirements of the Constitution, the election was determined by the House of Representatives, where each state cast one vote. Adams was elected President, and new party lines were in the making. In the next presidential campaign Adams was soundly defeated for reelection by Jackson, who had the support of the Crawford and Calhoun groups. The Jackson forces were known as the Democratic-Republicans, while the supporters of Adams and Clay had put together a coalition known as the National Republicans. (Jacksonian Democratic-Republicans are the forebears of the present Democratic party; in 1840 at the third national convention of the Democratic-Republican party, the word "Republican" was dropped from the party title.) Jacksonian democracy and a new era in party politics had begun.

In the spring of 1834 the National Republicans and others opposed to the Democratic-Republicans joined forces to form the Whig party, under the leadership of Clay and Daniel Webster. The Whig party had little but its opposition to the Jeffersonian Democrats to hold it together. Nevertheless, despite their inability to agree on a positive party program, the Whigs were able to capture the presidency in 1840 and 1848 by using the technique (honored before and since) of nominating military heroes—William Henry Harrison and Zachary Taylor. The technique did not work, however, in 1852, when politically inept General Winfield Scott was the candidate.

By this time the issues that separated the Whigs from the Democrats were beginning to change; coming to the fore and cutting across party lines was the irrepressible issue of slavery. As the nineteenth century approached the midpoint the slavery question found political expression in the Abolitionist, the Liberty, and the Free Soil third parties. Both the Whigs and the Democrats, however, wanted to sidestep the slavery issue and avoid offending either their northern or southern supporters. The result was the passage of the Compromise of 1850 (endorsed in 1852 by both Whig and Democratic parties), which was designed to remove the slavery issue from politics. However, with the passage of the Kansas-Nebraska Act in 1854, the issue of slavery was forcibly returned to politics and the Whig party violently split into pro- and antislavery wings. Out of the slavery turmoil emerged the "Anti-Nebraska" men, the seeds of the Republican party, and the American or "Know-Nothing" party.

With the presidential election of 1856 there came about another realignment of parties. That year the Republican party had its first national convention, and although the Democrats won the election, the Republicans emerged from it as the leading opposition party. Instead of being fragmented among a multitude of groups, opposition to the Democratic party became consolidated in the Republican party. During the administration of Democrat James Buchanan, the Dred Scott decision and the bloody battles in Kansas between free-soil and slave-soil settlers kept the slavery issue boiling and precipitated a split within the Democratic party. In the 1858 midterm elections, the Democrats lost control of the House and Abraham Lincoln lost the senatorial race to Stephen Douglas but emerged as a national figure. All of this was a prelude to the great schisms of 1860 and the Civil War.

In 1860, the Republicans held their second national convention and nominated Lincoln, and the Democratic party formally split between northern and southern factions. The northern Democrats nominated Douglas and the southern Democrats nominated John Breckinridge. The party situation was further confused when the remnants of the Whig and Know-Nothing parties nominated John Bell as the candidate of the Constitutional Union party. Though the outcome of the 1860 campaign was a Republican victory, Lincoln's election did not reflect a popular mandate. He entered into the presidency with the smallest percentage of the popular vote ever polled by a winning candidate. Lincoln's election and the rupturing of the union presaged a new orientation in American politics.

After the Civil War the Republican party emerged as the dominant party, and for nearly a century the Democratic party was out of power nationally more frequently than it was in. Yet the vote differential between the parties was small. During the Civil War and Reconstruction era the Republicans were in power. From 1875 to 1897 a balance existed between the two parties; presidential elections were closely contested, and simultaneous control of the executive branch and both houses of the legislature occurred for the Democrats only in 1893–1895, and for the Republicans in 1881–1883 and 1889–1891. New forces were now operating in the country. In the states that had formed the Confederacy, the Democrats reestablished their supremacy and the "Solid South" emerged as a potent political factor. Agrarian movements and third parties were organized manifestations of the revolution that was changing the American economy and political system. As the nineteenth century closed, the smoldering tensions of the Great Barbecue emerged in the election of 1896, leading to a realignment of political positions.

In the 1892 elections the third-party Populists, on a platform appealing mainly to farmers and laborers, had polled more than a million votes, over 12 percent of the vote. Four years later, economic protest forces in the South and West gained control of the Democratic convention, disavowed the policies of Grover Cleveland and the conservative eastern wing, and united the opposition to the established order behind their nominee, William Jennings Bryan. Bryan attempted to unite the western and southern farmers with the laborers behind a platform calling for free silver, tariff reform, a graduated income tax, and prosecution of the trusts. The Republicans nominated William McKinley, who ran on a platform of fiscal rectitude, the gold standard, and a protective tariff. Although the Democrats made a substantial showing, the Republicans won and a second period of Republican ascendancy had begun.

With the first decade of the twentieth century, Republican political hegemony began to feel strains. By 1910 there was an insurgent revolt within the Republican ranks against the conservative policies of President Taft. Taft, however, attempted to consolidate his position, thereby alienating former President Theodore Roosevelt and the progressive members of the party. After Taft secured for himself the 1912 Republican nomination, the progressives deserted the party and nominated Roosevelt on the Bull Moose Progressive party ticket. The strains of industrialization and urbanization were further reflected in the presidential candidacies of Socialist Eugene V. Debs and Democrat Woodrow Wilson. The disruption within the GOP gave the Democrats control of the presidency and the Congress, and, inaugurated by Wilson's New Freedom, a period of Democratic dominance began.

But uncontested Democratic dominance was shortlived. The Progressives and the Republicans united against the Democrats for the 1916 campaign, and although Wilson was reelected, largely on the basis of popular appeal, his coattails did not cover the House of Representatives, where the Democrats lost their commanding lead. Two years later, a Republican resurgence began which presaged the 1920–1932 period of Republican rule. The election of 1920 presaged significant changes in American politics. As prosperity eclipsed progressivism, the business elements gained control of the Republican party. Torn by internecine factionalism between rural and urban elements of the party—in 1924 it took 103 ballots at the Democratic convention before John W. Davis emerged as the compromise candidate—the Democrats could not campaign successfully against "Republican prosperity." Aside from the third-party candidacy of Robert M. LaFollette, the 1924 election was a dull one. Calvin Coolidge's 1924 victory was followed four years later by another Republican victory with Herbert Hoover. But the uneven affluence of the 1920's ended abruptly with the depression, and in the polemics of politics the Republicans were held responsible for the country's economic disaster. In 1932 the Democrats led by Franklin D. Roosevelt, swept into office in another critical election which marked profound party realignment.

Under FDR, the Democrats retained control of the presidency for four elections, and in 1948 Harry S. Truman, who became President upon Roosevelt's death, succeeded in winning the office in his own right. After the conclusion of World War II, a pattern of postwar political dislocations began in the midterm elections of 1946 when the Republicans gained control of both the House and the Senate for the first time since 1932. These dislocations reached their apogee in the 1948 election. Within the Democratic party Truman was faced with disaffection from the conservative southerners who resented his civil rights program and from the followers of former Vice-President Henry A. Wallace who disliked his foreign policy. In the election, the southerners ran Dixiecrat candidates on a states' rights and white-supremacy platform, and Wallace, with the backing of a hybrid collection of liberals and left-wing radicals, ran as the candidate of the Progressive Citizens of America on a platform that attacked the Marshall Plan and called for disarmament. The outcome looked painful for the Democrats, but in a hard-driving, whistle-stop campaign, Truman successfully appealed to farmers, laborers, Negroes, and minority groups with his Fair Deal platform, and the Republicans, despite pollster predictions to the contrary, suffered their worst congressional defeat since 1932. Once reelected, however, Truman was confronted with a congressional coalition of southerners and Republicans, and was unable to bring his Fair Deal to fruition.

Republican fortunes repaired somewhat in 1950 and two years later, after a bruising intraparty fight, the Republican national convention rejected conservative "Mr. Republican" Robert A. Taft and endorsed instead popular, apolitical General Dwight D. Eisenhower. Capitalizing on a benign image and the accumulated dissatisfactions and frustrations arising from domestic strains and the burdensome stalemate in Korea, the Republicans captured both the White House and the Congress. The Democratic candidate, Adlai E. Stevenson, tried with wit and urbanity to "talk sense to the American people," but his cerebral sophistication was drowned in the bland Eisenhower aura. Although the electorate may have liked Ike in 1952, the party's lead was only a one-seat majority in the Senate and an eight-seat majority in the House. The election was a triumph for Eisenhower, not the Republican party, a fact underscored in 1954, 1956, and 1958, when congressional Republicans suffered losses.

In 1956 the parties fielded the same presidential candidates, and Ike again won a personal triumph and the dubious distinction of being the first president in 108 years to win the presidency without carrying at least one house of Congress. The election had produced another paradox in American political history: a President of one party and a Congress of another. Constitutionally prohibited from serving a third term, Eisenhower was unable to be the Republican nominee in 1960; instead the nomination went to his Vice-President, Richard M. Nixon.

Nixon's Democratic opponent was John F. Kennedy, who had won the nomination by astute strategy and hard campaigning. After a campaign highlighted by the "Great Debates," Kennedy, by the narrowest of margins, returned the White House to the Democrats. Before Kennedy's New Frontier had much chance to develop, he was tragically assassinated and Vice-President Lyndon B. Johnson ascended to the presidency. As the Democratic party nominee in 1964, Johnson faced Barry M. Goldwater. Goldwater, a staunch right-winger, by persistence and skillful organization accumulated sufficient delegate strength to win the nomination. The "modern" Republicans were disheartened and dismayed, and rightfully so. After a riotous campaign, the Republicans were crushed and the triumphant Democrats under Johnson prepared to lead the country into the Great Society.

The reading which follows, "Issue Conflict and Consensus Among Party Leaders and Followers," illustrates sampling and statistical analysis techniques and presents a number of interesting conclusions about the relation of ideology to membership in the Republican and Democratic parties.

ISSUE CONFLICT AND CONSENSUS AMONG PARTY LEADERS AND FOLLOWERS *

Herbert McClosky, Paul J. Hoffmann, Rosemary O'Hara

AMERICAN political parties are often regarded as "brokerage" organizations, weak in principle, devoid of ideology, and inclined to differ chiefly over unimportant questions. In contrast to the "ideological" parties of Europe—which supposedly appeal to their followers through sharply defined, coherent, and logically related doctrines—the American parties are thought to fit their convictions to the changing demands of the political contest. According to this view, each set of American party leaders is satisfied to play Tweedledee to the other's Tweedledum.

I. PRESSURES TOWARD UNIFORMITY AND CLEAVAGE

Although these "conclusions" are mainly derived from *a priori* analysis or from casual observations of "anecdotal" data (little systematic effect having been made so far to verify or refute them), they are often taken as confirmed—largely, one imagines, because they are compatible with certain conspicuous features of American politics. Among these features is the entrenchment of a two-party system which, by affording both parties a genuine opportunity to win elections, tempts them to appeal to as many diverse elements in the electorate as are needed to put together a majority. Since both parties want to attract support from the centrist and moderate segments of the electorate, their views on basic issues will, it is thought, tend to converge. Like giant business enterprises competing for the same market, they will be led to offer commodities that are in many respects identical. It is one thing for a small party in a multi-party system to preserve its ideological purity, quite another for a mass party in a two-party system to do so. The one has little hope of becoming a majority, and can most easily survive by remaining identified with the narrow audience from which it draws its chief supporters; the other can succeed only by accommodating the conflicting claims of many diverse groups—only, in short, by blunting ideological distinctions.

Constraints against enlarging intellectual differences also spring from the loosely confederated nature of the American party system, and from each national party's need to adjust its policies to the competing interests of the

* From Herbert McClosky, Paul J. Hoffmann, and Rosemary O'Hara, "Issue Conflict and Consensus Among Party Leaders and Followers," in *American Political Science Review* (Vol. LIV, No. 2), pp. 406-427. Reprinted by permission of the authors. Thirty-seven footnotes in the original article have been omitted.

locality, the state, and the nation. Many party units are more concerned with local than with national elections, and prefer not to be handicapped by clear-cut national programs. Every ambitious politician, moreover, hopes to achieve a *modus vivendi* tailored to the particular and often idiosyncratic complex of forces prevailing in his constituency, an objective rarely compatible with doctrinal purity. Often, too, local politics are largely non-partisan or are partisan in ways that scarcely affect the great national issues around which ideologies might be expected to form. The development and enforcement of a sharply delineated ideology is also hindered by the absence in either party of a firmly established, authoritative, and continuing organizational center empowered to decide questions of doctrine and discipline. Party affiliation is loosely defined, responsibility is weak or non-existent, and organs for indoctrinating or communicating with party members are at best rudimentary.

Cultural and historical differences may also contribute to the weaker ideological emphasis among American, as compared with European, parties. Many of the great historical cleavages that have divided European nations for centuries—monarchism *vs.* republicanism; clericalism *vs.* anti-clericalism; democracy *vs.* autocracy, etc.—have never taken root in this country. Apart from the slavery (and subsequently the race) issue, the United States has not experienced the intense class or caste conflict often found abroad, and contests of the capitalism *vs.* socialism variety have never achieved an important role in American politics. In addition, never having known a titled nobility, we have largely been freed from the conflicts found elsewhere between the classes of inherited and acquired privilege.

Consider, too, the progress made in the United States toward neutralizing the forces which ordinarily lead to sharp social, and hence intellectual and political, differentiation. The class and status structure of American society has attained a rate of mobility equalling or exceeding that of any other long established society. Popular education, and other facilities for the creation of common attitudes, have been developed on a scale unequalled elsewhere. Improvements in transportation and communication, and rapid shifts in population and industry have weakened even sectionalism as a source of political cleavage. Rural-urban differences continue to exist, of course, but they too have been diminishing in force and have become less salient for American politics than the differences prevailing, for example, between a French peasant proprietor and a Parisian *boulevardier*. In short, a great many Americans have been subjected in their public lives to identical stimuli—a condition unlikely to generate strong, competing ideologies.

The research reported here was designed not to refute these observations but to test the accuracy of the claim that they are sufficient to prevent differences in outlook from taking root in the American party system. We believed that the homogenizing tendencies referred to are strongly offset by contrary influences, and that voters are preponderantly led to support the party whose opinions they share. We further thought that the competition for office, though giving rise to similarities between the parties, also impels them to diverge from each other in order to sharpen their respective appeals. For this and other reasons, we expected to find that the leaders of the two parties, instead of ignoring differences alleged to exist within the electorate, would differ on issues more sharply than their followers would. We believed further that even in a brokerage system the parties would serve as independent reference groups, developing norms, values, and self-images to which their supporters could readily respond. Their influence, we felt, would frequently exceed that of ethnic, occupational, residential and other reference groups. In sum, we proceeded on the belief that the parties are not simply spokesmen for other interest groups, but are in their own right agencies for formulating, transmitting, and anchoring political opinions, that they attract adherents who in general share those opinions, and that through a feedback process of mutual reinforcement between the organization and its typical supporters, the parties develop integrated and stable political tendencies. Other hypotheses will be specified as we present and analyze our findings.

II. PROCEDURES

The questions considered in this paper were part of a large field study made in 1957-1958 on the nature, sources, and correlates of political affiliation, activity, and belief in the American party system (hereafter referred to as the PAB study). Pilot studies on Minnesota samples had led us to suspect that many "settled" notions about party affiliation and belief in America would not stand up under careful empirical scrutiny; further, we felt that little progress would be made in the exploration of this subject until a comprehensive portrait of party membership in America had been drawn. Accordingly, a nationwide study was launched to acquire a detailed description of party leaders and supporters, gathering data on their backgrounds, political experiences, personality characteristics, values, motivations, social and political attitudes, outlooks on key issues, and related matters.

For our samples of party "leaders" we turned to the Democratic and Republican national conventions, largely because they are the leading and most representative of the party organs, their delegates coming from every part of the United States and from every level of party and government activity. Our samples ranged from governors, senators, and national committeemen at the one end to precinct workers and local officials at the other. In the absence of comprehensive information about the characteristics of the party élites in America, no one can say how closely the convention delegates mirror the total party leadership. We felt it fair to assume, nevertheless, that the delegates represented as faithful a cross section of American party leadership as could be had without an extraordinary expenditure of money and labor. Using convention delegates as our universe of leaders also held some obvious advantages for research, since the composition of this universe (by name, address, party, state, sex, place of residence, and party or public office) can usually be ascertained from the convention calls. Of the 6,848 delegates and alternates available to be sampled, 3,193 actually participated; 3,020 (1,788 Democrats and 1,232 Republicans) completed and returned questionnaires that were usable in all respects. The proportion of returns was roughly equivalent for both sets of party leaders.

The rank and file sample, which we wanted both for its intrinsic value and for its utility as a control group, was obtained by special arrangement with the American Institute of Public Opinion. In January 1958, Gallup interviewers personally distributed our questionnaire to 2,917 adult voters in two successive national cross-section surveys. Some 1,610 questionnaires were filled out and returned, of which 1,484 were completely usable. This sample closely matched the national population on such characteristics as sex, age, region, size of city, and party affiliation, and, though it somewhat oversampled the upper educational levels, we considered it sufficiently large and representative for most of our purposes. Of the 1,484 respondents, 821 were Democratic supporters (629 "pure" Democrats, plus 192 whom we classified as "independent" Democrats) and 623 were Republican supporters (479 "pure" Republicans, plus 144 "independent" Republicans). Forty respondents could not be identified as adherents of either party.

The lengthy questionnaire developed for the study was designed to be self-administered. It contained, in addition to questions on the respondents' personal backgrounds, a number of queries on their political history and experience, their attitudes toward the party system and toward such related matters as party organization, discipline and responsibility, their self-images with regard to social class and liberalism-conservatism, their reference group identifications, and their views on party leadership and ideology. The largest part of the questionnaire consisted of 390 scale items, randomly arranged, which when sorted and scored fell into 47 scales for measuring the personality, attitude, and value characteristics of each of the respondents. We had validated and used all but three of these scales in earlier studies.

The questions most relevant for the present article were those which asked each respondent to express his attitudes toward twenty-four important national issues, and to state whether he believed support for each issue should be "increased," "decreased," or "remain as is." The list of issues and the responses of each sample will be found in Tables II-a through II-e, where for convenience of analysis, the issues have been grouped under five broad headings: Public Ownership, Government Regulation of the Economy, Equalitarianism and Human Welfare, Tax Policy and Foreign Policy.

In tabulating the results, we first scored each individual on each issue and then computed aggregate scores for all the members of a given sample. To begin with, percentages were used to show the proportion who favored increasing, decreasing, or retaining the existing level of support on each issue. But as it was clumsy to handle three figures for each issue, we constructed a single index or "ratio of support" which would simultaneously take account of all three scores. The index was built by assigning a weight of 1.0 to each "increase" response in the sample, of 0 to each "decrease" response, and of .50 to each "remain as is" (or "same") response. Thus the ratio-of-support score shown for any given sample is in effect a mean score with a possible range of 0 to 1.0, in which support for an issue increases as the scores approach 1.0 and decreases as they approach 0. In general, the scores can be taken to approximate the following over-all positions: .0 to .25—strongly wish to reduce support;

.26 to .45—wish to reduce support; .46 to .55—satisfied with the *status quo;* .56 to .75—wish to increase support; and .76 to 1.00—strongly wish to increase support. Note that the differences in degree suggested by these categories refer not to the *strength of feeling* exhibited by individuals toward an issue but rather to the *numbers of people* in a sample who hold points of view favoring or opposing that issue.

Because they include "same" and "no code" as well as "increase" and "decrease" responses, our ratios of support sometimes flatten the differences between groups. Had we employed only the percentage scores for the "increase" or "decrease" responses, the differences between samples would in many instances have seemed larger. Nevertheless, the ratio of support offers so many advantages that we have employed it as our principal measure. For one thing, as the equivalent of a mean score, it takes into account all scores, omitting no respondent from the tabulation. For the same reason it enables us to assess the mount of dispersion or homogeneity exhibited by any sample and makes it easy to calculate significances of difference. Reliance upon a single, uniform statistic also allows us to make ready comparisons not only *between* but *within* samples, and to determine quickly how large the differences actually are. By observing whether a ratio of support is above or below .50 we can see at once whether a particular group predominantly favors or opposes the issue in question, and how strongly it does so. The use of ratio scores also makes it possible to compare issues as well as groups, *e.g.,* to see whether one issue is more preferred than another.

For further information on the meaning of the issue responses, we also compared samples on a number of related scales and items. Tabulating and statistical operations were carried out to control for demographic influences like education, occupation, age, and sectionalism; to ascertain homogeneity of opinion within the several samples; to rank the issues according to the magnitude of the differences between samples; to compare members' positions on issues against official platform statements; and to determine whether leaders and followers are able to name the issues which actually divide the parties. Some of the findings yielded by these operations will be considered here, while others, for reasons of space, will have to be reserved for future publications.

A word of caution before we turn to the findings. The respondents were offered only the twenty-four issues that impressed us in February, 1957, as most significant and enduring. However, they may not all be as salient today as they seemed at that time. Nor, within the limitations of a single questionnaire, could we explore every issue that informed observers might have considered important. Some presumably vital issues such as states rights, political centralization, and expansion of government functions could not be stated explicitly enough within our format to be tested properly. These are issues that are so generalized as to encompass many other specific issues, and so highly charged as to awaken a profusion of symbolic and emotive associations.

The *form* of our issue questions may also be open to criticism, for space limitations prevented our subjects from indicating how strongly they felt and how much they knew about each of the issues. This deficiency, however, may be less important than it appears, since for the groups we most wanted to compare (*e.g.,* Democratic *vs.* Republican leaders), the degree of political knowledge and intensity is likely to be rather similar. The difficulty is greater when comparing leaders with followers, but is somewhat offset by controlling for education and socio-economic status. Although some subtleties of interpretation are bound to be lost because these variables have been omitted, we are satisfied that our issue questions in their present form furnish a useful measure for assessing *group* (as distinguished from *individual*) opinion.

Finally, one may wonder about the value of opinions stated on a questionnaire compared with the worth of views formally expressed by an organization or implicit in the actions of its leaders. Advantages can be cited on both sides. The beliefs expressed in official party statements or in legislative roll calls, it might be claimed, represent the *operating* beliefs of the organization by virtue

TABLE I. AVERAGE DIFFERENCES IN THE RATIO-OF-SUPPORT SCORES AMONG PARTY LEADERS AND FOLLOWERS FOR FIVE CATEGORIES OF ISSUES

CATEGORY OF ISSUES	DEMOCRATIC LEADERS vs. REPUBLICAN LEADERS	DEMOCRATIC FOLLOWERS vs. REPUBLICAN FOLLOWERS	DEMOCRATIC LEADERS vs. DEMOCRATIC FOLLOWERS	REPUBLICAN LEADERS vs. REPUBLICAN FOLLOWERS	DEMOCRATIC LEADERS vs. REPUBLICAN FOLLOWERS	REPUBLICAN LEADERS vs. DEMOCRATIC FOLLOWERS
a. Public Ownership of Resources	.28	.04	.06	.18	.10	.22
b. Government Regulation of the Economy	.22	.06	.08	.10	.12	.16
c. Equalitarianism, Human Welfare	.22	.05	.08	.21	.06	.25
d. Tax Policy	.20	.06	.06	.20	.04	.26
e. Foreign Policy	.15	.02	.05	.08	.07	.10
Average Differences in Ratio Scores for all Categories	.21	.04	.07	.15	.08	.20

Sample Sizes: Democratic Leaders, 1,788; Republican Leaders, 1,232; Democratic Followers, 821; Republican Followers, 623.

of having been tested in the marketplace or in the competition of legislative struggle. Positions taken on issues on which a party stakes its future may be more valid evidence of what the party truly believes than are the opinions expressed by individual members under conditions of maximum safety. On the other hand, the responses to the issue and attitude questions in the PAB study represent the anonymous, private opinions of party leaders and followers, uncomplicated by any need to make political capital, to proselytize, to conciliate critics, or to find grounds for embarrassing the opposition at the next election. Hence they may for some purposes represent the most accurate possible reflection of the "actual" state of party opinion. The controversy over the value of the two approaches is to some extent spurious, however, for they offer different perspectives on the same thing. In addition, considerable correspondence exists between the party positions evident in congressional roll calls and the privately expressed opinions of the party leaders in our study.

III. FINDINGS: COMPARISONS BETWEEN LEADERS

No more conclusive findings emerge from our study of party issues than those growing out of the comparisons between the two sets of party leaders. Despite the brokerage tendency of the American parties, their active members are obviously separated by large and important differences. The differences, moreover, conform with the popular image in which the Democratic party is seen as the more "progressive" or "radical," the Republican as the more "moderate" or "conservative" of the two. In addition, the disagreements are remarkably consistent, a function not of chance but of systematic points of view, whereby the responses to any one of the issues could reasonably have been predicted from knowledge of the responses to the other issues.

Examination of Tables II-a-e and III shows that the leaders differ significantly on 23 of the 24 issues listed and that they are separated on 15 of these issues by .18 or more ratio points—in short, by differences that are in absolute magnitude very large. The two samples are furthest apart in their attitudes toward public ownership and are especially divided on the question of government ownership of natural resources, the Democrats strongly favoring it, the Republicans just as strongly wanting it cut back. The difference of .39 in the ratio scores is the largest for any of the issues tested. In percentages, the differences are 58 per cent (D) vs. 13 per cent (R) in favor of increasing support, and 19 per cent (D) vs. 52 per cent (R) in favor of decreasing support. Both parties

TABLE II-A. COMPARISON OF PARTY LEADERS AND FOLLOWERS ON "PUBLIC OWNERSHIP" ISSUES, BY PERCENTAGES AND RATIOS OF SUPPORT

ISSUES	LEADERS		FOLLOWERS	
	DEM. N = 1,788	REPUB. N = 1,232	DEM. N = 821	REPUB. N = 623
		(%s down)		
Public Ownership of Natural Resources				
% favoring: Increase	57.5	12.9	35.3	31.1
Decrease	18.6	51.9	15.0	19.9
Same, n.c.*	23.8	35.2	49.7	49.0
Support Ratio	.69	.30	.60	.56
Public Control of Atomic Energy				
% favoring: Increase	73.2	45.0	64.2	59.4
Decrease	7.2	15.3	7.1	10.0
Same, n.c.	19.6	39.7	28.7	30.6
Support Ratio	.83	.65	.79	.75
Mean Support Ratios for the Public Ownership Category	.76	.48	.70	.66

* n.c. = no code.

TABLE II-B. COMPARISON OF PARTY LEADERS AND FOLLOWERS ON "GOVERNMENT REGULATION OF THE ECONOMY" ISSUES, BY PERCENTAGES AND RATIOS OF SUPPORT

ISSUES	LEADERS		FOLLOWERS	
	DEM. N = 1,788	REPUB. N = 1,232	DEM. N = 821	REPUB. N = 623
		(%s down)		
Level of Farm Price Supports				
% favoring: Increase	43.4	6.7	39.0	23.0
Decrease	28.1	67.4	27.6	40.3
Same, n.c.	28.5	25.8	33.4	36.7
Support Ratio	.58	.20	.56	.41
Government Regulation of Business				
% favoring: Increase	20.2	0.6	18.6	7.4
Decrease	38.5	84.1	33.4	46.2
Same, n.c.	41.3	15.3	48.0	46.4
Support Ratio	.41	.08	.43	.31
Regulation of Public Utilities				
% favoring: Increase	59.0	17.9	39.3	26.0
Decrease	6.4	17.6	11.1	12.0
Same, n.c.	34.6	64.5	49.6	62.0
Support Ratio	.76	.50	.64	.57
Enforcement of Anti-Monopoly Laws				
% favoring: Increase	78.0	44.9	53.2	51.0
Decrease	2.9	9.0	7.9	6.6
Same, n.c.	19.1	46.1	38.9	42.4
Support Ratio	.88	.68	.73	.72
Regulation of Trade Unions				
% favoring: Increase	59.3	86.4	46.6	57.8
Decrease	12.4	4.5	8.9	10.6
Same, n.c.	28.3	9.2	44.5	31.6
Support Ratio	.73	.91	.69	.74
Level of Tariffs				
% favoring: Increase	13.0	19.2	16.6	15.2
Decrease	43.0	26.3	25.3	21.3
Same, n.c.	43.9	54.5	58.1	63.4
Support Ratio	.35	.46	.46	.47
Restrictions on Credit				
% favoring: Increase	24.8	20.6	26.1	25.7
Decrease	39.3	20.6	22.2	23.8
Same, n.c.	35.9	58.8	51.8	50.5
Support Ratio	.43	.50	.52	.51
Mean Support Ratios for "Government Regulation of the Economy" Category	.59	.48	.58	.53

TABLE II-C. COMPARISON OF PARTY LEADERS AND FOLLOWERS ON "EQUALITARIAN AND HUMAN WELFARE" ISSUES, BY PERCENTAGES AND RATIOS OF SUPPORT

ISSUES	LEADERS		FOLLOWERS	
	DEM. N = 1,788	REPUB. N = 1,232	DEM. N = 821	REPUB. N = 623
		(%s down)		
Federal Aid to Education				
% favoring: Increase	66.2	22.3	74.9	64.8
Decrease	13.4	43.2	5.6	8.3
Same, n.c.	20.4	34.5	19.5	26.8
Support Ratio	.76	.40	.85	.78
Slum Clearance and Public Housing				
% favoring: Increase	78.4	40.1	79.5	72.5
Decrease	5.6	21.6	5.8	7.9
Same, n.c.	16.0	38.3	14.6	19.6
Support Ratio	.86	.59	.87	.82
Social Security Benefits				
% favoring: Increase	60.0	22.5	69.4	57.0
Decrease	3.9	13.1	3.0	3.8
Same, n.c.	36.1	64.4	27.5	39.2
Support Ratio	.78	.55	.83	.77
Minimum Wages				
% favoring: Increase	50.0	15.5	59.0	43.5
Decrease	4.7	12.5	2.9	5.0
Same, n.c.	45.2	72.0	38.1	51.5
Support Ratio	.73	.52	.78	.69
Enforcement of Integration				
% favoring: Increase	43.8	25.5	41.9	40.8
Decrease	26.6	31.7	27.4	23.6
Same, n.c.	29.5	42.8	30.7	35.6
Support Ratio	.59	.47	.57	.59
Immigration into United States				
% favoring: Increase	36.1	18.4	10.4	8.0
Decrease	27.0	29.9	52.0	44.6
Same, n.c.	36.9	51.7	37.6	47.4
Support Ratio	.54	.44	.29	.32
Mean Support Ratios for "Equalitarian and Human Welfare" Category	.71	.50	.70	.66

preponderantly support public control and development of atomic energy, but the Democrats do so more uniformly.

V. O. Key, among others, has observed that the Republican party is especially responsive to the "financial and manufacturing community," reflect-

TABLE II-D. COMPARISON OF PARTY LEADERS AND FOLLOWERS ON "TAX POLICY" ISSUES, BY PERCENTAGES AND RATIOS OF SUPPORT

ISSUES	LEADERS		FOLLOWERS	
	DEM. N = 1,788	REPUB. N = 1,232	DEM. N = 821	REPUB. N = 623
		(%s down)		
Corporate Income Tax				
% favoring: Increase	32.3	4.0	32.0	23.3
Decrease	23.3	61.5	20.5	25.7
Same, n.c.	44.4	34.5	47.5	51.0
Support Ratio	.54	.21	.56	.49
Tax on Large Incomes				
% favoring: Increase	27.0	5.4	46.6	34.7
Decrease	23.1	56.9	13.8	21.7
Same, n.c.	49.9	37.7	39.6	43.6
Support Ratio	.52	.24	.66	.56
Tax on Business				
% favoring: Increase	12.6	1.0	24.6	15.9
Decrease	38.3	71.1	24.1	32.6
Same, n.c.	49.1	27.8	51.3	51.5
Support Ratio	.37	.15	.50	.42
Tax on Middle Incomes				
% favoring: Increase	2.7	0.8	4.5	3.0
Decrease	50.2	63.9	49.3	44.3
Same, n.c.	47.1	35.3	46.2	52.6
Support Ratio	.26	.18	.28	.29
Tax on Small Incomes				
% favoring: Increase	1.4	2.9	1.6	2.1
Decrease	79.2	65.0	77.5	69.6
Same, n.c.	19.4	32.1	20.9	28.3
Support Ratio	.11	.19	.12	.16
Mean Support Ratios for "Tax Policy" Category	.36	.19	.42	.38

ing the view that government should intervene as little as possible to burden or restrain prevailing business interests. The validity of this observation is evident throughout all our data, and is most clearly seen in the responses to the issues listed under Government Regulation of the Economy, Equalitarianism and Human Welfare, Tax Policy. Democratic leaders are far more eager than Republican leaders to strengthen enforcement of anti-monopoly laws and to increase regulation of public utilities and business. Indeed, the solidarity of Republican opposition to the regulation of business is rather overwhelming: 84 per cent want to decrease such regulation and fewer than .01 per cent say they want to increase it. Although the Democrats, on balance, also feel that

TABLE II-E. COMPARISON OF PARTY LEADERS AND FOLLOWERS ON "FOREIGN POLICY" ISSUES, BY PERCENTAGES AND RATIOS OF SUPPORT

ISSUES	LEADERS		FOLLOWERS	
	DEM. N = 1,788	REPUB. N = 1,232	DEM. N = 821	REPUB. N = 623
		(%s down)		
Reliance on the United Nations				
% favoring: Increase	48.9	24.4	34.7	33.4
Decrease	17.6	34.8	17.3	19.3
Same, n.c.	33.5	40.7	48.0	47.3
Support Ratio	.66	.45	.59	.57
American Participation in Military Alliances				
% favoring: Increase	41.5	22.7	39.1	32.3
Decrease	17.6	25.7	14.0	15.4
Same, n.c.	40.9	51.6	46.9	52.3
Support Ratio	.62	.48	.62	.58
Foreign Aid				
% favoring: Increase	17.8	7.6	10.1	10.1
Decrease	51.0	61.7	58.6	57.3
Same, n.c.	31.1	30.7	31.3	32.6
Support Ratio	.33	.23	.26	.26
Defense Spending				
% favoring: Increase	20.7	13.6	50.5	45.7
Decrease	34.4	33.6	16.4	15.4
Same, n.c.	44.8	52.8	33.0	38.8
Support Ratio	.43	.40	.67	.65
Mean Support Ratios for "Foreign Policy" Category (excl. Defense Spending)	.54	.39	.49	.47

government controls on business should not be expanded further, the differences between the two samples on this issue are nevertheless substantial.

The two sets of leaders are also far apart on the farm issue, the Democrats preferring slightly to increase farm supports, the Republicans wanting strongly to reduce them. The Republican ratio score of .20 on this issue is among the lowest in the entire set of scores. The magnitude of these scores somewhat surprised us, for while opposition to agricultural subsidies is consistent with Republican dislike for state intervention, we had expected the leaders to conform more closely to the familiar image of the Republican as the more "rural" of the two parties. It appears, however, that the party's connection with business is far more compelling than its association with agriculture. The Republican desire to reduce government expenditures and to promote independence from "government handouts" prevails on the farm question as it does on other issues, while the Democratic preference for a more regulated economy in which government intervenes to reduce economic risk and to stabilize prosperity is equally evident on the other side. Party attitudes on this issue appear to be determined as much by ideological tendencies as by deliberate calculation of the political advantages to be gained by favoring or opposing subsidies to farmers. Comparison of our findings with Turner's earlier data on farm votes in Congress suggests, in addition, that the sharp party difference on the farm issue is neither a recent development nor a mere product of the personal philosophy of the present Secretary of Agriculture.

Having implied that agricultural policies partly result from principle, we must note that on three other issues in this category (trade unions, credit, and tariffs), principle seems to be overweighed by old-fashioned economic considerations. In spite of their distaste for government interference in economic affairs, the Republicans almost unanimously favor greater regulation of trade unions and they are more strongly disposed than the Democrats toward government intervention to restrict credit and to raise tariffs. Of course, party cleavages over the credit and tariff issues have a long history, which may by now have endowed them with ideological force beyond immediate economic considerations. The preponderant Democratic preference for greater regulation of trade unions is doubtless a response to recent "exposures" of corrupt labor practices, though it may also signify that the party's perspective toward the trade unions is shifting somewhat.

The closer Republican identification with business, free enterprise, and economic conservatism in general, and the friendlier Democratic attitude toward labor and toward government regulation of the economy, are easily observed in the data from other parts of our questionnaire. Republican leaders score very much higher than Democratic leaders on, for example, such scales as economic conservatism, independence of government, and business attitudes. On a question asking respondents to indicate the groups from which they would be most and least likely to take advice, 41 per cent of the Democratic leaders but only 3.8 per cent of the Republican leaders list trade unions as groups from which they would seek advice. Trade unions are scored in the "least likely" category by 25 per cent of the Democrats and 63 per cent of the Republicans. Similarly, more than 94 per cent of the Republican leaders, but 56 per cent of the Democratic leaders, name trade unions as groups that have "too much power." These differences, it should be noted, cannot be accounted for by reference to the greater number of trade union members among the Democratic party leadership, for in the 1956 conventions only 14 per cent of the Democrats belonged to trade unions, and while an even smaller percentage (4 per cent) of the Republicans were trade unionists, this disparity is hardly great enough to explain the large differences in outlook. The key to the explanation has to be sought in the symbolic and reference group identifications of the two parties, and in their underlying values.

Nowhere do we see this more clearly than in the responses to the Equalitarian and Human Welfare issues. The mean difference in the ratio scores for the category as a whole is .22, a very large difference and one that results from differences in the expected direction on all six issues that make up the category. On four of these issues—federal aid to education, slum clearance and public housing, social security, and minimum wages—the leaders of the two parties are widely separated, the differences in their ratio scores ranging from .36 to .21. The percentages showing the proportions who favor increased support for these issues are even more striking. In every instance the Democratic percentages are considerably higher: 66 *vs.* 22 per cent (education); 78 *vs.* 40 per cent (slum clearance and housing); 60 *vs.* 23 per cent (social security); and 50 *vs.* 16 per cent (minimum wages). The Democratic leaders also are better disposed than the Republican leaders toward immigration: twice as many of them (36 per cent *vs.* 18 per cent) favor a change in policy to permit more immigrants to enter. The over-all inclination of both party élites, however, is to accept the present levels of immigration, the Democratic ratio score falling slightly above, and the Republican slightly below, the midpoint.

More surprising are the differences on the segregation issue, for despite strong Southern influence, the Democratic leaders express significantly more support for enforcing integration than the Republicans do. Moreover, the difference between the two parties rises from .12 for the national samples as a whole to a difference of .18 when the southern leaders are excluded. In his study of Congress, Turner found that the Republicans gave more support to Negro rights than the Democrats did. The reversal of this finding in our data does not necessarily mean that a change has occurred since Turner made his study, but only that the votes of the congressional parties do not always reflect the private feelings of the national party leadership. Then, too, Southern influence is disproportionately stronger in the Democratic congressional party than in the national Democratic organization as a whole, and disporportionately weaker in the Republican congressional party than in the Republican organization as a whole.

Examination of the actual magnitude of the ratio scores in this category reveals that the Republicans want not so much to abrogate existing social welfare or equalitarian measures as to keep them from being broadened. The Democrats, by comparison, are shown to be the party of social equality and reform, more willing than their opponents to employ legislation for the benefit of the underprivileged. Support for these inferences and for the greater liberalism of the Democrats can be found elsewhere in our data as well. Analysis of the scale results show Republican leaders scoring higher than Democratic leaders on such measures as chauvinism, élitism, conservatism, and right-wing values, and lower on tolerance, procedural rights, and faith in democracy. No differences worth noting, however, were found for ethnocentrism, faith in freedom, or the California F scale. The Democrats had a slightly higher average score on the left-wing scale, but the number of leaders in either party who scored high on this measure was fairly small.

The self-images and reference group identifications of the two parties also should be noted in this connection. For example, many more Democratic than Republican leaders call themselves liberal and state that they would be most likely to take advice from liberal reform organizations, the Farmers' Union, and (as we have seen) from the trade unions; only a small number consider themselves conservative or would seek advice from conservative reform organizations, the National Association of Manufacturers, or the Farm Bureau Federation. The Republicans have in almost all instances the reverse identifications; only a handful regard themselves as liberal or would seek counsel from liberal organizations, while more than 42 per cent call themselves conservative and would look to the NAM or to conservative reform organizations for advice. Almost two-thirds of the Republicans (compared with 29 per cent of the Democrats) regard the Chamber of Commerce as an important source of advice. Businessmen are listed as having "too much power" by 42 per cent of the Democrats but only by 9 per cent of the Republicans. The Democrats are also significantly more inclined than the Republicans to consider Catholics, Jews, and the foreign born as having "too little power." While self-descriptions and reference group identifications often correspond poorly with actual beliefs—among the general population they scarcely correspond at all, in fact—we are dealing, in the case of the leaders, with a politically informed and highly articulate set of people who have little difficulty connecting the beliefs they hold and the groups that promote or obstruct those beliefs.

Our fourth category, Tax Policy, divides the parties almost as severely as do the other categories. The mean difference for the category as a whole is .20, and it would doubtless have been larger but for the universal unpopularity of proposals to increase taxes on small and middle income groups. . . . The differences between the parties on the tax issues follow the patterns previously observed and tax policy is for the Democrats a device for redistributing income and promoting social equality. Neither party, however, is keen about raising taxes for *any* group: even the Democrats have little enthusiasm for new taxes on upper income groups or on business and corporate enterprises. The Republican leaders are overwhelmingly opposed to increased taxes for *any* group, rich *or* poor. This can be seen in their low ratio scores on the tax issues, which range from only .15 to .24. But while they are far more eager than the Democratic leaders to cut taxes on corporate and private wealth, they are less willing to reduce taxes on the lower income groups. These differences, it should be remarked, are not primarily a function of differences in the income of the two samples. Although there are more people with high incomes among the Republican leaders, the disproportion between the two samples is not nearly great enough to account for the dissimilarities in their tax views.

Of the five categories considered, Foreign Policy shows the smallest average difference, but even on these issues the divergence between Democratic and Republican leader attitudes is significant. Except for defense spending the Democrats turn out to be more internationalist than the Republicans, as evidenced in their greater commitment to the United Nations and to American participation in international military alliances like NATO. Twice as many Democrats as Republicans want the United States to rely more heavily upon such organizations, while many more Republicans want to reduce our international involvements. Both parties are predominantly in favor of cutting back foreign aid—a somewhat surprising finding in light of Democratic public pronouncements on this subject—but more Republicans feel strongly on the subject. Our data thus furnish little support for the claim that the parties hold the same views on foreign policy or that their seeming differences are merely a response to the demands of political competition.

Nevertheless, it would be incorrect to conclude that one party believes in internationalism and the other in isolationism. The differences are far too small to warrant any such inference. Traces of isolationism, to be sure, remain stronger in the Republican party than in the Democratic party—an observation buttressed by the finding that twice as many Republicans as Democrats score high on the isolationism scale. The pattern of Republican responses on both the issue and scale items signifies, however, that the leaders of that party generally accept the degree of "internationalism" now in effect, but shrink from extending it further. Consider too, the similarities in the leaders' scores on defense spending, for despite their greater leaning toward isolationism, the Republicans are no more inclined than the Democrats to leave the country defenseless.

In treating issues in the Elmira election study of 1948, Berelson, Lazarsfeld, and McPhee found it helpful to distinguish between "style" and "position" issues. "Style" issues principally yield symbolic, psychological, or subjective gratifications, and have relatively intangible consequences; "position" issues reflect direct, personal and material interests, and have more objective consequences. According to the Elmira report, "position" issues (or what politicians might call "bread and butter" issues) divide voters more sharply than style issues. Most of the issues tested in the present study would have to be classified as "position" issues, but five of them—United Nations, international alliances, foreign aid, immigration, and segregation—could be classified as style issues. Four others—natural resources, atomic energy, education, and slum clearance—contain both symbolic and material elements and can best be described as "mixed."

Although the classification is crude, the findings it yields are generally consistent with the claims of the Elmira study. On the fourteen position issues—taxes, trade unions, tariffs, minimum wages, farm prices, social security, credit restrictions, and the regulation of business, public utilities and monopolies—Democratic and Republican leaders show an average ratio score difference of .21. On the style issues the two parties differ by .13—a significantly smaller difference. Largest of all, however, are the differences for the "mixed" issues, which average more than .30. This result should occasion little surprise, for when ideology and interest are *both* at work, partisanship is likely to be intensified. Several considerations could account for the superiority of position over style issues as causes of political cleavage: they are "bread and butter" issues, and are thus more often subject to pressure by organized interest groups; they have immediate and tangible consequences, which may lead politicians to pay greater attention to them than they do to issues whose payoff is more uncertain; and, finally, they are not so likely to be part of the common core of values upon which the community structure rests.

Comparison of the magnitude of the differences between groups can be seen in Table III, p. 55, where we have ranked the issues, high to low, according to the size of the difference between the groups being compared. By presenting a rank-order of differences for the two leader groups, for the two follower groups, and for the leaders and followers of each party, this table makes it possible to observe not only which issues most and least divide the several party groups, but whether they divide the leaders and followers in the same way.

Notice that the issues commonly thought to be most divisive do not always evoke the greatest cleavage between the parties. Immigration, tariffs, civil rights, monopoly control, and credit regulation fall toward the lower end of the rank order, while farm supports, federal aid to education, slum clearance, social security, minimum wages, public housing, and issues dealing with the regulation and taxation of business fall toward the upper end. Though by no means uniformly, the older, more traditional issues appear to have been superseded as sources of controversy by issues that have come into prominence chiefly during the New Deal and Fair Deal.

IV. COMPARISONS BETWEEN FOLLOWERS

So far we have addressed ourselves to the differences between Democratic and Republican *leaders*. In each of the tables presented, however, data are included from which the two sets of party *followers* may also be compared.

The observation most clearly warranted from these data is that the rank and file members of the two parties are far less divided than their leaders. Not only do they diverge significantly on fewer issues—seven as compared with 23 for the leader samples—but the magnitudes of the differences in their ratio scores are substantially smaller for every one of the 24 issues. No difference is larger than .14, and on the majority of the issues the disparity is smaller than .05. Insofar as they differ at all, however, the followers tend to divide in a pattern similar to that shown by the leaders, the correlation between their rank orders being .72. All the issues on which the followers significantly disagree are of the "bread and butter" variety, the more symbolic issues being so remotely experienced and so vaguely grasped that rank and file voters are often unable to identify them with either party. Policies affecting farm prices, business regulation, taxes, or minimum wages, by contrast, are quickly felt by the groups to whom they are addressed and are therefore more capable of arousing partisan identifications. It should also be noted that while the average differences are small for all five categories, they are smallest of all for foreign policy—the most removed and least well understood group of issues in the entire array.

Democratic and Republican followers were also compared on a number of scales and reference group questions. The results, while generally consistent with the differences between the leaders, show the followers to be far more

TABLE III. RANK ORDER OF DIFFERENCES IN THE SUPPORT-RATIO SCORES OF PARTY LEADERS AND FOLLOWERS *

DEMOCRATIC vs. REPUBLICAN LEADERS — DIFF. BETWEEN RATIO SCORES***	ISSUES	DEMOCRATIC vs. REPUBLICAN FOLLOWERS — DIFF. BETWEEN RATIO SCORES	ISSUES	DEMOCRATIC LEADERS vs. FOLLOWERS — DIFF. BETWEEN RATIO SCORES	ISSUES	REPUBLICAN LEADERS vs. FOLLOWERS — DIFF. BETWEEN RATIO SCORES	ISSUES
+.39	1. Natural Resources	+.14	Farm Supports	+.25	Immigration	−.39	Fed. Aid to Edu.
+.38	2. Farm Supports	+.12	Gov't. Reg. of Business	+.15	Anti-Monopoly	−.32	Taxes-Large Income
+.37	3. Fed. Aid to Edu.	+.10	Taxes-Large Income	−.15	Taxes-Large Income	−.28	Taxes-Corp.
+.33	4. Taxes-Corp.	+.09	Minimum Wages	−.13	Taxes-Business	−.27	Taxes-Business
+.33	5. Reg.-Business	+.07	Taxes-Business	+.12	Reg. Pub. Util.	−.25	Natural Resources
+.28	6. Taxes-Large Inc.	+.07	Reg. Pub. Util.	−.11	Tariffs	−.23	Pub. Housing
+.27	7. Pub. Housing	+.07	Taxes-Corp.	−.09	Restrict. Credit	−.22	Reg. Business
+.26	8. Reg. Pub. Util.	+.06	Social Security	+.09	Natural Resources	−.22	Social Security
+.23	9. Social Security	−.05	Fed. Aid to Edu.	−.08	Fed. Aid to Edu.	−.22	Farm Supports
+.22	10. Taxes-Business	+.05	Reg. Trade Unions	+.08	Foreign Aid	−.18	Minimum Wages
+.21	11. Minimum Wages	+.05	Natural Resources	+.07	Reliance on U.N.	+.17	Reg. Trade Unions
+.21	12. Reliance on U.N.	−.04	Public Housing	−.05	Minimum Wages	+.13	Immigration
+.20	13. Anti-monopoly	+.04	Taxes-Small Income	−.05	Social Security	−.12	Reliance on U.N.
+.18	14. Atomic Energy Control	+.04	American Participation, NATO	+.05	Reg. Trade Unions	−.12	Enforce Integration
−.18	15. Reg. Trade Unions	−.03	Atomic Energy Control	+.04	Atomic Energy Control	−.11	Taxes-Middle Income
+.13	16. American Participation, NATO	+.02	Immigration	+.02	Farm Supports	−.10	Atomic Energy Control
+.12	17. Enforce Integration	+.02	Defense Spending	−.02	Reg. Business	−.10	American Participation, NATO
−.11	18. Tariffs	−.02	Taxes-Middle Income	+.01	Enforce Integration	−.07	Reg. Public Utilities
+.10	19. Foreign Aid	+.02	Reliance on U.N.	−.01	Taxes-Middle Income	−.04	Anti-Monopoly
+.10	20. Increase Immigration	−.01	Tariffs	−.01	Taxes-Corporation	−.03	Foreign Aid
−.08	21. Taxes-Small Income	+.01	Enforce Integration	−.01	Taxes-Small Income	+.03	Taxes-Small Income
+.08	22. Taxes-Middle Income	+.01	Restriction Credit	+.01	American Participation, NATO	−.01	Restriction Credit
−.07	23. Restriction Credit	−.01	Foreign Aid	−.01	Public Housing		Tariffs
+.03	24. Defense Spending	.00	Anti-Monopoly	**	Defense Spending	**	Defense Spending

N's. Democratic Leaders: 1,788; Republican Leaders: 1,232; Democratic Followers: 821; Republican Followers: 623.

* The plus sign means that the first group listed in the heading is more favorable to the issue named than the second group; the minus sign means that the second group is the more favorable.

** Leaders and Followers cannot be compared on defense spending [because response on this issue was obviously inflated at time of survey due to launching of Sputnik I in November, 1957].

*** Size of difference required for differences to be significant at .01 level: Democratic Leaders vs. Republican—.048; Democratic Followers vs. Republican Followers—.068; Democratic Leaders vs. Democratic Followers—.054; Republican Leaders vs. Republican Followers—.063.

united than their leaders on these measures as well. Even on business attitudes, independence of government, and economic conservatism, the differences are small and barely significant. No differences were found on such scales as tolerance, faith in democracy, procedural rights, conservatism-liberalism (classical), the California F scale and isolationism. The average Democrat is slightly more willing than the average Republican to label himself a liberal or to seek advice from liberal organizations; the contrary is true when it comes to adopting conservative identifications. Only in the differential trust they express toward business and labor are the two sets of followers widely separated.

These findings give little support to the claim that the "natural divisions" of the electorate are being smothered by party leaders. Not only do the leaders disagree more sharply than their respective followers, but the level of consensus among the electorate (with or without regard to party) is fairly high. Inspection of the "increase" and "decrease" percentage scores (Tables II-a–e) shows that substantial differences of opinion exist among the electorate on only five of the 24 issues (credit restrictions, farm supports, segregation, and corporate and business taxes). Of course, voters may divide more sharply on issues at election time, since campaigns intensify party feeling and may also intensify opinions on issues. Available data from election studies allow no unequivocal conclusion on this point, but even the party-linked differences found among voters during elections may largely be echoes of the opinions announced by the candidates—transient sentiments developed for the occasion and quickly forgotten.

V. LEADER CONFLICT AND FOLLOWER CONSENSUS: EXPLANATIONS

Considering the nature of the differences between the leader and follower samples, the interesting question is not why the parties fail to represent the "natural division" in the electorate (for that question rests on an unwarranted assumption) but why the party élites disagree at all, and why they divide so much more sharply than their followers?

Despite the great pressures toward uniformity we have noted in American society, many forces also divide the population culturally, economically, and politically. The United States is, after all, a miscellany of ethnic and religious strains set down in a geographically large and diverse country. Many of these groups brought old conflicts and ideologies with them, and some have tried to act out in the new world the hopes and frustrations nurtured in the old. Then, too, despite rapid social mobility, social classes have by no means been eliminated. No special political insight is needed to perceive that the two parties characteristically draw from different strata of the society, the Republicans from the managerial, proprietary, and to some extent professional classes, the Democrats from labor, minorities, low income groups, and a large proportion of the intellectuals. Partly because the leaders of the two parties tend to overrespond to the modal values of the groups with which they are principally identified, they gradually grow further apart on the key questions which separate their respective supporters. The Republican emphasis on business ideology is both a cause and a consequence of its managerial and proprietary support; the greater Democratic emphasis on social justice, and on economic and social levelling, is both the occasion and the product of the support the party enjoys among intellectuals and the lower strata. These interrelationships are strengthened, moreover, by the tendency for a party's dominant supporters to gain a disproportionate number of positions in its leadership ranks.

The differences which typically separate Democratic from Republican leaders seem also to reflect a deep-seated ideological cleavage often found among Western parties. One side of this cleavage is marked by a strong belief in the power of collective action to promote social justice, equality, humanitarianism, and economic planning, while preserving freedom; the other is distinguished by faith in the wisdom of the natural competitive process and in the supreme virtue of individualism, "character," self-reliance, frugality, and independence from government. To this cleavage is added another frequent source of political division, namely, a difference in attitude toward change between "radicals" and "moderates," between those who prefer to move quickly or slowly, to reform or to conserve. These differences in social philosophy and posture do not always coincide with the divisions in the social structure, and their elements do not, in all contexts, combine in the same way. But, however crudely, the American parties do tend to embody these competing points of view and to serve as reference groups for those who hold them.

Party cleavage in America was no doubt intensified by the advent of the New Deal, and by its immense electoral and intellectual success. Not only did it weld into a firm alliance the diverse forces that were to be crucial to all subsequent Democratic majorities, but it also made explicit the doctrines of the "welfare state" with which the party was henceforth to be inseparably identified. Because of the novelty of its program and its apparently radical threat to the familiar patterns of American political and economic life, it probably deepened the fervor of its Republican adversaries and drove into the opposition the staunchest defenders of business ideology. The conflict was further sharpened by the decline of left-wing politics after the war, and by the transfer of loyalties of former and potential radicals to the Democratic party. Once launched, the cleavage has been sustained by the tendency for each party to attract into its active ranks a disproportionate number of voters who recognize and share its point of view.

Why, however, are the leaders so much more sharply divided than their followers? The reasons are not hard to understand and are consistent with several of the hypotheses that underlay the present study.

(1) Consider, to begin with, that the leaders come from the more articulate segments of society and, on the average, are politically more aware than their followers and far better informed about issues. For them, political issues and opinions are the everyday currency of party competition, not esoteric matters that surpass understanding. With their greater awareness and responsibility, and their greater need to defend their party's stands, they have more interest in developing a consistent set of attitudes—perhaps even an ideology. The fol-

lowers of each party, often ignorant of the issues and their consequences, find it difficult to distinguish their beliefs from those of the opposition and have little reason to be concerned with the consistency of their attitudes. Furthermore, the American parties make only a feeble effort to educate the rank and file politically, and since no central source exists for the authoritative pronouncement of party policy, the followers often do not know what their leaders believe or on what issues the parties chiefly divide. In short, if we mean by ideology a coherent body of informed social doctrine, it is possessed mainly by the articulate leadership, rarely by the masses.

(2) Differences in the degree of partisan involvement parallel the differences in knowledge and have similar consequences. The leaders, of course, have more party spirit than the followers and, as the election studies make plain, the stronger the partisanship, the larger the differences on issues. The leaders are more highly motivated not only to belong to a party appropriate to their beliefs, but to accept its doctrines and to learn how it differs from the opposition party. Since politics is more salient for leaders than for followers, they develop a greater stake in the outcome of the political contest and are more eager to discover the intellectual grounds by which they hope to make victory possible. Through a process of circular reinforcement, those for whom politics is most important are likely to become the most zealous participants, succeeding to the posts that deal in the formation of opinion. Ideology serves the instrumental purpose, in addition, of justifying the heavy investment that party leaders make in political activity. While politics offers many rewards, it also makes great demands on the time, money, and energies of its practitioners—sacrifices which they can more easily justify if they believe they are serving worthwhile social goals. The followers, in contrast, are intellectually far less involved, have less personal stake in the outcome of the competition, have little need to be concerned with the "correctness" of their views on public questions, and have even less reason to learn in precisely what ways their opinions differ from their opponents'. Hence, the party élites recruit members from a population stratified in some measure by ideology, while the rank and file renews itself by more random recruitment and is thus more likely to mirror the opinions of a cross section of the population.

(3) Part of the explanation for the greater consensus among followers than leaders resides in the nature and size of the two types of groups. Whereas the leader groups are comparatively small and selective, each of the follower groups number in the millions and, by their very size and unwieldiness, are predisposed to duplicate the characteristics of the population as a whole. Even if the Republicans draw disproportionately from the business-managerial classes and the Democrats from the trade union movement, neither interest group has enough influence to shape distinctively the aggregate opinions of so large a mass of supporters. Size also affects the nature and frequency of interaction within the two types of groups. Because they comprise a smaller, more selectively chosen, organized, and articulate élite, the leaders are apt to associate with people of their own political persuasion more frequently and consistently

than the followers do. They are not only less cross-pressured than the rank and file but they are also subjected to strong party group efforts to induce them to conform. Because their political values are continually renewed through frequent communication with people of like opinions, and because they acquire intense reference group identifications, they develop an extraordinary ability to resist the force of the opposition's arguments. While the followers, too, are thrown together and shielded to some extent, they are likely to mingle more freely with people of hostile political persuasions, to receive fewer partisan communications, and to hold views that are only intermittently and inconsistently reinforced. Since, by comparison with the leaders, they possess little interest in or information about politics, they can more easily embrace "deviant" atttiudes without discomfort and without challenge from their associates. Nor are they likely to be strongly rewarded for troubling to have "correct" opinions. The followers, in short, are less often and less effectively indoctrinated than their leaders. The group processes described here would function even more powerfully in small, sectarian, tightly organized parties of the European type, but they are also present in the American party system, where they yield similar though less potent consequences.

(4) Political competition itself operates to divide the leaders more than the followers. If the parties are impelled to present a common face to the electorate, they are also strongly influenced to distinguish themselves from each other. For one thing, they have a more heightened sense of the "national interest" than the followers do, even if they do not all conceive it in the same way. For another, they hope to improve their chances at the polls by offering the electorate a recognizable and attractive commodity. In addition, they seek emotional gratification in the heightened sense of brotherhood brought on by the struggle against an "outgroup" whose claim to office seems always, somehow, to border upon usurpation. As with many ingroup-outgroup distinctions, the participants search for moral grounds to justify their antagonisms toward each other, and ideologies help to furnish such grounds. Among the followers, on the other hand, these needs exist, if at all, in much weaker form.

VI. LEADERS VERSUS FOLLOWERS

In comparing each party élite with its own followers we were mainly interested in seeing how closely each body of supporters shared the point of view of its leaders, in order to test the hypothesis that party affiliation, even for the rank and file, is a function of ideological agreement. In predicting that the parties would tend to attract supporters who share their beliefs, we expected, of course, to find exceptions. We knew that many voters pay little attention to the ideological aspects of politics and that, in Gabriel Almond's phrase, a party's more "esoteric doctrines" are not always known to its followers. Nevertheless we were not prepared for the findings turned up by this phase of the inquiry, for the differences between leaders and followers—among the Republicans at least—are beyond anything we had expected. Indeed, the conclusion is inescapable that the views of the Republican rank and file are, on the whole, much closer to those of the Democratic leaders than to those of the Republican leaders. Although conflicts in outlook also exist between Democratic leaders and followers, they are less frequent or severe.

If we turn once again to the table of rank order differences, we see that the Democratic followers differ significantly from their leaders on twelve of the 23 issues, and that the average difference in the ratio scores of the two samples is .07. Democratic leaders and Republican followers differ significantly on only eleven of the 23 issues, with an average difference between them of only .08. Notice, by contrast, that Republican leaders and followers diverge significantly on 18 of the 23 issues, and show an average difference of .16. To complete the comparison, the Republican leaders and Democratic followers were in disagreement on 19 of the 23 issues, their average difference being .20. As these comparisons make plain, there is substantial consensus on national issues between Democratic leaders and Democratic and Republican followers, while the Republican leaders are separated not only from the Democrats but from their own rank and file members as well.

Examination of the Democratic scores shows the leaders to be slightly more "progressive" than their followers on most of the issues on which differences appear. The leaders are, for example, more favorable to public ownership of natural resources, to regulation of monopolies and public utilities, to a reduction of tariffs, and to a liberalized credit policy. They are more internationalist on the foreign aid and United Nations issues and substantially more sympathetic to the maintenance and expansion of immigration. The results showing the relative radicalism of the two samples are not unequivocal, however, for on several issues—federal aid to education, minimum wages, and taxes on business enterprise and large incomes—the followers take the more radical view. Nor are the differences significant on such issues as atomic energy, slum clearance, segregation, farm price supports, government control of business and trade unions, and taxes on middle and small income groups. In general, the followers turn out more radical chiefly on a few of the bread and butter issues—a reflection, no doubt, of their lower socio-economic status. When we control for occupation, the differences between Democratic leaders and followers on these issues largely disappear.

Consideration of the scores of Republican leaders and followers shows not only that they are widely separated in their outlooks but also that the leaders are uniformly more conservative than their followers. Only on the immigration issue is this trend reversed. The followers hold the more "radical" ideas on the two public ownership issues, on five of the six equalitarian and human welfare issues, on four of the seven regulation-of-the-economy issues, and on four of the five tax policy issues. They are also more willing to place greater reliance upon the U.N. and upon international military alliances. Observe that the largest differences occur on those issues which have most sharply separated New Deal-Fair Deal spokesmen from the hard core of the Republican opposition—federal aid to education, redistribution of wealth through taxes on business, corporations and the wealthy, public ownership of natural resources, public housing, regulation of business, social security, farm price supports, minimum wages, and trade union regulations.

In short, whereas Republican leaders hold to the tenets of business ideology and remain faithful to the spirit and intellectual mood of leaders like Robert A. Taft, the rank and file Republican supporters have embraced, along with their Democratic brethren, the regulatory and social reform measures of the Roosevelt and Truman administrations. This inference receives further support from the scores on our Party Ideology scale where, on a variety of attitudes and values which characteristically distinguish the leaders of the two parties, the Republican followers fall closer to the Democratic than to the Republican side of the continuum. Thus, in addition to being the preferred party of the more numerous classes, the Democrats also enjoy the advantages over their opponents of holding views that are more widely shared throughout the country.

Assuming the findings are valid, we were obviously wrong to expect that party differentiation among followers would depend heavily upon ideological considerations. Evidently, party attachment is so much a function of other factors (e.g., class and primary group memberships, religious affiliation, place of residence, mass media, etc.) that many voters can maintain their party loyalties comfortably even while holding views that contradict the beliefs of their own leaders.

Still, we are not entitled to conclude that issue outlook has no effect on the party affiliation of ordinary members. It is conceivable, for example, that the Republican party has come to be the minority party partly because the opinions of its spokesmen are uncongenial to a majority of the voters. We have no way of knowing from our data—collected at only a single point in time—how many "normally" Republican voters, if any, have defected to the Democrats or fled into independency because they disapprove of Republican beliefs. At the present stage of the analysis, we have no grounds for going beyond the proposition that political affiliation without conformity on issues is possible on a wide scale. In future analyses we shall attempt to learn more about the nature of the relationship between belief and party affiliation by stratifying voters according to the frequency with which they conform to the beliefs of their party leaders. We hope, in this way, to discover whether those who conform least are also less firm in their party loyalties.

VII. THE HOMOGENEITY OF SUPPORT FOR LEADERS AND FOLLOWERS

So far we have only considered conflict and agreement *between* groups. We should now turn to the question of consensus *within* groups. To what extent is each of our samples united on fundamental issues?

In order to assess homogeneity of opinion within party groups, standard deviation scores were computed on each issue for each of the four samples. The higher the standard deviation, of course, the greater the disagreement. The range of possible sigma scores is from 0 (signifying that every member of the sample has selected the same response) to .500 (signifying that all responses are equally divided between the "increase" and "decrease" alternatives). If we assume that the three alternative responses had been randomly (and therefore equally) selected, the standard deviations for the four samples would fall by chance alone around .410. Scores at or above this level may be taken to denote extreme dispersion among the members of a sample while scores in the neighborhood of .300 or below suggest that unanimity within the sample is fairly high. By these somewhat arbitrary criteria we can observe immediately (Table IV) that consensus within groups is greater on most issues than we would expect by chance alone, but that it is extremely high in only a few instances. Although the Republican leaders appear on the average to be the most united and the Democratic leaders the least united of the four groups, the difference between their homogeneity scores (.340 vs. .310) is too small to be taken as conclusive. The grounds are somewhat better for rejecting the belief that leaders are more homogeneous in their outlooks than their followers, since the hypothesis holds only for one party and not for the other.

While generalizations about the relative unity of the four samples seem risky, we can speak more confidently about the rank order of agreement *within* samples. In Table IV we have ranked the issues according to the degree of consensus exhibited toward them by the members of each of the four party groups. There we see that the leaders of the Republican party are most united on the issues that stem from its connections with business—government regulation of business, taxes (especially on business), regulation of trade unions, and minimum wages. The Democratic leaders are most united on those issues which bear upon the support the party receives from the lower and middle income groups—taxes on small and middle incomes, anti-monopoly, slum clearance, social security, and minimum wages. The Republican leaders divide most severely on federal aid to education, slum clearance, U.N. support, segregation, and public control of atomic energy and natural resources; the Democratic leaders are most divided on farm prices, segregation, credit restrictions, immigration, and the natural resources issue. Among the followers the patterns of unity and division are very similar, as attested by the high correlation of .83 between the rank orders of their homogeneity scores. Both Republican and Democratic followers exhibit great cohesion, for example, on taxes on small and middle incomes, social security, slum clearance, and minimum wages. Both divide rather sharply on segregation, farm price supports, defense spending, U.N. support, and taxes on large incomes. The two sets of followers, in short, are alike not only in their opinions on issues but in the degree of unanimity they exhibit toward them.

Inspection of the homogeneity data furnishes additional evidence on the between-group comparisons made earlier. Whereas Democratic and Republican followers divide on issues in approximately the same way, the two sets of leaders differ from each other in this respect also (the correlation between their rank orders on homogeneity is only .28). Democratic leaders and followers tend to unite or divide on the same issues for the most part (r equals .77), but Republican leaders and followers are not parallel in this respect either (r equals

TABLE IV. CONSENSUS WITHIN PARTY GROUPS: RANK ORDER OF HOMOGENEITY OF SUPPORT ON TWENTY-FOUR ISSUES

AVERAGE RANK ORDER*	ISSUE	DEMOCRATIC LEADERS		REPUBLICAN LEADERS		DEMOCRATIC FOLLOWERS		REPUBLICAN FOLLOWERS	
		RANK ORDER	SIGMA	RANK ORDER	SIGMA	RANK ORDER	SIGMA	RANK ORDER	SIGMA
1	Tax on Small Incomes	1	.220	6	.270	1	.224	1	.250
2	Tax on Middle Incomes	3	.276	4	.248	6	.292	2	.278
3	Social Security Benefits	5	.282	8	.296	2	.266	3	.286
4	Minimum Wages	6	.292	5	.268	4	.276	4	.294
5	Enforcement of Anti-Monopoly	2	.246	13	.321	8	.324	7	.314
6	Regulation of Public Utilities	8	.307	10	.300	10	.336	5.5	.310
7	Slum Clearance	4	.276	23	.386	3	.274	5.5	.310
8	Regulation of Trade Unions	12	.356	3	.240	9	.331	15	.345
9	Government Regulation of Business	17	.376	1	.192	20	.363	8	.315
10	Tax on Business	9	.338	2	.236	19	.362	16	.348
11	Level of Tariffs	10	.350	16	.344	11	.338	9	.316
12	Public Control of Atomic Energy	7	.302	20	.362	7	.312	13	.340
13	Federal Aid to Education	13	.360	24	.394	5	.283	11	.322
14	Foreign Aid	19	.383	12	.317	12.5	.340	12	.340
15	Tax on Large Incomes	11	.356	9	.298	17	.358	22	.379
16	American Participation in Military Alliances, NATO	14	.370	18	.351	14	.350	14	.344
17	Immigration into U.S.	21	.399	17	.345	12.5	.340	10	.318
18	Corporate Income Tax	16	.375	7	.284	21	.371	17	.361
19	Restrictions on Credit	22	.400	14	.324	16	.358	18	.362
20	Defense Spending	15	.371	15	.334	22	.380	21	.366
21	Public Ownership of Natural Resources	20	.393	19	.354	15	.352	19	.362
22	Reliance on U.N.	18	.380	22	.384	18	.359	20	.365
23	Level of Farm Supports	24	.421	11	.306	23	.414	23	.397
24	Enforce Integration	23	.416	21	.382	24	.418	24	.399

* The range of sigma scores is from .192 to .421, out of a possible range of .000 (most united) to .500 (least united). Hence, the lower the rank order the greater the unity on the issue named.

.30). The pattern of homogeneity and dispersion among Republican followers is, in fact, much closer to that of the Democratic leaders (r equals .75).

In computing scores for homogeneity we were in part concerned to test the belief that political parties develop greatest internal solidarity on those questions which most separate them from their opponents. According to this hypothesis, external controversy has the effect of uniting the members further by confronting them with a common danger. Whether or not this hypothesis would be borne out in a study of small, sectarian parties we cannot say, but it receives no support from the present study of the American mass parties. Comparisons of the rank order data in Tables III and IV show that there is no consistent connection between inter-party conflict and intra-party cohesion. The correlations between the rank orders of difference and the rank orders of homogeneity are in every case insignificant.

SUMMARY AND CONCLUSIONS

The research described in this paper—an outgrowth of a nationwide inquiry into the nature and sources of political affiliation, activity, and belief—was principally designed to test a number of hypotheses about the relation of ideology to party membership. Responses from large samples of Democratic and Republican leaders and followers were compared on twenty-four key issues and on a number of attitude questions and scales. Statistical operations were carried out to assess conflict and consensus among party groups and to estimate the size and significance of differences. From the data yielded by this inquiry, the following inferences seem most warranted:

1. Although it has received wide currency, especially among Europeans, the belief that the two American parties are identical in principle and doctrine has little foundation in fact. Examination of the opinions of Democratic and Republican leaders shows them to be distinct communities of co-believers who diverge sharply on many important issues. Their disagreements, furthermore, conform to an image familiar to many observers and are generally consistent with differences turned up by studies of Congressional roll calls. The unpopularity of many of the positions held by Republican leaders suggests also that the parties submit to the demands of their constituents less slavishly than is commonly supposed.

2. Republican and Democratic leaders stand furthest apart on the issues that grow out of their group identification and support—out of the managerial, proprietary, and high-status connections of the one, and the labor, minority, low-status, and intellectual connections of the other. The opinions of each party élite are linked less by chance than by membership in a common ideological domain. Democratic leaders typically display the stronger urge to elevate the lowborn, the uneducated, the deprived minorities, and the poor in general; they are also more disposed to employ the nation's collective power to advance humanitarian and social welfare goals (e.g., social security, immigration, racial integration, a higher minimum wage, and public education). They are more critical of wealth and big business and more eager to bring them under regulation. Theirs is the greater faith in the wisdom of using legislation for redistributing the national product and for furnishing social services on a wide scale. Of the two groups of leaders, the Democrats are the more "progressively" oriented toward social reform and experimentation. The Republican leaders, while not uniformly differentiated from their opponents, subscribe in greater measure to the symbols and practices of individualism, laissez-faire, and national independence. They prefer to overcome humanity's misfortunes by relying upon personal effort, private incentives, frugality, hard work, responsibility, self-denial (for both men and government), and the strengthening rather than the diminution of the economic and status distinctions that are the "natural" rewards of the differences in human character and fortunes. Were it not for the hackneyed nature of the designation and the danger of forcing traits into a mold they fit only imperfectly, we might be tempted to describe the Republicans as the chief upholders of what Max Weber has called the "Protestant Ethic." Not that the Democrats are insensible to the "virtues" of the Protestant-capitalistic ethos, but they embrace them less firmly or uniformly. The dif-

ferences between the two élites have probably been intensified by the rise of the New Deal and by the shift of former radicals into the Democratic party following the decline of socialist and other left-wing movements during and after the war.

3. Whereas the leaders of the two parties diverge strongly, their followers differ only moderately in their attitudes toward issues. The hypothesis that party beliefs unite adherents and bring them into the party ranks may hold for the more active members of a mass party but not for its rank and file supporters. Republican followers, in fact, disagree far more with their own leaders than with the leaders of the Democratic party. Little support was found for the belief that deep cleavages exist among the electorate but are ignored by the leaders. One might, indeed, more accurately assert the contrary, to wit: that the natural cleavages between the leaders are largely ignored by the voters. However, we cannot presently conclude that ideology exerts no influence over the habits of party support, for the followers do differ significantly and in the predicted directions on some issues. Furthermore, we do not know how many followers may previously have been led by doctrinal considerations to shift their party allegiances.

4. Except for their desire to ingratiate themselves with as many voters as possible, the leaders of the two parties have more reason than their followers to hold sharply opposing views on the important political questions of the day. Compared with the great mass of supporters, they are articulate, informed, highly partisan, and involved; they comprise a smaller and more tightly knit group which is closer to the well-springs of party opinion, more accessible for indoctrination, more easily rewarded or punished for conformity or deviation, and far more affected, politically and psychologically, by engagement in the party struggle for office. If the leaders of the two parties are not always candid about their disagreements, the reason may well be that they sense the great measure of consensus to be found among the electorate.

5. Finding that party leaders hold contrary beliefs does not prove that they *act* upon those beliefs or that the two parties are, in practice, governed by different outlooks. In a subsequent paper we shall consider these questions more directly by comparing platform and other official party pronouncements with the private opinions revealed in this study. Until further inquiries are conducted, however, it seems reasonable to assume that the views held privately by party leaders can never be entirely suppressed but are bound to crop out in hundreds of large and small ways—in campaign speeches, discussions at party meetings, private communications to friends and sympathizers, statements to the press by party officials and candidates, legislative debates, and public discussions on innumerable national, state, and local questions. If, in other words, the opinions of party leaders are as we have described them, there is every chance that they are expressed and acted upon to some extent. Whether this makes our parties "ideological" depends, of course, on how narrowly we define that term. Some may prefer to reserve that designation for parties that are

more obviously preoccupied with doctrine, more intent upon the achievement of a systematic political program, and more willing to enforce a common set of beliefs upon their members and spokesmen.

6. The parties are internally united on some issues, divided on others. In general, Republican leaders achieve greatest homogeneity on issues that grow out of their party's identification with business, Democratic leaders on issues that reflect their connection with liberal and lower-income groups. We find no support for the hypothesis that the parties achieve greatest internal consensus on the issues which principally divide them from their opponents.

In a sequel to this paper we shall offer data on the demographic correlates of issue support, which show that most of the differences presented here exist independently of factors like education, occupation, age, religion, and sectionalism. Controlling for these influences furnishes much additional information and many new insights but does not upset our present conclusions in any important respect. Thus, the parties must be considered not merely as spokesmen for other interest groups but as reference groups in their own right, helping to formulate, to sustain, and to speak for a recognizable point of view.

3. The Minor Parties

THIRD parties have abounded in American political history. If one were to include city parties, local parties, and single-state parties the number could run into the hundreds. According to American political terminology, a minor party is any group which challenges the two major parties. This loose definition encompasses a colorful and heterogeneous collection of political "anti's," ranging from parties of striking political significance to those which are ephemeral and inconsequential. Other minor parties are not even protest groups and can be readily dismissed as vehicles for frivolous, exhibitionist candidacies. The late Henry Krajewski, a New Jersey tavern owner, ran for President in 1956, 1960, and 1964 on an American Third party, sometimes called the Poor Man's party, ticket. Despite their small vote, minor parties have played an important role. They have contributed to the continuation of a two-party system which emphasizes government by compromise. Somewhat quixotically, since by definition third parties are parties of protest, they have ultimately produced political harmony by suggesting new ideas or programs which the major parties may subsequently accept.

A minor party consists of a far less complex group of interests than does a major party. For this reason the minor party, with its more cohesive following, can avoid equivocation and squarely present issues and ideas which would be disastrously disruptive to the coalition of interests in a major party. Furthermore, minor parties are important not only as ideological barometers, but also as influences on electoral tactics and strategy. If the major-party candidates for President are prevented from gaining the necessary clear majority of electoral votes, the election is determined in the House of Representatives, a possibility that gives the minor party political power out of all proportion to its actual popular vote.

It should be noted that a minor-party movement has more leverage if it has strong sectional support, rather than if its votes are scattered throughout the states. If voting strength is geographically concentrated there is a possibility of capturing a number of state electoral votes; if it is dispersed, no state electoral votes may be won. In 1948, both J. Strom Thurmond's States' Rights party, or Dixiecrats, and Henry Wallace's Progressive party polled over a million popular votes, but whereas Wallace received no electoral college vote, Thurmond received 39 electoral votes. In actual fact, however, this tactic has rarely proven to be effective. The greatest height ever achieved by a third party in attempting to influence the party pattern through the electoral college was the 88 electoral votes which Theodore Roosevelt's Bull Moose party received in 1912.

What does happen more frequently is that the vote received by one or more third parties acts to deny the presidency to one of the major-party candidates, thereby giving the election to his opponent. This happened to Whig Henry Clay in 1844, Democrat Lewis Cass in 1848, Democrat Stephen A. Douglas in 1860, Republican James G. Blaine in 1884, and Republican William H. Taft in 1912. Thus, the minor parties have played, and may in the future again play, an important conditioning role by their position and presence in the political system and by their interaction with the major parties.

Since the birth of the Anti-Mason party in 1827, third-party patterns have emerged. One group of third parties is doctrinaire and has had a long political life, consistently presenting their nominees over the years. Aware that they have little chance of winning or even of influencing the party pattern, they are content to campaign in the hope that the public ultimately will accept their particular viewpoints and sets of solutions. In this category is the Prohibition party, whose symbol, the camel, has been ridden by more presidential candidates than any other third party symbol, having run alongside the Democratic donkey and the Republican elephant in every presidential race since 1872. Running in 1964 together with the Prohibition party (which, incidentally, is not a one-plank party; its long detailed platform advocates, among other things, uniform marriage and divorce laws, world peace, public morality, separation of church and state, etc., and only in its last plank does it deal with the "alcohol problem") were the Socialist Workers' party and the Socialist Labor party. Clifton DeBerry, the Socialist Workers' nominee, was the first Negro ever nominated for the presidency. Eric Hass, the Socialist Labor candidate, was making his fourth race. But the total vote of all three of these parties in 1964, when the major parties' presidential candidates polled over 70 million votes, was well under 100,000 votes. It is noteworthy that the most famous doctrinaire party, the Socialist party, disappeared from the political scene in 1956 when its candidate, Darlington Hoopes, attracted a meager 846 votes.

The demise of the Socialist party marks an end to an era. Ever since 1900, when its founder, Eugene V. Debs, ran in the first of his six races for the presidency, this party was stronger and more intellectually significant than any other contemporary group on the left. It elected national and state legislators and installed municipal administrations. Its leaders, Debs and Norman Thomas (who like Debs also ran six times for the presidency), carved for themselves a permanent and distinguished place in American history. Also in eclipse is the Communist party of the United States. Originally a splinter from the Socialist party, it has deviated from the Socialist ideal, becoming, by and large, an instrument of Soviet policy. In this respect, and to the extent that it has at times advocated revolution, it is outside the American party system.

In sharp contrast to the long-standing doctrine parties are the transient third-party movements. They light up the political sky like roman candles and darken and die just as quickly. It is these parties, more than the ideological parties, that affect election results or modify the tone of major-party pronouncements. In the turbulent thirty years preceding the Civil War and the establishment of the present biparty pattern, a number of minor parties briefly occupied the political stage: in the 1830's it was the Anti-Mason party, in the 1840's the Liberty and the Free Soil parties, in the 1850's the American or "Know Nothing" party and the Constitutional Union party. These transient minor parties in the post-Civil War period can be divided into economic protest and secessionist parties; but the lines dividing the types are blurred and the characteristics of each type are often blended. The post-Civil War depression led to the rise of the economic protest Greenback party and the Liberal

Republican secession movement of 1872. (That year was the low point for the Democrats: they accepted the Liberal Republican presidential nominee, Horace Greeley—the only time in American political history that a major party adopted the presidential candidate of a third party.) The agrarian discontent which led to the Greenbackers also led to the formation of the Populist or People's party and the events of 1896 in which there arose secessionist wings within the Democratic party.

The Populist party left a significant imprint on American political history. It contoured the ideological competition between the major parties for years after, forced major-party realignments, inspired subsequent reform and protest movements, called attention to the inequities of the then-dominant ethic of a free and unregulated competitive economy, and publicized a number of reforms (graduated federal income tax, postal savings banks, eight-hour workday, direct election of senators, secret ballot) subsequently enacted into legislation, as well as a number of ideas (public ownership of railroads, telegraph, and telephone) subsequently discarded.

In the twentieth century, secessionist movements took place in 1912 and 1948, and parties of economic protest appeared in 1924 and 1936. In 1912 the Republican party split, making the Democrats the beneficiaries of their disharmony. A dozen years later Robert M. LaFollette's Progressive party appeared as an economic protest movement which also had the support of the Socialist party and the Farmer-Labor party. The 1924 LaFollette party had tinges of populism and 1912 progressivism, and although it trailed badly, its presence was crucial in keeping alive the organized politics of protest and paving the way for subsequent political reforms. After the collapse of LaFollette's party, the American political scene was devoid of any spectacular minor-party pyrotechnics (aside from the swift appearance and demise of the Union party in 1936) until 1948 when the Wallaceites and the Dixiecrats seceded from the Democratic party. Since 1948 third-party activity in national politics has been noticeably quiescent, except for the Liberal party of New York, which still plays a part on the national, state, and local political scene. Nevertheless, as the pattern of past history demonstrates, the seeds of national third-party movements are omnipresent and, if nourished by the right combination of forces, can flower almost immediately.

The following selections concerning the New York Liberal party are not only descriptive of the very special politics of an influential local party, but also illustrative of some of the classic techniques and problems of a minor party: its potential for reform; its pivotal position and potential veto power which may influence major party policies and swing elections; its precarious position on the ballot; and, finally, the fact that a third party may have within itself the potential to inspire sufficient political reaction to thereby neutralize itself.

As a postscript to the readings in this section it should be noted that John V. Lindsay won New York City's mayoralty contest and that in the 1966 New York State gubernatorial election, the Liberal party decided not to support the Democratic party's candidate but instead nominated its own candidate, Franklin D. Roosevelt, Jr. Roosevelt received a substantial vote (507,234) for a Liberal candidate, but this was offset by the surprisingly large number of votes (510,023) received by Paul Adams, the Conservative party's nominee. The four-year-old Conservative party thus displaced the twenty-two-year-old Liberal party as New York's third-ranking political party and won the right to line C on future ballots.

NEW YORK POLITICS AND THE LIBERAL PARTY *

Bernard Rosenberg

EVER since 1944, when the Liberal party, but recently a minority within another minority party, delivered 330,000 votes for Franklin D. Roosevelt, it has been a force with which New York politicians of every stripe have had to reckon. A Republican Speaker of the State Assembly, if he covets the governorship—and who knows where that might lead?—will seek Liberal party endorsement as eagerly as his Democratic opponent. This little party, then, has power. Much of it is visible (and not only during election campaigns). As for that part of its power which is not visible, Liberal leaders like Alex Rose (vice chairman of the party and otherwise president of the United Hatters, Cap and Millinery Workers Union) and Ben Davidson (executive director of the party since its inception) protest that their best work must be quiet and informal. The influence they bring to bear cannot, they claim, always be publicized—for fear that office holders will be embarrassed and the party's influence thereby lost.

As with the many victories for which Liberal spokesmen take too much credit, there is nevertheless something in what they say here, and the "pros" from President Johnson on down know it. In New York City, in Albany, and in Washington, they listen respectfully to the Liberals. Whether the Liberals say enough is another question, but that their voices are heard, if not always heeded, is certain.

How did all this come about? Why is it that the Liberal party of New York has survived to celebrate its twentieth anniversary, when the several Labor parties, the Progressive party, the Epic Movement, the Farmer-Labor party, the Commonwealth party, and the Socialist party—to name only those recently singled out by Ben Davidson—have all gone into eclipse?

The chronology, at any rate, is clear. In 1936, the American Labor party came into being, spawned officially by Sidney Hillman and David Dubinsky of the two big garment unions, together with some ex- , quasi- , and demi-socialists and other "progressives." We have it from William B. Hesseltine, a close student of third-party movements in the United States, that "In the 1930's New York unions and the Social Democratic Federation which had split from the Socialists, formed the ALP for the thinly-veiled purpose of keeping Roosevelt from swinging too far to the right." This version is not inaccurate, but it tells less than half the story, for the prime mover in forming the ALP actually seems

* From Bernard Rosenberg, "New York Politics and the Liberal Party," in *Commentary*, Vol. 37, No. 2 (February, 1964), pp. 69–75. Reprinted by permission of Professor Rosenberg and *Commentary*. Copyright © 1964 by the American Jewish Committee.

to have been James Farley, who can hardly be said to have had any interest in keeping his chief from swinging to the right. Consummate strategist that he was, Farley understood, and so did Roosevelt, that an indeterminably large number of votes could be scooped out of New York in the year FDR was seeking his second term, by the simple expedient of creating a party through which people loyal to Roosevelt but hostile to the Democrats could vote for him.

At its point of origin, then, the ALP was centered more on helping Roosevelt at the polls than on pushing him in any direction. Presently, however, the Communists saw and seized an opportunity to penetrate the new party. They met with little resistance from Hillman or Jacob Potofsky of the Amalgamated Clothing Workers who believed then, and for too long thereafter, that it was possible to work with the Communists. Dubinsky, Rose, and Davidson knew better. By the time they saw their New York County branch in Communist hands, they were ready to withdraw. It had taken the C.P.U.S.A. eight years of bitter struggle to complete this little coup, whose success had fateful consequences for American politics at least until 1948.

The Liberal party was born in 1944. There were fewer midwives than the ALP had in 1936, but all of them stood in resolute opposition to the Communists, who have never again given them any trouble. (Indeed, the problem today is how to prevent *Republicans,* and to some extent, Democrats from infiltrating and dominating several clubs in upstate New York—while it is the Reform Democratic movement that is bedeviled by attempts at Communist takeover!) Ideological ballast, such as it was, came from a unique source, Columbia's Teachers College, which imparted a peculiar coloration to the party that has not yet disappeared. John Dewey lent his name and gave his blessing to the Liberals, and his disciples, John Childs and George S. Counts, each subsequently a state chairman, did likewise, in addition to devoting their services. (With interim exceptions, the chairman has always been a gentile, apparently on the principle that guided Freud when he selected Jung, *his* gentile, as president of the International Psychoanalytic Society.)

Childs presided over a committee charged with drafting the original Declaration of Principles in 1944. The general objective spelled out at that time was to fight reaction and corruption in both big parties, to promote the liberal wing of each, to steer clear of Stalinism, to help win the war, and to work steadily toward a basic political realignment. New York-based though they were, Childs and his colleagues strove to establish a national perspective. The Liberals' first political act was to nominate Roosevelt, whose name now appeared three times on every New York ballot. Democratic regulars, Popular Fronters (through the ALP), and dissident anti-Communists (through the Liberals) could all cast votes for the same man—votes which some would not have cast at all under auspices repugnant to them. Candidates ever since have seen the advantages inherent in this situation. Albany, still in the hands of a lopsidedly rural conservative legislature, could destroy the Liberal party, instead of just harassing it, by abolishing dual and multiple designation, but cooler heads (sometimes those of Republican governors) have prevailed against all ultra-conservative attempts to legislate the Liberals to death. There is every reason in the Eastern megalopolis for Republicans to save the Liberals from upstate hatchet men of their own party. New York City, for all its multifariousness, belongs to the Democrats, which means that few, if any, Republicans can realistically hope for election to municipal office without Liberal support. Neither are a Republican's chances very bright for statewide and national office unless the Liberals give him their seal of approval. Thus, both big parties stand to benefit from, and therefore put up with, a third party they could easily suffocate.

Up until the ALP was dealt a fatal blow in the humiliating defeat of Henry Wallace in 1948, the Liberals struggled with uneven success to differentiate themselves from their parent organization, and running behind it, remained a fourth party. They did, however, become legally established as a fixture on the ballot in 1946. State law requires that for this privilege a party must poll at least 50,000 votes in a gubernatorial election. Despite a relatively poor showing with a lackluster candidate in 1962, the Liberals have never had any real trouble in surpassing that figure.

The year 1945 was a crucial one, more for what did not occur than for what did. By then, Wendell Willkie had strayed so far from his Republican confreres that, although he had been their most recent standard bearer, they had not even invited him to the national convention of 1944. It struck the Liberals that if Willkie could be persuaded to run for Mayor of New York on a Fusion ticket, they might have a man in the mold of La Guardia who would continue to do battle against Tammany Hall—and much, much more. Liberal overtures were made to Willkie; he was said to be interested; and after a second conference with Childs, the political wheels were set in motion. The Liberal leaders who conceived this scheme thought, probably with good reason, that Willkie could have won New York City, and that his victory might just have started a revolution reverberating through the country.

How so? Here the public record is fragmentary, though the publication of Willkie's correspondence with FDR may some day fill in the tantalizing lacunae. We do know that both men were greatly dissatisfied with their parties, that they were drawn by personal and political bonds to each other, and that their talk about founding a nationwide third party was serious. Presumably, even after Roosevelt's death, Willkie's imagination was stirred by the prospect of winning an impressive victory in New York and subsequently organizing the broader movement; also, it was the Liberals' golden opportunity. But a few weeks after having more or less agreed to run, Willkie died, and the steam went out of all these ambitious plans. It has never been restored. Comptroller Mc-Goldrick of the La Guardia administration seemed willing to be a mayoral candidate, but he equivocated and finally declined the nomination. That left the Liberals with Jonah Goldstein, a Democrat acceptable to the Republicans, who bore no special relation to the Liberal party and who ran so poorly, garnering a mere 123,000 votes, that several Liberal leaders thought of giving up the ghost. But following a six-month respite from practical affairs, a period set aside for a comprehensive review through a "listening committee" of officers who, at open hearings, heard conflicting arguments from spokesmen of local clubs, they decided to persist against heavy odds in an uphill battle which could only yield slow progress. And they also resolved that they would henceforth be more careful and circumspect in approaching candidates.

The crisis of 1945 produced new financial problems, for many of those who like to support a winner and have no other basic commitment, dropped away with the Goldstein debacle. To run a political party is no paltry matter: it takes an enormous amount of money. The authorized version is that "liberal and labor forces" supply the necessary backing for the Liberal party. But mainly, one surmises, these "forces" boil down to the Hatters and the International Ladies' Garment Workers' Union. In any case, funds materalize and fairly expensive operations are undertaken even between campaigns; as of this year, the Liberal party's headquarters, previously rather shabby, are almost elegant, a new series of radio broadcasts has been launched, and more organizers are hard at work upstate. The party is growing—despite dips and rises, its relative proportion of state votes has increased every year since 1946. There is now much less talk than in late 1961 of merger with the Democrats, sloganized as "reappraising the Liberal party's role." That phrase, set afloat after Mayor Wagner had allegedly broken the back of Tammany Hall, has been discarded in favor of "continued independence."

Independence sometimes signifies repudiation of Democratic and Republican candidates in favor of a Liberal who runs all by himself, and sometimes, detachment from Tammany and support for a progressive Republican. The Liberals pursued this latter policy in 1949 when they endorsed Newbold Morris for mayor, passing their old ALP rivals for the first time, and besting Vito Marcantonio, a formidable vote-getter. Morris lost the election by a small margin, declaring that if the Republicans had done as much for his cause as the Liberals, he would have won.

The next such expression of local independence, and by far the most successful one to date, occurred in 1951. That year Rudolph Halley received 583,000 votes on the Liberal line as an independent candidate for President of the Council of the City of New York, and defeated two hacks, the Democrat Joseph T. Sharkey, and the Republican Henry J. Latham. In 1950, before proportional representation was abolished (and the Liberals are agitating to have it restored), two Liberal city councilmen had been elected. But neither their presence nor that of Halley changed the municipal scene in any significant way. The truth now universally admitted is that the Liberals embraced Halley without inquiring about his politics, just as the ADA—a non-party organization parallel to the Liberal party, and as flexible—found itself boosting General Eisenhower for President soon after World War II. Halley had sex appeal at the polls: millions of people knew him as a TV personality, a tireless chief counsel of the Kefauver Crime Commission who could be a forceful interrogator of criminals. The Liberals—who saw their chance to capitalize on a public image—

were just as disillusioned as the rest of us when Halley turned out to be a political cipher. Nevertheless, when they ran him for mayor in 1953, he made
an impressive showing. The year before, Dr. Counts, whose fame was somewhat more limited, had also scored impressively as the Liberal party's
independent candidate for U.S. Senator—with about half a million votes. These
results delighted the Republicans as much as they sobered the Democrats. From
now on, no one could seriously doubt that the Liberal party had veto power,
that it often occupied a pivotal position, and that it could prevent the big parties from heedlessly nominating men it considered unacceptable.

Although the moderate exercise of that power has in general proved more
welcome than not to political bigwigs, it has naturally annoyed others—especially those of the reactionary right. The result has been the formation of yet
another party in New York state, the Conservative party, which has deliberately modeled itself after the Liberal party, and which, by virtue of a surprisingly big vote for its gubernatorial candidate in the 1962 election, now has a
permanent place on the ballot. Already Republican office seekers soliciting Liberal endorsement do so at the risk of losing Conservative support. If these
tactics work, the two fringe parties are bound to neutralize and eventually force
each other out of business. It will be interesting to see how the Liberals meet
this challenge of the reverse mirror image.

From the beginning they have had to meet other challenges, those built so
solidly into our system that to survey them is to wonder how any minority
party can ever be established in the United States. State law, made and administered by Democrats and Republicans, is ingeniously designed to prevent political competition, and if it fails it can still be used most effectively to stifle a
minority party. When the law proves inadequate, moreover, there are extralegal
techniques available to men who, if no other recourse avails, do not hesitate to
use them. At the precinct level, politics is still a dirty business.

Obstacle number one for a new party in New York State consists of petitions
—sheets of paper on which fifty valid signatures must appear for each of sixty-
two counties. Any signature may be challenged for any number of reasons,
ranging from incorrect form or the use of initials to out-and-out fraud, and if a
single name is successfully challenged, all others on the same sheet are thrown
out. As might be expected, the petitions of an unwelcome minority party are
examined with a microscope. Thus, a dedicated functionary like Ben Davidson
knows his people should start ringing doorbells at 6:30 A.M. to make sure that
for every fifty signatures needed they will collect two hundred and fifty. With
much experience behind him, Davidson in '44 had his party's petition volumes
locked in a safe and had guards stationed around the safe. And when the petitions went to New York and then to Albany for processing, they went under
police protection.

A resourceful leader of a third party, if he has a pool of volunteer workers,
can overcome this obstacle—only to find that the path before him is still strewn
with mines. The Liberals today must contend with physical intimidation,

threats to livelihood (and worse) from racketeers and gamblers, a type by no means confined to New York City but likely to pop up in towns like Utica and Hudson. The underworld, no more a respecter of American party labels than Lord Bryce, is as active in Republican territory upstate as it is in Democratic urban centers. Liberal organizers, then, have their hands full. On top of all this, new bills are introduced into the State Legislature virtually every year with a view toward making life impossible for the Liberals. The election laws get more complicated, further technicalities are added, a greater percentage of signatures is proposed, extra committeemen must be added in every county.

To their great credit, the Liberals have fought back, refusing despite continued frustration and harassment to shut up shop, and we have them to thank more than anyone else for the possibility of electoral dissent in New York—a possibility that hardly exists in most of the other states. We have already seen why the two major parties tolerate the Liberals—it is by and large to their advantage to do so. But when the advantage looks dubious, when, for instance, Republican legislators find their posts in jeopardy, pressure invariably mounts to destroy the Liberal party, and at that point only a deal can insure its survival. Curiously, such a deal may involve an assertion of independence. When is independence not independence? When the Liberals agree to run a man of their own instead of throwing their support behind a particular Democratic candidate where a Liberal endorsement might tip the balance against his Republican opponent. Maneuverability is thus taken away from the Liberals in exchange for the privilege of being. So much has to be surrendered—in the interest of fighting good fights on other fronts. What are these other fights? And where are the other fronts?

Reflecting on such questions, the party's top tactician finds it ironic that he and his friends, who started out to change the world, have now come to stand for nothing more radical than "old-fashioned honesty." There is no doubt that the hope of municipal reform gave the Liberals their greatest impetus, and sustains them even now in a city whose people have every reason to be cynical about politics. Gus Tyler, intellectual leader of the ILGWU and a devoted Liberal, believes, for instance, that his party's primary function is to purify the Democratic party. If the Liberals' *raison d'être* is indeed to establish honesty in local government through the reconstruction of a corrupt old party, their work —as Lincoln Steffens, who knew all about the cyclical nature of reform and corruption, would have said—is cut out for them on a permanent basis.

Yet one wonders how the Democrats can be purified by a party, one of whose principal agents can announce, all unselfconsciously, as he did to me, "We have proved that there is nothing wrong with opportunism." Or again, and verbatim, "There is this paradoxical situation, you see: at times we have to make a coalition with crooked Democrats, at other times with reactionaries." No one is held in greater disdain by the Liberal hierarchy than your political purist who would stand aloof from compromising coalitions. Such a man is impractical, visionary, utopian, unfit for the rough and tumble of politics. Liberals contend that by compromising, by eschewing intransigent idealism, by renouncing sectarianism and embracing realism, they are able to get things done. Mindful, then, of its splendid aphorism—that politics is not just a matter of arithmetic but also of algebra—what can be said from a "realistic" point of view about the Liberal party? Does it stand up well when judged not by its roots but by its fruits?

Much has to be credited to the positive side, however ambivalent one's general reaction may be. In many cases, Liberals have forced the Democratic party to raise the caliber of its candidates. When they choose to be a counterforce in local and state affairs, their impact can be mildly beneficent. Each year the party draws up a state program (largely the handiwork of Louis J. Merrell, who is widely respected for his thoroughness and competence) which addresses itself intelligently to every major issue before the state legislature. Assemblymen and senators of both parties use this program and find it helpful to them in their deliberations. Apparently they have also welcomed, or have not greatly resented, an annual legislative conference at which specialists from inside or outside the party ranks present their views in Albany. (The conferences still take place, but now in New York.) Liberals did yeoman work in opposition to a power grab of the St. Lawrence and Niagara Rivers, helping to salvage 50 per cent of the power for public and cooperative use which would otherwise have been handed over to private capital. Their big gun on this issue was Adolph A. Berle, Jr. (a founder of the party, at present Honorary State Chairman, his warm friendship for and public support of Governor Rockefeller in 1962 notwithstanding). The Liberals pioneered in Albany on the question of consumer protection through Averell Harriman, the governor they considered very much their man (when he was not Carmine De Sapio's). Most recently they contributed to the campaign against Albany's relentless effort to impose tuition fees on students of the city colleges of New York. Their presence has been felt in the state capital under three governors: Dewey, Harriman, and Rockefeller. They can be relied on to make an occasional dent, "to have a detail here and a detail there adopted," as Davidson has put it.

The Liberal record, apart from a few serious blemishes, is, well—liberal, unexceptionable and unexciting. The Liberals favor rent control; they drafted the legislation which brought it into being; and since it lapses every two years, their representatives must testify that often at meetings where landlords assemble by the carload and the busload. Liberals have been active in urban renewal, in the economic integration of housing, in fostering disability and unemployment insurance, reapportionment, civil rights, medicare. They believe in doing good by their lights, which are those of the New Deal. They are never more than a baby-step ahead of the Democratic platform; sometimes they may even lag behind that platform or behind those charged with implementing it. And it is here, in the Liberal party's relation to the program of the Democrats, that we come to the negative side of the ledger in assessing its role from the "realistic" point of view.

A third party in the earliest American tradition, that of John Randolph who broke with both Jefferson and Hamilton (choosing to be neither a Federalist nor a Republican), is literally a "third something," a *tertium quid*. We have had a great profusion of such parties. In evaluating them retrospectively, the student of American politics rarely points to how long-lived many of them have been. Yet the Liberals' greatest pride is that after two strenuous decades, they are still there, a hard fact which strikes them as proof of their success. Can it be that nothing fails like such success, and that for a real *tertium quid* nothing succeeds like excess?

In 1932 the Socialist party offered a program far to the left of either big party, and a million voters who were counted, as well as something like another million who were not, cast their ballots that year for Norman Thomas. Newly installed in office and confronted with a great depression, the Democrats quickly acceded to every "minimum demand" made by Thomas, thus stealing his thunder and that of his party. Although there are other weighty reasons for the decline of the Socialists, none is more important than the fine showing they made in 1932. For this showing could only frighten the big parties into adopting a large part of the Socialist program and rendering the Socialist party itself superfluous. Thus it is that Thomas, the perennial Presidential candidate, can look back on the performance of a major historic service. Will Dubinsky or Rose ever be able to enjoy a similar satisfaction? So far, there is no sign that they will. The Liberals are too ready to remain a satellite party, they suffer from too much timidity to advance many of their own strongest convictions, and they are too fearful of excess, of proposals that may be "premature" or "unrealistic," to flutter the dovecots in any serious way.

Liberal leaders will tell you that their go-slow attitude derives in part from the sophistication they acquired as trade unionists. In collective bargaining you can't reach for the moon: give a little, take what you can, bide your time till the next round of negotiations, and above all, don't expect too much. But this philosophy, which can be questioned even as applied to the American labor movement, is simply not proper to a third-party movement whose purpose is to prod the big parties into taking the kind of action their own inertia keeps them from taking. A pressure group that is not actuated by some sense of urgency, which does not make outlandish demands, and refuses to ask for much more than it can reasonably expect to get, ceases to be a pressure group. Not only that, but it ceases to be attractive to its most important potential constituency— the intellectuals.

New York has tremendous intellectual resources, a nucleus of scholars and artists who are chronically troubled about the remediable ills in their environment and in the world at large. Among them are many of the non-voters who stay at home on election day, not out of apathy, but because they see no decisive difference in policy between the two big parties. Such men could probably be drawn into a real third party where they might freely air their views, unfold alternatives to the prevailing consensus, and generate new ideas. Early on, intellectuals like Adolph Berle and Reinhold Niebuhr did enlist in the Liberal ranks, but no notable addition has been made in the last ten years. As the party evolved along conventional lines, and "practicality" overwhelmed "idealism," many intellectuals came to feel that they were no longer entirely welcome, and the consequence has been a certain anemia in the party's approach to the political issues of the day.

The current state chairman of the Liberal party is Professor Timothy Costello, who teaches industrial psychology at the New York University School of Business Administration. He has no office, nor even a desk at party headquarters, yet he is fairly *au courant* with party affairs. For Costello, the Liberal party is "the cutting edge of the Democratic party," an agency by which "forward-looking concepts are fed into the larger community," and "electable as well as desirable candidates" can be brought to the fore. Liberals, with or without the capital "L," are living, he says, off the fat of previous generations. Times have changed and that fat affords very little nourishment. What, then, can replenish the supply? The answer, according to Chairman Costello, is applied social science. But is it? After all, large and, by any earlier standard, astronomical sums are being spent to study social problems in America—crime, delinquency, suicide, mental disorder, drug addiction, marital discord—and if anything, there has been a steady increase in the magnitude of these problems. On the other hand, since 1954 and the so-called sociological decision on desegregation (and would it not have been better if the Supreme Court had based the decision on legal or moral grounds instead of on problematic psychological data?), there has been a virtual moratorium on research in race relations accompanied by unparalleled progress in the direction of integration. Insofar as Costello's favored technique, conflict resolution, does work, it is more often than not an instrument used by management to manipulate workers. The truth is that social science will not do as a substitute for hard ethical and political judgments.

Timothy Costello is concerned about disarmament. He sees some merit in the unilateral initiatives idea, and has talked it up, but without striking a responsive chord in his party. Of course, there are Liberals with a more pronounced streak of pacifism, notably the Reverend Donald Harrington, successor to John Haynes Holmes at New York's Community Church. Harrington, however, was rapped on the knuckles this year by Albert Margolies, until recently a Liberal publicist, for allegedly favoring unilateral disarmament—which he denies—in the party's official publication. In this area, as in nearly all matters pertaining to foreign policy, the party has simply followed the Kennedy administration (which, in Liberal eyes, is even absolved of any responsibility for the disastrous Cuban invasion), and will now probably follow Johnson.

The Liberals are convinced that but for their support, Kennedy would not have captured New York and would therefore not have been elected President. In any election whose outcome was so close, any bloc may make such a claim. Some skeptics, indeed, may find Norman Mailer's whimsical argument as persuasive as that of the Liberals. (After the Democratic Convention of 1960, Mailer mistook Kennedy for a hipster, and said so with enthusiasm in *Esquire*.

He figures that perhaps a million people read the article, of whom a sizable number—enough, possibly, to have made a decisive difference—were influenced by it. Why not?)

In any case, the late President appreciated Alex Rose's help more than Norman Mailer's: Liberal party leaders had (and have) a calling card to the White House, and in general—being representatives of organized labor as well as spokesmen for a political party—they have no trouble whatever in reaching the decision-makers. The question is, what do they do with this disproportionately large voice of theirs? Melancholy observers fear that the answer, for domestic almost as much as for foreign policy, is: nothing really, at all.

Theoretically, the Liberal party favors "democratic economic planning" today as strongly as it did twenty years ago. The term does not frighten members, many of whom still regard themselves as socialists, even if they exemplify Norman Thomas's famous remark that he knows lots of people who are still socialists—*very still*. Still or not, however, they can hardly be indifferent to the ills of our economy. Their primary allegiance is to the working people of New York, a large percentage of whom suffer from underemployment, poor pay, inadequate relief, and all the miseries attendant thereon. The garment industry, for example, is plagued by runaway shops and the spectre of automation. If, as is all too possible, the needle trades should get into a condition similar to that which has come to plague coal mining, New York City will have a massive new problem on its hands. The Liberal party could begin addressing itself to that problem now, seeking some kind of solution as a model for the national economic planning it supposedly supports. But one's guess is that the national administration will come forward with a program for dealing with automation none too soon, and yet well in advance of any proposals the Liberals will find to make.

So, too, in the field of civil rights, where the Liberals were both passive and uncritical of the Kennedy administration instead of acting as a goad and a counterforce from the left. For several months before the Negro March on Washington, for example, the President was expressing public doubt about the advisability of such a march, holding to the line that "these matters are best settled in the courts, not on the streets." The Liberal party, which has no racist wing to pacify and one of whose better-known members is James A. Farmer, director of CORE, took no stand on the March. Finally, Kennedy reversed himself, under pressure from Negro leaders. Only then did the Liberals feel free to act on their best impulses by endorsing the March and organizing a delegation to join it in Washington.

So much for the state and national scenes. What about the third major arena in which the Liberals play a role—New York City? There, alas, the party is as overcommitted to the Wagner administration as it is to the Democratic administration in Washington. The Liberals' electoral exertions on behalf of "Fighting Bob," as Rose dubbed him in 1961, were most effective. They helped him make a clean break with the Democratic bosses, De Sapio, Buckley, and Sharkey. Although it is still unclear who rejected whom, and how much, the break did occur, and Wagner won a notable primary by attacking Tammany Hall, with signal assistance from the Liberal party and yet another union group, not heard from since, the Brotherhood party. Even before Wagner's reelection, on September 27, James A. Wechsler, editor of the New York *Post* and a Liberal party sympathizer, commented:

Political writers have held funeral rites for New York's Liberal party on many occasions, but it has invariably lived to fight again.

Now it is conceivable, however, that the end is in sight—not because of a crushing defeat but because of a famous victory. The new political circumstances created by Mayor Wagner's rout of the machine-men in the Democratic primary create the real possibility of the Liberal party's merger with both the Democratic reform movement and the large labor bloc represented in the newly-formed Brotherhood party.

Despite such talk, and more that came later, the Liberals decided against formal dissolution of their party. Instead they became deeply committed to Wagner, professing to see a great difference in the mayor before and after election day of 1961. Previously he had been a prisoner of the bosses; now he was a free man, and the Liberals had figured prominently in his emancipation. How is the new Wagner better than the old Wagner? His champions affirm that he works hard: "He has to. Decisions that used to be made in Tammany Hall now have to be made in City Hall." But the big change, they say, is a vast improvement in the quality of his appointments. Not a few of these appointments, perhaps a hundred, from judgeships on down, have gone to Liberals. This is novel—patronage going to a third party—but there is nothing inherently sinister about it, especially since in almost every instance the Liberals who have been appointed are good people, much to be preferred over the usual appointees.

All the same, grave questions must be raised. Wagner will not be mayor forever. He may run for the U.S. Senate (or the vice-presidency) this year, and in that event, one of his lieutenants, a man like Abraham Beame or Paul Screvane, will be the likeliest Democratic candidate for mayor. With such a big sprinkling of quondam county chairmen and other Liberal party personnel in Wagner's official family, will Liberals ever be able to oppose any member of that family? At least one voluble Liberal, Stuart Scheftel, is afraid that they may not. Scheftel came to the Liberal party as a Fusionist, and a Fusionist he has steadfastly remained. He doubts that New York, where, he estimates, illegal gambling constitutes a two-billion dollar a year industry, can ever be anything but a "payoff city" under Democratic rule. Accordingly, two years ago, Scheftel became the only insurgent in the Liberal party's twenty-year history. He declined to accept Wagner, his old school chum and a man he personally likes, as the Liberal nominee for Mayor, and entered his own name in the one important primary the Liberals have ever had. The attempt failed for lack of petitions, but Scheftel still refused to support Wagner. Lately things do seem to him to have picked up a bit in City Hall ("Bob's more energetic these days"), but he is disturbed by Wagner's appointment (with Liberal support) of Louis I. Kaplan to a judgeship after the New York Bar Association and the Citizens Union found Kaplan to be unqualified. In Scheftel's opinion, the Liberals have a bright future on the local scene if they stick to their original purposes. To betray them again, he thinks, is to risk extinction. Is he right? An acid test will be coming very soon, and it remains to be seen whether the Liberals will be able to summon up the resources to fight the Democratic party with a Fusion ticket such as Rose, with all his political wizardry, could put together and whose triumph could well have political consequences far beyond the bounds of New York City itself.

TEXT OF THE ADDRESS BY ALEX ROSE
ENDORSING REPRESENTATIVE
JOHN V. LINDSAY FOR MAYOR OF NEW YORK *

Fellow delegates:

While I will present to you the viewpoint of the policy committee of our party, I know there will be many other viewpoints expressed here tonight, and I hope that all of them will be discussed and debated with full respect for each other's opinion and that in the end we shall emerge from this conference united, as we did in the past.

Before I give you the recommendation of the policy committee in connection with the coming municipal election, I want to say at the very outset, that, contrary to all speculation, President Johnson did not call any of our party leaders, nor did we call him.

We regard our New York City election strictly as a local matter, dealing with local issues which have no bearing on national issues.

Mayor Wagner, on the other hand, rightfully so, has a special concern in our local government and expressed the hope that we might continue coalition with the Democrats. The Mayor, however, did not specify any one candidate, and assured us that he had confidence in the integrity of our party.

Historically, our party has worked with the Democrats in national and state elections, but in municipal elections we have always been independent.

We supported Fusion in 1937, and in 1941, and in 1945, and in 1949. And during those years, President Roosevelt and President Truman were in the White House. As a matter of fact, in 1937 Franklin D. Roosevelt supported

* From *The New York Times*, June 29, 1965, p. 20, col. 4. © 1965 by The New York Times Company. Reprinted by permission of *The New York Times*.

the Fusion candidate for Mayor, Fiorello LaGuardia against his own party's nominee.

There is no inconsistency in such a policy. We are for progressive government in the nation and we are for clean and good government in the city. On other occasions we had Rudolph Halley as our own candidate for Mayor and we have also supported Democratic candidates, Ferdinand Pecora and Robert F. Wagner.

Our support for Pecora and Wagner was not based on their party label, but on our confidence in them as individuals.

We know that in presenting the question of whether to go Fusion or to continue with a Democratic candidate, many within our party ranks still hear the echo of the last national election when we worked so hard and so faithfully to elect the Johnson ticket. Yet in 1949, only one year after the great Truman victory, when we also worked so hard, we nominated Republican Newbold Morris for Mayor and our party's treasurer, Harry Uviller, for City Controller on a Fusion ticket. Many in our ranks were in doubt at that time. Some even predicted the doom of the Liberal party. Yet we emerged from that election with a great moral influence and enjoyed a remarkable decade of political success.

Here is the record:

¶ In 1950 our vote elected Herbert H. Lehman to the United States Senate.

¶ In 1951 we elected Rudolph Halley City Council President.

¶ In 1952 we rolled up half a million votes for our former state chairman, George S. Counts, for United States Senate as our protest candidate.

¶ In 1954 we elected Averell Harriman Governor in a close contest.

¶ In 1960 we provided the margin of vote to carry the State of New York for John F. Kennedy and with it the margin for the nation.

¶ In 1961 we played a considerable role in the reelection of Mayor Wagner and in his great dramatic victory against the political bosses.

So you see, the Fusion campaign for Newbold Morris in 1949 did not hurt us at all. In fact, it established our independence and gave us the moral strength and quality image for all the campaigns that followed.

Let me also remind my fellow trade unionists that the A.F.L.-C.I.O. political policy, through its COPE (Committee on Political Education), urges the labor movement not to be beholden to any one political party, nor to be taken for granted by any one political party, and to display independence when dealing with candidates for high office, and to judge them irrespective of their party affiliation.

It is during national and state elections that a party such as ours may be deprived of its freedom of action and be compelled to make sacrifices and adjustments when naming its ticket, but on the other hand, in municipal elections, when good government is the issue, when honesty, efficiency, morality and imaginative leadership are required, party labels should be the last consideration.

It is the big city machines that live on party labels, and the voters are getting tired of them and growing more and more independent of them. In fact, cities like Los Angeles and Cleveland don't use any party labels in their municipal elections. And in the state of Minnesota they use party labels only in the Presidential and Congressional elections.

Nothing illustrates better the independence of the voters than the last municipal election of 1961, when Wagner, with the help of our party, defeated the combined efforts of all the county bosses and the entire Democratic party machine.

And although Wagner is a Democrat, the issue of that campaign was very much like the issue of all other Fusion campaigns. At stake were an unbossed administration and good government for New York City.

Important changes have taken place in the Democratic party of New York since the last Presidential election of 1964—changes not for the better, but for the worse. These changes in the Democratic party reflected themselves in the persistent and unrelenting obstruction against Mayor Wagner—in the recent struggle for legislative control, in the present fragmentation which is leading up to so many contests in the Democratic primary. In fact there are so many Democratic candidates in the race (with a few more standing by in the wings, waiting for encouragement) that it seems they are invoking the Supreme Court decision of "one vote, one candidate."

Are all these conflicts within the Democratic party meant for the good of New York, or are they struggles for the naked political power designed not only for immediate machine control, but also beyond the 1965 election?

Let me at this point say that the Democratic aspirants who appeared before our screening committee are all nice men, but in our judgment none of them have the political strength to stop the Democratic party from reverting to normalcy. By such normalcy we mean control, once again, by the political machine over public officials.

Without Robert Wagner in City Hall, partisan Democratic rule will mean a return to a political normalcy—with a vengeance—to make up for lost time.

The question before the Liberal party today is, shall we put our resources, our energies, and our honor behind a faction in the Democratic party and help nullify the achievements of the 1961 Wagner victory, or shall we go forward to fight for good government and clean politics to finish the job of 1961 where it needs to be finished?

Some Democratic politicians are naive enough to think that we will help to destroy what we helped to achieve. No, we will not help bring political power back to the club houses. Nor will we risk the fate of our city once again by subjecting it to boss rule. Nor will we relegate City Hall merely to official receptions for foreign dignitaries.

Yes, many Democratic politicians are yearning for the days of Carmine de Sapio's rule. His footsteps are again being heard.

Yes, the Democratic politicians would like the Liberal party's help for at least one more election—to embrace us for one more kiss—and then get rid of this Liberal party nuisance.

With such potential developments facing New Yorkers, the Liberal party's policy committee is of the opinion that this is the moment of great historic importance for our city and for the moral climate of our community. We feel that the Liberal party must act in accordance with its best traditions in municipal elections. We must join all good government-minded forces in all parties for a nonpartisan Fusion administration.

And tonight we earnestly recommend that you turn to the man who publicly advocates such a policy.

We feel that in this election the Liberal party must support a candidate for mayor who is bigger than his own party organization. Robert Wagner is such a man and John Lindsay is such a man.

Let us judge Congressman Lindsay by his enemies: He will be running in this election against TWO Buckleys—Boss Charles Buckley and Conservative William Buckley.

Can we, the Liberal party, ask for a better issue in the coming election? Can there be a more clearcut choice for the voters of New York?

With Mayor Wagner going out of office, the city administration will need an overhaul. There are weak spots—tired spots—in our city government. There are complacent elements hanging on to positions of power and authority from the old days of party machine rule.

We need a government not beholden to any political party. We need a nonpartisan administration of men and women imbued with a passion for public service and dedicated to the interest of its 8 million people.

We need at the head of that government a man of integrity and ability and imagination. Let us help elect such a Fusion administration.

Let us help elect Congressman John Lindsay as the next mayor of New York.

II. THE PARTY SYSTEM AND PRESIDENTIAL SELECTION

4. The Nominating Process

EVERY four years the American public witnesses one of the greatest shows on earth—the national party conventions. It is an amazing spectacle—merging the hoopla and fanfare of a circus, the fervent oratory of a revival meeting, and the importance, if not the solemnity, of a summit meeting. Americans have learned to accept the national convention method of selecting presidential and vice-presidential candidates as the logical outgrowth of the political system. But non-Americans ponder the proceedings—highly unorthodox to them—with incredulity and puzzlement. This is understandable, since the American nominating process, the product of pragmatic historic improvisation, is extralegal and unique. But more important, it is also functional.

The American nominating process is extralegal in that national conventions are not regulated by either state or federal law. It is unique in that party and government service are not a standard prerequisite for nomination. (In Great Britain, party leaders must follow the political path through Parliament.) The process is functional and flexible in that it responds not only to the decentralized politics caused by a constitutional provision for federalism and the separation of executive and legislative branches, but also to the centralizing influence of the presidency on the party system. Within the party it accommodates and reconciles diverse interests, factions, and ideologies, and imposes order on internal party government. And finally, it meets the supreme test: despite its deficiencies, it works.

National party conventions, as we know them, came into being in the early 1830's during Andrew Jackson's first presidential term. Prior to that two systems of selecting a President had been successively in effect. George Washington became President in 1789 and 1792 in the manner provided for in the Constitution (each state legislature appointed electors equal to the state's total congressional representation). The second system began with the 1796 election and utilized gatherings of party members in Congress—the beginning of the congressional caucus. In the elections at the turn of the nineteenth century, the congressional party caucus was used effectively by the Jeffersonian Republican party. But the Federalists had less success with it; they were declining in influence and congressional membership, and the congressional caucus was no longer representative of the Federalist party as a whole. To remedy this situation, secret meetings of Federalist leaders, in and out of Congress, were held to decide upon the nominations for the elections of 1808 and 1812. After the War of 1812 the political environment changed rapidly and so did the role of the congressional caucus. Popular suffrage was expanding and the frontier areas and the urban centers were becoming politically potent. The rise of Jacksonian democracy was accompanied by the decline of King Caucus. In 1824 the Jacksonians boycotted the Republican congressional caucus. The caucus nominee, William H. Crawford, received fewer electoral and popular votes than did Jackson. The election was decided in the House of Representatives and the caucus was no longer a major factor in the nominating process.

Four years later, presidential nominations were made by state nominating conventions, state legislative caucuses, and state legislatures. In 1831 the Anti-Mason party held the first national nominating convention, and later that year the National Republicans also assembled in convention. The following year the Jacksonian Democratic-Republicans adopted the practice of the other parties and held a national convention. The displacement of the congressional caucus was complete and the presidential nominating convention was an institutional aspect of the national party system.

Once firmly rooted, the convention expanded the number of its functions. One of its early functions, that of generating party enthusiasm among the faithful and the undecided, ultimately became an electioneering device within the party. In 1860 Abraham Lincoln's supporter Norman Judd, unknown to Lincoln, counterfeited tickets to the public gallery, thereby endowing Lincoln with a sizable cheering section. Carefully planned "spontaneous" demonstrations on behalf of the contenders for the party nomination are now standard procedure. By 1840 national nominations included the vice-presidential candidate and the party thus presented the electorate with a complete ticket. Around the middle of the nineteenth century the convention instituted a continuing national committee to serve as the party governing body. In 1852, in an attempt to impose intraparty harmony, the practice now generally followed of adopting platforms before selecting the nominees was instituted.

By the time of the Civil War, with the convention left entirely to self-regulation, abuses had begun to creep into the system. Crude and corrupt practices, a reflection of the boodle politics of the post-Civil War era, became rampant. Public criticism was now directed to the apportionment of delegate strength, the internal mechanics of delegate meetings, and the time and manner of selecting delegates. By the late decades of the nineteenth century there was a movement for political reform. "Bosses" and "machines" were no longer to be tolerated, and a populistic view of democracy which extolled the virtue and wisdom of the common man became a basic tenet of the reform impulse. One of the major institutional reforms which the progressives advocated as a means of returning control of the government to the people was the direct primary.

In 1905 Wisconsin adopted the first presidential primary law, requiring that delegates to the national party conventions be elected directly by the people. This started a trend which continued for the next two decades. In 1912 the Progressive party platform came out for "nationwide preferential primaries" and the Democratic platform endorsed state preferential primaries. The next year, in his first annual message to Congress, President Woodrow Wilson urged the adoption of a national direct primary law. But the idea never really caught on and the number of states using some form of presidential primary has declined.

The laws regulating primaries, which are held in about a third of the states, are extremely complicated and fall into five categories:

(1) Election to national conventions of delegates, who may or may not declare their presidential preferences. In Ohio, California, Florida, and South Dakota, the voter elects one or more delegates who he believes will support the candidate of his choice. (In certain states—for instance, California and South Dakota—the voter votes just once for a presidential aspirant whose name leads a slate of delegates pledged to him.)

(2) Election to national conventions of delegates who are barred by state law from

showing their presidential preferences. This type of primary is held in Alabama and New York and the results have little national significance. These primaries are of importance chiefly in reflecting interfactional party quarrels.

(3) Election of delegates, combined with *advisory* presidential preference polls. In New Hampshire, New Jersey, Massachusetts, Nebraska, Illinois, West Virginia, Pennsylvania, and in Washington, D.C., voters state their presidential preferences, but the results of the poll are not binding on the elected delegates. In some states delegates may pledge themselves to a candidate or not, or they may be required by law to be unpledged. In the nonpledged states the presidential poll assumes increased importance, as it demonstrates the vote-getting ability of the presidential aspirant.

(4) Election of delegates, combined with *mandatory* presidential preference polls. In Oregon, the entire delegation must support the candidate who wins the preference poll.

(5) *Mandatory* presidential preference polls only. In Indiana, Maryland, and Wisconsin, delegates are chosen by state conventions, rather than by the voters, but they must support the candidate who wins the preference poll. In 1967 Wisconsin became the first primary state to provide for a "no" vote. If a voter disapproves of a candidate put on the ballot by his party he can register his disagreement by voting "no." The "no" provision, it is argued, is designed to minimize cross-over and thereby make the primary more meaningful.

The table on page 90 may be found helpful.

The maze of primary laws is further complicated by variations in the eligibility to vote in the primaries, which is determined by state law. In most states, only voters who are registered party members may vote (the "closed" primary). In other states, a voter can enter the primary without declaring a party preference (the "open" primary). In Washington, a voter need not declare any party preference and may vote for any candidate of either party (the "jungle" primary). In recent years, the trend generally has been against the open primary, which many people feel violates party responsibility. (This was one of the arguments bringing about the abolition in 1959 of California's cross-filing primary law, which permitted a candidate to run on other party tickets as well as his own.) It is no wonder that there continue to be advocates of some form of nationwide direct primary. Such diverse senatorial types as George W. Norris of Nebraska, William Langer of North Dakota, Margaret Chase Smith of Maine, Estes Kefauver of Tennessee, and George Smathers of Florida tried at one time or another to generate support for a particular version of national primary reform. The prospects for the adoption of a nationwide primary, however, are remote. Other reform proposals are designed to bring about more uniformity in state presidential primary laws.

There have also been proposals for convention reforms. About two-thirds of the states choose delegates to the national party conventions by intraparty conventions or committees, and a voluntary change in party rules governing the designation of delegates has been suggested. Changes have also been urged in the structure, organization, and procedure of a national nominating convention.

Although the structural changes in the convention may have been minimal, the convention has continued to be a flexible instrument. Without formal or structural alteration, party methods are responding to twentieth-century mass democracy. Increasingly, presidential aspirants who have made successful preconvention campaigns, or who have become national figures, are in a position of greater strength when the convention meets than nonnationally known candidates are. This is so because presidential politics, as distinguished from congressional politics, has a

DELEGATES

Group	Presidential Preference Poll	Pledged to Candidate	Unpledged to Candidate	Pledged or Unpledged	Bound to Support Candidate Endorsed by Majority of Voters
I	No	Ohio		California* Florida South Dakota	
II	No		Alabama New York		
III	Yes (Advisory)		Nebraska Illinois West Virginia Pennsylvania Washington, D. C.	New Hampshire New Jersey Massachusetts	
IV	Yes (Mandatory)				Oregon
V	Yes (Mandatory)				Indiana Maryland Wisconsin

*Delegates bound to support pledged candidate at convention.

national constituency and involves mass appeal and requires a national image. The preconvention primaries, with a far different meaning then when they were first instituted, may provide national publicity for a previously unknown contender. No longer can a presidential hopeful seriously contend for the nomination unless he has the makings of a national image. In effect this is a political reaction to the expansion of mass communications and to computerized public opinion samplings. Other changes, not presently foreseen, will undoubtedly occur.

In the readings which follow, the nominating process in national politics is described and assessed. Some of the vagaries of accumulating nominating votes in the primaries are captured in "The 1964 Presidential Primaries," taken from the National Broadcasting Company's coverage of the campaign. In "Convention Decisions and Voting Records," Richard C. Bain discusses the pros and cons of the convention method of selecting presidential candidates. Nelson W. Polsby and Aaron B. Wildavsky address themselves to the various goals and preconvention strategies of the candidates in "The Nominating Process." In the fourth reading, some conclusions about "The Nominating Process and the Future of the Party System" are presented by Paul T. David, Ralph M. Goldman, and Richard C. Bain. And finally, Gerald Pomper discusses "The Nomination of Hubert Humphrey for Vice-President" and trends in the politics of vice-presidential nominations.

THE 1964 PRESIDENTIAL PRIMARIES *
Gene Shalit and Lawrence K. Grossman

PROLOGUE

SOME of the peculiar flavor of American politics can be seen in a scrutiny of . . . [a] photograph, one of the millions of frozen images left to us from an election year. It describes an encounter on a snowy residential street in New Hampshire in February—the ground, the neat clapboard houses, the leafless white birch and the sky behind it all about the same color as the snow. In the whiteness of this cold and quiet small town a little color is welcome; and equally welcome in the quiet cold is the noisy warmth the visiting politician always brings with him. He brings it with him because he must, because the temper of our country demands it. This visitor, [a] hulking blackness on the right, is Governor Rockefeller, a multi-millionaire trying not to look like one. His overcoat is an old, belted-back model out of style for years. The others at the scene wear gloves, but not the Governor. He is there to shake hands, and whatever it is that passes between two people in a handshake surely is diminished by two thicknesses of leather and wool. To [a] plump and well-fed little girl in [a] flowered parka, he offers: (1)A smile (His face is out of range, but

* From Somehow It Works, edited by Gene Shalit and Lawrence K. Grossman (Doubleday and Company, 1965). Copyright © 1965 by the National Broadcasting Company, Inc. Reprinted by permission of Doubleday and Company, Inc.

how else could an American politician greet a child when her parents are there and the photographers around?); (2)His ungloved hand for shaking; (3)A box of animal crackers; and (4) In his coat pocket for cases of special need, a hand of bananas. Baby kissing is laughably old fashioned and unsanitary. (It also means they have to be lifted up off the ground, which is hard on a man's back in a long day of campaigning.) But animal crackers are boxed and cleanly wrapped, and bananas are immaculate and germ-free in their own skins—a requisite quality in a country that won't buy a detergent until it is warranted to clean whiter than white. Leftward, an older girl holding [a Rockefeller] poster is laughing gaily (she is out of school, and there is a little excitement in town), at the Governor's witticism. A small packet of such witticisms is essential, and can be used over and over. But the little girl in the parka is not quite old enough to get the joke, and [a] lady in the center didn't hear it because she is looking away and her ears are covered. The poster is the standard political graphic art—red, white and blue, the photograph showing the candidate smiling but not overdoing it (remember what happened to Adlai Stevenson's too many jokes and too many laughs). How many photographs of this Governor did they pick through before they chose this one? In the poster's lower right corner can be seen the printer's union label. Just try to run for President without that. Fully visible here are only two people old enough to vote, and so if Rockefeller's handshakes, jokes, animal crackers and bananas won him the hearts of everybody in sight, he would have moved just two 70-millionths of the way to the White House. As things turned out, he lost the New Hampshire primary to Lodge. Lodge lost the Republican nomination to Goldwater. And Goldwater lost New Hampshire to Johnson just nine months after this picture of a greeting by warm people in a cold town.

DAVID BRINKLEY

FRANK MCGEE: There will be 1,308 delegates at the Republican Convention in July. Exactly 14 of these will come from New Hampshire. That is about one out of every 100. And even these 14, once they get to San Francisco, will not be bound to vote for the winner of this primary. Figured that way, the amount of time, energy and money being spent here by a pack of Presidential candidates makes no sense at all, but candidates do not and cannot figure it that way. They have a far larger objective in mind. Because it holds the first primary in the nation, New Hampshire offers the candidates their first chance to prove that they can get votes. Consequently, no voters in the nation will be politicked more, or polled as much, as those who live in this small corner of New England. And no voters will enjoy the fuss being made over them more. Once every four years they have the satisfying feeling that they are shaping momentous events. They are, for although they have only a small voice in deciding the ultimate winner, they have a decisive voice in sorting out the losers.

Since it must begin somewhere, let it begin in New Hampshire. Small matter that the State is not a good laboratory to test their solutions for the nation's problems. A State with only three Negroes for every thousand population may not share the candidates' feeling of urgency about civil rights. So other issues must be found and stressed.

MERRILL MUELLER: Politics comes naturally to many people, but few master the art of shaking hands with strangers in an attempt to turn them into voters. This gregarious blessing is one of Nelson Rockefeller's strongest assets. Whether it's in a bustling metropolis, or in a frozen village, the Governor campaigns as "Rocky, the regular guy." His blitz campaigning relies on the direct approach to men, women and children.

ROCKEFELLER: Hi, nice to have seen you.

BOY: Where are you going?

ROCKEFELLER: I'm going to a super market. Do you go shopping with your mommy? That's where I'm going.

BOY: Why?

ROCKEFELLER: Well, because I'm trying to get support to run for President of the United States.

BOY: Why?

ROCKEFELLER: Well, it's a good question. Because I'm worried about what's going on in the world and I want to do my part to help. That's why I'm doing it, so that nice boys like you will have a real chance to grow up in a country where there's freedom and where there's opportunity. And you are a wonderful boy.

ROBERT MACNEIL: Sen. Goldwater's campaign has been restrained. He seemingly prefers small, indoor groups to the more aggressive style of his rivals. He is not an easy man to advise. About the only concession he made was to eliminate the "damns" and "hells" which used to season his talks.

GOLDWATER: I'm not one of these hand-shaking candidates. And I don't kiss babies, because I lose track of their age too soon. And I don't like to insult the American intelligence by thinking that a loud whack on the back will get your vote.

Primary day arrives with freezing temperatures, snow and sleet. Taking the storm in stride, New Hampshire's voters drive, walk, slip and slide to the polls. On March 10, primary election night, NBC-TV reports.

RAY SCHERER: [In Washington, D.C.]: Here with me is Cliff White, director of field operations for Sen. Goldwater. The Senator said he hoped to get 40 percent of the votes in New Hampshire. He is not getting it. What happened?

WHITE: Ambassador Lodge is, in effect, a regional individual. I don't think he can get the nomination, and I suspect that the people in New England are merely paying tribute to a native son.

MCGEE: Campaign managers for Sen. Goldwater and Gov. Rockefeller are being left in the position of saying that the New Hampshire primary, where they had courted the vote so heavily, will actually prove nothing. Former New Hampshire Gov. Hugh Craig, a leader of the Rockefeller forces, is with NBC's Sander Vanocur in Concord.

SANDER VANOCUR: What do you think this election proves, so far as Gov. Rockefeller is concerned? Is he out of the Presidential race?

CRAIG: Gee, I don't see that at all. Gov. Rockefeller seems to be holding his own with Sen. Goldwater. He is our opposition, as far as I'm concerned. If we can do well against him, we've got a victory.

VANOCUR: Did his divorce hurt Gov. Rockefeller?

CRAIG: I can't understand what you mean by being hurt. We're holding our own here, except against Lodge, and we haven't been running against Lodge. He hasn't been a candidate. He's not an opponent. He hasn't campaigned.

VANOCUR: Do you think that Gov. Rockefeller will now go on into all the rest of the primaries?

CRAIG: I'm certain he will. He is leaving tomorrow for California to start his campaign there.

MCGEE: Our lady candidate, Sen. Margaret Chase Smith, has not done well in the returns so far. She is with NBC's Nancy Dickerson in Washington.

NANCY DICKERSON: How do you feel, Senator?

SEN. SMITH: Well, I'm very happy, but I'd be happier if I were getting more votes.

NANCY DICKERSON: Are you disappointed with the outcome so far?

SEN. SMITH: I wouldn't be human if I wasn't.

MCGEE: The write-in campaign for Ambassador Lodge appears to have been sharply stimulated in the past three weeks by statements from his son, George Lodge, suggesting rather firmly that his father was a candidate even though he remained in Vietnam. The younger Lodge has now arrived from Boston and is now in Concord.

GEORGE LODGE: I think it is a wonderful vote of confidence in my father. I know he will be surprised and gratified when he hears about it. He regards his responsibility in Saigon right now as extremely serious. He was Ambassador during the crucial days of transition in Vietnam and he sees it as his duty to see it through. He is not one to pull out of a fight. However, if his Party calls on him in Convention, there is no doubt in my mind but that he will answer that call and do it gratefully, humbly, enthusiastically.

HERB KAPLOW: Nixon hopes the other men will cancel each other out, and that he will make respectable showings in the primaries he will not be able to duck. He seems to be holding his own tonight as a less aggressive write-in candidate than Lodge. Nixon presents himself as the best team player. He will do everything he can for the Party. Finally, Nixon presents himself as the middle-of-the-roader, the man whose political philosophy comes closest to a Republican consensus.

MCGEE: Another campaign adding interest to the New Hampshire primary has been the late blooming write-in campaign for Robert Kennedy for the Democratic Vice Presidential slot. Gov. John W. King, who headed that campaign, talks to NBC.

VANOCUR: Governor, would you have been embarrassed if President Johnson received fewer votes tonight than Attorney General Robert Kennedy in the write-in ballot?

KING: I don't get embarrassed very easily. The vote is going pretty much the way we anticipated it.

VANOCUR: Wasn't there a drive during the past few days to make sure that people wrote in the name of the President so that the name of the Attorney General would not appear there all alone?

KING: Not really. It is what I recommended.

The results show: Lodge, 33,521 (35.4%); Goldwater, 21,775 (23%); Rocke-feller, 19,496 (20.6%); Nixon 15,752 (16.6%); Smith, 2,812 (3%); Stassen, 1,285 (1.4%). It is an upset victory for Ambassador Lodge. The candidates who campaigned strenuously and spent lavishly are overthrown by a man who is 10,000 miles away, who made not a single speech, shook not a single hand, and whose name was not even on the ballot.

"I goofed up some place," says Sen. Goldwater. Gov. Rockefeller says, "This is a victory for moderation." The winner's backers joyously proclaim, "Ambassador Lodge has emerged as the people's choice."

On Wednesday morning, the very day after the primary, Gov. Rockefeller flies to California to campaign in that all-important contest. Sen. Goldwater rests in Phoenix, but two days later he, too, is campaigning in California.

Meanwhile, Republican primaries are coming one after another. On April 28, Gov. Scranton sets a new Pennsylvania record, with 220,573 write-in votes on a primary ballot that does not list Presidential candidates. Far behind are Lodge (79,781); Nixon (36,686); Goldwater (32,305); and Rockefeller (7,160).

On May 1, Georgia Republicans gather in Atlanta for their State convention. Robert MacNeil reports.

MACNEIL: Georgia was one of the few Southern States in which Goldwater felt it necessary to woo delegates in person. It was necessary because it threatened to crack his solid Southern phalanx. Although he already had 18 of the State's 24 delegates, Goldwater flew all the way back from California to the Georgia convention to win the other six. He got four of them in the twenty-four hour visit, but psychologically, it was one of the lowest points of his campaign. He was exhausted by travel, and irritated by thrusting microphones and the increasing number of newsmen. Arriving late at night in Atlanta, the Senator woke up to find an unscheduled crowd of friends at the airport. He got annoyed, wanted to know who was responsible for arranging a demonstration and refused to leave the plane. Finally, campaign director Denison Kitchel went back to him and said, "Dammit, Barry, you're a national figure." Reluctantly, the national figure got out of the plane and suffered himself to be adored. But he was in good humor by the time he got to the convention itself.

On May 2, Texas holds its first Presidential primary ever. The Texas primary has no standing in law, and is merely a popularity contest sponsored by the pro-Goldwater Republican State Committee. When Gov. Rockefeller's name is placed on the ballot over his protests, he says: "I don't think it's a primary; I think it's a stacked deck and a rigged deal." Sen. Goldwater wins the election, piling up 100,909 votes to 23,552 for Lodge, Rockefeller and Nixon combined.

Although Sen. Goldwater is the only candidate on the Nebraska primary ballot of May 12, he gets only 49.5% of the vote. An intensive write-in campaign for Richard Nixon gives the former Vice President 31.5%, and Ambassador Lodge receives 16.2%. That same day, Gov. Rockefeller sweeps to a 100% victory in West Virginia: he is the only candidate on the ballot and no write-ins are permitted.

As for the Democrats, the Indiana primary on May 5 is Gov. Wallace's second venture into a Northern contest. And again a Democratic governor (this time, Indiana's Gov. Matthew Welsh) represents President Johnson on the ballot. On the Republican side, Sen. Goldwater faces only token opposition in Harold Stassen. Also on the Indiana ballot are Lar Daly, who campaigns in an Uncle Sam costume, and Mrs. Fay T. Carpenter-Swain, who says she wants "everything free." On primary night, Frank McGee reports from Indianapolis.

MCGEE: Indiana's Gov. Matthew Welsh, stand-in for President Johnson, has won this State's Democratic primary, beating back a determined drive by Alabama's fiery segregationist, Gov. George Wallace. But Wallace—by taking about 30 per cent of the vote—claims he has shaken the liberals in both parties. Wallace's showing here has been almost exactly the same as it was a month ago in the Wisconsin primary.

MCGEE: The Indiana Democratic organization campaigned on the slogan, "Clear the way for LBJ, vote for Welsh on the fifth of May." Here is how the Governor viewed the outcome:

WELSH: This cannot properly be called a Wallace victory. We had a massive cross-over of Republicans voting in the Democratic primary.

Gov. Welsh holds the State for President Johnson with 376,023 votes (65%). Gov. Wallace gets 172,646 (29.8%). Mr. Daly gets 15,160 votes (2.6%), and Mrs. Carpenter-Swain receives 7,140 votes (1.2%). On the Republican side, Sen. Goldwater overwhelms Mr. Stassen, 267,935 to 107,157—67% to 26.8%.

"We shook the eye-teeth of those people in Wisconsin," says Gov. Wallace, "and the noises you hear now are the teeth falling out in Indiana. We're going on to Maryland from here."

The Alabama Governor is to make his strongest showing in his third and final primary: Maryland, on May 19. Here, President Johnson's stand-in is Sen. Daniel Brewster. The Senator wins as Maryland Democrats vote in record numbers, but Gov. Wallace takes 16 counties to the Senator's seven. The Maryland vote is 267,104 for Sen. Brewster to 214,837 for the Alabama Governor. "Everyone knows we won a victory here tonight," Gov. Wallace says. "We have a majority of the white vote. If the Republicans could have crossed over, we'd have beaten the hell out of them, sure enough." Sen. Brewster responds: "There is no substitute for victory," and he notes with satisfaction that at the Democratic Convention, Maryland's votes will go to President Johnson.

OREGON

The climactic Republican primary fights take place on the Pacific Coast. There, attention focuses first on the battle for the 18 delegates from Oregon. On the eve of the May 15 Oregon primary, NBC News reports.

MCGEE: The Oregon primary is different. In the others, the candidates decide if they will run; in this one, the people decide—at least indirectly. Oregon's Secretary of State enters the names of the candidates most people are talking about for the Presidency. As a result, this is the first time the names of six candidates have been printed on the ballot, giving the voters a full choice.

Oregon is important to each contender, but for different reasons. Two of them—Gov. Scranton and Mrs. Smith—know they have no prospect of winning this primary. No one has campaigned here for them. Two others have not campaigned in person because they find it is better politics at the moment to claim they are not candidates: Ambassador Lodge and former Vice President Nixon. The remaining two candidates have campaigned in Oregon: Sen. Goldwater and Gov. Rockefeller. Both were hurt badly when they lost in New Hampshire to Lodge. All the polls show that Lodge will win this one also. Rockefeller's strategy calls for a handsome win over Goldwater in Oregon to help him in California, where their names are the only ones on the ballot. Oregon offers Ambassador Lodge the last chance to prove he has public support and pick up delegates to the Convention. What he earned in New Hampshire and may earn here will be almost all the real strength he could take to the Convention.

VANOCUR: Henry Cabot Lodge, the absentee candidate, is carrying on his work as Ambassador in Saigon. Despite his impressive victory in the New Hampshire primary, Lodge has made no effort to return home to campaign—a decision which reflects his assessment that his best strategy is to stay on the job in South Vietnam. In his absence, his work is being carried on by his son, George, and volunteers working in his behalf.

MCGEE: Oregon will send only 18 delegates to the Convention. California will send 86. A few weeks ago, Sen. Goldwater cancelled all further personal campaigning in Oregon. Reporting on this development is NBC's Robert MacNeil.

MACNEIL: Barry Goldwater believes that the primaries are not the important part of getting nominated. So far, he has been proving it. He loses primaries but he is piling up delegates elsewhere. In this process, Oregon is almost irrelevant to him, but not quite. The issues that betrayed him in New Hampshire came back to haunt him here. Would he hurt Social Security? Would he cause war? Vigorously, his organization refuted these themes. The machinery ground on, but so did the adverse polls. Money was short and so was time. The really crucial prize of California's 86 delegates glittered to the South. But Goldwater could not afford a bald retreat. It had to be a tactful as well as a tactical withdrawal. He found the means in the civil rights bill and, pleading duty, he suddenly cancelled all his remaining appearances. Still, the campaign could not simply be dismantled. The stunned Oregon workers had to convince themselves he had not written them off.

So, reinforcements came. Barry, Jr., an effective younger version of the Senator from jaw line to philosophy, campaigned hard to fight the Rockefeller line that Goldwater did not care enough to come back. Gen. Albert Wedemeyer, World War II Asia expert, came out to speak. The aim was to prevent a defeat so colossal that it would have a bad psychological effect on California.

MCGEE: The primaries are not important to former Vice President Nixon. His best chance for the nomination lies in a deadlock between the conservative forces of Sen. Goldwater and the moderate or liberal forces represented by all the other candidates. Nixon is keeping himself in circulation. Shortly after Ambassador Lodge won the New Hampshire primary, Nixon took off on a tour of Southeast Asia that included a stop at Lodge's post in Saigon. The tour and his speeches helped to keep Nixon's name alive. Just a couple of days after Nixon's return, some of his supporters in Oregon opened a campaign headquarters for him.

BRINKLEY: We are seeing here an unusual political campaign: six candidates, five of them absent—as though they were trying to run a beauty contest without girls. Rockefeller is doing himself some good by being here, but three of the others—Goldwater, Lodge and Nixon—are trying to win it without showing their faces. Some of their devices are interesting, possibly effective.

Lodge is trying to win it by mail order. His people are mailing cards to registered Republicans asking for pledges. And when they come back, the information is put on five-part carbon paper forms. Well, this makes for a lot of paper shuffling and it is, therefore, the kind of job that could be automated, with each voter becoming a set of holes in a punch card. We may all come to that.

Sen. Goldwater, who is not here either, is having his campaigning done for him by family and friends. They are holding rallies, making speeches and saying the things Goldwater would say if he were here. Families, of course, have been used in primaries before, but usually with the candidate and not in place of him. So that is new.

And Nixon has had fifty telephones installed upstairs out of sight, and hired fifty girls to call around drumming up votes for him. This was kept secret until NBC got pictures of it the other night. They told us then that they were taking a poll for some kind of magazine. Perhaps: "would the readers like more recipes or more fashions?" But now that it is out, they are saying their telephone girls find surprising support for Nixon. And, in the meantime, Rockefeller is himself out shaking hands, making speeches and doing it in the old fashioned way. So we have four kinds of campaigning—by mail, by telephone, by proxy, and in person. Friday night, we will find out the winning candidate and the winning system.

Fair weather covers Oregon on Friday, May 15, and the voters—aware that the eyes of the nation are upon them—go to the polls in large numbers. The result is a surprise victory for Gov. Rockefeller in the State. Ambassador Lodge, the predicted winner, is second, and Sen. Goldwater, third—just 2,163 votes ahead of Richard Nixon. The totals: Rockefeller, 93,032 (33%); Lodge, 78,227 (27.7%); Goldwater, 49,784 (17.6%); Nixon, 47,621 (16.8%); Smith, 8,268 (2.9%); and Scranton, 5,716 (2%). Paul Grindle, national director of the "Draft Lodge" movement, concedes victory to Gov. Rockefeller an hour after the polls close. He says: "There is not the slightest question that Oregon voters have seen one of the greatest finishes in political history. They have seen an incredible fighter with lots of guts, who has gone on slugging since New Hampshire. I think the Oregon voters have gone along with us in expressing their admiration for Nelson A. Rockefeller." In Los Angeles, Sen. Goldwater says: "I still have 325 delegates. I am glad he [Gov. Rockefeller] has some —it makes a better race."

CALIFORNIA

This is the last contested State primary prior to the Republican Convention. Ever since New Hampshire, Sen. Goldwater has said that if he is to be the Republican nominee, he must win in California. The battle between the Senator and Gov. Rockefeller is joined. The prize is 86 California delegates. One week before the June 2 California primary, an important Republican voice is heard. Gen. Eisenhower writes a statement for the NEW YORK HERALD TRIBUNE *describing the type of candidate he hopes the Republicans will nominate. It is generally agreed that his specifications fit every candidate except Sen. Goldwater. In a lighthearted mood, the Senator poses for a photograph with an arrow seemingly stuck in his back. He says the picture typifies "some of the problems I've had in the last few days." But in a formal statement, he says, "I endorse Gen. Eisenhower's excellent statement . . . I hail its forthright restatement of the basic Republican principles upon which I proudly stand." Questioned in Washington by a reporter who wants to know if Sen. Goldwater fits the statement's specifications, Gen. Eisenhower replies, "try to fit that shoe on that foot."*

On the Saturday preceding the primary, a son is born to the Rockefellers, thus focusing attention anew on the New York Governor's divorce and remarriage.

On June 1, the eve of the California primary, Gen. Eisenhower denies that his recent statement describing the ideal Republican candidate was anti-Goldwater. To read that into the statement, he says, is a "complete misinterpretation." "I never attempted to read anyone out of the Party."

On June 2, the voters in America's most populous State go to the polls. . . .

All night long, as the vote pours in, Sen. Goldwater clings to a precarious lead. It is so close that even after midnight, Gov. Rockefeller, in New York, refuses to concede. He congratulates the Senator on "the tremendous number of votes he is rolling up," but insists that "the show isn't over." In Los Angeles, when it appears evident to Sen. Goldwater he will win, the Senator says, "This is not a victory for Barry Goldwater. It's a victory for the mainstream of Republican thinking." He also predicts "a greater and greater 'Stop Goldwater' movement. I do not have this thing sewed up. We have a ways to go." He adds that his victory is "a giant step" towards the nomination.

The final California vote gives Sen. Goldwater 1,089,133, for 51.4% and Gov. Rockefeller 1,030,180, for 48.6%. Out of 2,119,313 votes cast, the Senator wins by 58,953. This is the only primary Sen. Goldwater has won in which he has had real competition. And because of California's 86 delegate votes and the Goldwater victory's enormous psychological impact, this final Republican primary provides the most important political victory of the year so far.

CONVENTION DECISIONS AND VOTING
RECORDS *
Richard C. Bain

THE PLACE OF THE CONVENTION IN THE POLITICAL CYCLE

THE national nominating conventions are the culmination of one phase of the political cycle and the beginning point of another. Analysis of convention strategy and tactics must take into account, on the one hand, that the composition of a convention, the power vectors involved, and the problems confronting it are the resultants of the long-term party process. Party factions and divisive problems frequently persist over long periods of time, despite personnel change and variance in relative strength patterns.

The Convention As End-Game. On the other hand, in each election year new factors enter the picture—rising new leaders and new combinations searching for factional stability or for new issues. The preconvention period gives

* From Richard C. Bain, *Convention Decisions and Voting Records* (The Brookings Institution, 1960), pp. 2–7. © 1960 by The Brookings Institution.

the new elements and the old a chance to try their strength and to jockey for position. When the convention opens, the situation is similar to that of an end-game in chess—the positions and relative strength of the antagonists is a resultant of the game that has gone on before.

As in chess, the variety of end-game situations is almost limitless, but there are nevertheless a limited number of general patterns. In many cases the question of victory or defeat is no longer at issue—one opponent is clearly in an overwhelmingly powerful position, and it remains simply to see how fast and in what way the position will be exploited and victory ratified. In other cases, some slight hope may be retained by the weaker opponent that the game can be pulled out of the fire by brilliant play on his own part, or by egregious error on the part of the stronger man. In still other cases, the game is wide open, with victory evenly in the balance, sometimes with the situation highly structured and with heavy pieces closely engaged, at other times with the situation so fluid that considerable development must occur before decisive moves can be made.

The first situation—that of one opponent being in an overwhelmingly powerful position—usually occurs when an incumbent President is seeking renomination, as in the 1956 Republican convention. The Democratic convention of 1956 illustrates the second situation, in which Adlai Stevenson clearly was far in the lead, but with Averell Harriman still hoping that a miracle would happen. The two 1952 conventions illustrate the two situations outlined in the third general type. The closely structured game, with the heavy pieces closely engaged, is typified by the Eisenhower-Taft situation; fast, hard-hitting action is almost a certainty under this condition. The situation was much more fluid in the Democratic convention, and the game required further development before the critical moves could be made. The pawn was queened when Stevenson became clearly available, and the game became more clearly structured.

While the contests for the nomination are going on, the party leaders must constantly keep in mind that the convention also is the starting point of the electoral battle to follow—indeed, is an integral part of that fight. To become so engrossed in the intra-party struggle that its effects upon the electoral campaign are disregarded can be fatal. The Republicans in 1912 and the Democrats in 1924 *learned* this to their sorrow.

Contests and Rational Choice. When looked at from the standpoint of the party leaders whose goal is party victory in the election rather than factional victory in the convention, the ultimate winners of contested nominations throughout the history of the convention system appear to have been remarkably rational choices. Even so maligned a nomination as that of Warren G. Harding, whose selection made the phrase "smoke-filled room" famous—or infamous—can be seen as a rational act when the information available to those making the choice is considered. A life of Harding up to his Inauguration Day, if written only from information available at that time, would have been quite different from the life of Harding that was actually written after the story was finished. For many other Presidents, this would also be true; incumbency in the Presidency is a test that can reveal previously unperceived weakness or call forth unexpected strength.

Any student who evaluates Abraham Lincoln or Franklin D. Roosevelt, for instance, strictly on the basis of what was written before and at the time of their nominations would arrive at conclusions remarkably different from those based on their later action in the presidential office. It is a matter of record that numerous contemporaries who became ardent followers of these two Presidents had originally expressed grave misgivings about and sometimes violent objection to them as nominees.

PROS AND CONS OF THE CONVENTION SYSTEM

From the first national party convention held in 1831 down to the present date, the system has been subject to continual attack. The focal points against which attack has been directed have varied, and corrective measures or alternatives proposed have received different emphases at different times, but the criticism has usually concentrated upon four main aspects of the conventions. Briefly, the charges are:

—Convention membership is not truly representative of the party and/or the national electorate.

—Actual decisions are made by only a few of the many delegates who attend the conventions.

—Conventions cannot—or at least do not—pick the best men.

—Conventions characteristically are undignified, and prone to indulge in meaningless displays.

Despite these persistent criticisms, the convention system for selecting national party nominees for the highest offices in the land has been amazingly virile. And it is noteworthy that the legitimacy of the convention choice has rarely been questioned—even in the face of the fact that throughout most of their history, conventions have had no legal status whatever, and even now are recognized in law only in peripheral ways.

Neither the virility of the system nor the general public acceptance of convention decisions as legitimate—for a period of one hundred and thirty years—can be attributed to chance. It would seem more logical to assume that there are underlying reasons which justify continuation of this method of choosing national party nominees—that, in fact, conventions fulfill a basic need of the American political system adequately enough so that no alternative system has yet been found to supplant them. If this is so, it may be well to examine in more detail the four charges outlined above.

The Convention Membership. Several studies have attempted to identify the convention delegates in terms of such factors as income level, age, religion and party position. Generally speaking, these studies indicate that the delegates are a broadly representative cross-cut of America, but with considerable weighting toward the upper levels of the socio-economic scale. It has been pointed out, however, that there is much evidence that this is the kind of representation the American public wants and tends to select whenever given the opportunity.

All of the delegates presumably are politicians, if we accept the broad definition of a politician as one who takes sufficient interest in public and party affairs to participate actively. It is important to note, however, that an individual may be a politician in this sense at one level, and an unpolitical citizen at another. Thus, one man may be very active in local politics, yet pay almost no attention to state or national politics, while another may be deeply implicated at the national level and almost completely disinterested at the lower levels.

Due to the structure of our state and national parties, the delegates frequently selected for national conventions are really politicians in the local or state sense only. Despite previous lack of interest in national politics, strong local leaders, if they decide they want to be delegates, cannot easily be denied. Thus, many delegates may be found in the conventions who know few if any outside of their own state delegation; others may have only limited previous connection even with members of their own delegation, other than those from their immediate local area.

The major stock-in-trade of a politician is the web of personal contact and influence with which he surrounds himself. On the one hand, he has contacts from whom he receives information, and upon whose judgment he relies; on the other, he has a following that relies upon him for information and for advice. A seasoned politician who moves outside his own web and into another area of political activity is little better off than a newcomer to politics. Through skills he has developed, he may be able to adjust quickly to the new scene, but he cannot do much within the span of the few days comprising the convention period. Accordingly, the delegate who is not already oriented to the national political scene cannot operate effectively in a national convention, and must depend for his communications upon others who have a place in the communication web. Generally, these are the key leaders in his own delegation.

The situation of the average delegate in depending upon someone he trusts to supply him with the political information he needs is not too different from the non-political situation of anyone faced with having to make decisions without adequate information. If a man is buying a house, for instance, he is likely to seek advice from a knowledgeable friend; if the friend is in the business of selling the commodity involved, his recommendations will be accompanied by a certain amount of pressure to have them accepted. So too, the politician is always in the business of persuading others to vote as he does.

Smoke-filled Rooms as Market Places. It is a commonplace that any gathering numbering more than a handful of people must develop a leadership structure, formal or informal, if it is to take any kind of action. Even apparently uncontrollable mobs are swung one way or another by the actions of a few who are accepted, at least temporarily, as leaders. Certainly, national nominating conventions from their earliest days have been too large to permit their operating as a town meeting where everyone had equal say, and equal time to say it. As they have grown larger through the years, this has become increasingly true.

It is obvious that negotiation on almost any subject at almost any level cannot be carried out in full view of all who are affected by the ultimate decisions. This is one of the greatest dilemmas of democracy. In the process of convention negotiation, propositions that are known by all parties to the negotiation to be unacceptable are advanced for the purpose of defining the outer boundaries of the area within which the ultimate compromise is to be made. The onlooker, to the degree he is uninformed of the questions at issue and the purposes for which bargaining proposals are made, may become unduly alarmed and create such a disturbance that further negotiation can be made impossible.

In recognition of this problem, the open sessions of the body as a whole, and even the open meetings of its subcommittees are fundamentally educational and ratification meetings. Even when, for political or technical reasons, open debates are held, these debates seldom change decisions made *in camera,* nor are they expected to by the leaders who permit and participate in the debates. This does not mean that open debates are irrelevant or unimportant. They frequently have tremendous implications to the future of political issues and to the individuals involved and sometimes to the subsequent acts of the convention. But they seldom change the vote substantially on the issue actually under debate.

Within every factional or subfactional group, whether oriented to an issue or a candidate, is a group of leaders, self-constituted, perhaps, but backed by the acceptance of their followers. Depending upon the kind of group it is, the leaders may or may not have members who have good communications with counterpart leaders in other groups. Those that do have a good chance of ending up in the winning coalition; those that do not are very apt to end up in the losing minority. It is this, perhaps more than any other factor, that militates against the success of candidates whose stand upon controversial issues is unequivocal. The thin line of distinction between *unequivocal* and *dogmatic,* though it may be recognized by the top leadership, is all too frequently not recognized by the loyal followers, and dogmatism and free communication do not live well together. Accordingly, communication contacts between the subleaders of such potential candidates may be, and generally are, quite poor.

On the other hand, factional leaders who are not deeply committed to any candidate or issue will tend to have wide communication with other groups of the same kind, and can even deal with the less fanatical followers of the more ideological groups. Being more or less in the center of the political spectrum they can bargain either to the right or to the left, if their own numbers are not sufficient, and make the best bargain they can. Whatever the outcome, if the middle groups form a major part of the coalition, the solution will be less extreme than if the coalition is dominated by a more extreme faction.

It is generally assumed by the public that an important part of the smoke-filled room process is negotiation by factional leaders for recognition by and access to the hoped-for administration, if not for actual positions in the administration structure. This negotiation is often attacked as insidious, invidious, and undemocratic. The assumption is correct, but the basis for the attacks needs further examination.

To understand this part of the process, one must first recognize that the President of the United States is not simply a man; he is the symbol and the representative of a more or less organized coalition, of which he may or may not be the actual leader and within which the members have a general understanding of their positions in the hierarchy. In forming a coalition strong enough to win the nomination—and looking forward to winning the election —leaders of groups that join the coalition quite legitimately want a clear understanding that the groups they represent will be given recognition by the new administration if the election is won. Indeed, they would not be representing their followers adequately if they did not seek this.

There is no question but that "deals" for support are sometimes too commercial or that administration appointees resulting from the process are sometimes unqualified for the jobs. However, it would be difficult to find any employment system, where human ambitions are involved, in which only those with the highest motivations and the best qualifications are universally selected. Instead, therefore, of categorically condemning the present appointee system because it does not always work perfectly, it might be well to consider the scope of the problem, and its relationship to the efficient functioning of the Executive Branch of the government.

When a new President assumes his office, several hundred people take office with him, all of whom he personally appoints, "by and with the consent of the Senate" in most cases. The success or failure of his administration depends in large part on the way this small host of appointees performs. He therefore has a tremendous personal stake in their ability and in their loyalty to himself.

But he must also depend upon other elements of the governmental structure. He certainly must have the cooperation of Congress, if he is to implement his program. Since many of his appointees have extensive dealings with Congress, it is of the utmost importance that they have good relations with individual congressmen, and particularly with the leaders. To the extent that the congressional leaders are consulted for approval of the appointments, it is reasonable to assume that the prospects of good relations will be increased.

If the President is to have widespread national support for his program, he will need the cooperation of party organization leaders and of leaders of important economic and social groups. If these individuals feel that they are represented within the administration councils, they will be more willing to extend cooperation.

Obviously, the influence of these various forces on the President's appointments can be at times carried too far—in which case a President may find himself dependent upon a staff whose basic loyalties are to others than himself, with the result that he cannot exert the leadership proper to his office. From this standpoint, the first major test of a man's adequacy for the Presidency is his ability to hold his own in the negotiations leading toward his nomination—providing satisfaction to competing leaders of the factions forming his nominating coalition and at the same time maintaining control of his administration components for the future.

The Nominees. Perhaps the principal criticism leveled at the system of nomination by conventions is that strong leaders are generally passed over in favor of relative nonentities or of men who have not made their positions on major public issues fully clear. In a sense this is true, but much of the criticism is based upon assumptions about leadership and the democratic process that should be examined carefully. Implicit in the criticism is the picture of a leader as one who is out in front of his followers directing the march toward, and the fight for, more or less concrete objectives. Implicit also is the idea that leaders of this type are best fitted to govern.

There is, however, another concept of leadership and another type of leader who may be better fitted to lead the government of a complex democracy, and it can be argued that this latter type more frequently than not emerges from the convention process. It is a leadership adept at reconciling conflicting goals and points of view, and adept also at creating a climate which permits a compromise program to be developed and carried out. The program may not be spectacular, and actually may be completely acceptable to no one, but if it is sufficiently acceptable to a majority of people to prevent them from bolting to more extreme leaders sponsoring more extreme programs, it may be adopted as the party program. The individual who engineers, or symbolizes the engineering of, the compromise solution will similarly be accepted as the party leader.

This is not to say that leaders of the first type do not play an essential part in the democratic process. They are indeed essential; by clarifying and dramatizing the issues, they force thought and re-evaluation on less energetic or more complacent citizens, and it is from this thought and re-evaluation that a climate is developed in which new goals become possible. Nevertheless, the leader of a faction whose views are considered relatively extreme by a majority of the people within and without the party is in a weak position to form a government acceptable to this majority.

The Campaign Rally Function. It has been endlessly charged that the frenetic displays of oratory and the riotous demonstrations that accompany the presentation of candidates and the nominations that follow are undignified and incompatible with the serious business of the conventions. There is considerable justification for the criticism, especially if conventions are thought of simply as agencies for making nominations and developing a party platform. These functions are indeed the central reason for the existence of the system as an institution—but they are also functions that must depend heavily on the enthusiastic and devoted participation of a vast number of people.

Throughout history, all institutions whose membership was widespread have found it useful, and often essential, to hold more or less regular convocations where representatives of "the laity" can mingle with the "professional" leadership, and all such gatherings have characteristically featured some sort of ritual or display. The kind of display is dictated by the apparent need of the organization, and may range from carefully staged monastic contemplation in a religious group to neanderthal orgies such as Hitler staged at Nürnberg. Of whatever kind, such manifestations are meant to instill in an organization's membership a sense of belonging to the group.

An American political party has a special need to find ways of making its membership feel "belonging," because party affiliations has so far scarcely ever been on a dues-paying, card-holding basis but depends almost entirely on the will of the individual member to become and remain a partisan. In this context, it can be said that the function of the convention as a campaign rally is a necessary one (which is not to say that the excess wildness of the rally is essential). Each leader, great or minor, who is given the convention stage for a few brief moments is at the same time given a feeling of participation, and his followers identify themselves in participation with him. So, too, the demonstrations give the rank-and-file delegates a sense of belonging to a dynamic movement—at least for the moment, whatever their more sober later reflections may be.

It should not be surprising that even the apparent irrelevancies of the conventions have meaning and function; indeed, it would be surprising if they did not. The American national nominating conventions are among the oldest quasi-official political institutions of importance in existence. That they and the ways in which they operate have survived with so little change for a hundred and thirty years should be proof enough that they satisfy real needs.

THE NOMINATING PROCESS *
Nelson W. Polsby and Aaron B. Wildavsky

STRATEGIC CONSIDERATIONS

Goals

The delegates to national party conventions are selected state by state, in conventions or primaries, or by a combination of the two methods. They represent the outcomes of processes that are slightly different in their legal requirements and political overtones in each of the states, the District of Columbia, and the territories—all of which send delegations to both party conventions. But when delegates arrive at the convention, they enter into a social system in which their roles are reasonably regularized. Not surprisingly,

* From Nelson W. Polsby and Aaron B. Wildavsky, *Presidential Elections* (Charles Scribner's Sons, 1964), pp. 59–64 and 70–77. Reprinted with the permission of Charles Scribner's Sons. Copyright © 1964 Charles Scribner's Sons.

they try to behave in a way that will maximize their political power. The rational dice player will place his bets in accordance with his chances of winning under the rules of the game he is playing. Similarly, the "rational" delegate will be expected to be reasonably well informed about how his behavior affects his chances of achieving his goals, and will behave in accordance with his information, his position in the game, and the goals he is intent upon achieving.

American national parties are loose federations of independent state parties representing somewhat different combinations of economic, ethnic, religious, sectional and other interests. Therefore, the great search at the convention is for "The Man Who Can Win," for without hope of victory, over the years there would be little reason for a heterogeneous party to stay together. Even if the parties were far more cohesive than they are today, they still could not disregard the need to get into office now and then by nominating a popular candidate.

The desire to nominate a winner is widespread but is not equally distributed among delegates. It is strongest among delegates from states with a high degree of party competition or where the party is weak. Both of these groups of delegates need a popular candidate, in close states to increase their vote, and in states where the party is weak to bring them some patronage. On the other hand, winners are least needed in areas where the party is overwhelmingly dominant, such as the South in the case of the Democrats, where local fortunes will continue to be good regardless of what happens in the national election. But the one-party areas have long since ceased to control the conventions and competition seems to be growing in many formerly one-party areas.

Capitalizing on the understandable desire to nominate a winner, candidates seek to demonstrate that they can win and others cannot. Candidates cite polls and make complicated electoral analyses in order to convince delegates on this point. Frequently, there appear to be several strong candidates and disagreements about which one is the most probable winner often take place because the delegates have private preferences and lack enough information about what the voters are likely to do.

Politicians seek to maintain or increase their own political power. In order to do so, most of them feel that they must, in general, increase the potential vote for candidates whom they sponsor. The more leaders who agree on a candidate and the more interest groups and state party organizations that are working for his election, the greater are the chances that he will win office and provide those politicians who supported him with access to political power. Party unity, therefore, is perceived by politicians as an important prerequisite to the achievement of victory. Unless party leaders achieve a consensus among themselves, the chances are diminished that they will be able to elect a President. Parties tend as a result to nominate candidates who at the least are not obnoxious to, and ideally, are attractive to as many interest groups and state party leaders as possible.

The members of each party may love their party on a sentimental basis. They certainly love the idea of getting into office. But do they love one another? The convention tests party unity by determining whether the disparate elements which make up each party can agree on one man to represent them— a man who cannot possibly be equally attractive to all of them. Party unity may aid in securing victory and this provides an incentive for keeping all the factions under the same party umbrella. But the differences among delegates may be so great that no one is quite sure whether they can agree. The much maligned party platform is exceedingly important in this regard not so much for what it makes explicit but for the fact that it is written at all. The platform tests and communicates the ability of the many party factions to agree on something, even if on some crucial points, major differences have to be papered over.

One of the important estimates which rival party leaders must make is how far they can go in attaining their preferences without completely alienating some faction, resulting in its withdrawal from the convention. This information may not be available until party factions begin to bargain at the convention.

Delegates not only want to unify the party around a probable winner; they also want to make certain that they have a claim on him so that he will consider their requests favorably. Thus, they seek either a candidate who is known to be friendly to them, whose policy views tend to coincide with theirs, or who will be indebted to them because they have provided support toward his nomination. Jim Farley's famous list establishing priorities for distributing patronage—FRBC (For Roosevelt Before Chicago)—illustrates this point. It helps to explain the rush to get on the bandwagon by delegates who wish access to the winning candidate. But more than one bandwagon may appear to be in the making and delegates and their political leaders may have difficulty deciding when the best time is to make the jump and gain the greatest bargaining advantages for themselves.

It must never be forgotten that delegates come from state parties with internal lives of their own. The delegates spend over 1400 days every four years as members of their state parties and less than a week at the national convention. To commit acts at the convention—supporting a candidate unpopular in that state, insisting on a unit rule for delegation voting against the intense opposition of a strong minority which would lead to years of bitter internal rivalry—would be unwise. Yet it is not always possible to avoid mistakes. Delegates may misjudge who will run well in their state and provide a "coattail effect." Sometimes nominees run better in states which opposed them at the convention than in those which gave them support. In any event, it is clear that in order to interpret or predict a state's behavior one may have to know a great deal about internal party conditions. One of the first requirements imposed on any Presidential aspirant is that he acquire information on internal party affairs which may prove indispensable to planning his strategy and may enable him to take advantage of or to avoid dangerous party splits.

Some delegates have strong policy preferences. Negroes and Southerners may care deeply about racial questions. Union officials and industrial executives may be unwilling to support candidates presumed to be hostile to the interests they represent. Delegates from the District of Columbia may consider home rule to be of paramount importance while the men from Tennessee may be adamant about public power. To some extent, therefore, intense policy preferences may restrict the actions of delegates who share them; they may seek the man who has the best chance of winning among those candidates who meet their specifications on crucial policies.

The major goal of the Presidential aspirant in the convention is to win the nomination; but in addition he rightly regards the nominating convention as the first part of the election campaign. This means that even while prospective candidates are belaboring one another in an attempt to get the nomination they must give due consideration to the necessity for party unity in case they win. There are several ways in which this party unity is achieved. One device available to the winner of a contested nomination is to select the disappointed Presidential aspirant with the second most votes in the convention as a Vice-Presidential nominee, as Kennedy selected Lyndon Johnson in 1960.

Incumbent Presidents and other obvious choices, such as Richard Nixon in 1960, are in a better position to treat the convention as the opening gun of their campaign. They can participate wholeheartedly in the party rituals, the speech-making, informal social gatherings, and the self-congratulation that give the party faithful at the convention a sense of identity and mission, and project over television an image of unity, purpose, and togetherness. Such nominees also can manipulate the party platform to offset their real or imagined weaknesses with the electorate and to capitalize on their strengths. In contested conventions, the platform must be negotiated among representatives of the leading contenders and major segments of the party, and so it is less easy to write a platform that the eventual winner can comfortably campaign on.

Thus, we can describe quickly the major goals of most delegates to national conventions. They want: to gain power, to nominate a man who can win the election, to unify the party, to obtain some claim on the nominee, to protect their central core of policy preferences, and to strengthen their state party organizations. . . .

PRE-CONVENTION STRATEGIES

The selection of a Presidential nominee is the business which dominates the convention. From this it follows that decisions preceding the Presidential nomination are important or unimportant largely depending upon their implications for the Presidential nomination. Decisions not taken unanimously which precede the Presidential nomination in the convention are almost always tests of strength between party factions divided as to the Presidential nomination. These decisions are usually more important for the information they communicate on the strength of the candidates than for their actual content.

Perhaps the first strategic decision facing an avowed candidate is whether to attempt to become a front-runner by entering primaries, barnstorming the country, and publicly seeking support at state conventions. The advantage of this strategy is that a candidate may build up such a commanding lead (or appear to do so) that no one will be able (or will try) to stop him at the national convention. The disadvantage is that an open campaign may reveal his inability to acquire support or may lead other candidates to band together in order to stop him. Adoption of this position depends for its success, then, upon the front-runner's ability to predict accurately both how he will fare compared to others in open competition, and what others will be able to do when they discover his lead. He may, for example, try to anticipate whether his activity will stimulate a coalition of opponents who are otherwise unlikely to get together. If such a coalition seems likely, the candidate may issue communications playing down the extent of his support. But this tactic may discourage new supporters who would have been attracted by a display of strength. Candidates can never be entirely certain that they are striking the right balance between reticence and aggressiveness, which may explain why unabashed attempts to use bandwagon or dark horse strategies in relatively undiluted form are quite common.

The dark horse is an avowed candidate who avoids primaries and much open campaigning. Like Stuart Symington in 1960, he is content to be everyone's friend and no one's enemy. As Abraham Lincoln wrote to a supporter in 1860 describing his dark horse strategy: "My name is new in the field, and I suppose I am not the first choice of a very great many. Our policy, then, is to give no offense to others—leave them in a mood to come to us if they shall be compelled to give up their first love." The strategy of the dark horse is to combine with others to oppose every front-runner. His hope is that when no front-runner is left he will appear as the man who can unify the party by being acceptable to all and obnoxious to none. The dangers the dark horse faces are that he will enter the convention with too little support to make a strong bid or that some other dark horse will prove preferable. How much support is enough to make a serious bid but not enough to be shot at as a front-runner? How far behind the front-runner can a candidate permit himself to get without becoming entirely lost from sight? Either an intuitive ability to guess or an exceedingly accurate apparatus for collecting information on the present strength of candidates, as well as on the likely effect of different levels of strength on other delegates, must be part of the serious dark horse's equipment.

Primaries. Primaries are important largely because the results represent an ostensibly objective indication of whether a candidate can win the election. The contestants stand to gain or lose far more than the small number of delegate votes which may be at stake. Thus a man situated as was Richard Nixon in 1960 would be ill-advised to enter a primary unless the information at his disposal led him to believe that he was quite certain to win. This stricture applies with special force to any candidate who is well ahead in delegate support. All he can gain is a few additional votes, while he can lose his existing support by a bad showing in the primary since this would be interpreted as meaning that he could not win in the election. The candidate who is far behind, or who has to overcome severe handicaps, however, has little or nothing to lose by entering a risky primary. If he wins, he has demonstrated his popularity; if he loses, he is hardly worse off than if he had not entered the primary at all. Such was the case when John Kennedy quieted the apprehensions of Democratic politicians about the religious issue by winning in Protestant West Virginia. The man who is ahead needs more certain information about how primaries are likely to turn out because he takes the greater risk.

The man who is behind in securing convention support or whose ability to win is in doubt engages in strategies of enticement in which he issues siren calls inviting the leading contenders into a primary. He suggests that they are cowardly, lacking in fighting spirit, afraid to face the public. By luring them into a primary, he hopes to deal a severe blow to their chances and thereby boost his own. In order to avoid this trap, it may be necessary for candidates to publicize their disdain for primaries, to specify in advance all the reasons why such a contest would be unnecessary, unfair, and a waste of time. The candidate who finds himself in a primary (and wishes to live and fight again another day) does well to have alibis ready to explain away seemingly disadvantageous results.

In a primary in which there are many contenders a defeated candidate may attempt to gain advantage from what may be regarded as an ambiguous result by claiming that the man who actually won was allied to him ideologically. The results may then be viewed as a victory for the ideology rather than defeat for the candidate. After La Follette had won an overwhelming victory in the 1912 Republican primary in North Dakota, Theodore Roosevelt issued a statement "claiming an immense progressive victory." He even went beyond this to count the La Follette delegation as part of the Roosevelt camp once it had cast "a complimentary vote for La Follette."

One strategy for primaries, the write-in, offers the maximum possibility of gain with the minimum possibility of loss. If a candidate gets virtually no votes, he can easily explain this by saying that he did not campaign and that it is difficult for people to write in names. If he receives 10 per cent of the vote, he can hail this as a tremendous victory under the circumstances. And if he should win, he can build it up to the sky, stressing the extraordinary popularity required to get people to go to all the trouble of writing in a name. But the man who is behind cannot rest content with being able to explain away a poor showing; he must win to establish himself as a contender. The strategy of the write-in, consequently, is most accessible to the man who is ahead and hopes to solidify his position while minimizing his risks.

The foregoing discussion should help us to understand why those who win primaries sometimes do not win the nomination. Part of the reason is that there are not many primaries and not all of those actually commit delegates to vote for a candidate. Of greater significance, however, is the fact that primary activity is often (though by no means always) a sign that a candidate has great obstacles to overcome and must win many primaries in order to be considered for the nomination at all. The image communicated to political professionals by a few primary victories, unless they are overwhelming, may be less that of the conquering hero than that of the drowning man clutching at the last straw.

Thus, entering and winning primaries may be of little value unless the results are widely interpreted in such a way as to improve a candidate's chances. The contestant who "loses" but does better than expected may reap greater advantage from a primary than the one who wins but falls below expectations. It is, therefore, manifestly to the advantage of a candidate to hold his claims down to minimum proportions. Kennedy tried in 1960 to follow this advice in Wisconsin—he claimed Humphrey had been Wisconsin's third Senator—but the press, radio, and TV took note of his extensive organization and of favorable polls, and in advance pinned the winner-by-a-landslide-label on the Senator from Massachusetts. The public media have taken some of the control over "expectations" from the candidates.

Yet there is more to the strategy of primaries than mere calculation of chances on the candidate's part. The desires of the existing state organizations may also have to be taken into account. The state organization may be sponsoring a favorite son who, it hopes, may be nominated in case of deadlock. It may wish to remain uncommitted in order to increase its bargaining power by making a claim on the winner in return for throwing last minute support to him. The party may be divided and fear internecine warfare over rival candidates which would leave it in a shattered condition. For all of these reasons, the state leadership may request candidates to stay out and may threaten to work against them in the primary and at the convention if they disobey. Presidential aspirants may have to rest content with second or third choice support unless their position is so desperate that they have little to lose by antagonizing the state party.

Paradoxically, the candidate who can show that he has no choice but to enter a primary may gain a bargaining advantage. The state leaders may then decide that it is worth making concessions to him to avoid the internal strife that would be caused by a primary contest. This is more or less what happened when John Kennedy, fortified by a poll claiming that he would win, insisted that he absolutely had to have Ohio's votes to have a chance at the national convention. Ohio Governor Michael DiSalle, who wanted to run as a favorite son, had to back down in order to avoid a primary fight that could have been extremely embarrassing to him, and so he ran on a slate pledged to Kennedy. The Governor's decision was prompted by the knowledge that the Cuyahoga County (Cleveland) party faction, which was hostile to him, would run a slate pledged to Kennedy and use this as a weapon to reduce the Governor's stature within the state. The struggle for power within a state may have much to do with its action at the convention.

State and District Conventions. Most of the delegates are still chosen, not by primaries, but by state and district conventions. This process provides relatively few contests over the selection of delegates, although these may be important. Most attempts to influence delegates chosen in this way are made after they are chosen. The first strategic requirement for the candidate seeking to influence these delegations is an intelligence service, a network of informants who will tell the candidates which delegations are firmly committed, which are wavering, and which may be persuaded to provide second or third choice support. Advance reports on the opportunities offered by internal divisions in the state parties, the type of appeal likely to be effective in each state, and the kinds of bargains to which leaders are most susceptible, may also be helpful. The costs of this information may come high in terms of time, money, and effort, but it will be worth it to the serious candidate who needs to know where to move to increase his support and block his opponents.

Aspirants for nomination vary greatly in the degree to which they know other politicians throughout the country. Men like former Vice-President Richard Nixon and Senator Barry Goldwater, who have travelled extensively and extended assistance to members of their party, may simply need to keep their files up to date in order to have a nationwide list of contacts. When the time comes, they know whom they can call upon for assistance in gathering information, persuading delegates, and generally furthering their cause. Candidates who lack this advantage, however, have to take special steps in order to build up their political apparatus. In paving the way for Franklin D. Roosevelt's nomination in 1932, James F. Farley began early by sending invitations to Governor Roosevelt's inauguration to party leaders throughout the country. Most invitations were refused but a valuable correspondence grew out of this approach. Farley next sent a small manual containing a few facts about the Democratic party organization to people throughout the country. The response encouraged a follow-up pamphlet which presented, without comment, the New York gubernatorial vote in every county since 1916. It was intended to be impressive testimony of FDR's vote-getting ability. When many people wrote back expressing an interest in FDR's candidacy, offering suggestions, or just saying "thanks," Farley replied with a personal message and endeavored to keep up the contact through further letters, phone calls, and even a phonograph record. Later, in 1931, Farley took a trip through the West, ostensibly to visit the Elks Convention in Seattle, but actually to contact over 1,000 party leaders in all but three states west of the Mississippi. Upon his return, every one of Farley's contacts received a personal letter.

The well-organized candidates contact the delegates personally or through close associates. They may show a winning personality, make implied promises of good things to come, discuss or avoid controversial issues of special importance to the locality, as seems best calculated to increase their support. If a favorable public opinion poll is handy or can be arranged, this will often be cited to substantiate the claims of victory which must be made to convey the impression that it would be a good idea to climb on the bandwagon. More than one can play at this game, however, and "pollsmanship" is becoming a common art whose practitioners know how to secure the desired impression and blunt harmful ones. There are good reasons to suppose that the number of polls taken exceeds the number made public since sometimes the news they disclose disappoints the candidate who paid for them.

THE NOMINATING PROCESS AND THE FUTURE
OF THE PARTY SYSTEM *
Paul T. David, Ralph M. Goldman, Richard C. Bain

THE nominating contests at the conventions and the elections that follow provide regular opportunities for decisive change in the ordering of political affairs. It is very possible that the decisions at the conventions are more critical than those left to the general election; certainly, if a systematic general theory of political change in the United States is ever constructed, it must give a central place to the nominating process.

Each successive convention helps to shape the future evolution of the party institution. It affects also the extent to which the party can bring cohesion and clear purpose to the work of government—or the extent to which it will retreat from this task, leaving a governmental vacuum to be filled by other mechanisms of some more obscure and less definable sort.

The conventions were created to cope specifically with the presidential and vice-presidential nominations and to remove the early dominance of Congress in this process. They have unavoidably become a central political mechanism with a potential for power far beyond anything their original sponsors dreamed. For each of their decisions they have an inescapable responsibility; questions for the future, concerning what can and should be done about both the nominating process and the party system, thus become largely synonymous with what can be done by the parties in convention assembled.

THE CENTRAL POSITION OF THE NOMINATING PROCESS

The principal and most clearly defined function of the presidential nominating process in each party is to identify the candidate who is entitled to be designated the party's nominee—with all this entails in the conferring of legitimacy, securing a place on the ballot, and assuring the loyalty and the votes of the party faithful. A much less clearly defined function, but an important one and seemingly in the process of becoming recognized, is to designate the candidate

* From Paul T. David, Ralph M. Goldman, and Richard C. Bain, *The Politics of National Party Conventions*, rev. ed. (Vintage Books, 1964), pp. 320–327. © Copyright 1960, 1964 by the Brookings Institution.

also as the chief party leader. The ambiguity of this second function results from the dependence of effective leadership on victory in the election.

At the beginning of the convention system, Andrew Jackson let no one doubt that he was his party's leader. But for many decades after 1840 the nominating act was merely the designation of a candidate for the ensuing election—a candidate to be discarded if he lost and to be disregarded as much as possible in party matters even if he won. Recently it has become settled custom that winning the Presidency entitles the incumbent to recognition as the chief leader of his party—in the government, in the party organization, and in the electorate. The defeated candidate, however, has no secure entitlements. He is generally known as the titular leader of his party, but the extent to which the label has meaning remains obscure.

Whatever the eventual fate of the candidate, the nomination—the last hurdle but one on the course that leads to the highest position open to an American citizen—is still a sufficient glory in itself to exercise a profound effect upon all political arrangements. The nominating process occupies its central position in the party system chiefly because it exerts a substantial influence on the behavior of all actors throughout the system, an influence much greater than they are able to exercise on it. Although the relationship is not exclusively one-way, it is primarily so. For this reason, certain basic questions about the legitimacy and effectiveness of the relationship are justified.

CANDIDATE COMPETENCE

Is the nominating process capable of selecting the most able candidates available in the two parties for a final choice by the electorate? Or, if not the most able, candidates who are at least fully competent to meet the responsibilities of the office? The question comes close to the issues of national and world survival, and is no more capable of a conclusive answer than most such questions. But it does suggest the importance of elements that may either move the process toward or push it away from the selection of competent candidates.

One such element is the choice that must be made between short-run and long-run considerations that compete for recognition. The choice is posed most vividly in the traditionally contrasted bases for candidate selection: ability to win the election—or ability to lead and operate the government. Obviously some thought has usually been given to both sets of considerations and to others as well, but there have been times in American history when the contrast has been starkly put. The Whig party hastened its own end by its penchant for selecting vice-presidential candidates without regard for whether they could provide party or governmental leadership if called upon to do so.

Only a system that seeks a balanced pattern of electoral and governmental success in its choice of top leaders could be said to have achieved the degree of maturity that is compatible with survival. The American political system has not yet reached full maturity in this respect, but there have been many recent indications that the balance of the short-run and long-run considerations has changed for the better. If it has so changed, three . . . factors for change . . .

may be given most of the credit.

One is the increasing influence throughout the nominating process of responsible elective officials of high rank, as distinguished from party bosses who can hold political power without becoming directly accountable for the conduct of government. The second factor is the recent tendency of public-spirited and intelligent citizens to join the party process in various states to an extent that did not exist when bossism was more rampant. This may be partly responsible for what seems to be a growing disposition in the whole electorate to judge candidates by qualities that are required for competence in office, and not merely by those conducive to proficiency in campaigning.

The third is an apparent tendency for elective office to be more attractive and more accessible to the members of each oncoming generation who are marked for success and have the widest field of choice in deciding on their careers. The remarkably numerous able young candidates for the elective offices of intermediate rank who have come over the horizon in recent years suggest that a public-service type of motivation may be spreading; if so, it would be one of the most hopeful signs for the future.

POPULAR CONTROL

Although the convention system was established in part as a revolt against the undemocratic aspects of nominations by the congressional caucuses, popular control continued for many years to be indirect, to say the least. To the extent that it existed, it was necessarily based on the most meager information about many of the candidates before their nomination. Clearly there has been a great increase since 1900 in popular participation—brought about by the spread of the mass media, the presidential primaries in certain states, the public opinion polls, and the responses of the candidates to these and other factors. The candidates have developed new attitudes on the extent to which it is appropriate and essential to appeal to the popular will, along with new attitudes on the kind and amount of campaigning that are legitimate in doing so.

Much of the struggle that used to occur in the conventions has been shifted to the preconvention period, and with the great modern access to information about delegate commitments and intentions, most of the losers in recent times have probably known that they were beaten before the convention opened. Generally they were too deeply committed to withdraw, but their power to make "deals" before admitting defeat was greatly reduced.

When public opinion is clearly developed in support of a majority choice, popular control now seems almost complete within either party. And even when a clear popular mandate is lacking, in practice there has been a considerable shift away from the traditional situations of convention stalemate in which a compromise candidate can or must be selected. The 1952 contests in both conventions and the Democratic contests of 1956 and 1960 were quickly resolved through clearly defined voting victories. The development and reporting of widespread public sentiment within the parties had much to do with this.

The values associated with popular control of the political system are deeply imbedded in the ethic of democracy but, by itself, popular control provides no complete answer to the problems of discovering the basis of a truly national consensus and of finding a leadership adequate to develop it. The dangers of the times demand a consensus that is not only broadly based, but also adapted to the requirements of national and world survival. Political leaders are clearly needed who will not merely follow their followers, but will assume the burdens of political education and grasp the nettle firmly when moral leadership is the country's greatest need.

These are the capacities of wisdom, yet men of wisdom also recognize their own limitations and may thus hesitate to volunteer for the rough-and-tumble of political life. Unless they have already been brought into political office at lower levels, they are unlikely to enter the race for the highest elective offices. When they do not volunteer, they may have to be drafted; and if the system fails to bring such men into positions where they can be recognized, the system itself may need to be changed.

CLARIFICATION OF PARTY ROLES

In choosing a candidate, a political party is also deciding its future, which depends mainly on its continuing success in developing the position it proposes to occupy in relationship to the needs of the times. This is a far more complicated problem than the writing of formal platform statements. Essentially it involves the clarification and adaptation of the party role.

By comparison with other types of organizations, political parties are relatively plastic, but each party is limited at any one time by its inherited character. The task of party leadership is to find a road to success through the prejudices of the past, the expediencies of the moment, and the demands of the future—a task especially beset by perils when a former top leadership is declining and a new top leadership has not yet come to full authority. It is a special characteristic of American political parties that large portions of their total life history are devoted to passing through such interregnums.

Many voices then speak on the future party role. They speak with unequal authority, and no one voice is likely to be decisive. The process goes on until some of the alternative concepts of the role begin to crystallize and candidates for the nomination begin to align themselves with one concept or another.

The act of choosing a candidate generally produces an immediate clarification for the time being of the party's future role: the candidate stands before the public as the most concrete expression of the direction in which the party has decided to move. As he campaigns, he continues to clarify the party position, mainly by expounding the party conception of the national position. This is his most important function in the period between convention and election.

Only in the event of victory can the wisdom of the party choice be fully tested. After the election a defeated candidate is committed at best to a holding operation in which he seeks to maintain his definition of the party role; the other leaders of the defeated party resume their accustomed activities, and the party awaits another opportunity for decisive action.

To the candidate who wins comes the great reward of consolidating the concept of the party role that he represents. As President of the United States, he has an unmatched opportunity to organize and direct his party as a basis for governmental power. When he performs with skill, the party learns how to make its greatest contribution to the national consensus. It also revitalizes itself for the future.

THE NOMINATION OF HUBERT HUMPHREY
FOR VICE PRESIDENT *
Gerald Pomper

THE nomination of Hubert Humphrey as the 1964 Democratic candidate for Vice-President constituted one of the most unusual incidents in recent political history. It was achieved through an active campaign, but one of limited public involvement. Humphrey's designation was achieved ostensibly through the deliberate choice of one individual, Lyndon Johnson, but only after an extensive effort to direct his choice to the Minnesota Senator. All of the participants in the decision were greatly influenced by the presence of Robert Kennedy, who was not even a candidate by the time of the Atlantic City Convention.

Moreover, the Vice-Presidential nominating contest was remarkable in that it existed at all. The office involved is one which has been the object of ridicule for almost all of American history. The common evaluation of the "second counsel" was most bitingly expressed by the famous Mr. Dooley:

Th' prisidincy is th' highest office in th' gift iv th' people. Th' vice-prisidincy is th' next highest and th' lowest. It isn't a crime exactly. Ye can't be sint to jail f'r it, but it's a kind iv a disgrace. It's like writin' anonymous letters. At a convintion nearly all th' dillygates lave as soon as they've nommynated th' prisidint f'r fear wan iv thim will be nommynated f'r vice-prisidint. . . . If ye say about a man that he's good prisidintial timber he'll buy ye a dhrink. If ye say he's good vice-prisidintial timber ye mane that he isn't good enough to be cut up into shingles, an' y'd bether be careful.

* From Gerald Pomper, "The Nomination of Hubert Humphrey for Vice-President," in *The Journal of Politics*, Vol. 28, No. 3 (August, 1966), pp. 639–659. © 1966 by the Southern Political Science Association. Reprinted by permission of Professor Pomper and the editors.

More recently, the office has been paid greater respect. Increasing governmental responsibilities have been placed upon the Vice-President, particularly since the passage of the National Security Act. The political importance of the office has increased as well, as demonstrated most strikingly by Richard Nixon's successful bid for his party's Presidential designation in 1960. Above all, the assassination of John Kennedy has made politicians and voters aware of the significance of the Vice-Presidency.

THE OUTLOOK IN 1964

Until November 22, 1963, no serious controversy existed in regard to the future national leadership of the Democratic party. Renomination of the successful 1960 ticket was certain. Senator Humphrey, for his part, seemed to have reached the culmination of his career. After unsuccessful attempts to win a national nomination in the past, he had become Senate party whip, and might expect eventually to be majority leader. The road to the White House, however, appeared blocked. John Kennedy, if re-elected, would be President until 1969. The principal alternative inheritors of his leadership appeared to be Attorney-General Robert Kennedy or Vice-President Lyndon Johnson. Certainly Humphrey had little reason to expect to be the center of activity in Atlantic City. Free of other commitments, he agreed to do a twice-daily commentary for the American Broadcasting Company during the convention.

The Dallas assassination necessarily brought great political changes. Johnson's accession to the Presidency carried with it the leadership of the party. His nomination for a full term was rapidly assured, but the question of a Vice-Presidential candidate was thrown completely open. The most obvious possibility was the Attorney-General. It is doubtful if Johnson ever wanted Robert Kennedy on the ticket with him. There were many differences of temperament and policy between them. A proud man, the new President naturally wanted to win the forthcoming election without debt to the name of his martyred predecessor. Moreover, the two men had been rivals in the past, and Johnson had suffered defeat in 1960 after a campaign directed by Robert Kennedy.

Despite his own feelings, however, Johnson had to take account of the great political strength of the Attorney-General. After the assassination, Robert Kennedy became the object of deep emotional support. In the three years that his brother had been President, moreover, the national party machinery had become dominated by those close to their family. Indeed, a movement to place the Attorney-General on the ticket began in earnest early in 1964. In the New Hampshire primary, through write-in votes, 25,000 Democrats indicated their preference for him as the Vice-Presidential candidate.

Johnson played a waiting game, expecting the emotional reaction to the assassination to subside, while he preserved his freedom of choice. To maintain that freedom, he began to create an extensive public list of possible running-mates. Inclusion of Sargent Shriver served to decrease the concentration on Robert Kennedy as the political heir of the late President. Addition of other names served to prevent a concentration of support or opposition on any other single possibility.

Hubert Humphrey had been mentioned as a possible candidate from the first. He had the advantages of a widespread and generally favorable public reputation, accumulated governmental experience and demonstrated ability in a wide range of subject areas. His political strength was equally important. The Minnesota Senator was an active participant at the four previous Democratic conventions. He led the successful fight for a stronger civil rights plank in the 1948 convention, and was a favorite son candidate in 1952. Four years later, he actively sought the Vice-Presidential nomination and in 1960 he fought John Kennedy in the presidential primaries. Through such experiences, he developed a wide acquaintanceship in the party, which he strengthened by a heavy schedule of attendance and speeches at the great variety of American political functions.

Humphrey's political assets were well suited to the campaign he was about to enter. He had the broad party support and personal friendships—including that with Johnson—that were to prove vital in 1964. In previous national campaigns, he failed because he lacked the resources necessary to win mass support—money, or "charisma," or professional advice. In this campaign, these deficiencies, where they still existed, were of less importance.

The Senator was also able to make good use of the unique position held by President Johnson. By the time the Democratic convention met, the delegates had accepted, almost as self-evident truth, the proposition that "the Presidential candidate selects his own running mate." An unbounded prerogative was assumed to exist. Historically, this was certainly not the case. Open contests for the Vice-Presidential nomination have been frequent, and internal party conflict over the choice has been common. Perhaps the only Presidential candidate who actually dictated the selection of a running-mate was Franklin Roosevelt in 1940. His preference for Henry Wallace aroused such antipathy within the party, however, that it was not a happy precedent for Johnson.

The freedom granted the President was historically unique. In part, it can be explained by the fact that he was still enjoying the "honeymoon" accorded a new President—a "honeymoon," moreover, occurring immediately before the expected consummation of the November election. The Kennedy assassination, too, had left its mark. Democrats remembered, in keynoter John Pastore's words, "that day four years ago in Los Angeles when John F. Kennedy said, 'I need you, Lyndon Johnson.'" They believed that the choice had been made by Kennedy alone and, as proven by the transfer of power after the assassination, that it had proven a wise choice. It therefore followed, in party logic, that the best choice would always be made by the Presidential candidate acting independently.

The President's freedom, however, while greater than in most conventions, was not unlimited. Other elements of the party at least retained the prerogatives Bagehot had accorded to the British Crown: the rights to be consulted, to encourage, and to warn. Johnson might have succeeded in forcing the convention to ratify even some outrageous choice, but it would have been very costly in political support, a cost he was not likely to assume.

For Humphrey, the limits on the President served to increase his own chances for the Vice-Presidential nomination. These limits brought Johnson's attention to focus on prominent political figures, such as the Minnesota Senator, and decreased his consideration of obscure "dark horses." At the same time, Humphrey had the favor of the President. Coming to the Senate in the same year, 1948, the two had always been friendly. They shared the intense experience of defeat by John Kennedy in 1960. After the assassination, the Minnesotan became virtual leader of the Senate Democratic party. Humphrey was particularly prominent during the three-month filibuster on civil rights legislation, which occupied the Senate during the very time the Vice-Presidential campaign was conducted.

Unlike Robert Kennedy, then, Humphrey did not have to pressure the President into making a choice he personally opposed. Instead, his task was to persuade Johnson to make a selection he found satisfactory, at least, or actually favored personally. The strategy decided upon, more by his staff than the Senator himself, was that of "the next best man." All efforts were directed toward convincing significant persons and groups that the running-mate should be selected strictly on grounds of ability, rather than narrow electoral appeal. A short document was distributed, usually without comment, to the press, prominent individuals, party personnel and others who might be able to influence the "attentive public" or the President himself. The theme of the document was simple:

The sudden death of President Kennedy, the subsequent succession of President Johnson, the present vacancy in the office of the Vice-Presidency, have all underlined the necessity for the Vice-President to be the man next-best-qualified for the Presidency itself. . . . [Other] factors—in the nuclear age—are overshadowed by the necessity of guaranteeing that, should tragedy befall the President, the nation would be under the most experienced and capable leadership available.

A small staff of the Senator's close friends and assistants was assembled to spread this message. Fewer than two dozen persons were continuously involved in the campaign.

PRE-CONVENTION CAMPAIGNING

The actual conduct of the campaign cannot be portrayed as following a logical and pre-established plan. Like most political efforts, it was marked by considerable innovation, intuition and improvisation. Chronology does not help greatly to order events, either, for several efforts were being conducted simultaneously. The organized campaign for Humphrey began in January, 1964. Commenting on a poll of Democratic county chairmen which showed him the leading candidate, the Minnesota Senator carefully showed his interest and deference: "It is, of course, an honor to be associated with President Johnson," he replied, "and it would be a singular honor to be with him on the Democratic ticket. . . . The decision for Vice-President, however, will be made by the Democratic convention, which I am confident will respect the wishes in this matter of President Johnson."

In the weeks following there was only one date of crucial importance. This was July 30, the day on which President Johnson formally excluded Robert Kennedy from consideration for the Vice-Presidency. Without further explanation, the President told the press he had decided against any "member of the Cabinet or those who meet regularly with the Cabinet." This criterion also ruled out of consideration Secretaries Dean Rusk, Robert McNamara and Orville Freeman, as well as Sargent Shriver and Adlai Stevenson. Until this time, Humphrey was only one of several possible candidates. After July 30, his backers shifted their emphasis toward building a consensus on behalf of the Senator.

The pre-convention campaign can best be analyzed by observing the efforts made to win support from three important elements: the major constituent interests of the Democratic party, the delegates and leaders of the national convention, and the general public. For purposes of analysis, the latter group is considered to include the President, although he was obviously the object of the other efforts as well.

As Will Rogers, once quipped, the Democrats constitute "no organized party." Rather, they are a heterogeneous assembly of divergent interests. Humphrey attempted to win support from all of these various groups. Labor backing was vital. In March, Walter Reuther blocked a movement at the annual convention of the United Automobile Workers to endorse Robert Kennedy for Vice-President. He then campaigned among his union colleagues for Humphrey. By July, all members of the AFL-CIO Executive Council had indicated their support of the Minnesotan, and George Meany, president of the labor federation, was particularly emphatic in his support. These endorsements were important not only as a direct aid to the Senator. They also indicated that Robert Kennedy lacked some of the support his brother held in 1960. Polls of labor leaders, taken at the behest of the Humphrey staff, also indicated strong labor endorsement of the Senator. Similarly, polls among Democratic farm leaders indicated wide backing for the Minnesotan, and this preference was reinforced by that of party leaders from farm areas.

The Senator had the early support of civil rights groups, because of his long championing of their cause and his current leadership of the Senate floor fight. When cloture was invoked and a strong civil rights act passed under Humphrey's leadership, his standing with these groups was further strengthened. This demonstration of legislative skill also caused Humphrey to exult that "an albatross has now become my greatest asset."

Humphrey strength was notable within the party organization. A June Gallup poll of 3,000 county chairmen showed him ahead of all other contenders as the personal preference of the chairmen. Leading Robert Kennedy, the runner-up in the poll, by nearly a 2-1 margin, Humphrey headed the field in all regions but the South. In that area, he trailed Stevenson and Senator William Fulbright. With these exceptions, the Minnesotan led all other possibilities by a 2-1 margin in Southern chairmen's preferences.

Opposition to Humphrey existed, but was restricted. As shown in the poll of chairmen, he was relatively weak in the South, where his liberalism alienated many, but not all, voters and leaders. Thus, most Southern Senators favored other candidates, but the majority whip did win the endorsement of some Southern colleagues. This support was rendered even as the protracted civil rights filibuster continued.

The Minnesotan also lacked support from the bulk of the remaining big city "machines," such as those of Chicago, New York, and Philadelphia. In part, this position was based on loyalty to Robert Kennedy and the desire to have a Catholic on the national ticket. Moreover, Humphrey's liberalism, intellectualism, and effusiveness, as well as his rural, Protestant heritage, were alien and suspect. These groups, however, were neither sufficiently concerned nor sufficiently powerful to attempt to block Humphrey. Significantly, they were not united. In New York, for example, while older "bosses," such as Charles Buckley of the Bronx personally opposed Humphrey, younger "reform" elements supported the Senator.

The only other element of the party potentially opposed to Humphrey was the business community. Normally, a Democratic ticket expects and seeks only limited support from industry. In 1964, however, the Republican party's nomination of Barry Goldwater and President Johnson's personal stress on national unity indicated increased importance for this group within the party. To gain its endorsement, Humphrey attended a series of private receptions for business leaders in July, seeking to allay suspicions that he was unfriendly to their interests, and accepted invitations to address groups such as the American Management Association.

No direct solicitations were made of those present at the business receptions, but volunteers were asked to let the President know their opinion of Humphrey. Others offered financial help or spoke to other businessmen on his behalf. Although all of them did not later support Humphrey, those attending the meetings included President Eisenhower's Treasury Secretary, the president of the New York Stock Exchange, and executives of such firms as Sears Roebuck, Metropolitan Life Insurance, General Dynamics, New York Central Railroad, Anaconda, and Inland Steel. Members of both parties and leaders of corporations of various sizes were included. The emphasis was toward proportionately greater representation of Democrats and middle-sized firms.

These various efforts were directed in part at gaining the support of the President. They were undertaken, however, in recognition of the fact that the President would be influenced by the opinions of the many elements in the Democratic coalition. That Johnson did not have a completely free choice was indicated by the elimination of Defense Secretary McNamara. This occurred well before the July 30 announcement. Labor leaders strongly objected to the inclusion of a former corporation president on the national ticket, particularly one associated with the Ford Motor Company, a traditional opponent of Walter Reuther's Automobile Workers. McNamara's rejection of a 1961 AFL-CIO nomination for a Defense Department position had also aroused resentment. Party organization leaders, particularly the Michigan state party and National Chairman John Bailey, also were severely critical of the possible nomination of a non-political figure and one, moreover, who had voted for and contributed large sums to the Republican party. Faced with these objections, the President recognized the political limits on his freedom of choice and rejected the Defense head.

The second major effort in the pre-convention campaign was directed toward the party convention delegates. This effort was carefully discreet. No "pressure" was applied, and the Humphrey group was extremely cautious to avoid any action which might seem to be an attempt to force the hand of the President. The basic purpose was defensive, to be prepared for any change in the situation.

Many of the actions in this period were directed toward preparing for a possible floor fight. In part, this preparation was due to memories of the 1956 convention, when Adlai Stevenson had allowed the convention a free choice of his running-mate. Surprised on that occasion, and conditioned by their past experience, Humphrey backers did not want to be caught off guard again should Johnson allow the delegates to make the decision. Few, however, expected the President to permit this freedom. Far more likely, it was thought, was an attempt to stampede the convention into the nomination of Robert Kennedy by an emotional invocation of the late President's memory. Such an attempt was feared even after the July 30 statement.

To prepare for any open contest, the Humphrey group began to canvass delegates. Although similar in many respects to a Presidential campaign, the effort was far more reserved. The friendships, contacts, and knowledge gained in four previous conventions were put to use. The Senator's supporters had learned, in Theodore White's words, "The root question of American politics is always: Who's the Man to See? To understand American politics is, simply, to know people, to know the relative weight of names—who are heroes, who are straw men, who controls and who does not."

Delegates were won without primary election contests or open attempts to win commitments from state parties. In a few cases, known supporters of the Senator were contacted and asked, if possible, to win designation as convention delegates. Since no contests were expected at the national convention, party leaders of moderate influence were able to win places without controversy. In order to judge the strength of the various candidates, a letter and informal poll was sent to pro-Humphrey leaders in each state. Dated July 30, the letter asked for the preferences of each delegate among four Vice-Presidential possibilities: Robert Kennedy, Humphrey, Shriver, and Stevenson. Space was left for indications of the past convention status of the delegates and remarks. Copies of the poll results were to be sent to a designated "local coordinator" and to the unnamed "resident" at a suburban Washington address. The anonymity of the poll indicates how careful the Humphrey group was to avoid an open campaign and to respect the freedom of the President. The date of the letter, and its list of names, indicates that the Senator's backers were not informed any considerable time before the President eliminated the major rivals of the Minnesotan.

In reply to the poll, varying assessments were received. A majority of the delegates were prepared to accept Johnson's Vice-Presidential preference, but among the contenders, Humphrey had the most support. With this information, his backers were reasonably well-informed as to the sources of support for each possible candidate. Robert Kennedy, in this informal poll, was shown to be the second strongest contender. However, his support was less broadly based than that of Humphrey, being centered in the northeast. Almost all southern delegations were strongly opposed to Kennedy's nomination. Significantly, while not enthusiastic about Humphrey, they were willing to accept his designation. Some delegates favorable to Humphrey not only answered the poll, but also announced their preference to the local press or wrote to the President on Humphrey's behalf.

Even the best of plans might go astray. Some preliminary thought was given to a convention organization, but these tentative plans ultimately were abandoned. Many in the Humphrey group feared that the convention would become "an emotional bath" in memory of John Kennedy, and that this would lead to the nomination of the Attorney-General for Vice-President. In news interviews and in a trip to Poland and Germany, Robert Kennedy seemed to be publicizing his qualifications. A poll taken by this writer indicated that he was the choice of a plurality of New Jersey delegates, and similar support in other states had been found by the Humphrey group. Rumors were current that Mrs. Jacqueline Kennedy would attend the convention to arouse emotional support for her brother-in-law.

To avert a Kennedy bandwagon, Humphrey backers hoped for public support of the Senator by President Johnson before the opening of the convention, and these wishes were partially met by the public disapproval of Robert Kennedy on July 30. Their anxieties were further relieved when the Democratic National Committee changed the convention program, deferring a special memorial tribute to President Kennedy, introduced by his brother, until after the nominations were made. The postponement was also announced on July 30, reportedly after a personal decision by the President. In the event, the memorial did become the occasion for a spontaneous emotional demonstration. Delay helped Humphrey.

The President's actions left the Humphrey staff free to concentrate on building support for their own candidate, rather than defending against any other possibility. After the July 30 statement, the White House, probably upon the personal direction of President Johnson, encouraged Humphrey to develop support in his own cause. The Senator and his staff then expanded the third phase of the campaign, seeking the support of the more general public. Best characterized by one aide as "a campaign not of silence, but of restraint," it was oriented toward gaining the endorsement of influential officials, public spokesmen and the press, without stimulating a mass movement which might offend the President.

One means of maintaining this delicate balance was to isolate Senator Humphrey himself from most of the overt activity. The sampling of delegate sentiment and other sensitive tasks were left to the staff and friends. The Senator kept himself before the public by his activities in the Senate. He accepted a number of invitations for television interviews, speeches and press conferences. Though non-political in inspiration and content, a half-hour television program on "My Childhood" was particularly effective.

Humphrey also continued his contract for television commentaries during the convention with A.B.C. The Minnesotan had many personal reasons, including financial need, for adhering to his earlier commitment. Politically, it would have been difficult to withdraw from the agreement without appearing to pressure the President. For similar reasons, Humphrey continued as a delegate to the convention and even appeared on the floor before his own nomination.

While the Senator remained available, discreet public support was stimulated. At this time, all politically important visitors to the White House were being asked their opinions on the ticket. Even Senator Humphrey was asked about his rivals. As he described the situation later to a reporter, "It's like a guy calling the girl next door—who he knows is madly in love with him—to ask the phone number of the newest broad in town." When friends of the Senator expressed a desire to aid his nomination efforts, they were provided with basic information. A diagram was prepared, comparing the biographies of the leading potential nominees. Without comment, it demonstrated the greater variety of experience and longer political services of the Senator. One could note, for example, that in 1948 Humphrey had been a leader in the Democratic convention and had been elected to the Senate. In the same year, Robert Kennedy had entered law school, McNamara had held a middle-level management position, and Eugene McCarthy had been elected to his first term in the lower house of Congress.

The Senator ultimately won the endorsement of a large number of opinion leaders, including some 40 Democratic Senators and, according to a White House survey, "nearly all significant party figures in 26 states and the District of Columbia, and a clear majority in six additional states." The mass media were also contacted discreetly, and some columnists and editorial writers virtually endorsed the Minnesotan. *The New York Times,* for example, while making the customary acknowledgement that "the power to choose his running mate lies, as it always has, with President Johnson," also pointedly described Humphrey as "a man with experience, broad interests and demonstrated integrity and capacity . . . a man of Presidential quality."

Through most of their campaign, the Humphrey group had emphasized the argument of "the next best man." As their campaign widened, they attempted to prove the electoral appeal of the Senator as well. At first, this was a purely defensive maneuver. Great suspicion was voiced about the members and staff of the Democratic National Committee, and their possible support of the Attorney-General. Members of the Senator's staff, in some cases, felt that the President might receive incorrect reports, warning him of possible defeat in November unless he ran with Robert Kennedy.

More positively, the Humphrey group attempted to demonstrate the political strength the Minnesotan would bring to the ticket. A poll taken by the White House showed that Robert Kennedy was indeed the most popular of the Vice-Presidential possibilities, but that Adlai Stevenson was considered the most qualified. Significantly, Humphrey placed second in both categories, indicating that he might be the best over-all choice. In late May, a national sample was questioned on the standing of a possible Republican ticket of Goldwater and William Scranton in opposition to Democratic tickets of Johnson and Humphrey and Johnson and Robert Kennedy. In these matchings, the Johnson-Humphrey ticket received 2.1% more of the "vote" than the Johnson-Kennedy slate. The Senator's advantage held in all subdivisions of the sample except among Catholics but, still, a Johnson-Humphrey ticket received 84.9% of that group's support.

The nomination of Goldwater was also turned to Humphrey's advantage. Geographically, the nomination made the Mid-West, where the Minnesotan was strongest, the crucial area for November. The Republican choice also centered the contest for marginal gubernatorial, senatorial and congressional seats on this area. The Democrats could now regard the East as relatively safe, making it unnecessary to nominate a candidate from that area, such as Robert Kennedy. Analyzing probable patterns of group voting, a number of political scientists found reasons to support Humphrey's candidacy. Seen as crucial to the party were a large increase in the number of Negro voters, a consolidation of union members behind the ticket and an appeal to farmers of the Mid-West and the Plains.

To win this support, it was argued, would require an intensive campaign by a well-known, popular and effective candidate. Since such an effort could not be mounted by an incumbent President, it would fall to the running-mate. Humphrey, it was said, did have the stamina and popularity to win new Negro support, curtail the "white backlash" among union members, encourage a defection among Republican farmers, and assume much of the campaign's duties for the President.

To be sure, Humphrey still represented some political liabilities. He was relatively weak in the South and among businessmen and Catholics. The importance of each of these groups was indicated, respectively, by Goldwater's "Southern strategy," his conservative ideology and his Catholic running-mate, William Miller. However, the long pre-convention campaign had lessened the opposition to Humphrey's nomination among all of these groups. As the Democrats prepared to open their convention, the Minnesota Senator was clearly in a leading, if not yet dominant, position.

AT THE CONVENTION

In Atlantic City, the attitude of the Senator and his staff was a combination of hope and anxiety. All were sure that Humphrey was the choice of the various elements of the party and that he was accepted by the delegates and the public as "the next best man." They believed, too, that he was the President's own personal preference. It was now clear that Robert Kennedy would not challenge his elimination from the contest, but was instead preparing to run for United States Senator from New York. Nevertheless, problems remained.

The first of these was keeping Humphrey activities within bounds. By the time of the convention, the support of the Minnesotan had become so obvious that it was dangerous. The Senator's group feared that the president would feel himself pressured and, in order to reassert his own power, would recommend another candidate. To avoid offending and alienating the President, plans for the convention were drastically revised. Humphrey's headquarters at the Shelburne Hotel became instead the Minnesota delegation's headquarters (and therefore available for use by Senator McCarthy as well). Reservations for large numbers of rooms were cancelled or forfeited. The staff, including Humphrey's administrative assistant, was scattered through many hotels in Atlantic City, with many listed as attached to A.B.C. rather than to the Senator.

Many efforts were made to dampen any overt campaign. A reception on the convention eve was sponsored by the Minnesota state delegation, rather than by the Senator. Staff members were told not to discuss the Vice-Presidential nomination in public. If asked, they were to reply that the President was free to make his own decision, and that all persons should support that decision. Humphrey took this position himself on the innumerable occasions he was asked for personal comments. In this atmosphere of uncertainty, rumor and anxiety flourished.

A second and more serious threat to Humphrey was the contest over the seating of the Mississippi delegation. The regular and all-white delegation was challenged by the "Mississippi Freedom Democratic Party." This integrated group had little legal claim to convention seats, based on state law and past practice. It did have a strong moral claim, however, considering the deliberate exclusion of Negroes from political participation in Mississippi, the spate of segregationist terrorism in the state during the summer, and the likelihood of disloyalty to the national ticket by the regular organization.

In terms of convention politics, the Mississippi contest did not really center on that state. Whatever the decision, it seemed unlikely that Negroes would be permitted political participation in the state, that the regular party would support the national ticket, or that Johnson would carry the state in the November election. The real concern of the party leadership, including Johnson and Humphrey, was to avoid a floor fight. They wished to present an image of unity and rationality to the national television audience, in contrast to the emotionalism and divisiveness of the Republican convention at San Francisco. They wanted also to prevent a walkout of other Southern delegations, and a consequent weakening of the party's strength in the region of Senator Goldwater's greatest appeal.

It fell to Humphrey, by dint of the President's request and his own prominence at the convention, to seek a formula which would satisfy these demands. The Senator was in a delicate position. Since he was relatively weak in the South, he had to conciliate that section. A walkout by Southern delegates, moreover, might convince the President and the party that the ticket required a more moderate candidate for Vice-President. Even if he had wanted to, however, Humphrey could not consider the Southern position alone. A floor fight could be obtained if eleven delegations on the Credentials Committee signed a minority report and if eight delegations requested a roll call vote. The Senator, therefore, had to find a settlement which would represent an overwhelming consensus, not merely a majority position.

At first, the Senator argued for a three-point proposal known as the "Wymong plan." The regular Mississippi delegation would be seated, if it took a loyalty oath to the party. The Freedom party would be welcomed as non-voting guests of the convention. Finally, in the future, state parties would "assure that voters in the state, regardless of race, color, creed or national origin, will have the opportunity to participate fully in party affairs." The proposal was presented to a subcommittee headed by Walter Mondale, Attorney-General of Minnesota and a Humphrey supporter. It won endorsement there by a 4-1 vote, but failed to win the necessary consensus in the full committee.

To leave time for more bargaining, the report of the committee was delayed for 24 hours. In this period, one change was made. "In recognition of the unusual circumstances presented at the hearing, and without setting any precedent for the future," two members of the Freedom Democratic party would be seated as voting "delegates-at-large." The Humphrey communications network was activated, every state delegation was contacted, and the influence of the White House was brought to bear. The new plan won the support of sufficient delegations to prevent an open convention conflict. The compromise was rejected by both Mississippi factions, but Humphrey's objectives had been fully met. The party had recognized the moral claims involved and had taken at least a token action against discrimination in party affairs. Party unity had been preserved and all but the intransigent Alabama and Mississippi delegations had remained loyal.

For the Senator, the result was a personal success. Dealing with an emotional issue in the frenetic atmosphere of the convention, he had solidified a broad coalition within the party. He had demonstrated his leadership without severely antagonizing any element. The solution of the credentials contest removed the last potentially serious obstacle to his nomination.

It was still conceivable that the President would indicate a different choice, and accomplish his selection. At this point, however, there would be an extremely high price to pay in disaffection and resentment. The President had preserved his freedom of action to meet any new development, but no such development had occurred. The Minnesotan had come to the convention as the leading candidate. While there he had retained, even strengthened, his position.

The remaining period was one of waiting on the part of the Senator and of managed drama by the President. By Tuesday, the day before the nomination, the Senator was informally notified of his selection. Buttons, signs, and hats with "Johnson and Humphrey" designations—in preparation for a week—were ordered for final delivery to a private home. Aides began writing an acceptance speech. Johnson, in Washington, continued to suggest names, to fence with reporters, and to build tension. Finally, on Wednesday, hours before the nomination itself was scheduled, he called Humphrey to the White House.

The final dramatic moment came that evening immediately after Johnson had been nominated by acclamation. In an unprecedented action, he appeared to announce his choice of a running-mate. His speech indicated the success of the Humphrey group's basic strategy. The President argued their thesis, that the Vice-President should be "a man best qualified to assume the office of President of the United States, should that day come. . . . This is not a sectional choice; this is not merely just a way to balance the ticket; this is simply the best man in America for this job." He indicated as well the success of the campaign to win public support for the Senator, when he noted that the choice was reached "after discussions with outstanding Americans in every area of our national life" and represented "the enthusiastic conviction of the great majority of the Democratic party." Humphrey's nomination by acclamation followed.

The political value of the long selection process was indicated the following week when the Harris survey asked voters their opinions of the Vice-Presidential nominees. Humphrey led the Republican candidate by a 7-3 margin. Moreover, he was preferred over Miller more than the President was preferred over Goldwater in every area of the country and among virtually every social group. Significantly, the major reason for Humphrey's support was that he was considered "better qualified, [more] experienced" than his opponent. The public, too, had accepted the thesis of the "next best man." The final test of this choice came on November 3, when Hubert Humphrey was elected Vice-President of the United States.

CONCLUSIONS

The nomination of Senator Humphrey points the way to the future of the Vice-Presidency. In the past, whatever attention was given to the office centered on its governmental, rather than political aspects. This focus was evident among politicians as well as academicians. The recent history of the Vice-Presidency should serve both to increase attention to the office in general and to foster particular interest in its political character.

It seems likely that we will find more campaigning for the office of "second counsel" in forthcoming elections. The Presidential nomination itself has gradually become the object of public and vigorous campaigning. As some candidates adopt these practices for the running-mate position as well, others will be required to follow their example. Such efforts will certainly be evident when an incumbent President is a candidate for renomination. With the top position on the ticket thereby foreclosed, ambitions will be directed toward the second slot. Campaigning is unlikely, however, to attain fully the intensive, openly competitive and mass character of a Presidential effort. The influence of the President and other party leaders will remain too great to enable a candidate to win nomination largely on the basis of popular backing. The attempt, rather, will be to gain the support of important factions and to use evidence of voter appeal to win such backing.

The campaigns for the two nominations will be alike in one other respect. They will be exercises in the building of coalitions. The entire nominating process is one of building a majority coalition. In the past, the Vice-Presidential nomination has been one of the prizes used to build a consensus in support of the ticket-leader. If the Humphrey case is indicative, the second spot will no longer be simply a trading device. There will be efforts to build a consensus behind this choice separately or, more likely, the same coalition will be evident in the elections of both candidates. We are less likely to see "balanced" tickets, in which the two running-mates represent distinctively different positions. In both parties in 1964, there was an ideological consistency to the tickets that is startling when compared to such combinations of the recent past as Dewey and Bricker or Stevenson and Sparkman.

The choice of a coalition, by definition, is different from the choice of a single individual, even one with the responsibilities and political acumen of the President. The common belief, constantly reiterated in 1964, is that the Presidential nominee selects his own running mate. This view, albeit with guarded qualifications, is also frequent in the scholarly literature. "The Presidential nominee ordinarily can, in fact, make the choice, although the range of his discretion may differ with circumstances," wrote V. O. Key. "When a presidential nominee is named, he and other party leaders sit around in a room and select the vice-presidential candidate," declared an experienced politician. "The opinion of the presidential nominee is always the most important influence," according to others.

A closer look at the record of vice-presidential nominations, however, results in a different conclusion. Paul David examined the four conventions since 1896 in which an incumbent President sought renomination when the Vice-Presidency was vacant. In all four cases, "the President was able to exercise only limited influence on the situation. . . . Seemingly the choice tended to be made by the convention, with other leaders exercising as much influence as the President." Even in 1964, there were limits on the President, though they were less constrictive than in the past.

Not only is this contention incorrect; it is wrong as a matter of principle. In a free society, there is nothing inherently objectionable in the nomination being "an instrument of compromise—compromise between factions, between sections, between interests and even perhaps between back room political bargainers." No democratic system can easily accept the proposition that the vital choice of future leadership is the prerogative of any single individual. In 1964, the President did endorse the individual who was the clear choice of the majority of delegates and of party factions. The outcome, then, did not violate fundamental democratic beliefs. The proposition of unlimited Presidential discretion, however, does violate these beliefs.

The emotions aroused by the assassination of John Kennedy permitted the unusual freedom accorded the new President. It was felt that he was entitled, in effect, to name a successor to his now-vacant office, and that Kennedy's successful choice of Johnson indicated the desirability of unlimited freedom. However, Kennedy did not act alone—he stated his preference and then worked among the leaders of his party to win agreement. This is far different from leaders passively accepting a designation. The Dallas tragedy should remind us of the significance of the Vice-Presidency and of the importance of the choice of a man to that office. In a democracy, important choices must be made through widespread participation, not through the personal preferences of a few leaders.

The nomination of Hubert Humphrey was accomplished in part through such participation, but it offends a democrat's sense of decency that any one individual should be accorded even the theoretical right to deny the popular choice. Whatever our reaction to the specific selection made in 1964, we should reject the premise. Consent, not dictation, is the basic process of free government.

5. The Electoral College

WHEN the nominating conventions are concluded, intraparty rivalries are muted, party lines are drawn, and the campaign for the greatest prize in the American political system, the presidency, begins. The basic strategy of presidential campaigns is shaped by the electoral college, which has been the subject of debate ever since the Constitutional Convention of 1787.

The convention was forced to choose among several ways of electing a chief executive: direct popular election or election by the Congress, by state legislatures, or by intermediate electors. As with other provisions of the Constitution, the method of election of the President and Vice-President was a product of compromise. It attempted to reconcile the problems inherent in differing state suffrage requirements, the existence of slaves, the fear of the small states that they would be dominated by the large states, and what the Framers considered to be the necessary balance and separation between both branches of government and the states and the national government.

The Constitution provides that each state appoint a number of electors equal to the total number of the state's senators and representatives and that each state legislature determine the method of their appointment. Since the popular suffrage movement of the early nineteenth century, however, the legislatures have left to the voters the actual selection of a slate of electors. (These slates are drawn up by the state's political parties.) When the voter casts his ballot for a presidential candidate, he is actually voting for the slate of electors chosen by the candidate's party. The function of the elector, therefore, is generally regarded as that of registering popular desire. But electors are not required in all states to follow their "instructions," or even to pledge themselves to a candidate. In 1948 and 1960, a few electors exercised their own judgment, and in 1960 to 1964, the "unpledged elector" movement attracted considerable attention. (In 1960, in particular, the presence of unpledged electors on the Alabama Democratic ballot created considerable confusion in calculating the vote.)

With no party system in 1787, it was logical that each elector cast his votes for two candidates, the candidate receiving the most votes to be President and the runner-up Vice-President. When George Washington was a candidate no problems arose, but with the beginnings of Federalist–anti-Federalist (Republican) competition, complications developed. In 1800, the anti-Federalist electors intended to elect Thomas Jefferson President and Aaron Burr Vice-President, but by casting an equal number of votes for both men they caused a tie in the electoral college. The election was decided in a lame-duck session of the House of Representatives. As a result, the electoral system was formally modified with the Twelfth Amendment.

Ratified in 1804, this amendment was designed to prevent a recurrence of the situation in 1800; henceforth election of the President and the Vice-President would take place separately.

In 1962, in an attempt to eliminate a long-standing inequity, the Twenty-third Amendment gave three electoral votes to the District of Columbia. However, it made no provision for the District's participation in a situation where no candidate received a majority of the electoral vote, in which case the President would be elected by the House of Representatives and the Vice-President by the Senate.

Other changes, also significant, but never achieving the status and formality of a constitutional amendment, have evolved in response to the political system over the years. Initially "popular" election took the form of electors being chosen from districts similar to congressional districts, the electoral votes of a state reflecting the wishes of the districts. However, under the district system, the dominant majorities in the state legislatures were often unable to carry their states for a given candidate. To alter this circumstance, the unit rule evolved under which all the state's electoral votes go to the political party winning a statewide plurality of the popular vote. By 1836 the district plan was firmly supplanted by the unit rule. Since both the rule of unit voting and the method of choosing presidential Electors are outside the purview of the Constitution, it is possible for a state legislature to alter the established pattern of choosing electors and alloting their votes.

It is the states' unit rule in the electoral college that determines the strategy of presidential campaigns. To win the election a candidate must receive a majority of "the whole number of electors appointed." Should no one receive such a majority, selection falls to the House of Representatives, where each state is given one vote which is cast according to the majority vote of all the state's representatives. Thus, the candidates are interested in winning the states' electoral votes, not the popular vote per se. All a candidate needs is a plurality (more votes than any other candidate) to win all the state's electoral votes. Consequently, candidates find it good strategy to spend most of their time campaigning in "swing" states—that is, states in which the vote could go to either party. Furthermore, the candidates are interested in the large, populous swing states. Campaign logic asks: Why concentrate on Nevada with only 3 electoral votes, when New York has 43? "Safe" states—that is, states which one party is reasonably certain to carry—also are often passed over. There is no point in raising one's margin of victory in a "safe" state from 60 percent to 80 percent of the popular vote when 60 percent is enough to secure the state's electoral votes. Similarly, there is no point in trying to raise the popular vote in a "lost" state from 15 percent to 25 percent when the state's electoral votes are certain to go to one's opponent.

The stress placed on winning in the states has at least two effects on the political system. First, presidential aspirants must appeal to the voters on both national and state issues; and second, because the presidential aspirant needs the help of the state party organizations, the latter are put in a strong position in which they may bargain for favors and act independently.

Traditionally, Democratic candidates have been able to count on the votes of the southern states, and Republican candidates on the votes of some New England and midwestern states. But party patterns are changing and two-party competition has reduced for both parties the number of "safe" states. (For a discussion of changing party patterns see Part VI.) Recent campaigning has been concentrated on the large doubtful states such as New York with 43 votes, California with 40 votes, Pennsylvania with 29 votes, and Illinois and Ohio with 26 votes each. Any candidate who wins all five of these states, with their 164 electoral votes, is virtually certain to win the election. (Since there are 538 electoral votes it takes at least 270 votes to win.) With the exception of Woodrow Wilson in 1916, who won the presidency by carrying just two of these states (and had only 11 electoral votes to spare), all other winners in close elections have carried at least 3 of these pivotal states. In 1948 President Truman carried California, Illinois, and Ohio, and in 1960 President Kennedy carried Illinois, New York, and Pennsylvania. Texas with 25 electoral votes and Michigan with 21 votes are also important states.

It is possible for a candidate to receive less of the popular vote than his opponent and still receive a majority of the electoral college votes. This occurred in 1876 and 1888. In 1876 Samuel J. Tilden, the Democratic candidate, polled 247,448 more votes than Rutherford B. Hayes, the Republican candidate, but returns from four states were contested and a congressionally created bipartisan electoral commission, voting along strict party lines, decided the contested returns in favor of Hayes, thereby giving him the election by one electoral vote. In 1888, the incumbent President, Grover Cleveland, led Benjamin Harrison by 100,476 popular votes, but Harrison received 233 electoral votes to Cleveland's 168 and was elected President. In twelve other instances in which more than two candidates ran, the result has been the election of a President who did not receive a majority of the popular votes.

The winner-take-all character of the states' electoral college unit rule has created a number of factors which influence the outcome of the voting. Joseph E. Kallenbach in *The Midwest Journal of Political Science* has listed and analyzed these factors. According to Kallenbach, they are (1) the electoral vote allocation formula, (2) the relative extent of popular participation in a presidential election, (3) the number of electors a voter may help to choose, and (4) the relative closeness of the popular vote for President. The electoral vote distribution formula (electors are given to the states on the basis of Senate seats as well as seats in the House of Representatives) considered alone tends to enhance the value of an individual popular vote in the less populous states. But the value of individual votes may be modified by the second variable—the number of people who actually vote in a given election. Voting participation varies from state to state and may be affected by any number of things, such as suffrage and registration requirements, or the intensity of the campaign. Since the electoral vote is fixed, while the number of popular votes is not, the individual vote has a variable influence on the state's electoral votes. If few votes are cast, each of those votes has more weight than if many votes are cast. Furthermore, the voters who live in the more populous states participate in determining large blocs of electoral votes (factor three). Finally, in the swing states, a small number of popular votes can decide the entire state's electoral vote. This means that the critical value of each popular vote in relation to the total number of votes cast is enhanced. These factors tend to balance each other out, and their impact varies from election to election. The one thing which does remain constant is that the balance of electoral power rests with the voters in the strategic high-value swing states.

The debate over the existing electoral college system generally raises the following pro and con arguments.

Pro: Aside from the constitutional amendments mentioned, the electoral college has withstood the test of time. Hayes was the only real "minority" President, Tilden being the only losing candidate who compiled an absolute majority. In all other cases the minority candidates who became President were opposed by men who also failed to achieve an absolute majority. Elections have been decided in the House of Representatives only twice. Further, the winner-take-all unit rule discourages the growth of splinter parties, and in 1860 and 1912, when major third-party candidates were in the field, insured political stability. The system's exaggeration of the winner's majority is not necessarily all bad. After a bitter election contest, the appearance of nationwide backing and the elimination of doubt about the outcome of the election foster acceptance of the victorious candidate as President. (In the 1960 election, despite John F. Kennedy's hairline margin of popular votes, he received 303 electoral votes to Richard M. Nixon's 219.)

Con: It permits the election of Presidents who receive fewer popular votes than their chief opponents. The unit rule was never contemplated by the Founding Fathers, and it has many drawbacks. Because the states cast their electoral votes in bloc, minority popular votes are discounted nationally. In the safe states there is little incentive for large voter turnout. In the swing states where the parties are fairly evenly divided, the unit rule inflates the bargaining power of pressure groups and splinter parties. The unit system may also encourage electoral fraud, since the manipulation of a few votes can change the electoral votes of an entire state. The current electoral system gives state legislatures complete discretion in the selection of presidential electors, and while the possibility of eliminating the popular vote for the electors is remote, it is nonetheless legally possible. Presidential electors in some states are not legally bound to vote for the candidate to whom they were pledged before the election. The possibility exists that in a close race a few electors might vote independently and alter the choice of President. In 1960, Senator Harry F. Byrd of Virginia (who was not running!) received 15 electoral votes—6 unpledged Alabama Democratic electors, 8 unpledged Mississippi Democratic electors, and one Oklahoma Republican elector who refused to vote for Mr. Nixon. Moreover, if an election is thrown into the House of Representatives, an archaic and totally unrepresentative system goes into operation.

Ever since January 6, 1789, when Representative William L. Smith proposed the first constitutional amendment intended to change the electoral college, the debate has continued. In the 1960's public interest in the subject was renewed by the extraordinarily close election, the activities of the unpledged electors, a series of precedent-breaking Supreme Court rulings by which the Court entered "the political thicket" of apportionment and redistricting (see Part V), President Johnson's messages on reform of the electoral college, an American Bar Association commission's recommendation that the electoral college system be abolished in favor of direct popular election, the electoral college hearings of the Senate Judiciary Subcommittee on Constitutional Amendments, and, finally, the 1966 Supreme Court decision not to review Delaware's claim that the winner-take-all system is, according to the Court's one-man, one-vote doctrine, unconstitutional discrimination against the voters of small states.

The following table shows the relationship of popular votes to electoral votes in the 1964 presidential election. In the reading, the late Senator Estes Kefauver, a longtime proponent of electoral college reform and former chairman of the Subcommittee on Constitutional Amendments, describes the operation of the existing electoral system and discusses its defects. He also analyzes the political implications of, and the arguments for and against, direct national election, the district system, and the proportional system—the three principal proposals for reform of the electoral college.

OFFICIAL 1964 PRESIDENTIAL ELECTION RESULTS

Total popular vote cast: 70,643,526

STATE	TOTAL POPULAR VOTE		
	JOHNSON	GOLDWATER	OTHER PARTIES
ALABAMA	‡	479,085	210,733
ALASKA	44,329	22,930	None
ARIZONA	237,753	242,535	482
ARKANSAS	314,197	243,264	2,965
CALIFORNIA	4,171,877	2,879,108	6,601
COLORADO	476,024	296,767	4,195
CONNECTICUT	826,269	390,996	1,313
DELAWARE	122,704	78,078	538
FLORIDA	948,540	905,941	None
GEORGIA	522,557	616,600	195
HAWAII	163,249	44,022	None
IDAHO	148,920	143,557	None
ILLINOIS	2,796,833	1,905,946	62
INDIANA	1,170,848	911,118	9,640
IOWA	733,030	449,148	2,361
KANSAS	464,028	386,579	7,294
KENTUCKY	669,659	372,977	3,469
LOUISIANA	387,068	509,225	None
MAINE	262,264	118,701	None
MARYLAND	730,912	385,495	50
MASSACHUSETTS	1,786,422	549,727	8,649
MICHIGAN	2,136,615	1,060,152	6,335
MINNESOTA	991,117	559,624	3,721
MISSISSIPPI	52,618	356,528	None
MISSOURI	1,164,344	653,535	None
MONTANA	164,246	113,032	1,350
NEBRASKA	307,307	276,847	None
NEVADA	79,339	56,094	None
NEW HAMPSHIRE	184,064	104,029	None
NEW JERSEY	1,867,671	963,843	15,256
NEW MEXICO	194,015	132,833	1,792
NEW YORK	4,913,156	2,243,559	9,488
NORTH CAROLINA	800,139	624,844	None
NORTH DAKOTA	149,784	108,207	398
OHIO	2,498,331	1,470,865	None
OKLAHOMA	519,834	412,665	None
OREGON	501,017	282,779	2,509
PENNSYLVANIA	3,130,954	1,673,657	18,079
RHODE ISLAND	315,463	74,615	None
SOUTH CAROLINA	215,700	309,048	8
SOUTH DAKOTA	163,010	130,108	None
TENNESSEE	635,047	508,965	34
TEXAS	1,663,185	958,566	5,060
UTAH	219,628	181,785	None
VERMONT	108,127	54,942	20
VIRGINIA	558,038	481,334	2,895
WASHINGTON	779,699	470,366	8,309
WEST VIRGINIA	538,087	253,953	None
WISCONSIN	1,050,424	638,495	2,896
WYOMING	80,718	61,998	None
DIST. OF COLUMBIA	169,796	28,801	None
TOTAL	43,128,956	27,177,873	336,697

Other Party Vote Breakdown: Independent Democratic Electors (Alabama only) 210,732; Socialist Labor (Hass and Blomen) 45,186; Prohibition (Munn and Shaw) 23,267; Socialist Worker (DeBerry and Shaw) 32,705; Constitution (Lightburn and Billings) 5,060; National States Rights (Kasper and Stoner) 6,953; Universal (Hensley and Hopkins) 19; Scattered 12,774.

Based on complete official vote totals reported to Congressional Quarterly by the Governmental Affairs Institute and state government sources.

PLURALITY	PERCENTAGES ⊕		ELECTORAL VOTE	
	JOHNSON	GOLDWATER	JOHNSON	GOLDWATER
268,353		69.5		10
21,399	65.9	34.1	3	
4,782	49.5	50.4		5
70,933	56.1	43.4	6	
1,292,769	59.1	40.8	40	
179,257	61.3	38.2	6	
435,273	67.8	32.1	8	
44,626	60.9	38.8	3	
42,599	51.1	48.9	14	
94,043	45.9	54.1		12
119,227	78.8	21.2	4	
5,363	50.9	49.1	4	
890,887	59.5	40.5	26	
259,730	56.0	43.6	13	
283,882	61.9	37.9	9	
77,449	54.1	45.1	7	
296,682	64.0	35.7	9	
122,157	43.2	56.8		10
143,563	68.8	31.2	4	
345,417	65.5	34.5	10	
1,236,695	76.2	23.4	14	
1,076,463	66.7	33.1	21	
431,493	63.8	36.0	10	
303,910	12.9	87.1		7
510,809	64.0	36.0	12	
51,214	58.9	40.6	4	
30,460	52.6	47.4	5	
23,245	58.6	41.4	3	
80,035	63.9	36.1	4	
903,828	65.6	33.9	17	
61,177	59.0	40.4	4	
2,669,597	68.6	31.3	43	
175,295	56.2	43.8	13	
41,577	58.0	41.9	4	
1,027,466	62.9	37.1	26	
107,169	55.7	44.3	8	
218,328	63.7	36.0	6	
1,457,297	64.9	34.7	29	
240,848	80.9	19.1	4	
93,348	41.1	58.9		8
32,902	55.6	44.4	4	
126,082	55.5	44.5	11	
704,619	63.3	36.5	25	
37,843	54.7	45.3	4	
53,185	66.3	33.7	3	
76,704	53.5	46.2	12	
309,333	62.0	37.4	9	
284,134	67.9	32.1	7	
411,929	62.1	37.7	12	
18,720	56.6	43.4	3	
140,995	85.5	14.5	3	
15,951,083	61.1	38.5	486	52

** Count from Schuylkill County not yet official.

‡ Democratic electors were not pledged to Johnson, thus their vote appears under Other Parties Column.

⊕ Percentages of total Presidential vote cast, including minor party vote.

"Politics in America: 1945–1964," reprinted from *Congressional Quarterly*, by permission of the editors. Copyright, 1965, by Congressional Quarterly, Inc.

THE ELECTORAL COLLEGE: OLD REFORMS
TAKE ON A NEW LOOK *

Estes Kefauver

THE PRESENT SYSTEM

THE 1960 Kennedy-Nixon election dramatically demonstrated some of the defects of our constitutional method of electing the President. As the electoral college lumbered like an oxcart through the selection of America's President for the space age, its machinations sounded several alarms. I do not refer to the razor-thin margin. The possibility of close elections will always be with us and in a federation of 185 million people spread from Maine to Hawaii, uncertainty and suspense will attend the final determination of a close contest under any system.

A collection of happenings throughout this crazy quilt system should have aroused us all to the need for change. In Oklahoma, Mr. Henry D. Irwin, a regular Republican elector who was expected to vote for Nixon, voted instead in the electoral college for Senator Harry F. Byrd, who, despite his merits otherwise, was not a candidate for the Presidency. Fourteen electors in Mississippi and Alabama also recorded votes for Senator Byrd. Unlike their Oklahoma counterpart, they had campaigned as unpledged electors and at least had some sort of mandate to exercise their own judgment. Louisiana's school segregation crisis produced an unsuccessful movement in its Legislature to suspend the state's election laws after Kennedy had won on November 8 so that unpledged electors could then be appointed. In Illinois, charges of election irregularities were accompanied by a threat that the state's Republican Election Board might refuse to certify the twenty-seven electoral votes cast by Democratic electors. An opposite result materialized in Hawaii where the votes of both Democratic and Republican electors were certified to Congress.

A divided ticket of Democratic electors in Alabama baffled election statisticians and demonstrated the myth of our so-called "popular vote." Voters who pulled the party lever for the Democratic ticket elected six unpledged electors who voted in December for Senator Byrd and five regular Democratic electors who voted for President Kennedy. Attempts to translate this into popular vote totals deserve passing mention because they expose the inherent fiction of the

* From Estes Kefauver, "The Electoral College: Old Reforms Take on a New Look," from a symposium, "The Electoral Process: Part I" in *Law and Contemporary Problems* (Vol. 27, No. 2, Spring 1962), pp. 188–212, published by the Duke University School of Law, Durham, N. C. Copyright 1962 by Duke University. Reprinted by permission.

popular vote concept.

Customarily, a candidate is awarded the popular vote figure received by the highest elector on his ticket. The six unpledged Alabama electors each received from 322,000 to 324,000 popular votes and the Kennedy electors received about 317,000 to 318,000 votes. The eleven Republican electors each drew 237,981 votes. Obviously, the latter group intended to register their preference for Mr. Nixon. But what of the 324,050 Alabamans who voted in varying combinations for Democratic electors? Most of them voted for the entire slate and thus were voting at the same time both for and against Mr. Kennedy. The Clerk of the House of Representatives in compiling his official statistics ignored the ticket split and merely listed the Democratic popular vote at 324,050. If the votes for Byrd were similarly treated, Alabama Democrats obviously would be recorded twice and the total Alabama vote would be correspondingly inflated. The *Congressional Quarterly* distributed 5/11 of the total Democratic vote to Kennedy and 6/11 to unpledged. This avoids duplication but it determines the popular vote from the electoral vote which is at odds with our basic assumption. Also, it leads to a hypothetical popular vote victory in Alabama (and the nation) for Mr. Nixon, a fact never claimed by the most zealous of his supporters.

The only conclusion which can be drawn is that there is a great gulf between our presidential election system as it is popularly viewed and as it actually exists. Gymnastics with the Alabama vote serve no purpose in attempting to measure the popularity of either candidate. Other features of the system prevent it from being accurate in this respect. But a realistic look a this and other peculiarities of our system would be useful if it drives home to the American people the myths under which they enthusiastically flock to the polls and exercise their democratic birthright every fourth November.

A renewed demand for electoral reform followed the 1960 election in at least one sense. Those of us in Congress who have worked for reform for years hopefully renewed our efforts. There was an increase in the number of proposed constitutional amendments to the Constitution introduced in the Eighty-seventh Congress, but after presiding over extensive hearings last year as Chairman of the Subcommittee on Constitutional Amendments, I am still waiting for evidence of substantially increased support for reform at the grass roots level.

Analysis of constitutional reforms should proceed from a realistic restatement of the constitutional foundation upon which presidential elections now rest. Unfortunately, much public discussion of the subject proceeds upon assumptions without basis in the Constitution.

The present system is embodied in article two, section one, and the twelfth amendment to the Constitution, which provide simply that the President and Vice President shall be chosen by electors appointed by each state in the manner directed by its legislature. Each state has a number of electors equal to the total of its senators and representatives. The electors are to meet in their respective states and ballot separately for the President and Vice President, at least one of whom shall not be an inhabitant of their state. A signed list showing their votes is certified and transmitted to the seat of the United States Government directed to the President of the Senate.

The votes are counted in the presence of the Senate and House of Representatives. A majority of the votes of the whole number of electors appointed is necessary for election. Absent a majority, the House of Representatives elects the President from the three candidates receiving the largest number of votes. In such an election, each state casts but a single vote, with a majority of the state's congressional delegation thus controlling the vote of the state. A majority of votes is necessary to elect, and in the absence of such majority the Vice President acts as President. In the absence of a majority of vice presidential electoral votes, the Senate elects the Vice President from the two highest candidates by simple majority vote.

The two-party system has produced an extra-constitutional elective process which is virtually uniform throughout the states, with the result that few Americans are aware of the meager nature of this constitutional scheme and the limited extent of their constitutional rights in the election of their President. Several popular misconceptions are apparent to the most casual student.

First, the people of the United States do not elect the President in the November election. He is elected by 538 individual electors meeting in fifty states and the District of Columbia on the first Monday after the second Wednesday in December. For the past eighty-five years, each state has appointed its electors by popular vote but this continues only at the sufferance of state legislatures and not as a matter of right.

Most people view the elector merely as a quaint procedural device for registering the will of the people. The fidelity of electors over the years has largely justified this faith but this assumption is also without legal basis.

Alexander Hamilton wrote that the electoral college system was intended to insure that the election of the Chief Executive "should be made by men most capable of analyzing the qualities adapted to the station, and acting under circumstances favorable to deliberation, and to a judicious combination of all the reasons and inducements which were proper to govern their choice." With characteristic distrust of the popular will, he added: "A small number of persons selected by their fellow citizens from the general mass will be most likely to possess the information and discernment requisite to such complicated investigation."

Hamilton's aspirations for the electors as a deliberative body were soon frustrated by the advent of the two-party system and the rise of popular democracy. Extra-constitutional devices such as pledges, statutory instructions and the short ballot have largely guaranteed elector fidelity but there is little doubt that each elector is still constitutionally free to vote for whomever he chooses in December, regardless of the manner in which he was "appointed" in November.

The most controversial feature of our present system is, of course, the so-called unit-rule or general-ticket method by which all of a state's electoral votes are cast in bloc for the candidate receiving a plurality of its popular votes. Like popular voting for electors and binding by pledge, this, too, is extra-constitutional. It results from our two-party system but is solely the product of state legislation. The plenary power of state legislatures resulted in a variety of methods other than election by state-wide general ticket in our early history. In addition to direct legislative appointment, electors were also chosen by the people voting in districts fixed by the legislature or by a combination of electors chosen by districts and electors chosen at large. In 1796 and 1800, the Tennessee legislature divided the state into three districts and designated three named individuals in each district to appoint electors.

We do not have to go back far to find a state legislature manipulating its system for partisan advantage in a particular election. In 1892, the Michigan legislature adopted a district system for the purpose of splitting the state's electoral votes in the coming presidential election. The Supreme Court of the United States upheld the legislature's power and quoted with approval the following statement which had been made in 1874 by a Senate Committee:

The appointment of these electors is thus placed absolutely and wholly with the legislatures of the several states. They may be chosen by the legislature, or the legislature may provide that they shall be elected by the people of the state at large, or in districts, as are Members of Congress, which was the case formerly in many states; and it is, no doubt, competent for the legislature to authorize the Governor, or the supreme court of the state, or any other agent of its will, to appoint these electors. This power is conferred upon the legislatures of the states by the Constitution of the United States, and cannot be taken from them or modified by their state constitutions any more than can their power to elect Senators of the United States. Whatever provisions may be made by statute, or by the state constitution, to choose electors by the people, there is no doubt of the right of the legislature to resume the power at any time, for it can neither be taken away nor abdicated.

The system produces two sorts of objections—pragmatic and philosophical. Pragmatic objections are concerned with the mechanics of the system's operation and are addressed primarily to the retention of the office of presidential elector, the method of resolving the election when no candidate obtains a majority of electoral votes, and the potential for manipulation of the system from state to state and from election to election. Philosophical objections are addressed to the fact that our system does not insure that the President is the candidate preferred by the largest number of Americans and to the distribution of political power under the present system, as between large and small states or as between rural and urban citizens.

It is safe to say that the pragmatic objections are a concern of all proponents of change. The uncertainties and dangers inherent in the present system have no vocal defenders although there is disagreement as to whether these defects alone merit correction by constitutional amendment.

The philosophical and political aspects of the problem result from two elements of the present system: the weighted electoral votes of the states and the operation of the state unit-rule method of casting those votes. At this point we reach the principal points of division among those who advocate substantial reform. Shall the states' electoral votes be retained at all? If so, what is to be substituted for the unit-rule method?

This may be somewhat of an oversimplification but it is a worthwhile basis for approaching the three principal proposals—direct national election, the district system, and the proportional system. Direct election eliminates the weighted electoral votes of the states. The district and proportional plans retain the electoral votes but differ significantly in their method and extent of eliminating the unit rule.

DIRECT NATIONAL ELECTION

When this method was proposed in the original Constitutional Convention, it was defeated by a vote of nine states to two. It has fared little better in Congress in the intervening years, although as early as 1826 a constitutional amendment for direct national election was introduced by Representative McManus of New York. In 1950, when the Senate approved the proportional system, Senator Langer of North Dakota offered as a substitute direct popular election along with national nominating primaries. The Langer substitute was rejected by a vote of 60 to 31. Senator Humphrey of Minnesota then offered as a substitute an amendment which provided only for election by direct national vote and it was defeated by a vote of 63 to 28. In 1956, when the Senate considered the proportional-district system compromise, Senator Langer again offered an amendment for nomination and election by national popular vote. This time it was defeated 69 to 13. Senator Lehman of New York then offered an amendment providing only for election by national popular vote and this was rejected by 66 to 17.

The chief advantage of this proposal is obvious; it would completely eliminate the possibility of a so-called "minority President," which cannot honestly be claimed for any other proposal. This term sometimes refers to a President who is elected without a majority of the popular vote although with more popular votes than any opponent. This has happened in fourteen elections. It is used more frequently to refer to a President who is elected with fewer popular votes than his leading opponent. This has happened three times. In 1824, although Andrew Jackson received more popular and electoral votes than did John Quincy Adams, the latter was elected by the House of Representatives. In 1876, although Samuel J. Tilden polled 247,448 votes more than Rutherford B. Hayes, the resolution of contested slates of electors by the Electoral Commission created by Congress resulted in Hayes being elected by one electoral vote. In 1888, although Benjamin Harrison received 90,728 fewer popular votes than did Grover Cleveland, Harrison was elected by 233 electoral votes to Cleveland's 168. We have had several "near-misses" where shifts of handfuls of popular votes in a few states would have produced a minority President.

This feature of the present system probably draws the most fire and arouses the most emotional objections. Yet a poll which I conducted last year of heads of the nation's political science departments showed only 34.2 per cent in favor of direct election. How do we account for the relative unattractiveness to political scientists of this simple straightforward reform which would place presidential elections under the purest democratic principle? By eliminating the state as an electoral counting unit every vote would be equally reflected in the national totals. The minority party in a state would not see its votes counted out at the state level as is now done by the unit-rule's operation. The "swing votes" of minority blocs in pivotal states would lose the special importance they now enjoy by virtue of their power to tip the electoral vote into one column or another in a close vote. The votes of any given group of Americans would look to a candidate like those of any other group.

Despite the objections to a minority President, there apparently is still a strong feeling that the federal principle should not yet be abandoned in presidential elections. State and regional interests are still sufficiently important that sheer numbers of votes on a national level should not determine the Presidency. Disproportionate weighting of the votes of citizens of less populated states may become increasingly distasteful as the Supreme Court's decision on representation in state legislatures is implemented; but for the time being the consensus is against a system which would ignore state lines and interests and cause campaigns to be directed to masses of voters.

A related objection is that direct election would necessarily nationalize our election machinery. Every voter would have an immediate interest in the fairness and accuracy of the election machinery in every state. Voters in Maine, for instance, could see their votes nullified by opposing votes in Alaska as readily as by votes cast in the same precinct in Maine. That this would require national election laws and federal administration of elections is not denied by most advocates of direct national election.

A weaker argument is that direct election would result in a race among the states to lower voting qualifications as each state sought the greatest possible voice in selecting the President. Some suggest that ridiculous voting ages might result and that all states would be driven to the lowest common denominator of voting qualifications. This could be avoided by providing in any amendment that voting qualifications in each state shall be those requisite for electing the most numerous branch of the state legislature, as is the case now for congressional elections. In order to generate a larger popular vote in presidential elections, a state would then have to adopt the same broadened suffrage requirement for electing its state legislators, senators, and representatives.

The most frequent argument made against direct national election in the Congress is that it would be futile for Congress to submit such an amendment to the states; that it would have no chance of ratification by three-fourths of the states because thirty-six of them have added weight in the election of the President by reason of the electoral college system. This theoretical advantage of voters in smaller states is shown by the table on the following page:

Yet can it truthfully be said that a voter in Alaska has five times the voice in electing the President as that of the voter in California or that a Nevadan has

RATIO OF ELECTORAL VOTES TO POPULATION FOR 1964 AND 1968 PRESIDENTIAL ELECTIONS (BASED ON 1960 CENSUS)

RANK AND STATE	RATIO	RANK AND STATE	RATIO
1. Alaska	75,389	28. Kansas	311,230
2. Nevada	95,093	29. Connecticut	316,904
3. Wyoming	110,022	30. Washington	317,024
4. Vermont	129,960	31. Tennessee	324,281
5. Delaware	148,764	32. Louisiana	325,702
6. New Hampshire	151,730	33. Alabama	326,674
7. North Dakota	158,112	34. Georgia	328,593
8. Hawaii	158,193	35. Wisconsin	329,315
9. Idaho	166,798	36. Virginia	330,579
10. Montana	168,692		
11. South Dakota	170,129	National average	333,314
12. Rhode Island	214,872		
13. Utah	222,657	37. Kentucky	337,573
14. New Mexico	237,756	38. Minnesota	341,386
15. Maine	242,316	39. North Carolina	350,473
16. District of Columbia	254,652	40. Florida	353,682
17. Arizona	260,452	41. New Jersey	356,870
18. West Virginia	265,774	42. Indiana	358,654
19. Nebraska	282,266	43. Missouri	359,984
20. Oklahoma	291,036	44. Massachusetts	359,984
21. Colorado	292,325	45. Michigan	372,533
22. Oregon	294,781	46. Ohio	373,325
23. Arkansas	297,712	47. Texas	383,187
24. South Carolina	297,824	48. Illinois	387,736
25. Iowa	306,369	49. New York	390,286
26. Maryland	310,069	50. Pennsylvania	390,323
27. Mississippi	311,163	51. California	392,930

four times the voice of a New Yorker? The opposite is nearer the truth because New York equals fifteen Nevadas where it really counts—in the electoral vote column as state units.

There were instances in our hearings where a witness would dismiss the practical chances of direct national election proposals as depriving the small states of their electoral vote advantage and then attack the present system as favoring the large states over the smaller ones.

The truth is that we have swung full circle and a system originally designed to favor the small states is now achieving the opposite result. This fact led former Presidents Truman and Hoover to sound similar notes in statements made for our hearings. President Truman described our problem as "the emergence of the big cities into political overbalance, with the threat of imposing their choices on the rest of the country." Mr. Hoover noted that our inquiry "confronts the same difficulties as were met by the Founding Fathers—that is, to prevent domination by a few large states."

If hope is ever abandoned for other reforms and we are faced with a choice between direct national election and the present system, this proposal might take on a different light. But for the present and the foreseeable future, I do not feel that direct national election is a serious possibility as a practical matter. It conflicts too greatly with our federal principles and some deep-seated facts of political life.

THE DISTRICT SYSTEM

Both the district and proportional plans are aimed principally at the unit rule, the former by dividing electoral votes among districts within each state and the latter by proportioning electoral votes in each state in accordance with its popular vote.

Some form of the district system of choosing presidential electors was employed by a number of states in the early history of the nation. It was favored in some form by such early statesmen as James Madison, Thomas Jefferson, John Quincy Adams, Thomas Hart Benton, Andrew Jackson, Martin Van Buren, and Daniel Webster. Madison wrote in 1823 that it "was mostly, if not exclusively, in view when the Constitution was framed and adopted." Four times between 1813 and 1824, constitutional amendments containing some form of the district system were approved by the Senate. In 1820, the House approved a district plan by a vote of 92 to 54. None has since been brought to a vote in either House.

Until the Eighty-seventh Congress, recent proposals of the district system provided that two electors corresponding to senators from each state would be elected at large and the balance (those corresponding to representatives) would be chosen by congressional districts. This form of the district system became known as the Mundt-Coudert plan. The current version sponsored by Senator Mundt differs in that it calls for independent presidential elector districts instead of using congressional districts.

Since the principal objective of the district system is to alleviate the consequences of the unit-rule or general-ticket system, it is relevant to consider the extent to which it will split state units of electoral votes. Historically, the district system had limited results in breaking up state unit votes. From 1789 to 1892, there were fifty-two instances of states using some form of district system. In thirty-six instances, the state's vote were still cast as a unit. Analysis of how the district system would have operated in 1960 indicates that a surprisingly high number of states' votes would have still been cast in bloc. If congressional districts had been used for a district plan in 1960, electoral votes would still have been cast in a bloc by these twenty-one states: Alaska, Arizona, Delaware, Georgia, Hawaii, Iowa, Kansas, Louisiana, Maine, Massachusetts, Nebraska, Nevada, New Hampshire, New Mexico, North Dakota, Oregon, Rhode Island, South Dakota, Utah, Vermont, and Wyoming. These states had a total of 119 electoral votes. In an additional seven states with a total of fifty-one electoral votes, only one vote in each would have been split from the state unit. They are Arkansas (1 of 8), Colorado (1 of 6), Connecticut (1 of 8), Idaho (1 of 4), Indiana (1 of 13), Montana (1 of 4), and Oklahoma (1 of 8). In six more states having a total of seventy-five electoral votes, the minority party would have captured no more than twenty-five per cent of the electoral vote. They are Kentucky (2 of 10), Ohio (5 of 25), South Carolina (2 of 8), Virginia (3 of 12), West Virginia (2 of 8), and Wisconsin (3 of 12).

This suggests that in many states, the division of political sentiment is sufficiently uniform throughout the state that voting by districts will produce the same result as voting by states. For the minority party to capture electoral votes, its strength must be localized in pockets large enough to carry districts. In many states (and all districts), minority party voters would still be "disfranchised" in the sense that their popular votes would not be reflected in the national vote totals.

In populous states with distinctive rural and urban areas, the district system very effectively splits state unit votes. Using the same analysis, in 1960 New York's vote would have split 25-20, California 19-13, Illinois 15-12, Pennsylvania 17-15, and Michigan 10-10. The large states would be drastically affected while most small states and essentially one-party states would see little change in the course of their electoral votes. One can see the truth to Thomas Hart Benton's 1834 prediction that "the district system would break the force of the large states."

In still another way, the district system's impact would vary between large and small states. This is in the weight of individual votes where the district system is claimed to correct disparities favoring large states. Under the unit-rule system each citizen has as many votes in presidential elections as his state has electors. A New Yorker voted in 1960 for all of his state's forty-five electors, but the Nevadan only voted for three. The district system is said to be an equalizer, limiting every person to voting for only three electors.

At first glance, this may appear valid but it ignores another vitally important factor—the number of voters sharing the choice in each instance. There is no equality if one set of three electors is elected by a group of 100,000 voters and three other electors are chosen by 1,000,000 voters. When the citizen of New York voted for his forty-five electors in 1960, he shared his choice with more than 7,200,000 other voters. In 1960, each electoral vote of New York corresponded to 162,018 popular votes, but in Nevada to only 35,756 voters. The district system would aggravate these state-to-state disparities. The one elector chosen corresponding to each voter's representative in Congress will roughly represent the same number of persons in every state. But the disparity in voters per elector is widened greatly for the two at-large senatorial electors who represent two-thirds of each voter's participation. In 1960, more than 7,200,000 New York voters would have shared in selecting the at-large electors under a district system, as against approximately 60,000 voters in Alaska—a ratio of 120 to 1, worse than the extremes of Georgia's much publicized county unit system.

Instead of equalizing voter representation, the district system therefore introduces a new inequality of voting weight in favor of smaller states' citizens far greater than that now operating against them. This demonstrates the fallacy of attempting to apply concepts of voter equality while retaining the system of electoral votes which flows from federal principles of state representation in our bicameral national legislature.

Another problem raised by the district system is the vast decentralization which it would introduce into presidential elections. Assuming the membership of the House is not increased, there will be 435 separate and independent single-elector districts and each state continues to be a district for choosing two at-large electors. In the District of Columbia and five states having only one representative, there will be no districting because the single-elector district corresponds with the two-elector district. Each will be a three-elector district. Within the forty-five states having more than one representative there will be created 430 single-elector districts corresponding to the representatives from these states. Thus, viewing a "district" as a distinct geographical area to which electoral votes are assigned as a unit, there will be six three-elector districts, forty-five two-elector districts, and 430 single-elector districts, or a total of 481 separate presidential election districts. The 538 electoral votes which would otherwise be cast in fifty-one state units of from three to forty-three votes will be scattered among 481 units of from one to three votes each. This fragmentation of a federal election carries obvious implications in terms of targeting campaign appeals, reporting election returns, contesting state and district results, and speedy ascertainment of the national results.

More troublesome than the plethora of 481 electoral districts is the possibility of manipulation and political abuses of the 430 districts which will be established by state legislatures. Prior to the Eighty-seventh Congress, proposals of the district system provided that electoral districts would be identical with congressional districts. If a state elected its congressmen at large, it would also choose its presidential electors at large. If congressional districts were gerrymandered or malapportioned for the benefit of a particular party in power, their effects would have been carried over into the election of the President.

In reintroducing this proposal in the Eighty-seventh Congress, its principal sponsors admitted that the past proposal (the Mundt-Coudert plan) was vulnerable on this point. It was therefore modified to require that electoral districts be of "contiguous and compact territory" and contain "as nearly as practicable the number of persons entitling the state to one Representative in the Congress."

This envisions either two state systems of federal electoral districts, one for congressmen and one for presidential electors, or that congressional districts will be re-constituted to meet these standards. There seems to be general agreement that although two sets of electoral districts are possible, they would not be desirable. Voters at the same polling place could be voting for the same congressmen but for different district presidential electors, or vice versa. (Elimination of the elector could cure this but still the district presidential vote could be included in a different district's returns.)

Instead of either reforming congressional districts or establishing separate presidential districts, state legislatures would be tempted to adopt existing congressional districts as their presidential elector districts. Many of the same political pressures and chances for partisan advantage would operate in both instances. In fact, it is possible for either type of district to meet the tests of compactness, contiguity and equality of population and still be drawn for political advantage. A common sort of example is the Kansas congressional redistricting after the 1960 census. The Republican state legislature split Democratic Kansas City between two rural strongly Republican districts. Neither party has a monopoly on this sort of thing but densely populated metropolitan areas are obviously more vulnerable to this divide-and-conquer partitioning.

The next question is whether the constitutional standards for presidential elector districts can be enforced as a practical matter. The Supreme Court's decision in the Tennessee apportionment case indicates that federal courts will no longer avoid the "political thicket" of districting and apportionment. In any event, the constitutional amendment could include a clause requiring the courts to take jurisdiction and enforce districting standards. Nonetheless, the suitability and practicality of judicial action in this area still raises many questions. What would be the allowable deviation of norms of population? Would the courts establish proper districts or merely enjoin certification of election results from improper districts? Would the state's two at-large electoral votes be validly cast in all events? Presumably, a court could not order an at-large election because the Constitution would specifically require that electors be chosen by districts. How would the cumbersomeness and delay of appeals affect elections?

An alternative method for enforcing district standards might be the power of Congress in counting the electoral votes to reject votes certified from states whose districts did not conform to constitutional standards. If this happened, the state would have lost its voice in the particular presidential election. The political implications obviously would cause a hesitancy in Congress to exercise such power. The strict party lines upon which the 1876 Hayes-Tilden election was resolved in Congress is indicative of the extreme reluctance which a party in power would hold towards rejecting electoral votes cast for its candidate. Another historical lesson may lie in the fact that Congress never refused to seat members elected from congressional districts which did not conform to federal statutory requirements during the period from 1842 to 1929 when there was pertinent federal legislation on the books. Some point also to the fact that Congress has never exercised its power under the fourteenth amendment to reduce a state's representation in Congress because of denial of voting rights.

Another possibility is simply to allow Congress to establish the districts or to give it a corrective power to modify districts established initially by the states. Once again is reared the ugly head of party politics. If our present system has any particular advantage, it is the certainty and inflexibility of fifty electoral districts. It is known from one election to the next just exactly what the system will be throughout the entire country. The complexities and uncertainties of the district system would be a considerable departure from this.

The conceptual basis of the district system raises an interesting question of political theory. It is called the "counterpart system" by some because it would put the Presidency and the Congress on the same political base. People would vote in the same combinations and with the same relative weight for the Presidency as they do for their share of the total representation in Congress where each voter is represented by his state's two senators and the representative from his congressional district.

Many feel that this is desirable and that it would produce a President whose program and political beliefs are more likely to be in harmony with those of the Congress. After twenty-three years in Congress, I am inclined to doubt that there is any such "consensus" among 535 legislators which could or should be a yardstick for measuring the Presidency. A President who had to appeal separately to the myriad of conflicting state and district interests represented in Congress would be less likely to have the positive and dynamic program for action which is needed for that high office under the demands of the cold war and space age.

A strong argument can be made, too, that the Presidency and the Congress should not necessarily be responsive to exactly the same electorates. The separation of powers doctrine may require not only a division of powers between the separate branches, but also having them responsive to different electorates—that is, the people voting in different combinations. Having the President elected upon a different political base helps to insure that conflicting interests are all represented in the federal government and the interplay of the executive and legislative branches helps towards ultimate accommodation of the legitimate interests of all segments of our society. . . .

Also, the concept underlying the election and functioning of Congress breaks down when one attempts to transfer it to the Presidency. Unlike electoral votes, senators and representatives cannot be equated to each other. The 435 members of the House are coordinate with only 100 senators. Yet no one suggests that the 100 electors corresponding to senators should have a weight in the presidential election equal to that of the 435 electors corresponding to representatives.

In another sense, the district system would not be a counterpart of congressional elections in the constitutional sense. The Constitution left the states free, subject to ultimate congressional regulation, to elect their representatives either at large or by districts. The framers did not specify how either electors or representatives would be chosen. The district system would make presidential elections a constitutional counterpart of an extra-constitutional method of electing representatives. That the framers did not contemplate true counterparts is suggested by the fact that the Constitution protects each state from having its representation in the Senate taken away without its consent but makes no similar provision for the two presidential electors corresponding to senators.

The truth is of course that the constitutional schemes for both presidential elections and congressional representation were necessary compromises between large and small states to secure ratification. They were hammered out as matters of necessity along similar lines by giving equal representation to states in the Senate and two bonus electors to each state in the poorly conceived electoral college, but here the similarity ceases. I think the demands upon and duties of the Presidency are so vastly different from those of senators and representatives that it serves no purpose to seek further common constitutional bases in their election. If the district system were a true counterpart, it would be more cause for criticism than for support.

THE PROPORTIONAL SYSTEM

Like the district system, this plan retains the states' electoral votes and seeks to eliminate the unit rule. Instead of using districts within states to split state units, it would divide every state's electoral votes among the candidates in proportion to their shares of its popular vote. Unlike the district system, it insures that the electoral votes of every state will be apportioned among the principal candidates, and it accomplishes this while still retaining the fifty states (and the District of Columbia) as the only separate electoral districts. This proposal is commonly called the "Lodge-Gossett" plan, for Senator Henry Cabot Lodge of Massachusetts and Representative Ed Gossett of Texas, who were its principal sponsors when it was approved by the Senate in 1950 by a vote of 65 to 27. Electors are eliminated and each state's electoral votes are divided to the nearest one-thousandth in the same proportion as the total popular vote of the state. Forty per cent of the total number of electoral votes is necessary for election. In the event no candidate receives forty per cent, election is by the House and Senate in joint assembly with each member having one vote and a majority of the votes being necessary for election.

If I appear to have some slight prejudice in favor of this approach, it is because I have supported it for a number of years, both in the House and Senate. It seems to me to be the reform which best meets the principal evils of the present system while introducing a minimum of new complications or inequities. The idea is not of recent vintage, although not so old as the district system, having first been proposed as a constitutional amendment by Representative Lawrence of New York in 1848. In the 1870's Representative Ashley of Ohio even advanced a proportional plan which retained the individual presidential electors.

In 1896, the classic essay of Dr. Herman V. Ames analyzed all proposed amendments to the Constitution of the United States during the first century of its history. Of those concerning presidential elections, he concluded that,

The proposition for the distribution of the electoral vote of each state among the candidates in the proportion the electoral ratio shall bear to the popular vote of each candidate seems the fairest and most desirable of all the plans presented, as it retains the relative importance of each state, and at the same time secures to the minority its due proportion of the vote.

When the Senate approved the "Lodge-Gossett" plan by the lopsided 65 to 27 vote in 1950, it was the first break-through for electoral reform in either house in 125 years. But the groundwork in the House had been poorly done. It was only considered under a motion to suspend the rules for its consideration and this was soundly defeated by a vote of 210 to 134.

The proportional plan bounced back in 1955 when the Senate Judiciary Committee again reported it favorably. Before it was considered on the floor of the Senate, a compromise was reached to secure the support of those who favored the district plan and a substitute amendment was offered by the principal sponsors under which each state would be given the option of using the proportional system or the district system. The substitute amendment was only agreed to by a vote of 48 to 37. This made it apparent that the requisite two-thirds approval could not be obtained and the principal sponsors moved to recommit the resolution to the Committee on the Judiciary. (This "neither fish nor fowl" hybrid proved more vulnerable in debate than either plan separately and it has not been seriously considered since. It has not even been reintroduced as an original resolution in the Senate.)

The proportional plan proved to be the most popular in the poll of political scientists which I mentioned earlier, drawing approval from 46.9 per cent as against only 16.2 per cent for the district system. Unless it has lost its steam from past reversals, it would still seem to be the most likely possibility for substantial reform. What are the objections to it?

The criticism most often made of the proportional system is that it would encourage splinter parties and endanger our two-party system. A splinter party could reflect its popular votes in the electoral college by polling small percentages of the popular vote within a state and could obtain roughly the same proportion of the national electoral votes as it obtains of the total popular vote.

Neither the assertion nor denial of this charge is susceptible of much proof or documentation. But the American voter characteristically wants a chance of voting with the winner. Whether his vote is counted out at the state or district level by a unit rule, or at the national level where it is insufficient by virtue of its total, he is not likely to waste his vote on a third party candidate who has no chance of winning.

The requirement of only a forty per cent plurality of the electoral votes for election is also a deterrent to third party movements. A third party could not expect to throw the election into Congress with less than twenty per cent of the total electoral vote. If an election is ever thrown into the Congress, the choice there is limited to the top two candidates (as against three under present constitutional provisions), which will prevent a third party candidate from being considered or holding the balance of power there.

Some criticize the forty per cent provision and call it a departure from traditional majority rule concepts and an implicit admission that candidates would be less likely to capture electoral majorities under the proportional system. But any elective system must provide in some way for an ultimate final choice, and any provision of this sort is at best a compromise. Election by the 535 individual members of Congress is generally regarded as the best contingent method but this is to be avoided if reasonable alternatives are available. I believe I speak for many members when I say that it is a function we would not relish. The forty per cent provision should cause elections in Congress to be very, very rare. Election of a candidate who has such a plurality is preferable to election by the Congress. This provision has much to commend it for any proposal.

The proportional system is often met by critics' cries of "proportional representation," or "P.R.," a system of representation which allows minority parties to elect delegates to parliamentary bodies. This term would certainly apply to the proportional plan if the electoral college were a deliberative body and individual electors were divided proportionally among all parties which polled popular votes. Any representation concept becomes irrelevant when the college of individual electors is eliminated. Electoral votes are retained only as a counting device for the federal purpose of weighting voting strengths among the various states. The object is to choose one Chief Executive for the nation, and as Senator Lodge stated in 1950: "Even the cleverest surgeon cannot divide one man up—proportionally or otherwise—and expect him to live." If this system involves proportional representation, then so do ninety-nine per cent of our elections in America because it only provides for counting all votes cast. Direct national election would do the same thing. Once it is recognized that "representation" is not involved and that "proportioning" is done so that our electoral counting device accurately projects the popular will of each state, then the proportional representation argument vanishes.

Indeed, dividing electoral votes to reflect the popular votes could minimize, rather than encourage, the influence of multiple parties and pressure factions. Small groups in large pivotal states now hold positions of great importance because they may add or withhold enough votes from either party to swing the state's entire block of electoral votes. Examples include the Liberal Party in New York and the candidacy of Henry Wallace in 1948, which is considered to have thrown two states to Mr. Dewey.

The district system may be equally or more vulnerable in this respect by its localizing effects. For instance, a Farm Party in agricultural sections, or a Labor Party in industrialized areas might capture enough single-elector districts to gain a balance of power position in the electoral vote.

In the 1956 Senate debates and again in our 1961 Hearings, it was argued that the proportional system would penalize two-party states and favor the so-called one-party states. One witness cited as an example that under the unit rule system, Mr. Kennedy won the states of Connecticut, New York, New Jersey, and Pennsylvania in 1960 by a combined margin of 613,000 votes. He won Georgia and Louisiana by a combined margin of 360,000 votes. If the proportional plan had been in effect, he would have gained a margin of 3.835 electoral votes in the larger group of states and a margin of 5.196 in the latter two states. In other words, a popular margin of 613,000 in closely contested states would have netted less than three-quarters as much electoral vote advantage as a popular margin of only 360,000 in one-party states.

This analysis is directed only to the net advantage in each group of states. Under the proportional system, Kennedy would have captured a total of 52.267 electoral votes from the first group of states but only 12.546 electoral votes from the latter. Under any system, a candidate must obtain a majority (or at least forty per cent) of the entire electoral vote of the nation and will seek an aggregate of electoral votes as well as aggregates of "advantages." Kennedy's votes in the first four states would still have contributed four times as much to his election as the votes of the latter two states.

Let us look at how important New York would still continue to be as a state. Under the proportional plan, Mr. Kennedy would have received 23.638 of New York's forty-five electoral votes in 1960, more than his combined share of the total electoral votes of Arkansas, Georgia, North Carolina, and South Carolina, where he would have won 22.911 of forty-two electoral votes. Under the proportional plan, one-half of New York's electoral votes is still greater than the combined electoral votes of seven states and would be eleven per cent of the total necessary for election.

Where the district system fragments New York's electoral vote into forty-five pieces, the proportional system still allows each New Yorker's ballot to count towards the state's entire block of electoral votes—but only in proportion to relative party strengths within the state. By contrast to the unit-rule system, each party's weight in the national totals would only be in accordance with the relative weights in the state popular vote. Since this same principle would apply to all states, New York would have the relative voice to which its electoral vote entitles it, but no more.

A similar argument has caused many Republicans to look upon the proportional plan with disfavor. It has been shown that in most past elections Democratic candidates would have profited from the proportional system because of the so-called "Solid South." Democratic candidates would have given up fewer electoral votes by proportional division in southern states than they would have gained by proportioning the more closely contested northern and western states.

This objection is fast losing its validity. In the last four elections, there are only six states which have not gone Republican at least once and nine states have gone Republican every time. Having seen Tennessee go Republican in 1952, 1956, and 1960, I am painfully aware that in presidential elections the two-party system seems to have arrived in the South. The Midwest is beginning to appear more solidly Republican than the South is Democratic. In any event, an argument based upon shifting patterns of sectional party strength should not control in evaluating the soundness of a constitutional system to be used over a long period.

Another objection often raised is that this plan would encourage disputed elections. In one sense, this is true. Any contest in any state which appreciably varied its popular vote totals would also vary the state and national electoral vote totals. Those seeking to change the apparent results of a close election could look anywhere in the country for a potential election contest. This would also be true under direct national election and shows that the proportional plan is a substantial movement in this direction. The district system's proliferation of election jurisdictions correspondingly increases the potential for contests but, like the proportional system, it reduces the effects of local irregularities.

The temptation to cry or commit fraud and to challenge election results will be much less when the shift of a handful of votes in a state can no longer tip inordinately great blocks of electoral votes from one column to another. Under the proportional system, the effect of accident or fraud in the electoral vote column would be only in proportion to its effect on the popular vote. Only in an extremely close election on the national scale would it be worth the trouble to contest local results. As 1960 demonstrated, such an election will always bring uncertainty in determining the final results.

The mathematics involved in computing each state's electoral vote to the nearest one-thousandth also troubles some observers. But when it is considered that 100 popular votes may be represented by one-thousandth of an electoral vote, this becomes a positive advantage. Again it illustrates that, except for retaining the electoral vote weighting of states' votes, the proportional system amounts to direct election.

Both the district and proportional systems would alleviate the great emphasis now placed upon the large pivotal states and relatively small organized groups of "swing voters" who may hold the balance of power in such states. The district system largely isolates voters' influence to the districts where they live and the proportional system limits their voice to its proportionate numerical weight. Under either system, campaigns would be directed more to the country as a whole. Citizens of smaller states are now less apt to see the candidates in person and they understandably may feel that their interests are of lesser importance to their President. . . .

Elimination of the unit rule by either the district or proportional system would thus go far towards truly "nationalizing" our presidential elections by restoring some balance to the roles of citizens in different sections of the country. The proportional system, however, would be less apt to swing the pendulum too far. The electoral votes of a large state would still be sought as a unit even though they are to be apportioned later in the counting process. The district system would partition large states' voters into small units and leave only two electors as the target of statewide efforts. Considering the small fraction which the two at-large electors account for in most states' electoral votes, it is safe to say that the state as such would become insignificant as an election unit. Real damage to our federal principles could result if parties and candidates become unconcerned with state interests. Continuing the state unit system to the extent the proportional system does is not only a fair price to pay for keeping the electoral vote advantage of small states, but is also good insurance that presidential elections will retain a sound balance between local, state, and national interests.

ELIMINATION OF ELECTORS

Doing away with the troublesome institution of individual presidential electors is a procedural reform which could be accomplished with or without other substantial reform and without touching the balance of political power in the country. One may well wonder why this was not done long ago apart from other controversies about the system.

This idea is almost as old as the electoral college itself. As soon as the rise of the two-party system and popular democracy caused electors to become mere "dummies," proposed amendments in the Congress began to include or center upon provisions for abolition of the office of elector. A Senate Committee headed by Senator Thomas Hart Benton in 1826 recommended a form of the district system under which people would vote directly for President without the intervention of electors. . . .

Also in 1826, Representative Haynes of Georgia was introducing the first proposed amendment to abolish electors and automatically award a state's entire electoral vote to the winner of its popular vote. At the same time, the legislators of Georgia, Alabama, and Missouri concurred in resolutions proposing amendments along the same line.

President Andrew Jackson, in his first annual message to Congress, urged that the people within the states should vote directly for the President, warning that "in proportion as agents to execute the will of the people are multiplied, there is danger of their wishes being frustrated. Some may be unfaithful, all are liable to err." Andrew Johnson, as Representative, Senator, and President, advocated direct election by districts without electors, as did Senator Oliver P. Morton, of Indiana, the leading advocate of electoral reform in the 1870's. In 1934 an amendment abolishing electors sponsored by Senator Norris of Nebraska passed the Senate 52 to 29, just short of the required two-thirds approval.

Concern with the constitutional independence of electors is considered trivial by some. From 1789 to 1960, in no more than eight instances of a possible 14,000 can it be said that individual electors departed from their mandates, and none of these affected the result of an election. However, three of these eight instances have occurred since 1948 and there is current evidence of substantial efforts to control election results by exploiting the elector's constitutional independence.

A 1948 Tennessee elector who was on both the Demoocratic and States' Rights tickets was elected as a result of popular votes cast for the Democratic ticket. Nevertheless, he voted in the electoral college for the States' Rights candidate. Although he had indicated his intentions before he was elected, his presence on the Democratic ticket of electors made it impossible for the voters of Tennessee to register the state's entire vote for the Democratic nominee. In 1956, one Alabama Democratic elector voted for a person other than the Democratic nominee. In 1960, Mr. Henry D. Irwin, a Republican elector from the state of Oklahoma, cast his vote for Senator Harry F. Byrd instead of Mr. Richard Nixon.

On July 13, 1961, Mr. Irwin testified before our Subcommittee on Constitutional Amendments concerning his actions. Without opposition in the Republican primary, he had been one of eleven electors nominated by the Oklahoma Republican Party. In order to qualify for the primary, he had been required to file a sworn written statement that he believed in the principles of the Republican Party and intended to vote for its nominees at the coming general election. (Since the electors, and not Nixon and Lodge, were the nominees of the Republican Party in the general election, Mr. Irwin technically carried out this pledge by voting for himself and the other Republican nominees for elector.) Mr. Irwin testified that he never intended to vote for Nixon if he were the nominee.

When the Republican ticket carried Oklahoma by over 160,000 votes, Mr. Irwin was elected to the exalted constitutional office of "elector of the President and Vice President." Irwin then helped spearhead an almost unbelievable "coalition movement" between the general election and the meeting of the College of Electors on December 19. It sought to combine Republican electors who would otherwise have cast useless votes for the defeated Mr. Nixon, with enough unpledged and defecting Southern Democratic electors to elect some third candidate in the electoral college.

Mr. R. Lea Harris, an attorney of Montgomery, Alabama, conceived the idea and wrote to all presidential electors on November 9 of plans for such a coalition. Irwin was attracted to Harris' idea and agreed to solicit all Republican electors for the plan. Irwin wired every elected Republican elector in the country urging them to join the coalition and vote for a third ticket. He received approximately forty responses from Republican electors. The great majority indicated a feeling of legal or moral obligation to vote for Nixon. About thirteen indicated interest in the coalition plan and a desire to participate if it had any chance of success. Three were interested if they were released from pledges by official party organizations.

Irwin then decided that the principal obstacle to the coalition was the "false assumption" by electors that they were obligated to vote for Nixon. He then wired each Republican National Committeeman and each State Republican Chairman and urged them to release the Republican electors from any feeling of moral obligation to vote for Nixon so they could join the coalition. He received six responses, three of which were sympathetic but none offering assistance. The high point of Irwin's effort was the New Mexico Committeeman's response that he had taken up the matter with party leaders at "the Republican National Committee level," and that although they favored the move, they felt it should not be sponsored by the party organization.

Irwin and Harris bombarded electors with literature urging them to cast "free votes" as their constitutional right and duty, but on December 19, all Republican electors except Irwin himself stood firm and voted for Nixon. Along with the fourteen unpledged electors of Alabama and Mississippi, Irwin voted for Senator Byrd.

Harris and Irwin concluded that his vote had served to educate people to the freedom of electors and immediately started working towards 1964. In a post-mortem form letter of December 30, 1960, Harris laid out plans for a similar effort for 1964 and urged "friends of the movement" to begin now to arrange to become presidential electors.

As a result of Irwin's actions, Oklahoma election laws were amended in 1961 to provide that electors shall be chosen by state party conventions, that each must sign an affidavit that he will vote for the party nominee, and that violation of the oath is a misdemeanor punishable by $1,000 fine. The fine is the only means of enforcing the oath. If an elector is willing to incur the fine or wishes to contest the constitutionality of the law, he could still vote for someone else and his vote would be so recorded. Mr. Irwin testified that the prospect of such a fine would not have deterred him if there had been such a law in Oklahoma in 1960.

In the emotionally-charged climate of presidential elections, circumstances are not at all inconceivable where enough electors might follow Irwin's example to change the result of an election. Considering the excess-baggage nature of the elector, why should any risk be taken that a few individuals could some day miscarry an election when they have long since ceased to serve their intended purpose and are at best an imperfect conduit?

It is too bad the elector cannot be eliminated by a constitutional amendment which said nothing more, but this is not possible. Any amendment which eliminates the elector but retains the states' electoral votes must include some means for translating popular vote pluralities into electoral votes.

The minimal amendment would seem to be one which provides that the state's electoral vote will be automatically awarded to the winner of its popular vote as has been the virtually uniform practice for 135 years. In much the same manner as electors' votes are now certified to the Congress, the vote of the people for the candidates could be certified directly. Ample time could still be allowed for resolving election contests at the state level before certification of results. In fact, more time could be allowed and the possibility of resolving disputes in the Congress could be reduced because of the elimination of the intermediate step of electors meeting and voting.

This straightforward proposal meets opposition from two sources. One school of thought resists incorporating the unit-rule system in the Constitution. They feel that this might freeze this system for a number of years and harm the chances for more substantial reform. I doubt this. The public's view of such an amendment would be that it was directed simply at the office of presidential elector and not at any broader problem. In any event, this improvement is sufficiently worthwhile of itself to justify the slight risk of hampering further reform.

A second source of opposition is the few who believe the presidential elector to be a worthwhile office which ought to be retained. These are not merely the tiny number of extremists who want the elector to exercise his independent judgment and choose the President. Some few believe the elector is essential to preserving state control and decentralization of presidential elections.

I have considered this argument carefully but cannot agree. Just as state law and the two-party system are now trusted to produce elections of presidential electors, they can also be trusted to produce elections of presidential candidates. A corrective amendment of the type I have mentioned would simply guarantee to the people of each state the right to vote directly for the President, just as they now do for congressmen and senators. Voting qualifications for presidential elections could also be left expressly to state control as could regulation of the times, places, and manner of elections. The nominating process is now extra-constitutional and would continue to be so. Just as state law now determines how electors get on the ballot, state law could as easily prescribe how the names of presidential candidates get on the ballot. In thirty-three states which have so-called "short ballots," it is the names of presidential candidates, not the electors, that now appear on the ballot.

If he functions as expected, the elector is only a conduit through which the popular will is conducted and a more reliable conduit is readily available. The popular vote of each state can be transformed directly into the electoral vote counting process. We now have four steps: (1) The people elect electors in November; (2) the electors meet and elect the President in December; (3) the states certify the electors' votes to Congress; and (4) the Congress counts and certifies the final result in January. This proposal simply eliminates the second step and requires the states to certify their popular vote totals to Congress where it is simple arithmetic to count the electoral votes accordingly. Legally and constitutionally, we do not have a President-elect until December. If the electors were eliminated, we would have a President-elect in November.

Should the elector be retained for the possible exercise of his constitutional discretion in this interim? There is no conceivable situation where the elector might exercise his discretion which could not be handled better in some other way. If the successful candidate dies between the November election and December electoral college meeting, party regulations and state law now provide methods which direct the elector how to vote. Once the electors meet and vote, we now have the same situation until Congress convenes as we would have without electors from the popular election until Congress meets. No new problem or vacuum would be created.

Eliminations of electors would also eliminate the use of unpledged electors as occurred in two states in 1960. In a sense, this was a return to the system contemplated by Hamilton and the Founding Fathers; but almost everyone today believes that the American people should elect their President. More important, unpledged electors should be precluded because of their potential for manipulation and balance-of-power bargaining in a close election.

An amendment which abolished electors could also improve the present provision for contingent elections in the House of Representatives. If the electoral vote fails to produce a majority for any candidate, the Constitution now places the election in the House of Representatives with the delegation of each state having one vote. In 1800 and 1824 our Presidents were elected in this manner. Since each state's vote is determined by the majority of its delegation, if a delegation is evenly split, the state would lose its vote. It is also unfair to give a one-member state delegation the same voice as the forty-one member delegation of New York. The opportunity for deadlock and third party balance of power is also apparent. Most proposed amendments would correct this inequity by substituting election by a joint session of the House and Senate with each member having one vote. This would give each state the same relative weight that it has in the electoral vote.

Indications are that the House would not object to sharing this responsibility with the Senate. In fact, after the Adams-Jackson-Crawford deadlock of 1824, the House adopted a resolution urging that some provision be made so that election of the President could never again devolve upon the Congress.

An amendment aimed at electors and contingent elections which accepted the unit rule would at least perfect the present system as it is generally expected to function. It would provide a certain and uniform system which could not be manipulated from state to state or from election to election. In urging such an amendment, one scholar calls it a "housekeeping amendment." This approach was supported by President Kennedy as a Senator and by the Department of Justice in our 1961 Hearings. It has also been endorsed by an influential bar association. This amendment would at least put out present electoral house in order while we continue the debate of whether to rebuild its basic structure.

CONCLUSION

I would not attempt to predict which of the possible reforms may become law or when this may occur. It has been 158 years since the constitutional method of electing the President was touched in any respect and it would be most presumptuous to make specific claims for the future. However, I do believe the climate for electoral reform is improving perceptibly and that some of the most serious past obstacles are being removed.

Division among proponents of reform should lessen as a result of the current consideration of the subject by the public and in the Congress. There will probably be lessened efforts for proposals which are shown to have no chance of success and their supporters will then be faced with a choice between the status quo and some other proposal. Through a process of narrowing the alternatives one of the basic proposed reforms should emerge as the only realistic alternative to the present system. What are now four or five opposing camps will become but two. When this occurs, but not before, I believe we can expect something substantial to be done.

III. ELECTORAL BEHAVIOR AND POLITICAL PATTERNS

6. Campaign Conduct and Electoral Behavior

THE nominating process is prelude to another critical phase of the political cycle, the campaign, and resulting electoral decision. In the United States, campaigns and campaign strategies are related to, and influenced by, the decentralized politics of federalism and such institutional factors as fixed dates for election, the absence of party responsibility, and the presence of the electoral college. Contributing to political decentralization and local political party autonomy are the federal system with its recognition of national, state, and local elections, and the electorate with their specialized requirements and clienteles. It is only quadrennially, for the presidential election, that the national political machinery is geared together for a supreme short-run effort. In some instances, not all the gears mesh. State party organizations or individual candidates, keenly aware of their own needs, may decide not to support the national ticket. Often, too, the candidate who has secured his party's nomination through his own machinery prefers his own organization to the existing regular party arrangement—a situation that may create intraparty disaffection or contribute to organizational inefficiency or duplication. Free of the demands of party responsibility and assured of fixed dates for elections, American politicians are able to build their own personal campaign organizations. (In contrast, in responsible-party parliamentary systems, such as Great Britain, the individual party member is dependent on the party leadership for scheduling elections, frequently on short notice, and on party backing for a place on the ticket, and is, of course, committed to the party program.) Furthermore, the winner-take-all result of both single-member districts and the states' unit rule for the electoral college means that state and local campaigns may be strategically and politically unrelated to national presidential campaigns. But though campaigns may be divorced, they are not necessarily separated. Other candidates on the ticket are only too happy to ride into office on the coattails of a strong presidential candidate.

American political campaigns, particularly presidential ones, are a cacophony of discordant elements: idealism coexists with cynicism and venality; attempts are made to educate the electorate about candidates and issues, but also to systematically manipulate the mass mind and attractively "package" the candidate. Although campaign styles and techniques have undergone considerable change (see Alexander Heard's essay which follows), certain techniques and problems have remained constant ever since the first parties contested for electoral office by waging campaigns. The candidate must follow a time-honored script which is designed to persuade as many voters as possible that he is first of all competent. Some candidates have even tried to demonstrate that they are wise, but excessive wisdom, especially if it borders on intellectuality, can be dangerous to a candidate, as Adlai Stevenson's experience demonstrated; the common touch is a prerequisite for any campaigner. He must also impress upon the voter his honesty. It helps if one can be also morally above reproach. The birth of a child to Governor Nelson Rockefeller and his second wife, on the eve of the California primary, is thought by some observers to have highlighted Rockefeller's divorce and remarriage and consequently to have cost him the primary and with it the Republican nomination in 1964. And finally, the candidate must convince the voter of his interest in him. Since there are many voters, often with conflicting interests, this presents a challenge to the candidate's political dexterity.

Mudslinging and fraud—although they are abjured by responsible candidates and although attempts have been made to suppress them—continue to manifest themselves. The Fair Campaign Practices Committee, a toothless private agency that attempts to referee election battles, is up against the ethic pithily expressed by an old-time boss: "The game of politics is not a branch of the Sunday school business." Political skulduggery is both ancient and bipartisan. While mudslinging and distortions demean the electoral process, destroying the public confidence, fraud attacks the process frontally and boldly. It takes many shapes—phony evidence, doctored photographs, etc.—but its classic form is cheating at the polls. In the heyday of the bosses it was established practice to pad the registration lists with false names and addresses; when the reformers went to check, they often found that the "voters" were dogs, children, insane or dead people, who, in many instances, had voted not once but several times! The classic tale concerns the paid "repeater" who, when confronted with evidence that he wasn't the prominent clergyman he impersonated, replied, "The hell I ain't you ————." But fraud was not confined to the actual act of voting. When the polls were closed, political mathematics came into play; it is said that many devoted precinct workers were able to deliver more votes than there were registered voters. The secret ballot, the voting machine, and permanent registration and voting procedures (poll tax, literacy and other voter-qualification tests), stuffing. Election fraud nowadays is mostly confined to "irregularities."

But a substantial number of the electorate never go to the polls. According to the report of the President's Commission on Registration and Voting Participation, "one-third of our adults do not vote in presidential elections, and more than half do not vote in Congressional elections." The comprehensive commission report studied the reasons why so many citizens failed to vote and concluded that low voter turnout in the United States (other democracies such as Italy, West Germany, Canada, Israel, and the Scandinavian countries have a significantly higher voter turnout) was caused by legal and administrative hurdles and inconvenient and burdensome registration, however, have eliminated massive election fraud and wholesale ballot-box restrictive residence and absentee voting requirements, and certain election-day difficulties (crowded and inaccessible polling places, early closing hours, and long ballots).

To improve voter turnout the commission called for sweeping electoral reform and made twenty-one specific recommendations: abolition of literacy tests, poll taxes, and other legal barriers to voting; changes in residence requirements (state residence requirements not to exceed six months, local residence requirements not to exceed thirty days, and new state residents to be allowed to vote for President); the facilitation of voter registration and actual voting at the polling places; the adoption of fair absentee balloting systems; the elimination of unreasonable requirements which make it difficult for minority parties to secure places on the primary and general election ballots; lowering the voting age (the minimum voting age in 46 of the 50 states is 21) to 18 along with establishing citizenship programs; and extending the vote to those living on federal reservations. These commission suggestions were directed to the states and localities; no recommendations requiring federal action were made.

An analysis of nonvoters shows that women, young people, and the "disadvantaged" are less likely to vote than others. The nonvoter is found primarily in the South where race, one-party politics, and obstacles to registration have combined to keep voting participation low. However, since the commission issued its report in 1963 there have been a number of developments which are likely to increase voter turnout. These include the ratification in 1964 of the Twenty-fourth Amendment, which abolished the poll tax as a requirement for voting in federal elections, and the 1966 Supreme Court decision in *Harper* v. *Virginia State Board of Elections,* which declared a local poll tax unconstitutional as a violation of the equal protection clause of the Fourteenth Amendment. The Civil Rights Act of 1964, going substantially beyond the voting rights protection included in the 1957 and 1960 Civil Rights acts, barred unequal application of voter-registration requirements, prohibited denial of the right to vote because of immaterial errors or omissions on application records, and made a sixth-grade education in English a rebuttable presumption of literacy. The Voting Rights Act of 1965 provided for the suspension of literacy tests and for the registration of Negroes at the discretion of federal registrars in those states and subdivisions where less than 50 percent of the voting age population was registered or voted in November, 1964. Moreover, the 1965 act also permitted Puerto Ricans to vote on the basis of Spanish literacy, despite any state law requiring literacy in English as a prerequisite for voting. This last clause, striking down a New York English literacy statute, was upheld by the Supreme Court in 1966 on the ground that Congress had the right to enforce the equal protection clause of the Fourteenth Amendment. With the encouragement of the Southern Regional Council and other civil rights organizations, southern Negroes who have never before had access to the ballot are now registering in large numbers throughout the South. The political implications of the expanding Negro franchise are substantial and will be discussed in Part VI.

Mudslinging, fraud, and restrictions on the right to vote are not the only areas of campaign conduct which give rise to serious public concern. Of equal concern, albeit in a different context, are the controversial issues relating to the economics of politics. Who gives what, when, how, and why is a study in itself. Of importance here, however, is the narrower issue of electoral expenditures. The fear that money can corrupt the democratic process is not new. To avoid situations in which legislators are obligated to contributors, political reformers have demanded legislation regulating campaign contributions and requiring candidates for public office to disclose the sources of their campaign funds. It was felt that regulation and disclosure would prevent special interests from exploiting the public for private gain. Toward the close of the nineteenth century and in the early part of the twentieth century, the first major state and federal laws were enacted to regulate political finance: New York passed a financial-reporting statute in 1890 and the Tillman Act of 1907 prohibited corporations and national banks from making money contributions in federal elections. Over the years additional state and federal legislation has been passed. Now nearly all the states have some form of statutory regulation of political finance and the Tillman Act has been strengthened by the federal Corrupt Practices Act and other supporting legislation.

Despite the absence of uniformity in state regulation of political finance, certain patterns on both state and federal levels have been observed. These patterns, according to political finance expert Herbert E. Alexander, take four basic forms: (1) The limitation of expenditures. (2) The prohibition against contributions from certain sources and the imposition of ceilings on individual contributions. (3) The interdiction on the government's soliciting contributions from government employees. (The first provision against political assessment of federal employees goes back to 1867. This protection was later extended in the Civil Service Reform Act of 1883; that same year New York became the first state to prohibit the solicitation of contributions from state employees and to prevent the levying of political assessments on officeholders.) (4) The enactment of legislation requiring public reporting of campaign contributions and expenditures.

On the federal level, the 1910 Corrupt Practices Act was modified in 1911 and substantially revised in the Corrupt Practices Act of 1925 (Clean Politics act). The latter required the national political committees or their subsidiaries to file periodic reports of contributions and expenditures, but made no provision for the publication of the filed reports. These reports were subject to no official audits; reported amounts were indicative, rather than complete; and primary expenditures were not included. Political committees working in a single state were not considered subsidiaries of the national political committee and could be excluded from the reporting provision. Absurdly low ceilings were established for campaign expenditures: $5,000 for candidates for the House, $25,000 for senatorial candidates. The Hatch Act of 1939 prohibited active participation in national politics by federal employees. A year later the Hatch Act was amended and limits were established at $5,000 for annual individual political contributions and $3 million for annual spending by political committees in federal elections. The $3 million ceiling was easily avoided by setting up a number of committees under different names, each of which was able to spend up to $3 million. In 1943 in the Smith-Connally War Labor Disputes Act, Congress extended, for the duration of the war, the 1907 prohibition on political contributions by national banks and corporations to include certain financial activities of labor unions. This prohibition was made permanent in 1947 in the Taft-Hartley Labor-Management Relations Act.

However, legal regulation of corporate and union political contributions has had minimal effectiveness. Large loopholes exist in the legislation. Federal prohibitions do not affect campaigns for state and local elections. And while direct corporate or union giving to federal campaigns is interdicted, nothing is said about bonuses received by corporate executives who may then donate them to campaign coffers as individuals, or furnish services "in kind"—office equipment, personnel, etc. Furthermore, ads may be placed in political publications appearing as educational books. Late in 1964 the Republicans published *Congress—The Heartbeat of Government*, charging $10,000 a page for ads; in 1965 the Democrats published *Toward an Age of Greatness*, charging $15,000 per page. The spirit, if not the letter, of the law restraining corporate giving is certainly violated here. Unions, too, know how to use the loopholes. Union treasuries are used for registration and get-out-the-vote drives, direct contributions within individual states for state and local campaigns, and educational expenditures (technically nonpartisan, but in practice generally in support of Democratic candidates).

Attempts to regulate campaign financing on the state and national levels have proven to be a farce. In fact, there has never been a single Justice Department prosecution under the Corrupt Practices Act since the law was enacted in 1925. A number of provisions of the 1951 Florida "Who Gave It—Who Got It" law (a law that was the result of the unsavory disclosures of the Kefauver committee and a newspaper crusade) have been incorporated into the Model State Campaign Contributions and Expenditures Reporting Law, prepared by the National Municipal League. But the Florida law and the Model State Campaign Law, which could have provided the basis for a substantial reform movement in the states, never attracted much attention. Although there have been considerable state revisions of election laws, these have been minor and not basic to the problem of money in elections.

This dismal record has been punctuated by journalistic exposures of financial mal-practices in campaigns and sporadic attempts to reform the regulatory legislation. In the post-World War II years Congress considered a number of proposals, but no significant legislation was enacted. In April, 1962, during the Kennedy administra-tion, the President's Commission on Campaign Costs (the Heard commission) issued its report. Recognizing the extraordinarily high costs of presidential campaigns and the probability that these costs would continue to rise, the commission made a num-ber of recommendations to help presidential candidates and the political parties sup-porting them to raise funds, increase public confidence in campaign financing, and bolster public respect for the system of legal regulation; the commission also made suggestions for the reduction of campaign costs. (The costs of political campaigns have rocketed during this century. According to a tabulation published by the *Con-gressional Quarterly*, in 1912 when the total vote was 15,037,000, the total reported expenditure was $2,876,816, amounting to 19¢ per vote; in 1964 when the total vote was 70,644,000, the total reported expenditure was $36,479,829, amounting to 52¢ per vote. In the 1966 elections, overall major-party spending hit an all-time midterm high. Furthermore, it should be remembered that funds reported as having been spent are only a fraction of the total actual spending.)

While the commission's report was directed toward presidential and vice-presi-dential campaign finances, the commission noted that its recommendations carried implications for campaigning for congressional, state, and local offices and expressed the hope that its proposals would have a desirable effect on all political fund-raising. The commission made several specific recommendations, among which were the following:

That for an experimental period extending over two presidential terms, individuals be given a credit against their federal income tax of 50 percent of political contribu-tions, up to a maximum of $10 in credits, or, as an alternative, a deduction from taxable income up to a maximum of $1,000 a year.

That an effective system of public disclosure be adopted which would require principal sources and uses of money to be reported to a Registry of Election Finance.

That the statutory ceiling of $3 million on the annual receipts and expenditures of interstate political committees and the $5,000 limit on annual individual contribu-tions to those committees be repealed, leaving no limit.

That all candidates for President and Vice-President and committees raising or spending at least $2,500 a year be required to report in detail expenditures in pri-mary and general election campaigns.

That, in an attempt to "institutionalize" the transition from one administration to another, when the party in power has changed, the government pay the reasonable and necessary costs of a President-elect's facilities and staff. It was felt that these costs are not partisan in nature and only increase the financial pressure on the political parties.

That Section 315(a) of the Federal Communications Act, the equal time provision, be suspended temporarily as it applies to presidential and vice-presidential nominees.

The recommendations of the commission bore little fruit. President Kennedy submitted to Congress several proposals embodying commission recommendations, but no legislation emerged.

Both before and since the Heard commission report, Section 315(a) has provoked considerable discussion and focused attention on the role of radio and television in campaign conduct and political finance. Radio and television time is expensive but necessary. In 1964 networks and stations earned $34.6 million for all political broadcasts; this was two and a half times the $14 million spent in 1960. Since 1952 when, for the first time, the national conventions of the two major parties were televised, television has played an increasingly important role in campaigning. In 1960, Kennedy and Richard M. Nixon, as Democratic and Republican presidential nominees, engaged in a series of four televised confrontations which came to be known as the "Great Debates." Many people believe that it was Senator Kennedy's performance in these debates that won him the election over Vice-President Nixon. The Kennedy-Nixon debates cost the major parties nothing and were held under a suspension of the equal time provision of Section 315(a). After the election and the publication of the Heard report, Congress, in 1962, discussed the possibilities of suspending the equal time restrictions for congressional candidates in the 1962 elections, but no legislation was enacted. Despite some agitation in favor of suspending the equal time provision in the 1964 presidential campaign, this was not done, and no Great Debates were held.

In 1966 President Johnson, noting that the regulations controlling political finance were "more loophole than law," submitted to Congress an Election Reform Act. The President requested detailed public disclosure of campaign finance; the inclusion of primaries in the law, so as to bring primary campaigns and convention nomination contests under the disclosure law; the application to the primaries of those criminal laws which apply to the general election; retention of the existing $5,000 limit on contributions from any one source, but repeal of the present unrealistic ceilings on total expenditures for federal office. In addition, in hope of broadening the financial base of the parties, it was proposed that a special tax deduction of any amount up to $100 be permitted for contributions to any candidate in any election—primary, federal, state, or local. The President's reform proposals were ignored, but in the final days of the 89th Congress, a campaign finance bill was passed.

The 1966 campaign finance law, which applied to presidential campaigns only, allowed a tax checkoff. Any taxpayer might, merely by checking a box on his income tax return, authorize the transfer of $1.00 ($2.00 on a joint return) of his taxes to a "Presidential Election Campaign Fund," a special Treasury account. The system was to have come into effect in the 1967 tax year, making funds available for the 1968 presidential campaign. Certain campaign expenses would have been certified under guidelines and controls to be established by the Comptroller General, and the parties would have received monies from the Campaign Fund. Payments were to be based on a voting formula pegged to the preceding presidential election; no party which received fewer than 5 million votes would have received money. If a third party received more than 5 million votes, it was to collect $1.00 for each voter over 5 million. The major parties were to divide the remainder of the fund equally. In actual practice, with more than 70 million votes cast in 1964, the Republican and

Democratic parties would each have received over $30 million, and no third party would have qualified for funds.

Although the object of this legislation was to provide a broader base of political giving, the law posed some serious questions. How could a political party legitimately collect $30 million from the government when another campaign regulation law put a $3 million ceiling on expenditures? Would the Campaign Fund encourage increases in campaign expenses? How was the use of this money by the national committees of the two major parties to be regulated? Would this discrimination against third parties freeze the present political system? Would the Supreme Court consider the discrimination against third parties constitutional? Furthermore, campaigns for congressional, state, and local office were not covered. Nothing in the law was done to correct the glaring inadequacies of the existing "regulatory" statutes.

These questions caused many people to have second thoughts about the adequacy of the 1966 Presidential Election Campaign Fund Act. President Johnson created a presidential advisory group to recommend changes in the law and Senator Albert Gore (Democrat of Tennessee) led a Senate movement to repeal it. The law, finally, was made inoperative until Congress could enact legislation establishing new administrative guidelines. In May, 1967, as a "corrective, remedying present inadequacies in the law," President Johnson proposed the Election Reform Act of 1967. The major provisions of the President's proposal were as follows.

Presidential campaign funds would be provided by direct congressional appropriation, rather than by individual tax checkoffs. There would be no formula governing the size of this appropriation, but the amount would be calculated by a special advisory board in consultation with the Comptroller General, who would disburse and audit the money.

The amount appropriated by Congress would be divided equally between the major parties and the funds would be used only to bring the issues of the campaign before the public, as in radio and television, newspaper and periodical advertising, preparation and distribution of campaign literature, and travel.

A "major party" would be defined as one which received 25 percent or more of the popular votes cast in the last election. A "minor party" would be defined as one which received between 5 percent and 25 percent of the popular vote in the current election. The minor parties would be reimbursed immediately after the election at the same per-vote rate as the major parties.

The percentage of federal funds received by a major or minor party which could be used in any one state would be limited on the basis of an established formula. This, the President noted in his message, "would prevent the concentration of funds in any particular state and would minimize the ability of national party officials to reduce the role and effectiveness of local political organizations."

However, even if Congress should enact election financing reform legislation, a basic problem would still exist. Aside from the presidency there are no exclusively national elections—only state elections at which national officials are chosen. This means that fund-raising committees do not have exclusive constituencies; smaller election districts drain off money and votes at lower levels. State and local party units compete for funds from many of the same sources, with the result that party revenue continues to be dependent on large contributions and fund-raising dinners (someone once called them the "cash and calorie plan"). One frequently suggested remedy is that the government provide a subsidy, graduated to conform to the office and size of the constituency, to candidates for federal and state offices. But no matter what action is taken, the fact remains that the problem of responsibility and adequacy of party finance, like so many other things basic to democratic government, is not susceptible to pat and easy solution.

Although the objective of any campaign is simple—to win office—the campaign is directly related to the more complex context of the voting behavior of a mass electorate and the larger political universe. Decisions reached at the polls have important effects throughout the entire political system. The President and the Congress as elected national public officials represent only a small number of the 500,000 public offices on all levels of government which are filled through the party process and elections. In the readings which follow, various aspects of campaign conduct and electoral behavior are discussed. Alexander Heard analyzes campaign trends, mass communication campaigning, the role of commercial politicians, and problems of campaign costs. Stanley Kelley, Jr., examines the role of mass media in the electoral process and raises a number of seminal questions concerning the influence of media on voters and politicians. In "Voters and Elections," Angus Campbell studies the flow of the total vote and advances a number of propositions regarding the size of voter turnout, party divisions, the pattern of circulation of votes, high turnout swing elections, the cyclical theory of American politics, and comments on the future of behavioral electoral research. In sharply contrasting terms, Murray B. Levin and Allen Schick discuss the social characteristics and mechanisms of political alienation as a form of electoral behavior.

HISTORY, ORGANIZATION, AND FUNCTIONS
OF CAMPAIGNS *
Alexander Heard

ALTHOUGH entirely unlike in external appearance, election campaigns may serve identical political functions. In their consequences, the torchlit, whooped-up speakings of 1860 may not differ from the klieglit, souped-up broadcasts of 1960. Boisterous campaigning at a crossroads tavern in one century may be equivalent to a televised carnival in another. The requirements for an effective television personality have been lampooned; but it has not been shown that these, while different, are more deleterious to political debate than the bull-horn voice and chautauqua talents that prospered in another era. One gathers that Mr. Lincoln's anecdotes, not all of which presumably were original with him, illuminated some issues and obscured some. Mr. Eisenhower's capsule simpli-

* From Alexander Heard, "The Organization and Functions of Campaigns," in *The Costs of Democracy: Financing American Political Campaigns* (Doubleday Anchor Books, 1962), pp. 351-77. © The University of North Carolina Press.

fications of public problems, not all of which presumably were original with others, achieved the same ends.

If political campaigns are functional, their functions may well be accomplished by different means under different conditions. Processes of communications and organization may change without altering significantly the functions themselves. To see the meaning of trends in campaign expenditures is harder than to detect the trends.

I. CAMPAIGN TRENDS

A change in American campaign habits always arouses foreboding. In the election of 1836 William Henry Harrison made the first public appeal by a presidential candidate that resembled a modern campaign speech. During the next four years the novel practice grew, and Representative John Quincy Adams, himself once a president, recorded his exasperation in his *Memoirs*:

Here is a revolution in the habits and manners of the people. Where will it end? . . .

Electioneering for the Presidency has spread its contagion to the President himself, to his now only competitor, to his immediate predecessor. . . .

One of the most remarkable peculiarities of the present time is that the principal leaders of the political parties are travelling about the country from State to State, and holding forth, like Methodist preachers, hour after hour, to assembled multitudes, under the broad canopy of heaven.

Nearly a century later, speaking through the president of the Southern Publishers Association, newspapers protested the growing use of radio broadcasting by the major parties. The arrival of television and the campaign airplane stimulated a fresh splash of commentary, some of it hopeful, but most of it apprehensive. Ability to gauge the consequences of changed campaign practices is severely limited. It is difficult enough to discern the effects on voters of particular campaign appeals. It is even more difficult to understand the import for the political system of altered ways of making the appeals.

The Evolution of Campaigns. American national campaigning has evolved through five broad periods, as measured by the things for which money has been spent.

Limited public campaigning characterized the Republic's first third century. Before the time of Jackson and Harrison, the presidential contest was a relatively staid procedure in both tempo and scope. The visible exertions of the candidates were slight, although organizational work was often of prime importance. Most of the canvassing, as it was called, took the form of preachments by supporters from stump and pulpit, of debate in the highly partisan press, of private correspondence, and of persuasive activities on election day. There was no lack of raucous contention for lesser offices, with due attention to the frailties of voters, but the suffrage was limited and the focus of presidential politics was as often on legislatures as on the people.

The torchlight era commenced with Jackson's election, symbolic of a shift in political power from the leadership of the eastern patriciate. The controversies surrounding Old Hickory deepened political competition. The United States Bank spent heavily in the campaign of 1832, but Jackson appealed directly to the masses against the "Money Monster." They understood and showed it in torchlight processions and hickory-pole raisings. The hard-cider campaign of 1840 demonstrated in full swing a new style of canvassing that would last until the end of the century.

The presidential stump speech grew in importance. After its first use by Harrison, other candidates occasionally took to the hustings, notably Douglas, Bell, and Breckenridge in 1860—but not Lincoln. Garfield spoke 70 times during the 1880 campaign, the most active stumper since Harrison and the only one aside from Tippecanoe to get elected. Not until 1928 did speeches by candidates on tour become a fixture of presidential campaigning.

Campaigning has always been concerned with two basic processes: communications and organization. Public attitudes are sensed and assessed in various ways, but chiefly through these processes are efforts made to mobilize popular support. In the flamboyant campaigning of the torchlight period, the emphasis lay on organization. Financial demands mounted and both parties began to draw on wealthy backers for funds. The municipal machine became the hallmark of American politics. These organizations sold their influence, and individuals sold their votes, on a massive scale. Appeals to the electorate were made through newspapers, broadsides, processions, public speaking, but field activities consumed the giant share of national and state campaign budgets, and election-day expenses consumed the largest share of local budgets. Travelling organizers arranged the support of local leaders, plotted ways to corral votes, negotiated the tactics of personalities and issues. It was said that in 1896 the Republican national committee hired 1,400 organizers and sent them wherever they were most needed.

The era of campaign literature began in 1880. Handbills and other printed materials had been campaign fixtures for decades, but a mounting number of printing presses and a fall in the price of paper produced an unprecedented torrent of printed words. In 1896, the Republican national committee alone was said to have distributed from its headquarters 300,000,000 pieces, weighing, somebody calculated, 2,000 tons. The torches literally went out that year, marking a transition to modern political-campaigning methods. Printed words came to supplement fiery oratory. The new century brought sharply mounting expenditures for communications, i.e., campaign publicity. Pollock reported in 1926 that the combined costs of advertising candidates, and printing and distributing their speeches and other tracts, constituted the most important item of campaign expense at national, state, and local levels. During the years 1912–24, something like 40 per cent of total expenditures went for newspaper and periodical advertising, news bureau services, outdoor billboards, lithographs, and the printing and sending of campaign literature. The profession of advertising grew, along with mass mailings and other techniques facilitating access to large publics. Politics followed business in making use of them.

Radio campaigning produced a sudden decline in 1928 of expenditures for newspaper advertising by the two national committees. Radio had been used but slightly in 1924, and at small cost to the parties. Four years later it emerged as a major campaign innovation, to remain until 1952 the distinctive medium of communications characterizing those years.

Television campaigning, after a limited initiation in 1948, began its dominance of campaign communications in 1952.

The Displacement Principle. Throughout the history of campaigning, a process of displacement has gone on. As new forms of campaigning develop, they displace older ones. It has already been suggested that the cost of national-level campaigning did not increase between the 1920's and 1950's, if allowances are made for changes in the price level and in the size of the electorate. Moreover, at the end of that period, publicity as a whole consumed no larger share of national campaign-committee expenditures, about one-half, than it had at the beginning. Yet in 1952, two-thirds of communications costs were attributable to radio and television, whereas in 1920 there had been no significant charges for these items. Expenditures were made for other kinds of communications. Even in 1928, in fact, radio accounted for only 18 and 10 per cent, respectively, of the expenses of the Democratic and Republican national committees. In other words, by 1952 broadcasting had significantly *displaced* other publicity devices in the campaign budgets of the national campaign organizations.

Between 1952 and 1956, however, the story was different. Radio and television broadcasting by *national-level* campaign groups not only further displaced other media of publicity but had the additional effect of increasing total costs. The percentages of total direct expenditures and the dollar amounts are shown below:

	1952			
	REP.	DEM.	OTHER	TOTAL
Radio and TV:	31%	34%	16%	30%
(in millions)	$2.0	$1.5	$0.2	$3.7
Other publicity:	16%	18%	33%	19%
(in millions)	$1.1	$0.8	$0.5	$2.4
Other expenditures:	53%	48%	51%	51%
(in millions)	$3.5	$2.2	$0.7	$6.4
Total:	100%	100%	100%	100%
(in millions)	$6.6	$4.5	$1.4	$12.5

	1956			
	REP.	DEM.	OTHER	TOTAL
Radio and TV:	37%	41%	11%	36%
(in millions)	$2.8	$1.7	$0.1	$4.6
Other publicity:	12%	17%	37%	16%
(in millions)	$1.0	$0.7	$0.4	$2.1
Other expenditures:	51%	42%	52%	48%
(in millions)	$3.8	$1.7	$0.6	$6.1
Total:	100%	100%	100%	100%
(in millions)	$7.6	$4.1	$1.1	$12.8

For both parties, the percentage and the dollars spent for broadcasting went up, and the percentage and the dollars spent for other types of publicity went down. The percentage also went down in both cases for the remaining campaign costs, although only in the case of the Democrats did the dollar outlays decline. The fall in these categories was nevertheless not sufficient to offset the broadcasting increases.

Separate radio and television data for 1952 and 1956 are not available for these or other groups of campaign committees. It is nonetheless clear from other information that the increase in 1956 can be attributed to television and that expenditures for radio declined as those for television rose. Generally comparable information about total expenditures made at *all political levels* for federal candidates was reported to Senate committess by stations and networks for these media in both years. The percentage of combined radio-television expenditures going for television rose from 49 in 1952 to 72 four years later:

	1952			1956		
	REP.	DEM.	TOTAL	REP.	DEM.	TOTAL
Radio:	52%	49%	51%	27%	29%	28%
(in millions)	$1.8	$1.3	$3.1	$1.0	$0.9	$1.9
Television:	48%	51%	49%	73%	71%	72%
(in millions)	$1.6	$1.3	$2.9	$3.0	$2.1	$5.1
Total:	100%	100%	100%	100%	100%	100%
(in millions)	$3.4	$2.6	$6.0	$4.0	$3.0	$7.0

While a degree of displacement had occurred, expenditures for radio broadcasting did not decline as much as those for television rose. Total broadcasting costs increased from $6,000,000 to $7,000,000 between the two elections. These are the costs of federal campaigns only, however. When all radio and television party broadcasts are taken into account (the estimates are dependable), the jump was about 20 per cent, or from $8,000,000 in 1952 to $9,600,000 in 1956. How much of this was offset by reductions in campaign expenditures for other than broadcasting cannot be said. A portion of it doubtless was offset, and even if it were not, $1,600,000 is only a tiny fraction of the total United States general-election bill. The data suggest, incidentally, that the jump in campaign costs after 1952 was probably not as sharp as is usually supposed.

2. MASS COMMUNICATIONS CAMPAIGNING

Politicians campaign at all governmental levels and for many offices. The changes that take place in campaign practices, however, do not occur equally in all kinds of elections. Many local candidates have been left relatively untouched by the shift from printed publicity to radio and television. For them, personal canvassing continues the chief requisite for success.

Campaigns are more likely to be altered by new media of communications in large constituencies. In large constituencies, also, changes in population and in social patterns are more likely to require new modes of campaign organization. Presidential campaigns seem to register most readily the innovations that periodically occur. The significance of such changes is more difficult to discern than the changes themselves, but what is true of presidential politics will often be true to varying extents of lesser offices.

Television: New Medium, Old Process? In 1960, the United States found itself deep in an era of mass communications campaigning. The era had commenced at the end of the previous century, and its most notable current manifestation was television. What the coming of television means to American politics and American society has been the subject of much foreboding and much optimism. The impact on the structure of American values and on the ability of the United States to understand its problems and meet them with consensus might well prove profound. Yet its impact on voting behavior was uncertain, and some of its other presumed consequences might be more apparent than real. Innovations in campaign practice have always prompted grave predictions by those accustomed to the old ways.

A large proportion of the people of the United States unquestionably follow politics over television; when questioned in polls, a large share of them assign it as the most important source of their campaign information. Not all the consequences claimed for its use might be as portentous, however, as seemed to some at first. It was pointed out, for example, that television enabled candidates to become quickly "known" throughout large constituencies. Adlai Stevenson was declared by many to have benefited accordingly in 1952. Nonetheless, the United States across its history has chosen many successful presidents who were not personally exhibited to a large share of the voters. Moreover, 56 years before, and sans microphones, William Jennings Bryan at the age of 36 had converted himself into a national figure in an equally short period of time.

It has been observed, too, that the speed and coverage of television also served Richard Nixon well in 1952. The vice presidential candidate was able to answer the Nixon Fund charges promptly, personally, and before a large audience. That the medium would reduce the incidence of campaign slander—the meaning some of Mr. Nixon's supporters saw in the episode—was, however, by no means assured. Critics held that the very tactics employed by Mr. Nixon then and on other occasions corrupted political debate. But the one-way feature of mass communications has always tempted ardent campaigners down lines less permissible in face-to-face colloquies. At the turn of the century, quantities of defamatory falsehoods, called "roorbacks," were printed and distributed in ways designed to influence the ignorant and thwart an adequate rejoinder. Some individuals clearly prospered before the television cameras. That Stevenson and Nixon and others possessed a set of personal skills denied other men less suited to the contemporary medium did not, however, seem significant. The same was true in other days, in the days of Franklin Roosevelt's radio voice, of Theodore Roosevelt's boisterous phrase-making, of Thomas Jefferson's agile pen. The types of persons equipped for successful political careers alter with the changing requirements of campaigning. It is difficult to see why at any given moment the random distribution of political talents would favor one politically significant group over another. It is difficult to conclude that the poor have fewer spokesmen or the rich are ridden over because the personal qualities that elected the father will hardly help the son.

The subtle and the lasting effects of television campaigning might in the end prove numerous and profound. As many feared, ability to project personality might, through television campaigning, acquire a primacy hitherto unknown. In the meantime, certain characteristics of the mass communications campaigning that had commenced half a century earlier were visibly accentuated by the use of the new medium. At one time, a candidate's organization consisted principally of a small group of personal aides and a set of treaties with other political leaders. As the importance of publicity mounted, the character of the campaign skills required and the ways they were assembled changed. Organization continued crucial as a campaign function, but the decline of old-style political machines and the growth of direct communications between candidates and voters evidenced the ascending significance of communications, especially its financial significance. The changes were, basically, technological in origin. Inventions in transportation and communications affected campaigning directly and underlay most of the profound alterations that occurred in social organization, in the character of the electorate, and in the nature of political issues. These forces combined to revolutionize the machinery of campaigning and its cost and to touch deeply other aspects of party procedure. Certain of these were especially noteworthy.

More Than a Pheidippides Needed. Pheidippides fell dead as he reached the outskirts of Athens. Modern mass communications have converted many presidential campaigns into marathon races, imposing an astonishing personal burden upon presidential candidates. Hard work is no novelty for American politicians, but candidates for high office have important responsibilities to meet, including the maintenance of good health, if they are to serve well the offices to which they are chosen. It was anomalous that as the ease of communicating to the electorate improved, the labor devoted to doing so increased. In the first year of full radio campaigning, 1928, stump speaking by the candidates became a *standard* feature of presidential campaigns. Curiously enough, television further increased the pressure on candidates to travel, and with the airplane, the time saved in the air multiplied the demands upon the candidates instead of reducing them. Not even his immense popularity and severe illnesses excused President Eisenhower from the stump in 1956, but rather they seemed to make his personal appearances necessary. In 1896, William Jennings Bryan, in an unprecedented orgy of oratory, travelled more than 18,000 miles to deliver some 600 speeches to 5,000,000 people in person. In 1956, Adlai Stevenson, who could be seen and heard by many times this number by going before a television camera—and on numerous occasions was—felt compelled to travel twice the distance by plane, train, and car.

The pressures on presidential candidates to hit the hustings stem from several sources. The spread of competition among the states increases the interest local and national leaders feel in their personal appearances. The visits made by Eisenhower and Stevenson to the South in 1952 and 1956 reflected a trend in evidence elsewhere. Candidates running simultaneously for other positions often want the leaders of the party ticket to visit their states—pleas likely to be treated with respect when the candidates might later assist in presidential relations with Congress. The airplane has limited the ability of the presidential aspirant and his managers to say no. They can no longer plead lack of time. Moreover, to be broadcast, a speech must be made. A hall of howling partisans adds punch. So candidates accept some of the sounding boards offered to them, and to avoid favoritism they race off to others. The mobility resulting from technological developments leads political interests of all types to press claims for the personal attention of candidates. The growth of organized interest groups has both reflected and created increased demands on government. The plight of the presidential candidate is not solely a product of planes and mikes but of a more complex structure of political interests as well.

The result of it all is a cruel, grueling personal experience that exhausts the candidate. The pace of his day and the multiplicity of his decisions exceed the capacities of the best. (They led one candidate to call his party's nominee for Congress by the name of an opponent, and another after a speech in Bethlehem to thank the good people of Allentown.) Decisions taken and commitments made in the heat of a campaign are always difficult enough. In a day when domestic politics and foreign policy are seldom separate, the campaign no longer constitutes a backyard play that can be forgotten as soon as it is over. Like a president, a presidential candidate needs to be informed, to be alert, to make decisions under such conditions that he may reasonably be held responsible for them. The organizational and staffing needs of the White House finally received attention; the corresponding needs of presidential candidates require attention too.

An Era of Specialists. Detailed study of the purposes for which modern campaign funds are used reveals a high degree of specialization in campaign operations. Campaign organizations are neither large nor complex by the standards of contemporary administrative structures in government and business, but the thousands of pages of itemized campaign payments reported for each election emphasize the multiplicity of goods and services called into use. The proliferation of skills employed in the political process extends beyond campaign organizations to all reaches of party and candidate activities.

As a result of this division of labor, a politician becomes a difficult person to define—which reveals, incidentally, that the door to political activity is open to a wide variety of persons. The concept of the politician as a mediator among conflicting interests embraces the broad functions of parties and factions. But not all individuals significantly active in parties and campaigns are engaged directly in mediating roles, nor are they all clothed with the ultimate attributes of political leadership, power, representativeness, accountability. In common parlance, all candidates, their managers, and party officers are accepted as politicians, although job descriptions of what even they actually do in different settings would expose many variations. In addition, necessary cogs in the wheels of modern politics include diverse types such as jingle writers, stage directors, public opinion pollsters, advance men, statistical researchers, precinct bosses, interest-group leaders, public relations advisers, contributors, solicitors, finance chairmen, career accountants, field representatives, confidential alter egos, advisers on an infinite number of special policy areas, the head of a women's division, and the head of a Negro division. These just begin the list that makes the campaign organization of the mid-twentieth century a wholly different phenomenon from that which sought Mr. Buchanan's election in 1856 or Judge Parker's in 1904.

Campaign Effectiveness and Party Bureaucracy. Waste of money has been acute in political campaigns as far back as the record runs. It is not simply that money may stick to the fingers through which it passes (or rather, through which it does not pass). Men of experience have at one time or another estimated that a fourth, a half, even a larger proportion of campaign expenditures went down a useless drain. Administrative inefficiencies have been gross (symbolized at the end of the last century by the million copies of a document directed to organized labor in New York that were printed without a union label, only to be junked and printed again). Political inefficiencies, more important to the effectiveness of the election process, have taken the form of poor judgments, piqued feelings, unneeded commitments, wretched failures to capitalize on opportunities to build public support. Most campaign headquarters are welters of confusion, a state of affairs inherent in modern conditions of campaigning.

The probabilities and penalties of campaign inefficiency have reached new peaks with the arrival of television. There is a new premium on campaign planning and efficient management. The large costs of network television, to be met in advance, alone require a new kind of timing in the planning and launching of campaigns. Failure to anticipate television needs apparently cost Republicans $300,000 to $400,000 in 1952. Pre-emption and other charges could have been avoided by advance arrangements, although it might be argued that the money was well spent if it permitted the Republicans to capture a significant part of the audience of the choice commercial shows whose time was pre-empted. The preparation required by modern campaigns often must commence before candidates are chosen, a condition, it may be well to remember, that makes difficult the shortening of campaigns.

Few if any party organizations possess the staff necessary to supply the technical and professional skills called for in modern campaigns. To fill this void, and in some localities to help fill larger voids created by generally weak party organizations, public relations people and others from outside the party structure have often stepped in. They claim to offer a steady set of diverse and expert skills that cannot be developed and sustained by party organizations. The parties are not, however, entirely devoid of stable administrative staffs.

In October of the nonelection years 1953, 1955, and 1957, the payrolls of the Republican and Democratic national committees averaged 97 and 64 employees, respectively. Taken as a whole, these were hardly career staffs and could not meet the full requirements of election-year campaigning, but compared with a generation before they were monstrous bureaucracies. The situation in the states is more difficult to assess, but some suggestive answers were supplied to a questionnaire by the chairman of each party in each of 48 states.

There is, first of all, a rapid turnover among the state chairmen themselves. While many who reach the post have served a long apprenticeship in other capacities, few linger long enough to provide much continuity in formal leadership. In 1958, over one-fourth of all state chairmen had been in office less than two years, and in both parties over three-fourths had held office less than five years. Only four Republican and three Democratic state chairmen had served as long as nine years.

Virtually all state party organizations take on paid staff during a campaign. At the peak in 1956, with practices about the same in both parties, there were 44 committees with between one and five employees, 35 with between six and 20, and eight with over 20. Yet well over one-fourth of the state chairmen said their committee's offices were not kept open throughout 1956 and 1957, and some who said they were clearly had in mind their personal offices and not a separate party quarters. Forty state chairmen stated that no *county* organization of their party kept an office open throughout 1952 and 1956.

The staffing of the 39 Republican and 29 Democratic state headquarters that *were* kept open is indicated by the number of paid personnel normally employed when no campaign was in progress:

NUMBER OF STATES WITH	REP.	DEM.
Secretarial staff only		
Part-time	2	3
Full-time	9	4
Professional-level personnel		
Part-time	2	3
Full-time		
1 person	16	12
2–3 persons	6	4
4–5 persons	2	1
over 5 persons	2	2
	—	—
	39	29

Each state chairman was asked how long these people had been employed by the state committee at the end of 1957. Counting the senior person only in each state, the results were as follows:

NUMBER OF STATES WITH	REP.	DEM.
Secretarial staff only		
Under 5 years	8	5
5–8 years	1	1
Over 8 years	2	1
Professional-level personnel		
Under 5 years	19	14
5–8 years	5	2
Over 8 years	4	6
	39	29

In some states, committees that employed persons of professional status had secretarial employees with greater longevity than the professional.

These are the hired hands of party organizations. In a few instances, politicians of personal influence get on the party payroll, but the personnel summarized here are mostly technicians. They, like their mentors among the political leaders of their areas, often possess experience and shrewdness in the pull and haul of factional and party competition. Their chief significance, however, lies in the contribution they make in meeting the requirements of contemporary political campaigning. What they do not do, it is fair to suppose, others will try to do.

3. COMMERCIAL POLITICIANS

The public relations man has replaced the political boss as an object of opprobrium. Whether rated good or bad, he has significance, like the boss, because he fills a functional need in political operations. Public relations is a recognized occupation, and for some it is a profession. Those who follow it seem, like other specialists in persuasion, on their way to a place among the elite corps of American society. All hands now seem to require help from public relations specialists. Fights for control of corporations are managed by them; the Farm Bureau Federation hires them; communities and states engage their services. Candidates are beginning to come from the public relations ranks, as they have from law and journalism, to wit, a candidate for mayor of Philadelphia and a congressman from California. The hired public relations counselors who trade in the coin of politics are commercial politicians.

Carl Byoir, the late, famed public relations consultant credited with the idea for the Roosevelt birthday balls, concluded that public relations "is whatever the individual practitioner thinks it is." For political purposes, a public relations man is whoever calls himself one. Public relations has become a label of convenience covering any kind of freewheeling political activity one takes a fancy to. Types who used to be known as lobbyists, campaign managers, press agents, confidential advisors, hangers-on, or simply as lawyers with a bent for politics, show up in every state bearing the new label. Indicative of the trend was the remark of California's "secret boss," Artie Samish, later jailed for his casual regard for the tax laws: "Who, me? I represent industry. I'm a lobbyist, a public relations man." One political freebooter of mediocre talents who had made his way to an important appointive job in Texas government insisted that his profession was public relations. In an earlier day he would have been called, by others at least, a patronage hog.

"Public relations" gives many kinds of operators a vocational base from which to sell their political services. Many of these are of the facilitating, mediating, intermediary kind that are traditionally associated with lawyers and lobbyists. Many are more technical in character, involving writing skills and knowledge of publicity techniques. And, increasingly it would seem, they include knowledge of personalities, of factional rivalries, of interest groups, and of local political history, necessary ingredients of effective political campaigning.

No census records the number of these commercial politicians, nor how numerous and varied are their skills. In 1957, the Public Relations Society of America, whose qualifications for membership are considered relatively strict, had more than 2,600 individual members. Two-thirds of these were employed in public relations departments of large organizations and one-third in public relations counseling firms, the latter numbering slightly over 500, scattered over 25 states. Many other firms as well as individuals practiced public relations, but PRSA's list of counseling firms constitutes the backbone of organized public relations activity.

The Financial Dimension. Since the appearance of mass advertising early in the twentieth century, political parties have made large payments to news and advertising agencies for arranging space. At times these agencies presumably added advice and counsel to their services, though the kind and significance is not apparent from the figures. Many modern public relations firms have advertising departments, and much of the money paid to them as well as to advertising agencies still goes for use of mass communications media. To understand the political roles of public relations firms, therefore, it is necessary to ask what they do, not simply how much political money they handle. Nevertheless, a high proportion of the funds of many campaign committees flows through public relations and advertising firms.

In 1952, at the national level, the three most important Democratic campaign committees reported paying nearly $1,000,000 to the Joseph Katz Company alone, and the three top Republican groups paid the Kudner Agency more than $1,200,000. When committees are examined at state and local levels, as much as 90 per cent of the total disbursements of some committees, and frequently more than 50 per cent, are found going through such firms. This is true of regular party organizations, *ad hoc* candidate committees, local and state committees, committees of both parties, committees in all sections of the country.

The Republican state chairmen in 18 states, and the Democratic chairmen in 15, said in 1958 that their state committees had employed a *public relations* firm at some time during 1956 or 1957. It seems probable in many states that candidate and volunteer committees are even more likely to employ public relations firms than are the regular party groups. Moreover, public relations services are made available in political campaigns via other channels. The Republican finance chairman in a large and important state volunteered that "the biggest loophole" through the statutes regulating campaign finance is the employment of public relations people by corporations on retainer. They do political-campaign work as part of their responsibility to their employer.

Public relations firms are active in many types of campaigns. A questionnaire was circulated to 200 public relations counseling firms represented in the membership of the Public Relations Society of America. These were the firms most prominent in their areas and thought to be most interested in political accounts. The responses received numbered 130 and covered activities during the years 1952-57. These firms said they rendered services of some kind in a total of 554 campaigns for nomination and election at all levels of politics. They claimed to have had over-all responsibility for the management of the campaign in 183 instances.

In 70 of the 554 instances, they had served candidates for president; in 40, for United States senator; in 47, for United States representative; in 47, for governor; in 55, for mayor; and so on. About half the campaigns involved were for a party nomination. These data do not pretend to be comprehensive. Many politically active public relations people are not members of PRSA. Yet the information demonstrates that in many parts of the country (the responses to the questionnaire came from 24 states) public relations firms (as opposed to advertising agencies) are importantly involved in the management of campaigns for elective office (not simply the management of initiative and referenda campaigns, lobbying, and related forms of political activity).

Services Rendered. Some notion of what public relations firms do in campaigns for public office was disclosed by the PRSA questionnaire. Sixty per cent of the 130 firms responding to the questionnaire had rendered some kind of service during the years 1952-57. These services ranged from the conventional advertising-agency function of arranging for advertising space or air time (44 per cent of the 130 had done this) to acceptance of full responsibility for the management of a campaign (32 per cent). Other services included fund-raising (28 per cent), counseling on strategy and tactics (54 per cent), preparation of publicity materials, and speechwriting (51 per cent).

The part played by public relations counselors in the 1952 presidential campaign has been described by Stanley Kelley, Jr., in a book opening up the whole subject of *Professional Public Relations and Political Power*. Mr. Kelley reported that the Katz Company's services to the Democrats were more confined to purely technical functions than were those of agencies retained by the Republicans, which had a hand in formulating grand strategy. The number of firms that are able and willing to take full responsibility for campaign management is limited. Forty-one of the PRSA members questioned placed themselves in this category, and it is the opinion of some experienced PR hands that the total number in the country is probably not much larger. The 41 were spread among 15 states, but over half of them were located in California, New York, and Texas. The head of a large Texas public relations organization sug-

gested that his state and California are so large, and their politics so heterogeneous, that really six or seven campaigns must be run at once, and to do
this requires professional planning and a large staff. When full management is
assumed, the budgets on which the public relations firms operate resemble those
of a political committee.

Many of the political tasks undertaken by public relations people have long
been the province of free-lance specialists. The new importance of the commercial politicians arose from their assumption of communications and organizational activities and associated processes that had traditionally been provided
from within parties and factions. The effects of the trend, however, are easy to
overjudge. So far, no wholesale displacement of party functionaries has occurred sufficient to convert political campaigns into contests between advertising firms, although the possibility was worth an amusing novel by John G.
Schneider called *The Golden Kazoo*. And the trend was not uniform among
the states. Two lines of change warranted special notice, however, both of them
evidence of the penetration of commercial politicians into the political process.

One of these has received considerable attention: the effect of a salesman's
philosophy of political campaigning on the definition of issues and the nature
of debate. Mr. Kelley's treatment of the broad implications of this aspect of
mass communications campaigning is especially interesting. The functions of
public relations people in building and maintaining party structures have also
been noticed. Both of these developments are compatible with the kind of bureaucracies that characterize American parties. The commercial politicians are
hired to do what the parties do not do for themselves. When wide discretion
is granted the political mercenaries, it usually reflects the inadequacy of party
officials and party staffs to handle modern campaign responsibilities.

Organizational Significance. The lush, chaotic politics of California afforded
enormous opportunities for anyone who could provide a sensible and economical way to run a political campaign. The presence of large numbers of referenda created contests in which *ad hoc* alignments shifted from one election
to the next. New campaign organizations had to be constructed to wage each
fight. The cross-filing system in the primaries confused whatever tendencies
existed toward stable factional lines within the parties. And there was not much
by way of party organization in the first place, a condition partly attributable to
California's nonpartisan municipal elections. Whitaker & Baxter and the others
responded to a market opportunity created by the frequent referenda and the
technical demands of the communications media. The inability of party and
factional structures to prosecute political campaigns even for their own candidates created a vacuum. Public relations firms stepped in to fill the vacuum.

Public relations firms seem to play their most important organizational roles
in states of weak party organization. One public relations man of considerable
Texas experience divided his firm's campaign activities into three phases: helping decide the "pitch" of the campaign; providing the "ammunition"; and
managing the field campaign through county and district organizations. As-

sistance from public relations firms with the first two of these activities is now a stable feature of presidential campaigning and is found in many state and local contests. The development by commercial politicians of personal structures of acquaintanceship and influence has, however, special significance. Some of these organizations claim such a knowledge of personalities, and such a network of relationships in the areas where they operate, that they are called to assist in assembling a candidate's campaign organization. They get to know who is politically active, what their preferences are, what types of candidate they are likely to support, what kinds of work they may be willing to do. Some of the public relations people bring new individuals into political life, activating them when opportune issues and candidates come along. Two or three wisely chosen persons can be the difference "between a county that produces and one that doesn't," said one public relations campaign manager. This is especially true where party committees at local levels are weak or inoperative. To maximize their ability to marshal field organizations, some public relations firms maintain card files on politically useful personalities. They know who can be employed to "cruise" an area, to watch over local efforts, to report shifts in sentiment. Firms that develop special familiarity with one section of a state may be called in by others, so that two or more may be active for the same candidate.

Organizing is not so packageable a commodity as scriptwriting. What kind of campaign organization can be energized depends largely on the candidate and the sources of personal, factional, and party support he begins with. The role a public relations firm plays depends also on the latitude the candidate and his aides are willing to give it. Whitaker & Baxter insist on control of the purse and of central decisions on the strategy of issues. They supervise and coordinate county and volunteer organizational efforts, but tight control of local efforts cannot be achieved. By the nature of their work, public relations firms often have knowledge of structures of influence and how to reach them. A public relations firm that has worked with the state medical association, to improve the community relations of the medical profession, not only increases the political potential of doctors, but also increases the ability of that firm to gain the political cooperation of doctors at later times. In all they do, moreover, public relations firms develop stable news outlets useful for many purposes.

Another aspect of commercial politicians adds to their significance. Most effective public relations experts have a recognizable political orientation. To be sure, some are willing to serve more than one party. Twenty-eight of 78 PRSA firms that said they had rendered some kind of political service—that is, over one-third—stated that they had worked for more than one party. Yet political sympathies frequently cross party lines. Particular commercial politicians tend to belong to one crowd and to work in the campaigns of that crowd. In Texas, in fact, some of the most prominent got started in the mid-1950's as the result of long and successful identification with the fortunes of particular individuals. Mr. Jake Pickle, a lawyer by training who found his way into a public relations and advertising firm, was clearly a Lyndon Johnson man. Mr.

John VanCronkhite, who had followed a miscellaneous political career in several states, fortuitously found himself attached to a winner in the person of Governor Allan Shivers (a profitable connection, but one that suffered its ups and downs as time went on). In California, Harry Lerner and Associates worked almost exclusively for Democrats, in contrast to Mr. Lerner's former employers, Whitaker & Baxter, who work the Republican side. In Georgia an advertising firm was identified with one of the governors. In other states, too, the recurring alliance of particular firms with one of the parties, or with a particular candidate, makes them look like components of a party or factional organization. They resemble mercenaries marching beside the regular army. If a public relations firm becomes a continuing component of a factional or party structure, it necessarily accrues influence.

Parties are already dependent on commercial politicians for the *expertise* required to use mass media effectively. They are dependent upon them in an increasing number of places for planning, budgeting, and supervising the administration of campaigns. Whitaker & Baxter may advance as much as $100,000 to keep operating expenditures flowing smoothly. Party politicians testify that a campaign run by public relations experts is economically more efficient. The $5,000 to $75,000 fee normally paid to manage a statewide race is well earned (one budget for a statewide race called for a fee of $5,000, plus a "bonus in the event of election" of $2,500!), and nobody seems to begrudge the standard 15 per cent commission paid for advertising services.

The Salesman's Philosophy. There is a manifest danger in employing professional propaganda specialists in political campaigns. Especially if their connection is a transitory one, their role can become highly irresponsible. They concentrate on the short-run goal of influencing votes in an immediate campaign—not, however, a new phenomenon, nor one confined to the United States. This they can do, or like you to think they can do, effectively. "My God, it's horrible," shuddered one practitioner recalling a television film of dubious ethical quality. "You can sell 'em anything, especially the women. You can sell half the women a bucket of kraut." He had done it and he knew. The candidate would benefit in the short run. If any boomerangs came sailing back in future years it would be the candidate and not his public relations counselors who would have to catch them. Commercial politicians commanding structures of influence are tempted to operate in the short run too. Their primary goal, after all, is the fee for the service rendered, or the pride of success, and they are less restrained, if restrained at all, by concern for consistencies in policy and by qualms of private conscience. *Their* concern, as one of them said, is whether they can "get a proposition through, or handle a matter, or get the guy in." If so, the fellows for whom they did it "call on you to help them out again."

While these reports are doubtless accurate, one is nevertheless reminded that few things are new under the sun. The political cartoon, great weapon of controversy during the latter part of the nineteenth century, found its strength in an oversimplified, visual presentation of a highly partisan viewpoint. Designed to be understood quickly, even by the illiterate, to get a wide circulation, and to trigger conditioned preferences and prejudices, the cartoon in many ways resembled the spot broadcasts and salesman's slogans of a later day.

Despite the hoary character of the problems growing out of such practices, neither the public relations profession nor the political profession has developed an effective code of campaign ethics. Yet, in all campaigns, men are restrained by standards of rectitude or by fear of the wages of sin. The line of restraint is set by community expectations and prevailing tastes as well as by personal habits. It seems inescapable that the prospects for improving party and community standards would be enhanced if the responsibility for political campaigns were clearly focused in a stable party bureaucracy. In the era of mass communications campaigning, the parties have not developed adequate campaign machinery. Nor are they always equipped to hold their own with the specialists hired to fill the void. The frequent result is inefficient spending, campaign bloopers, and confusion inside the parties in the performance of their electoral functions.

4.   WHAT SHOULD CAMPAIGNS COST?

In the present state of the craft, there is no conclusive answer. Despite vigorous criticism of the volume of campaign expenditures, no one has designed a model campaign that fixes optimum levels of expenditure under specified conditions. As a matter of fact, not much is said explicitly about what an election campaign ought to accomplish. Campaign theory goes little beyond the general notion that a well-informed electorate will behave more wisely than an ill-informed one.

Two-Bits per Vote. The difficulties of defining and determining total expenditures in particular campaigns have already been emphasized. In most localities, nevertheless, there is a limited sector of total costs that candidates or their backers must "see" a reasonable chance of meeting before a campaign can be undertaken. This is the money that must be assembled for use through one or more central headquarters. In many states, local campaign organizations are expected to raise and spend their own funds. In others, especially in primary campaigns, a state headquarters may help finance local campaign operations. The headquarters money must be raised by the candidate or his group of immediate supporters. In most campaigns, once they are underway, modest funds flow automatically to all significant candidates. But to launch a campaign and to keep its central organs functioning require a basic amount of money, and this is the money that must be seen at the outset.

Types of expenditures and levels of costs vary with the office sought, the locale, the candidate, the character of the competition, local financing habits, and other factors alluded to earlier. Yet *headquarters'* expenditures for statewide races in most of the country in the mid-1950's ran between 10 and 25 cents for every vote cast. Using information gathered informally by interview as well as from official reports, this range seemed to obtain in such states as Connecticut, New York, Virginia, Illinois, Montana, Oregon, and California.

(In several southern primaries, where heavy subventions were made to local campaign organizations from headquarters funds, the cost might run three or four times as high.) Candidates in all states may spend both more and less than the sums mentioned, but these sums are representative under typical conditions.

As long as present conditions obtain, sums on this order must be taken into account in legislative proposals for subsidizing or limiting state campaign costs. Except for those cases where large-scale local-level financing is required through state headquarters, 25 cents per vote cast is a reasonable working maximum of the money needed—or at least spent. For all national-level campaign committees combined in a presidential contest, the corresponding expenditures per party came to about one-half that amount in 1952 and 1956.

Is It Worth It? During the discussion of campaign costs that followed the 1956 elections, Louis Graves, a veteran southern newspaper editor, declared that most campaign money is wasted: "Ninety-five per cent . . . would be a low estimate of the waste. The voters could get all the information about issues that would do them any good, all that they could possibly understand, if the two parties would just agree, or be compelled by law, to limit their appeals for voters to a few amply circulated newspaper statements and a few radio and television broadcasts in the five or six weeks before the election." Thus is raised a central query. How useful, how functional, is the money that is spent?

The efforts made by public relations firms to rationalize political campaigning are normally guided by one criterion: the efficient influencing of voters. The energies they and others direct toward influencing voters, however, accomplish other purposes as well. There are latent as well as manifest functions in the use of campaign money. Campaigning is inescapable in a system of popular elections, so that candidates and parties may display themselves, their records, and their views to the scrutiny of the electorate. But the process achieves more than the election of some candidates and the defeat of others.

The socially useful functions of political parties are numerous, and election campaigning contributes substantially to many of them. They are part of what the nation buys with its election money and should be remembered in assessing the social utility of campaign expenditures.

The public and private discussion generated by election campaigns serves to organize agreement and disagreement on public matters. The campaign is a necessary part of the process by which parties and groups reach agreements within themselves and focus the disagreements that separate them. This process in turn is integral to the long-run processes through which public matters are aired, information about them is distributed, and conflicts about them are reconciled or put on the shelf. The political campaign is one of the chief means by which parties achieve the functions claimed for them in American society. An American election campaign is more than a contest between candidates. It is a forum for the representation of interests in which a significant share of the citizenry feels involved. It is one way the country goes about making up its mind about its common concerns. The sums required to facilitate this discussion and to encourage the myriad of narrower debates that proceed within it exceed those sufficient for candidates and parties to present their programs and personalities.

Large numbers of people relate themselves to the government through the activities of campaigns. They need not ring door bells nor make speeches to become importantly involved in the processes of self-government. The campaign and its surrounding events are, in fact, the one occasion that presses citizens to address themselves to the totality of their government. At other times they are concerned with the property-tax rate, a regulatory commission, a minimum-wage statute, the exercise of public domain, the decision of a revenue officer, the fate of a son overseas. These and other *particular* concerns thrust the citizen at random points into contact with the governments under which he lives. The political campaign asks him to think in larger categories of public concern; it asks him to decide what candidates—usually, which one of two candidates—will, on balance, serve his total interests best. To do this launches a harmonizing, reconciling process within individuals by which consciously or subconsciously they themselves decide what things are most important to them. Faced by the alternative candidates and parties they may perceive the depth of the absence of the choices before them. The processes that go on within individuals are stimulated by the variety and volume of communications that reach them. Some are touched by one medium, others by many; the bombardment of repetitive political messages of a campaign may stimulate *internal* self-governing processes of individuals that otherwise would lie dormant.

The vexed vent their wrongs, can have their say, or hear another say it for them. Their competitive and combative energies find outlet, vicariously and actively, in the conduct and excesses of campaigning. A campaign is sublimated violence and is part of the election process that achieves peaceful transition of authority. As such, those who enter the lists, and some of those whose support they seek and represent, exert or spend themselves to the maximum for victory. The psychological adjustments achieved by campaigns may require greater expenditures than needed for an informed and rational voting decision.

A unity of community, moreover, is bred by common campaign experiences. The bonds woven in politics run to allies. But the bonds even cross battle lines to link opponents with a sense of mutual fate. Old political enemies, like old prizefighters, often stand arm in arm, linked by a private bond more personal than they share with their own lieutenants. Thomas Jefferson and John Adams were even closer after their years of rivalry than before. Despite the raucous charges and frequent bitterness, the typical, eventual result of American elections is a greater sense of unity. Seldom does dispute cut deep enough to vitiate a sense of common process and confidence in it.

It seems likely, too, that the volume and character of communications stimulated by political campaigns contribute to a general sense of community. Sense of community must be fortified periodically if the common tasks of a community are to be met effectively. The mass media lace all hamlets, all cities, all sections of all states together in a common net of information, emotion, dispute. Many feel they are on their way to hell in a hack, but at least for the larger problems everybody is in the same hack. No pretense is offered that electioneering is an unblemished, golden vessel; on the contrary, the confusion of election processes may well contribute to the condition described by Joseph A. Schumpeter as the "reduced sense of responsibility and the absence of effective volition" characterizing many American citizens. The point is that political campaigns serve functions not apparent to the unaided eye and whose value cannot be measured soley in dollars and cents.

ELECTIONS AND THE MASS MEDIA *

Stanley Kelley, Jr.

THE purpose of this essay is to examine the role of the mass media in the electoral process: It will try to specify the character and dimensions of that role; try to outline, and sometimes to guess at, its consequences and potentialities. Because the activities of the media are so various, we can best begin this task, perhaps, just by noting and classifying the kinds of things the media do in elections.

First, the media transmit campaign propaganda to large numbers of people. In news broadcasts and news columns they report directly or in paraphrase what campaigners say. They sell campaigners time and space for advertising their wares. They make it possible for the politician to reach more people, quicker and more cheaply, than he could in any other way.

Second, the media transmit propaganda selectively. This is most apparent when media executives pare the propagandist's prodigious output to fit into the time and space they allot to reporting public affairs. They also exercise discretion when they sell time and space to political groups, however; they can refuse, and have refused, to accept advertising by minor parties and even major party groups. More than anything else, it is this ability of media personnel to determine media content that makes them political actors in their own right.

Third, the media transmit propaganda in certain conventional formats. Newspapers present campaign messages in news columns, news features, advertisements, and occasionally in full transcript. Television and radio present

* From Stanley Kelley, Jr., "Elections and the Mass Media," reprinted in part from a symposium, "The Electoral Process: Part I," appearing in Law and Contemporary Problems (Vol. 27, No. 2, Spring 1962), pp. 307–319, published by the Duke University School of Law, Durham, N. C. Copyright 1962 by Duke University. Reprinted by permission of Professor Kelley and the editors.

them in fifteen and five minute newscasts; in standard time periods offered for sale; and in interviews, documentaries, panel shows, and debates. Magazines feature weekly summaries, interviews, picture stories. This matters because the formats that the mass media provide for political communication are not just different ways to present the same things. They lead politicians to say things differently and to say different things.

Fourth, the media present campaign propaganda in the context of materials they themselves originate: their opinions about who ought to win; discussions of public policy issues; reports on campaign organization and methods; personality sketches of the candidates; lecturettes on the duties of voters and rules of fair play for candidates; observations on who seems to be winning and why. There is a mass of such material, although it probably occupies less space and time in the media then materials originated by campaigners. Implicit or explicit in it are a set of expectations about campaigns, notions of what is important in elections, a moral view of them, and sometimes partisan preferences.

In a narrow sense of the word "do," the activities just listed are what the media mainly do in elections and are the basis for whatever further functions they perform. A mere listing of such activities, however, gives us no hint of their impact. One way to assess that is to examine the relationship of the media to their audiences.

I

What influence have the media on voters? To ask this question is really to ask several. What attitudes are affected by the output of the various media? How strongly does it affect them? In what segments of the voting population does it affect them?

In trying to frame answers to these questions, it will be useful to distinguish between the influence the media may have in arousing interest in campaign discussion, affecting attitudes *in* elections, and affecting attitudes *toward* elections. The distinction between attitudes "in" and "toward" elections may at first glance seem unnecessary. It is an important distinction, however, because campaign discussion in the media tends to color the voter's view of the electoral process as such, not just of those contests with which it is manifestly concerned.

Why is that important? First, because elections are not just decisions—they are a way of making decisions, carrying with them an order, an ethic, and an etiquette. No one is quite certain of all the consequences that flow from this particular way of making decisions; but it is likely that it encourages in citizens a feeling of participation in governing and a readiness to accept the acts of government that lends stability to democratic regimes. Second, a democratic regime can derive these benefits from the electoral process only if elections are taken seriously; only if most people regard them as a good and important way to make decisions; only, that is to say, if most people adopt certain attitudes toward them.

The set of attitudes that lend support to elections as institutions is acquired. We do not expect the citizen of Ghana "naturally" to regard the winner of an electoral victory as his legitimate ruler, nor the Indian citizen naturally to regard voting as a better way to get what he wants from government than civil disobedience. We did not expect the immigrant who came to our shores to understand "our ways," and it is doubtful that most of us understand them now, in the sense that we have examined them critically and found them good. Our own views of elections, of the significance of the vote, of proper and improper forms of political action, are a faith.

The mass media are agencies for propagating this faith. Probably they propagate it most effectively simply by devoting a great deal of attention to election activities; few can, like Macbeth, conclude that anything to which so much sound and fury attaches may signify nothing. The coverage the media give elections conveys the notion that they are important, and the media reinforce this notion with themes that run repeatedly through their accounts of campaigns and campaign events. That voters have a choice; that a decision at the polls has profound results; that politicians have their ears to the ground and care what voters think; that Soviet elections are fictitious, ours real; that citizens ought to inform themselves about candidates and issues; that denial of the right to vote is the denial of a basic civil liberty. The well educated are likely to find some of these themes tedious. They do not need to be sold on the value of elections, however, while their less well educated fellow citizens may.

How many people does this media moralizing of elections affect and how strongly? The best guess would be that it encourages a more or less unquestioning faith in the significance of the electoral process, and of the citizen's role in it, among a great many people. It is, after all, an almost completely one-sided propaganda that the media are disseminating. By the same token, however, the faith may not go very deep; it may be held as dead dogma. There is some support for these observations in the results of the research that has been done on the relative effectiveness of one-sided and two-sided presentations of propaganda themes. As Joseph Klapper summarizes some of the findings of that research, "one-sidedness was more effective in converting the poorly educated . . . [and] more effective among men originally favoring the advocated view . . ." but not an efficient inoculator against subsequent exposure to counter-propaganda.

Media influence on the voter's attitudes in voting has inspired more interest and more research than the impact of the media on attitudes toward the electoral process. Undoubtedly this is because the potential significance of such influence is so immediately obvious—it may determine who wins and loses. In any event, there is a more solid base for generalization here.

Early researchers expected to find the mass media a direct and potent force in shaping and changing voting behavior. Their expectations were not borne out. How a person votes and whether he votes seems most closely related to his party affiliation, his perceptions of the interests of the groups with which he identifies himself, his opinions about several long-standing issues of public policy, his perceptions of the personal qualities of candidates, and his view of party performance in the management of governmental affairs. These affiliations, opinions, perceptions, and views are relatively stable. They are not easily altered by current communications of any kind and so perforce not by communications conveyed to the voter by the mass media. Campaign communication is, in fact, more likely to reinforce than to alter them.

The stability of party identifications, perceptions of group interest, and convictions about some policy issues among voters—and the high correlation of these factors with voting behavior—can be explained as follows: The voter is pressed to make a decision. He is asked, in effect, to predict the probable future behavior of rival candidates, to assess the impact of this behavior on interests he considers important, and to choose accordingly. He has only a little time to give to the matter; he is, after all, earning a living and doing other things required of him. Now, a candidate's party label, the character of the groups supporting him, and his views on a few time-worn issues are rough indicators of his probable future behavior in office. It is not surprising, therefore, that the voter seizes upon these bits of information to guide him in voting. It is an exceedingly economical, and, under the circumstances, not an irrational, way to arrive at a decision. To arrive at it in this way, however, means that the voter can and probably will remain relatively impervious to most of the communications campaigners are directing toward him.

A second reason for the failure of campaign communications radically to alter pre-existing political alignments is this: Such communications always find the voter in a context. He is tied to other people in an intricate set of relationships that serve to anchor his opinions and convictions, to mediate the impact of any communication on them. He has to fit the new ideas that come to him into a pattern of thought that his associates have come to expect of him: "Probably I will vote Democratic," a young man told one of Paul Lazarsfeld's interviewers, "because my grandfather will skin me if I don't." Group norms, group expectations, persons whose opinions are particularly valued— all these set limits on the ability of campaign discussion to induce opinion changes in the short run.

At this juncture, however, one point ought to be made clear. To say that campaign discussion in the media does not change voter behavior radically is not to say that it has no significant effect on voting. That it reinforces partisan allegiances is in itself a significant effect. That it induces marginal changes in opinions about parties, issues, and group interests is another. Finally, it is probable that the media exert a very considerable influence on the voter's perceptions of the personal qualities of candidates.

Klapper argues convincingly that the media can create opinion more easily than they can change opinion. Why? Because to "the degree that the issue is really 'new,' the communication [about it] is unlikely to run afoul of unsympathetic predispositions, unsympathetic group norms, or unsympathetic opinion leaders." To put it another way, all the factors that ordinarily operate to filter and bend mass media communications to reinforce existing opinion cease to do so, since there is no existing opinion for them to reinforce.

The relevance of this observation to the politics of personality should be obvious. The personal attributes of candidates as perceived by voters influence the voting decision independently of the other factors that help to determine it; a significant number of people, in fact, seem to bring no other criterion to bear in voting than their evaluation of "the man." The personal qualities of new candidates are, furthermore, new issues for a great many people. What newspapers and magazines say about a new candidate and the candidate's appearances on radio and television are likely, therefore, to be major factors in creating his public image—either to his damage or benefit.

In contests for nomination, the treatment the media give candidates may have even more important consequences than it does in general election campaigns. It may serve as an indication to the public of the candidacies that are to be taken seriously and those that are not. In their coverage of what candidates for nomination do and say, the media are, in Paul David's words,

. . . influenced by events, by whether a candidate already holds public office, and by the ability of the candidates to create news; but wide discretion remains, along with wide opportunities for differences in perception and judgment. The cumulative effect of these judgments may well be the point at which the media have their greatest independent impact on the nomination process; certainly it is the point at which they are most directly compelled to take responsibility for decisions of important political consequence.

What the media are contributing to is a definition of the alternatives in contests for the nomination; and, in "making decisions, recognition of the alternatives for choice is always a first and vital step."

Arousing interest in the electoral decision, and in discussion about it, is also a vital step in electoral decision-making. The mass media probably do as much as any institution to overcome voter apathy about campaign talk. To the extent that they succeed in doing so, they succeed because they dramatize elections, because they make them entertaining. This is conjecture, but highly plausible conjecture.

What difference does it make whether or not the voter's interest in elections is aroused? First, an interested voter, quite obviously, is likely to act differently from an uninterested one. He is more likely to expose himself to campaign discussion on his own initiative and more likely to participate politically in other ways as well. Second, both the outcome of particular elections and the functioning of the electoral system in the long run are in large part determined by the extent to which election contests arouse the interest of voters. Voter interest is an important factor in determining the scope of electoral conflict; and, as E. E. Schattschneider has observed, "the outcome of all conflict is determined by the scope of its contagion. The number of people involved in any conflict determines what happens; every change in the number of participants, every increase or reduction in the number of participants affects the result."

Arousing the voter's interest in elections in modern times has proved an exceedingly difficult task. If there is one thing known about the audience for campaign discussion in the mass media, it is that most of it is inconstant, inattentive, easily distracted. In campaign periods most voters expose themselves to the political output of the media to some extent. Few follow it closely. As newspaper readers, probably a majority of voters read little beyond the headlines. Most campaign speeches that are broadcast find a relatively small proportion of the potential electorate in their audiences. Many voters read about campaigns in magazines, but very few rate them as their most valuable source of information on campaigns.

This kind of reaction to campaign discussion is understandable if one puts oneself in the average voter's place. For him, involvement in electoral politics is necessarily a leisure time activity. It must be paid for by foregoing some alternative use of his leisure. Why should he pay this cost? Political discussion is not of much use to him. He may indeed learn that the outcome of an election will make a difference to him, but the chance that *his* vote, informed or uninformed, will affect that outcome in any very large constituency is obviously slight. He may derive some prestige from knowing the political score, but not in most segments of our society. He may get a sense of satisfaction from having done a civic duty, and, indeed, this does appear to be a significant factor in political participation.

The media seek to capture the voter's attention for campaign discussion by appealing to his sense of civic duty. They also inculcate in him an essentially unrealistic notion of the efficacy of his vote and so, probably, succeed in getting more of his attention than they would otherwise. More important, however, they present election stories in a manner calculated to dramatize elections, emphasizing their elements of conflict, their uncertainties, the personal fortunes that ride on their outcomes. The language of campaign reporting—"infighting," "counter-attack," "the next move," "homestretch"—is the language of sports, games, and military action. Stories about the early lives of candidates, about how their wives feel about the coming decision at the polls, about the tensions and frustrations of campaigning—these are for the most part irrelevant to anything but the presentation of elections as drama. Reporters and broadcasters present campaigns in this way, undoubtedly, simply because they do not want to carry dull stories or broadcast dull programs. If one were to try deliberately to conceive of a strategy that would arouse the voter's interest in campaign discussion, however, it would be difficult to conceive of a strategy more effective than that which the media have unconsciously adopted. To dramatize politics is to make paying attention to campaign discussion its own reward.

The public reaction to the television debates in the 1960 presidential race suggests that the power of campaign discussion may not only depend in large measure on its value as entertainment, but may vary radically when that value varies. Unlike most political shows, the debates were exceedingly well designed to exploit the drama inherent in a presidential election. They brought the two candidates face to face in an atmosphere of uncertainty, tension, and deadly seriousness. Whatever the outcome might mean for the voter, he could see and feel what it must mean for John F. Kennedy and Richard M. Nixon.

By any applicable standard each of the debates drew an enormous audience: bigger than that for the Sunday World Series game, bigger than that for the most popular regularly scheduled commercial show, bigger than that reached by either of the two national conventions in any given time period, far bigger than that attracted by any paid political telecast. They held their audiences more effectively than hour-long commercial entertainment shows and far more effectively than programs like *CBS Reports*. The average paid political broadcast in 1960 attracted seventy per cent of the audience normally attracted by the show it replaced. The debates, on the average, attracted 120 per cent of the audiences of the programs they replaced. In the 1956 campaign the number of persons expressing "very much interest" in the campaign rose from forty-six per cent in September to forty-seven per cent in October, an increase of one per cent. During the same period in 1960—the period of the debates—there was a twelve per cent increase in the number of persons expressing "very much interest" in the campaign.

If the argument that has just been made—that interest in politics varies strongly with the entertainment value of politics and that the media arouse interest in elections by exploiting their value as entertainment—if this argument is valid, then it also follows that the media have helped to create the normal disinterest in political discussion that they help to overcome. In the entertainment-starved small towns of the nineteenth century, politics seems to have been an inviting leisure time activity. Ostrogorski reported that,

The whole neighbourhood is invited to a "rally," a big meeting; the farmers generally come in large numbers, on horseback, in breaks, or on foot, often with their families. Political speakers sent down by committees hold forth in a covered enclosure to audiences which, especially in the West, are composed of both men and women. In the daytime a "procession" takes place: the faithful followers of the party, adorned with emblems, scour the country, headed by a band; the negro village barber, wearing a costume trimmed with gold, beats time with indescribable dignity. In the evening the houses of all the party faithful are illuminated and a torch-light procession concludes the "Chinese business." The fête, however, still goes on; the speakers reappear, and, in the open air, on the green, by the flickering glare of the torches, they harangue the assembled crowd. But the attention of the wearied public is distracted, there are only a few groups listening here and there, the rest are talking, the young people are flirting in the dim light.

What Ostrogorski was describing, of course, was a social and recreational, as well as a political occasion. Since his day, the mass media have made entertainment widely available and cheaply available, and the kind of occasion he reports has all but disappeared. Politics as a form of entertainment, it would seem, has suffered badly from the rising competition of other forms of entertainment.

II

The role of the mass media in the electoral process is not defined solely by the impact of media activities on the attitudes of voters. The media also do things both for and to politicians, and to modes of political action, organization, and discourse.

The modern candidate is acutely interested in gaining access to the media and in using that access effectively. He spends a large proportion of his campaign funds for the purchase of broadcast time. He adjusts the output of his statements to the rhythms of newspaper production. Even his whistle-stopping, and now his jet-stopping, is intended as much to capture the front pages of local newspapers as it is to expose the candidate to local crowds.

In view of what has been said about the relatively modest capabilities of campaign communication to change votes, all this concern with the media might seem misguided. Of course it is not. To win office in a competitive two-party system the campaigner normally must make marginal changes, but need not make more than marginal changes, in the political situation in which he finds himself. And that is what the realistic campaigner will try to do. He will try to increase the enthusiasm of his supporters in an effort to increase somewhat the numbers of them that go to the polls. He will try to give a somewhat wider currency to his name and project a more attractive image among independents, the undecided, and the uninterested. He will take stands on issues designed both to increase his appeal to the main body of his supporters and to "swing" groups in the population.

In realizing these objectives the sheer size of the audience he can reach is important to him, for the larger the audience he reaches, the more likely it is to include the most malleable elements of the population. Television and newspapers—the mass media *par excellence*—enable him to reach maximum audiences more cheaply than he could by any alternative means. In 1960 Vice President Nixon was seen in person by an estimated ten million people. In 1952 party workers solicited the votes of perhaps fifteen million people. Both these figures are less than the normal audience for one paid political telecast in a presidential campaign. Presumably candidates could reach as many voters by direct mail as they can *via* newspapers and television, but the cost per voter reached would be far higher.

The communications that the campaigner aims at the general public through the mass media are important not only for their direct effects, but also because they reinforce and support other campaign activities. The candidate may reach an understanding with farm leaders or business leaders; what farm magazines or business magazines say about the candidate help to translate such understandings into votes. He may reach an agreement with the leader of an opposing faction within his party—as President Eisenhower did in his Morningside Heights meeting with the late Senator Robert A. Taft—and the media will carry news of the agreement to the party rank and file. He may use the mass media to facilitate the efforts of party workers to get voters registered and to the polls, just as the commercial advertiser facilitates over-the-counter sales of his product by advertising in the media. The very fact of his ability to mount a campaign of impressive proportions in the media may contribute greatly to maintaining the morale of his campaign workers.

These are some of the things the mass media can do *for* politicians. As has already been noted, however, they also do things *to* politicians and to politics. The nature of these influences can be made clear if we contrast the properties of the media with the properties of the political communications systems that ante-dated their rise. Probably the most important of these was the political machine, and the contrast can be made the clearer because the rise of the mass media has been accompanied by the machine's gradual decay.

Both the machine and the mass media can enable the politician to establish a relationship with voters and to give a partisan direction to their opinions and actions. They perform these functions, however, in quite different ways. The machine's precinct workers sought direct, personal ties with the voter. They performed services and expected loyalty in return: Elections are won, Chicago's Jacob Arvey has observed, "by what you do all year round, by the day-to-day good will you generate in each precinct." However true this may once have been (and may still be in some localities), the media do not lend themselves to this kind of political action—one cannot fix parking tickets, keep a boy out of jail, or deliver food to the needy *via* newspapers and television. The mass media are useful to the politician as instruments of propaganda. The decline of the machine and the increasing dependence of politicians on the media, therefore, has meant a gradual shift in American political life from the politics of personal favors toward a politics of issues and images.

These same two events have tended to give candidates a greater voice in the affairs of the modern political organization and sometimes to make them its effective leaders. The test of the classic machine's power as an organization was its ability to deliver votes regardless of candidates and regardless of issues. To quote Arvey once more:

We won. In a ward where 90 per cent of the voters were Jewish, we beat the Jewish candidate, who was not only a very popular man but a very able governor. I don't think my father could have been any closer to me than Henry Horner was; but we beat him 2½ to 1.

The big majority that voted for Bundesen were not enthusiastic about Bundesen. They liked him all right; but they were voting for the prestige of the organization. And we, through our precinct captains, had made them conscious of why they should support the organization. To me, that's ward politics.

But it is not mass media politics. An attractive candidate is among the most salable commodities available to a political organization that must use the media as its primary means to reach the electorate. The proven vote-getter, therefore—a Thomas E. Dewey, a Robert F. Meyner, a Joseph Clark—becomes, if not the leader of the organization, at least one of its stars. And he must be treated as such.

New weapons systems bring new kinds of military specialists to the fore. The battleship admiral gives way to the carrier admiral, the airplane general to the missileman. New political communications systems act in a similar fashion. The rise of the mass media has altered the personnel of political organizations to include, and to give greater weight to the opinions of, those skilled in their use and in the politics of issues and images that their use entails. Among those with the required skills are the public relations man, the advertising man, the academic brain-truster, the editor, and the publisher.

Editors and publishers are not newcomers to the inner councils of political organizations, although their presence there undoubtedly has a different significance now than it did when the political machine was at the height of its power. Nor do all editors and publishers become actively involved in their parties' affairs. Those who wish to become involved, however, have three strong claims to the practical politician's attention: Their knowledge of the media and their use, the power of their editorial columns, and their power to give a partisan bias to the news. Probably a relatively small proportion of the nation's publishers exercise this last power in any flagrant manner—at least so one would conclude from one of the best recent studies of press campaign coverage. But all bias need not be flagrant: Newspapers and news magazines can devote comparable space to what campaigners are saying while emphasizing or de-emphasizing themes in their propaganda. They can, by carefully chosen words, subtly suggest the heroes and villains of the events they are reporting. The best judgment would seem to be that if most of the press uses its power to bias with moderation, it nevertheless uses it; that if it is a limited power, it is nonetheless real.

In arguing that the modern campaigner plays a politics of issues and of personality appeals, we have not, of course, meant to imply that issues and personality appeals assumed importance in politics only with the rise of the mass media. The argument is rather that they are of greater importance now than they were previously. Does the modern politician also treat issues differently than his pre-mass media counterpart? The answer would seem to be: In some respects, yes; in some important respects, no.

The mass media form a network of communication that transmits messages almost instantaneously to national audiences. The fact has at least two important consequences. First of all, it forces the politician to maintain consistency in his appeals; he cannot profitably pander to local prejudices by saying one thing in one place, another in another. Indeed, it has become a fashion for presidential candidates to make their first statements on civil rights questions in the South, to repeat them later (with suitable notice of their original source) to Negro audiences in the North. Second, the modern politician is compelled to give his campaign a pace, an appearance of movement. Before the rise of the mass media the campaign speaker could develop—just as the Chautauqua speaker developed—an act in which he could use repeatedly all his most successful rhetorical embellishments. The modern campaigner still uses a basic speech which he repeats with variations, but he must search day after day for new pegs to hang it on, if he is to furnish newsmen with new headlines and voters with new topics of conversation. Vice President Nixon, whose basic speech became so well known to newsmen that many could repeat it almost verbatim, nevertheless managed to vary it by promising, on three successive days in late October 1960, a manned flight around the moon in 1966–69, a possible summit talk with Premier Nikita Khrushchev, and a tour of the Eastern European captive nations.

As has already been noted, the formats that the media provide for political expression not only serve as its vehicles, but also discipline it. A campaigner must make a series of decisions as to the way he will handle issues. He must decide what issues to stress, which (if possible) to avoid; with what degree of specificity to state his positions; how much attention to give to his opponent; how to portray his opponent's record and positions on policy problems. The form in which he expects his communications to reach the public will be an important factor in determining the nature of these decisions.

Propaganda designed to capture the headlines or to reach the public through spot announcements, for instance, is normally characterized by gross distortions and a failure to define party differences. It is so characterized because the propagandist works on the assumption that communications distributed in this manner will reach many voters whose attention is so sporadically attracted to campaign discussion that they are unlikely to hear the answers of one side to the assertions of the other. It is good strategy, therefore, for propagandists on both sides to present their opponent's position in as poor a light as possible and to ignore attacks on their own weaknesses. With a debate, however, good propaganda strategy becomes quite a different thing. Both sides have equal and simultaneous access to the same audience, an audience that includes the partisans of both and of neither. In this situation to distort the position of one's opponent is to invite a quick and authoritative reply. To fail to answer challenges is to invite a conclusion by the audience that a good answer is not possible. To fail to define differences with one's opponent is to invite him to define them in the way most advantageous to himself. Debates thus tend to increase the accuracy, specificity, and relevance to the voting decision of statements in campaign discussion.

The media sometimes put campaign discussion into a question-and-answer format by means of press conferences, panel shows, interviews, and other devices. This format, too, affects the character of campaign discussion. It tends to force candidates to take responsibility for arguments made on their behalf or to disavow such arguments. It was in a press conference that President Eisenhower declined to endorse the notion that the Democratic Party had been the party of wars, a notion that the Republican National Committee had been seeking to cultivate. The question-and-answer format forces candidates to discuss issues they most probably would prefer to avoid, as when the *Farm Journal* solicited and got President Kennedy's reply to the following inquiry, "You announced in Los Angeles at the Democratic Convention that you would introduce emergency farm legislation in August. Since there was a large Democratic majority in both Houses to support such action, why didn't you introduce the legislation as promised?" If editors, reporters, and panelists make their questions specific, they tend to get specific answers to them; one can evade a direct question, but only at the cost of appearing to be evasive.

Once these sorts of media influence on political discourse have been acknowledged, however, it remains true that the revolution in communication has not been accompanied by any comparable revolution in the way campaigners treat issues. James Bryce's description of campaign discussion applies in its essentials equally well to such discussion both before and after the rise of the mass media:

> The object of each party naturally is to put forward as many good political issues as it can, claiming for itself the merit of having always been on the popular side. Any one who should read the campaign literature of the Republicans would fancy that they were opposed to the Democrats on many important points. When he took up the Democratic speeches and pamphlets he would be again struck by the serious divergences between the parties, which however would seem to arise, not on the points raised by the Republicans, but on other points which the Republicans had not referred to. In other words, the aim of each party is to force on its antagonist certain issues which the antagonist rarely accepts, so that although there is a vast deal of discussion and declamation on political topics, there are few on which either party directly traverses the doctrines of the other. Each pummels, not his true enemy, but a stuffed figure set up to represent the enemy.

Today, as in Bryce's day, the campaign discussion that the media convey to their audiences is, in very large measure, a discussion where the candidates talk past each other, one that is filled with distortions, ambiguities, and meaningless generalities.

Why? Among other reasons, because the potentialities of the media for altering the quality of campaign discussion have just begun to be explored.

VOTERS AND ELECTIONS: PAST AND PRESENT *

Angus Campbell

INTRODUCTION

TO the mystification of most politicians and the agonized protest of many scholars, much research on the vote in recent years has devoted itself to a

* From Angus Campbell, "Voters and Elections: Past and Present," a paper presented at the annual meeting of the Southern Historical Association, Asheville, N. C., November 7, 1963. Reprinted in *The Journal of Politics*, Vol. 26, No. 4 (November, 1964), pp. 745-757. Copyright, Southern Political Science Association. Reprinted by permission of Professor Campbell and the editors.

detailed examination of the behavior of the individual voter, in apparent disregard of the collective decisions of the electorate. Paul Lazarsfeld set the pace in 1940 when he undertook in his famous Erie County study to "follow the vagaries of the individual voter along the path to his vote." For twenty years the major studies of the vote have followed in this general pattern, some of them placing the emphasis on sociological setting, others on perceptions, attitudes and other psychological variables, but mainly preoccupied, as Lazarsfeld was, with the motives, the conflicts and the decisions of the individual voter. Many interesting facts have come from these studies and much has been learned about voting but there has been recurrent criticism that in concentrating on the voter Lazarsfeld and his successors have ignored "the vote," that they have not come to grips with the "important" problems in politics.

It was perhaps inevitable that the entry of the behavioral scientist into the study of politics should have concentrated as it did on the individual member of the polity. This was the point closest to his own intellectual habits and most readily comprehended in terms of his previous research experience. It was a necessary point of departure from which progress toward a bridging of the conceptual gap between the voter and the vote could be made. It should now be recognized, however, that we are moving beyond this phase of our inquiries into the nature of voting. Within the last few years a number of attempts have been made to move "upward" from the study of micro-political units to an understanding of the flow of the total vote, to apply the insights gained from the study of the individual voter to the explanation of the behavior of the electorate. The results of these studies represent the beginning of a new phase in political analysis.

ARGUMENT

Our intention in this paper is to present several attempts to apply information drawn from contemporary studies of voting to the illumination of certain regularities in the collective vote as recorded in the election statistics of the past hundred years. It will not be possible to describe in any detail the actual studies which underlie the analysis to be presented. As a minimum it may be said that since 1948 the Survey Research Center of The University of Michigan has conducted a series of detailed surveys of the perceptions and motives of the national electorate. These have been sample surveys but they do not bear a very close resemblance either in methods or intent to the newspaper polls. We are not primarily interested in predicting the vote, as the polls typically are. On the contrary, we have been trying to come to an understanding of the individual voting decision and, as we extend the number of elections studied, to an understanding of American elections as collective acts.

Our program of study of the American voter has led us to a considerable number of descriptive facts about the present-day electorate. Many of these may seem quite commonplace; others depart rather dramatically from popular beliefs about American politics. The following short list of general statements drawn from our research findings will lead us to our subsequent discussion of the characteristics of elections.

1. Two underlying political attributes characterize the members of the electorate. One is their level of intrinsic interest in politics. People differ greatly in this trait, from the activist who is ready to respond to everything political to the disengaged person who lives in a wholly nonpolitical world. This intrinsic interest level, whether high or low, is relatively stable over time for each individual and is one of the standing predispositions which underlie individual response to ongoing political events.

2. The second basic political attribute is party identification. Most members of the electorate feel some degree of psychological attachment to one of the major parties. This partisan identification is remarkably resistant to passing political events and typically remains constant through the life of the individual. It exercises an important influence on perceptions, attitudes, and behavior.

3. These two political predispositions, intrinsic interest and party identification, are related. Generally speaking, the people most concerned and most responsive to political stimuli are also the most strongly party identified. Most people who call themselves independent or nonpartisan are relatively disinterested in politics.

4. These basic predispositions determine the standing position from which the individual moves as he responds to contemporary political conditions. National and international events, the personal characteristics of the major candidates, the current image of the major parties, and issues of national policy create short-term political forces. These short-term forces assume importance for the individual citizen as they occur and are perceived by him. His behavior at any particular point in time derives from the interaction of his political predispositions and the short-term forces generated by the current political situation.

5. Extent of information concerning political affairs varies greatly within the electorate. Most people are poorly informed on questions of national policy and show little evidence of organized ideology regarding governmental action. They do not associate the two parties with clear alternatives on national issues. Level of information is associated with both interest in politics and strength of party identification. Highly informed people tend to be interested in politics and identified with a party.

Now, transposing these characteristics of voters to the characteristics of the collective vote, we come to the following propositions regarding the elections themselves:

1. The size of the turnout in national elections depends on a combination of intrinsic political interest and the impact of short-term political forces. People with a high level of intrinsic interest vote in most or all national elections; people with little intrinsic interest vote only when additionally stimulated by impelling short-term forces. The weaker the total impact of the short-term forces, the smaller will be the total turnout.

2. The smaller the turnout in a national election, the greater the proportion of the vote which is contributed by people of established party loyalties and the more closely the partisan division of the vote will approach the basic underlying division of standing commitments to the two parties, what Lord Bryce referred to years ago as the "normal voting strength."

3. The larger the turnout, the greater the proportion of the vote which is made up of marginal voters, people who have relatively weak party identification, relatively little intrinsic political interest, and relatively little political information.

4. If the sum of the short-term forces is approximately balanced in its partisan impact, the total vote will not vary from the vote division to be expected from the underlying "normal party strength." If the sum of the short-term forces favors one candidate-party alternative over the other it will swing the vote division toward that alternative, with the greatest movement occurring among the marginal voters. The greater the total impact of the short-term forces, the greater will be the potential deflection from the "normal party strength."

If these assumptions regarding the nature of our national elections have validity they should obviously fit the facts of American electoral history. Of course we do not have interview survey data to draw on for more than the last few years but we do have reasonably accurate aggregative turnout and partisanship data for the presidential and congressional elections for at least the last one hundred years. These voting statistics have been the subject of much scholarly analysis and numerous regularities in the movement of the vote over time have been pointed out. Let us now consider a selection of these recurring relationships or cycles in terms of the general understanding of the nature of the vote which we have briefly outlined.

1. When we look at the two-party division of the national vote over the past seventy years we find that the fluctuations in the two-party division of the vote in the presidential years are much greater than those in the off years. Donald Stokes and Warren Miller have recently pointed out that the variation in the proportion voting Republican in the presidential elections between 1892 and 1960 is over twice as great as the variation in the proportions voting Republican in the off-year elections during this period and that the variation of the Republican vote for Congressmen in the presidential years is almost half again as great as that of the vote in the off years. The greater stability of the off-year votes over this seventy-year period must reflect some underlying difference in these two kinds of elections.

The most immediately apparent difference in the presidential and off-year elections is the greater turnout in the presidential years. In terms of our earlier language this is brought about by the presence of short-term forces in the presidential elections which are stronger than those in the mid-term elections. The electorate is under stronger pressure in the presidential years than it is in the off years. This pressure brings to the polls in the presidential elections a large number of marginal voters who do not bother to vote in the less impressive off-year elections. These people are less party-identified and therefore more mobile than the regular core voters who have enough intrinsic interest in political matters to participate in all national elections. As the fortunes of politics vary from year to year these marginal people shift their votes from one party to another and contribute a substantial part of the large variability in the vote in the presidential years which we have noted. In the off-year elections these people do not turn out; the decision is left largely to the core regulars whose greater degree of party loyalty makes them less mobile.

It is true, of course, that deflections from the basic "normal" vote do occur in off-year elections; the party balance in Congress obviously does not remain constant. It is also true that local circumstances sometimes create dramatic swings in individual congressional districts and that a swing in one direction in one district may be offset by an opposite swing in another district. But we know that in recent elections the total amount of party-crossing has been less in the off-year elections than in the elections of the President. The people who vote in off-year elections are difficult to move and the short-term forces that might move them are relatively weak. Party loyalty plays a more dominant role than it does in most presidential elections and party loyalty changes very little from one year to the next.

2. It is well-known to every politician that since the Civil War the party which wins the White House almost invariably loses seats in the House of Representatives in the following off-year election. "This normal off-year reaction against the party in power," as one widely-read historian calls it, is usually attributed to a natural disillusionment with the President's party as it fails to come up to the expectations created during the enthusiasm of the campaign. Since winning Presidents commonly poll a higher vote in their second campaign than they do in their first, however, this is not a fully satisfying explanation.

We would suggest that the familiar off-year loss does not depend on an inevitable cooling of the public ardor for the President's party, although this undoubtedly occurs in particular years. It depends rather on a pattern of circulation of votes which is characteristic of presidential and off-year elections. In the relatively stimulating circumstances of a presidential election the turnout is high. As we have just noted, the regular voters whose intrinisic political interest is high enough to take them to the polls even under less stimulating conditions are joined by marginal voters who are less concerned with politics but may be activated if the stakes seem high. Ordinarily one of the two candidates standing for the presidency will be benefited by the political circumstances of the moment more clearly than the other, either because of embarrassments of the party in power, the personal qualities of the candidates, domestic or international conditions, or for other reasons. The advantaged candidate will draw to him the votes of a majority of the marginal voters, who have relatively little party attachment and are responsive to such short-term influences. He will also profit from some defections by regular voters from the opposition party who are sufficiently tempted to break away from their usual party vote at least temporarily. In moving toward the advantaged candidate both the regular and the marginal voters, especially the latter, tend to support both the candidate and his party ticket. In the off-year election which follows, two movements occur. The regular voters who moved across party lines to support a presidential candidate they preferred are likely to move back to their usual party vote when that candidate is no longer on the ticket. The marginal voters who had given the winning candidate a majority of their votes in the presidential election do not vote in the election which follows. Both of these movements hurt the party of the candidate who benefited from the votes of the two groups in the presidential election. The loss of congressional seats is the result.

The 1934 election, the only exception to the law of off-year loss, offers an interesting test of the explanation we are proposing. It would appear from such retrospective information as we can obtain in our surveys that the small gain the Democrats achieved in 1934 depended on the fact that the two types of movement we have described as characteristic of off-year elections were blunted by the massive realignment of partisan orientations which was taking place at that time. Mr. Roosevelt and the New Deal brought many new adherents to the Democratic Party, some of whom had previously been Republican and many of whom had been politically inactive. This type of realignment, which in the 1930's displaced the Republican Party as the majority party in this country, has been an uncommon occurrence in the nation's political history, however.

3. Professor V. O. Key has pointed out in one of his books that since the election of 1892 whenever there has been a significant increase in the turnout in a presidential election the increment of votes has always gone very largely to one party; it is not divided between the two. To quote his statement, "An unusually rapid rate of growth in the total number of voters from one election to the next is accompanied by an exceptionally high rate of increase in the number of supporters of one of the parties but not the other." He cites the elections of 1896, 1916, and 1952.

What are the characteristics of these high turnout swing elections? We have detailed information on only one such election, 1952, but it may provide a key to the understanding of the others as well. The most striking fact about the flow of the vote in the 1952 election was the universality with which the various segments of the electorate moved toward the Republican candidate. It was not a situation in which some groups became more Democratic than they had been in 1948 but were offset by other groups moving in the other direction. There was virtually no occupational, religious, regional or other subdivision of the electorate which did not vote more strongly Republican in 1952 than it had in 1948.

A second impressive fact about the 1952 election was the relative insignificance of policy issues in the minds of the voters. There were no great questions of policy which the public saw as dividing the two parties. Instead the voters were thinking about "the mess in Washington," the stalemate in Korea, and

General Eisenhower's heroic image. It would appear that the flow of the vote from the Democratic majorities of the previous twenty years to the Republican victory in 1952 was the response to short-term forces which were largely unilateral. They favored the Republican alternative and they were not offset by balancing forces favoring the Democrats. Having little policy content they did not set interest group against interest group, class against class, region against region.

The third important characteristic of the 1952 election was the fact that, despite the decisiveness of the Eisenhower victory, the underlying Democratic advantage in the basic party attachments of the elecorate was not disturbed. We know from our national surveys that the proportions of the electorate identifying themselves as Democrats or Republicans did not change throughout the eight years of the Eisenhower administration. In 1960, when the candidacy of Mr. Eisenhower was no longer a consideration, the vote swung strongly back toward the "normal" Democratic majority, despite the severe handicap to the Democrats of a Catholic candidate at the head of their ticket.

What kinds of forces have the capacity to produce this surge phenomenon, with an upswing in turnout moving unidirectionally toward one party and a subsequent decline to a normal division of the vote? . . .

It is our belief that the more basic quality of these surge elections is the absence of great ideological issues. The fact that so many of them have been dominated by persons of military background dramatize this lack. If Mr. Eisenhower may be taken as an example, the public image of these gentlemen has little to do with great issues of public policy. With certain notable exceptions, the dramatic swings of turnout and partisanship during the last hundred years do not give the impression of an aroused electorate taking sides in a great debate on national policy. On the contrary these swings in the vote appear to be more a reaction to circumstances and personalities than to issues in the usual sense. Public interest in these immediate events and persons is translated into political action, with a high turnout of voters and a general movement toward the party which happens to be in a position to profit from the situation. The movement is unidirectional because the circumstances which produce it are not seen as favorable by one section of the electorate and unfavorable by another. They tend rather to create a generally positive or negative attitude throughout the electorate, resulting in the almost universal type of shift which we observed in 1952.

4. This conclusion brings us to the consideration of a theory of American politics which enjoys a certain respectability, the belief that the major oscillations in the presidential vote over the last hundred years reflect a cyclical movement from a conservative to a liberal mood in the minds of the voters. This theory was originally identified with Professor Arthur Schlesinger and has been implicit in much political commentary for many years.

Professor Schlesinger contended in 1939 that electoral history since 1841 could be divided into epochs of some fifteen or sixteen years duration which alternated between conservative and liberal governmental policies, resulting from shifts in predominant public sentiment. "Apparently the electorate embarks on conservative policies until it is disillusioned or wearied or bored and then attaches itself to liberal policies until a similar course is run." By examining the legislation enacted over the previous hundred years he found it possible to identify succeeding periods in which these sentiments seemed to dominate.

Like many another student of society, Professor Schlesinger is led to explain the cycles he observes in collective behavior (in this case the legislative acts of Congress) by speculations regarding the motives of the individual members of the collectivity. Social theorists commonly feel the need of an underlying psychology to support their explanations of the behavior of the total society. As long as no direct evidence from the individual level is available their psychological suppositions cannot be tested and some of them have passed into the domain of what Professor Galbraith calls the "conventional wisdom." For the past twenty years, however, it has been possible to assess the motives of the individual members of society directly. One need not be overly confident about the precision with which these assessments are carried out; measuring the human mind undoubtedly has its problems. But there is no doubt that we have learned enough to know that some of the speculations about why people behave as they do do not accurately describe people as they actually are.

In our view Professor Schlesinger's theory of electoral cycles is based on just such an erroneous assumption regarding the characteristics of the electorate. He apparently believes that the voters go to the polls with some relatively clear intention regarding the legislation they want their representative to enact. For a period they want what he calls "liberal" legislation; then with an apparent sense of appropriate limits they choose a government which will take them back toward the conservative side of the scale. So by the use of the franchise the citizenry guides the ship on a zigzag course within the shoals of ideological extremity.

This description of the motivation of the vote, congenial as it is with the traditional theories of democratic government, bears very little resemblance to the facts of the case. Consider 1952 as an example. This was a year which many people interpreted as a swing to the right, a conservative reaction to two decades of liberal government. In fact it was a rare person indeed among the people we interviewed in 1952 who had a program of legislation he wanted the new government to undertake. They wanted to get the crooks out of the Internal Revenue Service and the troops out of Korea and they certainly admired General Eisenhower. But far from voting for a conservative program, only a small percentage had any apparent comprehension of what a conservative-liberal, or left-right dimension in politics implies. And, as we have observed earlier, those voters who contribute the greatest part of the shift in surge elections like 1952 are even less well-informed about politics than the average.

If the flow of the vote in 1952 did not express a conservative mood in the electorate, how is it to be explained? It would be much more parsimonious and much more in keeping with the evidence at hand to say that it simply expressed a desire for a change in stewardship of the federal establishment. Accumulating grievances and dissatisfactions over the last years of Democratic government finally led to a vote for a new administration. The voters were not asking for any specific platform of legislation; they just wanted a new bunch of fellows to run things better.

We do not have the kind of information about earlier swings in the national vote that we have about 1952 and one cannot be sure how closely the 1952 pattern fits the earlier experience. We know there have been occasions when national crisis have polarized the electorate around a major issue and brought about far-reaching realignments in party strength. Such occasions have been infrequent, however, and it seems highly probable that the election of 1952 was more representative of the American elections than the highly charged situations of 1856–60, 1896, and 1932–36 were. The electorate seems quite capable of expressing its intolerance of circumstances it finds exasperating and it sometimes responds strongly to the personal qualities of an attractive candidate but it is not well enough informed to follow a deliberate program of choice between conservative and liberal alternatives in governmental policies.

CONCLUSION

The attempts of sociologists and psychologists over the last twenty years to apply new methods of quantitative research to the study of political phenomena have not been very well received by some students of American politics in other academic disciplines. They have thought we have been asking the wrong questions and they have some doubts as to whether we can ever answer the right questions.

It would be foolish to deny that behavioral studies of the vote have their limitations. They are certainly lacking in time depth although this fault should become less serious as present programs of research are extended. They undoubtedly have greater applicability to some kinds of problems than to others and there are some kinds of questions to which they have nothing whatever to say. Granting these and other restrictions on his scope, what does the behavioral scientist have to offer the scholar who is primarily interested in the collective behavior of society? The burden of this paper has been the argument that he is uniquely equipped to provide a realistic statement of the nature of the individual acts which make up the collectivity. He need not accept on faith the hypothetical man invented by social and economic theorists. He has devised ways of finding and measuring men as they are and he often finds that in real life they do not closely resemble the man who has been deductively created.

The question is, of course, whether or not this specialized information can be fruitfully applied to the illumination of questions of collective behavior. Can it extend our understanding of the workings of our political system? The history of attempts to find the connection between aggregative events and the component individual acts is not reassuring. Arnold Toynbee has recently deplored our "ignorance of the relation between collective results and the underlying individual human acts" and asserts that it has characterized all scholarly effort since Aristotle.

Despite this authoritative observation it is possible to feel a cautious optimism for the future, at least within the narrow field of political behavior which we have been discussing. Tentative feelers are being put out from both sides of the gap. The efforts of Sellers and other historians to find new insights in behavioral studies for the identification of patterns in presidential elections are most intriguing. From the other side, behavioral researchers are increasingly moving from their preoccupation with the individual voting decision to a concern for the characteristics of the total vote. It would be hazardous to predict where these converging interests will lead but the integration of historical evidence from the elections of the past with survey data from the elections of the present seems a natural intellectual enterprise and it is not totally unrealistic to hope that something worthwhile will come from it.

THE ALIENATED VOTER *
Murray B. Levin

THE FORMS OF POLITICAL ALIENATION

POLITICAL alienation is the feeling of an individual that he is not a part of the political process. The politically alienated believe that their vote makes no difference. This belief arises from the feeling that political decisions are made by a group of political insiders who are not responsive to the average citizens—the political outsiders. Political alienation may be expressed in feelings of political powerlessness, meaninglessness, estrangement from political activity, and normlessness.

Political powerlessness is the feeling of an individual that his political action has no influence in determining the course of political events. Those who feel politically powerless do not believe that their vote, or for that matter any action they might perform, can determine the broader outcome they desire. This feeling of powerlessness arises from and contributes to the belief that the community is not controlled by the voters, but rather by a small number of powerful and influential persons who remain in control regardless of the outcome of elections. This theory of social conflict between the powerful and powerless is not identical to the Marxian theory of social conflict between capitalists and proletarians. The powerful are not necessarily capitalists, they may be professional politicians, labor leaders, underworld figures, or businessmen.

Many voters believe that the powerful, who are most often identified as politicians, businessmen, and the underworld, continuously exploit the public. The politician needs campaign contributions, the businessman needs licenses, tax abatements, and city contracts, and the underworld needs police immunity. This provides the setting for the mutually satisfactory relationships among the powerful, from which the average voter is excluded. The feelings of powerlessness among the electorate are sharpened by the view that regardless of the outcome of the election, the powerful remain in control by realigning themselves with the newly elected. These voters view the political process as a secret conspiracy, the object of which is to plunder them.

Political alienation may also be experienced in the form of meaninglessness. An individual may experience feelings of meaninglessness in two ways. He may believe that the election is without meaning because there are no real differences between the candidates, or he may feel that an intelligent and rational decision is impossible because the information upon which, he thinks, such a decision must be made is lacking. The degree of meaninglessness will vary with the disparity between the amount of information considered necessary and that available. If the candidates and platforms are very similar or identical, it will be difficult to find "meaningful" information on which to base a voting decision.

In municipal politics another source of meaninglessness is likely to be present in the nature of city government. In theory, and to a large extent in practice, there are no issues in a controversial sense. Indeed, in the usual textbook version, a city government is a "bundle of services." In practice the political choices available to the administrators of a city government are severely circumscribed by economic realities and by state law. There exist only a small number of ways in which revenue can be raised and these are generally exploited to their fullest. At the same time the services which the city must maintain pre-empt almost all of the city's budget. The police force, the fire department, and the school system must maintain the standards of a going social system. Therefore the minimal facilities which a city must provide to maintain its viability tend to be not much less than the maximal facilities it can achieve with available funds. The municipal public official necessarily operates within a narrow range of alternate programs.

Municipal elections therefore tend to center around the inefficiency or dishonesty of the administration, not its program. Consequently, the "honesty" of the candidate is often the variable about which most information is demanded by voters who wish to make a "meaningful" decision. However, information concerning the honesty of the candidate is difficult to secure because corrupt and dishonest activities are carefully hidden from the public. It is precisely the absence of information on this problem which brings about feelings of meaninglessness.

Under these circumstances an individual who feels alienated in the "meaningless" sense will tend either not to vote, to believe his vote makes no difference, or to make his decision in terms of what he believes are inadequate standards. Since relevant factors are absent, many voting decisions are based on "gut reactions"—intuitive emotional responses to the candidate's physical appearance, voice, and personality. "Don't like his looks," "tough," "ugly looking," "smug—looks crooked," "something about his eyes."

Feelings of political meaninglessness give rise to a low sense of confidence among many voters that their voting decision was correct: that their candidate would be a better mayor. When relevant facts are not available, voters cannot predict the future course of political action with any sense of certainty. This also contributes to feelings of powerlessness.

Feelings of political alienation may also be experienced in the sense of the lowering of an individual's political ethics. This occurs when standards of political behavior are violated in order to achieve some goal. This is likely to occur when the political structure prevents the attainment of political objectives through institutionally prescribed means. An example of this would be an individual who believes that paying off a public official is legitimate, yet does so. The fact that the individual may be reluctant to bribe a public official does not alter the fact that he is lowering his standards of political ethics.

When individuals believe that corrupt practices are the only ways to achieve political goals and when they feel that corruption is widespread, there will be a greater tendency to resort to it. If the corruption becomes the generally accepted method of dealing with public officials, the stigma attached to it tends to disappear and the political community becomes normless, i.e., anomic.

Political estrangement refers to the inability of an individual to find direct satisfactions in political activity itself, that is, gratification from fulfilling his obligations as a responsible citizen. Both politically active and politically inactive individuals may be politically estranged. Political activists are estranged if their activity is motivated by goals of personal monetary gain rather than a sense of their obligation as citizens. Individuals who do have a sense of community responsibility are likely to find other community activities, such as support of a symphony orchestra, charities, or clubs, a more rewarding way of fulfilling this obligation than being politically active. This is political estrangement.

SOCIAL CHARACTERISTICS OF POLITICAL ALIENATION

Four aspects of political alienation—powerlessness, meaninglessness, the lowering of norms, and estrangement—have been distinguished. The extent to which a particular individual is affected by any one of these forms can be related to such variables as social class, age, and religion.

Separation of a population according to income tends to include separation according to education and occupation as well. Data on income was obtained in this survey and will be used as a gross measure of social-class difference.

The majority of the Boston electorate, who are elementary or high-school graduates, employed in blue-collar or white-collar jobs, and in the lower-income group, might be expected to feel alienated primarily in the sense of powerlessness. It is this group which is in fact furthest removed from the seats of political power. They have relatively little contact with the city as compared to home owners and businessmen, and when they do have contact, they lack the economic means to participate in the "business" of politics. Collins' major campaign appeal was directed to those who feel powerless. His campaign slogan was "Stop Power Politics," and he presented himself as leading a battle against the politicians. Powers' prolific use of political endorsements did not hinder the image Collins was creating. The data collected in our survey shows that the lower-income groups switched from Powers to Collins in larger proportions than did the middle- or upper-income groups. This implies that feelings of powerlessness were greater in the lower-income groups.

In contrast to the lower-income groups, the upper-income groups, who have more economic power, might be expected to experience political alienation in the forms of meaninglessness, lowering of norms, and estrangement more than in the form of powerlessness. Upper-income groups have more education, which tends to develop more rigorous standards of clarity of information on which to base decisions. The data shows that this group had greater interest in political programs and expressed fewer "gut reactions" than did lower-income groups. With higher standards of clarity there is likely to be stronger feelings of political meaninglessness.

The upper-income groups include businessmen and property owners who necessarily have more contact with the city because they may require licenses of various kinds, tax abatements, and building inspection certificates. Since they have economic power, they are in a position to purchase special political consideration. Those who do this will experience political alienation in the form of lowering of political norms.

Upper-income groups include some individuals with a sense of community responsibility. Because of the disjunction of their political values and the political structure, they are likely to be active in nonpolitical civic activities such as charities or service organizations.

Age is another variable related to political alienation. Older persons, who have lived in Boston for many years and have observed the political structure over a long time, might be expected to show greater feelings of alienation. This age group had largest proportion of individuals who thought that the man they supported would be no better than his opponent. Having observed more elections, they seem to feel more strongly that the effect of their vote makes little difference in the long run.

Religion is another sociocultural variable to be considered. Since Boston is a strongly Catholic city, it might be expected that Protestants and Jews, having less political power, would have stronger feelings of political alienation. In support of this are the facts that a smaller percentage of Protestants and Jews voted than did Catholics and that a greater proportion voted for Collins, whose campaign was largely an appeal to the politically alienated.

MECHANISMS OF EXPRESSION OF POLITICAL ALIENATION

Feelings of political alienation may be expressed through rational activism, withdrawal, projection, or identification with a charismatic leader. These are conscious or unconscious mechanisms by which an individual may handle the uncomfortable feelings of political alienation. Some forms of alienation lead to specific mechanisms, for example, feelings of estrangement inevitably lead to withdrawal because gratification is found only in nonpolitical activity. Other forms may result in one or more of several mechanisms, for example, feelings of powerlessness may lead to political activism or to projection and identification with a charismatic leader.

Rational activism is political action based on a realistic evaluation of the political situation, the object of which is to promote a political structure consonant with political values. The frustration arising from political alienation can be a spur to rational activism; feelings of powerlessness can lead to increased political activity. Feelings of meaninglessness can lead to demands for more information rather than withdrawal or "blind" voting. And guilt, resulting from normlessness, can result in activity directed toward raising political standards. Mature individuals, who are those able to tolerate frustration and to act on their beliefs, are those most likely to handle their feelings of political alienation through rational activism. This activity may occur within existing political institutions or it may be directed toward the creation of a new set of political institutions. Rational activism is more likely to be the response to feelings of political alienation when individuals believe that their activity has a reasonable chance of bringing about a change.

Political withdrawal is the removal of an individual's interest and activity from politics. This may occur as a result of a conscious rational decision based on a realistic estimate of the political situation or as an effective, unconscious response. In the latter case the anger and resentment of political alienation may be internalized within the individual rather than expressed outwardly. This mechanism is more likely to occur when the individual feels that any political effort on his part has little chance of producing an effect.

Although an individual may have withdrawn from political interests, he is not likely to escape entirely from politics. Municipal problems of education, traffic, and taxes may affect him personally, or he may note the recurrent exposure of corruption in newspapers. Consequently, additional mechanisms of expression of political alienation are likely to be used. There may be projection, identification with a charismatic leader, or rational activism.

Feelings of anger and resentment which arise from political alienation may be projected on to some other individual or group. This group is seen as participating in a hostile conspiracy. Political leaders may use this mechanism because it establishes a sense of identity between them and the voters to whom they are appealing.

The conspiratorial theory is particularly appealing to individuals who have feelings of powerlessness and normlessness because it accounts for the absence of power and the lowering of values in a simple and easily understood fashion. The individual who projects sees himself as powerless because sinister forces have successfully conspired to destroy the traditional political rules in such a way that he is excluded from exercising his rights. Hofstadter has observed that:

this kind of thinking frequently occurs when political and social antagonisms are sharp. Certain audiences are especially susceptible to it—particularly, those who have obtained a low level of education, whose access to information is poor, and who are so completely shut out from access to the centers of power that they feel deprived of self-defense and subjected to unlimited manipulation by those who wield power.

Another mechanism for dealing with feelings of political alienation is identification with a charismatic leader. This is the attempt of an individual to feel powerful by incorporating within himself the attitudes, beliefs, and actions held by a leader whom he perceives as powerful. "Charismatic" refers to an extraordinary quality of a person regardless of whether this quality is actual, alleged, or presumed. In taking over the attributes of a charismatic leader, the individual may enter into activity he would otherwise abhor. German *bourgeoisie* who identified with Hitler approved of and took part in behavior their consciences would otherwise not allow them to do.

Rational activism is behavior based on logical reasoning and an undistorted perception of political realities. Withdrawal may be a rational response in some situations and an irrational, affective response in other circumstances. The mechanisms of projection resulting in conspiratorial thinking and identification with a charismatic leader are irrational, affective responses. They are also regressive, in that they are more characteristic of a child's than of an adult's handling of a problem.

When feelings of political alienation are widespread, individuals will adopt one or more of the mechanisms we have described to handle the frustration and anxiety associated with them. The political behavior of each individual will be affected by the particular mechanism or mechanisms he selects.

We have described the forms of political alienation and the mechanisms by which they may be expressed. When political alienation is widespread, it may be a major factor in determining the outcome of an election. The astute politician is aware of this; consequently his strategy takes these factors into account.

ALIENATION AND POLITICS *

Allen Schick

A COMMON feature of virtually all political alienation studies is the combination of meager research and bold conclusions. Somehow the notion has taken hold that this complex phenomenon can be packaged into a handful of standard questions which yield up, the mysteries of political behavior. In this section I will appraise several studies, each of which encapsulates the alienation idea in its own set of fragile questions.

The writings of Murray Levin are the most elaborate application of the alienation hypothesis to politics. His two books have forcefully introduced the concept of "the alienated voter" into the lexicon of politics. His findings, moreover, are drawn from public opinion polls of two electoral contests, the 1959 mayoralty election in Boston and the 1960 gubernatorial race in Massachusetts.

In *The Alienated Voter* Levin defines alienation as "the feeling of an individual that he is not part of the political process. The politically alienated believe that their vote makes no difference." Levin then constructs a four-fold political alienation scheme which is derived from Seeman's typology. The four cognate feelings which he associates with political alienation—powerlessness, meaninglessness, estrangement, and normlessness—will be explored when we turn to problems of meaning, but it is important to note that Levin makes no use of these concepts in the questions he asked voters or in his interpretations. They stand as an admirable framework of potential utility for future researchers.

Levin's concept of alienation is expanded (albeit less systematically and with some crucial inconsistencies) in *The Compleat Politician*. There Levin writes that "a citizen who is alienated believes that whatever the political system is, it is not democracy, or perhaps more cynically, that democracy is only what the current political reality shows it to be." At another point Levin comments, "The alienated voter believes that he has been cheated of his political birthright and stripped of his political power by corrupt and self-seeking politicians."

It is difficult to pin down the percentage of voters who fall into Levin's alienation categories. Thus in *The Alienated Voter* he concludes: "a large proportion of the electorate feels politically powerless . . ."; "the average voter believes that he is not part of the political structure and that he has no influ-

---

* From Allen Schick, "Alienation and Politics," a paper delivered at the 1964 meeting of the American Political Science Association, September 9–12, 1964. Reprinted by permission of Professor Schick.

ence upon it"; and in *The Compleat Politician,* "perhaps 30 to 40 per cent of the electorate" feels "alienated, powerless, cynical, cheated, and potentially disloyal."

These conclusions are barely supported by any evidence. Nowhere in his published studies is there any indication that Levin asked voters what they think democracy is, whether they believe it exists in Massachusetts, what they feel their rightful role should be, whether they feel powerless, cheated, estranged, etc. In fact, Levin has done little more than ask voters why they support one candidate rather than his opponent. That he found as many as 50 per cent reporting that they voted against an opponent (rather than for their candidate) may be evidence of widespread cynicism and certainly merits further investigation. But on the basis of this negativism (which may be only a transitory reaction—do Massachusetts voters feel the same way about a Kennedy?) Levin has constructed a theory which purports to probe deeply the relationship between citizen and government. Had he inquired more thoroughly into the attitudes of his respondents, Levin might have found that the same persons who feel that it doesn't make much difference whether one candidate or another wins may nevertheless feel it does make a big difference whether the election is held at all or whether they have a right to vote. The very ambivalence of Levin's key term, "the alienated voter"—a person who is disenchanted yet votes—suggests the wide spectrum of relevant political attitudes untapped by his research.

Because the American political system furnishes many more opportunities for the expression of political discontent than for expressions of satisfaction, one must be careful not to take the standard indications of discontent as prima-facie evidence of alienation. Levin, however, has collected commonplace reactions to politics and categorized them under the rubric of "alienation," neglecting all the while to consider the probability that these cynical reactions are expressed by persons who experience overriding satisfaction from, and loyalty to, the political system. In so doing, he has misused the concept of political alienation. After all, it is not a new discovery that many citizens manifest feelings of apathy, cynicism, disinterest, distrust, and negativism toward politics. What is new is the packaging of these sentiments under the term "alienated voter." This term conveys the impression that there is far more amiss than the older concepts of apathy and cynicism indicate. But Levin's usage makes it virtually impossible to distinguish between conventional cynicism and feelings which border on disloyalty and rejection of the political order. There are no criteria of differentiation between a NAACPer and a Black Muslim, between a cynical worker and a non-voter. This failure to distinguish various forms of dissatisfaction leads Levin to his unwarranted, and sometimes absurd, conclusions.

In sum, Levin has taken a quick peek and mistaken it for the full view. What he calls *alienation* can be termed more properly *cynicism* and a commonplace, low-tension cynicism at that. Neglected altogether are the myriad shadings and variations in political attitudes.

7. Party Patterns in the United States

CAMPAIGNS and electoral behavior are reflections of many factors: historical forces, the nature and temper of America's pluralist society, the character and relationship of the parties, the constitutional arrangements through which the parties compete for the exercise of power, regional variations, city-country dichotomy, and the complexities of urban politics. Of particular interest in studying collective national electoral decisions are the influences of federalism, regionalism, and urbanism on the party patterns.

Federalism, the constitutional division of power between the national government and the state governments, is of basic importance to the American party process. The Constitution mandated the states with their senators and representatives, permitted state legislatures to prescribe the manner of elections, and created the electoral college. As a result, political party localism and its concomitant decentralization have become distinguishing characteristics of the political system. Structural confederation causes the national party organization to depend on city, county, and state organizations for local, state, and congressional nominations. Only in presidential elections does the national party headquarters assume leadership. A member of the legislative branch also acts autonomously and cannot be compelled by a President of the same party to vote in compliance with the President's wishes. The President may cajole, promise, intimidate, and resort to any number of devices, but he must stop short of compulsion. A President, even one whose party is in the majority in both houses, has no guarantee of support for his program. Organizational decentralization allows for ideological diversity and, furthermore, since it has its roots in local politics, decentralization provides a strong base for a minority party during years of absence from national executive power.

Although political parties find a focal point in the Congress and in the executive branch, federalism assures local party decentralization and the allocation of powers among the nation, the states, and, increasingly, the localities. In this juristic separation of powers and functions, political parties act as a crucial link, providing channels of access not only to the scattered decision-making points in the governmental structure, but also to the pressure groups which are the articulators of America's pluralism. (For a discussion of pressure groups, see Part IV.)

Federal-state relations and political party adjustments to them, particularly since the demise of dual federalism, are primary elements in the political process. When, in the spring of 1937, the Supreme Court retreated from its former rigid adherence to the doctrine of dual federalism, it marked the end of one era and the beginning of another, the era of cooperative federalism. (The theory of dual federalism held that, according to a strict construction of the Constitution, the federal government and the states constituted two sovereign systems, each with its own powers and re-sponsibilities, and that neither could intrude upon the other's sovereignty.) None-theless, intergovernmental cooperation did exist, particularly in such areas as internal improvements, land-grant programs, and a variety of federal service programs. It remained, however, for the Court to sanction cooperative federalism before there occurred a permanent and pervasive enlargement of federal power.

Under the New Deal the federal government moved into agriculture, labor, hous-ing, and welfare, areas traditionally left to the states. After World War II, along with the expanding federalization in economic and social fields, there occurred the altogether new federalization of political and civil rights (see Parts V and VI). This provoked considerable political comment and reaction. Many Republicans and south-ern Democrats were disenchanted with the continued growth of federal activity and sought to restrain it, if not roll it back, while most northern Democrats and liberal Republicans felt that increased federal programs were a partial answer to pressing national problems. The postwar debate over the proper constitutional design of federalism reached its climax in the 1964 presidential election. The Republican plat-form, faithfully reflecting Barry Goldwater's views on states' rights, warned that "individual freedom retreats under the mounting assault of expanding centralized power." President Johnson took an opposite stance and expressed the philosophy that government activity liberated man "from the enslaving forces of his environment."

The new thrust of federal activity involved a change in the traditional structural and political arrangements of federalism. No longer was the structural relationship solely a federal-state one; there was a direct federal-local relationship as well. Such terms as "creative federalism," "direct federalism," and "private federalism" have come increasingly into use in the 1960's. There has been increasing federal assistance to the localities for such projects as slum clearance, urban renewal, water and air pollution control, and airport construction. The problems of urbanization and metro-politanization, because of their scope, disregard of jurisdictional boundaries, financial and technical complexity, and interrelationship with the national scene, have resulted in new political patterns.

Creative federalism goes beyond old-line federal-state or federal-local (direct fed-eralism) arrangements. To deal with regional or local problems and programs, it may utilize private federalism (government grants to private institutions, businesses, agencies, or foundations) or quasi-public "umbrella" organizations or institutions. (The war on poverty program, based on the Economic Opportunity Act of 1964 and subsequent legislation, is an example of creative federalism and new political patterns.) This new federalism is certain to create new centers of power and decision-making, opening new avenues for political parties, popular control, and public accountability.

Another important influence on party patterns is sectionalism. Sectionalism has been defined by Daniel J. Elazar as "the more or less permanent arrangements that tie groups of continuous states or segments of states together with bonds of shared economic and social interests." Sectionalism in politics, with its deep historic roots, is in part responsible for the dualism of American parties. As far back as the debates over the ratification of the Constitution there was a conflict of interests between the frontier and the seaboard, the advancing West and the settled East. With the adop-tion of the Constitution, economic-sectional politics became a determinant of public policy formulation. The Federalists secured their support from the seaboard com-mercial interests, while the Jeffersonian Democratic-Republicans were endorsed by the back-country grain growers. These general lines, with modifications and exceptions, were carried over to the Jacksonian period. But with the rise of slavery as a major national issue, the East-West cleavage became a North-South dichotomy, with the West being torn apart and used as a free-versus-slave-soil battleground. Politics was inadequate to resolve the multitude of economic and social conflicts, and the result was the Civil War, which left in its wake a new pattern of political sectionalism.

The Democratic party became entrenched in the South (the Solid South), the Republican party in certain sections of the North (particularly rural New England), and the West, with some indigenous problems, produced the parties of protest, the Greenback and the Populist parties. The national party system thus reflected sectional forces. After the Civil War the Democrats began each presidential campaign with a bloc of southern electoral votes, while the Republicans had many northern areas already committed to them. In the twenty years from 1876 to the decisive election of 1896, it seemed as if the major political parties had struck a natural balance. In two of the five presidential elections of this period—the elections of 1876 and 1888—the winner failed to secure a popular vote margin, and in three others the margin of victory for the President was exceedingly small; for eighteen of those years, the Republicans controlled the Senate, and for sixteen years the Democrats controlled the House. The critical McKinley-Bryan election in 1896 introduced the political patterns which were to dominate the twentieth century.

In his masterful *Southern Politics,* the late V. O. Key, Jr., has shown that in the South the position of the Negro became central to the voting. (Election returns were also conditioned by two great historical crises, the Civil War and the Populist revolt of the 1890's.) Key effectively demonstrated that the individual states of the South had distinctive political cultures that varied "roughly with the Negro proportion of the population," a proposition likely to hold true through the 1960's and 1970's. The South is undergoing real and rapid change (industrialization and urbanization) and fundamental shifts are taking place in the technological, economic, social, and legal bases of the region. These changes, discernible in outline in the sixties, will probably become clearer in the seventies. Predictions of Republican-Democratic realignment or the possibility, meanwhile, of a new third party seem risky. It should be remembered that despite Goldwater's capture of five states of the Deep South in 1964, Republican victories were equivocal. The one thing that seems certain in southern politics is the continued importance of the Negro vote. (For a discussion of Negro voting trends see Part VI.) Up to 1930 the Negro vote in the South was negligible. In 1940 in his *American Dilemma,* Gunnar Myrdal estimated the number of Negro voters in eight Deep South states at 80,000 to 90,000. Twenty years later, in 1960, the Southern Regional Council estimated that about 1,400,000 Negro voters were registered in eleven southern states. In 1964 that figure rose to about 2,174,000. It seems reasonable to assume that Negro voting participation and political activities will continue to increase.

The Midwest and the West, after the Civil War, also demonstrated their own regional political syndromes. The Midwest and West had the land to settle and the frontier to conquer. The midwesterner had to contend with the post-Civil War revolution in agriculture and a host of economic problems—transportation, money and credit, and tariffs—all with political implications. Out of this background came populism and a brand of indigenous middlewestern progressivism that affected the national ideology and the major parties. As John Fenton notes, vigorous two-party competition was commonplace in Ohio, Indiana, and Illinois, whereas from the Civil War to the Great Depression, Michigan, Wisconsin, and Minnesota were one-party Republican states. Only after the New Deal did the Democratic party inherit the protest movements that produced viable two-party systems in the latter three states.

Presidential voting in the West has, from the beginning of the century until the 1960 elections, generally reflected national trends. The one exception to this occurred in 1960 when John F. Kennedy won the presidency without the western states. In that year Richard M. Nixon carried ten western states—all but Hawaii, Nevada, and New Mexico. In 1964 Lyndon Johnson carried all thirteen western states with the exception of Barry Goldwater's home state of Arizona. Contemporary state politics throughout the West is characterized by weak party organizations, growing auxiliary, extralegal party organs, periodic spontaneous grass-roots movements, and increasing two-party competition within the states.

The broad political and social patterns associated with sectionalism, however, should not obscure the dissident minority that exists within the dominant electoral bloc of each region. Furthermore, the economic and cultural bases of sectionalism have been steadily eroding ever since 1910, when the census showed that the population in the cities had been increasing and the rural population, though at that time still in the majority, decreasing. Specifically, the technologically and economically induced decline of historic yeoman agriculture, the revolutions in transportation and communication with their nationalizing effects, rapid industrialization, and the movement of population to the cities are factors which have contributed to the softening of the sectional impact on the political process. And of these factors it is urbanization alone which, with its extensions of suburbanism and metropolitanization, has independent political significance.

The shift toward the cities can be seen most easily by looking at some statistics. In 1790, there were only 24 urban places with populations of 2,500 or more, and urban residents composed only about one-twentieth of the population. The previously mentioned 1910 census indicated the twentieth-century movement toward the cities. And by 1920, for the first time more than one-half of the nation's population lived in urban areas. Forty years later, according to the 1960 census, some 69.9 percent of America's then 179 million population were urbanites, with some 112 million living in the standard metropolitan statistical areas (SMSA): 58 million Americans lived in cities with populations of 50,000 or more, and 54 million other Americans lived immediately adjacent to these cities. In about 24 states, a majority of the population live in metropolitan areas. This urban orientation is a phenomenon to be found, albeit in varying degrees, in the North, the South, the central states, and the West. It is significant to note that the South had, after the West, the biggest percentage increase in metropolitan population between 1950 and 1960. Flowing from this urbanization trend is metropolitanism, suburbanism, and a new regionalism, the megalopolis, each with its own intrinsic metro-politics.

The population movement from rural to urban and suburban locales has had, by itself, enormous political consequences because residence influences politics. Each locale—rural, urban, suburban—has a characteristic political style. Traditionally, state legislatures were dominated by the rural populations, while urban and suburban populations were underrepresented. This representation imbalance was checked in 1962 when the Supreme Court held, in the landmark case of Baker v. Carr, that inequitable apportionment was a denial to the voters of the equal protection of the laws guaranteed by the Fourteenth Amendment. The effects of Baker v. Carr and subsequent reapportionment cases are still being felt, and new state political patterns are being created. (For the text of Baker v. Carr and a discussion of the problems and implications of reapportionment see Parts V and VI.)

In the following essays the major party patterns in the United States are discussed. In "The Politics of the Federal System," the late Morton Grodzins enumerates the causes contributing to the dispersal of power in the American federal system and discusses the effects of federalism on national politics and the party system. John H. Fenton, in "Midwest Politics," addresses himself to the pattern of two-party politics in six midwestern states. He outlines a method of analyzing state political parties according to whether they are issue-oriented or job-oriented political systems. Fenton's analysis of party competition and his issue-oriented–job-oriented distinction have a significance transcending regional lines and are useful tools for comparative state politics. In "The South in National Politics," O. Douglas Weeks presents an excellent history of southern political patterns, describes the changes occurring within the South, relates the 1948 Dixiecrat movement to southern and national politics, analyzes presidential electoral trends, and concludes with some provocative thoughts about the future of southern politics. In "Urbanism and National Party Organizations," Francis E. Rourke points out the vital interrelationship between local and national politics. Edward C. Banfield and James Q. Wilson, in "Urban Cleavages," list and discuss four types of divisions found within the urban setting. In a far-ranging essay, "The Changing Pattern of Urban Party Politics," Fred I. Greenstein presents the characteristics and determinants of urban party organizations, discusses the decline of the old-style machine, and analyzes the varieties of contemporary urban politics.

THE POLITICS OF THE FEDERAL SYSTEM *

Morton Grodzins

MANY causes contribute to dispersed power in the federal system. One is the simple historical fact that the states existed before the nation. A second is in the form of creed, the traditional opinion of Americans that expresses distrust of centralized power and places great value in the strength and vitality of local units of government. Another is pride in locality and state, nurtured by the nation's size and by variations of regional and state history. Still a fourth cause of decentralization is the sheer wealth of the nation. It allows all groups, including state and local governments, to partake of the central government's largesse, supplies room for experimentation and even waste, and makes unnecessary the tight organization of political power that must follow when the support of one program necessarily means the deprivation of another.

In one important respect, the Constitution no longer operates to impede centralized government. The Supreme Court since 1937 has given Congress a

* From Morton Grodzins, "The Federal System," in Goals for Americans, The Report of the President's Commission on National Goals, by The American Assembly, 1960, pp. 271–276. © 1960. Reprinted by permission of Prentice-Hall, Inc., Englewood Cliffs, N. J.

relatively free hand. The federal government can build substantive programs in many areas on the taxation and commerce powers. Limitations of such central programs based on the argument, "it's unconstitutional," are no longer possible as long as Congress (in the Court's view) acts reasonably in the interest of the whole nation. The Court is unlikely to reverse this permissive view in the foreseeable future.

Nevertheless, some constitutional restraints on centralization continue to operate. The strong constitutional position of the states—for example, the assignment of two senators to each state, the role given the states in administering even national elections, and the relatively few limitations on their lawmaking powers—establish the geographical units as natural centers of administrative and political strength. Many clauses of the Constitution are not subject to the same latitude of interpretation as the commerce and tax clauses. The simple, clearly stated, unambiguous phrases—for example, the President "shall hold his office during the term of four years"—are subject to change only through the formal amendment process. Similar provisions exist with respect to the terms of senators and congressmen and the amendment process. All of them have the effect of retarding or restraining centralizing action of the federal government. The fixed terms of the President and members of Congress, for example, greatly impede the development of nation-wide, disciplined political parties that almost certainly would have to precede continuous large-scale expansion of federal functions.

The constitutional restraints on the expansion of national authority are less important and less direct today than they were in 1879 or in 1936. But to say that they are less important is not to say that they are unimportant.

The nation's politics reflect these decentralizing causes and adds some of their own. The political parties of the United States are unique. They seldom perform the function that parties traditionally perform in other countries, the function of gathering together diverse strands of power and welding them into one. Except during the period of nominating and electing a president and for the essential but non-substantive business of organizing the houses of Congress, the American parties rarely coalesce power at all. Characteristically they do the reverse, serving as a canopy under which special and local interests are represented with little regard for anything that can be called a party program. National leaders are elected on a party ticket, but in Congress they must seek cross-party support if their leadership is to be effective. It is a rare president during rare periods who can produce legislation without facing the defection of substantial numbers of his own party. (Wilson could do this in the first session of the sixty-third Congress; but Franklin D. Roosevelt could not, even during the famous hundred days of 1933.) Presidents whose parties form the majority of the congressional houses must still count heavily on support from the other party.

The parties provide the pivot on which the entire governmental system swings. Party operations, first of all, produce in legislation the basic division of functions between the federal government, on the one hand, and state and local governments, on the other. The Supreme Court's permissiveness with respect to the expansion of national powers has not in fact produced any considerable extension of exclusive federal functions. The body of federal law in all fields has remained, in the words of Henry M. Hart, Jr. and Herbert Wechsler, "interstitial in its nature," limited in objective and resting upon the principal body of legal relationships defined by state law. It is difficult to find any area of federal legislation that is not significantly affected by state law.

In areas of new or enlarged federal activity, legislation characteristically provides important roles for state and local governments. This is as true of Democratic as of Republican administrations and true even of functions for which arguments of efficiency would produce exclusive federal responsibility. Thus the unemployment compensation program of the New Deal and the airport program of President Truman's administration both provided important responsibilities for state governments. In both cases attempts to eliminate state participation were defeated by a cross-party coalition of pro-state votes and influence. A large fraction of the Senate is usually made up of ex-governors, and the membership of both houses is composed of men who know that their re-election depends less upon national leaders or national party organization than upon support from their home constituencies. State and local officials are key members of these constituencies, often central figures in selecting candidates and in turning out the vote. Under such circumstances, national legislation taking state and local views heavily into account is inevitable.

Second, the undisciplined parties affect the character of the federal system as a result of senatorial and congressional interference in federal administrative programs on behalf of local interests. Many aspects of the legislative involvement in administrative affairs are formalized. The Legislative Reorganization Act of 1946, to take only one example, provided that each of the standing committees "shall exercise continuous watchfulness" over administration of laws within its jurisdiction. But the formal system of controls, extensive as it is, does not compare in importance with the informal and extralegal network of relationships in producing continuous legislative involvement in administrative affairs.

Senators and congressmen spend a major fraction of their time representing problems of their constituents before administrative agencies. An even larger fraction of congressional staff time is devoted to the same task. The total magnitude of such "case work" operations is great. In one five-month period of 1943 the Office of Price Administration received a weekly average of 842 letters from members of Congress. If phone calls and personal contacts are added, each member of Congress on the average presented the OPA with a problem involving one of his constituents twice a day in each five-day work week. Data for less vulnerable agencies during less intensive periods are also impressive. In 1958, to take only one example, the Department of Agriculture estimated (and underestimated) that it received an average of 159 congressional letters per working day. Special congressional liaison staffs have been created to service this mass of business, though all higher officials meet it in one form or another.

The Air Force in 1958 had, under the command of a major general, 137 people (55 officers and 82 civilians) working in its liaison office.

The widespread, consistent, and in many ways unpredictable character of legislative interference in administrative affairs has many consequences for the tone and character of American administrative behavior. From the perspective of this paper, the important consequence is the comprehensive, day-to-day, even hour-by-hour, impact of local views on national programs. No point of substance or procedure is immune from congressional scrutiny. A substantial portion of the entire weight of this impact is on behalf of the state and local governments. It is a weight that can alter procedures for screening immigration applications, divert the course of a national highway, change the tone of an international negotiation, and amend a social security law to accommodate local practices or fulfill local desires.

The party system compels administrators to take a political role. This is a third way in which the parties function to decentralize the American system. The administrator must play politics for the same reason that the politician is able to play in administration: the parties are without program and without discipline.

In response to the unprotected position in which the party situation places him, the administrator is forced to seek support where he can find it. One ever-present task is to nurse the Congress of the United States, that crucial constituency which ultimately controls his agency's budget and program. From the administrator's view, a sympathetic consideration of congressional requests (if not downright submission to them) is the surest way to build the political support without which the administrative job could not continue. Even the completely task-oriented administrator must be sensitive to the need for congressional support and to the relationship between case work requests, on one side, and budgetary and legislative support, on the other. "You do a good job handling the personal problems and requests of a Congressman," a White House officer said, "and you have an easier time convincing him to back your program." Thus there is an important link between the nursing of congressional requests, requests that largely concern local matters, and the most comprehensive national programs. The administrator must accommodate to the former as a price of gaining support for the latter.

One result of administrative politics is that the administrative agency may become the captive of the nation-wide interest group it serves or presumably regulates. In such cases no government may come out with effective authority: the winners are the interest groups themselves. But in a very large number of cases, states and localities also win influence. The politics of administration is a process of making peace with legislators who for the most part consider themselves the guardians of local interests. The political role of administrators therefore contributes to the power of states and localities in national programs.

Finally, the way the party system operates gives American politics their overall distinctive tone. The lack of party discipline produces an openness in the system that allows individuals, groups, and institutions (including state and local governments) to attempt to influence national policy at every step of the legislative-administrative process. This is the "multiple-crack" attribute of the American government. "Crack" has two meanings. It means not only many fissures or access points; it also means, less statically, opportunities for wallops or smacks at government.

If the parties were more disciplined, the result would not be a cessation of the process by which individuals and groups impinge themselves upon the central government. But the present state of the parties clearly allows for a far greater operation of the multiple crack than would be possible under the conditions of centralized party control. American interest groups exploit literally uncountable access points in the legislative-administrative process. If legislative lobbying, from committee stages to the conference committee, does not produce results, a cabinet secretary is called. His immediate associates are petitioned. Bureau chiefs and their aides are hit. Field officers are put under pressure. Campaigns are instituted by which friends of the agency apply a secondary influence on behalf of the interested party. A conference with the President may be urged.

To these multiple points for bringing influence must be added the multiple voices of the influencers. Consider, for example, those in a small town who wish to have a federal action taken. The easy merging of public and private interest at the local level means that the influence attempt is made in the name of the whole community, thus removing it from political partisanship. The Rotary Club as well as the City Council, the Chamber of Commerce and the mayor, eminent citizens and political bosses—are all readily enlisted. If a conference in a senator's office will expedite matters, someone on the local scene can be found to make such a conference possible and effective. If technical information is needed, technicians will supply it. State or national professional organizations of local officials, individual congressmen and senators, and not infrequently whole state delegations will make the local cause their own. Federal field officers, who service localities, often assume local views. So may elected and appointed state officers. Friendships are exploited, and political mortgages called due. Under these circumstances, national policies are molded by local action.

In summary, then, the party system functions to devolve power. The American parties, unlike any other, are highly responsive when directives move from the bottom to the top, highly unresponsive from top to bottom. Congressmen and senators can rarely ignore concerted demands from their home constituencies; but no party leader can expect the same kind of response from those below, whether he be a President asking for congressional support or a congressman seeking aid from local or state leaders.

Any tightening of the party apparatus would have the effect of strengthening the central government. The four characteristics of the system, discussed above, would become less important. If control from the top were strictly applied, these hallmarks of American decentralization might entirely disappear. To be specific, if disciplined and program-oriented parties were achieved: (1) It would make far less likely legislation that takes heavily into account the desires and prejudices of the highly decentralized power groups and institutions of the country, including the state and local governments. (2) It would to a large extent prevent legislators, individually and collectively, from intruding themselves on behalf of non-national interests in national administrative programs. (3) It would put an end to the administrator's search for his own political support, a search that often results in fostering state, local, and other non-national powers. (4)It would dampen the process by which individuals and groups, including state and local political leaders, take advantage of multiple cracks to steer national legislation and administration in ways congenial to them and the institutions they represent.

Alterations of this sort could only accompany basic changes in the organization and style of politics which, in turn, presuppose fundamental changes at the parties' social base. The sharing of functions is, in fact, the sharing of power. To end this sharing process would mean the destruction of whatever measure of decentralization exists in the United States today.

MIDWEST POLITICS *

John H. Fenton

THE Midwest is both a geographical location and a state of mind. It is neither East nor West, neither South nor North. It is the population center of America and in many respects it is the heart of the nation. The people are heterogeneous in their origins, but perhaps more homogeneous in their Americanism than the residents of other sections of the nation. Unlike the citizens of Texas, Mississippi, or Vermont, who identify strongly with the Lone Star State or the South or New England, most Midwesterners think of themselves as Americans. They do not live in the Midwest. Rather, they live in America, for the Midwest is America.

Given the heartland character of the Midwest, the findings concerning two-party politics in Ohio, Indiana, Illinois, Michigan, Wisconsin, and Minnesota have a significance that transcends regional lines. In the past, the two-party job-oriented politics that typified the American party system was rooted most firmly in the villages of Ohio, Indiana, and Illinois. The two-party issue-oriented politics of the post–World War II period, similarly, is nationally identified with developments in Michigan, Wisconsin, and Minnesota.

The foregoing inquiries into the politics of six Midwest states largely revolved around assessments of the degree to which the theoretical benefits of two-party

* From John H. Fenton, Chapter 8, "Conclusions," in *Midwest Politics* (Holt, Rinehart and Winston, Inc., 1966), pp. 219–231. © 1966 by Holt, Rinehart and Winston, Inc. Reprinted by permission with a change in the chapter title.

competition are realized in issue-oriented as opposed to job-oriented political systems. An eminently practical reason for the inquiry was to assess the desirability of the turn taken by American politics after World War II. The notion or hypothesis around which the studies of the states' politics revolved was that two broad aspects of two-party competition must be present before the theoretical benefits of two-party competition . . . may be realized: (1) a fairly equal division of the electorate between the two parties roughly along the lines of contemporary problems; and (2) a leadership of the parties which makes them distinct entities, competes at every level of government, advocates alternative approaches to issues, and attempts to carry through after election by translating the programs into public policy. In the following pages we will review the findings concerning the degree to which the two requisites of two-party competition were present in the six states studied, the reasons for their presence or absence, and the consequences on the governments of the states.

(1) A FAIRLY EQUAL DIVISION OF THE ELECTORATE
BETWEEN THE TWO PARTIES
ALONG THE LINES OF CONTEMPORARY PROBLEMS

In the six Midwest states studied, the electorate was rather narrowly divided between the Democratic and Republican parties. Although some of the states tended Republican and others tended Democratic, there was little difference between them in the competitiveness of their state politics when competitiveness is defined to mean the narrowness of the vote division between the two parties. There were important differences, however, in the nature of the divisions between the parties. In Ohio, Indiana, and Illinois, the Democratic party was an alliance of rather conservative rural people, whose Democratic loyalties dated from their great grandparents' pro-Southern inclinations during the Civil War, and the more recent immigrants to the cities from eastern Europe and the American South.

The Republican parties in Ohio, Indiana, and Illinois consisted largely of the white, Protestant, more prosperous Americans. The traditional centers of Republican strength in the three states were the areas settled by New Englanders. The Yankee Republican voting strength was supplemented by the votes of people who prospered in the cities and the corn belts. The Republicans in the three states were largely people who had invested their blood and sweat and money in their lands and enterprises and had prospered. They resisted the demands of more recent immigrants for a larger share of the material goods of the state.

In summary, the voters of Ohio, Indiana, and Illinois were rather evenly divided between the Democratic and Republican parties. However, in all three states the division was, in part, along lines which had little or no relationship with twentieth-century issues.

The dominant political trend, 1920-1960, in the three states was for urban disadvantaged elements (foreign, non-white, urban) to enter the Democratic party and for traditional rural Democrats to leave the party. As a result, voters were more and more likely to take political sides for reasons related to twentieth-century problems, but the Civil War continued to exert an important influence on voting habits.

In contrast to Ohio, Indiana, and Illinois, the two-party divisions of voters in Minnesota, Wisconsin, and Michigan were closely related to differences of opinion on twentieth-century issues. The lines along which the Democratic and Republican parties divided were remarkably similar in Minnesota and Wisconsin. In the two states there was a history of issue-oriented divisions of the voters within the dominant Republican party. In Minnesota the intraparty Republican division between liberals and conservatives was institutionalized by the creation of a Farmer-Labor party which competed with the Republican party in state elections. Following the New Deal and World War II, the Farmer-Laborites joined the urban disadvantaged groups in a Democratic-Farmer-Labor party. Similarly, in Wisconsin the Republican intraparty division between liberal La Follettes and conservatives was institutionalized during the 1930s in a Progressive party which competed with the Republican party in statewide elections. The Progressive party disbanded in 1946; and with the defeat of Robert La Follette by Joseph McCarthy in the 1946 Republican U.S. senatorial primary, the Wisconsin Progressives tended to join the urban immigrants in a liberal Democratic party.

Therefore in both Minnesota and Wisconsin the affiliation of groups to the Democratic and Republican parties was related to twentieth-century issues. In large part, the immigrants of Milwaukee and Minneapolis and St. Paul cast their lot with the Democratic party because of Franklin Roosevelt's New Deal. Similarly, the Farmer-Laborites and Progressives of the two states left the Republican party in the 1920s and 1930s because they felt that its approach to social and economic problems was overly conservative. The merging of these groups in the Democratic party brought together farmers, laborers, immigrants, and liberals, all of whom demanded positive governmental action to redress their grievances. Mainly in the form of a more egalitarian distribution of goods and opportunities. This left the Republican parties of Minnesota and Wisconsin with most of the people who felt relatively comfortable with the given distribution of goods and opportunities and who felt threatened by the demands of the urban and rural disinherited; that is, the native, Protestant, non-Scandinavian, stalwart or conservative Republicans.

Michigan is the sixth of the Midwest states studied, and the divisions of people between the two parties in Michigan breaks more markedly along urban disadvantaged versus less-urban advantaged group lines than in any of the other five states. The combined impact of the New Deal plus the "Soapy" Williams administration, 1948-1960, drew into the Democratic party large numbers of Negro and eastern European immigrants, most of whom lived in the cities. At the same time, the liberal Democratic policies at both the national and state levels drove most conservative Democrats into the Republican party. Urban eastern European Catholic and Negro people in Michigan voted overwhelmingly Democratic and the less-urban western European Protestant white people voted Republican. The result was a division of groups along the lines of problems that currently faced them. Michigan's urban disadvantaged sought improved job and educational opportunities, along with a greater share of the good things of life, and they were largely in the Democratic party; on the other hand, the more well-to-do native white elements were relatively content with the given share of goods and opportunities or wanted an even larger share, and resisted the attempts of the disadvantaged to chip away at their privileges through progressive taxes and generous welfare and public education programs.

In summary, the Ohio, Indiana, and Illinois electorate were divided along both Civil War lines and along urban disadvantaged versus advantaged lines. This resulted in populations which, in large part, adhered to a political faith for reasons which were irrelevant to the problems that confronted them. The Minnesota and Wisconsin voters divided between the Democratic and Republican parties along cleavages marked out by the La Follette Progressives and the Farmer-Laborites, as well as along the urban disadvantaged versus advantaged "faults" which were exploited by the New Deal. In most cases, the Progressive and New Deal lines dividing the electorate paralleled or supplemented one another. The outcome was a division of the electorate along issue lines which were relevant to the problems the people of the states faced in mid-twentieth century America. Some of these issues were, conservation, welfare, employment, tax policies, parks, education, mental health, and farm programs. In Michigan the division between the two parties tended to be along the urban disadvantaged versus advantaged lines marked out by the New Deal. The Republican party maintained a strong grip on the traditional political loyalties of the sons and daughters of the settlers of the state, regardless of their economic status. The result was the division of the electorate between parties roughly along the lines of contemporary problems. The political trends in Ohio, Indiana, and Illinois were in the direction of a Michigan-type division of the electorate.

We turn next to a summary of the effects of the nature of the vote divisions in the six states on the style of their political leadership. The discussion will be in terms of the second condition for effective party government.

(2) LEADERSHIP OF THE PARTIES
WHICH MAKES THE PARTIES DISTINCT ENTITIES,
COMPETES AT EVERY LEVEL OF GOVERNMENT,
ADVOCATES ALTERNATIVE APPROACHES TO ISSUES,
AND ATTEMPTS TO CARRY THROUGH AFTER ELECTION
BY TRANSLATING THEIR PROGRAMS INTO PUBLIC POLICY

The analyses of political organization in the six Midwest states dealt largely with political leadership in the traditional two-party states of Illinois, Indiana, and Ohio, as opposed to the programmatic party leadership in Minnesota, Wisconsin, and Michigan. Perhaps the most interesting finding was the process by which programmatic political leadership emerged in Minnesota, Wisconsin, and

Michigan. The dates and occasions for the emergence of issue-oriented politics in the northern tier of states were as follows: (1) In Minnesota it occurred in 1944 with the merger of the Democratic and Farmer-Labor parties; (2) in Wisconsin, the key date was 1946, when the Progressive party disbanded and Robert La Follette, Jr., was defeated by Joseph McCarthy in the Republican senatorial primary; and (3) in Michigan, programmatic politics developed out of the formal entrance into the Democratic party of the United Auto Workers and the capture of the Democratic party organization by an alliance of labor and liberals in 1948.

In each of the three states the pattern of events and the dynamics of transition to a programmatic type of two-party politics was similar. First, the Democratic party was an empty shell. Many of the traditionally Democratic but relatively conservative German and Irish Catholic voters had deserted the Democratic party in the 1930s and early 1940s because of the liberal economic policies pursued by Franklin Roosevelt and because of their disapproval of American involvement in World War II. In company with the desertion of their party by traditional Democrats, job-oriented politicians in the three states lost interest in political activity because of the adoption of strict civil service laws and the outbreak of World War II, which dimmed the luster of political jobs and appointments by providing better-paying employment opportunities elsewhere.

Therefore, the Democratic party was weak and disorganized in the three states in the early 1940s. However, the party retained a substantial untapped vote base which voted for Franklin Roosevelt and the New Deal, but ignored the state Democratic party's candidates because of their conservatism and corruption. In Minnesota and Wisconsin these liberal votes were cast for the Farmer-Labor and Progressive party candidates in state elections, leaving the Democratic party a weak third party. In Michigan much of the liberal vote was not cast at all.

The moribund condition of the Democratic parties attracted the attention of astute political and interest-group leaders. In every instance the kind of political leadership which moved to fill the vacuum in the three state Democratic parties was issue-oriented rather than job-oriented. In Minnesota, many professors moved into positions of political leadership; in Wisconsin the new programmatic-oriented leaders were largely labor leaders, ex-Progressives, and Socialist leaders; and in Michigan the new issue-oriented leadership came largely from the ranks of labor, from liberals in business, and from the professions. In all three states women also played an important part in providing new political leadership.

The professors, women, labor leaders, socialists, and liberals who captured the three state Democratic parties encountered little opposition, because of the disinterest of traditional job-oriented politicians in an activity that promised little in the way of jobs or other traditional perquisites of political power after the enactment of civil service laws. The key to the successful exploitation of the situation and seizure of the Democratic party by issue-oriented people was the existence of organized groups of liberals in the three states who were in a position to provide direction, lend luster to, and in some instances financially support the efforts of liberals. In Minnesota the most important organized group of liberals was the Farmer-Labor party; in Wisconsin the key liberal groups were the Progressive party, labor unions, and Socialists in Milwaukee; and in Michigan it was the United Auto Workers. In each state, then, liberals had an institutionalized power base from which to operate. They were not lonely and atomized. Rather, they interacted frequently through the Farmer-Labor party, Progressive party, Socialist party, the United Auto Workers, or through tangential groups such as Americans for Democratic Action, where leaders from all these segments of liberalism came together and in turn interacted with otherwise atomized liberals in business and the professions.

Once installed, this new Democratic leadership provided a distinctly different face from the Republican leadership. The differences derived basically from the motives which impelled people to desert the Republican party and join the Democratic party. Fundamentally, the motive was dissatisfaction with the existing power structure and the distribution of goods and opportunities which accompanied it. Consequently, the leadership which precipitated the move into the Democratic party was also most firmly committed to policies and programs which would alter the status quo by providing a larger share of goods and opportunities for the less privileged members of the society. Often these people were white, native, privileged, Protestant Anglo-Saxons. Nevertheless, they were committed by reason of ideology to alterations in the power structure.

The Republican party was largely left with the people who were relatively happy with the existing power structure. These tended to be the more successful farmers, professional people, and businessmen. Frequently, as in Minnesota, the wives of the businessmen belonged to the League of Women Voters and interlarded their conservatism with a desire for improvements in the existing political, economic, and social systems (for example, civil rights, honest government, public education, and mental health). In the Republican party, as in the Democratic party, the traditional job-oriented politician tended to disappear in the 1940s, to be replaced by businessmen, as in Wisconsin and Michigan, and the wives of businessmen, as in Minnesota.

The outcome was the development of parties which were distinct entities. There was none of the mutual esteem that Republican and Democratic "pros" professed for one another in Ohio, Indiana, and Illinois. After all, the Democratic and Republican "pros" in traditional two-party states wanted the same thing—jobs! But in Minnesota, Wisconsin, and Michigan the political leaders sought different ends and the result was meaningful competition at every level of government and an absence of the bipartisan collusion that characterized the politics in other states. After election, no urging was required to persuade the issue-oriented politicians of Minnesota, Wisconsin, and Michigan to earnestly attempt to translate their programs into public policy. Their only reason for participation in politics was commitment to issues. The businessmen left good-paying jobs with American Motors or General Motors because they felt that their notions concerning the proper role of government would best serve the interests of the nation. Similarly, wealthy liberals, such as Neil Staebler, or university professors, such as Hubert Humphrey, were not attracted to government by patronage jobs but rather by a commitment to certain ideals and a desire to see them incorporated into the day-to-day activities of government.

In Indiana and Illinois the traditional job-oriented politicians held sway in the 1960s. Their continued organizational dominance was due to the presence in the Republican and Democratic parties of people whose party allegiance was unrelated to contemporary problems. In addition, both parties contained large numbers of adherents whose allegiance represented a response to the policies of Franklin Roosevelt and Dwight D. Eisenhower. The job-oriented politician emerged out of the traditional segment of the party but found a useful niche in the parties in mediating conflicts between the factions of the party and by nominating candidates who were acceptable to conservatives and liberals alike. In these states neither party was an empty shell and the job-oriented politician was rewarded by patronage for his activities. Consequently, the leadership of both parties sought jobs through political activity rather than public policy ends. Therefore, the parties were not distinct entities, but rather they were engaged in bipartisan collusion for corrupt ends. They often failed to compete, as in the Illinois legislature. And after election they seldom made an earnest attempt to translate their election programs into public policy.

Ohio political organization or disorganization was substantially different from that of the issue-oriented states or the traditional two-party states. In a sense, Ohio's political organization was similar to Michigan's before the UAW—liberal seizure of the Democratic party in 1948. There was no statewide Democratic party in Ohio. Rather, there were many city-based and county-based Democratic machines which were sustained through patronage at the local level. Each resisted the development of a strong state party because it would threaten their independence. Why was it then that issue-oriented groups did not seize the Ohio Democratic party as in Minnesota, Wisconsin, and Michigan? The answer is that there was no institutional base for Ohio liberals comparable to the UAW in Michigan, the Farmer-Labor party in Minnesota, or the Progressive party in Wisconsin. Ohio's liberals were atomized and seldom interacted with one another.

Ohio's Republican party was well organized under the direction of the very able Republican State Chairman Ray Bliss. One explanation for the existence of a cohesive Republican party in Ohio was the concentration of Republican votes, money, and jobs in the Cincinnati area, which enabled the Cincinnati Republican leaders to dominate and provide guidance for the party. In addition, Republicans in Ohio were well organized out of necessity. Lou Harris' polls indicated that the Democrats enjoyed an advantage in the stated party preferences of Ohioans. However, the Republicans were ahead in numbers of registered voters due to good organization.

The end product of Ohio's political disorganization was that the parties' candidates did not consistently advocate alternative approaches to the problems of government and were not distinct entities. For example, Senator Frank

Lausche, Democrat of Ohio, was more conservative than most Republican candidates. In addition, because of Democratic disorganization little was done to translate into public policy the programs advocated in the election campaigns. The Republican party deliberately attempted to keep "divisive" issues out of elections for fear that they would activate urban Democrats.

In summary, the issue-oriented two-party states of Minnesota, Wisconsin, and Michigan had a fairly even division of voters along the lines of twentieth-century issues and an issue-oriented leadership of the two major political parties which competed at every level of government, advocated alternative approaches to problems facing the people of the states, and attempted to translate their political programs into law after election. These conditions for meaningful two-party competition were not met in Ohio, Indiana, and Illinois. We now turn to comparisons between the actual performance of government as a result of two-party issue-oriented politics as practiced in Minnesota, Wisconsin, and Michigan, and government performance where the more traditional job-oriented politics was practiced, as in Ohio, Indiana, and Illinois.

COMPARATIVE STATE PROGRAMS

... The more competitive two-party states tend to spend more on welfare and education than the less competitive states. Inquiry also led to the hunch that another important determinant of the amount and direction of state expenditures is the degree to which the politics of the state is issue-oriented. It remains now to pull together some of the material concerning job-oriented and issue-oriented political systems in order to test the validity of the hypothesis that states with programmatic political parties tend to spend more on government, and especially on welfare and education, relative to the wealth of the people than do states with traditional job-oriented political parties.

Data concerning the total amount spent on state government and on welfare and education programs relative to the amount of money earned by the people of the state show that in every instance the governments of the three states with programmatic parties made a greater effort (spent more relative to income) than the governments of the three states with traditional job-oriented two-party competition (see Table for the comparative figures for the six states). The dollar expenditures per pupil in average daily attendance and the per-capita welfare expenditures also tended to be higher in the three issue-oriented states than in the three traditional two-party states (not included in Table).

There were no profound differences between the states with respect to their two-party competition scores, 1946–1958; per-capita income, 1959; per cent urban, 1960; and per cent rural-farm, 1960. Therefore, the hypothesis that issue-oriented two-party politics encourages a diversion of resources from private to public expenditures in order to divide goods and opportunities more equitably has been strengthened by the results of the study. Six equally competitive two-party states were studied, and the governments of the states where issue-oriented politics prevailed invariably levied higher taxes and spent more on welfare and education relative to the wealth of the state. The study does provoke some

COMPARATIVE GOVERNMENTAL PROGRAMS, DEMOGRAPHIC AND POLITICAL DATA FOR SIX MIDWEST STATES

	TWO-PARTY COMPE-TITION SCORE 1946–1958*	TOTAL EFFORT % PER-CAPITA STATES LOCAL TAX REVENUE 1959, OF PER-CAPITA INCOME 1959	WELFARE EFFORT % PER-CAPITA PUBLIC WELFARE EXPENDITURES LESS FEDERAL, 1959, OF PER-CAPITA INCOME, 1959	EDUCATION EFFORT % PER-CAPITA EXPENDITURES IN AVERAGE DAILY ATTENDANCE 1959–1960, OF PER-CAPITA INCOME, 1959	PER-CAPITA INCOME 1959	% URBAN 1960	% RURAL-FARM 1960
Traditional Two-Party States							
Ohio	77	6.9	0.55	15.7	$2328	73.4	5.4
Indiana	83	8.0	0.34	16.9	2102	62.4	10.4
Illinois	89	6.7	0.45	15.4	2610	80.7	5.6
Issue-oriented States							
Minnesota	—	10.3	0.76	20.6	1962	62.2	17.2
Wisconsin	73	9.3	0.62	18.2	2116	63.8	14.0
Michigan	80	8.7	0.60	18.9	2253	73.4	5.6

* The two-party competition score is derived from the average percentage divisions between the two parties in the gubernatorial elections and in the two houses of the state legislature, 1946–1958. For example, if the average percentage division in all the gubernatorial contests, 1946–1958, were 55–45, and if the average two-party division of seats in the State Senate were 70–30 and in the state House of Representatives 60–40, leaving an average division in the state legislature of 65–35, 1946–1958, the two-part competition score would be the sum of the two lesser percentages (45 plus 35), or 80.

questions concerning the social utility of traditional two-party competition where the divisions of the voters are partially along Civil War lines. The traditional parties would seem to serve few of the theoretical ends of two-party competition and to exact a rather large price for their services. In addition, they tend to institutionalize divisions of the voters along lines which have no relationship to the problems the people face.

The people of Minnesota, Wisconsin, and Michigan were found to be in the enviable position of owning state governments which were genuinely responsive to the public will. The question that remains is whether political conditions in the three states represent aberrations from the two-party norm or a trend in a new direction for American politics. The data on the six Midwest states clearly indicated that the development of issue-oriented political parties in the 1940s in the northern Midwest was no accident. It was the result of forces that were in operation throughout American society. In the states of Ohio, Indiana, and Illinois it was observed that the traditional conservative Democrats were deserting their party in opposition to disadvantaged urban elements in the Democratic party. Outside Michigan, Wisconsin, and Minnesota this redivision of the electorate along issue lines was furthest advanced in Ohio. However, no catalyst had appeared in Ohio to transform the state's politics into an issue-oriented form.

The division of voters along lines related to twentieth-century problems appeared to be working to the long-run advantage of the Republican party. The Republicans benefited by this division because the flow of immigrants from eastern Europe was reduced to a trickle by discriminatory immigration laws, and the new immigrants to the cities were either Negroes who voted Democratic (but were less likely to vote than other groups or people from neighboring farm areas who often brought with them rather strong pro-Republican biases. The outcome was a gradual plus-Republican trend concentrated especially in the medium-sized cities where the rural-farm immigrants to the cities often settled. If the Republican party responded to this opportunity with sensitivity, it would almost inevitably return to majority party status. However, if it pursued reactionary policies it would frighten its urban adherents into the Democratic party, as in 1964.

In any event, the future holds the prospect of continuing two-party competition in all the Midwest states with a growing tendency for the electorate to divide between the parties along issue lines. The result should be healthy for the future of American democracy.

THE SOUTH IN NATIONAL POLITICS *

O. Douglas Weeks

THE present moment is a most difficult time to say anything definitive about the South in national politics—1950 to 1970. It is perhaps too soon to place any final interpretations on what the political events and changes of the 1950's and early 1960's have meant in the political life and institutions of the South and on its present place in national politics. It is hard to prophesy what confronts the Nation as a whole, as well as the South, for the next year, let alone the remainder of the decade. The present is no doubt a very critical time in the history of what has always been the controlling issue in the South and the chief shaper of her politics and political system. Are the organized Negroes and their friends about to force their way into full equality, or will their persistence produce a reaction in politics and otherwise which will set back their cause for years to come both in the North and South?

The race issue is always uppermost in Southern politics, but economic issues are never far behind. The South in general has in recent times undergone in effect an extensive economic revolution, which has not been completed by any means, but which has had and will have profound effects upon its political system and its place in national politics. To some extent the two revolutions are interrelated. What this will lead to by 1970 is difficult to foresee. . . .

THE SOLID SOUTH

From the end of Reconstruction and for nearly thirty years into the Twentieth Century, the eleven states of the South, except for a few areas and a few elective places, supported the Democratic ticket "from president to constable." Even though the Democratic party, because of its cleansing baths in Bryan populism in 1896 and Wilson progressivism in 1912, was considered the more liberal of the two major parties, the conservative South remained staunchly loyal to it and showed no signs of revolt until 1928, when its solidity or solidarity was cracked for the first time and the Republicans carried a majority of its vote for the presidency. The section had been two-party in the days before the Civil War, but for sixty years after Reconstruction and for the four times the Democrats attained the presidency in 1884, 1892, 1912, and 1916 and in many congressional elections the party was beholden to the support of the undivided South.

* From O. Douglas Weeks, "The South in National Politics," in Avery Leiserson, ed., *The American South in the 1960's* (New York: Frederick A. Praeger, Inc., 1964), pp. 221–240. Reprinted by permission of the publishers.

The Republican party, which had figured importantly during Reconstruction, continued on among the white voters in parts of Virginia, North Carolina, and Tennessee, and in certain smaller areas and counties of other Southern states where it still polls a considerable traditional vote and elects local officials, legislators, and members of Congress. The party was also generally supported by those Negroes who could vote until the period of Franklin D. Roosevelt and the New Deal. On the whole, the Republican party ceased to be important in most parts of the South after Reconstruction except as an occasional ally of the Greenback and Populist parties which gave the Democrats serious opposition throughout the South in the depression periods of the 1870's and 1890's.

After the elections of 1900 these third parties disappeared. At about the same time, many of the Southern states by a series of constitutional and legal devices largely eliminated the Negro from participation in politics. Thus, the Republican party was further reduced in importance. State-wide Republican organizations survived, but in all save the states with considerable Republican votes these organizations became machines for choosing and controlling delegations to Republican national conventions and for dispensing federal patronage when the party held the presidency. Thus, for the most part, these organizations became rotten or pocket borough affairs to be manipulated by Republican national leaders like Mark Hanna in 1896 in the nomination of McKinley and by Presidents Theodore Roosevelt and Taft in dictating the Republican nominations of 1908 and 1912. Republican nominating and campaigning functions were de-emphasized except where the party had local areas of strength. In most areas and for most election places the field of elections became frankly recognized as a Democratic monopoly. While incomplete Republican tickets were nominated usually for some of the state-wide and district elective places, the party took little interest in campaigning for their election.

A factor which further solidified the Democratic South in the early Twentieth Century was the full emergence of the direct primary system of nomination which came to be invariably employed by the Democratic party, whether legally mandatory or not, to make state-wide and district nominations, and, therefore, applied to all congressional nominations, and might even apply to the choice of delegates to Democratic national conventions. For one reason or another the Republicans frequently did not hold primaries, and thus the voters tended to drift into the Democratic primaries and to regard them as the elections, which they came to be in effect, since the nominees of the Democratic primaries almost always won in the increasingly neglected general elections. Moreover, about half the Southern primary laws required parties to finance their own primaries, and this obviously proved to be a hardship on a minority party like the Republican. In approximately the same states the law required parties to administer their own primaries. These and other legal handicaps discouraged the growth of the Republican party and caused more and more voters to participate in the Democratic primaries. The run-off primary, which came to be required in many Southern states where a majority choice was not made in the first primary, was a perfect substitute for the general election. Also the white primary rules devised by party authorities to bar Negroes from participation in Democratic primaries proved more effective than the earlier registration and suffrage restrictions in keeping the Negro out of the political picture. In the black belt states, however, "custom" and "common knowledge" largely took care of the situation without need to invoke law or party rule.

This, then, was the shell or container for most of the politics of the Southern states built up by the Democratic party and within which most political decisions were in effect made. That is, United States senators, governors and other state-wide elective officers, and district and county elective officers were in effect chosen in the Democratic primaries except for the mountain areas of Virginia, North Carolina, and Tennessee and in a few areas in other states. Within the one-party system thus developed there evolved within each state a factional system which varied from state to state and served as a substitute for a party system. In Virginia, for instance, conservative and liberal factions came to operate somewhat like opposing parties nominating complete slates all the way from governor to constable, united by common platforms and campaigning like parties. At the other extreme in states like Texas and Florida, no such permanent factionalism developed. The candidates for each office in the Democratic primary came to stand on their own legs, setting up their own campaign organizations, and adopting their own platforms. Most of the real interest in such systems has centered upon the principal state-wide races like those for United States Senate and governor. In most states the Democratic party as such did no campaigning and its primary was really nothing more than a mechanism for electing public officials and scarcely a partisan affair at all.

While Democratic primaries are concerned with congressional, state, district, and county politics, with what at the national level James MacGregor Burns would call the Congressional Democratic party, the South was scarcely less solid at the presidential level for many years. Certainly, between the turn of the present century and 1928 the Republican presidential vote was at a low ebb. In that year, however, the Solid South experienced its first real split and at that level. The split was a real one, with Virginia, North Carolina, Tennessee, Florida, and Texas deserting the fold. Southern Democrats had never before divided in any very serious way over the Democratic nominees for the presidency, not to the extent at any rate of bolting the ticket. In this case the Catholicism of Al Smith, the Democratic candidate, his opposition to prohibition, and his urbanism, were too much for a staunchly Protestant, dry, and still predominantly rural South. The states which bolted were all ones with relatively small Negro populations; Louisiana, Mississippi, and South Carolina with high Negro percentages produced very small Hoover votes. They were perhaps even more intensely prejudiced against what Smith stood for, but they could not go back on the chief reliance, the Democratic party. In the states that bolted it is also true that the largest traditional Republican areas were to be found, and the beginnings of the economic developments which were later to sweep the South were under way. This phenomenal first split of 1928 was engineered by very little Republican effort and converted few voters permanently to Republicanism. Moreoever, its underlying causes were quite remote, for the most part, from those that were to produce the later splits. The conditions which in the thirty-odd years since were to render insecure the superstructure and the very foundations of the "Solid South" had not as yet developed.

STRAINS ON DEMOCRATIC SOLIDARITY

These conditions are familiar to everybody. They have revolutionized the whole country as well as the South—economically, socially, constitutionally, and politically. We need only to mention the Depression, the New Deal, World War II and its continuous aftermath, the Fair Deal, New Republicanism, the New Frontier, and the Nuclear Age to know what is meant. In the South, agricultural diversification, industrialization, population shifts, urbanization and suburbanization have done their work. Wholesale political adjustments have been inevitable. The Negro and the Latin American have made progress politically, labor has become a real power, a great white-collar class has grown up, and many new immigrants from beyond the South have come in with the developments. In many respects these changes have made the South more like the rest of the country.

With this came the general expansion of government power at all levels, with phenomenal increases in the sphere of the national government and a complex intermeshing of national and state government and politics. The fact that the Democratic party, the traditional friend and protector of the South and the historical defender of states rights and rugged individualism, should have been the author of most of these political innovations did not ease the situation in the South or conduce to harmony within the Democratic party in the Southern states. While the "New Deal," the expansions and restraints of wartime controls, the "Fair Deal" and the "New Frontier" have had their friends among Southern Democrats, the traditional loyalty to the party, so strong in the past, could not be expected to survive and flourish with the same vigor. The party shell, certainly, could no longer serve as adequately as a commodious container within which all political struggles could take place.

Obviously all this multiplied the special interests and created many more powerful groups whose demands needed to be satisfied or compromised politically. In a growing community with many new interests and forms of wealth appearing, the predominant tone of politics tends to be conservative, although it is also true that liberal interests emerge to counteract and combat the more powerful conservative ones. This new emphasis on the extremes of right and left produced a more pronounced pattern of conservatism *versus* liberalism. The moderate center remained as the strongest element. In fact, it has even been greatly enhanced in importance, what with urbanization, suburbanization, and the growth of a white-collar class in general. Also, the many changes in agriculture toward diversification and mechanization and the progressive elimination of tenant farmers and unprofitable types of farming have made their contribution to the growth of the political center.

Political institutions and practices are more resistant to change, however, than those in other areas. In spite of all the stresses and strains, those of the South seem to hang on tenaciously and to retain much of their form and spirit. In short, the South still has substantially its one-party system in spite of many alterations and adjustments. Many are the signs that something different is on its way, but the South is adept at applying a delaying process in political matters which reduces greatly the rate of change. The system is by no means what it was in 1928 or even when V.O. Key, Jr. described it in 1949. The changes, however, have been slow in coming and may well continue to be in the immediate future or at least for the remainder of the present decade.

The real beginning of the process of change in the political system of the South and its place in national politics did not fully get under way until the 1940's. In 1932 the South was engulfed in the depression along with the rest of the country, and reacted favorably to the first stages of Roosevelt's New Deal as the country in general did. It provided many outstanding leaders in Congress and elsewhere who were staunch supporters and lieutenants of the President. By 1936 considerable extreme right and left fringe group opposition had developed, some of which came from the South, but when the election of that year was over, Roosevelt was seen to have swept the whole country by an unprecedented landslide. In his second term, he shifted definitely to the left because the business interests had deserted him and leftists had given considerable support to minority groups in 1936. This did not gain him support in the South.

In 1940 the sidetracking of Vice President Garner of Texas and the substitution of the leftist Henry Wallace as the President's choice for Garner's office, as well as his own candidacy for a third term, were not too popular in the South. Moreover, Senator Glass of Virginia had opposed Roosevelt's renomination and Senator Bankhead of Alabama had been Wallace's chief opponent for the vice presidential nomination. Wendell Willkie, the Republican candidate for president, attracted supporters in the South among economic conservatives and opponents of a third term for Roosevelt which resulted in a considerable increase in the Republican popular vote in the South. In 1940 it was almost equal to that of the later Republican vote of 1948.

The first real rift in the South which was to lead to more or less chronic cleavage came in 1944. In this year the Supreme Court of the United States invalidated the Texas white primary in *Smith v. Allwright* which was met immediately in South Carolina by an elaborate attempt to circumvent the decision by repealing all references in the state constitution and statutes to political parties and primaries and thus taking them out from under any restraints of the Fourteenth and Fifteenth amendments. Real Democratic opposition to Roosevelt's nomination for a fourth term developed in some Southern states including Texas, Mississippi, and South Carolina. Here conventions withheld the pledging of party presidential electors pending the outcome of the Democratic National Convention. Conditions were laid down to be met by the National

Convention in return for electors being bound to vote for Roosevelt. These were: restoration of the old two-thirds rule for nominations; rejection of Henry Wallace as nominee for the vice presidency; and a "white supremacy" plank in the Democratic platform. Needless to say, except for the nomination of Harry S Truman in the place of Henry Wallace for the vice presidency, the Convention did not meet these conditions. The rival delegations from Texas were both seated and the State's vote divided between them. The so-called Texas Regulars, who bolted after the Democratic National Convention, ran a separate electoral ticket in Texas pledged to Senator Byrd of Virginia which polled 135,439 votes as opposed to 821,605 cast for the Democratic electors. The South, however, again remained solid. While the racial issue made an entering wedge into the 1944 situation, the opposition within the Southern Democratic party came more from economic than racial issues. The racial issue had never really been forced by Roosevelt and the New Deal. That was to be the work of Truman and the Fair Deal, and it came in 1948. The Negro had been the real cause of the Solid South. The Democratic party had been the chief protector of the Solid South. When it ceased to be, the real split had come. How long would it remain one-party?

The presidential election of 1944 was the last one in which the South gave its entire electoral vote to the Democratic party. In the subsequent ones—1948, 1952, 1956, and 1960, the Solid South if not broken has at least been cracked. In fact after the death of President Roosevelt in 1945 the great coalition he had built up over the country in 1932 and had fairly well held together to 1944 seemed to be in the process of disintegration. Both houses of Congress went to the Republicans in the off-year election of 1946 for the first time in 18 years. If the usual signs held true, this would mean a Republican president in 1948.

Not until 1948 arrived, however, did the South show any serious indication of deserting the Democratic fold. In fact, late in 1947 it appeared as though President Truman might be in serious need of the old-time solid support of the Southern states if he were to remain in office. On December 29, 1947, former Vice President Henry A. Wallace, who had broken with Truman, announced he would seek the presidency on a third-party ticket which presumably would draw off the extreme left wing of the Democratic party. In spite of this defection, on February 2, 1948, the President sent a special message to Congress urging action upon a ten-point civil rights program not designed to hold the conservative Southern wing in line. It was based upon the proposals of his Committee on Civil Rights, submitted to him in October, 1947. The South was soon heard from. In March, 1948, seven of the fifteen members of the Conference of Southern Governors condemned the program and pledged themselves to oppose the nomination of any candidate who did not disavow it. They urged the selection of Convention delegates and presidential electors committed to this line of action. Southern state delegations to the Democratic National Convention were generally pledged not to support the Truman program. In the Convention, after much Southern maneuvering to sidetrack it, an amendment was adopted endorsing the civil rights program and demanding that Congress enact anti-poll tax, fair-employment practices, anti-lynching and anti-discrimination legislation. The Truman platform was thus victorious, and the Mississippi delegation and half the Alabama delegation walked out. Truman was nominated by 947½ votes. Senator Russell, the Southern choice, received a unanimous vote from each Southern state except North Carolina, which gave 13 of its 32 votes to Truman. Thus the Convention was split practically along the Mason-Dixon line, with the radical left of the Northern segment of the party organized into the so-called Progressive party. In the end, however, would the Southern Democrats split off in a solid block? There was not much chance of it.

As it turned out, the Southern revolt of 1948 was from the deep South and not from the rim as in 1928. It soon became organized and took the name of "States Rights Democrats," but was more familiarly known as the "Dixiecrats." In Alabama, Mississippi, Louisiana and South Carolina, it captured the machinery of the Democratic party; in the rest it was forced to assume the status of a third party. Most of the important Democratic leaders over the South refused to have anything to do with it. While the Dixiecrats ran tickets in all Southern states, their electors won only in Alabama (where the regular Democratic ticket was denied a place on the ballot), Mississippi, South Carolina, and Louisiana; in the first three by very large majorities; in the last by a smaller one. Only the states which had bolted in 1928 showed sizeable Republican votes, which was to have been expected, because they long had produced such votes. In this election the quarrel was within the Democratic party. The states which broke with the party were not yet ready to support the Republican candidates. The bolters tried to maintain the fiction that they were not bolting the Democratic party but that it was bolting them. The election of 1948 was a family quarrel among Democrats as was that of 1928. Shifting to the Republican party was still in the future, but its beginnings were soon to come. An amazing result of this election was that against all polls, prophecies, and expectations Mr. Truman was elected to a second term without the benefit of a left wing and a Solid South.

THE SOLID SOUTH CRACKS

Since 1948, the South had never settled back to its customary solidarity and political tranquility. The fifteen years since that date have witnessed more changes than even the previous fifteen and certainly more unsettling to the South's customary ways. Accelerated economic and social developments greatly altered the political outlook and disturbed political behavior patterns more than ever. The developments previously noted in the late thirties and early forties were multiplied: more new industries, more growth of cities, more population shifts, more immigrants from other parts of the country with ideas both liberal and conservative, more middle class, more effective labor and Negro political participation. This meant more complex and intense factionalism within the dominant Democratic party, much more activity on the part of powerful groups, and the emergence of the Republican party as a factor particul-arly in the part played by the South in national politics.

It might have been expected, perhaps, that under all the new conditions aris-ing the peculiar race relationships long established in the South would not remain unquestioned and undisturbed. As a matter of fact, President Truman and his ten-point civil rights program really had set the ball rolling in 1948, followed by the United States Supreme Court putting the *coup de grace* on the white primary in *Rice v. Elmore* and the Dixiecrat movement later in the year. From then on the civil rights question really never died down as a central issue in the politics of the South. The whole complex pattern of racial segregation and discrimination has been attacked and defended in every branch of the na-tional government and of the governments of the Southern States.

The United States Supreme Court's decisions decreeing racial integration in the schools have led to the most continuous and widespread controversy and to varied and elaborate legislative subterfuges in some states designed to get around national policy. Executive action, both national and state, both civilian and military, have entered into the picture. Republican President Eisenhower had his Little Rock and Democratic President Kennedy his Oxford, Mis-sissippi. Latterly, the whole controversy has gone beyond the South and has moved more or less out of the legal and governmental sphere into that of direct action. The practical results, one way or the other, had been so meager that the Negro grew restive and impatient and resorted to a variety of methods of mass demonstration . . .

A most important result of all these economic and ethnic problems of the 1950's and 1960's has been the entry of the Republican party in a bigger and more permanent way not only into the rim but to some degree even into the black belt states of the South. National politics in the South between 1928 and 1948 was to a large extent still confined within the Democratic party and con-sisted of intra-party family quarrels. True, the Solid South was cracked in those two presidential election years. In 1928 five states—nearly half of the eleven—had voted Republican, and in 1948 four had deserted the national Democratic ticket but they had not gone Republican. The first five were rim states; the last four from the black belt. Only two states, Arkansas and Georgia, refused to bolt in both years, and have since refused in all subsequent elections. In the four presidential elections between 1928 and 1948 the provocations were great, but the old Confederacy stayed solid and the six states still held the record of never having gone Republican since Reconstruction.

Beginning with the presidential election of 1952, the Republican party seems to have moved in at the level of presidential politics on a rather permanent basis, because its presidential tickets have piled up immense popular votes in 1952, 1956 and 1960 and have carried some states each election. Four states (Florida, Tennessee, Texas, and Virginia) voted Republican the first year, five (Florida, Louisiana, Tennessee, Texas, and Virginia) the second year, and three (Florida, Tennessee, and Virginia) the last year. Also in 1960 Alabama had six independent electors and Mississippi eight, all of whom voted not for Republican candidate Nixon but for conservative Democratic Senator Byrd of Virginia. While Republican popular presidential votes in black belt states have tended to mount in the last three elections, Louisiana is the only state of this group that has so far gone over the line. The three consistent bolters to the Republican presidential ticket beginning in 1952 have been Florida, Tennessee, and Virginia. They also voted Republican in 1928. Texas went Republican in 1952 and 1956 and also in 1928. North Carolina has not voted Republican since 1928.

To a very large extent the activities in support of the Eisenhower ticket in 1952 were the work of dissident Democrats. "Democrats for Eisenhower" or temporary organizations with some such names came rapidly into existence and bore the brunt of the campaign. In most cases the Republican organization was inadequate to the task. In Texas "Republicans for a day," who favored Eisenhower, in many cases swamped local Republican conventions and in the end took over the State party machinery. Two years later Hodding Carter complained that even in the four states that went for Eisenhower in 1952 (Virginia, Florida, Tennessee, and Texas) very little effort had been made to build up a two-party system even down to the congressional level. In other words, the sweeping victory in these states and big votes even in other states seemed to mean no more than the election of 1928. Would the South return to its normal Democratic loyalty as it had in 1932? Had it merely been swept off its feet by the personality and reputation of Eisenhower?

Analyses of the election of 1952 in the South seemed to indicate, however, that there were possibilities for building up something of a permanent Republican presidential opposition if people who professed to be Republicans or who said they wanted to see a two-party system would get to work. It was noted that a liberal versus conservative alignment was definitely discernible in most of the Southern urban areas. The facts showed that the Eisenhower strength was largely concentrated in these areas in Alabama, Arkansas, Florida, Georgia, Louisiana, Mississippi, North Carolina, Tennessee, and Texas. Only in South Carolina and Virginia was the city support of Eisenhower less pronounced. In some of the cities the pattern of voting was that of a strong Eisenhower vote in the upper income white precincts, a predominant Stevenson vote in the lower income white precincts, and a heavy Stevenson vote in the white laboring class and Negro precincts. The newer and more rapidly developing geographical areas added their strength to the cities in support of Eisenhower—the southern and newer half of Florida and the western, Gulf Coast, and Rio Grande Valley areas of Texas as well as the newly industrialized areas in various other states. Also, the traditionally Republican areas of western Virginia, western North Carolina, eastern Tennessee, and the German counties of south central Texas added their weight. Joined with these elements were the black belt whites in some counties of Alabama, Louisiana, Mississippi, and South Carolina, although similar areas in Georgia, North Carolina, Tennessee, Texas, and Virginia remained loyal to Stevenson.

However, by 1954, it was felt by many that the Eisenhower coalition had disintegrated. Its constituent elements had by no means been converted to Republicanism or to Eisenhower. The vast majority dutifully returned to the Democratic primaries in 1954 and 1956. With the restoration of relative harmony in the national Democratic party in the latter year, many of the urban Eisenhowerites returned to the fold. Most of the Texas voters, for example, who were with the Shivers conservatives in 1952 shifted back to a shaky union with the liberal-loyalists in the 1956 conventions and primaries and shifted again to vote for Eisenhower in the general election. These people were not Republicans, nor were they about to become Republicans. As one writer put it:

The Republicans did not convert the hosts of crusading amateurs who fought for Ike in '52 into a deep-going grass-roots organization, and the Republican "party" in Texas today could hold its caucus in a broom closet.

In fact, the Democratic party in the South had remained as usual huge and all-embracing since 1952; nowhere had the Republican party become a party in any complete sense. It had made little progress in congressional, state and local elections. Even in Florida, North Carolina, Tennessee, Texas, and Virginia, where respectable Republican organizations existed in certain areas, the one-party system still obtained. It was true that in 1956 more Republicans ran for Congress than in 1954 and 1952. They sought election to the House in 38 of the 94 congressional districts in nine Southern states as against 32 in 1954 of which they won seven and 30 in 1952 of which they won eight. In 1954 they gained only two seats and lost one they had won in 1952. In state and local politics, the monopolistic position of the Democratic party remained unassailed. Its primaries were still the determining elections.

Only the presidential break of 1956 was satisfactory to would-be Republican organizers, for it was even better than 1952 when Eisenhower had polled 48 per cent of the Southern popular vote. Now it was 49 per cent and was a plurality. These percentages stood out in strong contrast to Republican Dewey's 26 per cent in 1948 and his 25 per cent in 1944. The location of Eisenhower's support for 1956 followed that for 1952. In 1956 the Republican nominee did best in all states in the metropolitan counties and not quite as well in counties with smaller cities. Between 1952 and 1956 two shifts should be noted. Black-belt whites who were attracted to Eisenhower fell away in 1956, and Southern Negroes moved from a strong Democratic support in 1952 to about a 50-50 split in 1956. It has also been noted that Eisenhower did better in both elections in growing prosperous cities.

Was the presidential election of 1956 another Republican victory to be explained largely on the popularity of Eisenhower? What would happen in 1960 when he could not be a candidate? This was the big question in the late fifties and as the election of 1960 approached. Both major parties put on the most steam ever in the history of national campaigns, and the efforts in the South were far more extensive and intensive than in 1952 or 1956. National Democratic and Republican headquarters looked upon much of the South as

doubtful. Polls indicated several states safe for Nixon, only two or three leaning toward Kennedy and the rest uncertain. In previous campaigns the candidates for president and vice president did not make as many appearances. In
1960 Nixon appeared in every Southern State and Kennedy visited six. Senator
Lyndon Johnson made a whistle-stop tour of eight Southern States covering
2,500 miles, a feat before unheard of in the South. This and the intensive
efforts of Johnson and Speaker Rayburn in saving Texas by a hair's breadth,
are as good an explanation for the election of Kennedy as anything else. Moreover, the campaign of 1960 showed the Southern state and many of the local
Republican party units as better organized and Democratic party organizations
and Democrats for Nixon organizations as more effective than in the previous
two elections.

Most noteworthy for 1960, however, were the facts that the voter increase
was highest in the South and that the Nixon-Lodge ticket of the Republicans
polled around a half-million more votes than the Eisenhower-Nixon ticket of
1956. Moreover, more votes were cast in 1960 for the former in nine of the
eleven Southern states than before; only Arkansas and Louisiana fell behind.
Like the rest of the nation, margins were close in most Southern states and
very narrow in South Carolina and Texas. It is estimated that for the South as
a whole there were 4.6 Republican votes for every five Democratic votes.

In the nation at large it was estimated that Kennedy won 65 per cent of the
vote of the large cities whereas Stevenson in 1956 won only 52 per cent. Even
suburban areas, a source of Republican strength in recent elections, produced
decreased Republican votes. The South followed this trend. The most important explanations for this were the strong Roman Catholic support of Kennedy, most notable in the cities, the solidification of the Negro vote for the
Democrats, and the increased activity of organized labor in getting out the
working-class vote and holding it for Kennedy. To a lesser extent did the religious issue unite the Protestants. Many Protestant ministers wore out the
issue before the campaign was over. Also Kennedy's disarming statements
about his faith overcame considerable Protestant opposition. Kennedy appealed
strongly to the Negroes, while Nixon and the Republican campaigners neglected the Negro voters and muffled the civil rights issue in their eagerness to
win conservative whites. The Eisenhower administration must have appeared
in part responsible for the slow progress of integration. So far as white voters
were concerned, the civil rights issue was somewhat neutralized. Both parties
seemed to take about the same stand in their platforms and in the pronouncements of their candidates. Segregationists, having failed to get much consolation
out of Eisenhower and eight years of Republicanism in the White House,
settled down to contenting themselves with strong statements in state party
platforms and returning to their traditional Democratic loyalty.

It should be noted that there was a greater degree of Democratic harmony
among Southern party leaders in 1960 than there had been in 1952 or 1956.
Arthur Krock attributes to Lyndon Johnson a great deal of the credit for creating this harmony:

Johnson used his great influence to convince every important Southern party leader except Senator Byrd of Virginia that by party regularity they could restrain the "liberal" Democratic majority. Since they also depend on Democratic national victory and the seniority system for their powerful places in Congress and their states organizations, and on local party regularity for the offices they hold or seek, Johnson could use these arguments effectively. Also they "got the strong impression" (quoting one of them) and managed to persuade their resentful constituents, that Johnson would somehow see to it that the extreme proposals they bitterly resented in the Los Angeles platform would never become acts of Congress during a Kennedy-Johnson administration.

Thus the hope of a continued Republican-Southern Democratic coalition in Congress emerged once again as the last ditch defense of the South together with the rule of seniority in a Congress with somewhat diminished Democratic majorities. Hunger for federal patronage after eight years of Republican control of the presidency was a further unifying factor.

There were signs of encouragement for the Republicans in the presidential politics of the South in 1960. The three old habitual bolters—Florida, Tennessee, and Virginia—were again in the Republican column. Texas was extremely close, and in all the other states except Alabama and Mississippi the Republican minority vote was quite large. Also, there were larger votes for Nixon in 1960 than for Eisenhower in 1956 in all eleven Southern States except Arkansas and Louisiana. This last fact definitely expelled the myth that Eisenhower's personality was the chief cause for breaking the Solid South in 1952 and 1956.

Not so encouraging was the Republican record in congressional, state-wide, and local elections in the eight years from 1952 to 1960. While the Republicans had gradually contested more elective places, their accomplishments had not been impressive. During the Eisenhower era, only five United States House seats had been gained. In 1960 none was added. Virginia in that year retained her two, and only Florida, North Carolina, and Texas had one each. There were no Republican United States Senators and the Republican gains in state and local elective places were negligible. It seemed, therefore, by the beginning of the 1960's that two-party rivalry had come to stay in presidential elections, but that in other elections the Solid South was still largely intact and the Democratic primaries were still in effect the elections for most congressional seats and statewide and local elective offices.

A TWO-PARTY SYSTEM?

This situation, however, began to show some signs of change in 1961 and in the results of the congressional and state elections of 1962. The tremendous vote for Nixon in 1960 greatly encouraged Southern Republicans to think that they had a permanent chance thereafter to carry the South in presidential contests. A further boost came in the election of a Republican United States senator in Texas in a runoff of May 27, 1961, to fill the vacancy left by Lyndon Johnson's election to the vice presidency. In this election, John G. Tower won by a vote of

448,217 to 437,874 over interim Senator William A. Blakley. Tower had polled an unprecedentedly large vote against Johnson in the regular election of 1960 (926,653 votes as against 116,367 received by the Republican candidate for United States senator in 1958). Johnson, however, was candidate for Vice President as well as Senator in 1960 and many Texas Democrats resented this dual candidacy. In the special election run-off of 1961 both Tower and Blakley were ultra-conservative, and liberal Democrats were left with no choice, except to refrain from voting or vote for Tower. Presumably many of them did the latter. In any event the election of Tower seems to have been a shot in the arm to Republicans all over the South. Texas Republicans as a result ran candidates in 1962 for many more places than ever, but their victories were disappointingly few. Their candidate for governor, however, drew a very heavy vote, but he had only very recently been converted to the party, having run only in 1960 as a candidate for governor in the Democratic primary.

In November, 1961 a very significant conference of Republicans from 12 Southern States met in Atlanta. It consisted of 130 delegates. The Republican National Chairman, the Chairman of the Republican National Congressional Campaign Committee, and Senator Barry Goldwater of Arizona were present and addressed the meeting. Senator Goldwater was by then considered the South's favorite Republican presidential possibility for 1964. The conference talked much about building up a two-party system and concerned itself chiefly with the coming congressional election of 1962. Much evidence was also produced to indicate that healthy Republican organizations existed in most of the states, that many counties were in the process of being organized by businessmen and many young persons. It was admitted that many of the local leaders were political amateurs. However, much growing enthusiasm and many permanent conversions were reported.

Although the results in the election of 1962 in the South were quite meager so far as actual Republican gains were concerned, there were some reasons for advocates of a two-party system to feel some encouragement. For one thing, the Republicans contested 62 U. S. House seats as against 42 in 1960 and 24 in 1958. Their candidates were, on the whole, abler and more influential people, in some cases converted Democrats of considerable prominence. Their party organization undoubtedly had been extended and improved and their leaders more competent. The Republicans also made a much more extensive effort to win state and local offices.

The results, however, were not impressive. In the congressional elections, the seven Republican U. S. House members held on and four new seats were gained (Florida, North Carolina, Tennessee and Texas). In a number of other districts Republicans lost by narrow margins. In all serious congressional contests, however, the races were between conservative Democrats and conservative Republicans as in the earlier Blakley-Tower case, and where liberal Democrats voted Republican because of hatred for conservative Democrats. One writer believes that this will work to the advantage of a Democratic national administration whose main troubles in the past have come usually from Southern

Democrats in Congress. Defeating Southern Democrats with seniority in the end can only release committee chairmanships for Northern Democrats. He feels also that an ultraconservative bloc of Southern Republican senators and representatives might come to be as embarrassing to Republican leaders as such a bloc often is to the Democrats. It may be noted, however, that the congressional delegations of six states are still solidly Democratic and only Texas has a Republican U. S. Senator. . . .

In the election of 1962 Republican gains in statewide offices were nil even though Republican candidates for governor in Texas and South Carolina polled large votes. The meager legislative gains in a few states were negligible. Practically no dent was made in the Democratic monopoly in local offices. These places are held by people who are mostly moderate, conservative, and reactionary Democrats. They constitute after all the backbone of politics in all the Southern states and are sustained by a deep tradition still strong with many Southerners, and a well-established habit that makes Democratic primaries in effect the state and local elections.

All this would seem to indicate that the South is after all faced with a long slow process toward the realization of a two-party system. There is a great deal of disagreement as to what such a system is or ought to be. Many seem to have a rather idealistic picture of a two-party system as it is supposed to exist and operate outside the South. Some would insist that there can only be a genuine grass-roots two-party situation where both parties function effectively in congressional, state, district, county, and local elections, maintaining effective organizations, nominating candidates, staging opposing campaigns, and winning against each other at fairly frequent intervals. Such a system, however, exists in little more than one third of the fifty states. It exists nowhere in the South. The South seems to have attained the essence of this kind of rivalry so far only on the level of presidential politics. It may never come at lower levels except in some areas of some states. Certainly, no complete transformation will come anywhere by 1970, except perhaps in a few metropolitan counties. The matter that raises the most doubt is the impact of continuing Negro pressure through racial demonstrations and federal enforcement of strengthened civil rights legislation. The rising tide of presidential and urban Republicanism may well be contained within the sharp reefs of law-and-order symbolism successfully monopolized by the Democrats. It is by no means certain that moderate leadership of the state Democratic parties (outside Alabama and Mississippi) will be obliged to surrender to extreme segregationist elements, however much Freedom Marches may increase that possibility. If the disappearance of the one-party South seems no longer in doubt, the development of two-party, competitive politics is still contingent upon the ability of the two rivals to take somewhat ambiguous, not-too-opposed positions on fundamental questions.

URBANISM AND THE NATIONAL PARTY
ORGANIZATIONS *
Francis E. Rourke

AMONG the fondest dreams of the municipal reform movement in this country was the hope of developing an autonomous system of urban politics—entirely divorced from shifting tides and sentiments on the national political scene. From the perspective of urban reform, such a separation was necessary to prevent local elections from turning on national issues and personalities that were quite irrelevant to the needs and problems of the municipality itself. Moreover, there was a widespread conviction that Tammany and a great many other corrupt city machines had been able to strengthen their power by trading on the loyalties of the voter to a national political party of which they were the local representatives. This effort to isolate urban from national politics took the direction of separating the date of local and national elections, or—a more drastic remedy—banishing national party labels from municipal ballots altogether.

On the surface at least the efforts of reformers to effect a separation between local and national politics have met with considerable success. It has today become common practice to hold municipal elections on a different date from national contests. Across the country, but particularly in the West and Mid-West, such elections have become increasingly nonpartisan in legal form. As a recent study of nonpartisanship points out: "During the half-century which has passed since the development of the nonpartisan ballot in the United States the abolition of the party label in local elections has been extended to almost two-thirds of American cities—65,000,000 citizens."

And yet, as Eugene Lee and a variety of other observers indicate, the nonpartisan ballot does not prevent the persistence of strong national party identifications in local elections. Freeman, for example, argues that "institutional devices are not likely to abolish a local two party system in a city where attitudes toward the two major national parties are strongly structured and the relations between national and local party organizations are durable and persistent." The evidence he cites on the experience of Massachusetts, as well as that presented by Lee for California, and Williams and Adrian for Michigan, would suggest that national party alignments remain highly durable and on occasion even decisive factors in urban politics.

* From Francis E. Rourke, "Urbanism and the National Party Organizations," in *The Western Political Quarterly,* Vol. XVIII, 1965, pp. 149–163. Copyright © 1965 by the University of Utah. Reprinted by permission of the University of Utah, copyright owners.

Not least among the institutions that have made it difficult to maintain any hard-and-fast boundaries between national and local affairs are the national political parties themselves. For in the strategies and calculations of these institutions, the actors and actions of national and local politics have, from time immemorial, been indissolubly linked. Success in local gives the promise of success in national politics, both for men and political organizations, and it is not uncommon for a national political reputation to be turned to advantage in a state or local election. Conversely, failure is often regarded as contagious in either direction, and where this appears imminent, national prestige may be employed in behalf of a local candidate, or local power used to shore up an unpopular national ticket.

President Kennedy's appointment in 1962 of Cleveland Mayor Anthony J. Celebreeze as Secretary of Health, Education, and Welfare was widely interpreted as an adroit maneuver in the politics of federalism, designed to strengthen simultaneously (a) the Democratic party in Ohio by the honor thus bestowed upon one of its principal leaders; (b) the Kennedy administration in Washington with voters of Italian extraction across the country who were alleged to be dissatisfied with the recognition thus far accorded to them by the administration; and (c) the candidacy of the President's younger brother, Edward Kennedy, in Massachusetts, locked in a primary duel for the Democratic nomination to the United States Senate and anxious to obtain the support of Italian voters in that state.

Today, the emergence of a national grant-in-aid system for urban communities has opened up new opportunities for the interplay of national and local politics. The nationally sponsored urban renewal program, for example, has provided the resources upon which substantial mayoralty reputations have been built at the local level. Mayor Richard C. Lee of New Haven has won resounding electoral victories at home as well as being catapulted into the national limelight as a result of the urban redevelopment projects he launched with federal financial assistance. In Pittsburgh, Mayor David Lawrence used the same source of support not only to strengthen his political position in the city, but to go on and become the first Pittsburgh mayor ever elected governor of the state. The grant-in-aid program has thus had an innovating effect in promoting political as well as administrative interdependence in the American federal system.

But while local political careers may thus be built on assets made available in Washington, the political resources of urban areas are in turn of no less value to national politicians. It has long been clear to the leaders of each of the major political parties that presidential elections and, to a lesser extent, the balance of power in congressional elections may largely turn on the votes cast in the principal urban centers of the country. The effort of the reform movement to create an autonomous system of urban politics was thus limited from the start by the fact that each of the major parties has an enormous interest in creating and maintaining national party identifications in the major cities of the country. The importance of this national stake in the urban vote, which has long been recognized in the activities of the major parties, was dramatically highlighted by the results of the 1960 presidential election.

THE QUEST FOR URBAN SUPPORT

For many years the Washington headquarters of each of the major political parties has made a continuing effort to cultivate the urban vote in national elections. At the center of this effort in the case of both the Democratic and Republican parties have been the units set up to attract support from nationality or racial groups. As far as the major parties are concerned, the most easily identifiable segment of the urban vote is the vote of so-called minority groups clustered in the major cities of the country. Other urban voters are presumably reached by the party's general campaign effort, or by its specialized attempts to gain support from labor, business, professional, and other occupational groups.

Each of the major parties has made a sharp organizational distinction between its effort to appeal to nationality groups and its attempt to win over the Negro vote. The nationalities divisions of the two major parties appeal to what the national organizations regard as an "ethnic vote," a demographic classification bearing some relation to the Census Bureau's definition of "foreign stock," which includes within its scope residents who are foreign-born as well as those who have foreign parentage. According to the 1960 census figures, over 18 per cent of all Americans are now contained within the category of foreign stock, of whom over 83 per cent are urban residents. The total vote in the country susceptible to being influenced by so-called ethnic considerations is presumably much larger than this, since it is reasonable to expect that many voters born of native parentage may still feel bound to the country of their ancestry by ties of sentiment.

Perhaps as important as any other characteristic of urban ethnic voters is the fact that a great many of them are either Catholics or Jews, for Will Herberg among others has argued that a strong sense of religious cohesion persists among many nationality groups even after their ethnic tie has faded. As Herberg put it: "It is as members of a religious group that the great mass of Americans tend to identify themselves to establish their social location once they have really sloughed off their immigrant foreignness." The returns from the 1960 presidential election lend support to this hypothesis, since in that election Poles, Italians, and other Catholic groups voted heavily for Kennedy, in spite of the fact that as an Irish Catholic he belonged to a community with which these groups were often in bitter rivalry for the achievement of their own political aspirations in major urban centers of the country.

There is, in fact, an important political advantage attached to any appeal to the urban voters of foreign extraction which is based—implicitly at least—upon religious rather than ethnic affiliation. This is the fact that ethnic communities are often in conflict not only in terms of competition for advancement in domestic politics, but also as a result of national antagonisms inherited from the Old World. As both parties have recently discovered, it is extremely difficult to frame a policy on the Oder-Neisse frontier in central Europe which will simultaneously satisfy the German and Polish minorities in this country—not to mention the foreign ministries of West Germany and Poland. An appeal rooted in religion which transcends these national jealousies thus provides an effective means of unifying a large segment of ethnic support.

The national apparatus of each of the major parties is a highly fluid structure, varying from campaign to campaign and from election to off-year activity. But each of the national parties has found a place for a nationalities division in its organizational structure. In the case of the Democrats, it dates back to 1948, in which year it is said to have made a substantial contribution to President Truman's upset victory. The Republicans established a similar unit in their Washington headquarters in 1950. In recent decades, Republican activity in this area has been an uphill effort, since the Democratic party has enjoyed a preponderance of support among ethnic voters living in cities during much of the period since World War I. However, in both of his presidential campaigns and particularly in 1956, Eisenhower was able to make strong inroads within these ethnic communities.

The attempts of the major political parties to attract this so-called hyphenated vote in election years long antedate the establishment of specialized units in national party headquarters designed to attain this objective on a continuing basis. An appeal to the German vote, for example, figured prominently in Republican strategy in the election of Abraham Lincoln in 1860, and similar efforts to win Irish support were not uncommon in subsequent presidential contests in the nineteenth century. Presidents themselves were directly involved in these maneuvers. One of his biographers gives an amusing description of one of Theodore Roosevelt's less adroit attempts to play on the ethnic sentiments he affected to despise:

The dinner, the story goes, celebrated Roosevelt's appointment in 1906 of Oscar Straus as Secretary of Commerce and Labor. The President explained his choice. He had selected Straus without regard to race, color, creed or party. His concern had been only to find the most qualified man in the United States. This Jacob Schiff would confirm. Schiff, presiding at the celebration, good-naturedly senescent, wealthy, respectable, and, regrettably for Roosevelt, now quite deaf, nodded. "Dot's right, Mr. President," he acknowledged. "You came to me and said, 'Chake, who is der best Jew I can appoint Secretary of Commerce?'"

Aggressive as these efforts to woo the ethnic voter have been in the past, they were much less institutionalized in earlier periods than they have since become.

One of the great advantages the Democrats have always had over the Republicans in working with ethnic communities in cities is the fact that the Democratic leadership at the municipal level generally includes far more Americans of foreign stock. Without straining the credulity of ethnic voters, the Democratic party is thus able to picture itself as in some sense the party of the urban immigrant. In 1962, for example, Mayor Wagner of New York was designated as chairman of the Nationalities Division in national party headquarters. This appointment to a high party office of the German-Catholic mayor of the nation's largest city was only a contemporary illustration of the party's long-standing ability to exemplify its concern for the immigrant by pointing to the preferment that "ethnics" have won under the banners of the Democratic party in major urban centers of the country.

The Republicans, on the other hand, suffer from the disadvantage that while they can compete with the Democrats in espousing policies which will presumably be attractive to ethnic voters in cities and elsewhere—as, for example, the liberation of Eastern Europe theme which has figured strongly in the party's election effort since World War II—they have not had an equal capacity in this century to demonstrate their concern for the foreign born by pointing to the immigrants or sons of immigrants to whom the party has given political preferment in municipal politics. As Samuel Lubell put it: "The Republicans, by political necessity, became sensitive to the aspirations of the 'old' immigrant elements, who settled so largely on the farms. The Democrats, in turn, have been more alive to the aspirations of the 'new' immigrant elements who crowded the teeming cities."

To be sure, the Republican party has made impressive strides in some areas in capturing the urban vote by nominating and electing candidates who have their roots in ethnic communities, such as Senator Jacob Javits in New York, and Governor John Volpe in Massachusetts. And there have been Republican mayors—Fiorello La Guardia in New York and Theodore McKeldin in Baltimore—who achieved notable success in identifying themselves with the cause of the ethnic in politics. But the Anglo-Saxon predominance in the party's leadership cadres still remains a problem for Republicans in urban areas. In 1961 Albert B. Hermann, the director of political organization for the Republican National Committee, pointed out to his Republican colleagues that while 60 to 75 per cent of the big city vote was non–Anglo-Saxon, the leadership of the party in these areas was about 90 per cent Anglo-Saxon.

For each of the major parties there is some embarrassment attached to this effort to win a voter's support on the basis of his ethnic affiliation, presumably because it leaves the party organization open to the charge of considering some segments of the population as less than American in their loyalties. This embarrassment is reflected in the effort that is sometimes made to attach labels to these ethnic groups that will avoid the suggestion that the party looks upon them as having "foreign" sympathies.

The Republicans, for example, adopted the expedient of referring to these communities as the "language-culture" groups. Witness, for example, the statement in a 1962 party publication that "consistent efforts should be made to see that party organizations, in distributing such political patronage as may be available, give due consideration to the various language-culture groups." Not to be outdone, the Democrats in the same year announced their intention of rechristening the nationalities section in the national party headquarters the "All-Americans Division." But in spite of this semantic window-dressing, the communications both parties address to ethnic voters are very openly designed to appeal to feelings of national pride or patriotism which attach to their homeland.

Each of the major parties has also maintained a special unit in its Washington headquarters for appealing to the Negro vote. By and large the shape of Negro voting in presidential elections has tended to resemble that of the major urban ethnic groups. Predominantly Democratic in modern times, it shifted somewhat to Eisenhower in 1956, but returned to roll up substantial majorities for Kennedy in 1960 and gave overwhelming support to Johnson in 1964. In congressional elections, the Democratic advantage is equally impressive. All six Negro congressmen today are Democrats.

Generally speaking, the Negro population is somewhat less urban in residence than the principal ethnic communities. According to the 1960 census, only a little more than 72 per cent of Negroes lived in urban areas, as opposed to 83 per cent of the ethnics. However, as the Republican National Committee pointed out in a survey undertaken after the 1956 election: "The Negro voter is an urban dweller. In the Northern States the bulk of the Negro population lives in metropolitan cities. In the South, although a large part of the Negro population lives in rural areas, the voting Negroes live in the cities." In a recent study of Negro voting Oscar Glantz concludes that as a result of the migration of Negroes into northern and western industrial cities, the Negro has achieved "a balance-of-power position in local, state, and national politics."

The size of the ethnic and racial minority group vote for which the two major parties are contending in the major cities of the country is suggested by the Table.

PERCENTAGE ETHNIC AND NON-WHITE POPULATION
15 LARGEST CITIES IN U.S. 1960*

	(1)	(2)	(3)
			TOTAL PER CENT
CITY	PER CENT ETHNIC	PER CENT NON-WHITE	MINORITY GROUP
New York	48.6	14.7	63.3
Chicago	35.9	23.6	59.5
Los Angeles	32.6	16.8	49.4
Philadelphia	29.1	26.7	55.8
Detroit	32.2	29.2	61.4
Baltimore	14.8	35.0	49.8
Houston	9.7	23.2	32.9
Cleveland	30.9	28.9	59.8
St. Louis	14.1	28.8	42.9
Milwaukee	30.0	8.9	38.9
San Francisco	43.5	18.4	61.9
Boston	45.5	9.8	55.3
Dallas	6.9	19.3	26.2
New Orleans	8.6	37.4	46.0
Pittsburgh	30.3	16.8	47.1

* Excluding Washington, D.C.

SOURCE: U.S. Department of Commerce, Bureau of the Census. U.S. Census of Population 1960, U.S. Summary. *General Social and Economic Characteristics,* Table 153, and *General Population Characteristics,* Table 64.

Never in our national political history has either of the major party organizations made a more explicit effort to win over the urban vote than that undertaken by the Democrats in the presidential election of 1960. Certainly no presidential candidate in the party's long history except for Al Smith was more clearly identified with urban areas by personal and political background than John F. Kennedy. Moreover, the platform adopted at the Democratic national convention in that year was the first major party platform to contain specific planks designed to meet the problems of the city as a governmental unit. Party platforms in previous years had dealt with matters of concern to urban dwellers, such as housing, unemployment and public health. But on no prior occasion had the urban community itself received the careful attention bestowed upon it by the 1960 Democratic platform.

In a section of the platform entitled "Cities and Their Suburbs" the party called attention to the fact that "the United States is now predominantly an urban nation," and it promised that a "new Democratic Administration will expand Federal programs to help urban communities clear their slums, dispose of their sewage, educate their children, transport suburban commuters to and from their jobs, and combat juvenile delinquency." Charging the Republican administration with having "turned its back on urban and suburban America," the Democratic platform pledged that "we will give the city dweller a voice at the Cabinet table by bringing together within a single department programs concerned with urban and metropolitan problems."

Soon after the convention, Representative Frank Thompson of New Jersey was designated by the Democrats to head a nation-wide voter registration drive. It was felt that one of the keys to victory would be the ability of the party to register as many as possible of the unregistered voters, particularly in the cities, since the unregistered were believed to be predominantly Democratic in predisposition. A preliminary canvass undertaken by the Thompson organization in one ward in the city of Baltimore showed 3,267 registered and 1,692 unregistered voters, with a substantial majority of the unregistered regarding themselves as Democrats. For a period approximating two months, the Democrats pushed this registration drive with great vigor, and even before the election had taken place, Republican officials were reported as "privately and glumly" conceding that the Democratic effort "scored important gains in the big cities in key states—New York, Pennsylvania, Ohio, California, New Jersey, Michigan."

At the same time Democratic politicians at the local level were said to be somewhat apprehensive over the impact these newly registered voters might have upon primary elections and patterns of control in municipal politics. The disruptive effects that such efforts to organize support in national campaigns might have on local political arrangements had been dramatically pointed up by the New York experience, where the Volunteers for Stevenson organizations in the 1952 and 1956 elections underwent a metamorphosis into reform clubs bent on overthrowing "boss control" in New York city politics—an aim in which they ultimately achieved more than a minor degree of success.

In any event, when the returns from the 1960 presidential election were in, they seemed to provide ample justification for the efforts the Democratic party had made to organize urban support. The Kennedy victory rested heavily upon the majorities he garnered in the major cities of the country. He carried 27 of the 41 urban centers in the country with a population in excess of 300,000. Moreover, of the twelve states having the largest percentage of their population living in standard metropolitan areas, Kennedy carried all save one. And the one he lost, California, went against him by the narrowest of margins only after the absentee ballots were counted. The eleven metropolitan states carried by Kennedy gave him a total of 173 electoral votes of the 268 he needed for election.

The result of this election triggered unprecedented soul-searching within the ranks of the Republican national organization with respect to the urban vote. Kennedy had not yet been inaugurated as President when, on January 7, 1961, the Republican National Committee approved a plan to close the "big-city gap" that the election returns had revealed. Ray C. Bliss, the chairman of the Republican party in Ohio, was named to head a Special Committee on Big Cities, which was assigned the task of improving the party's election prospects in the major urban centers of the country.

The designation of Bliss as chairman of this new group was largely inspired by the fact that the Republican party had, under his direction, done much better in Ohio than in any of the other heavily urbanized states of the East and Mid-West. As a result, Ohio very quickly became a symbol of Republican success in an environment otherwise characterized by dismal failure. In fact, one of President Kennedy's first steps at a post-election conference with his Republican opponent, Richard Nixon, was to ask the Vice President what had happened in Ohio, a state Kennedy had confidently expected to win.

In announcing the establishment of the Bliss committee, Senator Morton, the Republican National Chairman, indicated that it would be composed of "National Committee members who are familiar with big city politics, plus Republican winners who have found the key to victory in metropolitan areas." The committee was set up, he said, to study big-city politics, survey and analyze the formulas that have won, and "tell us what steps have to be taken everywhere to erode the monolithic Democratic big-city vote." If this vote could be reduced, Morton declared, "We'll win a lot of the states we lost by narrow margins last time."

It soon became clear that Republican organization officials were far from agreed as to how this quest for additional votes should be pursued in urban areas. Senator Goldwater, who was then chairman of the Republican Senatorial Committee, publicly asserted that the Republican party should end its vain effort to attract block support from Negro and other minority groups clustered in large cities. This view was quickly disputed by the chairman of the Republican party in New York. In a report submitted to the Special Committee, he argued that the key to Republican failure in urban areas lay in the fact that the party "has not reflected the needs and aspirations of a majority of big-city voters, of whom Negroes are an important group." Referring to Senator Goldwater directly, he declared: "The Senator from Arizona has, I fear, proposed a Republican requiem in the cities when the challenge and the times require a Republican reveille."

When the Special Committee's Report on Big City Politics was released in January 1962, it did not end the dispute over the tactics to be pursued by the Republican party in urban areas. The report laid major stress upon organizational and technical weaknesses in Republican operations in the major cities of the country. The theme of the report, as stated by Bliss, was that the party had been "out-manned, out-organized, out-spent and out-worked" by the Democrats in competing for the urban vote. Graphic evidence of this organizational breakdown was cited by Bliss in releasing the report, including the fact that there were 5,000 urban precincts along the Eastern seaboard from Maine to Maryland in which the party had not had a single precinct worker during the previous election campaign.

The prescription of the Bliss committee for this state of affairs was a strengthening of the sinews of party organizations in urban areas. The Committee recommended the establishment of full-time paid professional staffs in urban political organizations, the maintenance of close relations with labor, business, professional and other groups in urban centers in an effort to recruit support for the Republican party, the organization in the National Committee of a special activities division which would attempt to build support among urban minority groups, and finally a more extensive and better financed use of public relations and political education techniques in urban areas.

Critics of the report were quick to point out that this focus on organizational reform overlooked entirely the importance of shaping a program and a platform designed to carry an appeal for urban voters. Democratic National Chairman John Bailey, for example, commented: "The Republican party can have the Bliss report and any other kind of report it wants, but until they [sic] stand for the things the people in the cities want, their organization won't do them a bit of good."

Some Republican officials were equally skeptical of the value of a report which they regarded as little more than a manual for precinct organization. From New York, the Republican state chairman said with respect to the Committee's organizational emphasis that this was "the same subject on which Republicans have concentrated for the past 20 years without any noticeable improvement in the Republican party." He charged that Bliss and a majority of the Committee members had sat on demands for a discussion of issues that might appeal to the urban voter.

Much of this dispute within the Republican organization reflected efforts by the conservative and liberal wings of the organization to point the party in directions from which they might gain a factional advantage in preparing for the 1964 presidential campaign. Supporters of Governor Nelson Rockefeller in

New York, for example, had a vested interest in urging the party to take stands which might attract urban voters, since this kind of posture would enhance the likelihood that the Republican national convention would give the presidential nomination in 1964 to a governor like Rockefeller who had achieved political success in a heavily urbanized state.

Conversely, conservative Republicans were opposed to reshaping the issues in any way which would make it more difficult to nominate a conservative like Goldwater in the next presidential election. A program geared to attracting urban voters would virtually rule out a conservative candidate in 1964. In essence, therefore, the organizational orientation of the Bliss report was dictated by the necessity of avoiding an open break in the ranks of the party. The authors of the report sought agreement among Republicans on the only terms in which it could easily be secured—the necessity for improved party organization in urban areas.

Following the publication of the Bliss report, the Republican party moved in essentially two directions with respect to the urban vote. In the first place the National Committee attempted to carry out the recommendations of the report by organizing a major effort to win over big-city voters. This campaign was concentrated on the development of better rapport with minority groups. At the same time Republican spokesmen vigorously attacked what they alleged to be the influence exercised in the Democratic party by big-city machines. This tactic, traditional with Republicans in national as well as local politics, was designed to appeal to the anti-machine element in cities, along with the rural and increasingly important suburban voters to whom urban "bossism" was expected to be repugnant.

With the nomination of Senator Barry Goldwater as the Republican candidate for president in 1964, the GOP effort to win over the urban vote focused on such issues as the growth of crime in the streets and parks of American cities, as well as public concern over the racial disorders that had flared up in urban areas in the wake of the civil rights movement. From the perspective of conservative politics, this attempt to fix the attention of the urban electorate upon local issues was sound strategy, since studies have indicated that lower and middle class voters in cities are much more conservative in their political attitudes and behavior on purely local matters than they are with respect to national policy. But neither the Bliss reforms nor the Goldwater strategy achieved much for the Republican cause in urban America. In most of the larger cities of the country the Democratic majorities in the presidential election of 1964 were greater than they had been four years earlier, and Senator Goldwater even lost some cities which Nixon had carried in 1960.

URBAN ORGANIZATION AND POLITICAL STRENGTH

While the Bliss report was well designed to preserve party unity, its exclusive preoccupation with organization as the key to political strength in the cities is open to several objections. In the first place the Republican vote in the presidential elections from 1948 to 1956 had been climbing steadily in most of the big cities of the country under the same local organizational structure that was now being held responsible for the party's 1960 failure in urban areas. Some factors other than organization would thus seem to have played a significant part in the party's poor urban showing in the 1960 presidential election.

Moreover, an analysis prepared by the Republican National Committee following the 1960 election showed that in the principal metropolitan regions of the country the Republican share of the 1960 vote fell off just about as much in suburban areas in which the Republicans had, if anything, an organizational advantage over the Democrats, as it did in the cities in which their organizational resources were so meagre. As the National Committee put it: "The decline of the Republican vote in the big cities was coupled with a decline in their suburbs. In the nineteen suburban areas studied the magnitude of the decline in the Republican percentage of the vote was about the same as in the city adjoining each area."

As a matter of fact, the complete returns from the major metropolitan areas of the country did not entirely support Bliss' contention that "the Republican party lost the 1960 election in the big cities of the country." To be sure Kennedy's victory in 1960 would have been impossible without his urban majorities. At the same time, however, it can be maintained that the Republican party lost the election in the outlying areas as well as the city, since even his top-heavy urban support would not have given Kennedy his victory in 1960 if the Republicans had been able to hold on to the rural and suburban pluralities they had attained in previous elections.

In Maryland, for example, the Democratic vote in the city of Baltimore went from a 37,000 deficit in 1956 to a 88,000 plurality in 1960—the largest majority given any presidential candidate in the city's history up to that time. But this vote only achieved a decisive effect because the Republicans were not able to match their 1956 plurality in the rest of the state of 149,484, or their 1952 plurality of 115,971. Instead, their lead outside of Baltimore fell to 11,777, and it was this decline as well as the Democratic margin in the city of Baltimore which put the state in the Kennedy column in the 1960 presidential election.

The same pattern of voting manifested itself in several other urbanized states dominated by one large city, including Illinois, Michigan, and New York. If Nixon had been able to hold on to Eisenhower's 1956 pluralities in these states in the areas outside of the big cities, he would have been elected President in 1960 in spite of Kennedy's urban majorities. In the end Kennedy's victory in 1960 was a matter of cutting Republican margins in the outlying areas as well as maximizing his support in the urban Democratic strongholds—the politics of subtraction as well as addition.

Finally, it should be noted that a study undertaken by Charles Gilbert found that Democratic support in presidential elections prior to 1964 was not appreciably greater in those cities in which the party was highly organized than it was in those in which the party had no such organizational strength. Gilbert argued that "differences in cohesiveness and effectiveness of local party organizations are not systematically associated with the size of Democratic presidential pluralities or with the degree of local Democratic electoral dominance; in most cities these outcomes appear primarily to depend upon cultural and socio-economic determinants of party identification." Two of the large cities studied by Gilbert (Cleveland and St. Louis) were very strongly Democratic in both local and presidential elections in spite of the fact that the Democratic organization in those areas was regarded as being relatively weak and ineffective.

In any case, the nature of Kennedy's victory in the 1960 election, and the resulting agonizing reappraisal by Republicans of the position of their party in urban areas has tended to obscure somewhat the fact that the Republican party is not altogether bereft of resources in urban America. The growing strength of Republicanism in Southern cities has been well documented. And Republican strength in urban areas is by no means confined to the South. Across the country, Republicans often do better in national elections in Western and farm-state cities than in the Northeastern strongholds of the Democratic party. In the presidential election of 1960, for example, however badly they fell down in urban areas elsewhere, the Republicans still managed to carry such non-Eastern cities as Seattle, San Diego, Indianapolis, Columbus, Phoenix, Portland (Oregon), and Omaha. William B. Prendergrast, the former director of research for the Republican National Committee, explained the difference between Democratic and Republican cities in terms of demographic factors. He argued that "the cities where Republicans are weakest are distinguished from the strongest by having a substantially higher percentage of Catholics, Jews, Negroes and peoples of southern and eastern European origin in their population."

Illustrative also of the existence of a reservoir of urban Republicanism is a table of Republican mayors compiled by the GOP National Committee in June of 1962. It showed Republican mayors in 13 of the 40 cities in the country with a population in excess of 300,000, and in 30 of the 76 cities with a population between 100,000 and 300,000. Many of these mayors were elected on a nonpartisan ballot, and the suggestion has sometimes been made that this nonpartisan system works to the advantage of the Republicans in national as well as local politics by helping to reduce party identification among normally Democratic voters in urban areas. However, the evidence on this point is inconclusive. There are significant differences in turn-out between local and national elections, and there are Democrats who also do well in nonpartisan local contests. In any case there is no clear indication that the vote in national elections is appreciably affected by the kind of electoral system used in local politics.

URBANISM AND THE PARTY BATTLE

From the point of view of the national party organizations, the stakes of urban politics are high. The significance of the big city vote in presidential elections was clearly spelled out in 1949 in an analysis by Samuel J. Eldersveld in which he pointed out that the Democrats would have lost the presidential elections of 1940, 1944 and 1948 without the urban pluralities which they received in each of these contests. As Eldersveld put it: "The big city vote was not a definitive factor in major party success and party supremacy in the twenties.

Since 1932, it has become well-nigh indispensable."

Eldersveld's findings with respect to urban ascendancy in the Democratic party confirmed the prophecy of Charles Beard many years before, that "the center of gravity in the Democratic party is passing, has already passed from the open country to the cities. . . . It is perhaps no exaggeration to say that the Democratic party, founded by Jefferson to represent the agricultural interest, has become the organ of 'the mobs of the great cities' which he feared and despised." Although Beard was writing prior to the 1928 election, most observers credit the presidential candidacy in that year of an Irish Catholic Democrat, Alfred E. Smith, with initiating the strong affinity between the ethnic voter and the national Democratic party that was later to become one of its greatest assets in urban areas. John D. Hicks, for example, has stated: "The election of 1928 marked a significant change in the attitude of the urban masses. Both in 1920 and in 1924, the twelve largest cities in the United States had, taken together, given a decisive majority to the Republicans; now the tables were turned, and the Democrats came out ahead. This, as later elections were to prove, marked the beginning of a long-term urban trend." With the benefit of hindsight, the Republican triumph in the 1928 presidential election looms as one of the most Pyrrhic victories either party has ever won in national politics. And the Democratic gain was not confined to national elections. Gilbert argues that since the 1920's "party identifications mainly oriented to presidential elections have led the way to local Democratic dominance." Moreover, this local dominance has in turn given some urban political leaders in the Democratic party a substantial voice in such national decisions as presidential patronage appointments.

Arthur Holcombe was among the first to call attention to the great impact which urbanization would have upon our national elections. Writing shortly after the 1920 population report of the Bureau of the Census had revealed that for the first time in our history the majority of Americans were living in urban rather than rural territory, Holcombe argued that this population shift seriously endangered the traditional domination of American politics by rural interests. Or, as he was later to say: "the original body politic, with its rural habitat, agrarian pursuits, and rustic way of life, has yielded to a new species of body politic with a predominantly urban habitat, urban occupations, and presumably urban point of view."

Initially at least, it was Holcombe's view that it would be the urban middle class which would exercise primary influence in American politics as a result of this population shift. As already indicated, however, the calculations of the major party organizations have been far different. From their perspective, the critical element in the urban electorate is rather represented by the minority groups concentrated in the large cities. It is these urban minorities—primarily the so-called ethnic and racial groups—which are in a strategic position to turn the tide in the urbanized states upon which the election of a President may well depend.

While the efforts of the major party organizations to win votes in urban areas for presidential and congressional candidates are motivated by considerations of self-interest, they may also be looked upon in a somewhat more altruistic light from the point of view of the results they accomplish. Writing shortly after an outbreak of riots in Philadelphia and New York, De Tocqueville foresaw the day when the growth of cities might represent a source of violent turbulence and instability for American politics. "In cities," he declared, "men cannot be prevented from concerting together and awakening a mutual excitement that prompts sudden and passionate resolutions."

While De Tocqueville's reputation as a prophet is a formidable one, it is not above reproach. Even as each decade has shown a growing concentration of population in urban areas, the urban vote has remained largely confined within the traditional framework of the two-party system, shunning not only revolutionary doctrine but even the third-party ferment by which rural America has so often been agitated. And down through American history, the violence which De Tocqueville feared has been as much a characteristic of rural as of urban politics in this country. Thus, while urbanization has been a source of internal change within each of the major parties, Jefferson's "pestilential city" has not disturbed the basic equilibrium of the political system itself. In the light of De Tocqueville's warning, the efforts of the national Democratic and Republican party organizations to cultivate urban support may thus be regarded as a contribution not only to their own partisan fortunes but also to the stability of American democracy.

URBAN CLEAVAGES *

Edward C. Banfield and James Q. Wilson

WITHIN the cities and metropolitan areas the most important cleavages are those between (1) haves and have-nots, (2) suburbanites and the central city, (3) ethnic and racial groups, and (4) political parties. These tend to cut across each other and, in general, to become one fundamental cleavage separating two opposed conceptions of the public interest.

HAVES AND HAVE-NOTS

Disparity in kinds and distribution of property, James Madison said, is the most fundamental cause of parties and factions in all ages and places. In the city, it is useful to think in terms of three income groups—low, middle, and high. Surprising as it may seem to Marxists, the conflict is generally between an alliance of the low-income and high-income groups on the one side and the

* From Edward C. Banfield and James Q. Wilson, *City Politics* (Harvard and M.I.T. Presses, 1963), pp. 35–46. © 1963 by the President and Fellows of Harvard College and the Massachusetts Institute of Technology. Reprinted by permission of the publishers.

middle-income groups on the other. The reason is not hard to find. The poorest people in the city favor a high level of expenditure for welfare, housing, and sometimes schools, and rarely oppose expenditure for any purpose whatever. They favor expenditures even for services that they are not likely to use—municipal opera, for example—because they pay no local taxes, or hardly any. Upper-income people also favor a high level of expenditures. They want good public services for the same reason that they want good private ones—they can afford them. But they also want good, or at any rate adequate, services for others, and they willingly support—although no doubt at levels lower than the poor would like—welfare services which they themselves will never use. Table I shows how our largest cities vary with respect to this upper-income group; the percentage of families with $10,000 or more income ranges from about 25 to 10 percent.

TABLE I.   CITIES OVER 500,000 POPULATION RANKED BY THE PERCENTAGE OF FAMILIES WITH INCOMES OF $10,000 A YEAR OR MORE, 1960

RANK	CITY	PERCENT	RANK	CITY	PERCENT
1	Los Angeles	25.1	12	Cincinnati	15.8
2	Seattle	22.9	13	Baltimore	15.0
3	San Francisco	22.6	14	Pittsburgh	14.3
4	Washington	21.7	15	Philadelphia	14.2
5	Chicago	21.3	16	Boston	13.6
6	San Diego	20.9	17	Buffalo	13.1
7	Dallas	18.9	18	Cleveland	13.0
8	New York	18.5	19	New Orleans	12.9
9	Detroit	17.8	20	St. Louis	10.8
10	Houston	17.5	21	San Antonio	9.6
11	Milwaukee	16.7			

Source: 1960 Census.

The middle-income group generally wants a low level of public expenditures. It consists of people who are worrying about the mortgage on their bungalow and about keeping up the payments on the new car. Such people are not especially charitable, no doubt partly because they feel they cannot afford to be, but partly, also, perhaps, because they feel that if others are less well off than they it is mainly because the others have not put forth as much effort as they. Many of these people want to spend their money in status-giving ways, and obviously a new car is more status-giving than a new school or a better equipped police force.

The United Auto Workers has tried for years without success to take control of Detroit's nonpartisan government. Detroit is largely a one-industry and one-union town, and the UAW has been extraordinarily successful in state politics, as evidenced by the fact that G. Mennen Williams, the workingman's friend, was elected governor five times. Nevertheless the mayor of Detroit for four terms was Albert E. Cobo, a conservative businessman who opposed public housing and favored economy and efficiency. Why did the working people who voted for

Williams for governor vote for Cobo for mayor? The answer may be that Detroit is a predominantly lower-middle-class homeowning town. In partisan state and national elections, a UAW member votes as a "liberal" because the costs of measures he supports will not be assessed against his bungalow. In nonpartisan city elections, however, he votes as a property owner and taxpayer, and in all probability (if he is white) as one who fears that a progressive city government might make it easier for Negroes to move into his neighborhood.

SUBURBANITES AND THE CENTRAL CITY

The spectacular recent growth of the suburbs and the not unrelated deterioration of the central city have tended to deepen a long-standing line of cleavage between the city and its suburbs. Today many central cities find that their principal antagonist in the legislature is not the rural hinterland but an alliance of the hinterland and the suburbs.

The suburbs are not all of one kind, of course; they are industrial as well as residential, lower-income as well as upper. Not very far from upper-class suburbs where garbage is collected in paper bags and put in fly-proof trucks and where high school teachers are paid as much as many Ivy League college professors, there may be communities (often unincorporated) in which most people cannot afford or else do not want even such basic amenities as sidewalks, police protection, and community sewage disposal. The upper-income suburbanite fears that by annexation or the creation of a metropolitan-area government he may be brought within the jurisdiction of the central city's government and receive a lower level of government service in consequence. The low-income suburbanite also fears being brought within the jurisdiction of the city, but for an opposite reason: it would insist upon providing him with—and taxing him for—services that he would rather do without.

This is not the only basis for the cleavage between city and suburb. Central-city residents often think that the city is being exploited by suburbanites, who use its facilities without paying taxes to it. Because the suburbanite comes to the city to work and shop, the city must spend more than it otherwise would for certain public services—traffic control and police protection, for example—but none of this extra expense, the city resident points out, can be charged against the suburbanite. To this, the suburbanite may reply that by coming to the city to work and shop he creates enough taxable values to make the city a net gainer. He may even assert that it is the suburbanite who is the victim of injustice since suburbs must provide expensive public facilities, particularly schools, even though most of the tax base created by suburbanite spending is in the city. When central cities try to annex suburbs or impose taxes upon the earnings of suburbanites who work in the cities, there is always a howl of protest and usually the effort fails.

ETHNIC AND RACIAL GROUPS

Ethnic and racial differences have been, and still are, basic to much of the conflict in the city. Here it will be convenient to speak of three such lines of cleavage: that between native Protestant and all others, that among the various nationality groups of foreign stock, and that between the Negro and all others.

Although the largest waves of immigration ended long ago, some cities, such as New York and Boston, still have, as Table II indicates, a sizable number of persons of foreign stock. Other cities, such as Dallas, have scarcely been touched by immigration at all.

Until the latter part of the last century, native Protestant industrialists and businessmen ran most cities. Then, in the Northern cities, when the tide of immigration swelled, the newly arrived ethnic groups began to challenge the natives for political control. For a time there was a sharp conflict, but in most cities the natives soon retired from the scene, or, more precisely, they transferred their activity from one sector of the scene to another.

TABLE II.   CITIES OVER 500,000 POPULATION RANKED BY THE PERCENTAGE OF PERSONS FOREIGN-BORN OR WITH AT LEAST ONE FOREIGN-BORN PARENT, 1960

RANK	CITY	PERCENT	RANK	CITY	PERCENT
1	New York	48.6	12	Philadelphia	29.1
2	Boston	45.5	13	San Antonio	24.0
3	San Francisco	43.5	14	San Diego	21.5
4	Chicago	35.9	15	Baltimore	14.8
5	Buffalo	35.4	16	St. Louis	14.1
6	Los Angeles	32.6	17	Washington	12.6
7	Detroit	32.2	18	Cincinnati	12.0
8	Seattle	31.4	19	Houston	9.7
9	Cleveland	30.9	20	New Orleans	8.6
10	Pittsburgh	30.3	21	Dallas	6.9
11	Milwaukee	30.0			

Source: 1960 Census. The term "foreign-born" does not, of course, include Puerto Ricans.

In Boston, for example, the Irish were able to command a majority beginning about 1890 and the native Protestants thereafter ran the city from the state house. Boston's police commissioner was appointed by the governor and so was its licensing board; a finance commission, also appointed by the governor, was set up to make continuing investigations of the city's affairs and was given the power of subpoena. Much of the interference of the legislatures in the affairs of other large cities at this time and afterward reflected the same cleavage between the outnumbered native Protestants and what Mayor James M. Curley of Boston used to call the "newer races."

In a good many cities, where several new ethnic groups competed for control, the old native Protestant elite might conceivably have retained its control by serving—as the Irish so often have—as a neutral force on which all elements of the ethnic struggle could agree. But the elite was incapacitated for this role by its distaste for the political culture of the new immigrant, a distaste that it did not try to conceal. As Peter and Alice Rossi have shown in an unpublished paper on "Bay City," Massachusetts, local politics, which was a source of prestige for the local industrialists until the immigrants became numerous, was "dirty business" afterwards. Accordingly, the old elite turned from elective office and took up instead the control of a relatively new set of institutions, the community service organizations. The local hospital, Red Cross chapter, Community Chest, and Family Welfare Society became the arenas in which the "old families," who of course now asserted that there was no prestige in public office, carried on their public activities.

One can see today in many places elements of informal government that have been produced by this cleavage between the "old family" Protestants and the "newer races." A study in 1947 indicated that in "Jonesville," Illinois, the Rotary Club was handpicking the members of the school board. The interviewer was told: "This school board around here has been looked upon as the private property of the Rotary Club for about twenty-five years. The fact is, the school board has been kind of a closed corporation. . . . The boys decide who they want to run. The fact is, they invite them to run." For at least fifteen years prior to 1947, all members of the "Jonesville" school board were Protestant Republicans; only twice in that period did candidates for the board face any opposition.

The Rossis, who are sociologists, in their report on "Bay City" interpret the change in the character of the old elite's public service as a redirection of its drive for status and recognition. Unwilling to play the status game in the same set with the immigrant, the old elite (according to the Rossis) set up its own game and in effect said that henceforth that was to be *the* game.

We prefer a different explanation. The native middle-class Protestant inherited from his Anglo-Saxon ancestors a political ethos very different from that which the new immigrants brought with them. The ethos of the native could not mix with that of the immigrant, and therefore the natives, who were in the minority, retired to a sphere in which they could conduct public affairs in the manner their culture prescribed.

Richard Hofstadter described the difference of ethos very well in *The Age of Reform:*

Out of the clash between the needs of the immigrants and the sentiments of the natives there emerged two thoroughly different systems of political ethics. . . . One, founded upon the indigenous Yankee-Protestant political traditions, and upon middle class life, assumed and demanded the constant, disinterested activity of the citizen in public affairs, argued that political life ought to be run, to a greater degree than it was, in accordance with general principles and abstract laws apart from and superior to personal needs, and expressed a common feeling that government should be in good part an effort to moralize the lives of individuals while economic life should be intimately related to the stimulation and development of individual character. The other system, founded upon the European background of the immigrants, upon their unfamiliarity with independent political action, their familiarity with hierarchy and authority, and upon the urgent needs that so often grew out of their migration, took for granted that the political life of the individual would arise out of family needs, interpreted political and civic relations chiefly in terms of personal obligations, and placed strong personal loyalties above allegiance to abstract codes of law or morals.

The Anglo-Saxon Protestant middle-class style of politics, with its emphasis upon the obligation of the individual to participate in public affairs and to seek the good of the community "as a whole" (which implies, among other things, the necessity of honesty, impartiality, and efficiency) was fundamentally incompatible with the immigrants' style of politics, which took no account of the community.

The native elite withdrew to the community service organizations because these constituted the only sphere in which their political style could prevail. The boards of these organizations were self-perpetuating; they could not be "crashed" by "outsiders." Because of the nature of their political ethos, Protestants and Jews have been in the vanguard of every fight for municipal reform. In Worcester, Massachusetts, for example, according to Robert Binstock:

> Yankees are the cultural, business, and social leaders—in short, "the first families of Worcester." They are not numerous enough to control the governmental apparatus of the city, yet by forming an alliance with the Scandinavians, they manage to place two representatives on the City Council. The influence of the Yankee within the city government is limited, but participation in a strong and active citizens association, the CEA, enables this group to enlarge its role in the political process.
>
> The Jews, more often than not, are political allies of the Yankees and Scandinavians. . . .

Conflict as between one immigrant ethnic group and another has tended to be over "recognition"—the prestige that accrues to a nationality group when one of its members is elected to public office. Since in the nature of the case there cannot be enough recognition to go around (if all were equally recognized, none would be recognized at all), the question of which groups are to get it must inevitably lead to conflict. The avidity of the "newer" ethnic groups to see their kind in office has been, and still is, of great importance, both as a motive force in the political system and because of certain incidental effects.

When one recalls the contempt with which "micks," "wops," and "polacks" were once—and to some extent still are—treated by some other Americans, no further explanation of the appeal of ethnic "recognition" is needed. But an additional reason is that ethnic politics, like sports, entertainment, and crime, provided a route of social mobility to people who were to a large extent excluded from power in business and industry. Mayor Daley of Chicago was born behind the stockyards. John E. Powers, the president of the Massachusetts Senate, began life as a clam digger.

One would expect that as the "newer" ethnic groups became assimilated to the middle class, they would become assimilated to the Anglo-Saxon Protestant political ethos as well, and that their interest in ethnic politics would decline accordingly. This seems to be happening, but at different rates among different groups. Jews, particularly those in the reform tradition, seem to acquire the Protestant political ethos very readily. It is interesting that the Jews have not sought ethnic "recognition" in city politics to the extent that other groups have. It may be that they have never doubted their worth as a group, and therefore

have not felt any need for public reassurance. More likely, however, their political ethos is such that a politics of ethnic appeal strikes them, as it does the
Anglo-Saxon Protestant, as uninteresting and even immoral.

Other ethnic groups also seem to be taking on the middle-class political ethos,
but to be doing it more slowly. Third-generation Poles, for example, usually
show a decided preference for Polish candidates, and third-generation Italians
usually prefer Italian candidates. Middle-class Irish Catholics who seem entirely to have shed the mentality that caused the immigrant to vote on the basis
of personal loyalty to a ward politician are nevertheless rarely found in the
ranks of the civic reformers; these are almost all Protestants and Jews.

Where the taste for ethnic recognition persists, it is for a special kind of recognition, however. The candidate must not be *too* Polish, *too* Italian, or *too* Irish
in the old style. The following description of Jewish candidates in Worcester
suggests the trend:

> Israel Katz, like Casdin, is a Jewish Democrat now serving his fourth term on
> the Worcester City Council. Although he is much more identifiably Jewish than
> Casdin, he gets little ethnic support at the polls; there is a lack of rapport between
> him and the Jewish voter. The voter apparently wants to transcend many features
> of his ethnic identification and therefore rejects candidates who fit the stereotype
> of the Jew too well. Casdin is an assimilated Jew in Ivy-League clothes; Katz, by
> contrast, is old world rather than new, clannish rather than civic-minded, and penny-
> pinching rather than liberal. Non-Jews call Katz a "character," Casdin a "leader."
> It is not too much to say that the Jews, like other minorities, want a flattering, not
> an unflattering, mirror held up to them.

Apparently, nowadays, the nationality-minded voter prefers candidates who
represent the ethnic group but at the same time display the attributes of the
generally admired Anglo-Saxon model. The perfect candidate, then, is of Jewish, Polish, Italian, or Irish extraction and has the speech, dress, manner, and
the public virtues—honesty, impartiality, and devotion to the public interest
—of the upper-class Anglo-Saxon.

The cleavage between white and Negro is pervasive in city politics. Until
World War II, few Northern cities had many Negroes. As we have already
seen, the Negro population of most Northern cities now is growing at a very
rapid rate, partly from natural increase and partly from migration from the
rural South. The new arrivals go into the Negro slum, which almost everywhere is the oldest part of the central city, where housing has been swept by
successive waves of low-status and low-income migrants. For many years restrictive covenants, written into deeds and prohibiting sale of property to Negroes, made it difficult or impossible for Negroes to buy in districts that were
not already Negro; their districts therefore became more and more crowded.
But after 1948, when the Supreme Court declared such covenants to be un-
enforceable in the courts, the Negro community began to spread more rapidly.

In many Northern cities, the question of where Negroes are to live lies behind almost every proposal for civic action. Will locating a major highway here

prevent them from "invading" that white neighborhood? And where will those Negroes who are displaced by an urban renewal project resettle? If a school or a hospital is placed here or there, will it bring Negroes to the neighborhood? And if it does, will the neighborhood eventually "tip" and become all Negro?

Many whites have fled to the suburbs to get away from the Negroes. One reason why many suburbanites want to remain politically separate from the central city is that they think this will make it easier for them to resist "invasion" by Negroes.

In all this, upper-class Negroes exhibit much the same attitude as do whites. Everything that we have said of the reaction of whites to Negroes can also be said of the reaction of upper-class Negroes to lower-class ones.

POLITICAL PARTIES

The central cities are almost all heavily Democratic; the suburbs tend to be heavily Republican, although there are many exceptions, and their Republicanism is nowhere near as solid or stable as the Democracy of the central cities.

The Democratic ascendancy is so great in most central cities that cleavage along party lines within the cities is not of great practical importance. Party cleavage is important, however, in matters that involve both the central city and the area which lies outside of it. Table III shows how the biggest cities voted in the Presidential election of 1960.

About 60 percent of all cities (but fewer large ones) are nonpartisan, which means that candidates are not chosen in party primaries and are not identified by party on the ballot. In some places, there are purely local parties—the "blues" and the "yellows," so to speak—and in other places local politics is carried on without anything that could properly be called a party (it is "unorganized"). Some cities are nominally nonpartisan and actually partisan (Chicago is an example) and others are nominally partisan and actually nonpartisan in the sense of having no connection with the *national* parties (La Guardia, for exam-

TABLE III. CITIES OVER 500,000 POPULATION* RANKED BY THE DEMOCRATIC PERCENTAGE OF THEIR 1960 PRESIDENTIAL VOTE

RANK	CITY	PERCENT	RANK	CITY	PERCENT
1	Boston	74.7	9	Baltimore	63.9
2	Detroit	71.0	10	Chicago	63.6
3	Cleveland	70.9	11	New York	62.8
4	Philadelphia	68.1	12	Milwaukee	61.8
5	Pittsburgh	67.0	13	San Francisco	58.0
6	St. Louis	66.6	14	Cincinnati	50.4
7	New Orleans	64.9	15	Seattle	48.8
8	Buffalo	64.9			

* No data available on Dallas, Houston, Los Angeles, San Antonio, or San Diego. Residents of Washington, D.C., could not vote.

Source: Richard M. Scammon, *American Votes 4* (Pittsburgh: University of Pittsburgh Press, 1962).

ple, was a nominal Republican who ran on a Fusion ticket, and so was in this sense nonpartisan).

The most interesting thing about party, with respect to the present analysis, is that it is an *artificially-created* cleavage which cuts across all other cleavages and often supersedes them in importance: party "regularity" requires that the voter ignore all cleavages except the party one. The party cleavage *has* to cut across others because in the nature of things there are no general organizing principles under which all cleavages can be subsumed. The nearest thing to general organizing principles, perhaps, are "conservatism" and "liberalism." But the cleavages in the city do not fall logically into this or any other pattern; each side of each cleavage stands by itself and ought, in logic, to have its own party. The attachment to party, then, *must* cut across issues. If people were divided into fat men and lean (or Guelfs and Ghibellines, as in medieval Florence) and party feeling were than whipped up, the result would be not unlike the American political party. Indeed, in Salt Lake City the party division is said to have been formed in a way as arbitrary as this. The Mormon hierarchy, obliged to liquidate its church political party when it was admitted to the Union, is said to have told people on one side of the street to vote Republican and those on the other side to vote Democratic. Their descendants, some people insist, still vote the same way.

M. I. Ostrogorski wrote on the development of American parties:

The problems preoccupying public opinion being numerous and varied, it was necessary, instead of grouping the men in accordance with the issues, to adapt the issues to fixed groups of men. With this object confusion of the questions of the day was erected into a system; they were huddled together into "omnibus" programmes; they were put one on top of another; they were shuffled like a pack of cards, some being played at one time and some at another; at a pinch those which caused irreconcilable divergencies were made away with.

This suggests something about the social function of cleavage in general. If cleavages run across each other (so to speak), they may serve to moderate conflict and to prevent "irreconcilable divergencies," because those who are enemies with respect to cleavage *a* are close allies with respect to cleavage *b* and indifferent (and therefore in a position to mediate) with respect to cleavage *c*. The "artificial" cleavage represented by party is especially functional in this respect because it cuts across *all* other cleavages. What Ostrogorski regarded as defects may therefore be great virtues.

Although logically all of these cleavages—between the haves and have-nots, the suburbanites and the central city, the natives and the immigrants, and the major political parties—are separate and often cross-cutting, there is a tendency for them to coalesce into two opposed patterns. These patterns reflect two conceptions of the public interest that are widely held. The first, which derives from the middle-class ethos, favors what the municipal reform movement has always defined as "good government"—namely efficiency, impartiality, honesty, planning, strong executives, no favoritism, model legal codes, and strict enforcement of laws against gambling and vice. The other conception of the public interest (one never explicitly formulated as such, but one all the same) derives from the "immigrant ethos." This is the conception of those people who identify with the ward or neighborhood rather than the city "as a whole," who look to politicians for "help" and "favors," who regard gambling and vice as, at worst, necessary evils, and who are far less interested in the efficiency, impartiality, and honesty of local government than in its readiness to confer material benefits of one sort or another upon them. In the largest, most heterogeneous of our cities, these two mentalities stand forth as distinctly as did those which, in another context, caused Disraeli to write of "The Two Nations."

THE CHANGING PATTERN OF URBAN PARTY
POLITICS *
Fred I. Greenstein

HIGHLY organized urban political parties are generally conceded to be one of America's distinctive contributions to mankind's repertory of political forms. Just as the two major national parties in the United States are almost universally described in terms of their *dis*organization—their lack of an authoritative command structure—the municipal parties have, until recently, been characterized by most observers in terms of their hierarchical strength. E. E. Schattschneider once summarized this state of affairs in the memorable image of a truncated pyramid: a party system which is weak and ghostlike at the top and solid at the bottom.

This essay deals with the disciplined, largely autonomous local political parties which sprang up in many American cities in the nineteenth century. Much of the literature on these political configurations is heavily pejorative, concerned more with excoriation than explanation. Even the basic nomenclature, "boss" and "machine," is laden with negative connotations, although recently there has been a turn toward nostalgic romanticization of the "vanishing breed" of city bosses.

Here, for reasons which I shall indicate, the attempt shall be to delineate rather than to pass moral judgment: What was the nature of old-style urban party organization? Why did this political pattern develop and how did it operate? What contributed to its short-run persistence in the face of reform

* From Fred I. Greenstein, "The Changing Pattern of Urban Party Politics," in *The Annals*, May, 1964, pp. 2–13. © 1964 by the American Academy of Political and Social Science. Reprinted by permission of Professor Greenstein and the editors.

campaigns? Under what circumstances have such organizations disappeared and under what circumstances have they continued into the present day—or even undergone renaissances? What are the present-day descendants of old-style urban party organizations?

Analytic delineation invariably involves oversimplification. This is doubly necessary in the present case, because our knowledge of the distribution of types of local party organization is scant. We have no census of local political parties, either for today or for the putative heyday of bosses and machines. And there is reason to believe that observers have exaggerated the ubiquity of tightly organized urban political parties in past generations, as well as underestimated somewhat their contemporary prevalence.

OLD-STYLE PARTY ORGANIZATION:
DEFINITIONAL CHARACTERISTICS

Ranney and Kendall have persuasively argued that the imprecision and negative connotations of terms like "boss" destroy their usefulness. What, beyond semantic confusion, they ask, can come from classifying politicians into "bosses" versus "leaders"? Such a distinction leads to fruitless preoccupation with the purity of politicians' motives rather than the actuality of their behavior; it overestimates the degree to which figures of the past such as Richard Croker, William Tweed, and Frank Hague were free of public constraints; and it obscures the fact that *all* effective political leaders, whether or not they are popularly labeled as bosses, use quite similar techniques and resources.

Granting these points, it still seems that a recognizable and noteworthy historical phenomenon is hinted at by the venerable terms "boss" and "machine." If the overtones of these terms make us reluctant to use them, we might simply speak of an "old style" of party organization with the following characteristics:

(1) There is a disciplined party hierarchy led by a single executive or a unified board of directors.

(2) The party exercises effective control over nomination to public office, and, through this, it controls the public officials of the municipality.

(3) The party leadership—which quite often is of lower-class social origins —usually does not hold public office and sometimes does not even hold formal party office. At any rate, official position is not the primary source of the leadership's strength.

(4) Rather, a cadre of loyal party officials and workers, as well as a core of voters, is maintained by a mixture of material rewards and *nonideological* psychic rewards—such as personal and ethnic recognition, camaraderie, and the like.

THE RISE OF OLD STYLE
PARTY ORGANIZATION

This pattern of politics, Schattschneider comments, "is as American as the jazz band . . . China, Mexico, South America, and southern Italy at various times have produced figures who played roles remotely like that of the American boss, but England, France, Germany, and the lesser democracies of Europe have exhibited no tendency to develop this form of political organization in modern times." What then accounted for the development of old-style party organization in the United States?

The Crokers, Tweeds, and Hagues and their organizations probably could not have arisen if certain broad preconditions had not existed in American society and culture. These include the tradition of freewheeling individualism and pragmatic opportunism, which developed in a prosperous, sprawling new society unrestrained by feudalism, aristocracy, monarchy, an established Church, and other traditional authorities. This is the state of affairs which has been commented on by countless observers, even before de Tocqueville, and which has been used to explain such disparate phenomena as the failure of socialism to take hold in the United States, the recurrence of popularly based assaults on civil liberties, and even the peculiarly corrosive form which was taken by American slavery.

It also is possible to identify five more direct determinants of the form that urban party organization took in the nineteenth century, three of them consequences of the Industrial Revolution and two of them results of political institutions and traditions which preceded industrialization.

Massive Urban Expansion. Over a relatively brief span of years, beginning in the mid-nineteenth century, industrial and commercial growth led to a spectacular rise in the number and proportion of Americans concentrated in cities. A thumbnail sketch of urban expansion may be had by simply noting the population of urban and rural areas for each of the twenty-year periods from 1840 to 1920:

	URBAN POPULATION	RURAL POPULATION
	(in millions)	
1840	1.8	15.2
1860	6.2	25.2
1880	14.1	36.0
1900	30.1	45.8
1920	54.2	51.6

These statistics follow the old Census Bureau classification of areas exceeding 2,500 in population as urban. Growth of larger metropolitan units was even more striking. In 1840 slightly over 300,000 Americans lived in cities—or, rather, a single city, New York—with more than a quarter of a million residents; by 1920 there were twenty-four cities of this size, containing approximately 21 million Americans.

The sheer mechanics of supporting urban populations of this magnitude are, of course, radically different from the requirements of rural life. There must be extensive transportation arrangements; urban dwellers are as dependent upon a constant inflow of food and other commodities as an infant is on the ministrations of adults. A host of new administrative functions must be performed as the population becomes urbanized: street construction and maintenance, bridges, lighting, interurban transportation, sanitary arrangements, fire-fighting, police protection, and so forth. Overwhelming demands suddenly are placed on governments which, hitherto, were able to operate with a minimum of effort and activity.

Disorganized Forms of Urban Government. The forms of government which had evolved in nineteenth-century America were scarcely suitable for meeting the demands of mushrooming cities. Governmental structures reflected a mixture of Jacksonian direct democracy and Madisonian checks and balances. Cities had a multitude of elected officials (sometimes they were elected annually), weak executives, large and unwieldy councils and boards. The formal organization of the cities placed officials in a position permitting and, in fact, encouraging them to checkmate each other's efforts to make and execute policies. Since each official was elected by appealing to his own peculiar constituency and had little incentive to co-operate with his associates, the difficulties caused by the formal limitations of government were exacerbated. In a period when the requirements for governmental action were increasing geometrically, this was a prescription for chaos.

Needs of Businessmen. A third aspect of mid-nineteenth-century American society which contributed to the formation of old-style party organizations was the needs of businessmen. There was an increasing number of merchants, industrialists, and other businessmen, licit and illicit, who needed—and were willing to pay for—the appropriate responses from city governments. Some businessmen wanted to operate unrestrained by municipal authority. Others desired street-railway franchises, paving contracts, construction work, and other transactions connected with the very growth of the cities themselves.

Needs of Dependent Populations. The needs of the bulk of the nineteenth-century urban population were not for profits but for the simple wherewithal to survive and maintain a modicum of dignity. It is difficult in the relatively affluent society of our day to appreciate the vicissitudes of urban life several generations ago: the low wages, long hours, tedious and hazardous working conditions, and lack of security which were the lot of most citizens. Even for native-born Americans, life often was nasty and brutish. But many urbanites were first- and second-generation immigrants who, in addition to their other difficulties, had to face an alien culture and language. Between the Civil War and the First World War, the United States managed somehow to absorb 25 million foreigners.

Unrestricted Suffrage. Urban dwellers were not totally without resources for their own advancement. The American tradition of unrestricted male franchise was, in the long run, to work to their advantage. Although it doubtless is true that few city dwellers of the day were aware of the importance of their right to vote, politicians *were* aware of this. Because even the lowliest of citizens was, or could become, a voter, a class of politicians developed building upon the four conditions referred to above: the requirements of organizing urban life, the inability of existing governments to meet these requirements, and the presence of businessmen willing to pay for governmental services and of dependent voting populations in need of security from the uncertainties of their existence.

The old-style urban party leader was as much a product of his time and social setting as was the rising capitalist of the Gilded Age. Building on the conditions and needs of the day, the politician had mainly to supply his own ingenuity and co-ordinating ability in order to tie together the machinery of urban government. If a cohesive party organization could control nominations and elect its own agents to office, the formal fragmentation of government no longer would stand in the way of municipal activity. The votes of large blocs of dependent citizens were sufficient to control nominations and win elections. And the financial support of those who sought to transact business with the city, as well as the revenues and resources of the city government, made it possible to win votes. The enterprising politician who could succeed in governing a city on this basis was a broker *par excellence;* generous brokers' commissions were the rule of the day.

The importance of out-and-out vote-buying on election day as a source of voter support can easily be overestimated. Party organizations curried the favor of voters on a year-long basis. In a day when "better" citizens espoused philosophical variants of Social Darwinism, urban politicians thought in terms of an old-fashioned conception of the welfare state. In the familiar words of Tammany sachem George Washington Plunkitt:

What holds your grip on your district is to go right down among the poor families and help them in the different ways they need help. I've got a regular system for this. If there's a fire in Ninth, Tenth or Eleventh Avenue, for example, any hour of the day or night, I'm usually there with some of my election district captains as soon as the fire engines. If a family is burned out I don't ask whether they are Republicans or Democrats, and I don't refer them to the Charity Organization Society, which would investigate their case in a month or two and decide they were worthy of help about the time they are dead from starvation. I just get quarters for them, buy clothes for them if their clothes were burned up, and fix them up 'til they get things runnin' again. It's philanthropy, but it's politics, too—mighty good politics. Who can tell how many votes one of these fires bring me? The poor are the most grateful people in the world, and, let me tell you, they have more friends in their neighborhoods than the rich have in theirs.

With numerous patronage appointees (holders not only of city jobs but also of jobs with concerns doing business with the city), party organizations could readily administer this sort of an informal relief program. And, unlike many latter-day charitable and governmental relief programs, the party's activities did not stop with the provision of mere physical assistance.

I know every man, woman and child in the Fifteenth District, except them that's been born this summer—and I know some of them, too. I know what they like and what they don't like, what they are strong at and what they are weak in, and I reach them by approachin' at the right side.

For instance, here's how I gather in the young men. I hear of a young feller that's proud of his voice, thinks that he can sing fine. I ask him to come around to Washington Hall and join our Glee Club. He comes and sings, and he's a follower of Plunkitt for life. Another young feller gains a reputation as a baseball player in a vacant lot. I bring him into our baseball club. That fixes him. You'll find him workin' for my ticket at the polls next election day. Then there's the feller that likes rowin' on the river, the young feller that makes a name as a waltzer on his block, the young feller that's handy with his dukes—I rope them all in by givin' them opportunities to show themselves off. I don't trouble them with political arguments. I just study human nature and act accordin'.

This passage reflects some of the ways in which party activities might be geared to the *individual* interests of voters. *Group* interests were at least as important. As each new nationality arrived in the city, politicians rather rapidly accommodated to it and brought it into the mainstream of political participation. Parties were concerned with the votes of immigrants virtually from the time of their arrival. Dockside naturalization and voter enrollment was not unknown.

But if the purpose of the politicians was to use the immigrants, it soon became clear that the tables could be turned. In Providence, Rhode Island, for example, a careful study of the assimilation of immigrant groups into local politics shows that, within thirty years after the arrival of the first representative of a group in the city, it began to be represented in the councils of one or both parties. Eventually, both of the local parties came to be dominated by representatives of the newer stocks. Thus, in 1864 no Irish names appear on the lists of Democratic committeemen in Providence; by 1876 about a third of the names were Irish; by the turn of the century, three-quarters were Irish. In time, the Republican party became the domain of politicians of Italian ancestry. Perhaps the most dramatic example to date of urban party politics as an avenue of upward social mobility was in the antecedents of President Kennedy, whose great-grandfather was an impoverished refugee of the Irish potato famine, his grandfather a saloon keeper and a classical old-time urban political leader, his father a multimillionnaire businessman, presidential advisor, and ambassador to the Court of St. James's.

When the range of consequences of old-time party organizations is seen, it becomes apparent why moral judgments of "the boss and the machine" are likely to be inadequate. These organizations often were responsible for incredible corruption, but they also—sometimes through the very same activities —helped incorporate new groups into American society and aided them up the social ladder. The parties frequently mismanaged urban growth on a grand scale, but they *did* manage urban growth at a time when other instrumentalities for governing the cities were inadequate. They plied voters, who might otherwise have organized more aggressively to advance their interests, with Thanksgiving Day turkeys and buckets of coal. But, by siphoning off discontent and softening the law, they probably contributed to the generally pacific tenor of American politics. It seems fruitless to attempt to capture this complexity in a single moral judgment. One can scarcely weigh the incorporation of immigrant groups against the proliferation of corruption and strike an over-all balance.

WHY REFORMERS WERE
"MORNIN' GLORIES"

Stimulated by high taxes and reports of corruption and mismanagement on a grand scale, antiboss reform movements, led by the more prosperous elements of the cities, became increasingly common late in the nineteenth century. Compared with the regular party politicians of their day, reformers were mere fly-by-night dilettantes—"mornin' glories." They lacked the discipline and the staying power to mount a year-long program of activities. Perhaps more important, the values of the reformers were remote from—in fact, inconsistent with—the values of the citizens whose support would be needed to keep reform administrations in office. Reformers ordinarily saw low taxes and business-like management of the cities as the exclusive aim of government. To the sweatshop worker, grinding out a marginal existence, these aims were at best meaningless, at worst direct attacks on the one agency of society which seemed to have his interests at heart.

THE DECLINE OF OLD-STYLE
PARTY ORGANIZATION

Although in the short run old-style party organizations were marvelously immune to the attacks of reformers, in recent decades the demise of this political form has been widely acclaimed. Because of the absence of reliable trend data, we cannot document "the decline of the machine" with precision. The decline does seem to have taken place, although only partly as a direct consequence of attempts to reform urban politics. Events have conspired to sap the traditional resources used to build voter support and to make voters less interested in these resources which the parties still command.

Decline in the Resources of Old-Style Urban Politicians. Most obviously, job patronage is no longer available in as great a quantity as it once was. At the federal level and in a good many of the states (as well as numerous cities), the bulk of jobs are filled by civil service procedures. Under these circumstances, the most a party politician may be able to do is seek some minor form of preferment for an otherwise qualified job applicant. Furthermore, the technical requirements of many appointive positions are sufficiently complex to make it inexpedient to fill them with unqualified personnel. And private concerns doing business with the cities are not as likely to be sources of patronage in a day when the franchises have been given out and the concessions granted.

Beyond this, many modern governmental techniques—accounting and auditing requirements, procedures for letting bids, purchasing procedures, even the existence of a federal income tax—restrict the opportunities for dishonest and "honest" graft. Some of these procedures were not instituted with the explicit purpose of hampering the parties. Legislation designed deliberately to weaken parties *has,* however, been enacted—for example, nomination by direct primary and nonpartisan local elections, in which party labels are not indicated on the ballot. Where other conditions are consistent with tight party organization, techniques of this sort seem not to have been especially effective; old-style parties are perfectly capable of controlling nominations in primaries, or of persisting in formally nonpartisan jurisdictions. But, together with the other party weakening factors, explicit antiparty legislation seems to have taken its toll.

Decline of Voter Interest in Rewards Available to the Parties. Even today it is estimated that the mayor of Chicago has at his disposal 6,000 to 10,000 city patronage jobs. And there are many ways of circumventing good government, antiparty legislation. An additional element in the decline of old-style organization is the increasing disinterest of many citizens in the rewards at the disposal of party politicians. Once upon a time, for example, the decennial federal census was a boon to those local politicians whose party happened to be in control of the White House at census time. The temporary job of door-to-door federal census enumerator was quite a satisfactory reward for the party faithful. In 1960 in many localities, party politicians found census patronage more bother than boon; the wages for this task compared poorly with private wages, and few voters were willing to put in the time and leg work. Other traditional patronage jobs—custodial work in city buildings, employment with departments of sanitation, street repair jobs—were becoming equally undesirable, due to rising levels of income, education, and job security.

An important watershed seems to have been the New Deal, which provided the impetus, at state and local levels as well as the federal level, for increased governmental preoccupation with citizen welfare. The welfare programs of party organizations were undercut by direct and indirect effects of social security, minimum wage legislation, relief programs, and collective bargaining. And, as often has been noted, the parties themselves, by contributing to the social rise of underprivileged groups, helped to develop the values and aspirations which were to make these citizens skeptical of the more blatant manifestations of machine politics.

VARIETIES OF CONTEMPORARY
URBAN POLITICS

Nationally in 1956, the Survey Research Center found that only 10 per cent of a cross section of citizens reported being contacted personally by political party workers during that year's presidential campaign. Even if we consider only nonsouthern cities of over 100,000 population, the percentage is still a good bit less than 20. This is a far cry from the situation which would obtain if party organizations were well developed and assiduous. But national statistics conceal a good bit of local variation. A survey of Detroit voters found that only 6 per cent of the public remembered having been approached by political party workers; in fact, less than a fifth of those interviewed even knew that there *were* party precinct officials in their district. Reports from a number of other cities—for example, Seattle and Minneapolis—show a similar vacuum in party activity.

In New Haven, Connecticut, in contrast, 60 per cent of the voters interviewed in a 1959 survey reported having been contacted by party workers. The continuing importance of parties in the politics of this municipality has been documented at length by Robert A. Dahl and his associates. New Haven's Mayor Richard C. Lee was able to obtain support for a massive urban redevelopment program, in spite of the many obstacles in the way of favorable action on such programs elsewhere, in large part because of the capacity of an old-style party organization to weld together the government of a city with an extremely "weak" formal charter. Lee commanded a substantial majority on the board of aldermen and, during the crucial period for ratification of the program, was as confident of the votes of Democratic aldermen as a British Prime Minister is of his parliamentary majority. Lee was far from being a mere creative creature of the party organization which was so helpful to him, but he also was effectively vetoed by the party when he attempted to bring about governmental reforms which would have made the mayor less dependent upon the organization to obtain positive action.

Further evidence of the persistence of old-style party activities came from a number of other studies conducted in the late 1950's. For example, in 1957 party leaders from eight New Jersey counties reported performing a wide range of traditional party services, in response to an ingeniously worded questionnaire administered by Professor Richard T. Frost.

SERVICES PERFORMED BY NEW JERSEY POLITICIANS

THE SERVICE	PERCENTAGE PERFORMING IT "OFTEN"
Helping deserving people get public jobs	72
Showing people how to get their social security benefits, welfare unemployment compensation, etc.	54
Helping citizens who are in difficulty with the law. Do you help get them straightened out?	62

There was even some evidence in the 1950's of a rebirth of old-style urban party activities—for example, in the once Republican-dominated city of Philadelphia, where an effective Democratic old-style organization was put together. Often old-style organizations seem to exist in portions of contemporary cities, especially the low-income sections. These, like the reform groups to be described below, serve as factions in city-wide politics.

Why old-style politics persists in some settings but not others is not fully clear. An impressionistic survey of the scattered evidence suggests, as might be expected, that the older pattern continues in those localities which most resemble the situations which originally spawned strong local parties in the nineteenth century. Eastern industrial cities, such as New Haven, Philadel-

phia, and many of the New Jersey cities, have sizable low-income groups in
need of traditional party services. In many of these areas, the legal impedi-
ments to party activity also are minimal: Connecticut, for example, was the
last state in the union to adopt direct primary legislation, and nonpartisan
local election systems are, in general, less common in industrial cities than in
cities without much manufacturing activity. Cities in which weak, disorganized parties are reported—like Seattle, Minneapolis, and even Detroit
(which, of course, *is* a manufacturing center of some importance)—are quite
often cities in which nonpartisan institutions have been adopted.

SOME NEW-STYLE URBAN POLITICAL PATTERNS

In conclusion, we may note two of the styles of politics which have been
reported in contemporary localities where old-style organizations have become weak or nonexistent: the politics of nonpartisanship and the new "reform" factions within some urban Democratic parties. Both patterns are of
considerable intrinsic interest to students of local government. And, as contrasting political forms, they provide us with further perspective on the
strengths and weaknesses of old-style urban politics.

The Politics of Nonpartisanship. The nonpartisan ballot now is in force in
66 per cent of American cities over 25,000 in population. Numerous styles of
politics seem to take place beneath the facade of nonpartisanship. In some communities, when party labels are eliminated from the ballot, the old parties
continue to operate much as they have in the past; in other communities, new
local parties spring up to contest the nonpartisan elections. Finally, nonpartisanship often takes the form intended by its founders: no organized groups contest
elections; voters choose from a more or less self-selected array of candidates.

In the last of these cases, although nonpartisanship has its intended effect,
it also seems to have had—a recent body of literature suggests—a number of
unintended side effects. One of these is voter confusion. Without the familiar
device of party labels to aid in selecting candidates, voters may find it difficult
to select from among the sometimes substantial list of names on the ballot.
Under these circumstances, a bonus in votes often goes to candidates with a
familiar sounding name—incumbents are likely to be re-elected, for example—
or even candidates with a favorable position on the ballot. In addition, campaigning and other personal contacts with voters become less common, because candidates no longer have the financial resources and personnel of a
party organization at their disposal and therefore are dependent upon personal financing or backing from interest groups in the community.

Nonpartisan electoral practices, where effective, also seem to increase the
influence of the mass media on voters; in the absence of campaigning, party
canvassing, and party labels, voters become highly dependent for information
as well as advice on the press, radio, and television. Normally, mass communications have rather limited effects on people's behavior compared with face-
to-face communication such as canvassing by party workers. Under nonpartisan circumstances, however, he who controls the press is likely to have much

more direct and substantial effect on the public.

Ironically, the "theory" of nonpartisanship argues that by eliminating parties a barrier between citizens and their officials will be removed. In fact, nonpartisanship often attentuates the citizen's connections with the political system.

The Reform Democrats. The doctrine of nonpartisanship is mostly a product of the Progressive era. While nonpartisan local political systems continue to be adopted and, in fact, have become more common in recent decades, most of the impetus for this development results from the desire of communities to adopt city-manager systems. Nonpartisanship simply is part of the package which normally goes along with the popular city-manager system.

A newer phenomenon on the urban political scene is the development, especially since the 1952 presidential campaign, of ideologically motivated grass-roots party organizations within the Democratic party. The ideology in question is liberalism: most of the reform organizations are led and staffed by college-educated intellectuals, many of whom were activated politically by the candidacy of Adlai Stevenson. In a few localities, there also have been grass-roots, Republican organizations motivated by ideological considerations: in the Republican case, Goldwater conservatism.

New-style reformers differ in two major ways from old-style reformers: their ideological concerns extend beyond a preoccupation with governmental efficiency alone (they favor racial integration and improved housing and sometimes devote much of their energy to advocating "liberal" causes at the national level); secondly, their strategy is to work within and take control of the parties, rather than to reject the legitimacy of parties. They do resemble old-style reformers in their preoccupation with the evils of "bossism" and machine politics.

There also is an important resemblance between the new reform politician and the old-style organization man the reformer seeks to replace. In both cases, very much unlike the situation which seems to be stimulated by nonpartisanship, the politician emphasizes extensive face-to-face contact with voters. Where reformers have been successful, it often has been by beating the boss at his own game of canvassing the election district, registering and keeping track of voters, and getting them to the polls.

But much of the day-to-day style of the traditional urban politician is clearly distasteful to the new reformers: they have generally eschewed the use of patronage and, with the exceptions of campaigns for housing code enforcement, they have avoided the extensive service operations to voters and interest groups which were central to old-style party organizations. For example, when election district captains and other officials of the Greenwich Village Independent Democrats, the reform group which deposed New York Democrat County Leader Carmine DeSapio in his own election district, were asked the same set of questions about their activities used in the New Jersey study, strikingly different responses were made.

SERVICES PERFORMED BY NEW YORK REFORM DEMOCRATS

THE SERVICE	PERCENTAGE PERFORMING IT "OFTEN"
Helping deserving people get public jobs	0
Showing people how to get their social security benefits, welfare unemployment compensation, etc.	5
Helping citizens who are in difficulty with the law. Do you help get them straightened out?	6

The successes of this class of new-style urban party politician have vindicated a portion of the classical strategy of urban party politics, the extensive reliance upon canvassing and other personal relations, and also have shown that under some circumstances it is possible to organize such activities with virtually no reliance on patronage and other material rewards. The reformers have tapped a pool of political activists used by parties elsewhere in the world—for example, in Great Britain—but not a normal part of the American scene. One might say that the reformers have "discovered" the British Labor constituency parties.

It is where material resources available to the parties are limited, for example, California, and where voter interest in these resources is low, that the new reformers are successful. In practice, however, the latter condition has confined the effectiveness of the reform Democrats largely to the more prosperous sections of cities; neither their style nor their programs seem to be successful in lower-class districts. The areas of reform Democratic strength are generally *not* the areas which contribute greatly to Democratic pluralities in the cities. And, in many cities, the reformers' clientele is progressively diminishing as higher-income citizens move outward to the suburbs. Therefore, though fascinating and illuminating, the new reform movement must at least for the moment be considered as little more than a single manifestation in a panorama of urban political practices.

CONCLUSION

The degree to which *old-style* urban party organizations will continue to be a part of this panorama is uncertain. Changes in the social composition of the cities promise to be a major factor in the future of urban politics. If, as seems possible, many cities become lower-class, nonwhite enclaves, we can be confident that there will be a continuing market for the services of the service-oriented old-style politician. Whether or not this is the case, many lessons can be culled from the history of party politics during the years of growth of the American cities—lessons which are relevant, for example, to studying the politics of urbanization elsewhere in the world. In the nineteenth century, after all, the United States was an "emerging," "modernizing" nation, facing the problems of stability and democracy which are now being faced by countless newer nations.

IV. POLITICAL PARTIES AND THE GOVERNMENTAL PROCESS

8.   Political Parties and Pressure Groups in the Government Process

IN the preceding comments and readings, attention has been given to the overall character of the American party system—its nominating processes, campaign methods, electoral behavior, and the resulting patterns of party activities. In this section the emphasis will be on the legislative processes of the party system, which involve the role of the President, party politics, and the crucial position of interest groups.

The office of President is the centralizing force in the fragmented, localized American party system. The President and Vice-President are the only officials elected to represent the entire national constituency. The President (and in a different sense the Vice-President) has an organic connection with the Congress and the party system. The dynamics of the presidential-congressional relationship, a product of constitutional arrangement, historical trend, and presidential personality, determine the effectiveness of American national government. Since the Constitution was written in 1787 the formal powers of the presidency have undergone little change, yet the office of the presidency has grown in prestige, power, and authority to the point where the President is today the pivotal figure in the American political system. This history of presidential aggrandizement, albeit discontinuous, has been a response to the challenges of industrialization, internationalism, and crisis situations. Of particular importance in the growth of the office are the President's roles as the preeminent participant in the legislative process and as leader of his party. The President recommends measures to Congress, secures the necessary voting majorities in the House and Senate, and then approves or vetoes bills enacted by the Congress.

The written text of the Constitution makes the President the chief executive (though "executive power" is a term of uncertain meaning), and the unwritten customs and conventions of the Constitution and the political system provide him with an opportunity, if he so desires, to be the chief legislator. The President's own conception of his office determines, in large measure, how he will behave toward Congress and his party. The strong Presidents (Lincoln, both Roosevelts, Wilson, Truman, Kennedy, Johnson), in contrast to weak Presidents (Buchanan, Taft, Harding, Hoover, Eisenhower), usually attempted to implement an ideology (New Freedom, New Deal, New Frontier, Great Society) with a supporting legislative program. To this end the vigorous Presidents were willing to marshal all the extensive techniques and devices in their arsenal, including the judicious distribution of patronage among the party faithful. But although the presidency has become the fountain of public policy leadership, the President's control over his own political party has not grown correspondingly. This disparity between the President's tremendous executive power and his inability to exert tight sustained control over his own party has given rise to demands for, and counter-arguments against, a more responsible party system. (See "Toward a More Responsible Two-Party System" and "Party Responsibility—A Critical Inquiry," which follow.)

The development of the chief executive into the chief legislator has been accompanied by a number of important changes in party politics and in the position and role of Congress. The federal system, it should be repeated (see Comment 7 and "The Politics of the Federal System"), encourages a variety of state political systems and nourishes party decentralization, but the balance between state, local, and federal government and politics is constantly being altered. This changing balance, in the direction of nationalization in some areas, has created an interdependence between state and local politicians and party organizations and has had a substantial effect on congressional behavior. The impact of presidential politics on state and local politics, and vice versa, is particularly strong in urban politics. (See Comment 7 and "Urbanism and National Party Organizations.") The President presides over a structurally decentralized party system which is constantly subjected to national concerns—civil liberties, labor, education, welfare, to name but a few—and to concomitant pressures from national interest groups. The President's task is further complicated because, in addition to being the leader of his own party, he must be "above" party as a national symbol and as the representative of the public at large. These two roles can be both conflicting and complementary. It is in dealing with Congress that the distinction emerges most clearly between the President as titular and the President as actual head of his party.

The President was not, according to the intent of the Framers, to have been chief legislator; Congress was to have been the source of national legislation. Indeed, extensive executive power and authority were anathema to the generation that had witnessed the Revolutionary War. The men who met in Philadelphia to frame the Constitution desired a federal government of limited and divided powers, incorporating a series of checks and balances, with governmental powers retained by the states and the people. The legislature was to initiate policy and program, while the President, who was to be chosen indirectly, was armed with a veto power with which he could block, or at least delay, any potentially dangerous and radical acts. But in the years since the Constitutional Convention there has been a reversal of the roles contemplated by the Framers. The office of the President has become the major source of the initiative of action, planning, policy, and program, while Congress, more often than not, is cast in the negative role of inhibiting proposals and programs of the executive.

This reversal of roles has come about for a number of reasons. Functionally, executive activities and responsibilities have increased in number and complexity. Institutionally, the presidency lends itself to an effective organizational structure because it allows for a chain of command and a unity of authority. Politically, although the electoral college magnifies the importance of urban areas, the President is still forced to respond to the complex requirements of a fifty-state constituency with nationally generalized needs and pressures. In contrast Congress is a large and diffuse bicameral body lacking cohesion and an organizational hierarchy and as such is unable to follow and supervise adequately the myriad of technical and specialized functions and services carried out by the bureaucracy. Institutionally the Senate and House of Representatives are organized on a factional basis with power dispersed among majority and minority leaders and whips and a multiplicity of committee and subcommittee chairmen who, because of safe seats, accumulate seniority and with it technical specialization and, ultimately, legislative fiefdoms. Politically, traditional districting has magnified the importance of rural areas (this is now changing because of *Baker* v. *Carr;* see Parts V and VI); furthermore, a congressman's constituency is a state or a district, with its frequently specialized needs and pressures. These elements, which have militated against the exercising of its legislative initiative by Congress, have led to both conflict and collaboration between the executive and legislative branches and are, in part, responsible also for the presidential and congressional party systems.

The decision of the Framers to establish a bicameral legislative body consisting of an upper and a lower chamber was one of the compromises of the Constitution that had far-reaching effects. The Senate, unlike most other upper chambers, enjoys legislative power equal to that of the lower body, the House of Representatives (which enjoys the technical privilege of originating all revenue bills), and has in addition the power to approve and disapprove treaties and the appointment of important executive officers. The latter power adds to the authority of the Senate and also offers a potential for conflict with the executive. According to "senatorial courtesy" the Senate will reject a nominee to a federal office (judge, district attorney, customs official, postmaster, etc.) if the nominee has been objected to by a senator of the President's party from the state in which the federal office is to be filled. Thus patronage distribution within the states has been transferred from the President to the senators of his party. In the House of Representatives, too, there is potential conflict with the President. The Speaker of the House has very considerable power—though his power stems from his strategic position rather than from House parliamentary rules. Until the 89th Congress changed House parliamentary regulations, the House Rules Committee exerted pivotal control over legislation coming to the House floor. Under the old rules, bills recommended for passage by other House committees ordinarily had to be approved by the Rules Committee; under the new provisions, the Speaker may remove a bill from the jurisdiction of the Rules Committee after twenty-one days. The Rules Committee has long been dominated by its conservative members and has thwarted liberal bills sponsored by the President and liberal congressmen.

The legislative work in both houses is carried on by the committees and subcommittees. Senate and House versions of bills are reconciled (and often radically altered) by conference committees composed of the ranking members of both parties of the standing committees that reported the bill. Committee and subcommittee chairmen wield extraordinary power and are capable of blocking executive wishes. Consequently they are carefully courted by the President, the bureaucracy, and pressure groups. In this legislative milieu of undisciplined parties, the President must often appeal to like-thinking members of the opposition party for support of his programs. In times of crisis and national emergency, however, the President's prerogatives as commander-in-chief are enormous, congressional and partisan animosities are generally muted, and judicial review of executive actions tends to be relaxed. Congress may even go so far as to delegate some of its powers to the President for the duration of the emergency.

The ceaseless interplay between President and Congress rests on constitutional and party systems in which authority and responsibility are at the same time autonomous, interdependent, and potentially in conflict. But interests cut across policy and program; among these are executive versus legislative interests, national and generalized versus local and specialized interests, and Democratic versus Republican interests, which in our party system may be confused in coalitions that cross party lines. Adding to the complexity of the American governmental system is the vital relationship of political interest groups to the political process.

Political interest groups thrive in America's highly pluralistic society. Since people realize social values through groups and because organized groups can concentrate their resources for self-expression, security, and the attainment of common ends, organized groups are structures of power. In the United States, where political and governmental power is dispersed and the party system is undisciplined, political interest or pressure groups are functional actors in the formulation of public policy. Pressure groups vary in size, strength, form, visibility, techniques utilized, and objectives, but they all have, in contrast to ordinary interest groups, a desire to influence government decisions. Organized interest groups articulate demands and provide channels of communication within the context of political-institutional decision-making.

The large universe of interest groups is diverse and is characterized by group conflict in which most groups confront a variety of shifting opponents rather than a consistent monolith of opponents. Increasing specialization has fostered a multitude of specialized groups within such general areas as agriculture, labor, business, and the professions. Thus, farmers may be members of a number of commodity groups as well as general agricultural groups (American Farm Bureau Federation, National Farmers' Organization); businessmen may be members of any number of trade associations as well as general business groups (U.S. Chamber of Commerce, The National Association of Manufacturers); laborers may be members of their own particular trade or labor unions as well as the general labor organization (AFL-CIO). If the specialized groups indulge in intragroup conflict, their efficacy is weakened. The lengthy, acrimonious squabbling between the leaders of the American Federation of Labor and the Congress of Industrial Organizations prior to their merger only served to tarnish organized labor's image and weaken its overall position. On the other hand, if specialized groups join forces and consolidate their strength, their efficacy is tremendously increased and their position considerably enhanced.

Given the fact that American politics is highly pragmatic and nonideological and that the major parties perform brokerage functions, organized interest groups feel free to be militant with both major parties. Certain groups, however, are more closely associated with one or the other of the major parties, for example, the U.S. Chamber of Commerce or the National Association of Manufacturers with the Republican party and the AFL-CIO and the Farmers' Union with the Democratic party. But the association of a group with a party on one issue does not prevent that group from identifying with the opposing party on a different issue. The American Medical Association consistently opposed Democratic efforts to bring about the adoption of Medicare, but it just as consistently favored Democratic measures to strengthen federal aid to medical education. The U.S. Chamber of Commerce and the American Farm Bureau Federation, groups usually identified with the Republican party, frequently opposed Democratic-sponsored legislation; nonetheless they supported the Kennedy administration's trade policy.

The multiplicity of decision centers within the political process affords interest groups an expanded range of opportunities and obstacles on both national and state levels. Failure or success at one level, or in some states, or with one branch of government, does not preclude the possibility of failure or success at other points. While the chief executive nowadays is the chief legislator, the Congress is always capable of initiating, altering, and rejecting legislation and influencing the bureaucracy's implementation of it. In situations where effective executive leadership is absent, interest groups have a particularly susceptible legislative environment.

Almost every bill considered by Congress or the state legislatures has its contingent of interest groups. Group representation before Congress and the state legislatures offers both benefits and liabilities. Organized groups inform the legislatures and the public, stimulate debate and provide direct access to those affected. But it has been pointed out that pressure groups may pursue their specialized objectives to the detriment of the general public. The degree of influence an organization exerts does not reflect the validity of its position, but the strength of its resources, and lurking in the background is the fear that pressure groups will resort to unethical practices to secure their ends.

The fear of corrupt activities on the part of pressure groups has its basis in historic fact. During the nineteenth and early twentieth centuries, self-seeking pressure groups displayed a cavalier indifference to the general public. This flagrant disregard precipitated a series of congressional investigations, though lobbyist registration and reporting bills were not passed until 1935 and 1936. But neither these laws, nor the 1938 Foreign Agents Registration Act, nor some provisions of the Revenue Act of 1939 were able to adequately control lobbying at the federal level; and so, in 1946 the Federal Regulation of Lobbying Act was enacted.

The Lobbying Act of 1946, the major legal control of federal lobbying, attempts to interdict dishonest activities of interest groups without restricting the constitutional rights of free speech and petition and without curtailing the beneficial contributions of pressure groups. The 1946 Act is predicated on the principle of exposure. No restrictions were imposed on the financial or general activities of pressure groups or their agents (though bribery, of course, was already illegal), but the Act required any person who received payment for the purpose of influencing Congress to register with the clerk of the House and the secretary of the Senate, so as to reveal who was paying him and what his declared objectives were, and to file quarterly financial statements regarding his activities. However, although the Federal Lobbying Act was somewhat helpful in revealing certain activities of organized groups, its effectiveness was minimal. A considerable number of loopholes exist because the Supreme Court has ruled that the law applies only to groups and individuals that collected or received money for the principal purpose of exerting influence through direct contacts with Congress. The qualifications of collecting and receiving money, principal purpose, and direct contact with congressmen have vitiated the strength of the statute because expenditures of funds which were not solicited expressly for lobbying were exempted; the groups and lobbyists were, to a large extent, permitted to determine what proportion of total expenses was to be reported as lobbying expenditures; the principal purpose of the organization had to be the influencing of Congress; peripheral activities such as trying to influence administrative agencies and the executive branch or the general public were not subject to the law; and, finally, there were no provisions for investigating the veracity of lobby registrations and reports. It remained for the Justice Department to adopt a policy of investigation only upon receipt of complaints. In the two decades since the passage of the law only four prosecutions have been undertaken by the Justice Department. In short, current federal legislation to regulate lobbying, although better than none, still fails to prevent abuses by unprincipled pressure groups or to preclude sophisticated attempts to secure privilege at the expense of the general interest. This generalization is also applicable to the regulation-of-lobbying legislation passed by approximately four-fifths of the states.

In the following readings various interrelated aspects of the government process are presented. Peter H. Odegard, in "Presidential Leadership and Party Responsibility," discusses the presidency as it relates to the Congress and the operation of the political process. "Toward a More Responsible Two-Party System," from the Report of the Committee on Political Parties of the American Political Science Association, is the classic presentation of the arguments in favor of a more disciplined party structure in the United States. Balancing this is the article by Murray S. Stedman, Jr., and Herbert Sonthoff, "Party Responsibility—A Critical Inquiry," which, as its title suggests, is in disagreement with the report as well as the underlying questions and assumptions of the doctrine of responsible parties. James MacGregor Burns' description of the congressional and presidential party systems is taken from his book *The Deadlock of Democracy: Four-Party Politics in America.* Frank J. Sorauf in "Patronage and Party" presents a seminal and balanced discussion of the nature of patronage in the political system. "Political Parties and Pressure Group Politics," by Hugh A. Bone, discusses the points of contact between interest groups and the political parties. And in the final selection, David B. Truman analyzes interest-group operations against the institutional backdrops of the Congress, the presidency, the judiciary, the parties, and the states versus the nation.

PRESIDENTIAL LEADERSHIP AND PARTY RESPONSIBILITY *

Peter H. Odegard

IN spite of vast powers, the office of the Presidency can become a mere masquerade of power if Congress chooses to make it so. It is not only that many of the powers of the President are derived from acts of Congress, and what Congress gives it may also take away. Even those Presidential powers derived directly from the Constitution depend in large measure for their effectiveness upon congressional co-operation. Without congressional approval of men and money, the President may be Commander in Chief, but of a phantom force. Even the President's foreign policy requires congressional support if it is to succeed, particularly in the period since World War II when economic and military assistance to underdeveloped areas and the associated powers of the free world have loomed so large. Thus it is literally true that, while the President proposes, Congress ultimately disposes. Hence the importance of good relations between the President and the legislature if an administration is to succeed. In this respect the governments of the United States and Great Britain stand in sharp contrast.

* From Peter H. Odegard, "Presidential Leadership and Party Responsibility," in *The Annals*, September, 1956, pp. 66–81. © 1956 by the American Academy of Political and Social Science. Reprinted by permission of Professor Odegard and the editors.

PARTY UNITY IN GREAT BRITAIN

The Prime Minister of Great Britain is not only a Minister of the Crown but a Member of Parliament, as is every member of his Cabinet. If the Prime Minister derives his constitutional authority from his appointment as a Minister of the Crown, he derives his *political* power from his membership in, and control of, the majority party in Parliament, that is, the House of Commons. Elected as a simple member of the House of Commons at the same time his 620-odd colleagues are chosen, he becomes the Queen's Prime Minister solely because of his party leadership in Parliament. This integration of the executive and legislative branches of government ensures control of both by the same party. Party discipline and unity are inescapable requirements of such a system. Without such unity the government falls; with it, the Prime Minister and his government are in complete command, not only of the executive branch but of the legislature too.

In one sense the Prime Minister and his Cabinet are creatures of Parliament, since they must resign when they lose the confidence and control of a majority of that body. But it is also true that Parliament is at the mercy of the Prime Minister, since, if his policies are defeated in the legislature, he may ask the Queen to dissolve Parliament before the expiration of its term. Thus the Prime Minister, "standing at the apex of a disciplined party machine, holds the power of political life and death over his followers." So great is the power of a Prime Minister that Ramsay Muir in his book on the British government describes this office as a "dictatorship."

PAROCHIAL TENDENCIES IN CONGRESS

Contrast this with the situation under our government. The President is, as we say, independent of Congress, elected for a term different from that of either house and from a different constituency. But Congress is also independent of him. Of all the 433 elected officers of the United States the President and Vice President alone are chosen by all of the voters, from coast to coast and border to border. Senators and Congressmen, on the other hand, are essentially local officers responsible to the voters of a single state or congressional district. Only once in four years do members of the House of Representatives and the President "go to the country" together and even then only one-third of the Senators go with them. At the so-called midterm elections, both Representatives and Senators must in effect "go it alone" without support from the booming guns of a presidential campaign. They must win or lose not so much in terms of national issues, as these issues relate to the general welfare of the country as a whole, but as they relate to the dominant interests of their state or district.

Hence the tariff is viewed in the light of its effect not on our total economy or our international relations but on the woolgrowers in Montana, the sugar interests of Utah and Idaho, the textile mills of New England, and so forth.

These parochial tendencies are increased by the vast scope and diversity of the economic, ethnic, and sectional interests in the United States. What pleases the Democratic Irish voters of Boston and New York may be anathema to the Democratic Negro voters of Chicago or the nativist Protestant voters of the South and Middle West. And a policy designed to please Republican hard-money bankers and investors in New York and Chicago may displease Republican farmers in Iowa, Maine, and North Dakota. The overridng sectional cleavages between North and South, East and West, cut across party lines on many important issues. The Republican party of Oregon or Nebraska is consequently not the same as the Republican party of New York or even of Maine and Vermont. And the Democratic party of New York certainly differs on many vital issues from that of Texas and South Carolina.

At midterm elections these sectional differences are likely to be paramount, and every Congressmen or Senator runs on his own platform. When in 1941 the Republicans looked forward to the midterm elections of 1942, Senator Taft was asked what Republican policy would be on foreign affairs in the campaign. He said:

No Republican National Convention can be held to make any binding declarations regarding policy before next year's elections (1942) and the party's National Committee clearly has no authority to make such declarations. *I see no reason why each senator should not run on his own foreign policy.*

Obviously such a system places a premium not on party unity but on diversity, not on discipline but on independence—independence not only of the President but also of the party organization of which the President is the formal leader.

PARTY LEADERSHIP

The President's position as party leader, moreover, is strikingly different from that of the British Prime Minister. His leadership of his party derives from his position as President, or as presidential candidate, rather than the other way around. In the United States, with the possible exceptions of Jefferson and Jackson, American Presidents have become party leaders only after their nomination and election, whereas in Great Britain the party leader becomes Prime Minister. Even after his election the relations between a President and his party are largely informal, irregular, and tenuous. As for the party in opposition, we indulge in the fiction that the defeated candidate for the Presidency is the party leader. But normally, with no official position either in the government or the party, his "leadership" is but a shadow of that represented by the Leader of the Opposition in Parliament. Even the President's influence as party leader is vitiated by the generally loose character of party organization in this country.

PRESSURE GROUPS

Candidates for Congress or for state elective offices are often more dependent upon powerful pressure groups than upon the party of which they are nominal members. There is many a congressional district in which support of organized labor or of the Farm Bureau Federation or the Chamber of Commerce is more important than the support of the regular Republican or Democratic organization. The American Legion with its ten thousand local posts throughout the country, the American Farm Bureau Federation reaching into thousands of counties and into most congressional districts—these, and hundreds more, constitute political forces often more powerful than the parties themselves. . . .

TEMPORARY PARTY UNITY

Although one or both of our two major parties reach into every town and hamlet, they function as effective national organizations only every four years, when control of the White House is at stake. During these quadrennial campaigns sectional differences and factional cleavages are temporarily submerged in support of the party's presidential candidate.

These differences often burn with an incandescent fire before and during the nominating conventions. But once the convention has picked the party candidate, the party hosts close ranks at least until the votes are counted. It is thus only around the President, first as candidate and later as Chief Executive, that our major parties achieve any substantial degree of unity.

Normally, too, a presidential election will sweep into office not only a President but a majority in Congress of the same party. Under such circumstances, the President can, if he is a strong man and understands the party system, enforce some degree of party unity and discipline on major administration measures. By consultation and co-operation with the Big Four in Congress (the Vice President, the Speaker of the House, and majority leaders in the House and Senate) such a President can often have his way.

But this honeymoon period is normally short-lived, and by the time of the second Congress in a presidential term the familiar pattern of factional conflict reappears and the discipline of pressure groups tends to displace that of the parties. The counterfeit of party unity and discipline enforced during the honeymoon period weakens and falls away.

PATRONAGE

It falls away first because it is enforced as much by a judicious distribution of patronage and party favors as by any basic agreement on matters of policy. With thousands of appointments to be made, appointments for which every Congressman has a candidate or two, the President is in a good bargaining position, and he uses jobs and other patronage to buy support for his legislative program.

Yet even under the best of circumstances it would be easy to exaggerate the influence of Presidential patronage as a "big stick" in securing congressional support for administration measures. The gradual extension of the merit system, "senatorial courtesy," and an emerging tradition of nonpartisanship even in the appointment of officials not formally covered by civil service rules have had a corrosive effect upon this weapon of Presidential leadership. In any case, once the appointments have been made and the favors distributed, the honeymoon cools and Congressmen tend to revert to their local, sectional, or other special loyalties.

In this mood they bargain not so much with the President as party leader as with other members of their own party and even with members of the Opposition. We call this process "log-rolling" or "back scratching." Thus votes in Congress after the honeymoon rarely show Republicans and Democrats lined up solidly on opposite sides, but rather conservatives of both parties joining against liberals of both parties, or high-tariff representatives, Republican and Democrat, united against those of both parties who seek to reduce or abolish protective rates. Indeed, differences within the party on some issues are almost as sharp as the differences between Republicans and Democrats. So numerous are these various groups and blocs that emerge in the process of legislation that on most measures party loyalty is meaningless and party discipline nonexistent.

"Like dancers in a vast Virginia reel," writes Professor Burns, "groups merge, break off, meet again, veer away to new combinations." There is an almost continuous crossing and recrossing of party lines, so that it is not unusual for a Democratic administration to rely on Republican votes to save its program or for a Republican administration to rely on Democrats. Obviously under these circumstances it is difficult to know which party is really responsible for any given policy.

MIDTERM CONGRESSIONAL ELECTIONS

A second reason for the falling off of party unity after the honeymoon is the fact that the term of office of members of the House of Representatives and of one-third of the Senators expires midway in the term of the President. This fact compels Representatives even of the President's own party to give their attention to their local or sectional political fences, often to the subordination or disregard of national interests. "I glory in the fact," said one Congressman, "that men who come from Peach Tree Creek have Peach Tree Creek at heart." And of course the midterm elections not infrequently return a Congress controlled not by the President's own partisans but by the Opposition.

If the members of the House of Representatives served terms coextensive with the President the possibility of a unified administration under united party leadership would be improved. The party in control of the White House would also be in control of the legislature, with two consequences: (1) the President would be able to compel or induce greater unity among his own party in Congress since they would have to stand or fall together;

(2) the voters could then force on the party some semblance of responsibility for public policy.

LACK OF PARTY UNITY AND DISCIPLINE

As matters now stand, the separation of powers, the staggered terms of the President, House of Representatives, and Senate, the decentralization of powers under the federal system, plus the growth of powerful pressure groups outside the party system, all combine to prevent the kind of party unity and discipline characteristic, for example, of the English parliamentary system. Short of certain unlikely and probably undesirable basic changes in our constitutional and social system, this situation is not likely to change, and the President will continue to be plagued by conflicts within his own party as well as by the official party in opposition.

Presidential efforts to enforce party discipline under existing conditions have never been conspicuously successful. Indeed there are no very clear standards by which to measure party loyalty in the American political system. Adherence to the party platform is one possible standard. But the separate planks that go to make up the platform are either too vague to mean very much or too narrow to allow for that diversity of interpretation required by the extent and variety of interests included in both major parties. Besides, there is no effective machinery for interpreting or applying this test in practice. Compliance with the decisions of the party caucus in Congress has been another test of party loyalty. But except on matters of organization and patronage, selection of the Speaker, appointments to committees and ratification of Presidential nominees for federal jobs, the party caucus rarely takes a stand. Nor have the steering committees of the two major parties been any more effective in enforcing party discipline on matters of policy. As someone has said, "They seldom meet, and never steer." Furthermore, the President has no very effective control over these and other agencies of party government in Congress; indeed those who compose the ruling clique in the House (the Speaker, the Rules Committee, the majority floor leader, the party whip, the chairmen of important standing committees) are less dependent on the President than he is on them. The fact is that the reins of party discipline rest lightly on most members of Congress. . . .

Both major parties contain members who can be classified as Republicans or Democrats only by the most generous interpretation of the party label. In general, everyone who calls himself a Democrat or a Republican, whatever may be his principles or his behavior in electoral campaigns or in Congress, is normally regarded as a member of the party with which he inscribes himself. . . .

. . . Take the case of Fiorello La Guardia, who in 1924 was elected to Congress as candidate of the Republican, American Labor, and Socialist parties. Or that redoubtable Marxist and fellow traveler, Vito Marcantonio, also from New York. In 1942 he succeeded in winning the nomination for Congress not only of the American Labor party but of the Democratic and Republican parties as well.

If one cannot be sure just when a Republican is a Republican and when he is a Democrat, Socialist, or Mugwump, how can a President enforce any great measure of party discipline upon those who march under his banner? Unless he can pick up considerable support from the opposition party, the average President must be content to see his policies falter and fail.

Democratic Party. The conflicts within the Democratic party are well known. Every aspiring Democratic candidate for President and every Democratic President must "walk on eggs" if he is not to offend some important and militant minority within the party, be it the Negro voters in the North or the Dixiecrats of the South, the Catholic voters of the northern cities or the nativist anti-Romanists of the West and South.

Republican Party. But the Republican party, too, has been torn by internal conflict and dissension. During the Civil War, Lincoln's agony as President was increased by the continual harassment to which he was subjected by congressional guerrillas bearing the Republican label. I pass over the Reconstruction period when the Republican factions in Congress made life miserable not only for that ambivalent Republican President, Andrew Johnson, but also for his successor, General Grant. During Grant's administration, smoldering rebellion within the party broke into open revolt in the so-called Liberal Republican party of the early 1870's. Some of the names now most honored among Republicans—Lyman Trumbull, Charles Sumner, Carl Schurz, Francis P. Blair, Jr.—were, in December, 1872, formally read out of the party by the Republican congressional caucus. In the turbulent eighties and nineties Greenback and Populist revolts broke out in both Democratic and Republican ranks. Most of us remember Bryan's attack on the gold-standard wing of the Democratic party in 1896. But not so many remember that a similar fight took place in the Republican Convention that year when Senator Teller of Colorado, leading a goodly number of so-called Silver Senators and Representatives, bolted the convention and campaigned against McKinley. And the Teller rebellion of 1896 was mild by comparison with the revolution of 1912 led by Theodore Roosevelt.

Republican Presidents were plagued with these insurgents for over thirty years. Even when the party returned to power in Congress in 1918 and in the White House in 1921, they faced the continuing resurgence of La Follette Progressives and their successors. In 1924 many of them followed La Follette into a new Progressive party, and when Mr. Coolidge was re-elected with a fairly strong majority in Congress, the rebels who survived were promptly read out of the Republican party.

Although the caucus could thus exclude them it could not silence them or their numerous friends and allies who remained in the party. Borah posed the problem of party discipline in terms not easy to answer:

I would not know where to establish the line of loyalty or party devotion under conditions as they have prevailed in this country for the last ten or fifteen years. I do not know what the test is. . . . The fact is that about 90 per cent of the present Republican voters are sons and daughters of renegades. . . . These are times . . . of wide differences of view as to what constitutes Republicanism. . . . Let us recognize these conditions and deal with them as broadminded leaders and not as narrow partisans.

In the saddle and riding hard, Mr. Coolidge and the Old Guard paid scant attention to Borah. But by 1926 when Republican control of the Senate was in danger and every vote counted, all the rebels then serving, including Senator Brookhart, and Senator Frazier, were invited back into the fold. Even in the years of "prosperity" from 1926 to 1929 there was serious thunder on the Republican left as Borah, Bob La Follette, Jr., Norris, La Guardia, John M. Nelson and Schneider of Wisconsin, McFadden of Pennsylvania, and William Lemke of North Dakota continued to snipe at Coolidge and Herbert Hoover, the titular heads of their party. And in the 1928 campaign three Republicans, Norris, Blaine, and La Follette, came out openly for Al Smith as against Hoover. It was this action that inspired Senator Moses to describe the rebels as "sons of the wild jackass."

After 1930 when the Democrats took control of Congress, the "sons of the wild jackass" in the Republican ranks began to multiply. Indeed so unstable were the Republican ranks that the Chicago *Tribune* said of the Eightieth Congress, "The so-called Republican majority in the Senate isn't a majority, because it comprises half a dozen different brands of self-styled Republicans." If this was true of the Eightieth Congress it was no less true of the Eighty-third, in which a narrow Republican majority included "half a dozen different brands of self-styled Republicans."

Presidential Difficulties. The complex, almost chaotic, character of American political parties, the intensity of intraparty as well as interparty conflicts, make the President's position as party leader extraordinarily difficult. No President who hopes to see his legislative program succeed can safely rely exclusively upon his own partisans in Congress, not even when they comprise a "safe" majority in both houses. During the honeymoon period the prospect of federal patronage may help to firm the wavering ranks. But what Cleveland once called the "cohesive power of public plunder" is no longer the "big stick" it once was. And even the so-called coattail effect of presidential leadership in a national campaign every four years, however important it may or may not be, has been weakened. The adoption of the Twenty-second Amendment limiting a President to two terms will inevitably impair this aspect of his leadership during his second and last term. Moreover, the seniority rule in Congress, by awarding key committee posts to members who come from "safe" districts or states, in effect gives control to those who are least dependent on such Presidential support. These factors, plus the tradition of congressional independence inherent in the separation of powers and resentment against being a "rubber stamp" for the White House, help to explain why as party leader the President's lot is not a happy one.

PRESIDENTIAL VETO

There are, however, other weapons in the Presidential arsenal that help to fortify his position. His power to recommend to Congress "such measures as he shall judge necessary and expedient" together with his power to veto measures sponsored by forces hostile to his own aims gives him a control of public policy that no other officer or officers of the government can match. Indeed the mere threat of a veto may serve to stifle Opposition measures "in the cradle" and prevent them from reaching a vote on the floor. But the veto, as a political instrument, reaches beyond merely stopping "bad" legislation. On important matters of policy it serves as a dramatic device for appealing over the heads of Congress to the people. To be sure, it requires great political "savvy" to use the veto well, for it is a two-edged sword. The Opposition can and, not infrequently, does seek to embarrass the President by presenting him with legislation which he can veto only at the cost of offending factions in his own party as well as powerful interest groups upon whose support even his own adherents may depend. Legislation dealing with farm benefits, veterans' pensions, tariff rates, general appropriations, immigration, education, and welfare lends itself to this kind of political maneuver. Nevertheless, an astute President can use his veto power to provide campaign material for himself and his party and to strengthen his own power and prestige in the country. It is not surprising, under these circumstances, that "political" vetoes are more frequent where the White House and Congress are controlled by rival parties.

THE PRESIDENT AND FOREIGN POLICY

Beyond his power to initiate and to veto legislation, beyond the political power arising from patronage and a place on the presidential coattail at election time, the President as a political leader has other sources of strength. As the sole official voice of the nation in foreign affairs he can, particularly in times of emergency or crisis, command support, even from the Opposition. But to do so he must give more than lip service to the belief that "politics stops at the water's edge." The President, and those who speak for him, cannot plead for "nonpartisanship in foreign policy" with one breath and denounce the opposition party as a compound of incompetence, corruption, and disloyalty in the next. The President must himself assume leadership in defining his policies with clarity and firmness and in resisting with all the vigor he can command those in his own party who seek to sabotage or subvert not only foreign policies to which the President is committed, but the Presidency itself, as the sole official voice in this vast field.

ACCESS TO THE PEOPLE

On the domestic front also the President as party leader enjoys advantages over any opposition leader. He more than any other person in the nation, perhaps in the world, has access to the eyes and ears of the people. The press, radio, television, are, if not at his beck and call, ever alert to report what he says or does or proposes to do. Nowhere is his skill as a political leader more clearly revealed than in the use he makes of these facilities to mold and mobilize public opinion.

LEADER OF THE NATION, LEADER OF THE PARTY

In final analysis the President's strength as a party leader derives from his power and prestige as President, and the office of President can exalt a man of character and vision as it can inflate a man of mean dimensions. "The President is at liberty," said Woodrow Wilson, "both in law and conscience to be as big a man as he can." For weal or woe the American President is the spokesman, sign, and symbol of the American people. He is an image both of what the nation is and of what it aspires to be, a father image, if you please, but one in which most of us see ourselves revised, enlarged, and illuminated.

His best success as a party leader thus will often depend on his success in rising above party in the service of the nation. As Wilson said:

Let him once win the admiration and confidence of the country, and no other single force can withstand him, no combination of forces will easily overpower him. His position takes the imagination of the country. He is the representative of no constituency, but of the whole people. . . . He cannot escape being the leader of his party, except by incapacity and lack of personal force, because he is at once the choice of the party and of the nation. He can dominate his party by being spokesman for the real sentiment and purpose of the country. . . . He may be both the leader of his party and the leader of the nation, or he may be one or the other. If he leads the nation, his party can hardly resist him.

These comments of Woodrow Wilson, like Cleveland's aphorism that "he serves his party best who serves his country best," are not simply copybook generalities. They harbor political wisdom of a very practical sort. Jackson added to the strength and prestige of the Democratic party as much by defying the nullificationists within its ranks as by his war on "Nick" Biddle, the Whigs, and the Bank. Who can say that the Republican party would not have been better served had Lincoln lived to win his war on the Radicals with their demand for a Draconian peace? The fact is that those Presidents who have translated the slogans of Cleveland and the counsel of Wilson into maxims of practical politics have not only been our great Presidents but also our great party leaders.

Party Drag. To be sure, a President, and still more a presidential candidate, is a creature of his party, for the party nominates and elects him. But if he is shaped by the party as President he can be the instrument for shaping the party in turn, for giving it direction, for leading it, as Walter Lippmann might say, from Drift to Mastery. As President he derives great strength from his position as party leader. But the party can be a source of frustration as well as strength. Lesser party leaders will admonish him, as Professor Rossiter says:

. . . [to] be careful not to plunge too far ahead or lag too far to the rear of his allies in Congress . . . [to] select his chief lieutenants from [party] ranks, act as "honest broker" among its squabbling wings, and endure silently attacks upon his integrity, by men who roam the outer reaches of party loyalty. In doing all these things for the sake of harmony, and for the sake of victory in the next election, he cannot help losing some of his zest for bold experiment. . . . The party, as we know from the history of a dozen administrations, is more likely to tame him than he is to reshape it. Franklin Roosevelt, supposedly the most dominant of political leaders, felt the drag of his own party through most of his years in office. . . . And even Mr. Eisenhower, who has little taste for adventure, has been hampered rather than invigorated by his leadership of the Republican party.

Whatever may be true of Mr. Eisenhower and the Republican party, the Democratic party of 1956 bears the unmistakable marks of Franklin Roosevelt and Harry Truman, just as at an earlier date it reflected the influence of Jefferson, Jackson, and Woodrow Wilson, and as the Republicans felt the impact of Lincoln and Theodore Roosevelt. And in Franklin Roosevelt's case, when the Democratic leaders in Congress, notably on the House Rules Committee and the Senate Judiciary Committee, blocked his program, he did not hesitate openly to ask for their defeat at the polls. Most Presidents unfortunately have been content either to ignore the intraparty battles of their own party by refusing to take sides or to compromise them on terms that kept the party at dead center on the theory that "if we cannot all move together, we'll not move at all." In other words, most Presidents have not been conspicuously successful as party leaders, being content at best to be party managers and at worst party hacks. Those who, on the contrary, have been dynamic party leaders have also been our most conspicuously creative Presidents. In fairness one should, I suppose, add that great Presidents and great party leaders are as much products of crisis as they are of personality or ideology. Yet crisis alone is not enough, as the examples of Madison, Buchanan, and Hoover show, nor is lack of crisis a bar to great leadership, as Jefferson and Theodore Roosevelt testify.

IMPORTANCE OF PRESIDENTIAL PARTY LEADERSHIP

All that I have said points to the importance of the President as a party leader. Father image he may be, symbol of the state he surely is, but being these is not enough. The President of the United States is no constitutional monarch, he is not Queen Elizabeth, away from and above the battle. He is at the heart and center of both policy and administration at a time and in a place fraught with grave significance not only for America, but for the human race. To avoid or to evade his responsibilities as party leader is in effect to abdicate his leadership as President. For neither of our major parties deprived of a strong hand at the helm is fit to govern. Neither is a united party. Both are torn by internal conflict. The issues between them are real and of far-reaching significance. On taxation, conservation, welfare, education, labor, business, and agriculture, even on foreign policy, Democrats and Republicans represent sharply different points of view. But these interparty differences are too often obscured by intraparty battles. If our two major parties are to offer the voters meaningful alternatives of men and measures they need spokesmen who can translate and clarify these issues. If the President fails to do this for the party in power, he will fail in what is probably his most important task. . . .

PRESIDENTIAL LEADERSHIP FOR PARTY UNITY

No one who cherishes the American passion for freedom will want a President who can enforce party unity only at the price of uniformity. The Communist and Fascist parties achieve unity by harsh internal discipline, and those who dissent are destroyed. This is the unity of the slave pens. Yet stable and effective government in these days cries out for greater unity in our major parties. And we must look to the President if it is to be achieved.

Our two great parties are in many ways like Tweedledee and Tweedledum. They agree on vastly more issues than they disagree on. Yet fundamentally they differ not only in detail but on important matters of public policy. Out of the internal struggle within them as well as the struggle between them the parties will find their direction in the days to come. In what direction will they move? The answer to this question will depend primarily on Presidential leadership.

TOWARD A MORE RESPONSIBLE TWO-PARTY
SYSTEM *

The Committee on Political Parties of the
American Political Science Association

I. THE ROLE OF THE POLITICAL PARTIES

1. *The Parties and Public Policy.* Throughout this report political parties are treated as indispensable instruments of government. That is to say, we proceed on the proposition that *popular government in a nation of more than 150 million people requires political parties which provide the electorate with a proper range of choice between alternatives of action.* The party system thus serves as the main device for bringing into continuing relationship those ideas about liberty, majority rule and leadership which Americans are largely taking for granted.

For the great majority of Americans, the most valuable opportunity to influence the course of public affairs is the choice they are able to make be-

* From a report of the Committee on Political Parties of the American Political Science Association. This material appeared as a Supplement to the *American Political Science Review*, vol. XLIV, No. 3, Part 2 (September, 1950). Copyright, 1950, by the American Political Science Association.

tween the parties in the principal elections. While in an election the party alternative necessarily takes the form of a choice between candidates, putting a particular candidate into office is not an end in itself. The concern of the parties with candidates, elections and appointments is misunderstood if it is assumed that parties can afford to bring forth aspirants for office without regard to the views of those so selected. Actually, the party struggle is concerned with the direction of public affairs. Party nominations are no more than a means to this end. In short, party politics inevitably involves public policy in one way or another. *In order to keep the parties apart, one must consider the relations between each and public policy.*

This is not to ignore that in the past the American two-party system has shown little propensity for evolving original or creative ideas about public policy; that it has even been rather sluggish in responding to such ideas in the public interest; that it reflects in an enlarged way those differences throughout the country which are expressed in the operation of the federal structure of government; and that in all political organizations a considerable measure of irrationality manifests itself.

Giving due weight to each of these factors, we are nevertheless led to conclude that the choices provided by the two-party system are valuable to the American people in proportion to their definition in terms of public policy. *The reasons for the growing emphasis on public policy in party politics are to be found, above all, in the very operations of modern government.* With the extraordinary growth of the responsibilities of government, the discussion of public affairs for the most part makes sense only in terms of public policy.

2. *The New Importance of Program.* One of the most pressing requirements of contemporary politics is for the party in power to furnish a general kind of direction over the government as a whole. *The crux of public affairs lies in the necessity for more effective formulation of general policies and programs and for better integration of all of the far-flung activities of modern government.*

Only large-scale and representative political organizations possess the qualifications needed for these tasks. The ascendancy of national issues in an industrial society, the impact of the widening concern of government with problems of the general welfare, the entrance into the realm of politics of millions of new voters—all of these factors have tended to broaden the base of the parties as the largest political organizations in the country. *It is in terms of party programs that political leaders can attempt to consolidate public attitudes toward the work plans of government.*

Modern public policy, therefore, accentuates the importance of the parties, not as mere brokers between different groups and interests, but as agencies of the electorate. Because it affects unprecedented numbers of people and because it depends for its execution on extensive and widespread public support, modern public policy requires a broad political base. That base can be provided only by the parties, which reach people touched by no other political organization.

3. The Potentialities of the Party System. The potentialities of the two-party system are suggested, on the one hand, by the fact that for all practical purposes the major parties monopolize elections; and, on the other, by the fact that both parties have in the past managed to adapt themselves to the demands made upon them by external necessities.

Moreover, in contrast with any other political organization today in existence, the major parties even now are forced to consider public policy at least broadly enough to make it likely for them to win elections. If public esteem of the parties is much less high than it might be, the depressed state of their reputation has resulted in the main from their past indifference to broadly conceived public policy. This indifference has fixed in the popular mind the idea of spoils, patronage and plunder. It is hence not astonishing when one hears a chosen representative assert for the public ear that in his state "people put principles above party." Much of the agitation for nonpartisanship—despite the impossibility of nonpartisan organization on a national level—is rooted in the same attitudes.

Bad reputations die hard, but things are no longer what they used to be. Certainly success in presidential campaigns today is based on broad national appeals to the widest possible constituencies. To a much greater extent than in the past, elections are won by influences and trends that are felt throughout the country. *It is* therefore *good practical politics to reconsider party organization in the light of the changing conditions of politics.*

It appeared desirable in this report to relate the potentialities of the party system to both the conditions that confront the nation and the expected role of the parties. *Happily such an effort entails an application of ideas about the party system that are no longer unfamiliar.*

Consideration of ways and means of producing a more responsible party system leads into the hazards of political invention. This is a challenge that has usually been accepted with misgivings by political scientists, who are trained to describe what is and feel less well qualified to fashion innovations. We hope that our own effort will stimulate both other political scientists and participants in practical politics to attempt similar undertakings on their own account. Only by a continuous process of invention and adjustment can the party system be adapted to meet the needs of our day.

2. WHAT KIND OF PARTY SYSTEM IS NEEDED?

There is little point to talking about the American party system in terms of its deficiencies and potentialities except against a picture of what the parties ought to be. Our report would be lacking in exactness without an indication of the sort of model we have in mind.

Americans are reasonably well agreed about the purposes served by the two major parties as long as the matter is discussed in generalities. When specific questions are raised, however, agreement is much more limited. We cannot assume, therefore, a commonly shared view about the essential characteristics of the party system. But we can and must state our own view.

In brief, our view is this: *The party system that is needed must be democratic, responsible and effective*—a system that is accountable to the public, respects and expresses differences of opinion, and is able to cope with the great problems of modern government. Some of the implications warrant special statement, which is the purpose of this section.

I. A STRONGER TWO-PARTY SYSTEM

1. *The Need for an Effective Party System.* In an era beset with problems of unprecedented magnitude at home and abroad, it is dangerous to drift without a party system that helps the nation to set a general course of policy for the government as a whole. In a two-party system, when both parties are weakened or confused by internal divisions or ineffective organization it is the nation that suffers. When the parties are unable to reach and pursue responsible decisions, difficulties accumulate and cynicism about all democratic institutions grows.

An effective party system requires, first, that the parties are able to bring forth programs to which they commit themselves and, second, that the parties possess sufficient internal cohesion to carry out these programs. In such a system, the party program becomes the work program of a party, so recognized by the party leaders in and out of the government, by the party body as a whole, and by the public. This condition is unattainable unless party institutions have been created through which agreement can be reached about the general position of the party.

Clearly *such a degree of unity within the parties cannot be brought about without party procedures that give a large body of people an opportunity to share in the development of the party program.* One great function of the party system is to bring about the widest possible consent in relation to defined political goals, which provides the majority party with the essential means of building public support for the policies of the government. Democratic procedures in the internal affairs of the parties are best suited to the development of agreement within each party.

2. *The Need for an Effective Opposition Party.* The argument for a stronger party system cannot be divorced from measures designed to make the parties more fully accountable to the public. *The fundamental requirement of such accountability is a two-party system in which the opposition party acts as the critic of the party in power, developing, defining and presenting the policy alternatives which are necessary for a true choice in reaching public decisions.*

Beyond that, the case for the American two-party system need not be restated here. The two-party system is so strongly rooted in the political traditions of this country and public preference for it is so well established that consideration of other possibilities seems entirely academic. When we speak of the parties without further qualification, we mean throughout our report the two major parties. The inference is not that we consider third or minor parties undesirable or ineffectual within their limited orbit. Rather, we feel that the minor parties in the longer run have failed to leave a lasting imprint upon both the two-party system and the basic processes of American government.

In spite of the fact that the two-party system is part of the American political tradition, it cannot be said that the role of the opposition party is well understood. This is unfortunate because democratic government is greatly influenced by the character of the opposition party. The measures proposed elsewhere in our report to help the party in power to clarify its policies are equally applicable to the opposition.

The opposition most conducive to responsible government is an organized party opposition, produced by the organic operation of the two-party system. When there are two parties identifiable by the kinds of action they propose, the voters have an actual choice. On the other hand, the sort of opposition presented by a coalition that cuts across party lines, as a regular thing, tends to deprive the public of a meaningful alternative. When such coalitions are formed after the elections are over, the public usually finds it difficult to understand the new situation and to reconcile it with the purpose of the ballot. Moreover, on that basis it is next to impossible to hold either party responsible for its political record. This is a serious source of public discontent.

II. BETTER INTEGRATED PARTIES

1. *The Need for a Party System with Greater Resistance to Pressure.* As a consciously defined and consistently followed line of action keeps individuals from losing themselves in irresponsible ventures, so a program-conscious party develops greater resistance against the inroads of pressure groups.

The value of special-interest groups in a diversified society made up of countless groupings and specializations should be obvious. But organized interest groups cannot do the job of the parties. Indeed, it is only when a working formula of the public interest in its *general* character is made manifest by the parties in terms of coherent programs that the claims of interest groups can be adjusted on the basis of political responsibility. Such adjustment, once again, calls for the party's ability to honor its word.

There is little to suggest that the phenomenal growth of interest organizations in recent decades has come to its end. Organization along such lines is a characteristic feature of our civilization. To some extent these interest groups have replaced or absorbed into themselves older local institutions in that they make it possible for the government and substantial segments of the nation to maintain contact with each other. It must be obvious, however, that *the whole development makes necessary a reinforced party system that can cope with the multiplied organized pressure.* The alternative would be a scheme perhaps best described as government by pressure groups intent upon using the parties to deflect political attention from themselves.

By themselves, the interest groups cannot attempt to define public policy democratically. Coherent public policies do not emerge as the mathematical result of the claims of all of the pressure groups. The integration of the interest groups into the political system is a function of the parties. Any tendency in the direction of a strengthened party system encourages the interest groups to align themselves with one or the other of the major parties. Such a tendency is already at work. One of the noteworthy features of contemporary American politics is the fact that not a few interest groups have found it impossible to remain neutral toward both parties. To illustrate, the entry of organized labor upon the political scene has in turn impelled antagonistic special interests to coalesce in closer political alignments.

In one respect the growth of the modern interest groups is exerting a direct effect upon the internal distribution of power within the parties. They counteract and offset local interests; they are a nationalizing influence. Indeed, the proliferation of interest groups has been one of the factors in the rise of national issues because these groups tend to organize and define their objectives on a national scale.

Parties whose political commitments count are of particular significance to interest organizations with large membership such as exist among industrial workers and farmers, but to a lesser extent also among businessmen. Unlike the great majority of pressure groups, these organizations through their membership—and in proportion to their voting strength—are able to play a measurable role in elections. Interest groups of this kind are the equivalent of organizations of voters. For reasons of mutual interest, the relationship between them and the parties tends to become explicit and continuing.

A stronger party system is less likely to give cause for the deterioration and confusion of purposes which sometimes passes for compromise but is really an unjustifiable surrender to narrow interests. *Compromise among interests is compatible with the aims of a free society only when the terms of reference reflect an openly acknowledged concept of the public interest.* There is every reason to insist that the parties be held accountable to the public for the compromises they accept.

2. *The Need for a Party System with Sufficient Party Loyalty.* It is here not suggested, of course, that the parties should disagree about everything. Parties do not, and need not, take a position on all questions that allow for controversy. The proper function of the parties is to develop and define policy alternatives on matters likely to be of interest to the whole country, on issues related to the responsibility of the parties for the conduct of either the government or the opposition.

Needed clarification of party policy in itself *will not cause the parties to differ more fundamentally or more sharply than they have in the past.* The contrary is much more likely to be the case. The clarification of party policy may be expected to produce a more reasonable discussion of public affairs, more closely related to the political performance of the parties in their actions rather than their words. *Nor is it to be assumed that increasing concern with their programs will cause the parties to erect between themselves an ideological wall.* There is no real ideological division in the American electorate, and hence programs of action presented by responsible parties for the voter's support could hardly be expected to reflect or strive toward such division.

It is true at the same time that ultimately any political party must establish some conditions for membership and place some obligations on its representatives in government. Without so defining its identity the party is in danger of ceasing to be a party. To make party policy effective the *parties have the right and the duty to announce the terms to govern participation in the common enterprise.* This basic proposition is rarely denied, nor are precedents lacking. But there are practical difficulties in the way of applying restraints upon those who disregard the stated terms.

It is obvious than an effective party cannot be based merely or primarily on the expulsion of the disloyal. To impose discipline in any voluntary association is possible only as a last resort and only when a wide consensus is present within the association. Discipline and consensus are simply the front and rear sides of the same coin. *The emphasis in all consideration of party discipline must be,* therefore, *on positive measures to create a strong and general agreement on policies.* Thereafter, the problem of discipline is secondary and marginal.

When the membership of the party has become well aware of party policy and stands behind it, assumptions about teamwork within the party are likely to pervade the whole organization. Ultimately it is the electorate itself which will determine how firmly it wants the lines of party allegiance to be drawn. Yet even a small shift of emphasis toward party cohesion is likely to produce changes not only in the structure of the parties but also in the degree to which members identify themselves with their party.

Party unity is always a relative matter. It may be fostered, but the whole weight of tradition in American politics is against very rigid party discipline. As a general rule, the parties have a basis for expecting adherence to the party program when their position is reasonably explicit. Thus it is evident that the disciplinary difficulties of the parties do not result primarily from a reluctance to impose restraints but from the neglect of positive measures to give meaning to party programs.

As for party cohesion in Congress, the parties have done little to build up the kind of unity within the congressional party that is now so widely desired. Traditionally congressional candidates are treated as if they were the orphans of the political system, with no truly adequate party mechanism available for the conduct of their campaigns. Enjoying remarkably little national or local party support, congressional candidates have mostly been left to cope with the political hazards of their occupation on their own account. *A basis for party cohesion in Congress will be established as soon as the parties interest themselves sufficiently in their congressional candidates to set up strong and active compaign organizations in the constituencies.* Discipline is less a matter of what the parties do *to* their congressional candidates than what the parties do *for* them.

III. MORE RESPONSIBLE PARTIES

1. *The Need for Parties Responsible to the Public. Party responsibility means the responsibility of both parties to the general public, as enforced in elections.*

Responsibility of the party in power centers on the conduct of the government, usually in terms of policies. The party in power has a responsibility, broadly defined, for the general management of the government, for its manner of getting results, for the results achieved, for the consequences of inaction as well as action, for the intended and unintended outcome of its conduct of public affairs, for all that it plans to do, for all that it might have foreseen, for the leadership it provides, for the acts of all of its agents and for what it says as well as for what it does.

Party responsibility includes the responsibility of the opposition party, also broadly defined, for the conduct of its opposition, for the management of public discussion, for the development of alternative policies and programs, for the bipartisan policies which it supports, for its failures and successes in developing the issues of public policy, and for its leadership of public opinion. The opposition is as responsible for its record in Congress as is the party in power. It is important that the opposition party be effective but it is equally important that it be responsible, for an irresponsible opposition is dangerous to the whole political system.

Party responsibility to the public, enforced in elections, implies that there be more than one party, for the public can hold a party responsible only if it has a choice. Again, unless the parties identify themselves with programs, the public is unable to make an intelligent choice between them. The public can understand the general management of the government only in terms of policies. When the parties lack the capacity to define their actions in terms of policies, they turn irresponsible because the electoral choice between the parties becomes devoid of meaning.

As a means of achieving responsibility, the clarification of party policy also tends to keep public debate on a more realistic level, restraining the inclination of party spokesmen to make unsubstantiated statements and charges. When party policy is made clear, the result to be expected is a more reasonable and profitable discussion, tied more closely to the record of party action. When there is no clear basis for rating party performance, when party policies cannot be defined in terms of a concrete program, party debate tears itself loose from the facts. Then wild fictions are used to excite the imagination of the public.

2. *The Need for Parties Responsible to Their Members. Party responsibility includes also the responsibility of party leaders to the party membership, as enforced in primaries, caucuses and conventions.* To this end the internal processes of the parties must be democratic, the party members must have an opportunity to participate in intraparty business, and the leaders must be accountable to the party. Responsibility demands that the parties concern themselves with the development of good relations between the leaders and the members. Only thus can the parties act as intermediaries between the government and the people. Strengthening the parties involves, therefore, the improvement of the internal democratic processes by which the leaders of the party are kept in contact with the members.

The external and the internal kinds of party responsibility need not conflict.

Responsibility of party leaders to party members promotes the clarification of party policy when it means that the leaders find it necessary to explain the policy to the membership. Certainly the lack of unity within the membership cannot be overcome by the fiat of an irresponsible party leadership. A democratic internal procedure can be used not merely to test the strength of the various factions within a party but also to resolve the conflicts. The motives for enlarging the areas of agreement within the parties are persuasive because unity is the condition of success.

Intraparty conflict will be minimized if it is generally recognized that national, state and local party leaders have a common responsibility to the party membership. Intraparty conflict is invited and exaggerated by dogmas that assign to local party leaders an exclusive right to appeal to the party membership in their area.

Occasions may arise in which the parties will find it necessary to apply sanctions against a state or local party organization, especially when that organization is in open rebellion against policies established for the whole party. There are a variety of ways in which recognition may be withdrawn. It is possible to refuse to seat delegates to the National Convention; to drop from the National Committee members representing the dissident state organization; to deny legislative committee assignments to members of Congress sponsored by the disloyal organization; and to appeal directly to the party membership in the state or locality, perhaps even promoting a rival organization. The power to take strong measures is there.

It would be unfortunate, however, if the problem of party unity were thought of as primarily a matter of punishment. Nothing prevents the parties from explaining themselves to their own members. The party members have power to insist that local and state party organizations and leaders cooperate with the party as a whole; all the members need is a better opportunity to find out what party politics is about. The need for sanctions is relatively small when state and local organizations are not treated as the restricted preserve of their immediate leaders. National party leaders ought to have access to party members everywhere as a normal and regular procedure because they share with local party leaders responsibility to the same party membership. It would always be proper for the national party leaders to discuss all party matters with the membership of any state or local party organization. Considering their great prestige, wise and able national party leaders will need very little more than this opportunity.

The political developments of our time place a heavy emphasis on national issues as the basis of party programs. As a result, the party membership is coming to look to the national party leaders for a larger role in intraparty affairs. There is some evidence of growing general agreement within the membership of each party, strong enough to form a basis of party unity, provided the parties maintain close contact with their own supporters.

In particular, *national party leaders have a legitimate interest in the nomination of congressional candidates,* though normally they try hard to avoid the appearance of any intervention. Depending on the circumstances, this interest can be expressed quite sufficiently by seeking a chance to discuss the nomination with the party membership in the congressional district. On the other hand, it should not be assumed that state and local party leaders usually have an interest in congressional nominations antagonistic to the interest of the national leaders in maintaining the general party policy. As a matter of fact, congressional nominations are not considered great prizes by the local party organization as generally as one might think. It is neglect of congressional nominations and elections more than any other factor that weakens party unity in Congress. It should be added, however, that what is said here about intraparty relations with respect to congressional nominations applies also to other party nominations.

3. THE INADEQUACY OF THE EXISTING PARTY SYSTEM

The existing party system is inadequately prepared to meet the demands now being made upon it chiefly because its central institutions are not well organized to deal with national questions. The sort of party organization needed today is indirectly suggested by the origin of the traditional party structure. This structure developed in a period in which local interests were dominant and positive governmental action at the national level did not play the role it assumed later.

I. BEGINNING TRANSITION

1. *Change and Self-examination.* Having outlined the kind of party system we accept as our basic model, we are now able to list briefly some of the principal deficiencies of the existing national party institutions. At the same time we can identify some of the conspicuous failings that show up in the operations of the two parties, in particular their failure to bring about adequate popular participation in politics and to develop satisfactory relations between the central and the local party organizations.

Marked changes have occurred *in the structure and processes of American society* during the twentieth century. Here it will be enough to point out that most of these changes *have necessarily affected the party system.* In many respects the party system is today far from what it was fifty years ago, even though there has not been as yet a conscious and planned adjustment. When a party system is undergoing such a slow transformation, it is difficult to describe its operation accurately or to enumerate its deficiencies precisely as they now exist. The Democratic party is today almost a new creation, produced since 1932. Some of its leaders have given much thought to its present-day characteristics. On the opposite side, the Republican party has been the subject of extensive and repeated self-examination for nearly two decades. It is *the prevailing climate of self-examination as well as the current tendencies toward change in the party system* that *give point to inquiries like that represented by our report.*

2. *Burden of the Past.* Despite these tendencies toward change, however,

formal party organization in its main features is still substantially what it was before the Civil War. Aside from the adoption of the direct primary, organizational forms have not been overhauled for nearly a century. The result is that the parties are now probably the most archaic institutions in the United States.

Under these circumstances, it is not surprising that *the main trends of American politics,* especially the emphasis on effective national action, *have tended to outflank the party system.* Until rather recently neither of the two parties has found it necessary to concern itself seriously with the question of adequate party organization at the national level. The familiar description of the parties as loose confederations of state and local machines has too long remained reasonably accurate.

PARTY RESPONSIBILITY—A CRITICAL INQUIRY *

Murray S. Stedman, Jr., and Herbert Sonthoff

INTEREST in the question of reorganization of American political parties is probably at an all-time high. Since the end of World War II, most of the dozen or more new books dealing with Congress have touched on the problem; and innumerable books and articles have dealt with the parties and the problem directly. The Report of the Committee on Political Parties of the American Political Science Association is one of the most recent contributions. It suggests the need for more centralized parties, and rests its arguments on assumptions usually made by proponents of such reform. Some of these assumptions will be examined in this article and frequent reference made to the *Report.* The purpose, however, is to approach the study of these assumptions broadly, rather than merely to center attention upon the *Report.*

I

There may be wide agreement with the *Report's* assumption that *the present two party system is irresponsible,* although the precise meaning of "irresponsible" may vary greatly. Yet the essence of the assumption is that the American party system is an inadequate mechanism for translating popular wishes into action or specific policy. This charge rests on several beliefs which are open to considerable doubt. It assumes that the problem of popular responsibility is largely the mechanical one of organization, i.e., that responsibility is "effective" only when there exist clear lines of responsibility. If, as the allegation presupposes, responsibility is a matter of

* From Murray S. Stedman, Jr., and Herbert Sonthoff. "Party Responsibility—A Critical Inquiry," in *Western Political Quarterly,* Vol. IV, No. 3 (September, 1951), pp. 454–68. © 1951 by the University of Utah. Permission to reprint granted by the University of Utah, copyright owners.

discipline, it becomes a fairly narrow and rigid premise.

There is also an implied assumption that majority rule is preferable to consensus rule, and that anything less than majority rule is, in a technical sense, irresponsible. It is presumably held, therefore, that a majority established by consensus, either as legislative or sectional consensus, is not true majority rule and is hence irresponsible. This argument is tenable only if we identify majority rule with majority party rule. Such an identification, however, raises the central problem of popular government. Is it empirically true that all sectional interests are increasingly negligible? Is foreign policy a matter of majority party determination? Does the election of a President mean that the electoral majority approves of the platform of the winning party? And why, most importantly, is rule by compromise less efficacious and less democratic than rule by one party, even though it be the majority party? A host of problems arise here. They, as well as the charge of party irresponsibility, pose the ancient question of the meaning of majority rule. What does "majority rule" mean? Does it mean local basis of representation, method of constituting and reconstituting the lawmaker, rule of legislative procedure, agreement of and by public opinion, mandate for the executive, or government by plebiscite? Majority rule in its strict, arithmetical sense refers to the degree rather than to the mode of agreement. It means merely opposition to the idea of minority rule, and needs by no means to be considered, therefore, as an alternative to the rule by consensus. Consensus has been the framework of American party politics, as witness most of the more significant legislative acts which were the product not of party rule but of party consensus, i.e., of agreement between major groups within the parties. In this country, therefore, "consensus" is an important procedural concept, rather than a philosophical one aiming at fundamental agreement in Mill's sense of the word. Before we undertake to streamline the party machinery to facilitate majority rule it would be wiser, and in the long run of greater benefit, to define the Constitutional task which this machinery is to serve.

II

Another assumption is that *more responsible parties would require a very high degree of centralization of the internal party structure.* It has long been noted by students of Congress that party discipline on important issues is either weak or nonexistent. One of the most popular plans advanced for the strengthening of congressional parties calls for the creation of a legislative cabinet. Yet this plan, with its many possible variations, falls far short of what the advocates of party government are seeking. This is not to argue that a legislative cabinet and party centralization are incompatible; it is merely to point out that they are not the same thing. The advocates of party government desire not only to facilitate executive-legislative co-ordination, but also to guarantee such co-ordination through highly centralized national parties.

Such a degree of centralization would be unprecedented in American history. However, only a centralized organization could possibly commit itself to and subsequently execute a specific program. To be successful, the national party would have to control rigidly such matters as patronage, finances, the nominating processes, and local party subsidiary organizations. The locus of power would be at the national rather than at the state or local level, as is the case today.

To make this change in power relationships, the national parties would have to possess sanctions to penalize recalcitrant state and local party leaders whose faith in the national "line" might otherwise waver. Such control would go far beyond the kind envisaged, for example, by the unsuccessful "purges" of 1938, since it would not be limited merely to congressional candidates. It would affect the nominating process generally. Quite logically, therefore, the advocates of party government stress the need for great control over local party organizations, including the power to refuse to seat "disloyal" elements at national conventions, and to exclude such elements from the national committees. Furthermore, as the *Report* states, ". . . consideration should be given to the development of additional means of dealing with rebellious and disloyal state organizations."

From this line of reasoning it follows that only the closed primary could be endorsed, for only if the national party could control the local nominating process could it choose candidates loyal to itself. It is clear that such a change would require tremendous revision of existing primary statutes. For example, the four states of Pennsylvania, New York, California, and Washington all use different procedures to nominate to statewide offices. It is hardly possible to determine objectively which of the four systems produces the best qualified candidates. Yet, most proposals for party centralization imply a drastic change of the primary, perhaps in the face of hostile public opinion.

The logic of the argument carries much further, however, than merely urging the closed primary or some particular form of it. It also implies a threat to the direct primary as an institution. If nominations are to be determined in accordance with criteria established by the national party, it is difficult to see what, if any, purpose is served by retaining the direct primary. But the abolition of the primary would have particularly serious effects in those states, counties, and cities which are essentially one-party areas. In those localities, the only meaningful choice for the voter is between candidates of the same party. This may be true not only of the choice between candidates, but also of the choice between programs. The net effect of the disappearance of primaries in such a situation would be to take from the voter his only effective weapon for registering protest. In two-party areas the ending of the direct primary would presumably have less serious results, but such an action might create more problems than it would solve.

Proponents of stronger national parties usually contend that such parties would weaken the hold of local bosses and pressure groups, thus achieving a separation of national from local issues. To be sure, if local organizations lost control of the nominating process, their power would be drastically reduced. It does not follow, however, that a greater separation of national from state and local politics would be achieved. Neither as a matter of principle nor as a matter of applied psychology is there any great support for the contention that the national parties would lose interest in local patronage. It is probable that the first of the existing national parties to reorganize itself would be able to extend its patronage power into hitherto sacrosanct areas. In passing, the question may be raised whether the whole idea of party government is compatible with any kind of nonpartisan approach to local government. If the answer is negative, one can visualize a vast new area of spoils opening up for the benefit of national organizations.

The danger of the idea of party government is not that stronger national parties per se would be created. The danger is that the national leaders, in order to build an ever more extensive base for their own operations, might take over, so far as possible, all existing state and local organizations. Such a development would clearly imply more than the death of the direct primary. To propose it raises very serious challenges to the federal pattern itself and to many real advances made in state and local governments during the past half-century. Quite possibly, because of its widespread character the centralized type of bossism, even under the name of "party government," might be even more objectionable than the existing local bossism.

In view of the almost proverbial contempt in which many professional students of politics hold party machines, a word in their defense may appear unusual. Still, we need to reflect on the positive services they perform in terms of the organization of local voter interest; and we should also consider the extent to which the usual connotation of the term "politician," which has become almost an expletive, impedes a realistic understanding of the functional role the politician plays in the crystallization of political opinion and in the political process on the grass roots level generally. It is an open question whether greater responsibility of the political party to the voter is obtained by strengthening the internal chains of party command through closer adherence to an obligatory party platform. The role of the local leader also requires examination; for another belief seemingly held by the proponents of stronger parties is that the public will abandon the idea of the politician as a broker. It is urged that the public will prefer an automaton committed beyond all else to the party program, and thus will cast aside the traditional politician's role of middleman. The implications of this line of thought are far-reaching. What is being urged is nothing less than a revolutionary transformation in the role and function of the party, of the candidates, and of the electorate.

III

It is further assumed that *centralized parties would be more democratic than the present parties.* Of the various writers who urge greater party centralization, Schattschneider expresses himself the most clearly on this point. "The essence of democracy," he says, "is to be found *between,* not *within* the parties. The fact that the parties compete for public support is the principal safeguard against any tendency they may have to become oppressive." This view possibly rests on too close an analogy between our comparatively decentralized parties and contemporary British parties; yet its meaning is quite clear. The line of reasoning is of particular significance for the problem of independency. Schattschneider, who states the issue more precisely than does the *Report,* says: "In the folklore of politics the greatest virtue of public officials is 'independence.' Thus, independent candidates are better than party candidates. . . . We cling to this notion in spite of the demonstrable fact that the greater the number of independents the smaller will be the number of partisans able to control Congress, for independence is a synonym of ineffectiveness in a game in which teamwork produces results." The attack continues by criticizing those, especially college professors, who stress non-partisanship. It is not clear, however, whether the author refers only to Congressional levels or includes nonpartisanship at the municipal level as well.

It is not quite clear, either, what is meant here by "independency." As a matter of fact, not of theory, very few candidates of minor parties—and very few independents—ever get elected to Congress. . . . The same observation is also generally true of state legislatures. Only in various municipal, school board, and judicial elections is independence in the sense of nonpartisanship stressed. If "independency" means absence of party labels, the attack is largely aimed at a straw man. If, however, the term refers to the shifting of voters from one party to the other in general elections, it is difficult to see the basis for the objection to this practice. A voter who changes parties in elections can hardly be termed "independent" in the sense that he repudiates parties. To the contrary, such a voter is presumably responsible for forcing the parties to commit themselves to programs at all. A third meaning of "independency" could be that it refers to persons who split ballots promiscuously. With strongly centralized parties this practice would undoubtedly be less widespread. But given the present structure of American government (which neither Schattschneider nor the *Report* specifically condemns), it is difficult to see why voting Taft-Lausche or Dewey-Lehman-Impellitteri is less effective in terms of securing competent officials than voting a straight party ticket.

Advocates of stronger parties also assume that pressure group activity is inferior to activity taken within the party itself. Strong parties are held to be the natural foes of pressure groups. But is the transference of pressure group activity into the party fundamentally compatible with the idea of *two* strong parties? There can be no doubt that such transference of influence is logically compatible with the existence of many *small* relatively fanatical parties. The farmers could organize a farmers' party; the veterans, educators, labor unions, and small businessmen could do the same. Such a development, however, is the antithesis of the strong *two-party* system which the proponents of more centralized parties are urging. The real choice is between a relatively weak two-party system with many outside interest groups or a very strong multi-party system with few nonpartisan interest groups. The latter development involves a fundamental reconstruction and reorientation of American socioeconomic life which might easily threaten the stability of the Republic. This would be too high a price to pay for the subjugation of pressure groups.

One of the major suggestions for the reform of the American parties is the establishment of a central party council which would function as the prime agent in the co-ordination of party policy; its purpose, in other words, would be to maintain party responsibility. The suggestion illustrates the increasingly administrative or even quasi-military approach to the study of political problems; and though this discussion is not a methodological one, we may note, and perhaps question, the organizational emphasis of this particular suggestion for party reform. Such an emphasis, seemingly priding itself on its "practicality," points necessarily to the two prime requirements of organization: force and discipline. The *Report,* entirely true to its premises, therefore stresses repeatedly the need of nationally enforced party discipline. It suggests the use of presidential power in the maintenance of that leadership and discipline, and it argues with admirable and revealing candor that "greater program responsibility at the level of political parties is likely to appeal to administrators and the career officialdom."

We may well resort to a different kind of "practicality" and inquire how acceptable such a far-reaching reform of the party system would be to the electorate, let alone to the members of both parties. Can the political behavior of the average American, who is so obviously a traditionalist and a gradualist, be altered by mere organizational reconstruction of what are, after all, voluntary associations? By this we do not mean to wave the flags of history and national uniqueness, the most pedestrian of all arguments against change. We are merely concerned with what appears to be a hierarchical and mechanistic approach to the problem of party responsibility.

The proposal for greater party centralization is further justified by its proponents with the argument that public policy, both on the legislative and executive levels, is becoming increasingly national in character. It is held, therefore, that party policy, to be effective and responsible, must comply with this trend; that, as sectionalism as a conscious political interest is dying out in national life, party interest must follow the same trend. No one will deny the increasingly national scope of government responsibilities and obligations. Yet that does not necessarily mean an automatic and corresponding decline either of sectional interests or of regional and local political problems. If that were so, regional and local political concerns and interests would long since have declined in American life, spurred on during the last two wars when considerations of national strength and survival were paramount.

The question therefore arises whether the insistence upon greater national party organization and a more "national" scope of party platforms is based on the assumption (which the *Report* seems clearly to suggest) that party programs will be the more "meaningful" as they become more national in scope. It is perhaps this assumption which is the ultimate justification for the call for greater party discipline. Hypothetically, national party programs need not conflict with sectional interests. A program which is the result of compromise between sectional interests, or even between interest groups, is not necessarily less "meaningful" than a program aimed exclusively at the level of national policy. A foreign policy program *is* meaningful because it is concerned only with the national interest; but even and particularly there, we are conscious of the strength of domestic regional and group interests and of their influence upon the determination of policy. Does the strength of that influence *necessarily* make for national weakness? That it may contribute to an indeterminate foreign policy with lamentable frequency cannot be denied. But does the answer then lie in as radical a change of domestic political processes as is suggested? A growth of general political intelligence may well be a better and more convincing answer.

Perhaps the central question is simply whether democracy is best realized through strong parties ("strong" meaning highly disciplined) or by a strong electorate organized in a variety of ways, including political parties. Such a variety of organization may be an expression of democratic strength of a different kind, representing and expressing the variety of ideas and desires of a people as diverse and as active as are Americans. A further, if subsidiary and tactical, question which should not be ignored is whether *legislative* responsibility, which in this country is responsibility by *both* parties, would be actually increased by greater internal party responsibility and by two party programs. The latter may be sufficiently distinct to offer a "meaningful" choice, but would be bound to impede the kind of interparty agreements upon which the smooth functioning of Congress and of the state legislature depends. For "on its official side, the party is unitary; on its unofficial side, it is pluralistic. It is consensus while it tries *to create* consensus. Its success in America has depended on its maintaining the double role."

IV

Many party reformers, including the authors of the *Report,* agree that *a multiparty system would be unfortunate.* It is an axiom of American politics that American political institutions and processes rest upon the two-party system whose benefits, as compared with a multiparty pattern, are evident. The *Report* therefore rightly stresses the danger of disintegration of the two parties either by direct presidential appeal to the voters or by the voters' dissatisfaction with the vagueness of party programs. Approval of the two-party system must, however, not be an uncritical one. It must rest on a proper awareness of the federal principle which, on the one hand, makes possible virtual one-party rule over large sections of the country, and, on the other hand, permits the rise to power on a local or regional scale of third parties. If we therefore consider the problem of party reform and party responsibility from the point of view of the two-party system and its maintenance, it resolves itself into these two seemingly conflicting questions:

1. What kind of reform does the American party system require in order to extend the two-party system into sections of the country where the voter has little, if any, meaningful choice; where the growth of second, third, and perhaps even more parties is highly desirable in order to offer the voter purposeful, alternative programs in terms of specifics?

2. How must the party system be reformed in order to prevent the growth of a nationwide multitude of parties?

The *Report* warns of the danger inherent in the rise of extremist parties due to "the incapacity of the two parties for consistent action based on meaningful programs." Even if we assume knowledge of what is "meaningful" (which American history hardly corroborates) and grant the somewhat alarmist premise that the mere vagueness and inconsistency of the policies of the two major parties cause the rise of new extremist parties, can that particular fire be fought with anything but fire? In short, more "meaningful programs" of the two parties can mean little else but more specific though perhaps not necessarily more doctrinaire programs. It must be admitted that the dividing line between "specificness of policy" and "program according to doctrine" is a thin one, as a glance at the European party systems shows. Another glance at those systems, warning examples of the erosion of the political grass roots through political doctrine, indicates that the splitting of the electorate into a multiplicity of parties which occurred through the increasing radicalization of party programs, in turn was the logical result of what we might call competitive program specificness. The Scandinavian multiparty system is often cited as counterevidence, and is at times suggested. as a model for a more "meaningful" American party system. However, the stability of the Scandinavian party system rests upon general agreement as to the positive social and economic functions of government, a subject which is the very core of party dissent in the United States. The practical obstacles to greater concreteness of programs of the American parties are immense in view of the diversity of regional and sectional interests. Since these interests are the major obstacle to program concreteness, the assumption is not too farfetched that any serious attempt at its attainment might threaten the very existence of the party at the national level. Another quite practical reason why competition between parties is carried on in terms other than those of specific programs is that the party leaders are fearful "of doing anything that would give the other party a good 'issue,'" a disposition which probably explains the lack of contrast between the parties better than the charge of party irresponsibility or voter apathy.

v

It seems evident that a major premise of the *Report* is that *voting behavior will fairly easily accommodate itself to the new concept of party*. It has been generally assumed by the proponents of more centralized parties that the job of selling the politicians on the idea would be more difficult than selling the electorate on it. This assumption, if in itself not antidemocratic, at least implies that voting behavior—voting habits and attitudes—constitutes no large obstacle in the path of party reconstruction. It is based largely on faith, for there exist little data to support it at this time. The principal studies of voting behavior show that voters are remarkably consistent, and that they are consistent in relation to their socioeconomic status. To refer to such consistency as "ancestor worship," as Brogan and others have done, is beside the point.

The similarity between major party platforms has led many to believe that there is no difference between the major parties. The electorate, they argue, has no real choice; and, in any event, whatever choice a majority of the voters may make has little significance. However, various studies of voting behavior attest to a marked difference in social composition of the major parties in two-party areas. It would seem reasonable, in view of this difference, to expect that the performance of Congress would differ according to the party in control. In actual fact, the qualitative output in Congress varies considerably *over a period of time.* The Congresses of the Wilsonian and New Deal eras passed numerous great regulatory acts; yet few such acts were placed on the statute books during the period of "normalcy." In short, while the electorate may show a fairly high degree of party consistency, a sufficient percentage of the electorate changes its view from time to time so that legislative changes do, in fact, occur.

If the voters can influence changes in the tenor of congressional legislation at intervals, what may be said for the success of party leaders in attempting to accelerate such change through control over party personnel? Here again the comparative consistency of voting habits is relevant. The failure of the famous 1938 "purge" showed that Democratic voters generally preferred the primary candidate who was opposed by President Roosevelt. The preference of the electorate for the present major parties *as they are,* is another important factor when considering the possibility of change in voting behavior. Public opinion polls show no great dissatisfaction with the present party system. The public generally adopts a negative attitude when the questions of reconstruction along liberal versus conservative lines or the creation of new parties are raised.

Proponents of stronger parties usually assume further that the public may be easily induced to prefer programs to personalities in particular elections. Both for the parties in and out of power, the prime objective is held to be the creation of specific programs. This assumption runs counter to existing practice. The fact that, over a period of time, the *tenor* of legislative acts will vary does not indicate that in specific elections the public supports or desires to support a specific *party* program. A study by Woodward and Roper implies that personality is a very strong factor in determining the outcome of a given election. From the long-range point of view, Louis Bean concludes that the trend of the business cycle is the most significant single factor in determining party control of the presidency and of Congress. Bean's study is concerned, of course, with party control, and not with qualitative differences in program. Yet both studies show how relatively insignificant is specificness of party program as a factor in existing voting behavior.

The demands upon the parties for more specific commitments to the electorate, the call for more definite national programs, for a perpetual state of preparedness to assume the burden and responsibility of the government, appear at first glance to be nothing but common sense. They are the heart of every criticism of the American party system. They imply, however, nothing short of a complete change of voting behavior. They may be "realistic" so far as efficiency in policy determination is a criterion, yet they are illusory as regards the disposition of the electorate. The question is how anxious are we to alter this disposition, even if such alteration were possible by some formula of social psychology. That disposition of the average voter has made possible the present system of constituent-representative relationship, which is one of remarkable closeness considering the size of the country and of the electoral districts. It has kept the voter close to and interested in the Government. It is that disposition which has made for a more tangible basis of popular government in this country—for a more "personal" basis, in several senses of the word—than would be possible by a system of increased party control. The greater the party control, the more the legislator is bound to the "boys in the back room" rather than to the "boys on the front lawn."

VI

Criticisms of the existing party system often imply that under a reconstructed and centralized system *the same party would normally control both executive and legislative departments.* The idea of fusion of executive and legislative departments through the instrumentality of party is basic to cabinet government. Such advocates of cabinet government as Elliott and Hazlitt have built a case largely upon the alleged unworkability of any system of a separation of powers. But in this study our concern is not with the case presented by the avowed advocates of cabinet government; it is rather with those who argue that greater party responsibility and centralization can be achieved without reckoning conclusively with the separation of powers principle.

Such an argument necessarily assumes that normally the same party will control both Congress and the presidency. Whether this is to be accomplished through the establishment of national party councils, coincidence of terms of office, or some other means, is not important. What is important is that, short of Constitutional amendment, there is no *guarantee* that the President and either house might not be of different parties. In terms of representation, the distinction between President and Congress is similar to that drawn by Rousseau in his comparison of the general will and the will of all. It is, of course, the latter which Congress now often represents. In any case, the proposals to establish party government would alter this pattern.

Let us hypothesize a very strong, disciplined party system in this country. Furthermore, let us imagine that for one reason or another the President and one or both houses represent different parties. What might be expected to occur in the highly important area of foreign affairs? Bipartisanship on foreign policy is often criticized on three principal grounds: First, that it is undemocratic in that the minority party by its acquiescence may contribute to its own demise; second, that it is immoral in that a totally false and misleading impression of national unity may be created; third, that it is incompatible with party government.

It is the last charge which concerns us here and needs examination. Under our present party arrangement, with one or two exceptions the major parties have always co-operated in periods of external crisis. Co-operation was never a hundred per cent complete; but a working majority of each major party usually agreed with its counterpart as to the basic policies to be followed. Whatever opposition existed was likewise usually bipartisan; that is, it was not confined to a single party. A most significant demonstration of approval of bipartisan foreign policy, so obvious as often to be overlooked, occurred in the 1948 elections. Whatever else the presidential election of that year showed, it conclusively demonstrated support for Truman's "bipartisan" foreign policy by repudiating the proposals of Henry A. Wallace.

In principle, the proponents of party government are driven to the position that bipartisanship is per se an evil. They condemn the present practice where, instead of aligning themselves solidly on different sides of great policy issues, Senators and Representatives split into pro and con bipartisan blocs. Party allegiance becomes subordinate to sectional and regional interests.

Few would argue that such an arrangement is an unmixed blessing. On the credit side, however, it offers the tremendous advantage of very great flexibility. It does not suffer from the rigidity which the existence of a really strong, well-organized opposition party would entail. The basis of consensus is broad enough to allow for compromise and thus, among other things, plays down any process of aggrandizement by the President at the expense of Congress. Some critics of the existing system express the fear that our traditional form of government may break down as the result of a series of crises in which congressional inability to co-operate with the executive is followed by presidential dictatorship. These fears appear grossly exaggerated. Nevertheless, in the absence of cabinet responsibility under a parliamentary type of government, the prospect of a breakdown in democratic procedures would surely be aggravated rather than lessened by the existence of strongly disciplined and highly dedicated parties. If such a doctrinaire congressional-presidential impasse would be unfortunate in domestic affairs, it could conceivably be disastrous in the area of foreign policy.

VII

Finally, we are assured that *no fundamental Constitutional changes are necessary*. The *Report* argues that federalism and the separation of powers are not insuperable obstacles to the reform of American parties and the increase of party responsibility. Yet it is hard to escape the conclusion that the authors of the *Report* consider federalism the source of many of the ills of the present party system. Perhaps we are not going too far afield in saying that the suggested reforms of parties here discussed rest on a certain misunderstanding of the nature of federalism, a misunderstanding indicated by the organizational, administrative approach. Is the belief, long held by some, that federalism is an outmoded political form, valid in any but an organizational sense? From the viewpoint of efficiency and smoothness of administrative operation (and, alas, policy-making), the argument is doubtless cogent. But is functional efficiency, after all, the most valid criterion in adjudging a constitutional system? In a way we are putting the cart before the horse when we aim, by whatever method, at an increase of party responsibility (in terms of a particular meaning of "responsibility") at the cost of a profound alteration of the constitutional system. Instead, we might first inquire into the objectives of that system and then consider how a change of party structure would aid in accomplishing these objectives. Federalism, as Madison's classic argument asserted, still is an effective guarantee against the threat of unlimited, undivided power, regardless of where concentrated. To be sure, concentration of power in the hands of parties supporting a list of programmatic demands is not the same thing as concentration of all political power; and the Hitlerian lesson-experience, while not comparable, is nevertheless impressive. To prevent the former from leading to the latter requires a constitutional order of the kind which has served this country well for an impressive length of time. It has done so because it has made possible peaceful change with a minimum of internal and external party strife—a state of affairs eminently worth perpetuating.

The present debate on party organization is greatly needed. It may lead to constructive action. Yet the advocates of greater party centralization, in neglecting or sidestepping the issues of profound Constitutional revision, have not made an effective case. Their prescription may cure or kill the patient. To the patient, if not the prescriber, this is a matter of some importance. An alternate approach of long standing has been the suggestion to create cabinet government outright through Constitutional amendment. The separation of powers would have to go; the Senate would have to be abolished or in some manner shorn of most of its powers; the electoral system would require great alterations. The wisdom and practicality of such a remedy go as far beyond the confines of political feasibility as they do of this paper. Yet, if the party system is as ill as many appear to believe, it seems probable that only drastic action has any hope of producing happy results. But then, the severity of the illness is still open to question.

CONGRESSIONAL AND PRESIDENTIAL PARTY SYSTEMS:

FOUR-PARTY POLITICS *

James MacGregor Burns

THE CONGRESSIONAL PARTY SYSTEM

I HAVE noted the heavy impact of national politics on state and local politics—how a presidential sweep of the nation, for example, can upset the competitive balance of parties in the states and leave a swath of one-party states

* From James MacGregor Burns, "The Congressional Party System," in *The Deadlock of Democracy: Four-Party Politics in America* (Englewood Cliffs, N. J.: Prentice-Hall, Inc., 1963), pp. 241–264. © 1963 by James MacGregor Burns.

and districts, with the resultant disintegrating and fragmentizing of state and local parties. Now we must look at the reverse process—how the structure of state and local politics, comprising personal organizations surrounding fairly autonomous politicians, reacts back on national party politics. The peculiar interplay in America of national political forces and state-to-local forces makes for a structure of politicians' motives, roles, expectations, and goals that comprise two political systems, the congressional and the presidential.

The base of the congressional system is the one-party district, as established and protected by the state legislatures. Though we hear much about congressmen's "safe seats," it is still hard to grasp the extent of non-competition in congressional elections. Almost half of the House seats never change party hands. Another quarter, roughly, switch only on rare occasions. Aside from great sweeps such as those of 1920 and 1936, about 150 Republican seats and about the same number of Democratic seats never switch to the other party. Reasonably competitive districts number about 125 out of a total of 435. Many Senate seats are also one-party, especially in the South, but not to the same extent as in the House.

These safe seats are only partly accidental in origin. They are also a planned result of the alignment of party forces in the states. The drawing of election districts (congressional as well as state) is in the hands of state legislatures. Most state legislatures are controlled year after year and decade after decade by the same party (at least in one house), and legislators naturally carve up the districts to benefit their own party. Actually, the hottest fights take place mainly within the dominant party as congressmen, to protect their districts, bring influence to bear on state legislators, state legislators maneuver for their own electoral advantage (especially if they have congressional ambitions), and intra-party factions engage in their horse-trading. Sometimes state legislators act positively to protect the congressional party. In 1962 the Mississippi legislature drove a pro-Kennedy congressman out of office by combining his district with a highly rural and conservative one.

Note the difference between this kind of manipulation and the shenanigans of gerrymandering. A state legislature can make every congressional district approximately equal in population—and hence absolve itself of the charge of gerrymandering—and at the same time carve up the state with such expertness that some districts remain, or become, hopelessly non-competitive. Indeed, there is a quiet but recurrent battle between state party leaders trying to strengthen the state party as a whole, and the congressmen and their legislative allies trying to fortify themselves in their part of the state. The state leaders want to make as many districts as possible fairly secure for their party, but not overwhelmingly safe, for they seek to spread their party's strength widely in order to win as many congressional and legislative elections as possible. The congressman, on the other hand, is a bit greedy; remembering the occasional horrible examples of "entrenched" congressmen being unseated, he usually wants to build up his majorities as high as possible. And given the diffusion of power in the state party, the congressman can often get his way.

Most one-party districts are made up of villages, small towns, and small cities.

They have a heavily rural bias. Compared to the larger metropolitan areas, these districts tend to be more homogeneous in social make-up and political attitude. They usually lack the political competition and vitality that characterize more urban or mixed areas. The major party, the local business interests, press and pulpit, the community leaders combine loosely to represent the dominant interests in the area. Possible centers of dissent, most notably the opposition party, trade unions or ethnic groups, cannot carry the burden of competition. The opposition, such as it is, fades away. The result in these areas is not so much a loud and clear conservatism (which might be logical in such a social and economic context) as confusion, conformity, and negativism. But the congressman does not see it this way. To him the grass roots are the source of common sense; he would agree with Rousseau that there was more wisdom in small bands of Swiss peasants gathered under oak trees to conduct their affairs than in all the governments of Europe.

We must not exaggerate these urban-rural differences, given the blurring of social forces in America. Rather we must see how the political mechanisms are linked to dominant social forces in typical areas. The link is the politician—in this case the congressman. He does not relate himself to his district impersonally. He deals with its political life on his own terms, kindling some forces and tranquillizing or ignoring others. Thus he contributes to the political tone of the district as well as expressing it. The manner in which he does this turns on his perception of how his political behavior, given the political materials he must work with, can advance his political career.

Typically such a congressman has two major career choices. He can seek to stay in his congressional post and hence rise through the hierarchy in Congress. Or he can use his office as a stepping stone to bigger offices, such as governor or senator. Usually this is not a free choice, for it is influenced by the nature of his district as well as by his own motives and expectations. A man in a safe district often finds himself, as in upstate New York or downstate Illinois, representing a constituency quite different from the state as a whole. Rural districts in particular are likely to be more conservative than the state generally, or at least more opposed to prevailing political and governmental trends in the state. Republican congressmen from the upstate districts of New York, for example, are often at odds with their party's governor and senators. Hence it may be hard for such congressmen to "go statewide"; most of them hesitate to risk a safe seat for the arduous and risky job of appealing to the independents and moderates who might hold the balance of power in a statewide contest.

So the congressman from a safe seat usually follows the easy alternative: he stays put. He placates the dominant social forces in the district; "protects" his district against hostile outside forces; does a great many individual favors; lobbies for benefits for the district; maintains a friends-and-neighbors political organization that scares would-be opponents out of the primary or trounces them if they come in; and comfortably overwhelms the opposition party's candidate—if there is one—on election day. His main commitment politically is to the status quo. He wishes nothing to disrupt his easy relationships with the public officials and private interests that rule the area. He views with alarm the great issues that sweep the nation and threaten to disrupt the familiar and comfortable politics of his district. He does not want to broaden the franchise or encourage more voting, because this might disturb existing arrangements.

Naturally the one-party congressman fares best in the "off-year" (non-presidential) election. In presidential years the vote in congressional races is over one-third again as large as the comparable turnout in the off-years. Since presidential candidates arouse hosts of independent or apathetic voters who then stay at home in the congressional elections two years later, the one-party congressman faces his greatest risk when the opposition party offers a strong presidential candidate, like Roosevelt or Eisenhower. But such presidential candidates are exceptional, so that in presidential as well as off-year elections the typical one-party congressman is quite safe. And he remains invincibly local. By remaining in the orbit of his congressional area, he stays politically in the orbit of his party's local candidates and officeholders. Thus he operates in a world of political localism, for the electoral and other political forces in the area are largely activated by other local candidates. Hence the congressman, though a national officeholder, is almost as locally oriented as the district attorney or county commissioner, and almost as much beyond the reach of influence by the President or the national party. And this is one more reason he achieves his key aim: unbroken longevity in office.

Longevity in office—this is the crucial nexus between the man in the safe rural district and the congressional party in Washington. The mechanism is well known—the rule of seniority, which promotes congressmen up the committee ladder toward the chairmanship in accordance with his unbroken tenure on the committee. Our man in the safe seat has a wonderful incentive to stay put. He can, with any kind of luck, expect steady promotion to the top councils of the congressional party, regardless of merit. No other major Western democracy rewards its politicians with so much power for so little relevant accomplishment.

But it is dangerous to focus too much on the seniority rule in the committees alone, for this committee rule is merely one instrument, though a central one, in the allocation of power in Congress. Again we must think in terms of a system of power. And that system is today, and has been since 1938, essentially the same as it was in the 1850's, the 1890's, in 1910, and at other turning points in American history.

The leaders of the congressional party are, of course, men who have climbed the seniority ladders and hence the men who come from the safe, usually rural, districts. They are the chairmen, or ranking majority or minority members of the more important committees: the committees that tax and spend, that seek to control other central economic policies, such as prices and investment, that have major influence on the political status and personal privileges of other members of Congress (i.e., special appropriations for members' districts, or special bills affecting individual constituents), and that influence the traffic of legislative business—most notably the House Rules Committee. The statistics are conclusive. In a recent Congress the 217 most urban districts produced 26 per cent of the House chairmen in general, while the 218 least urban accounted for 74 per cent. But the imbalance of rural-urban power becomes even more significant if one notes the relative importance of the committees rather than simply their total number.

This imbalance of urban-rural control of committees is not accidental. The congressional party leaders are the same persons who make assignments to committees. In the House these choices are made by Democratic and Republican committees-on-committees, which are largely composed of rural representatives. Conservative influence in these selection committees is self-perpetuating; by taking on only those members who have already attained some seniority, the committees-on-committees automatically exclude freshman members from the more urban and mixed "swing" districts. Both committees, a careful study concludes, "are so constituted as to be virtually immune to immediate pressures brought about by electoral changes." Using this selection machinery, the congressional parties control access to positions on the key substantive committees and on the Rules Committee. Moreover, House members seeking committee assignments channel their requests through the "dean" or senior member of their state party delegation—one more concession to seniority.

The seniority system is pervasive. It shapes not only key committee memberships and leadership but the whole life and tone of the Congress. Freshman members find themselves treated like freshmen. As they learn the ropes—if they can survive their early re-election campaigns—they learn that the things they need for political survival, such as constituent favors and home-town projects, and the little considerations they want as employees on the Hill, such as office space or congressional patronage, depend on their cooperating with the congressional party leadership. "If you want to get along you've got to go along"—this hoary adage is one of the working principles of congressional life.

How the congressional party operates on a specific and vital front of public policy can be seen in the House Appropriations Committee. This committee, like the party as a whole, has its own set of roles and norms, rewards and penalties. Its ruling elements consider themselves guardians of the taxpayer's money; they are more prone to cut Administration requests than to shape positive policies of their own, though of course they allow themselves and their congressional allies local appropriations. They operate less as Democrats or Republicans than as elements of a coalition dealing with one another through bargaining, reciprocity, and a united front on the House floor. And appointments to the committee are mainly controlled, of course, by the chairman and senior members. Membership on the committee is not just a job, its members like to say, but a way of life.

The seniors are expert at compounding their influence. Consider Representative Francis E. Walter of Pennsylvania. Not only is he chairman of the Judiciary Committee Immigration Subcommittee, but also of the Un-American Activities Committee and of the House Patronage Committee. Hence he can withhold Capitol Hill patronage jobs from erring members, block private immigration bills (a special problem for urban congressmen trying to get around general immigration restrictions), all the while serving as an astute parliamentarian and as chief guardian of Americanism on Capitol Hill. Other, less noted congressional party leaders operate in the subcommittees of the Appropriations and other committees to compound their influence on the Hill.

I have been emphasizing the House seniority system here, but the Senate shows the same forces at work, though sometimes less visibly. Most Senators, like most Representatives, are lawyers, and about half the Senators in a recent session had begun their careers as state legislators or prosecuting attorneys. In the upper chamber like the lower, men from the safe rural states are more likely to get the choice committee assignments and more likely to acquire greater influence on the committees. Senators "table-hop" from committee to committee over the years to gain better berths, and a senior Senator requesting a vacant committee seat almost always gets it, unless, like Estes Kefauver, he has defied Senate norms. Senators from more competitive states are, of course, less likely to build influence in the upper body.

The Senate, like the House, has a set of standing committees that not only provide for division of legislative labor but, as Ralph Huitt says, are part of the allocation of political power. As in the lower chamber, committee chairmen control subcommittee appointments. Effectiveness on the Hill depends greatly on conforming with one's elders. The Senate's seniority system "results in the under-representation of liberals among the chairmen of both parties . . . ," Donald R. Matthews concludes, "The seniority system's bias against urban liberals of both parties tends to be self-perpetuating." And the right to filibuster —which is the power of a very few Senators to bargain effectively with all the rest—represents the Madisonian tradition in its most extreme form.

Helping to unite the congressional party is a common ideology. This ideology is, of course, generally conservative (defining conservatism as opposition to the increased use of government to redistribute income in favor of lower-income groups) and isolationist (defined as opposition to greater political, diplomatic, and economic concessions and commitments to other nations). But this ideology is intrinsically negative; that is, it is hostile to major governmental trends in the 20th Century, although it offers grudging acceptance of welfare programs and other measures that have won wide support among voters. But on one matter the congressional party ideologists are most articulate and positive— defense of the congressional party system. States' rights, local elections, restricted franchise, minority rights, rural over-representation, checks and balances, congressional power, the danger of majority or "mass" rule, judicial review (at least in the old days), powerful committees, the seniority system, the filibuster—in short, the Madisonian system in all its ramifications—arouse their stout support. And the ideologists in Congress are buttressed outside it by able political thinkers, like James Burnham, by perceptive journalists like William S. White and David Lawrence, and by a host of newspapers, magazines, and commentators.

Congressional party leaders in both houses can exert a wide, though sometimes tenuous, discipline outside their chambers too. Congressmen report cases of Southern members being threatened with primary opposition backed with outside money unless they toed the line. In each house the Republican and Democratic congressional campaign committees, which for decades have operated largely apart from the national party committees, allot money to congressional candidates; and while the sum is not large, there are cases where the committees have given money to conservative candidates from safer districts at the expense of more needy aspirants from more competitive constituencies. The main party discipline of the congressional party, however, is internal. Significantly, the congressional party rarely takes prized committee assignments from members of Congress who bolt the presidential nominee.

Still, the main bulwark of the congressional party system is not this kind of conscious manipulation but, as I have indicated above, a whole system of local power patterns, electoral arrangements, voting behavior, career lines, and institutional arrangements and norms in Congress that together form an operating political system. For we must understand what the congressional party system is not, as well as what it is. It is not a tight, cohesive group of men, conspiring together in a secret chamber and pushing the buttons on a nation-wide machine. It is a loose cluster of men, sharing a common concept of the public interest, convinced that they are protecting the nation against radicalism, benefitting from and in turn protecting a set of rules and institutions that bolster their power, and the product of local political patterns. These men deal with one another by bargaining and accommodation rather than by direction and command. They are often divided over specific policies. They have the problem of cooperating across formal party lines between Democrats and Republicans, and across the physical and psychological gap separating Senate and House. And they must share some power with the formally elected leaders in each house, as we will see later. But what unites them is the common defense of a system that consolidates their influence on Capitol Hill. And that system, while not monolithic, is composed of social forces and political mechanisms that are mutually supporting and hence cumulative in their impact. Power in one part of the system can be parlayed into power in another. "The committees with their chairmen," a freshman congressman said recently, "are like a ring of forts."

THE PRESIDENTIAL PARTY SYSTEM

The head of the presidential party is the President. He sets its policies, confirms its ideology, appoints its leaders, and carries its hopes in the quadrennial crisis of the presidential election. Just as other parties are organized around other officeholders, so a party is organized around the Chief Executive. Beginning with Jefferson and Jackson the man in the White House has acted in varying degrees as "party leader." But he is not head of the whole Democratic or Republican party. . . . But of that section of the whole party that we call the presidential party, the President is undisputed leader.

The President runs his party through a small political staff in the White

House and through the chairman of the party's national committee. That chairman, like his own aides, is chosen by him and remains in office only as long as the President wishes. Other leaders of the President's party also remain at his sufferance: Cabinet members, top agency chiefs, and hundreds of administrative aides and operatives in the higher echelons of the Administration. These officials often appear to be non-political but in the final test they will support the presidential party. In the 1930's Harry Hopkins had a clear understanding of the close relation of relief activities to Roosevelt's re-election campaigns. In 1960, according to the testimony of the government official concerned, the Interior Department cancelled the sale of surplus tungsten in an effort to help Vice-President Nixon's election campaign. Some officials, such as the Secretary of Defense and heads of independent commissions, are less in the presidential party orbit, while others like the Attorney General or the Postmaster General hold offices that are much more partisan by tradition. And a few Administration officials may not be in the presidential party at all.

From Washington the presidential party fans out widely. Hundreds of Administration political appointees in the states and cities—federal attorneys, collectors of customs, federal marshals, and the like (except those who mainly owe appointment to Senators at odds with the President)—are expected to protect the Administration's local interests, at least where called on. Both in Washington and in the field the President's men also maintain close relations with many of the state party leaders, though some state committees are the possession of a potent Governor or Senator or big-city mayor, or are hopelessly divided between the President and the state leaders. The organizational reach of the presidential party typically does not extend below the state level, except perhaps in the choosing of national convention delegates.

The national convention shows the presidential party in its full splendor and power. The convention always endorses its leader in the White House, if he wishes it to—a fact of 20th Century history that Harry Truman remembered in the spring of 1948 and his adversaries in the party seemed to forget. The President's men write the platform, determine the content of the major speeches, decide which contested delegations will be seated, control the order of the business on the floor, and roll up the President's endorsement on the first ballot, followed by nomination by acclamation. Rebels are easily put down. The President also controls the nomination of his running-mate. If it is worth his while to make changes in the Vice-Presidency, as Roosevelt did in 1940, he can do so. Usually he does not make the effort, because the Vice-Presidency is not that important. All in all, the presidential party controls the convention as fully as the congressional party controls Congress.

The heart of national politics, Arthur Holcombe wrote, is the presidential campaign. So it is of the presidential party. Its candidate is the focus of the party's effort and the center of national attention. He dominates the national media and sharpens the national debate. He arouses and motivates millions of voters. The campaign is his supreme opportunity to arouse and shape mass opinion, to cut through the babel of voices, to show the voter the direct link between a national problem and doing something about it (i.e., voting for him).

This, indeed, has been the historic achievement of the presidential party—the immense widening of the electorate. "The rise of political parties and the extension of the suffrage produced the plebiscitary Presidency," Schattschneider says. ". . . The Presidency has in turn become the principal instrument for the nationalization of politics"—the destruction of old local power monopolies and sectional power patterns. From Harrison and Jackson in the last century to Eisenhower and Stevenson in 1952 and Kennedy and Nixon in 1960, it has been the presidential party contests that have spectacularly broadened the voting rolls. The reason is clear. The great incentive of the presidential candidates is to widen and "flatten out" their vote, to win states by dependable but not wasteful popular majorities, while the congressional party "bunches" its vote in safe districts.

The stunning impact of the presidential campaign is partly organizational. Roving through the nation, the President's men shake up sleepy committees, set up campaign organizations, raise money, recruit local party leadership. But the regular party organizations, no matter how efficient, are not able to mobilize the majorities that the presidential party seeks. So presidential party candidates establish auxiliary organizations to reach the millions of independents that the regulars disregard. This is an old practice; Horatio Seymour in 1868 set up the "Order of the Union Democrats" to bolster the listless Democrats with a vigorous new organization that could cut across party lines. More recently, the Willkie Clubs, Citizens for Eisenhower, Volunteers for Stevenson, Citizens for Kennedy and similar groups have conducted big campaigns separate from, and sometimes at conflict with, the regular organizations. Often they ignore or even "cut" the state and local candidates of the regular parties. Bad feelings always develop between volunteers and regulars. Sometimes the regulars slight the presidential candidate in return. Candidates for governor have been known to hold rallies without a single sign or poster for the presidential candidate of their own party—but the reverse also happens. Sometimes this uneasy marriage ends in disaster. In 1940 Willkie organized a huge force of volunteers through the Willkie clubs; during the war the regulars deserted him, in part because of his war-time support of Roosevelt, and they denied him renomination in 1944. Despite all the bickering, however, this bifurcation of presidential campaigns will continue as long as our parties retain their present character, for the presidential candidate must have machinery for winning independent and even opposition party votes.

Just as the congressional parties benefit from gerrymandered congressional districts, so the presidential party benefits from its own form of gerrymandering. This is the electoral college, which, by allotting all the electoral votes of a state to the candidate winning most popular votes in that state, puts a premium on the big urban states with their handsome electoral-vote plums. Since the big states tend to be highly competitive states, the winner-take-all arrangement plays up the importance of the organized groups, such as Negroes, Catholics, union labor, Jews, ethnic groups that supposedly control the balance of electoral power in the state. This control may be exaggerated, and usually is, but to the presidential parties, locked in fierce combat, this huge, supposedly deliverable vote, looks increasingly irresistible as election day nears. Kennedy's eleventh-hour emphasis on this vote in 1960, and Nixon's apparent unconcern for it when he flew to Alaska at the climactic moment, is bound to enhance the mythology of the electoral-college balance of power. The distortion resulting from the winner-take-all device further separates the bases of the presidential and congressional parties. But even without it, there would be some electoral bifurcation, for the presidential parties, as the more urban, liberally oriented party system, naturally direct their main appeals to the urban and suburban vote.

The career lines in the presidential party are significantly different from those in the congressional. The traditional path to the Presidency has been through a big-state governorship, the party organization around which is likely to be fairly parallel with the presidential party organization in that state (Stevenson in Illinois in 1952, for example). Few governors, on the other hand, rise to high places in the congressional party. Few Senators have become President in the past century, but we now know that the old rule that "Senators don't become President, with Harding as the exception that proves the rule," had a flaw in it (besides the notion that exceptions somehow prove rules). It was not Senators in general but Senators who were committed members of the congressional party that were ineligible for presidential party leadership (Harding *was* an exception to the rule). As if realizing this, John Kennedy moved steadily out of the orbit of the congressional party into that of the presidential during his years in the Senate. It was Lyndon Johnson's failure to do this, and Robert Taft's similar failure earlier, that fatally handicapped them in their quest for the nomination.

The career lines in the presidential and congressional systems seem to diverge at a deeper level too. While evidence on this is limited, it may well be that the presidential party draws on men who have risen through the bureaucracies of big business, universities, unions, large law firms, and state and federal executive departments. Many of these men are "political outsiders," as Mills has defined them; they have spent most of their working life outside strictly political organization. Congressional party leadership is mainly composed of one-time independent entrepreneurs, small-town lawyers, local law enforcement officials, and state legislators. We can guess that the differing vocational, ideological, and institutional worlds of the two groups—one more bureaucratic, hierarchical, and managerial, the other more individualistic and prone to negotiate and bargain—would have a significant impact on the nature of the parties.

All the foregoing discussion presupposes one crucial fact about the presidential party—that its leader is President. What about the presidential party that does not possess the White House? Things then, of course, are very different. There is no office around which the party can be organized, no office to lead it, discipline it, reward it. Defeated at the polls, the presidential party becomes apathetic and disorganized. No one speaks for it with a clear voice. The national chairman, as the executor of the defeated candidate's political estate, is powerless and must yield to the congressional party. The presidential party does not disappear, of course. Its head cut off, the body still lives, waiting for a new head and a new vitality. For the time being, however, it is impotent.

Such, at least, has been the traditional state of the out-of-office presidential party, but there has been an interesting change. After their defeat in 1956, notable presidential Democrats under the leadership of national chairman Paul Butler decided to establish a council to shape party policy and to focus attack on the Eisenhower Administration. Its members came from the presidential party: Harry Truman, Adlai Stevenson, Herbert Lehman, Averell Harriman, among others, with Eleanor Roosevelt as consultant. The committee had little direct influence on policy and was ignored by the congressional Democratic party. But it helped keep alive presidential party doctrine among Democrats and posed well-publicized alternatives to the Eisenhower politics. Much more than the congressional Democrats, the council served as Eisenhower's Loyal Opposition.

That Senator Hubert Humphrey and other liberal Democratic legislators were members of the Advisory Council points up a puzzling but important fact: a large minority of congressmen belong to their presidential party rather than to the congressional. Many of these congressmen are freshmen who represent marginal districts, and perhaps were elected in a presidential sweep with the head of their presidential party. Kept in essentially a freshman status by the congressional parties, these members of Congress turn to the presidential parties for a political home. Otherwise, the congressional makeup of the two presidential parties varies considerably. Democratic members are mainly those who represent urban dwellers and who are not at home in the rural atmosphere of the congressional parties—for example, Democrats Emanuel Celler of New York, John E. Fogarty of Rhode Island, Chet Holifield of California, Edith Green of Oregon. Republican congressmen in their presidential party are much less numerous and represent more competitive constituencies; Jacob Javits of New York and Clifford P. Case of New Jersey are the outstanding examples. One reason some congressmen move into the orbit of the presidential party is that they see the need for the President's help in gaining re-election. The more marginal and competitive the congressman's district, the closer he will ordinarily be to the presidential party.

The borders between the congressional and presidential parties in Congress are not clear-cut. Many a congressman hedges his bets by shifting back and forth between the two camps, or by keeping a foot in each. And nothing is fuzzier than the role of the elected leadership of Congress—the Speaker of the House, the majority and minority leaders, and the various party conferences and policy committees. Indeed, an interesting question is whether the formal leadership belongs to the presidential or congressional parties. The answer is: it depends.

It depends mainly on whether or not the presidential party is in power. When it is, the leadership ordinarily lines up behind the President. It retains some bargaining power, as Taft did with Eisenhower in 1953. It can always revolt if put under excessive pressure, as Alben Barkley did against Roosevelt in 1944. But generally it goes along, and the meeting of the congressional "Big Four" or "Big Six" with the President has become one of the most durable institutions in Washington. A President's prestige is so great that his fellow partisans in Congress will rarely choose leadership hostile to him. Sometimes he is powerful enough to determine the choice himself. But usually the decision is made largely independent of the White House, as in the selection of Charles Halleck as Republican House leader in 1959 and the election of John W. McCormack as Speaker in 1962. This semi-independence can be of some importance, though, as Neustadt says, "the more an officeholder's power stems from sources outside the President, the stronger will be his potential power *on* the President."

When the presidential party does not occupy the White House, the elected congressional leaders usually move closer to the seniority leadership of the congressional party. This was evident in both Taft's and Johnson's majority leadership in the Senate, . . . The difficulty for the elected-leaders, in contrast to the other sets of leaders, is that they lack firm institutional bases of support of their own. The policy committees, caucuses, and other party devices are insubstantial compared with the standing committees. If the majority leader and his whips lack a President to back them up, they are generally, and over the long run, drawn into the vortex of the senior leaders. Consider, for example, Rayburn's and Johnson's refusal to join the Democratic Advisory Council. They treated it as part of a somewhat different party—as indeed it was. Or consider Republican leader Halleck's attitude toward the Republican party platform of 1960. "We will take it out and read it from time to time," he said. "But the congressional people generally have very little to do with writing party platforms."

In this three-way tug of war much also depends on the skill of the elected leader. At times Taft through his experience and doggedness was able to act virtually as a third force in the Senate, as was Lyndon Johnson through his superb parliamentary skill and his grasp of the nuances of Senate life. But when the chips are down the elected leaders usually do not hold the levers of power. Sam Rayburn, despite all his prestige and support in the House, was never really able to vanquish Howard W. Smith, chairman of the Rules Committee. And, as we have seen, Henry Cabot Lodge finally had to yield to the Senate Irreconcilables in his fight against Wilson's League. One problem is that the Senate leader is not sure of his own constituency, as in the case of Senate Democratic majority leader Scott Lucas, who was defeated for re-election to the Senate in 1952. Another inhibiting factor is the fear of failure to be re-elected majority leader—the unhappy blow that Republican House leader Joseph W. Martin suffered in 1959. Unlike the seniority leaders, the elected leaders always face possible repudiation at the hands of one or both of their constituencies.

Another type of congressman who has a somewhat equivocal position is the member from a metropolitan, one-party district. He is ordinarily a Democrat responsive to urban interests and hence takes a liberal position on economic issues. At the same time he is the beneficiary of a seniority system that gives him special influence on Capitol Hill—though not so much influence as it gives rural representatives, who usually gain the most powerful chairmanships. Many such representatives of one-party urban districts end up in the awkward position of supporting the congressional power system at the same time that they support liberal policies, such as civil rights, that are blocked by that system. But the city men usually win by such big margins that their conflicting role positions on the Hill are not an electoral embarrassment, except possibly in a Democratic primary.

What of the freshmen congressmen and other congressional members of the presidential party? Sometimes they can turn to the elected leadership for help, but more often they are on their own. The freshman congressman quoted earlier as seeing the committee leadership like a ring of forts went on to evaluate his own side: "A coalition of Northerners, without interior lines of strength, is a tenuous thing. . . . We have no unifying philosophy. . . . We have no White House to cajole, threaten and promise. . . . The analogy with warfare that I have used is an accurate one. . . . The northern coalition, as the attackers, are spread out, with poor communications between one another and hence poor coordination. We have no base of power, with which to menace the chairmen on the one hand, or to discipline our own members on the other."

The President, as head of the presidential party, has no more vital task than to lead his presidential forces in Congress, to unify them, to give them interior lines of strength. For no section of the presidential party is more dependent on the President, nor more crucial to him.

FOUR-PARTY POLITICS

We can conclude that the pattern of national politics is essentially a four-party pattern. The Democratic and Republican parties are each divided into congressional and presidential structures, with all the elements that comprise the American type of party.

The division of Democrats and Republicans into two parties each is of course the immediate cause of the national four-party pattern. The four parties would not last long, however, if they lacked strong attitudinal bases in the electorate. They might not continue, for example, if people divided only over economic issues, for such a situation, combined with the tendency of politicians toward combinations, would normally produce two groupings, presumably of those who got smaller slices of the economic loaf against those who got bigger. At least two factors operate against such a simple two-way division in America.

One is the obvious fact that people divide over issues other than economic ones and—a crucial point—that the economic divisions are not congruent with the others. By "other issues" I mean those that have been variously called "moral" or "style" issues but that I will call "way-of-life" issues—that is, issues that pose choices about a nation's whole culture and way of life and that cannot be calculated in terms of immediate and tangible economic return for specific groups of people. Taxes, wages, social security, farm prices, tariffs, public housing are examples of economic issues; while civil liberties, women's rights, disarmament, immigration, corruption in government, defense strategy, racial tolerance and integration, government, and religion are examples of way-of-life issues. The presumed motivational appeal of the former, Berelson, Lazarsfeld, and McPhee suggest, is self-interest of a relatively direct and tangible kind, while that of the latter is self-expression and self-gratification of a more subjective, symbolic, and projective kind. Issues do not fall neatly into two categories. An expansion of civil rights, such as job opportunity, or of immigration of certain types of workers, or of certain types of defense activities, could mean economic benefits or deprivations for various groups as well as psychic benefits or deprivations for a wider public. But the difference between the two seems sharp enough to affect the shape of our party structure.

Data on the non-congruence of economic and way-of-life issues are limited but highly suggestive. Polls indicate that there has been in recent years little if any relationship between persons' relative positions on domestic and foreign issues. "An interventionist position in foreign affairs was as likely to be taken by a domestic conservative as by a domestic liberal" in 1956, report Campbell and associates, "and the relative isolationist was as likely to favor social welfare activities in Washington as he was to oppose them." By cross-tabulating distributions of responses in 1952 to an "international involvement" question and a "social welfare activity" question, Key finds four combinations of opinion: isolationist-liberal, internationalist-liberal, isolationist-conservative, internationalist-conservative (with the last the smallest of the four in numbers).

Evidence on the non-congruence of economic and domestic way-of-life issues is even more limited but still suggestive. Much of it stems from historians' observations. The political parties have usually had their "conscience" and "cotton" wings. Under Theodore Roosevelt the Republican party numbered hosts of high-income business and professional men who looked on their party mainly as a weapon to attack the moral and social evils of the day. The Democratic party in Bryan's and Wilson's days and also more recently has numbered not only hosts of economic reformers but also workers and farmers who took a hostile or stunted view of civil liberties, women's rights, civil rights, civic betterment, and other way-of-life problems.

A second root cause of the four-party pattern is the disarticulation of the national and state party systems, stemming from the workings of federalism in a sectional society combined with some of our special political arrangements. The impact of national politics on state and local politics in our sectional nation has been noted in these pages—the creation of one-party states and districts. Balance and competition at the national level, especially in presidential contests, helped produce local noncompetition and imbalance, most notably in the South and rural North. These one-party areas tended to be ignored by presidential candidates, who concentrated on the swing areas, and hence the one-party areas became less important to the presidential parties, but they received extra representation in Congress because of the seniority system, and hence became the buttress of the congressional parties.

This double cleavage, institutional and attitudinal, between the presidential parties and the congressional parties is largely responsible for the conflicting positions that a President, whether Democratic or Republican, and a Congress, whether Democratic or Republican controlled, take on the crucial affairs of state.

Willmore Kendall has pointed to the curious fact that the Executive "is able, with good show of reason, to put itself foward on any particular issue as the spokesman for . . . lofty and enlightened principle. . . . The Executive tends, that is to say, to have the nation's ministers and publicists with it on 'peace,' the nation's professors and moralizers with it on desegregation, the nation's economists with it on fiscal policy and redistribution, the nation's political scientists with it on political reform and civil rights, etc. . . . The Executive is for world government, for the outlawry of war, for unselfishness in our relations with the outside world, for the brotherhood of man, for majority-rule, for progress, for generosity toward the weak and lowly, for freedom of thought and speech, for equality, for the spreading of the benefits of modern civilization to 'underdeveloped' lands, for science and the 'scientific outlook,' for civil rights. . . ." Congress, according to Professor Kendall, stresses other values: small group discussion in the community, deference to highly prestiged and presumably wiser citizens, and an anti-quixotic concern for the "realities, problems, the potential benefits and potential costs (and for whom?)" of presidential proposals.

Why this gap between President and Congress over way-of-life issues? Why, in Professor Kendall's own terms, do the two presidential parties win a much larger share of the "moralizers" and reformers and utopians than do the two congressional parties? Possibly—and here I can only speculate, for we do not have adequate data—because the most persisting major conflicts in American politics have been over economic issues; hence the national parties have offered the most meaningful alternatives in the realm of economic policy; so that if divisions of the voters over economic and way-of-life issues are not congruent, as we have reason to think they are not, millions of voters more concerned with way-of-life issues than economic ones have had to operate on a party limbo. They are simply not aroused by the state and local contests, including congressional contests, that turn on the old bread-and-butter issues; they have not been geared into the local two-party alignment over the years because they have had no meaningful alternatives presented to them on the issues that mean most to them: corruption, human rights, social reform, and the rest. Hence the voices of the mugwumps have often been ignored in the obscure politics of the local, often non-competitive struggle. But the presidential contest does reach and arouse such independents because their collective voice nationally is loud, and because in the sharply competitive presidential race the two candidates must move beyond the traditional economic issues and find way-of-life issues that may reach the uncommitted.

The consequence of the four-party system is that American political leaders, in order to govern, must manage multi-party coalitions just as heads of coalition parliamentary regimes in Europe have traditionally done—as the French did, for example, before De Gaulle. But the task of governing in a sense is harder in the United States, for the leaders' job is not simply to pick up enough parliamentary votes to form a cabinet, or even just to pass a bill. They must bring together the right combination of presidential party and congressional party strength to accomplish a great variety of tasks day after day and year after year. And the leaders' job is further complicated by the fact that continuous, effective government policy-making is impossible without a strong working alliance between at least some combination of presidential and congressional parties. For the presidential side and the congressional side each wields power not only in its own "constitutional" orbit but in the opposite side's orbit as well.

The extent to which the congressional and presidential parties share the same powers and hence can block each other is extraordinary. The President has a broad range of legislative power besides his veto: he can issue executive orders that have the force of law; he can draw up with other nations executive agreements that are as controlling under international law as treaties ratified by the Senate; he can make war "by the push of a button" and let Congress ratify it later, if at all. But Congress inserts itself into the executive process too. The Senate can refuse to confirm appointments—even one lone Senator can induce the whole upper body to withhold approval through the device of "senatorial courtesy." The standing committees closely affect administrative arrangements through their control of policy, and the appropriations committees and sub-committees have a profound impact through their control of funds. The more "independent" an agency or commission may be of the President, the more dependent it may be on a committee or faction of Congress. The relation, of course, changes over time. After the Civil War Congress tried to control the Administration through such means as the Tenure of Office Act; the act is long since gone but not some of the motivation behind it. Today the Army Chief of Engineers has legislative authority to plan public works and report to Congress without clearing with the President.

In less obvious fields too, the two-party coalitions, the congressional and the presidential, maintain countervailing institutional apparatus. The President can publicize an issue and influence public opinion by appointing a "blue-ribbon" presidential commission controlled by the President's men, and he and his lieutenants can set into action other varieties of Administration inquiries, probes, and explorations. Congress at the same time has its standing committees including the Un-American Activities Committee, which can investigate at the drop of a hat, and it can set up special committees to conduct grand investigations.

The President can call Congress back into special session after it adjourns, but the houses can recess instead of adjourn and thus retain more control of their own operations. If the President can act on many matters through executive orders not subject to congressional veto, Congress can legislate, at least to a modest extent, through Concurrent Resolutions, which are not subject to presidential veto. Congress can limit White House legislative power by setting statutory expiration dates in the original act, as Ernest Griffith has noted, "as a device to circumvent a possible presidential veto of some future measure designed to change a particular policy to which it has given reluctant or experimental agreement." On the other hand, Congress has had to delegate to the President an immense amount of policy-making power. The bureaucracy of the executive department has grown enormously—but so has that of Congress. The General Accounting office, which has a theoretically executive duty, supplies information on administrative lapses to congressional watchdogs.

An executive impetus and a legislative tendency confront each other at every junction. The executive impetus is to combine legislative and administrative power, to coordinate functions, to exert control from the top. Whether it is Elihu Root, Theodore Roosevelt's Secretary of War, trying (unsuccessfully) to nationalize the state guard, or Hoover and Truman trying to centralize administration, or Kennedy trying to reorganize the executive branch, the instinct of the executive is to integrate government for the sake of better control. The legislative instinct is pluralistic. Congress and the state legislatures, under the control of the legislative parties, seek to fragmentize the executive by means of individual or committee influence over administrative units, or control of specific budgetary items, or through hobbling the executive's power to reorganize. State legislatures have in some instances kept whole sections of the executive branch out from the governor's control, and have resisted efforts to shorten the long ballot, which gives state officials electoral strength independent of the governor.

This bewildering array of countervailing and overlapping powers compels American political leaders to piece together a new patchwork of party fragments, factional chieftains, congressional votes, constitutional usage, and bureaucratic officials in order to put through each major new program. Presidential party leaders do this through endless persuading, pressuring, manipulating, and bargaining. Congressional party leaders use the same methods to balk or modify Administration proposals, and their task is all the easier because of the many points at which action can be slowed or stopped in the narrow, twisting, and crowded legislative channels. Since each set of parties, congressional or presidential, is a coalition itself, action depends on the alignment of coalition with coalition.

Not that the presidential and congressional party coalitions are of the same type. The former, to use Dahl's apt expression, is an "executive-centered coalition." The President has means of direction and discipline unmatched by the congressional parties or by the presidential party out of power. He has a public position, a command of the media, a control over personnel, and a direct electoral link with the people that enable him to maintain and exploit a somewhat hierarchical system in the presidential party. The congressional party is led by a coalition of parties, allied through their common attitudes and mutual dependence, and with an internal party system marked more by bargaining than by hierarchy. The essential operational process differs: the congressional reliance on committees, with their tendency to protect an existing consensus over the status quo, contrasts with the executive emphasis on single-leader activism. The out-of-power presidential party, to use Dahl's terminology, is a network of "independent sovereignties with spheres of influence." But even this network, inchoate though it is, has the attributes of party—ideology, program, leadership, machinery, and existing or potential electoral support.

Any one of the four parties can—and does—coalesce with any one of the others. We take for granted the coalition of the Democratic presidential and congressional parties, and of the two Republican parties—though often we should not. The durable alliance of the congressional parties has long been publicized by liberals as the "unholy alliance of Old Guard Republicans and Dixie Democrats" in Congress. Less obvious is another alliance, holy or unholy, between presidential Democrats and presidential Republicans. These parties occasionally combine in Congress, as Republicans from urban and suburban districts support the proposals of Democratic Presidents. But the main focus of the presidential party alliance is in the foreign policy and fiscal agencies. Roosevelt's enlistment of Stimson and Knox in his Cabinet in 1940, Truman's appointment of a host of Republicans to foreign-policy and foreign-aid agencies, Eisenhower's choice of Texas Democrat Robert Anderson as Secretary of the Treasury, and Kennedy's retention of Douglas Dillon and other Republicans from the Eisenhower Administration and his selection of an internationalist Republican, McGeorge Bundy, as an assistant, reflect a wide community of interest between the two parties. The alliance is consecrated in the name of "bipartisanship in foreign policy," or the hoary slogan "Party politics stops at the water's edge." What mainly stops at the water's edge is not party politics in general but congressional party politics in particular. The real "unholy alliance" to a good congressional Republican is the historic coalition between the internationalists in both parties. And the internationalist newspapers that approve so highly of foreign-policy bipartisanship today were never so enthusiastic about it in the 1920's and the early 1930's, when it represented a coalition of isolationists.

No political system is neutral—certainly not the congressional and presidential. Power is inseparable from structure. It is not by chance that liberal and internationalist Presidents in this century have been "strong" Presidents, and that men like Taft and Harding are relegated to the ranks of the weak. The stronger the exertion of presidential power, the more liberal and internationalist it will be because of the make-up and dynamics of the presidential party. The stronger the exertion of congressional power, the more conservative and isolationist will be our national policy because of the structure of the congressional forces. The man who is all for liberalism and internationalism "as long as the President's power is not increased" (as for example in the trade agreements act) is a man who has not grasped the relation of ends and means, of power and structure. The man who favors cutting down the powers of Congress because it is "slow and inefficient" is cutting down conservative influence, whether he wants to or not. The structure of coalition politics is inevitably the structure of "who gets what, when and how" in American national politics. As the Madisonian system in being, it is also the structure of slowdown and stalemate in American government.

PATRONAGE AND PARTY *

Frank J. Sorauf

IT was not long ago that political scientists reacted instinctively against political patronage much as they reacted against slavery, aggressive war, and divine right monarchy. Reminders of that older, more moral day linger even today—in, for instance, the activities of civic and better-government organizations, and in the Library of Congress's subject classification of "spoils system" under corruption (in politics)." But I suspect that the issue of patronage, even among those scholars not yet willing to endorse or condone it, is no longer the highly-charged moral issue it once was.

Undoubtedly the rise in prestige and status that political parties have enjoyed has done a great deal to elevate the institution of patronage to semi-respectability, at least among academics. In this era of strong, positive government, scholars have seized upon the party as an instrument through which discipline and responsibility may be achieved within the Leviathan. Party joins with government to generate the political power for achieving broad social ends. The stock of patronage rises concurrently with party's prestige on the general assumption that patronage is essential to a strong and vital party organization. In brief, we have succumbed to the lean but forceful logic of George Washington Plunkitt:

First, this great and glorious country was built up by the political parties; second, parties can't hold together if their workers don't get the offices when they win; third, if the parties go to pieces, the government they built up must go to pieces, too; fourth, then there'll be h--l to pay.

There doubtless remain other reasons for the decline in the crusading enthusiasm against patronage. The whole thrust of the political science of this generation has been toward a realistic acceptance of the political facts of life, a willingness to study and participate in grass-roots politics. The interest of political scientists in programs such as that of the Citizenship Clearing House is indicative. Furthermore, patronage no longer dominates public personnel

---

* From Frank J. Sorauf, "Patronage and Party," in *Midwest Journal of Political Science,* Vol. III, No. 2 (May, 1959), pp. 115–126. Copyright 1959 by Wayne State University Press. Reprinted by permission of Professor Sorauf and Wayne State University Press.

policy as once it did, and consequently it does not present a problem of the magnitude it did.

Where patronage remains today, two chief justifications or rationales generally support it. In the first place, its friends argue that patronage remains an essential aid to party responsibility and control of public policy. Republicans after 1952 bemoaned their inability to appoint a full "Republican team" to top administrative posts in Washington; the removal of some 130,000 jobs from Civil Service protection was said to be a move to restore unity to policy-making at the national level. Secondly, it is widely held that patronage contributes to, and may even be vital to, an energetic party system by providing a system of rewards and incentives for party service. It is this second justification that furnishes the focus of this paper.

The brief observations that follow grow out of research and thought about the uses of patronage and are concerned mainly with at least raising some questions about the assumed values and utilities of patronage to the party. Patronage has for long remained a tail tied to the kite of party; once its importance to party was conceded, its fortunes rose with those of party. To attack patronage was to challenge party and to appear to be burning the barn to kill the mice. It seems to me likely, however, that the basic political usefulness of patronage as either reward or incentive may be overestimated or misunderstood. At any rate the traditional justification of the benefits of patronage to party demands a re-evaluation in the light of new knowledge about the political process and recent developments in parties and politics in America. The main body of this paper contains brief examinations of the more important assumptions underlying (and, in fact, creating) the more explicit rationalization of patronage as a bastion of party. They are set down in the conviction that it ill behooves political science to accept any untested assumptions, much less public policy based on them.

THE ASSUMPTIONS

(1) *The Ability of Parties to Administer Patronage.* In the first place, one may seriously question the implicit assumption that the parties are able to use the patronage at their disposal. "The fiction prevails," writes V. O. Key, "that while party leaders may not always manage the public service well they are wizards in the conduct of party business." Too often we fail to realize that the effective administration of a patronage system demands administrative skills that very few county chairmen or precinct leaders can command. The unyielding application of political criteria, the systematic extraction of partisan service, and the ruthless firing that follows election victories require a high degree of administrative will and finesse. Especially in the small, closely-knit rural and small-town areas across the country the use of patronage becomes even more difficult and unlikely. Ties of friendship, blood, and community militate against the political discipline essential to the administration of patronage. The resulting lax and ineffective use of political jobs, the failure to appoint jobholders and supervise their activities with only the welfare of the party in mind, points

to the possibility that one may very well need more of the arts of public administration to run a patronage than a civil service system.

Furthermore, patronage systems offer just one more example of an old social fact—just as it takes money to make money, it takes political power to achieve greater power. The party long out of office and desperately in need of new reservoirs of strength is precisely the party that, should it suddenly find itself in office, would be least able to use patronage for rebuilding. Weak parties lack the discipline, the trained leadership, and the surplus of potential jobholders to use the system to their maximum advantage. It is, in other words, the dominant party that can muster the discipline and strength necessary to administer the apparatus of patronage. So capably do the strong build on strength that one is tempted to say that patronage does not build parties quite so much as parties build patronage systems.

(2) *The Necessity of Patronage for Effective Parties.* Students of politics and parties have too often accepted without empirical evidence the assumption that a certain amount of patronage is vital to the parties as a motivator of political activity. But the fact remains that in states such as Wisconsin political parties have survived and achieved a certain measure of strength and discipline without the inducement of political appointments. Patronage is not, in brief, a universal concomitant of the political process; it is rooted deeply in a particular set of social conditions and traditions.

The implication that party loyalties and activity rest on so slender a reed as the promise of political spoils is at least open to question. Recent studies have indicated that ties to the major parties rest heavily on the conserving force of tradition and on the present appeal of candidates and issues. At least some of this traditional and programmatic loyalty has been converted into work for the party. A generation or two ago patronage flourished among the uprooted, illiterate, and unassimilated groups in the urban centers of America. Without political tradition and involvement in the issues of the day, and constantly beset by economic insecurity, they could be wooed and their political allegiance shaped by offers of political reward. Patronage was under these circumstances a valuable aid in the pragmatic majority-building of American politics.

Rather than universalize the importance of patronage to party, however, one might suggest that its role is declining and that it survives in many places as a mere shadow of its former self. The politics of Messrs. Plunkitt and Dooley have been curtailed by the political education and assimilation of migrant and foreign-born populations. Furthermore, with the help of the mass communications media the parties have created loyalties to candidates by retailing their personalities to all corners of the political cosmos. And by centralizing political issues and appeals, the parties have diminished the importance of the local political activity that patronage once bought. Since the 1930's American parties have also become involved in social and economic politics to an extent quite new in our politics and have attracted new attention to the relevance of policy alternatives. Finally, one should mention that well-organized interest groups, such as labor unions, have begun to provide the parties with an alternate source of political workers. The result has been an inevitable decline in the necessity of patronage to the political party.

At the same time that party dependence on patronage has, as I have indicated above, declined steadily, the incidence of patronage has itself declined. Government, for instance, has stolen much of patronage's social and charitable function with its social welfare programs. Steadier economic prosperity, and the expansion of educational opportunities, have reduced the importance of patronage as job security. The need for greater specialization and skills within the public service has in its way contributed to the waning of patronage. But whatever the reason, the most casual glance will indicate the recession of patronage in our time, and that decline in itself—accompanied by no perceptible weakening of the parties—may be taken as evidence that the classic rationale for patronage no longer has the same validity it might once have had.

(3) *The Vitality of Patronage as Reward or Incentive.* Implicit in the whole argument on behalf of the patronage system is the assumption, related to the previous one, that the political job offers inducement enough to spur men to give money or service to the party. Unless the job carries high value and desirability as a reward, it can hardly serve as either "payment" for past work or incentive for new labors. Many more empirical studies must be made to determine the value of patronage as a political reward. Is it the main or only motive behind political activity? Does the patronage holder perform political service for the party? Does he even vote the party ticket, and does he lead his family, friends, and neighbors to the polls as well? Is patronage, in other words, a really effective means for securing organization and campaign activity for the party? The answer is at least uncertain.

In the first place, the poor pay and generally dismal future prospects that attend most patronage jobs discourage many potential jobholders. Especially in a period of full employment, qualified men and women can find more attractive career possibilities than those which patronage systems offer. More especially, the upper social, economic, and educational levels on which the parties increasingly rely for leadership will find little to tempt them in patronage as it exists in most states today. As a result most patronage jobs fall to the lower skill groups who also lack the political skills the parties need. Political jobs in many areas, because of low pay and the considerable insecurity involved, have been consequently debased as a political currency. They simply cannot attract first-rate political leadership nor extract party service from what jobholders they attract. Where pay is low, the worker may well feel that he "owes" nothing for his salary other than a good day's work. Very possibly, too, he may not be fully aware of the rationale and obligations of the system. As unlikely as it might seem to the sophisticated, he may recognize the party as the appointing agency without understanding his informal debt to it in return for the job.

Undesirable as these jobs may be in times of full employment, they might conceivably become attractive in a period of recession or in a pocket of high unemployment. But, paradoxically, in those very areas of economic hardship where the political job achieves its greatest desirability, the job insecurity also works to the party's disadvantage. A man removed from his position for parti-san reasons may find it difficult or impossible to obtain re-employment, particu-larly if he is beyond his 40's, and he may turn against party and patronage in a rage of disenchantment that more than destroys any gratitude he may have had for the initial appointment. Employment and economic security no longer are accepted as the subjects of political charity that patronage would have them, and dismissal for political reasons strikes the average employee today as unfair, if not immoral. Thus, the very conditions that give a political job its greatest value on appointment probably create the greatest hostility at dismissal, a hostil-ity directed not only at the "other party," but at politics and patronage in general as well.

(4) *The Single Use or Purpose of Patronage.* We tend to assume (and, in-deed, this paper has thus far assumed) that patronage serves only the function of reward for the recipient's past or future service to the party. Even at that, parties often must choose between patronage as either reward or as incentive. Were the Republicans after 1952, for instance, to reward the defecting Demo-crats for Eisenhower in the South or were they to use available patronage to build a Republican party in the South? But the greatest dilemmas facing a party in the administration of a patronage system may arise from the presence of nonpolitical uses or purposes of patronage.

For instance, patronage may become an inverted reward system, rewarding the rewarder rather than the recipient. The mere opportunity to dispense pa-tronage favors may soothe and flatter the ego of the party official to an extent great enough to reward him for his work on behalf of the party. But when the disposal of political jobs becomes the private suzerainty of the local politico, and when he gives the jobs to friends, relatives, and neighbors rather than to the politically worthy, he destroys the value of patronage as a device for enlist-ing party workers. In this respect I recall often being told by party officers that they cared not who really made the patronage appointments so long as the ap-pearances of their dispensation were maintained, and so long as they could carry the word to the lucky recipient and claim his gratitude.

The patronage system may also, surprisingly, serve a combination recruit-ment and "civil service" function. While at heart patronage and merit may be incompatible personnel selection systems, political parties may have to make their peace with efficiency and capability in administration. The party whose appointees, for instance, maintain a rural road network has a genuine political interest in maintaining public approval of the road system. It may have to com-promise the use of patronage as reward by appointing and retaining skilled em-ployees, regardless of their political qualifications, for the road crews. Even where this sort of *ad hoc* merit system does not flourish, the party at least functions as a decentralized, local recruitment and job placement agency.

Under usual conditions, therefore, patronage fills many roles. Within any system some balance and compromise among conflicting goals and claims must be struck. What emerges within any patronage system is in reality many sys-tems: some of the more attractive positions may actually serve as rewards, or possibly for policy coordination; some of the most specialized may be subsumed into a quasi-merit system; and some of local concern may be set aside for the self-satisfaction of the local party hierarchy.

(5) *The Nature of the Party Using Patronage.* No scholar of any perception would indulge himself in the illusion that American political parties are great unified, monolithic structures. Yet, we assume all too often that "the party" benefits from the use of patronage, that "the party" curries favor with its appointments. What we overlook is that only one organ of the party is apt to gain from any one specific political appointment. And it is a matter of vital concern in understanding the effects of patronage to know just which party organ or leader, on what level of the party structure, reaps the reward. Patronage, therefore, by bolstering local centers of power and entrenching the political lords in their local fiefs, by preventing unity on candidates and policy, may be used as a weapon in intra-party squabbles just as easily as it may be used to create intra-party cohesion or vitality.

To state the assumption another way, we assume, contrary to the preponderance of evidence, that political parties have just one internal interest. They indeed have many interests, and patronage may serve one to the detriment of others. The very existence of the institution of "senatorial courtesy" illustrates the war between national party and state party over the use of federal patronage. . . . In any event, patronage, like any other form of partisan power, may be used in destructive, internal wars as well as in the great interparty battles.

IN CONCLUSION

These remarks on the assumptions undergirding a patronage system indicate how we build a somewhat unreal image of patronage. The result is a view of patronage that dwells on its political uses, while ignoring its inadequacies and disadvantages. It has been largely on the basis of this simplified and overly charitable appraisal of the political values of patronage that the system has been weighed against merit systems. One could even suggest that in addition to overestimating the political constructiveness of patronage, we underestimate its power to destroy both itself and partisan strength.

The self-destructive tendencies of patronage are most virulent when patronage is laxly administered. Where only some workers are replaced following a change of parties, the group replaced will in most instances be the group that has been politically the most active. In other words, the workers who have been least identified with the appointing party become most acceptable to a new administration; accordingly, the apolitical and the "bi-political" survive. Such lessons are not lost on workers who realize they can cheaply purchase job security with political inactivity. A denaturing of patronage results.

Similarly, the retention of workers for personal reasons or for reasons of skill and experience works the same havoc on the patronage system. When personal rather than party considerations dictate political job-giving, as they so often do in closely-knit communities, the political nature of the job is obscured, as is the political obligation and discipline that it demands. Eventually, the very political essence of the positions becomes unclear and impotent. Community expectations about patronage are reshaped and altered, and woe then to him who tries to reestablish a tight political rein over the patronage positions. In fact, anything less than the greatest virtuosity in the management of spoils will invite these self-destructive tendencies. That fact represents the truth in the oft-quoted plaint of the party functionary that with each political appointment he makes nine enemies and one ingrate.

This willingness to accept the conventional assumptions about patronage may reflect some sort of "intellectual lag." The assumptions were no doubt truer 20 or 30 years ago and in the heyday of spoils than they are today. Much of the writing on patronage stems from that period and reflects not only the times but the particular urban conditions under which patronage flourished most vigorously. Political scientists and students of public administration have failed in this respect to heed the advice of the historian to reformulate their generalizations for their own generation. Their failure to do so may be due in part to the decline of patronage and to the triumph of merit civil service systems. But it may also be the result of the delicacy and touchiness of the subject; they may fear to tread where ordinarily voluble politicians become silent and evasive. So, the land in which "fat cats" eat "pie" and in which public servants are "maced" remains largely *terra incognita* for academic political science.

One final problem remains. If the rewards of patronage are so meager and the problems so great, why do parties fight to maintain the patronage system? Political leaders deprecate the value of patronage both publicly and privately, yet do little to divest themselves of it. Their reasons are no doubt complex, and one can only tentatively suggest a few. The parties need the strength of patronage, however minor and irregular it might be, and they realize, as does any great nation, that in matters of empire one does not willingly surrender even the most barren desert. Above all, patronage has generally been the political way of life and the political ally of the local centers of political power in their losing battle for political superiority in America. It survives to a great extent in their protest against the growth of national politics and centralized parties in the United States.

POLITICAL PARTIES AND PRESSURE GROUP
POLITICS *
Hugh A. Bone

POLITICAL interest groups and political parties share political power and influence in running American politics. Their interests, objectives, and techniques overlap in so many ways that they appear indistinguishable at times. Nevertheless, most students of government see a pressure group as "issue or policy oriented," and a political party as "election or personality oriented." A party is seen as primarily motivated toward capturing and operating the government; the interest group's motivation is to shape public policy.

These observations on differences undoubtedly contain a large grain of truth. But a party which controls the government is expected to shape policy and to assume responsibility for it. If a pressure group wishes to shape policy to its interests it can hardly ignore the necessity for electing persons sympathetic to its views. Parties and private groups both seek access to government and must perforce have contacts and relationships with each other. Both afford channels by which the citizen may participate in the control of his government. Both complement and supplement each other. There is a constant two-way process of influence and relationship from interest group to party and from party to interest group.

Although many persons are active in a party and in a pressure group, the professional bureaucracies of the two have usually remained separate. The same is true of the leadership. A state or county chairman is seldom the president of a chamber of commerce or of a labor union. But the leadership, active workers, and enthusiastic supporters of parties and groups have so much in common that they remain in touch with each other much of the time. Major opportunities for contacts are afforded by nomination, campaigns, campaign finance, party programing, and infiltration.

NONPARTISAN AND PARTISAN ELECTIONS

In the United States some 800,000 public offices are filled by election. A considerable number of local officers such as clerks, councilmen, judges, treasurers, park and education board members are nonpartisan. Party intrusions into these elections are usually denounced and may actually hurt the candidacy of the ones

* From Hugh A. Bone, "Political Parties and Pressure Group Politics," in *The Annals,* September, 1958, pp. 74–83. © 1958 by The American Academy of Political and Social Science. Reprinted by permission of Professor Bone and the editors.

receiving party support. In nonpartisan elections, therefore, the support of interest groups is often of paramount importance and eagerly sought. Because a nonpartisan nominee lacks the organizational and financial backing of a political party, interest groups have an excellent chance to influence the outcome of these elections and may aid candidates without being charged as being pro-Republican or pro-Democratic. . . .

In a number of large cities, citizens groups publicly rate the various candidates for local offices. Recommendations are eagerly sought by candidates for nonpartisan offices, and they are usually willing to appear before the "candidates committees" of the civic groups in the hope that they will receive favorable comment. Newspapers often carry the statements on candidates prepared by the associations so that the influence or the association carries far beyond its limited membership. In the absence of a party label, a number of voters are guided by the endorsements—or lack of them—given by a municipal league to candidates for nonpartisan offices.

Private interest groups are no less concerned with numerous other state and local offices where a partisan ballot is used. Insurance and land commissioners, sanitary engineers, port officials, and so on often run as Republicans or Democrats but, for various reasons, receive little more than nominal help from the party organization. These officials have the power to make decisions which vitally affect certain private groups, and it becomes understandable that the latter should take an active part in securing the election of officials whose rulings and orders may influence their membership. The multiplicity of offices and the long ballot are confusing to the voter. This situation plays into the hands of pressure groups and also makes it imperative for them to take an interest in who is elected to administer the diverse state functions.

NOMINATIONS

In addition to its mixture of nonpartisan and partisan elections, the American electoral system has another feature which has encouraged political activity on the part of numerous interest groups—the direct primary system of nomination. In parts of the United States the party organizations are forbidden by law or party rules to endorse a candidate where there is a contest in the primary. In many other places it is customary for the parties to remain neutral in the primaries. Those entering the primary, therefore, cannot hope to receive financial or other help from either the national or the local party committees. Under the circumstances the nominee must finance his own primary campaign or seek help from personal friends—neither of which may be sufficient. Hopefuls are likely to find pressure groups ready to assist them in the primaries provided the latter feel the prospective nominee will be friendly to their cause. It stands to reason that those candidates who appear to have some chance of winning the primary will receive more help than those less likely to capture the nomination. Occasionally, however, an interest group will support a candidate even though he has little chance of winning. This is done because the group wishes to use the primary campaign as a forum for criticizing an incumbent or championing certain issues. Labor unions have done this on occasion where anti- or non-union views appear to predominate. In this sense the primary campaign is run as an "educational" program rather than as a potentially successful electoral venture.

Interest groups of diverse objectives often co-operate in getting persons registered. The officials or special committees of interest groups may decide to make endorsements among the candidates in the primary. Where there are contests in both party primaries, interest groups sometimes make an endorsement in each, but it is more likely that approval will be given to only one candidate. Endorsements are made known to the membership through the channels of the press and more particularly in the official newspaper or magazine of the organization. Some of these publications carry information on all candidates, but the material is presented in such a way as to show favoritism for one of them. Candidates may be invited to speak before a meeting of the group and given access to the pages of the journal to present views of interest to the membership. Literature on the primaries is often distributed to the members and a door-bell ringing or telephone corps is used to get out the vote on primary day. Activities by interest groups on behalf of candidates have undoubtedly swelled the numbers of persons participating in the primaries.

Nominations for President and Vice-President are made at party conventions. Over half the delegates in the national convention are selected by conventions in the states. In some states party conventions also designate certain candidates for public office. Where an interest group feels that the nominees of the convention may have views strongly for or against something it stands for, the group becomes vitally concerned with the choice of delegates and may seek either to have some of its own members chosen to the convention or to influence the selection. Delegates also adopt the party's platform, a matter in which the interest groups are most interested. . . .

National conventions are dominated by certain powerful political leaders such as governors, senators, congressmen, and local party chairmen. The majority of delegates are persons with a record of active partisan politics. For this reason pressure groups find they must operate most of the time off the convention floor. But the leaders of the private groups maintain contacts during conventions with the influential delegates, and hotel lobbies in the convention city teem with representatives of private groups.

GENERAL ELECTIONS

The activities of pressure groups in a general election differ only in emphasis and detail from that of the primary Perhaps most important is that in the general election the group must work out its relationship and modus operandi with the party organization. Three alternatives are possible. First the pressure group may develop its own campaign organization paralleling to some extent the precinct and other organization of the party. The group remains quite independent from the party. Labor unions have done this on numerous occasions. Party leaders are not invariably enthusiastic about this. They feel that the campaign run by the pressure groups may be too amateurish and operate at cross purposes with the strategy of the party. If the candidate wins, the pressure group may ask for patronage or certain concessions.

A second alternative is for the interest group to operate closely with the party organization with the campaign direction largely in the hands of the latter. In this instance the pressure group furnishes personnel to the party head-quarters, providing doorbell ringers and speakers as requested by the party chairmen and campaign managers. It co-operates with and in general takes its orders from the party. This arrangement appeals to the party leaders.

A third arrangement is a combination of the two with the interest groups maintaining considerable autonomy, but working closely with the party and perhaps providing direct assistance to the party headquarters. Which of these three alternatives is to be followed is determined by expediency, local conditions, the leadership of the party and the interest group and, of course, the preference of the candidate. Pressure groups are usually less interested in the entire ticket and prefer to concentrate on certain candidacies. What often takes place in practice then is more a pressure group-candidate relationship than a pressure group-party relationship.

The alleged successes of interest groups in primary and general elections may perhaps belong in the category in which Mark Twain once placed reports of his death—as highly exaggerated. Voting behavior is not likely to be explained exclusively by the activities or the lack of them of pressure groups. Endorsement of a candidate by one group is frequently offset by endorsement of his opponent by another. Reliable data, moreover, is scanty. . . . Interest-group support may be important and significant but not necessarily determinative.

A recurrent theme . . . is the desire of pressure groups to gain access to government. A highly important method of access is through the public elected official. It follows then that the pressure group must function in one way or another in campaigns. Campaigns bring the pressure group in direct contact with the candidate and/or his managers and party officials. In the long run these relationships are more important than the precise degree to which the group contributes to the election itself.

CAMPAIGN FINANCE

One of the most important developments in recent years is the increasingly large role of nonparty groups in the financing of campaigns. With the cost of campaigns increasing, parties and candidates are looking for additional sources of revenue and also agencies through which money can be expended without exceeding the 3 million dollars limitation imposed by the Hatch Act for one committee. Corporations and labor unions are forbidden by law from making direct contributions to political campaigns. These various laws, often referred to collectively as corrupt practices legislation, have not kept political-interest groups from giving donations but made them somewhat more circumspect. There are several ways by which groups may raise funds for candidates and still remain within the law.

The first is to form a "political action committee" illustrated by the Machinist Non-Partisan Political League, the United Automobile Workers–CIO Political Action Committee, and the AFL-CIO Committee on Political Education (COPE). Political funds are raised and expended separately from the treasuries of the labor unions. . . .

The now defunct Peoples Committee to Defend Life Insurance and Savings offered an analogous opportunity for insurance executives and stockholders to contribute to campaigns. "Healing arts committees" have provided a channel for doctors, nurses, dentists, and pharmacists to contribute to campaigns.

A host of "citizens" and "volunteers" groups crop up all over the nation during campaigns. . . . A careful analysis of some of these local groups will often reveal important economic interests as dominant in both the leadership and finance of the organizations. In only a relatively few instances is a title used (except for labor) which clearly identifies the interest group involved. . . .

By creating separate political committees, the organizations themselves remain officially neutral in partisan politics. This is less offensive to those members who do not believe that campaigns should be financed out of the organization's treasury or who may hold political views at variance with the majority of the membership.

Governmental Investigation Committees. The United States House and Senate usually create special campaign investigating committees for every biennial election. Over the years they have amassed much data on sources of revenue in political campaigns. . . .

Interest groups are heavy donors to state and local parties and candidates. There are several states which require no statement of campaign expenditures and others which require only statements of spending in a direct primary. As a result the public generally has less knowledge of the role played by groups in financing local elections than for federal offices.

PLATFORM INFLUENCING

The fact that party platforms are usually ambiguous and general has not kept the pressure groups from trying to influence them. National party platforms are drafted by the national convention's committee on resolutions composed of one person from each state delegation. The committee members even before they arrive in the convention city receive communications and personal requests from interest groups on diverse planks and proposals. A preliminary draft is prepared by a group appointed by the national committee, and this group is also the recipient of requests from certain interests.

After the resolutions committee is convened, it is often divided into subcommittees according to subject matter such as foregn policy, civil rights, veterans', and agriculture. The subcommittees then hold public hearings. Witnesses distribute copies of their prepared addresses to the committee members, answer questions, and elaborate upon their statements. . . .

Party platform formation on the state and county level also affords the pressure group an opportunity both for publicity and influence. It is not unusual for the local press to record a state party platform as "strongly pro-labor," "a victory for the conservatives" or "a bid for the minorities vote," thus suggesting victories for dominant factors and interests.

The making of a party platform is a way by which a political party can build a coalition of supporting interest groups. Platform drafters can remind an interest group that it was "heard" and point to a plank or clause contributed by a group. At the same time a pressure group can remind office holders of platform pledges.

INFILTRATION

Infiltration of the party organizations by members of interest groups is not unusual. The reverse also takes place though it is less publicized and obvious. A former party chairman in metropolitan Seattle made it a studied policy to encourage his precinct committeemen to join pressure groups and to become active as well in philanthropic and cultural societies. The chairman felt that his workers would have many opportunities to bring the "gospel" to the various nonparty groups and thereby build up favorable sentiment for the party among those who were perhaps unresponsive to partisan publicity. The chairman pointed out to would-be candidates that one of the best ways to become known was to be active in civic improvement and various other private groups.

In 1956 the Republican National Committee created a special labor division to counteract the tendency of union labor to vote Democratic. One of its projects was to try to locate members of unions who were sympathetic to the Republican cause and who might be willing to take a position in the local party organization. These persons could be used to pass out literature at union meetings. During Presidential campaigns it is customary for both national headquarters to create special interest divisions such as farm, veterans, Negro, and national resources.

If a party is able to have some of its members active in nonparty groups, other values may be realized. Party members can help to engineer invitations to party candidates and officials to speak to the group. The minorities division of the national committees have their members in nationalities societies; they notify the office of important dates so that the national chairman or some other prominent person may send appropriate congratulations. Additional members of the group may be won over and recruited for party activity. Active partisans can serve as a source of intelligence on views, attitudes, and sentiments of the pressure groups on public policies and candidates. Political parties have the perennial problem of raising money, and prospective donors may be found in the membership of the pressure group.

As parties desire to broaden their strength and support among interest groups, the latter wish to extend their influence within the party organization. In most parts of the nation, party organization is loose, making it relatively easy for members of interest groups to become active members of parties. Willing and eager persons soon have opportunities for positions in the precinct, district, and county party organizations or in party clubs. This in turn affords the opportunity to attend party conventions, participate in campaigns, draft resolutions and, at times, to run for public office.

It is unusual, however, for wholesale infiltration to take place. There have been times nonetheless when a nonparty group has, by design, set about to capture control of the party organization. The Non-Partisan League in North Dakota employed the tactics of infiltration rather than third-party politics. League nominees were placed in the Republican primaries and were successful in capturing the Republican State Committee. By 1918 the Republican party, platform, and state government were taken over completely by the League and much of its legislative program was enacted.

Michigan provides another success story of interest group infiltration. The state has been traditionally Republican and there was no permanent Democratic organization until the New Deal. In 1948 the CIO-PAC observed that "progressives" in the Democratic party leadership were outnumbered by "reactionaries," but that the Democrats afforded the best channel for supporting the interests of Michigan labor and liberalism. Accordingly the PAC advised all CIO members "to become active precinct, ward, county, and congressional district workers and attempt to become delegates to Democratic conventions." The CIO built a coalition with certain ethnic, liberal, and other labor groups and captured control of the state Democratic committee. It did this by training and electing precinct captains and taking control of the party conventions. The coalition, therefore, was able to have a noticeable influence on both primary and convention nominations.

The CIO coalition brought about many changes in the Democratic party. One of these was the emphasis upon state party platforms. The platforms were oriented toward specific liberal, social programs, and potential candidates were evaluated in terms of their attitude toward the platform. . . . The coalition continued to govern the selection of party officers, eject the conservative Old Guard, and appoint liberals to policy-determining patronage jobs. . . .

Advantages and Liabilities of Infiltration. . . . An internal party relationship gives a pressure group a chance to breathe vigor and life into a party and to strengthen its organizational base. It helps to further its legislative program and to inform the other officials of the party about the needs of the group.

There are also potential liabilities to the internal party relationships both for the party and the interest group. The interest group may find that its activity within a party may heighten factionalism within its own ranks. The Teamsters Union in Michigan fought the liberal coalition and some of its membership went over to the rival party. In very few organizations are all of the members Republicans or Democrats, and the minority is likely to resent the partisan activities of the majority. Control of a party requires financial resources, sustained effort, and other activities. It is not easy to keep up the activity necessary to control the party year in and year out and may divert energies of the group's leadership away from problems of internal group organization and program.

Party politics require concessions and compromises which may be unpalatable to many members of the group. Charges of betrayal and "double-crossing" are not unusual. If the interest group fails to elect candidates or to obtain programs from the party it has infiltrated, some of the membership is bound to become disgruntled and to request that the efforts to control the political party be abandoned. Nevertheless, infiltration is a tempting tactic for it gives the group a chance to influence nominations and platforms from the inside rather than from outside the organization.

CONCLUSION

The nature of the American political system provides pressure groups many opportunities to influence political parties and their candidates at all levels of government. Federalism and separation of powers have caused a decentralization of party organization with congressmen looking more to their own congressional and senatorial campaign committees than to the national committees. The direct primary system has removed from the party organization itself the historic function of designation. The cost of running for office is rapidly increasing so that many candidates must look outside of the party for assistance. Added to this complex picture is the high degree of voter independence and a large number of nonpartisan offices.

All of these factors have tended to make candidates more dependent upon nonparty sources for money, votes, and services. Party leaders have seen potential voters brought together in thousands of economic, political, social, and ethnic associations. If they can deal with the leaders of these groups, it may be easier and more effective than dealing with them as isolated individuals.

If parties have become dependent upon pressure groups, the reverse is also true. As Donald Blaisdell has pointed out:

The organization which the parties set up and maintain for the purpose of gaining control over the governing personnel is thus the vehicle by which interests are able to share power with the titular leaders. As a means of gaining the power of governing, party structure and organization serve not only the leaders nominally in official and party positions but also the pressure groups.

Pressure groups at times have tried to operate through the channels of minor parties. The abolitionists and "dry" forces were active at times through third parties. Organized labor, though divided, achieved some limited successes in New York State through the American Labor and Liberal parties. Agrarian malcontents used the Greenback, Populist, and Farmer-Labor parties to further their ends. But the pressure groups found that third parties seldom gave them the desired access to government. With a few exceptions, pressure groups today regard the influencing of the two major parties the better strategy and tactic.

Persons who become influential and active both in a party and a group become valuable members to both because of their access to each. They become aware of the problems of each and understand the limitations and strengths. Members of interest groups who become active partisans learn what a party can and cannot do and what its potential is likely to be. Similarly a party member who joins a pressure group comes to know its viewpoints and demands. An infiltrator in time may serve as a valuable mediator and interpreter. As Ivan Hinderaker has stated:

as the infiltrator becomes more active in party affairs, he gains an education in the realities of party politics, and in his party role his pressure group loyalties must take second position behind his party loyalty. Though he still works for his pressure group objectives, now he begins to understand why the broad-based major party cannot accede to his pressure group's every demand.

Pressure groups serve society in many useful and valuable ways. They provide a type of political self-expression, formulate policies and seek their fulfillment, provide public officials with information, and help to define the public interest. At the same time the pressure group must be watched so that it does not subvert the public interest. Political parties have the function of accommodating the demands of private interests into the larger public interests. Our major parties are combinations of great interests, but they are also an entity apart from any one pressure group. The interests of the American society and of the interest group itself are best served when a pressure group makes no permanent identification with either major party. Each can best make its contribution to politics by remaining separate. But the realities of American politics make it necessary for them to have close contact with each other.

INTEREST GROUPS AND THE POLITICAL
PROCESS *
David B. Truman

THE CONGRESS

IN the popular view the prime centre of interest-group activity is the Congress. The legislature is assumed to be the home of the lobby. Although this view rests on an oversimplified conception of policy-making, underestimates discretionary authority at other points in the structure, notably the executive, it is not entirely in error. Few matters of policy, especially in the domestic sphere, do not require Congressional approval, at least in general terms, and virtually

* From David B. Truman, "Organized Interest Groups in American Politics," in Alfred J. Junz, ed., *Present Trends in American National Government*, pp. 132–139. © Hansard Society for Parliamentary Government. Reprinted by permission of the publishers, Frederick A. Praeger, Inc., New York.

none are entirely beyond its powers of inquiry. The relations of interest groups with the Congress, and especially with its standing committees are, moreover, a good deal more extensive than a casual acquaintance with Washington affairs would indicate. Over a large number of comparatively routine and non-controversial matters one will normally find on closer examination a quiet collaboration among groups, Congressional committees, and executive agencies that does not, and ordinarily need not, receive public attention.

In looking at these routine matters and even more in examining issues of high controversy it is critically important to bear in mind that neither the Senate nor the House of Representatives is an assembly of equals. Seniority in the chambers and on the standing committees implies influence as well as authority. Equally important, the principal positions within the legislative parties, especially the Speaker of the House and the minority and majority floor leaders in both chambers, are sources of variable but often considerable influence. The significance of these positions is that they constitute focal points in a structure with which any organized group must reckon. Ordinarily a group cannot directly create a majority in support of its demands; it must work through some or all of these leaders as well as with ordinary members. The occupants of leadership posts rarely can be mere brokers. They have broader obligations—to maintain their followings within the chamber, to improve the legislative party's "record," and to protect the prestige of the President if he is of their party— which may not be consistent with the demands of an interest group.

Consequently a group's legislative fortunes will rise, not only to the extent that its claims are running with the currents of popular opinion, but also as they are consistent with the broader objectives of the more influential members of Congress. It follows that a group may be most effective when it is least conspicuous, when it is furthest from the deliberate use of "pressure," when it need not resort to propaganda and letter-writing campaigns. These familiar tactics are not useless, especially when the group's intention is to prevent rather than to promote action; they are valuable if they can indicate to the wavering Congressman that opposing the group will be more costly to his objectives, whatever these may be, than supporting it will be. But the possibility of establishing such a preponderance of risk must exist. Where it is obvious, either for or against the group, "pressure" tactics are futile. They are effective where they can displace uncertainty with probability, especially uncertainty concerning reelection. But almost of necessity uncertainty implies the existence of competing demands upon the Congressman, in the constituency and in Washington, which may not be resolved in the group's favour.

If a group can obtain information on the inclination of a wavering Congressman, as on his voting within an important standing committee, and if it can adroitly stimulate influential elements within his constituency to protest these tendencies, it may be able to confront the legislator with the threat he most fears, opposition in the primary election, where his party label is of little value to him. The terms of the primary contest often lack certainty of definition, and a determined minority, even when it cannot directly control the outcome, may be able to affect how the competing candidates are perceived and to compel the Congressman to contest the primary on issues that he would prefer to avoid. These situations are not numerous, however. The concerns of an electorate are many, and, even if an issue can be made so salient as to threaten a Congressman's tenure, the chances are that the incumbent will have taken the desired view without prompting. A senator from a major oil-producing state such as Oklahoma need not be pressured into support for the industry's projects; one from a consuming or minor producing state may be beyond the group's reach or only tenuously within it.

THE PRESIDENCY

The White House is also an arena of group action, but one of quite different qualities. A President is generally free to accept what demands he will and to use the incomparable resources of his position to neutralize or to undermine those that he rejects. He must, however, have advice, and a group may find the powers of his office on its side if its leaders enjoy the confidence of the President. In addition or alternatively, a group may affect the advice a President hears from members of the Congress, from his cabinet, from elsewhere in the executive branch, and from outside the government proper through its connections in any of these quarters.

It would be inaccurate to describe the forces responsible for a President's nomination and election as a coalition of organized groups, yet almost inevitably the Presidency is a prize of such importance that differences of interest are discernible among the forces at one or both of these stages. Hence groups which can cast themselves as spokesmen for these forces can reasonably expect a receptive hearing in the White House. But not invariably, for the demands of groups within his coalition may be incompatible, and a perceptive president may be more concerned, if a choice is open to him, to accommodate groups whose loyalty to his cause is uncertain than to follow those that are committed. "Safe" groups, like "solid" states, may have less leverage than doubtful ones.

Although group spokesmen before the President thus are cast more as petitioners than as creditors, they are not incapable of independent action, especially of a negative sort. A President seeking a compromise solution to a controverted question, facing an irreconcilable opposition whose proportions he is anxious to minimize by the terms of his proposed solution, may be obliged to solicit the willingness of groups among his allies to "go along" with a formula that falls short of their full objectives. Even a Franklin Roosevelt on occasion faced this necessity, for example, in his dealings with organized labour; faced, that is, the probability that a refusal by the leaders of friendly groups to accept his designs would doom them to failure. If the project is important enough, a President occasionally can go over the heads of such group leaders by direct appeals to their followers and to the whole body of citizens, but this device is not infallible and it loses its effectiveness if too often used. A President thus may be obliged to accept the veto of a group spokesman as in effect and for the time being an accurate reflection of the group's attitudes.

The Executive Agencies. Most units of the executive branch exist in a setting dominated by a particular clientele of organized and unorganized groups immediately affected by their activities. Characteristically the relations between the agencies and these clientele groups are collaborative, involving an interchange of advice and information and a useful mutuality of outlook. The reasons for this intimacy may lie in the group's initial sponsorship of the activity or in its gradual acceptance of the agency, a regulatory bureau for example, as insurance against a less desirable arrangement such as public ownership. In either case the clientele groups will be more than casually concerned with appointments to the principal posts in the agency and may be of considerable value to it in fighting, for example, its budgetary battles in the Executive Office of the President and particularly in the Congress.

The vast majority of these clientele relations fortunately constitute stable subsystems, routinized, uncontroversial, and "unpolitical." Almost by definition they are resistant to change. Demands for alteration in policy emerge now and again, however, in a dynamic society. When the Presidency is the principal channel for these new demands, the agency executives may face an awkward choice between support of the Chief Executive—at the price of hostility from some of their clientele groups and from the latters' allies within the Congress—and a silent or open resistance to his wishes. Presidents come and go, and they may reflect weak or temporary political demands, but the make-up of Congressional committees usually changes slowly, and an agency may find itself in an indefensible position, facing punitive investigations and reduced appropriations, if a President cannot or a new Chief Executive does not give it effective support against groups made hostile by its initiatives and enjoying the confidence of influential members of the legislature. For the agencies of the executive are in fact responsible both to the Congress and to the President, and the system does not insure harmony between the views of the two superiors. As groups may exploit the separation of President and Congress, they may protect their positions in the administering agencies by using the alternative lines of responsibility.

THE JUDICIARY

The "political" segments of the government are the most active and the most conspicuous arenas of group activity, but the power involved in the system of judicial review inevitably means that the courts too are objects of group concern. The strong and honoured tradition of judicial independence excludes, of course, some tactics taken for granted in dealings with the executive and the legislature. Interest groups, to be sure, including the organized bar, attempt to influence both executive and senatorial action on appointments to the bench, especially to the Supreme Court. When the Court, as it has on several occasions in recent years, hands down constitutional or statutory interpretations that are objectionable to important interests, these groups with complete propriety will instigate or support efforts to amend the affected statute or to alter the Court's appellate jurisdiction. These efforts are distinguishable only in degree from those aimed at restraining executive agencies, but they are considerably less frequent and, given the prestige of the Court, normally less effective.

The chief means of group activity in the judiciary is litigation. Groups that are temporarily or chronically under-represented in the legislature and the executive may rely on the constitutional precedents established by the Court to negate unfavourable decisions by the other branches or even to establish their claims as public policy. Thus conservative groups, at odds with the Roosevelt Administration and with the majority in Congress, successfully used litigation to invoke prevailing constitutional interpretations against several early New Deal statutes. More recently the National Association for the Advancement of Coloured People, whose constituents are but weakly represented in the Congress and are little more influential in the executive branch, has placed primary reliance upon litigation to achieve its objectives. Especially since the 1954 decision on school segregation, the N.A.A.C.P. and its allies have used litigation to establish and with some success to enforce as constitutional doctrine a public policy that neither the affected state governments nor the Congress would have placed in the statute books. Groups are not always able to cast their claims in justiciable terms, but the courts undeniably are a significant arena of group activity. Their powers, their independence, and on occasion the repercussions of their decisions, contribute, moreover, to the visibility of organized groups in the American system.

THE PARTIES

The party organizations also in varying degrees provide a setting for group activity, in connection with both nominations and elections, but generalization about these relations is hazardous. The loose integration of the parties reflects a diversity of form and function that defies quick summary and produces a parallel variety in the actions of organized groups. In the states and localities organized groups may stand on the periphery of the parties, except as they or their members are courted by the organizations; they may intervene more or less openly in the primaries; or in some instances one group or an alliance may "capture" one of the parties and dominate its actions. Thus in Michigan in recent years the United Automobile Workers seem to have become the dominant force in the state's Democratic Party. This sort of open penetration, however, is probably exceptional. Strong groups in politically homogeneous states ordinarily can rely on the electoral machinery to produce receptive officials without open involvement by the group, and in closely contested areas containing a variety of groups the more characteristic relation is one of bargaining with the party whose policy tendencies the groups find congenial.

The national parties, as they assemble quadrennially to nominate candidates for the Presidency, are not leagues of organized interest groups but coalitions of state parties and factions with group ties of varying intimacy. Formal affiliation of groups with parties is not the American pattern. Yet most major groups display a stronger affinity for one of the two parties than for the other. Not all union members are Democrats, but labour leaders are considerably more conspicuous at Democratic than at Republican conventions. Nor are all corporate executives Republicans, yet most business groups are likely to find themselves more at home in Republican than in Democratic gatherings. These affinities, however, are rarely if ever the product of the action or design of particular groups. The class, occupational, and other politically relevant dispositions of the modal followings of the two major parties are more deeply rooted, and group leaders, characteristically sharing those dispositions, are likely to work within the party in which long association and the prevailing tendencies of their members give them the greatest chance of being influential.

The bipartisan complexion of the membership in most national groups, the old and widespread attitude that partisanship as such is un-civic, the presence of "sound" candidates in both major parties, and the tactical advantages in a group's appearing to influence elections by granting and withholding support all combine to encourage at least a pose of group non-partisanship in most national elections. They or their members may contribute their resources in money and energy largely to one of the parties, and their endorsements of candidates for the Congress, if they follow the practice, may accrue primarily to the advantage of one party, but normally they will avoid explicit party identification. . . .

THE STATES V. THE UNION

These comments on the national political scene would be incomplete if they did not record the additional fact that the states themselves are arenas in which group activity may have important national consequences. No less today than in the years before the Civil War, championship of "states rights" represents the invocation of federal principles to defend established positions. It is no accident that few labour unions or partisans of the welfare state are numbered among those who fear the eclipse of the states by the federal government. For a variety of reasons, including antiquated systems of representation, most of the states, even some of the most industrialized, have been less responsive than the federal government and particularly the Presidency to the demands for change symbolized by the New Deal. Proposals to return responsibilities in these areas to the states or to increase the discretionary and concurrent power of state officials in federally supported programmes thus imply in most cases reduction in the vigour of administration and alteration in the interests benefited. The efforts of groups working toward these objectives through the state governments and through organizations of state officials, such as the Association of State Attorneys-General, are of course reinforced by the localized partisan risks of the members of Congress, especially the Representatives. . . .

V. POLITICAL PARTIES AND THE JUDICIARY

9. The Political Process and the Judiciary

NO discussion of the American party process would be complete without some mention of the role of the federal and state courts in the regulation of political parties and the influence of the courts on the political process. The importance of the courts in the American political system stems from their authoritative position as official decision-making agencies. Ever since 1803 when Chief Justice John Marshall, a Federalist, articulated the doctrine of judicial review in *Marbury* v. *Madison,* a case with strong partisan political overtones, the courts, and particularly the Supreme Court, have been inescapably involved in the political process.

Some notable political storms were created in the nineteenth century by the Supreme Court's decisions in the Dred Scott case, the Greenback cases, and the Income Tax case of 1895. In the twentieth century the Supreme Court's power of review again evoked major political turmoil. In the 1930's the Court's invalidation of many New Deal measures resulted in President Franklin D. Roosevelt's abortive attempt to "pack the court" by increasing its membership. While Congress thwarted the President's proposal to enlarge the Court and thereby change its philosophy, the Court itself by the end of the decade had abandoned its laissez-faire tenets, ultimately accepting various forms of government regulation of economic activity as constitutional. But new ideological conflict, this time in noneconomic areas, again pushed the Supreme Court into the center of the political arena.

In the 1950's the Supreme Court came under intensive attack for its decisions outlawing racial segregation in the public schools and upholding the civil rights of Communists and accused Communists in national security cases. As a result of the segregation decisions eight southern state legislatures resurrected and enacted so-called interposition statutes, and in 1956 a Southern Manifesto accusing the Supreme Court of "a clear abuse of judicial power" was signed by nineteen senators and seventy-seven members of the House of Representatives. The high Court's decisions in national security cases prompted the introduction of bills designed to deprive the Supreme Court of federal preemption and appellate jurisdiction in specific areas dealing with national security. In the 1960's decisions in the politically sensitive area of congressional and state legislative apportionment and districting again served to remind the public that the Supreme Court plays a role in the political process. However, before discussing these momentous cases and the political reaction to them, some brief comments on the functional relationship of political parties to the judiciary and on judicial regulation of political parties are in order.

In the American constitutional system the Supreme Court acts to define the scope of legitimate governmental authority, the relationship between the states, the nation, and the citizen, and serves as the highest reviewing authority of executive and congressional action. But although under our system of separation of powers the judiciary functions independently of the executive and the legislature, under our system of checks and balances it is the executive which makes appointments to the courts and the legislature which confirms them. Furthermore, Congress retains some additional powers which it can exercise in restraint of the judiciary. The federal judiciary below the Supreme Court is beholden to Congress for its size, pay, operating funds and scope of jurisdiction. And the Congress retains the right to circumscribe the appellate jurisdiction of the Supreme Court (for example, the bills mentioned above). Congress can override the Court's invalidation of a congressional enactment by proposing a constitutional amendment (for example, the income tax amendment); Congress can also institute impeachment proceedings against federal judges (this power has been invoked only once against a Supreme Court justice). Congress can alter the number of judges sitting on the Supreme Court; throughout our history there have not always been nine justices. However, it is in appointments and confirmations that the interrelationship between the partisan party process and the nonpartisan judicial process is most frequently manifest.

On the federal level political considerations enter into judicial appointments. The federal bench offers some patronage opportunities, and appointments are confirmed in accordance with "senatorial courtesy." (See Comment 8.) Most federal judicial appointments are approved without undue controversy, primarily because the President's concern for his own image inhibits him from nominating obviously unqualified men. Political pressures, nonetheless, occasionally result in poor nominations, and in rare instances the Senate refuses to confirm a nominee. President Hoover's nomination of John J. Parker to the Supreme Court was rejected by the Senate. President Johnson's nomination of Francis X. Morrissey to a federal district judgeship provoked decided criticism and resulted in the nominee's requesting that his name be withdrawn. In Supreme Court appointments, prior experience on the bench is not always considered a requisite. Supreme Court Justice Felix Frankfurter, recognizing the essential political character of the Supreme Court, once commented that "the correlation between prior judicial experience and fitness for the functions of the Supreme Court is zero." This assertion is borne out by fact. Among the distinguished justices who had not been judges before coming to the high bench were John Marshall, Story, Taney, Hughes, Brandeis, and Warren.

Most state judicial offices are filled by popular election. Nominations to these posts are made through the political party selection process. State and local party organizations, accordingly, use judicial nominations for purposes of patronage and other political considerations such as ethnic balancing of a ticket or as a reward for political participation or backing. The mechanisms by which the political process staffs the federal and state judiciary is but one aspect of the political-judicial nexus; another facet is the means whereby the judiciary regulates the political process.

Judicial regulation of the political process is predicated on an interpretation of the Constitution, state constitutions, and congressional and state statutes. Traditionally, control of elections and political parties has rested largely with the states. State courts, accordingly, have dealt with such issues as the legality of state regulation aimed at protecting parties from raiding (voters of one party vote in the opposing party's primary, their object being to secure the nomination of the most vulnerable opposition candidate), whether a party can command loyalty to its ticket, party convention disputes, placing a party on the ballot, candidate eligibility, and issues arising out of the actual balloting in primaries and general elections. However, although the Constitution makes no mention of political parties and there is no specific grant of power to Congress to regulate the parties, the Fourteenth and Fifteenth Amendments have caused the federal judiciary to become involved in the constitutional politics of Negro suffrage.

The Fourteenth Amendment provides that "no State shall make or enforce any law which shall abridge the privileges or immunities of citizens of the United States, nor shall any State deprive any person of life, liberty, or property, without due process of law; nor deny to any person within its jurisdiction the equal protection of the laws." And the Fifteenth Amendment provides that "the right of citizens of the United States to vote shall not be denied or abridged by the United States or by any State on account of race, color, or previous condition of servitude." Congress was given the power to enforce these prohibitions by "appropriate legislation."

Theoretically the Fourteenth and Fifteenth Amendments should have enfranchised the Negro. In the South, however, four methods were used to prevent Negro voting: (1) the "grandfather clause"; (2) the "white primary"; (3) discriminatory administration of literacy and "understanding" tests; and (4) the poll tax. A welter of litigation resulted. In 1915 the Supreme Court invalidated the "grandfather clause" of the Oklahoma constitution. But although the "white primary" litigation involved only a simple constitutional question, it took two decades to resolve. In 1927, in *Nixon* v. *Herndon,* the Supreme Court held a Texas white primary unconstitutional under the equal protection clause of the Fourteenth Amendment. The Texas legislature, following the decision, repealed its white primary law and substituted an act authorizing political parties within the state to prescribe the qualifications of their own members. The Democratic state executive committee thereupon adopted a white primary rule. This rule was challenged, and in 1932 in *Nixon* v. *Condon* the Supreme Court ruled that a party committee acting under state authority could not adopt a white primary since it was a denial of equal protection by the state. Undaunted, in 1932 the Democratic party's state convention adopted a white primary rule. Three years later, in *Grovey* v. *Townsend,* the Supreme Court ruling on the legal character of political parties found them to be "voluntary associations for political action," rather than "creatures of the state." As a "private association" political parties could exclude Negroes. In 1944, in *Smith* v. *Allwright,* the Supreme Court overruled itself and invalidated the white primary. The reasoning in this case was that the primary was an "integral part" of the electoral mechanism. Although the state convention had acted under its own authority in excluding Negroes, the primary in other aspects was regulated by state law and was related to the general election. The state was barred by the Fifteenth Amendment from discriminating against Negroes. There were various other attempts to deny Negroes access to the primaries, but the federal courts, following the doctrine of *Smith* v. *Allwright,* thwarted them.

The protection of Negro voting rights, through federal judicial interpretation of the Constitution, continued in the 1960's. In 1960 the 1957 Civil Rights Act was upheld, and the Supreme Court decided *Gomillion* v. *Lightfoot,* which held that racial gerrymandering was violative of the Fifteenth Amendment. In 1964, in *Anderson* v. *Martin,* the Court ruled that a Louisiana state requirement that a candidate's race be stipulated on a local election ballot violated the Fourteenth Amendment's equal protection clause. The Civil Rights acts of 1957, 1960, 1964, and 1965, based on the Fifteenth Amendment, attempted to vitiate discriminatory administration of literacy and understanding tests. The Twenty-fourth Amendment, ratified in 1964, abolished the poll tax in federal elections. And in *Harper* v. *Virginia State Board of Elections* (1966), the Supreme Court, relying on the equal protection clause of the Fourteenth Amendment, held state poll taxes to be illegal. (For a discussion of the Civil Rights acts and the poll tax case, see Comment 6.)

Contemporary with these liberalizing changes were the Supreme Court's momentous decisions affecting congressional and state legislative apportionment. These controversial cases, which touch the power centers of the party system, had a most inauspicious precedent in *Colegrove* v. *Green*. In 1946 Kenneth Colegrove, a political scientist, challenged Illinois' districting of its membership in the House of Representatives. Colegrove charged that gross malapportionment denied him the equal protection of the laws. Colegrove's contention was not sustained by the Supreme Court, which handed down a decision split four to three. Justice Felix Frankfurter, long famous for his concept of judicial self-restraint, stated in his opinion that apportionment cases were not appropriate for resolution by courts (i.e., were nonjusticiable) and warned that "courts ought not to enter this political thicket." Justice Wiley B. Rutledge in his opinion agreed with the minority that federal courts did have the power to adjudicate such cases, but he nonetheless voted with the majority because of the "shortness of the time remaining" before the election. Since only seven justices participated in *Colegrove,* and because their opinions were divided, a number of other suits were appealed to the Court. None, however, was accepted for review until *Baker* v. *Carr* in 1962.

In the years between *Colegrove* and *Baker* certain changes had taken place. The Court, as in the 1954 school desegregation decisions, systematically extended its interpretation of the Constitution's protection of individual rights. There were changes in the Court's membership; by the early 1960's there was a decidedly liberal majority. And finally, the population movement from rural to urban and suburban areas (see Comment 7) had created a representation imbalance that was difficult to ignore.

On March 26, 1962, the Supreme Court, in *Baker* v. *Carr,* ruled that (1) the question of state legislature apportionment is reviewable by federal courts, and (2) some legislature apportionments might violate the equal protection clause of the Fourteenth Amendment and thus be unconstitutional. The Court, however, refused to specify the degree of population disparity in apportionment which would be unconstitutional, nor did it suggest possible remedies. Of the justices who remained from the *Colegrove* Court, Justices Black and Douglas, formerly dissenters, were now with the majority, while Justice Frankfurter reaffirmed his original dissenting position in *Colegrove* and wrote his last great opinion. Frankfurter pointed out that the absence of a clear basis of relief "catapults the lower courts" into a "mathematical quagmire." Appeal for relief from political mischief should be made not to the courts, but "to an informed, civically militant electorate."

The impact of *Baker* v. *Carr* on the political system was extraordinary. Within two years, court cases demanding an end to malapportionment were filed or prosecuted in forty-one states; within five years some form of reapportionment action had taken effect or was being considered in all states except Oregon, which had been apportioned on a population basis since 1952. *Baker* had spawned a complex progeny; new cases and new issues arose and with them political response. Some unresolved questions were: What degree of legislative malapportionment violates the Fourteenth Amendment? How equal in population would districts have to be? Did both houses of a state legislature have to be apportioned on the basis of population, or would a "little federal plan" (in which one house would be apportioned on the basis of population, and the other house according to other factors, such as geography) be considered constitutional? (In Virginia a federal court ruled that a "federal plan" was not acceptable; in Delaware another federal court ruled the opposite.)

Could initiative and referendum laws affect the constitutionality of apportionment plans? How would court orders be enforced? Would the federal courts write their own apportionment rules?

Some of these questions were answered in subsequent cases. *Gray* v. *Sanders,* decided in 1963, struck down the Georgia county-unit system of voting in state and congressional primaries. The Court established the fact that "within a given constituency there can be room for but a single constitutional rule—one voter, one vote." In *Wesberry* v. *Sanders,* another Georgia case decided in February, 1964, the Court followed *Baker* in holding districting questions justiciable, and *Gray* in maintaining the principle of "one man, one vote." But the Court did not base its holding on the Fourteenth Amendment as in *Baker* and *Gray,* but on Article I, Section 2, of the Constitution which requires representatives "to be apportioned among the states according to their respective numbers." *Wesberry* v. *Sanders* applied the "one man, one vote" rule on a national basis; henceforth congressional districts must be as equal in population as practicable. This ruling, which was destined to have a fundamental impact on the composition of the House of Representatives, did not establish permissible population disparities. That question remained open. What did seem likely was that as a result of *Wesberry* more states would redistrict following each decennial census. In June, 1964, however, in a group of appealed cases, the Supreme Court handed down its most sweeping reapportionment decisions and answered some of the questions raised by the previous cases.

The appealed cases, known collectively by the name of the leading case, *Reynolds* v. *Sims,* established a number of principles. The equal protection clause of the Fourteenth Amendment requires that the seats in both houses of a bicameral state legislature must be apportioned on a population basis. While "mathematical exactness of precision" in determining legislative districts may be impossible, apportionment must nonetheless be "based substantially on population." The federal analogy was inapplicable as a precedent for state legislative apportionments. In addition, a referendum or initiative that approved an apportionment based on any principle other than population had no standing because a "citizen's constitutional rights can hardly be infringed upon because a majority of the people choose to do so." A week later, on June 22, 1964, the Court applied its population rule and declared that the legislative districts in nine more states were unconstitutional. Although these decisions did not spell out specific guidelines, they served to quicken the pace of reapportionment action throughout the country, simultaneously unleashing a good deal of criticism of the Court.

The *Reynolds* decisions created a political storm far more furious than either *Baker* or *Wesberry,* because *Reynolds* was hitting against traditional power positions. State legislative districts are usually the basis of political power within the states. (The effects of the reapportionment cases on the party process will be discussed in Part VI.) Furthermore, the decisions were opposed by some who thought the application of the "one man, one vote" formula to state legislatures less logical than the application of the same formula to congressional districts. Others were worried about the increasing interference of federal courts in state affairs, and the spectre of further federal invasion of states' rights.

This new wave of anti-Court feeling, as in previous instances, brought forward many proposals to curb the Court. One of the most discussed proposals was sponsored by the ranking Republican member of the House Judiciary Committee, Representative William M. McCulloch, who proposed a constitutional amendment permitting bicameral state legislatures to apportion one house on factors other than population. Representative William Tuck of Virginia, a former Democratic governor, introduced a bill which would have denied federal courts any jurisdiction over state legislature reapportionment. The Tuck bill passed the House, but died in the Senate amid a welter of other Senate Court-curb bills. In the Senate, Everett McKinley Dirksen, the minority leader, tried first to attach to the vital foreign aid bill a rider directing a two- to four-year stay in federal court proceedings in state reapportionment cases. This tactic failed, and so, in 1965, Dirksen introduced a constitutional amendment designed to permit states with bicameral legislatures to apportion one house of its legislature on a nonpopulation basis. After considerable debate on it, the amendment failed to pass. Senator Dirksen, hoping to win additional support by modification of his original amendment, then offered a revised amendment, which was rejected by the Senate in 1966. By the time of the Senate's rejection of the second Dirksen amendment, the controversy over reapportionment had subsided. A majority of the states were already committed to reapportionment of their legislatures, and resentment against the Court's "legislating" had diminished. The high Court had weathered another storm. The fight over the reapportionment cases was merely an episode in the continuing struggle—so far unsuccessful—to curb the Court.

Excerpts from *Baker* v. *Carr* and *Reynolds* v. *Sims* follow.

BAKER v. CARR

369 U.S. 186 (1962)

MR. JUSTICE BRENNAN delivered the opinion of the Court.

This civil action was brought . . . to redress the alleged deprivation of federal constitutional rights. The complaint, alleging that by means of a 1901 statute of Tennessee apportioning the members of the General Assembly among the State's 95 counties, "these plaintiffs and others similarly situated, are denied the equal protection of the laws accorded them by the Fourteenth Amendment to the Constitution of the United States by virtue of the debasement of their votes," was dismissed by a three-judge court convened . . . in the Middle District of Tennessee. The court held that it lacked jurisdiction of the subject matter and also that no claim was stated upon which relief could be granted. . . . We noted probable jurisdiction of the appeal. . . . We hold that the dismissal was error, and remand the cause to the District Court for trial and further proceedings consistent with this opinion.

The General Assembly of Tennessee consists of the Senate with 33 members and the House of Representatives with 99 members. . . .

. . . Tennessee's standard for allocating legislative representation among her counties is the total number of qualified voters resident in the respective counties, subject only to minor qualifications. Decennial reapportionment in compliance with the constitutional scheme was effected by the General Assembly each decade from 1871 to 1901. The 1871 apportionment was preceded by an 1870 statute requiring an enumeration. The 1881 apportionment involved three statutes, the first authorizing an enumeration, the second enlarging the Senate from 25 to 33 members and the House from 75 to 99 members, and the third apportioning the membership of both Houses. In 1891 there were both an enumeration and an apportionment. In 1901 the General Assembly abandoned separate enumeration in favor of reliance upon the Federal Census and passed the Apportionment Act here in controversy. In the more than 60 years since that action, all proposals in both Houses of the General Assembly for reapportionment have failed to pass.

Between 1901 and 1961, Tennessee has experienced substantial growth and redistribution of her population. In 1901 the population was 2,020,616, of whom 487,380 were eligible to vote. The 1960 Federal Census reports the State's population at 3,567,089, of whom 2,092,891 are eligible to vote. The relative standings of the counties in terms of qualified voters have changed significantly. It is primarily the continued application of the 1901 Apportionment Act to this shifted and enlarged voting population which gives rise to the present controversy.

Indeed, the complaint alleges that the 1901 statute, even as of the time of its passage, "made no apportionment of Representatives and Senators in accordance with the constitutional formula . . . , but instead arbitrarily and capriciously apportioned representatives in the Senate and House without reference . . . to any logical or reasonable formula whatever." It is further alleged that "because of the population changes since 1900, and the failure of the Legislature to reapportion itself since 1901," the 1901 statute became "unconstitutional and obsolete." Appellants also argue that, because of the composition of the legislature effected by the 1901 Apportionment Act, redress in the form of a state constitutional amendment to change the entire mechanism for reapportioning, or any other change short of that, is difficult or impossible. The complaint concludes that "these plaintiffs and others similarly situated, are denied the equal protection of the laws accorded them by the Fourteenth Amendment to the Constitution of the United States by virtue of the debasement of their votes." They seek a declaration that the 1901 statute is unconstitutional and an injunction restraining the appellees from acting to conduct any further elections under it. They also pray that unless and until the General Assembly enacts a valid reapportionment, the District Court should either decree a reapportionment by mathematical application of the Tennessee constitutional formulae to the most recent Federal Census figures, or direct the appellees to conduct legislative elections, primary and general, at large. They also pray for such other and further relief as may be appropriate.

I. THE DISTRICT COURT'S OPINION AND ORDER OF DISMISSAL

. . . In light of the District Court's treatment of the case, we hold today only (a) that the court possessed jurisdiction of the subject matter; (b) that a justiciable cause of action is stated upon which appellants would be entitled to appropriate relief; and (c) because appellees raise the issue before this Court, that the appellants have standing to challenge the Tennessee apportionment statutes. Beyond noting that we have no cause at this stage to doubt the District Court will be able to fashion relief if violations of constitutional rights are found, it is improper now to consider what remedy would be most appropriate if appellants prevail at the trial.

II. JURISDICTION OF THE SUBJECT MATTER

The District Court was uncertain whether our cases withholding federal judicial relief rested upon a lack of federal jurisdiction or upon the inappropriateness of the subject matter for judicial consideration—what we have designated "nonjusticiability." The distinction between the two grounds is significant. In the instance of nonjusticiability, consideration of the cause is not wholly and immediately foreclosed; rather, the Court's inquiry necessarily proceeds to the point of deciding whether the duty asserted can be judicially identified and its breach judicially determined, and whether protection for the right asserted can be judicially molded. In the instance of lack of jurisdiction the cause either does not "arise under" the Federal Constitution, laws or treaties (or fall within one of the other enumerated categories of Art. III, § 2), or is not a "case or controversy" within the meaning of that section; or the cause is not one described by any jurisdictional statute. Our conclusion . . . that this cause presents no nonjusticiable "political question" settles the only possible doubt that it is a case or controversy. Under the present heading of "Jurisdiction of the Subject Matter" we hold only that the matter set forth in the complaint does arise under the Constitution . . .

Article III, § 2, of the Federal Constitution provides that "The judicial Power shall extend to all Cases, in Law and Equity, arising under this Constitution, the Laws of the United States, and Treaties made, or which shall be made, under their Authority . . . ." It is clear that the cause of action is one which "arises under" the Federal Constitution. The complaint alleges that the 1901 statute effects an apportionment that deprives the appellants of the equal protection of the laws in violation of the Fourteenth Amendment. Dismissal of the complaint upon the ground of lack of jurisdiction of the subject matter would, therefore, be justified only if that claim were "so attenuated and unsubstantial as to be absolutely devoid of merit," . . . or "frivolous," . . . Since the District Court obviously and correctly did not deem the asserted federal constitutional claim unsubstantial and frivolous, it should not have dismissed the complaint for want of jurisdiction of the subject matter. And of course no further consideration of the merits of the claim is relevant to a determination of the court's jurisdiction of the subject matter. . . .

An unbroken line of our precedents sustains the federal courts' jurisdiction of the subject matter of federal constitutional claims of this nature. . . .

The appellees refer to *Colegrove* v. *Green*, . . . as authority that the District Court lacked jurisdiction of the subject matter. Appellees misconceive the holding of that case. The holding was precisely contrary to their reading of it.

Seven members of the Court participated in the decision. Unlike many other cases in this field which have assumed without discussion that there was jurisdiction, all three opinions filed in *Colegrove* discussed the question. Two of the opinions expressing the views of four of the Justices, a majority, flatly held that there was jurisdiction of the subject matter. . . .

Two cases decided with opinions after *Colegrove* likewise plainly imply that subject matter of this suit is within District Court jurisdiction. In *Mac-Dougall v. Green,* . . . the District Court dismissed for want of jurisdiction, . . . a suit to enjoin enforcement of the requirement that nominees for state-wide elections be supported by a petition signed by a minimum number of persons from at least 50 of the State's 102 counties. This Court's disagreement with that action is clear since the Court affirmed the judgment after a review of the merits and concluded that the particular claim there was without merit. In *South v. Peters,* . . . we affirmed the dismissal of an attack on the Georgia "county unit" system but founded our action on a ground that plainly would not have been reached if the lower court lacked jurisdiction of the subject matter, . . .

We hold that the District Court has jurisdiction of the subject matter of the federal constitutional claim asserted in the complaint.

III. STANDING

A federal court cannot "pronounce any statute, either of a State or of the United States, void, because irreconcilable with the Constitution, except as it is called upon to adjudge the legal rights of litigants in actual controversies." . . . Have the appellants alleged such a personal stake in the outcome of the controversy as to assure that concrete adverseness which sharpens the presentation of issues upon which the court so largely depends for illumination of difficult constitutional questions? This is the gist of the question of standing. It is, of course, a question of federal law.

The complaint was filed by residents of Davidson, Hamilton, Knox, Montgomery, and Shelby Counties. Each is a person allegedly qualified to vote for members of the General Assembly representing his county. These appellants sued "on their own behalf and on behalf of all qualified voters of their respective counties, and further, on behalf of all voters of the State of Tennessee who are similarly situated . . . ." The appellees are the Tennessee Secretary of State, Attorney General, Coordinator of Elections, and members of the State Board of Elections; the members of the State Board are sued in their own right and also as representatives of the County Election Commissioners whom they appoint.

We hold that the appellants do have standing to maintain this suit. Our decisions plainly support this conclusion. Many of the cases have assumed rather than articulated the premise in deciding the merits of similar claims. And *Colegrove* v. *Green, supra,* squarely held that voters who allege facts showing disadvantage to themselves as individuals have standing to sue. . . . These appellants seek relief in order to protect or vindicate an interest of their own, and of those similarly situated. Their constitutional claim is, in substance, that the 1901 statute constitutes arbitrary and capricious state action, offensive to the Fourteenth Amendment in its irrational disregard of the standard of apportionment prescribed by the State's Constitution or of any standard, effecting a gross disproportion of representation to voting population. The injury which appellants assert is that this classification disfavors the voters in the counties in which they reside, placing them in a position of constitutionally unjustifiable inequality *vis-à-vis* voters in irrationally favored counties. A citizen's right to a vote free of arbitrary impairment by state action has been judicially recognized as a right secured by the Constitution, when such impairment resulted from dilution by a false tally, . . . or by a refusal to count votes from arbitrarily selected precincts, . . . or by a stuffing of the ballot box, . . .

It would not be necessary to decide whether appellants' allegations of impairment of their votes by the 1901 apportionment will, ultimately entitle them to any relief, in order to hold that they have standing to seek it. If such impairment does produce a legally cognizable injury, they are among those who have sustained it. They are asserting "a plain, direct and adequate interest in maintaining the effectiveness of their votes," not merely a claim of "the right, possessed by every citizen, to require that the Government be administered according to law . . . ." They are entitled to a hearing and to the District Court's decision on their claims. "The very essence of civil liberty certainly consists in the right of every individual to claim the protection of the laws, whenever he receives an injury."

IV. JUSTICIABILITY

In holding that the subject matter of this suit was not justiciable, the District Court relied on *Colegrove* v. *Green, supra,* and subsequent *per curiam* cases. . . . The District Court misinterpreted *Colegrove* v. *Green* and other decisions of this Court on which it relied. Appellants' claim that they are being denied equal protection is justiciable, and if "discrimination is sufficiently shown, the right to relief under the equal protection clause is not diminished by the fact that the discrimination relates to political rights." . . . To show why we reject the argument based on the Guaranty Clause, we must examine the authorities under it. But because there appears to be some uncertainty as to why those cases did present political questions, and specifically as to whether this apportionment case is like those cases, we deem it necessary first to consider the contours of the "political question" doctrine. . . .

. . . Deciding whether a matter has in any measure been committed by the Constitution to another branch of government, or whether the action of that branch exceeds whatever authority has been committed, is itself a delicate exercise in constitutional interpretation, and is a responsibility of this Court as ultimate interpreter of the Constitution. To demonstrate this requires no less than to analyze representative cases and to infer from them the analytical threads that make up the political question doctrine. . . .

[A lengthy analysis of cases involving the political question doctrine in the areas of foreign relations, dates of duration of hostilities, validity of enactments, status of Indian tribes, and republican form of government follows.]

We come, finally, to the ultimate inquiry whether our precedents as to what constitutes a nonjusticiable "political question" bring the case before us under the umbrella of that doctrine. . . . We find none: The question here is the consistency of state action with the Federal Constitution. We have no question decided, or to be decided, by a political branch of government coequal with this Court. Nor do we risk embarrassment of our government abroad, or grave disturbance at home if we take issue with Tennessee as to the constitutionality of her action here challenged. Nor need the appellants, in order to succeed in this action, ask the Court to enter upon policy determinations for which judicially manageable standards are lacking. Judicial standards under the Equal Protection Clause are well developed and familiar, and it has been open to courts since the enactment of the Fourteenth Amendment to determine, if on the particular facts they must, that a discrimination reflects *no* policy, but simply arbitrary and capricious action. . . .

We conclude that the complaint's allegations of a denial of equal protection present a justiciable constitutional cause of action upon which appellants are entitled to a trial and a decision. The right asserted is within the reach of judicial protection under the Fourteenth Amendement.

The judgment of the District Court is reversed and the cause is remanded for further proceedings consistent with this opinion.

Reversed and remanded.

Mr. Justice Whittaker did not participate in the decision of this case.

Mr. Justice Douglas, concurring.

While I join the opinion of the Court and, like the Court, do not reach the merits, a word of explanation is necessary. I put to one side the problems of "political" questions involving the distribution of power between this Court, the Congress, and the Chief Executive. We have here a phase of the recurring problem of the relation of the federal courts to state agencies. More particularly, the question is the extent to which a State may weight one person's vote more heavily than it does another's.

So far as voting rights are concerned, there are large gaps in the Constitution. . . .

I agree with my Brother Clark that if the allegations in the complaint can be sustained a case for relief is established. We are told that a single vote in Moore County, Tennessee, is worth 19 votes in Hamilton County, that one vote in Stewart or in Chester County is worth nearly eight times a single vote in Shelby or Knox County. The opportunity to prove that an "invidious discrimination" exists should therefore be given the appellants. . . .

With the exceptions of Colegrove v. Green, . . . MacDougall v. Green, . . . South v. Peters, . . . and the decisions they spawned, the Court has never thought that protection of voting rights was beyond judicial cognizance. Today's treatment of those cases removed the only impediment to judicial cognizance of the claims stated in the present complaint.

The justiciability of the present claims being established, any relief accorded can be fashioned in the light of well-known principles of equity.

MR. JUSTICE CLARK, concurring.

One emerging from the rash of opinions with their accompanying clashing of views may well find himself suffering a mental blindness. The Court holds that the appellants have alleged a cause of action. However, if refuses to award relief here—although the facts are undisputed—and fails to give the District Court any guidance whatever. One dissenting opinion, bursting with words that go through so much and conclude with so little, contemns the majority action as "a massive repudiation of the experience of our whole past." Another describes the complaint as merely asserting conclusory allegations that Tennessee's apportionment is "incorrect," "arbitrary," "obsolete," and "unconstitutional." I believe it can be shown that this case is distinguishable from earlier cases dealing with the distribution of political power by a State, that a patent violation of the Equal Protection Clause of the United States Constitution has been shown, and that an appropriate remedy may be formulated. . . .

Although I find the Tennessee apportionment statute offends the Equal Protection Clause, I would not consider intervention by this Court into so delicate a field if there were any other relief available to the people of Tennessee. But the majority of the people of Tennessee have no "practical opportunities for exerting their political weight at the polls" to correct the existing "invidious discrimination." Tennessee has no initiative and referendum. I have searched diligently for other "practical opportunities" present under the law. I find none other than through the federal courts. . . .

MR. JUSTICE STEWART, concurring.

The separate writings of my dissenting and concurring Brothers stray so far from the subject of today's decision as to convey, I think, a distressingly inaccurate impression of what the Court decides. For that reason, I think it appropriate, in joining the opinion of the Court, to emphasize in a few words what the opinion does and does not say.

. . . the Court today decides only: (1) that the District Court possessed jurisdiction of the subject matter; (2) that the complaint presents a justiciable controversy; (3) that the appellants have standing. My Brother CLARK has made a convincing prima facie showing that Tennessee's system of apportionment is in fact utterly arbitrary—without any possible justification in rationality. My Brother HARLAN has, with imagination and ingenuity, hypothesized possibly rational bases for Tennessee's system. But the merits of this case are not before us now. The defendants have not yet had an opportunity to be heard in defense of the State's system of apportionment; indeed, they have not yet even filed an answer to the complaint. As in other cases, the proper place for the trial is in the trial court, not here.

MR. JUSTICE FRANKFURTER, whom MR. JUSTICE HARLAN joins, dissenting.

The Court today reverses a uniform course of decision established by a dozen cases, including one by which the very claim now sustained was unanimously rejected only five years ago. The impressive body of rulings thus cast aside reflected the equally uniform course of our political history regarding the relationship between population and legislative representation—a wholly different matter from denial of the franchise to individuals because of race, color, religion or sex. Such a massive repudiation of the experience of our whole past in asserting destructively novel judicial power demands a detailed analysis of the role of this Court in our constitutional scheme. Disregard of inherent limits in the effective exercise of the Court's "judicial Power" not only presages the futility of judicial intervention in the essentially political conflict of forces by which the relation between population and representation has time out of mind been and now is determined. It may well impair the Court's position as the ultimate organ of "the supreme Law of the Land" in that vast range of legal problems, often strongly entangled in popular feeling, on which this Court must pronounce. The Court's authority—possessed of neither the purse nor the sword—ultimately rests on sustained public confidence in its moral sanction. Such feeling must be nourished by the Court's complete detachment, in fact and in appearance, from political entanglements and by abstention from injecting itself into the clash of political forces in political settlements.

A hypothetical claim resting on abstract assumptions is now for the first time made the basis for affording illusory relief for a particular evil even though it foreshadows deeper and more pervasive difficulties in consequence. The claim is hypothetical and the assumptions are abstract because the Court does not vouchsafe the lower courts—state and federal—guidelines for formulating specific, definite, wholly unprecedented remedies for the inevitable litigations that today's umbrageous disposition is bound to stimulate in connection with politically motivated reapportionments in so many States. In such a setting, to promulgate jurisdiction in the abstract is meaningless. It is as devoid of reality as "a brooding omnipresence in the sky," for it conveys no intimation what relief, if any, a District Court is capable of affording that would not invite legislatures to play ducks and drakes with the judiciary. For this Court to direct the District Court to enforce a claim to which the Court has over the years consistently found itself required to deny legal enforcement and at the same time to find it necessary to withhold any guidance to the lower court how to enforce this turnabout, new legal claim, manifests an odd—indeed an esoteric—conception of judicial propriety. One of the Court's supporting opinions, as elucidated by commentary, unwittingly affords a disheartening preview of the mathematical quagmire (apart from divers judicially inappropriate and elusive determinants) into which this Court today catapults the lower courts of the country without so much as adumbrating the basis for a legal calculus as a means of extrication. Even assuming the indispensable intellectual disinterestedness on the part of judges in such matters, they do not have accepted legal standards or criteria or even reliable analogies to draw upon for making judicial judgments. To charge courts with the task of accommodating the incommensurable factors of policy that underlie these mathematical puzzles is to attribute, however flatteringly, omnicompetence to judges. The Framers of the Constitution persistently rejected a proposal that embodied this assumption and Thomas Jefferson never entertained it.

Recent legislation, creating a district appropriately described as "an atrocity of ingenuity," is not unique. Considering the gross inequality among legislative electoral units within almost every State, the Court naturally shrinks from asserting that in districting at least substantial equality is a constitutional requirement enforceable by courts. Room continues to be allowed for weighting. This of course implies that geography, economics, urban-rural conflict, and all the other non-legal factors which have throughout our history entered into political districting are to some extent not to be ruled out in the undefined vista now opened up by review in the federal courts of state reapportionments. To some extent—aye, there's the rub. In effect, today's decision empowers the courts of the country to devise what should constitute the proper composition of the legislatures of the fifty States. If state courts should for one reason or another find themselves unable to discharge this task, the duty of doing so is put on the federal courts or on this Court, if State views do not satisfy this Court's notion of what is proper districting.

We were soothingly told at the bar of this Court that we need not worry about the kind of remedy a court could effectively fashion once the abstract constitutional right to have courts pass on a state-wide system of electoral districting is recognized as a matter of judicial rhetoric, because legislatures would heed the Court's admonition. This is not only a euphoric hope. It implies a sorry confession of judicial impotence in place of a frank acknowledgment that there is not under our Constitution a judicial remedy for every political mischief, for every undesirable exercise of legislative power. The Framers carefully and with deliberate forethought refused so to enthrone the judiciary. In this situation, as in others of like nature, appeal for relief does not belong here. Appeal must be to an informed, civically militant electorate. In a democratic society like ours, relief must come through an aroused popular conscience that sears the conscience of the people's representatives. In any event there is nothing judicially more unseemly nor more self-defeating than for this Court to make *in terrorem* pronouncements, to indulge in merely empty rhetoric, sounding a word of promise to the ear, sure to be disappointing to the hope. . . .

In sustaining appellants' claim, based on the Fourteenth Amendment, that the District Court may entertain this suit, this Court's uniform course of decision over the years is overruled or disregarded. Explicitly it begins with *Colegrove* v. *Green, supra,* decided in 1946, but its roots run deep in the Court's historic adjudicatory process. . . .

The *Colegrove* doctrine, in the form in which repeated decisions have settled it, was not an innovation. It represents long judicial thought and experience. From its earliest opinions this Court has consistently recognized a class of controversies which do not lend themselves to judicial standards and judicial remedies. To classify the various instances as "political questions" is rather a form of stating this conclusion than revealing of analysis. Some of the cases so labelled have no relevance here. But from others emerge unifying considerations that are compelling. . . . The doctrine of political questions, like any other, is not to be applied beyond the limits of its own logic, with all the quiddities and abstract disharmonies it may manifest. . . . What is actually asked of the Court in this case is to choose among competing bases of representation—ultimately, really, among competing theories of political philosophy—in order to establish an appropriate frame of government for the State of Tennessee and thereby for all the States of the Union.

In such a matter, abstract analogies which ignore the facts of history deal in unrealities; they betray reason. This is not a case in which a State has, through a device however oblique and sophisticated, denied Negroes or Jews or red-headed persons a vote, or given them only a third or a sixth of a vote. That was *Gomillion* v. *Lightfoot,* . . . What Tennessee illustrates is an old and still widespread method of representation—representation by local geographical division, only in part respective of population—in preference to others, others, forsooth, more appealing. Appellants contest this choice and seek to make this Court the arbiter of the disagreement. They would make the Equal Protection Clause the charter of adjudication, asserting that the equality which it guarantees comports, if not the assurance of equal weight to every voter's vote, at least the basic conception that representation ought to be proportionate to population, a standard by reference to which the reasonableness of apportionment plans may be judged.

To find such a political conception legally enforceable in the broad and unspecific guarantee of equal protection is to rewrite the Constitution. See *Luther* v. *Borden, supra.* Certainly, "equal protection" is no more secure a foundation for judicial judgment of the permissibility of varying forms of representative government than is "Republican Form." Indeed since "equal protection of the laws" can only mean an equality of persons standing in the same relation to whatever governmental action is challenged, the determination whether treatment is equal presupposes a determination concerning the nature of the relationship. This, with respect to apportionment, means an inquiry into the theoretic base of representation in an acceptably republican state. For a court could not determine the equal-protection issue without in fact first determining the Republican-Form issue, simply because what is reasonable for equal-protection purposes will depend upon what frame of government, basically, is allowed. To divorce "equal protection" from "Republican Form" is to talk about half a question.

The notion that representation proportioned to the geographic spread of population is so universally accepted as a necessary element of equality between man and man that it must be taken to be the standard of a political equality preserved by the Fourteenth Amendment—that it is, in appellants' words "the basic principle of representative government"—is, to put it bluntly, not true. However desirable and however desired by some among the great political thinkers and framers of our government, it has never been generally practiced, today or in the past. It was not the English system, it was not the colonial system, it was not the system chosen for the national government by the Constitution, it was not the system exclusively or even predominantly practiced by the

States at the time of adoption of the Fourteenth Amendment, it is not predominantly practiced by the States today. Unless judges, the judges of this Court, are to make their private views of political wisdom the measure of the Constitution—views which in all honesty cannot but give the appearance, if not reflect the reality, of involvement with the business of partisan politics so inescapably a part of apportionment controversies—the Fourteenth Amendment, "itself a historical product," *Jackman* v. *Rosenbaum Co.,* . . . provides no guide for judicial oversight of the representation problem. . . .

Contemporary Apportionment. Detailed recent studies are available to describe the present-day constitutional and statutory status of apportionment in the fifty States. They demonstrate a decided twentieth-century trend away from population as the exclusive base of representation. . . .

Manifestly, the Equal Protection Clause supplies no clearer guide for judicial examination of apportionment methods than would the Guarantee Clause itself. Apportionment, by its character, is a subject of extraordinary complexity, involving—even after the fundamental theoretical issues concerning what is to be represented in a representative legislature have been fought out or compromised—considerations of geography, demography, electoral convenience, economic and social cohesions or divergencies among particular local groups, communications, the practical effects of political institutions like the lobby and the city machine, ancient traditions and ties of settled usage, . . . The practical significance of apportionment is that the next election results may differ because of it. Apportionment battles are overwhelmingly party or intra-party contests. It will add a virulent source of friction and tension in federal-state relations to embroil the federal judiciary in them.

Although the District Court had jurisdiction in the very restricted sense of power to determine whether it could adjudicate the claim, the case is of that class of political controversy which, by the nature of its subject, is unfit for federal judicial action. The judgment of the District Court, in dismissing the complaint for failure to state a claim on which relief can be granted, should therefore be affirmed.

Dissenting opinion of MR. JUSTICE HARLAN, whom MR. JUSTICE FRANKFURTER joins.

The dissenting opinion of MR. JUSTICE FRANKFURTER, in which I join, demonstrates the abrupt departure the majority makes from judicial history by putting the federal courts into this area of state concerns—an area which, in this instance, the Tennessee state courts themselves have refused to enter. . . .

Once one cuts through the thicket of discussion devoted to "jurisdiction," "standing," "justiciability," and "political question," there emerges a straightforward issue which, in my view, is determinative of this case. Does the complaint disclose a violation of a federal constitutional right, in other words, a claim over which a United States District Court would have jurisdiction . . .

It is at once essential to recognize this case for what it is. The issue here relates not to a method of state electoral apportionment by which seats in the *federal* House of Representatives are allocated, but solely to the right of a State to fix the basis of representation in its *own* legislature. . . .

I can find nothing in the Equal Protection Clause or elsewhere in the Federal Constitution which expressly or impliedly supports the view that state legislatures must be so structured as to reflect with approximate equality the voice of every voter. Not only is that proposition refuted by history, as shown by my Brother FRANKFURTER, but it strikes deep into the heart of our federal system. Its acceptance would require us to turn our backs on the regard which this Court has always shown for the judgment of state legislatures and courts on matters of basically local concern.

In the last analysis, what lies at the core of this controversy is a difference of opinion as to the function of representative government. It is surely beyond argument that those who have the responsibility for devising a system of representation may permissibly consider that factors other than bare numbers should be taken into account. The existence of the United States Senate is proof enough of that. To consider that we may ignore the Tennessee Legislature's judgment in this instance because that body was the product of an asymmetrical electoral apportionment would in effect be to assume the very conclusion here disputed. Hence we must accept the present form of the Tennessee Legislature as the embodiment of the State's choice, or, more realistically, its compromise, between competing political philosophies. The federal courts have not been empowered by the Equal Protection Clause to judge whether this resolution of the State's internal political conflict is desirable or undesirable, wise or unwise. . . .

The claim that Tennessee's system of apportionment is so unreasonable as to amount to a capricious classification of voting strength stands up no better under dispassionate analysis. . . .

Thus reduced to its essentials, the charge of arbitrariness and capriciousness rests entirely on the consistent refusal of the Tennessee Legislature over the past 60 years to alter a pattern of apportionment that was reasonable when conceived.

A Federal District Court is asked to say that the passage of time has rendered the 1901 apportionment obsolete to the point where its continuance becomes vulnerable under the Fourteenth Amendment. But is not this matter one that involves a classic legislative judgment? Surely it lies within the province of a state legislature to conclude that an existing allocation of senators and representatives constitutes a desirable balance of geographical and demographical representation, or that in the interest of stability of government it would be best to defer for some further time the redistribution of seats in the state legislature.

Indeed, I would hardly think it unconstitutional if a state legislature's expressed reason for establishing or maintaining an electoral imbalance between its rural and urban population were to protect the State's agricultural interests from the sheer weight of numbers of those residing in its cities. . . .

In conclusion, it is appropriate to say that one need not agree, as a citizen, with what Tennessee has done or failed to do, in order to deprecate, as a judge, what the majority is doing today. Those observers of the Court who see it primarily as the last refuge for the correction of all inequality or injustice, no matter what its nature or source, will no doubt applaud this decision and its break with the past. Those who consider that continuing national respect for the Court's authority depends in large measure upon its wise exercise of self-restraint and discipline in constitutional adjudication, will view the decision with deep concern.

I would affirm.

REYNOLDS, JUDGE, ET AL. *v.* SIMS ET AL.

377 U.S. 533 (1964)

MR. CHIEF JUSTICE WARREN delivered the opinion of the Court.

Involved in these cases are an appeal and two cross-appeals from a decision of the Federal District Court for the Middle District of Alabama holding invalid, under the Equal Protection Clause of the Federal Constitution, the existing and two legislatively proposed plans for the apportionment of seats in the two houses of the Alabama Legislature, and ordering into effect a temporary reapportionment plan comprised of parts of the proposed but judicially disapproved measures. . . .

III

A predominant consideration in determining whether a State's legislative apportionment scheme constitutes an invidious discrimination violative of rights asserted under the Equal Protection Clause is that the rights allegedly impaired are individual and personal in nature. . . .

Legislators represent people, not trees or acres. Legislators are elected by voters, not farms or cities or economic interests. As long as ours is a representative form of government, and our legislatures are those instruments of government elected directly by and directly representative of the people, the right to elect legislators in a free and unimpaired fashion is a bedrock of our political system. It could hardly be gainsaid that a constitutional claim had been asserted by an allegation that certain otherwise qualified voters had been entirely prohibited from voting for members of their state legislature. And, if a State should provide that the votes of citizens in one part of the State should be given two times, or five times, or 10 times the weight of votes of citizens in another part of the State, it could hardly be contended that the right to vote of those residing in the disfavored areas had not been effectively diluted. It would appear extraordinary to suggest that a State could be constitutionally permitted to enact a law providing that certain of the State's voters could vote two, five, or 10 times for their legislative representatives, while voters living elsewhere could vote only once. And it is inconceivable that a state law to the effect that, in counting votes for legislators, the votes of citizens in one part of the State would be multiplied by two, five, or 10, while the votes of persons in another area would be counted only at face value, could be constitutionally sustainable. Of course, the effect of state legislative districting schemes which give the same number of representatives to unequal numbers of constituents is identical. Overweighting and overvaluation of the votes of those living here has the certain effect of dilution and undervaluation of the votes of those living there. The resulting discrimination against those individual voters living in disfavored areas is easily demonstrable mathematically. Their right to vote is simply not the same right to vote as that of those living in a favored part of the State. Two, five, or 10 of them must vote before the effect of their voting is equivalent to that of their favored neighbor. Weighting the votes of citizens differently, by any method or means, merely because of where they happen to reside, hardly seems justifiable. One must be ever aware that the Constitution forbids "sophisticated as well as simple-minded modes of discrimination." . . . As we stated in *Wesberry* v. *Sanders, supra:*

"We do not believe that the Framers of the Constitution intended to permit the same vote-diluting discrimination to be accomplished through the device of districts containing widely varied numbers of inhabitants. To say that a vote is worth more in one district than in another would . . . run counter to our fundamental ideas of democratic government. . . ."

State legislatures are, historically, the fountainhead of representative government in this country. A number of them have their roots in colonial times, and substantially antedate the creation of our Nation and our Federal Government. In fact, the first formal stirrings of American political independence are to be found, in large part, in the views and actions of several of the colonial legislative bodies. With the birth of our National Government, and the adoption and ratification of the Federal Constitution, state legislatures retained a most important place in our Nation's governmental structure. But representative government is in essence self-government through the medium of elected representatives of the people, and each and every citizen has an inalienable right to full and effective participation in the political processes of his State's legislative bodies. Most citizens can achieve this participation only as qualified voters through the election of legislators to represent them. Full and effective participation by all citizens in state government requires, therefore, that each citizen have an equally effective voice in the election of members of his state legislature. Modern and viable state government needs, and the Constitution demands, no less.

Logically, in a society ostensibly grounded on representative government, it would seem reasonable that a majority of the people of a State could elect a majority of that State's legislators. To conclude differently, and to sanction minority control of state legislative bodies, would appear to deny majority rights in a way that far surpasses any possible denial of minority rights that might otherwise be thought to result. Since legislatures are responsible for enacting laws by which all citizens are to be governed, they should be bodies which are collectively responsive to the popular will. . . . Our constitutional system amply provides for the protection of minorities by means other than giving them majority control of state legislatures. And the democratic ideals of equality and majority rule, which have served this Nation so well in the past, are hardly of any less significance for the present and the future. . . .

To the extent that a citizen's right to vote is debased, he is that much less a citizen. The fact that an individual lives here or there is not a legitimate reason for overweighting or diluting the efficacy of his vote. The complexions of societies and civilizations change, often with amazing rapidity. A nation once primarily rural in character becomes predominantly urban. Representation schemes once fair and equitable become archaic and outdated. But the basic principle of representative government remains, and must remain, unchanged—the weight of a citizen's vote cannot be made to depend on where he lives. Population is, of necessity, the starting point for consideration and the controlling criterion for judgment in legislative apportionment controversies. A citizen, a qualified voter, is no more nor no less so because he lives in the city or on the farm. This is the clear and strong command of our Constitution's Equal Protection Clause. This is an essential part of the concept of a government of laws and not men. This is at the heart of Lincoln's vision of "government of the people, by the people, [and] for the people." The Equal Protection Clause demands no less than substantially equal state legislative representation for all citizens, of all places as well as of all races.

IV

We hold that, as a basic constitutional standard, the Equal Protection Clause requires that the seats in both houses of a bicameral state legislature must be apportioned on a population basis. Simply stated, an individual's right to vote for state legislators is unconstitutionally impaired when its weight is in a substantial fashion diluted when compared with votes of citizens living in other parts of the State. Since, under neither the existing apportionment provisions nor either of the proposed plans was either of the houses of the Alabama Legislature apportioned on a population basis, the District Court correctly held that all three of these schemes were constitutionally invalid. Furthermore, the existing apportionment, and also to a lesser extent the apportionment under the Crawford-Webb Act, presented little more than crazy quilts, completely lacking in rationality, and could be found invalid on that basis alone. . . .

V

Since neither of the houses of the Alabama Legislature, under any of the three plans considered by the District Court, was apportioned on a population basis, we would be justified in proceeding no further. However, one of the proposed plans, that contained in the so-called 67-Senator Amendment, at least superficially resembles the scheme of legislative representation followed in the Federal Congress. Under this plan, each of Alabama's 67 counties is allotted one senator, and no counties are given more than one Senate seat. Arguably, this is analogous to the allocation of two Senate seats, in the Federal Congress, to each of the 50 States, regardless of population. Seats in the Alabama House, under the proposed constitutional amendment, are distributed by giving each of the 67 counties at least one, with the remaining 39 seats being allotted among the more populous counties on a population basis. This scheme, at least at first glance, appears to resemble that prescribed for the Federal House of Representatives, where the 435 seats are distributed among the States on a population basis, although each State, regardless of its population, is given at least one Congressman. Thus, although there are substantial differences in underlying rationale and result, the 67-Senator Amendment, as proposed by the Alabama Legislature, at least arguably presents for consideration a scheme analogous to that used for apportioning seats in Congress.

Much has been written since our decision in *Baker* v. *Carr* about the applicability of the so-called federal analogy to state legislative apportionment arrangements. After considering the matter, the court below concluded that no conceivable analogy could be drawn between the federal scheme and the apportionment of seats in the Alabama Legislature under the proposed constitutional amendment. We agree with the District Court, and find the federal analogy inapposite and irrelevant to state legislative districting schemes. Attempted reliance on the federal analogy appears often to be little more than an after-the-fact rationalization offered in defense of maladjusted state apportionment arrangements. The original constitutions of 36 of our States provided that representation in both houses of the state legislatures would be based completely, or predominantly, on population. And the Founding Fathers clearly had no intention of establishing a pattern or model for the apportionment of seats in state legislatures when the system of representation in the Federal Congress was adopted. Demonstrative of this is the fact that the Northwest Ordinance, adopted in the same year, 1787, as the Federal Constitution, provided for the apportionment of seats in territorial legislatures solely on the basis of population.

The system of representation in the two Houses of the Federal Congress is one ingrained in our Constitution, as part of the law of the land. It is one conceived out of compromise and concession indispensable to the establishment of our federal republic. Arising from unique historical circumstances, it is based on the consideration that in establishing our type of federalism a group of formerly independent States bound themselves together under one national government. . . . The fact that almost three-fourths of our present States were never in fact independently sovereign does not detract from our view that the so-called federal analogy is inapplicable as a sustaining precedent for state legislative apportionments. The developing history and growth of our republic cannot cloud the fact that, at the time of the inception of the system of representation in the Federal Congress, a compromise between the larger and smaller States on this matter averted a deadlock in the Constitutional Convention which had threatened to abort the birth of our Nation. . . .

Political subdivisions of States—counties, cities, or whatever—never were and never have been considered as sovereign entities. Rather, they have been traditionally regarded as subordinate governmental instrumentalities created by the State to assist in the carrying out of state governmental functions. . . .

Thus, we conclude that the plan contained in the 67-Senator Amendment for apportioning seats in the Alabama Legislature cannot be sustained by recourse to the so-called federal analogy. Nor can any other inequitable state legislative apportionment scheme be justified on such an asserted basis. This does not necessarily mean that such a plan is irrational or involves something other than a "republican form of government." We conclude simply that such a plan is impermissible for the States under the Equal Protection Clause, since perforce resulting, in virtually every case, in submergence of the equal-population principle in at least one house of a state legislature.

Since we find the so-called federal analogy inapposite to a consideration of the constitutional validity of state legislative apportionment schemes, we necessarily hold that the Equal Protection Clause requires both houses of a state legislature to be apportioned on a population basis. The right of a citizen to equal representation and to have his vote weighted equally with those of all other citizens in the election of members of one house of a bicameral state legislature would amount to little if States could effectively submerge the equal-population principle in the apportionment of seats in the other house. If such a scheme were permissible, an individual citizen's ability to exercise an effective voice in the only instrument of state government directly representative of the people might be almost as effectively thwarted as if neither house were apportioned on a population basis. Deadlock between the two bodies might result in compromise and concession on some issues. But in all too many cases the more probable result would be frustration of the majority will through minority veto in the house not apportioned on a population basis, stemming directly from the failure to accord adequate overall legislative representation to all of the State's citizens on a nondiscriminatory basis. In summary, we can perceive no constitutional difference, with respect to the geographical distributon of state legislative representation, between the two houses of a bicameral state legislature.

We do not believe that the concept of bicameralism is rendered anachronistic and meaningless when the predominant basis of representation in the two state legislative bodies is required to be the same—population. A prime reason for bicameralism, modernly considered, is to insure mature and deliberate consideration of, and to prevent precipitate action on, proposed legislative measures. Simply because the controlling criterion for apportioning representation is required to be the same in both houses does not mean that there will be no differences in the composition and complexion of the two bodies. Different constituencies can be represented in the two houses. One body could be composed of single-member districts while the other could have at least some multi-member districts. The length of terms of the legislators in the separate bodies could differ. The numerical size of the two bodies could be made to differ, even significantly, and the geographical size of districts from which legislators are elected could also be made to differ. . . .

VI

By holding that as a federal constitutional requisite both houses of a state legislature must be apportioned on a population basis, we mean that the Equal Protection Clause requires that a State make an honest and good faith effort to construct districts, in both houses of its legislature, as nearly of equal population as is practicable We realize that it is a practical impossibility to arrange legislative districts so that each one has an identical number of residents, or citizens, or voters. Mathematical exactness or precision is hardly a workable constitutional requirement.

In *Wesberry* v. *Sanders, supra,* the Court stated that congressional representation must be based on population as nearly as is practicable. In implementing the basic constitutional principle of representative government as enunciated by the Court in *Wesberry*—equality of population among districts—some distinctions may well be made between congressional and state legislative representation. Since, almost invariably, there is a significantly larger number of seats in state legislative bodies to be distributed within a State than congressional seats, it may be feasible to use political subdivision lines to a greater extent in establishing state legislative districts than in congressional districting while still affording adequate representation to all parts of the State. To do so would be constitutionally valid, so long as the resulting apportionment was one based substantially on population and the equal-population principle was not diluted in any significant way. Somewhat more flexibility may therefore be constitutionally permissible with respect to state legislative apportionment than in congressional districting. Lower courts can and assuredly will work out more concrete and specific standards for evaluating state legislative apportionment schemes in the context of actual litigation. For the present, we deem it expedient not to attempt to spell out any precise constitutional tests. What is marginally permissible in one State may be unsatisfactory in another, depending on the particular circumstances of the case. Developing a body of doctrine on a case-by-case basis appears to us to provide the most satisfactory means of arriving at detailed constitutional requirements in the area of state legislative apportionment. . . .

VII

One of the arguments frequently offered as a basis for upholding a State's legislative apportionment arrangement, despite substantial disparities from a population basis in either or both houses, is grounded on congressional approval, incident to admitting States into the Union, of state apportionment plans containing deviations from the equal-population principle. Proponents of this argument contend that congressional approval of such schemes, despite their disparities from population-based representation, indicates that such arrangements are plainly sufficient as establishing a "republican form of government." As we stated in *Baker* v. *Carr,* some questions raised under the Guaranty

Clause are nonjusticiable, where "political" in nature and where there is a clear absence of judicially manageable standards. Nevertheless, it is not inconsistent with this view to hold that, despite congressional approval of state legislative apportionment plans at the time of admission into the Union, even though deviating from the equal-population principle here enunciated, the Equal Protection Clause can and does require more. And an apportionment scheme in which both houses are based on population can hardly be considered as failing to satisfy the Guaranty Clause requirement. . . . In any event, congressional approval, however well-considered, could hardly validate an unconstitutional state legislative apportionment. Congress simply lacks the constitutional power to insulate States from attack with respect to alleged deprivations of individual consitutional rights.

VIII

That the Equal Protection Clause requires that both houses of a state legislature be apportioned on a population basis does not mean that States cannot adopt some reasonable plan for periodic revision of their apportionment schemes. Decennial reapportionment appears to be a rational approach to readjustment of legislative representation in order to take into account population shifts and growth. . . . While we do not intend to indicate that decennial reapportionment is a constitutional requisite, compliance with such an approach would clearly meet the minimal requirements for maintaining a reasonably current scheme of legislative representation. And we do not mean to intimate that more frequent reapportionment would not be constitutionally permissible or practicably desirable. But if reapportionment were accomplished with less frequency, it would assuredly be constitutionally suspect. . . .

X

We do not consider here the difficult question of the proper remedial devices which federal courts should utilize in state legislative apportionment cases. Remedial techniques in this new and developing area of the law will probably often differ with the circumstances of the challenged apportionment and a variety of local conditions. It is enough to say now that, once a State's legislative apportionment scheme has been found to be unconstitutional, it would be the unusual case in which a court would be justified in not taking appropriate action to insure that no further elections are conducted under the invalid plan. However, under certain circumstances, such as where an impending election is imminent and a State's election machinery is already in progress equitable considerations might justify a court in withholding the granting of immediately effective relief in a legislative apportionment case, even though the existing apportionment scheme was found invalid. In awarding or withholding immediate relief, a court is entitled to and should consider the proximity of a forthcoming election and the mechanics and complexities of state election laws, and should act and rely upon general equitable principles. With respect to the timing of relief, a court can reasonably endeavor to avoid a disruption of the election process which might result from requiring precipitate changes that could make unreasonable or embarrassing demands on a State in adjusting to the requirements of the court's decree. . . .

We feel that the District Court in this case acted in a most proper and commendable manner. . . . We affirm the judgment below and remand the cases for further proceedings consistent with the views stated in this opinion.

It is so ordered.

Mr. Justice Clark, concurring in the affirmance.

The Court goes much beyond the necessities of this case in laying down a new "equal population" principle for state legislative apportionment. . . .

It seems to me that all that the Court need say in this case is that each plan considered by the trial court is "a crazy quilt," clearly revealing invidious discrimination in each house of the Legislature and therefore violative of the Equal Protection Clause. See my concurring opinion in *Baker* v. *Carr,* . . .

I, therefore, do not reach the question of the so-called "federal analogy." But in my view, if one house of the State Legislature meets the population standard, representation in the other house might include some departure from it so as to take into account, on a rational basis, other factors in order to afford some representation to the various elements of the State. . . .

Mr. Justice Harlan, dissenting. . . .

PRELIMINARY STATEMENT

Today's holding is that the Equal Protection Clause of the Fourteenth Amendment requires every State to structure its legislature so that all the members of each house represent substantially the same number of people; other factors may be given play only to the extent that they do not significantly encroach on this basic "population" principle. Whatever may be thought of this holding as a piece of political ideology—and even on that score the political history and practices of this country from its earliest beginnings leave wide room for debate. . . . Stripped of aphorisms, the Court's argument boils down to the assertion that appellees' right to vote has been invidiously "debased" or "diluted" by systems of apportionment which entitle them to vote for fewer legislators than other voters, an assertion which is tied to the Equal Protection Clause only by the constitutionally frail tautology that "equal" means "equal."

Had the Court paused to probe more deeply into the matter, it would have found that the Equal Protection Clause was never intended to inhibit the States in choosing any democratic method they pleased for the apportionment of their legislatures. This is shown by the language of the Fourteenth Amendment taken as a whole, by the understanding of those who proposed and ratified it, and by the political practices of the States at the time the Amendment was adopted. It is confirmed by numerous state and congressional actions since the adoption of the Fourteenth Amendment, and by the common understanding of the Amendment as evidenced by subsequent constitutional amendments and decisions of this Court before *Baker* v. *Carr, supra,* made an abrupt break with the past in 1962.

The failure of the Court to consider any of these matters cannot be excused or explained by any concept of "developing" constitutionalism. It is meaningless to speak of constitutional "development" when both the language and history of the controlling provisions of the Constitution are wholly ignored. Since it can, I think, be shown beyond doubt that state legislative apportionments, as such, as wholly free of constitutional limitations, save such as may be imposed by the Republican Form of Government Clause (Const., Art. IV, § 4), the Court's action now bringing them within the purview of the Fourteenth Amendment amounts to nothing less than an exercise of the amending power by this Court.

So far as the Federal Constitution is concerned, the complaints in these cases should all have been dismissed below for failure to state a cause of action, because what has been alleged or proved shows no violation of any constitutional right. . . .

I have tried to make the catalogue complete, yet to keep it within the manageable limits of a judicial opinion. In my judgment, today's decisions are refuted by the language of the Amendment which they construe and by the inference fairly to be drawn from subsequently enacted Amendments. They are unequivocally refuted by history and by consistent theory and practice from the time of the adoption of the Fourteenth Amendment until today.

The Court's elaboration of its new "constitutional" doctrine indicates how far—and how unwisely—it has strayed from the appropriate bounds of its authority. The consequence of today's decision is that in all but the handful of States which may already satisfy the new requirements the local District Court or, it may be, the state courts, are given blanket authority and the constitutional duty to supervise apportionment of the State Legislatures. It is difficult to imagine a more intolerable and inappropriate interference by the judiciary with the independent legislatures of the States. . . .

Records such as these in the cases decided today are sure to be duplicated in most of the other States if they have not been already. They present a jarring picture of courts threatening to take action in an area which they have no business entering, inevitably on the basis of political judgments which they are incompetent to make. They show legislatures of the States meeting in haste and deliberating and deciding in haste to avoid the threat of judicial interference. So far as I can tell, the Court's only response to this unseemly state of affairs is ponderous insistence that "a denial of constitutionally protected rights demands judicial protection," *ante*, p. 566. By thus refusing to recognize the bearing which a potential for conflict of this kind may have on the question whether the claimed rights are in fact constitutionally entitled to judicial protection, the Court assumes, rather than supports, its conclusion.

It should by now be obvious that these cases do not mark the end of reapportionment problems in the courts. Predictions once made that the courts would never have to face the problem of actually working out an apportionment have proved false. This Court, however, continues to avoid the consequences of its decisions, simply assuring us that the lower courts "can and . . . will work out more concrete and specific standards," *ante,* p. 578. Deeming it "expedient" not to spell out "precise constitutional tests," the Court contents itself with stating "only a few rather general considerations." *Ibid.*

Generalities cannot obscure the cold truth that cases of this type are not amenable to the development of judicial standards. No set of standards can guide a court which has to decide how many legislative districts a State shall have, or what the shape of the districts shall be, or where to draw a particular district line. No judicially manageable standard can determine whether a State should have single-member districts or multimember districts or some combination of both. No such standard can control the balance between keeping up with population shifts and having stable districts. In all these respects, the courts will be called upon to make particular decisions with respect to which a principle of equally populated districts will be of no assistance whatsoever. Quite obviously, there are limitless possibilities for districting consistent with such a principle. Nor can these problems be avoided by judicial reliance on legislative judgments so far as possible. Reshaping or combining one or two districts, or modifying just a few district lines, is no less a matter of choosing among many possible solutions, with varying political consequences, than reapportionment broadside.

The Court ignores all this, saying only that "what is marginally permissible in one State may be unsatisfactory in another, depending on the particular circumstances of the case," *ante,* p. 578. It is well to remember that the product of today's decisions will not be readjustment of a few districts in a few States which most glaringly depart from the principle of equally populated districts. It will be a redetermination, extensive in many cases, of legislative districts in all but a few States.

Although the Court—necessarily, as I believe—provides only generalities in elaboration of its main thesis, its opinion nevertheless fully demonstrates how far removed these problems are from fields of judicial competence. Recognizing that "indiscriminate districting" is an invitation to "partisan gerrymandering," *ante,* pp. 578–579, the Court nevertheless excludes virtually every basis for the formation of electoral districts other than "indiscriminate districting." In one or another of today's opinions, the Court declares it unconstitutional for a State to give effective consideration to any of the following in establishing legislative districts:

(1) history;
(2) "economic or other sorts of group interests";
(3) area;
(4) geographical considerations;
(5) a desire "to insure effective representation for sparsely settled areas";
(6) "availability of access of citizens to their representatives";
(7) theories of bicameralism (except those approved by the Court);
(8) occupation;

(9) "an attempt to balance urban and rural power."
(10) the preference of a majority of voters in the State.

So far as presently appears, the *only* factor which a State may consider, apart from numbers, is political subdivisions. But even "a clearly rational state policy" recognizing this factor is unconstitutional if "population is submerged as the controlling consideration. . . ."

I know of no principle of logic or practical or theoretical politics, still less any constitutional principle, which establishes all or any of these exclusions. Certain it is that the Court's opinion does not establish them. So far as the Court says anything at all on this score, it says only that "legislators represent people, not trees or acres," *ante,* p. 562; that "citizens, not history or economic interests, cast votes," *ante,* p. 580; that "people, not land or trees or pastures, vote," *ibid.* All this may be conceded. But it is surely equally obvious, and in the context of elections, more meaningful to note that people are not ciphers and that legislators can represent their electors only by speaking for their interests—economic, social, political—many of which do reflect the place where the electors live. The Court does not establish, or indeed even attempt to make a case for the proposition that conflicting interests within a State can only be adjusted by disregarding them when voters are grouped for purposes of representation.

CONCLUSION

With these cases the Court approaches the end of the third round set in motion by the complaint filed in *Baker* v. *Carr.* What is done today deepens my conviction that judicial entry into this realm is profoundly ill-advised and constitutionally impermissible. As I have said before, *Wesberry* v. *Sanders, supra,* at 48, I believe that the vitality of our political system, on which in the last analysis all else depends, is weakened by reliance on the judiciary for political reform; in time a complacent body politic may result.

These decisions also cut deeply into the fabric of our federalism. What must follow from them may eventually appear to be the product of state legislatures. Nevertheless, no thinking person can fail to recognize that the aftermath of these cases, however desirable it may be thought in itself, will have been achieved at the cost of a radical alteration in the relationship between the States and the Federal Government, more particularly the Federal Judiciary. Only one who has an overbearing impatience with the federal system and its political processes will believe that that cost was not too high or was inevitable.

Finally, these decisions give support to a current mistaken view of the Constitution and the constitutional function of this Court. This view, in a nutshell, is that every major social ill in this country can find its cure in some constitutional "principle," and that this Court should "take the lead" in promoting reform when other branches of government fail to act. The Constitution is not a panacea for every blot upon the public welfare, nor should this Court, ordained as a judicial body, be thought of as a general haven for reform movements. The Constitution is an instrument of government, fundamental to which is the premise that in a diffusion of governmental authority lies the greatest promise that this Nation will realize liberty for all its citizens. This Court, limited in function in accordance with that premise, does not serve its high purpose when it exceeds its authority, even to satisfy justified impatience with the slow workings of the political process. For when, in the name of constitutional interpretation, the Court *adds* something to the Constitution that was deliberately excluded from it, the Court in reality substitutes its view of what should be so for the amending process.

I dissent in each of these cases, believing that in none of them have the plaintiffs stated a cause of action. To the extent that *Baker* v. *Carr,* expressly or by implication, went beyond a discussion of jurisdictional doctrines independent of the substantive issues involved here, it should be limited to what it in fact was: an experiment in venturesome constitutionalism.

VI. PARTY TRENDS AND PROSPECTS

10. The Party Process in the Sixties and Seventies: An Overview

THE analysis of contemporary political events and patterns is a task whose intellectual perils are surpassed only by the hazards of attempting to perceive future events. Proximity to events has its advantages, but journalistic chronicling is too frequently a substitute for substantive analysis, and the headline of the moment obscures the less dramatic, deep-running trend. Predicting future happenings is at best a chancy adventure; there are too many "if's" and too many "unexpected's." At the beginning of the 1960's one could have reasonably expected that John F. Kennedy and the politics of the New Frontier would have been the focal point for American political analysis during the decade, but instead it became Lyndon B. Johnson and the politics of the Great Society. But although an assassin's bullet in Dallas or Saigon can irrevocably alter the names of history, it cannot for long deflect fundamental political, social, and economic currents. The civil rights revolution, a prime ingredient in mid-twentieth-century American politics, would have had its effect on the New Frontier or the Great Society. Each election and the politics centering about it bear a heritage from the preceding election and become, in turn, the inheritance of the next election. Elections are not isolated episodes; they are markers in the political cycle.

Elections in the democratic process, are collective decisions that select government officials, determine party patterns, and give some direction—not always clearcut or meaningful—to public policy. One useful typology of elections (based on V. O. Key Jr.'s Theory of critical elections and extended by professors Campbell, Converse, Miller, and Stokes), is predicated on the pattern of party identification. This typology utilizes the terms "maintaining," "deviating," "reinstating," and "realigning" elections. Maintaining elections reflect the "normal" majority and balance between the parties. (The elections of 1900, 1904, 1908, 1924, 1936, 1940, 1944, and 1948 would be classed as maintaining elections because the normal majority retained power.) Deviating elections are those in which the normal majority is displaced; the electorate deviates or departs from established party identifications, though the pattern itself is not basically altered. (The elections of 1952 and 1956 in which General Eisenhower, the Republican candidate, captured the presidency while the Congress remained predominantly Democratic are examples of deviating elections.) A reinstating election follows a deviating election and returns the normally dominant party to office. (The elections of 1920 and 1960 are examples of reinstating elections.) In the final category, a realigning election, there is a lasting shift in the party identifications of the electorate. As in the election of 1932, what was formerly a minority coalition becomes the majority. Another concept useful in electoral analysis is that of the "critical period" or "critical election." These terms refer to periods of basic changes in party allegiances, leading ultimately to a realigning election. One can, of course, take issue with these classifications of elections. The terms, however, do emphasize the fact that electoral decisions are part of a continuing political process. (For a study of the flow of the total vote see "Voters and Elections: Past and Present" in Part III.)

American politics in the 1960's has been conditioned by a number of socioeconomic factors, and these were mirrored in the presidential elections of 1960 and 1964. A steady rise in living standards has occurred throughout the nation, and the minority not sharing in this rise have been promised that poverty will be lessened. (Compare this essential fact of politics in the 1960's with the overriding political fact of the 1930's—the corrosive effect of the Great Depression.) This generally affluent society supports a countrywide mass market in standardized goods, services, and communications. The erosion of rigid sectionalism, a high population mobility rate, the diversification of industry and its movement into new areas, the reduction of differences between the farmer and the city-dweller, the acceptance of organized labor as a pressure group equal in respectability and responsibility to business, the spreading suburban smear, the increase in metropolitan areas, the new megalopolis, the decline in mass immigration and the "coming of age" in politics of the old ethnic minorities, the restiveness of the Negro, a general acceptance of the basic principles of the welfare state, and the need for America to accept its international responsibilities (against an omnipresent backdrop of a "Cold War" replete with "hotspots") are all factors that have contributed to the nationalization of American politics and the overall pattern of the party process in the 1960's.

Party politics in the 1960's must be viewed from the perspective of the period preceding it, a period which ran from the end of World War II to the presidential election of 1960. During this time the Democrats have seemed to be the normal majority. In contrast, from the start of this century until the critical election of 1932, the Republicans held the presidency for twenty-four years as against eight for the Democrats. From 1932 through 1968, the Democrats will have held it for twenty-eight years as against eight for the Republicans. Moreover, the only man to be elected President under the Republican banner during this period was not a party regular or professional politician, but an apolitical hero-soldier whose coattails did not extend to the Congress. Paralleling the pattern of presidential politics was a pattern of congressional politics. From the turn of the century until 1932 the Republicans controlled the Senate for twenty-six years and the House for twenty-two; the Democrats for only six and ten years. But between 1932 and the 1966 midterm, the Democrats were dominant in both houses for thirty years, and the Republicans for only four. These statistics, however, while revealing, are also misleading. They indicate the pattern of normal Democratic party ascendancy, but they ignore the long-standing ideological and voting coalition between southern Democrats and conservative Republicans, as well as the fact that in 1960 Mr. Kennedy received 49.7 percent of the popular vote to Mr. Nixon's 49.6 percent, and finally the shifting balance between the parties in the states.

In the postwar years, with the exceptions of the brief periods of 1947–1948 and 1951–1954, the Democrats held a majority of state governorships and maintained regular majorities in most state legislatures. At the same time there has been, throughout the states, a decline in one-partyism and an increase in two-party competition. With this as background, some details about the elections in the 1960's are now in order.

As the presidential election of 1960 approached, certain political facts came to the foreground. President Eisenhower was precluded from running by the Twenty-second Amendment's two-term limitation on the presidency, and his Vice-President, Richard Nixon, appeared to have inherited the presidental nomination. In the Democratic camp four leading contenders, all senators, indicated an interest in the nomination. They were Hubert H. Humphrey of Minnesota, John F. Kennedy of Massachusetts, Stuart Symington of Missouri, and Lyndon B. Johnson of Texas. Of these four, only Kennedy and Humphrey decided to seek the nomination by way of the primaries. Kennedy, with an efficient organization and seemingly unlimited financial resources, accumulated an impressive number of delegates, and after the crucial West Virginia primary Humphrey withdrew, leaving the field to Symington, Johnson, and possibly Adlai Stevenson. Symington's candidacy never picked up momentum and Stevenson's started too late. Despite Johnson's support from the large southern-conservative bloc he was unable to secure widespread delegate endorsement. After Kennedy received the nomination, in a surprise move, he offered the vice-presidential spot to Johnson, who, in an equally surprising move, accepted it.

The Nixon-Kennedy contest centered on the record of the Eisenhower administration and the personalities of the candidates. Kennedy asserted the need for a vigorous executive and attacked Eisenhower's programs in space exploration, defense, and economics. Nixon, as part of the Eisenhower administration, was forced to defend its record, yet he also described it as "something to build on." In an unprecedented series of four nationally televised programs dubbed the "Great Debates," the candidates faced the nation. Kennedy seemed to project better than Nixon, and the debates also gave Kennedy a chance to become better known nationally. The issues of religion and civil rights were important in the campaign. Kennedy's Catholicism, in the opinion of many observers, turned out to be an advantage, as did his forceful stand on civil rights, because the Catholic and Negro votes helped Kennedy capture the cities. Despite the loss of almost the entire West and the farm belt, and despite defections to the Republicans in the traditionally Democratic southern states, Kennedy, by concentrating his efforts in the cities, states, and regions whose votes counted most in the electoral college, was able to put together a winning coalition of eastern states, central industrial states, and most of the South. His campaign strategy thus paid off: despite his hairline popular-vote victory over Nixon, his electoral college margin was quite substantial. The Kennedy-Johnson ticket carried 23 states with 303 electoral votes, to the Nixon-Lodge ticket's 26 states with 220 electoral votes. (Johnson's presence on the ticket turned out to be an adroit political maneuver; Johnson's southern background and overall conservatism tended to balance Kennedy's New England background and overall liberalism and was an important factor in holding most of the South to the Democratic ticket.)

Complementing this picture of presidential electoral preference were the congressional results. Although the Democrats retained their control of both houses, the significant fact to emerge was that the Democrats lost some of their seats in the House of Representatives while the Repulicans made a net gain of 20 seats. In the states, party competition seemed to be the trend. The Democrats captured 7 gubernatorial seats from the Republicans and the Republicans captured 6 from the Democrats, making 34 Democratic and 16 Republican governors, a net gain of one for the Democrats.

In the 1962 elections, Republicans, counting on the traditional pattern of midterm gains for the party out of power, were disappointed when the results proved to be an endorsement of Kennedy's New Frontier. The Democrats enlarged their Senate majority by 4 seats, thus putting the Senate beyond the Republican grasp before 1968, and suffered only a nominal loss of 4 seats in the House. The balance between Republican and Democratic governors remained the same as in 1960. But new trends were emerging. Vermont elected its first Democratic governor in more than a century, and Oklahoma voted in the first Republican governor in its history. In the California gubernatorial race, Richard Nixon, who two years before had nearly won the presidency, was soundly defeated by a Democrat, Edmund G. (Pat) Brown, but the state reelected Republican Senator Thomas H. Kuchel by a quarter-million-vote margin. In northern New England, the Democrats made inroads in traditionally Republican areas, and in the South, the Republicans made inroads in Democratic territory. The pollsters and the political prophets were preparing to chart the political waters of 1964 when one of the "unexpecteds" of history occurred. On November 22, 1963, John F. Kennedy was assassinated and Lyndon Baines Johnson succeeded to the presidency.

By virtue of his position as President, Johnson was certain of receiving the Democratic nomination for President in 1964. The only speculation centered on the President's choice of a running mate. After some suspense, Johnson announced as his choice Senator Hubert H. Humphrey. (For a discussion of the changing importance of the vice-presidency and the politics involved in the 1964 vice-presidential nomination see Gerald Pomper's "The Nomination of Hubert Humphrey for Vice-President" in Part II.) In contrast to the Democrats' easy path to the nominating convention, the Republicans were beset with strife. They were further hurt when a number of prominent Republicans refused to support the convention decision. The road to the Republican national convention was a virtual donnybrook and the outcome of the election, for the Republicans, a debacle. (For a description of the primaries and the conventions see "Somehow It Works: A Candid Portrait of the 1964 Presidential Election" in Part II.)

The seeds of the Republican disaster were nurtured by conservative and right-wing elements within the party who advocated a strictly limited federal government, a resurgence of states' rights, a nonactivist civil rights policy, and a militantly uncompromising stand against communism. This element, long dissatified with the overall Republican policy of moderation, early in the 1960's fostered the myth of a huge, dormant conservative vote and began a campaign for Senator Barry M. Goldwater. The Goldwater group believed that the Republican party's losses were attributable to a policy of "me-tooism" and a failure to speak out for "constitutional conservatism." Goldwater's showings in the primaries were not particularly impressive, but by nosing out Governor Nelson Rockefeller of New York in the California primary for its 86 convention votes, and by accumulating considerable delegate strength among the party regulars in state and district conventions throughout the South, Midwest, and West, Goldwater was able to enter the convention with a commanding lead in delegate strength. The moderates failed to stop Goldwater, who selectd as his running mate the Republican National Chairman, Representative William E. Miller, a strong conservative.

For the first time in many years the voters were presented with "a choice, not an echo." The Republican candidate had departed from the middle ground of American politics, while Johnson campaigned on the platform of a Great Society, designed to appeal to the entire spectrum of the electorate. The election results were clear: Johnson led the Democratic party to its greatest national victory in nearly three decades. Johnson and Humphrey ran nearly 16 million votes ahead of Goldwater and Miller.

The Democrats' electoral vote total was 486 to the Republicans' 52. The Democrats carried 44 states and the District of Columbia, while the Republicans carried only 6 states. Johnson and Humphrey swept New England, the East, the midwestern heartland, and all the mountain and Pacific states except Goldwater's home state of Arizona, which Goldwater carried by only 50.4 percent of the vote to Johnson's 49.5 percent. Goldwater's strength was only in the Deep South.

The GOP showing in Congress was no better. Republican membership in the House dropped to its lowest point since 1936. In general the conservative Republicans lost their seats, while the liberal Republicans retained theirs. The Republicans gained in the South: for the first time since Reconstruction, Republican representatives were elected to the House from Georgia, Alabama, and Mississippi. In the Senate, Republican membership dropped to its lowest point since the elections of 1940. In the state gubernatorial races the Republicans gained one state, but the Democrats still held 33 governorships to the Republicans' 17. Both parties then looked to the midterm elections of 1966.

The 1966 elections were held against a backdrop of spiraling inflation, increasing anxiety about the war in Vietnam, and uneasiness over the slogan "Black Power." The Republicans made unusually large gains even for an out-party in a midterm election: they added 47 seats in the House and 3 in the Senate. Of perhaps more importance was the fact that the Republicans captured 8 state houses, thus balancing the number of Democratic and Republican governors. In the 1966 election the Republicans took political control of five of the seven most populous states (those states which cast more than half the electoral vote needed to select a President)— California, New York, Pennsylvania, Ohio, and Michigan; only Illinois and Texas remained to the Democrats. Most of the Republican winners, significantly, were moderates who displaced liberals holding marginal seats that they had won in the Johnson sweep. (In general, in landslide elections, marginal candidates are able to dislodge well-entrenched members of the opposition party but have a hard time retaining their seats.) Although the GOP had cause for rejoicing, the Democrats soberly reminded them that the new lineups still showed a very substantial Democratic majority. As a result of the 1966 elections there were 67 Democrats and 33 Republicans in the Senate and 248 Democrats and 187 Republicans in the House.

But again the statistics do not tell the entire story. Aside from the numerical change, the trend in the Congress was toward moderate conservatism and away from some of the liberal programs of the Great Society. The Republicans seemed to have broken through in the cities and among the minority groups—traditionally Democratic areas—but the GOP further reasserted its strength in the Middle West, a traditional Republican stronghold, and continued its penetration of the South, where it won another 6 seats and 2 governorships.

The 1964 and 1966 elections seem to indicate that both major parties are increasingly issue-conscious and nationally oriented. Historically, America has sustained cycles of reform and consolidation, and their synthesis has generally produced new trends in party direction. One can be reasonably certain, allowing for "unexpecteds," that the Negro presence in politics will be felt, along with other influences such as reapportionment and metropolitanization. (For a discussion of these trends see the readings which follow.)

Reapportionment along population lines will, within the states, most likely make the suburbs the chief beneficiaries; thus, the shift will not be simply from rural to urban dominance, but will involve party conflict against intraurban and metropolitan region political bases. This, in turn, should revitalize state governments, reinvigorating party competition and federal-state relations. On the national level major shifts in population will continue the trend charted by the 1960 census in which the eastern and midwestern states lost seats to the West (primarily California), Texas, and Florida. These changes, however, will not necessarily make party responsibility more attractive or more effective, and in the absence of a major national crisis, public policy will continue to be determined by an intricate system of political brokerage.

The readings which follow present an overview of the party process in the sixties and seventies. Philip E. Converse, Angus Campbell, Warren E. Miller, and Donald E. Stokes in "Stability and Change in 1960: A Reinstating Election" discuss the surface characteristics of the election, the basic voting strength of the two major parties, and the place of the election in historical perspective. The 1964 presidential election is analyzed in "Electoral Myth and Reality." Aaron Wildavsky, in "The Goldwater Phenomenon: Purists, Politicians, and the Two-Party System," dissects the special political conditions that brought about Mr. Goldwater's nomination, the "privatization of politics," and some aspects of the future of the parties. Robert E. Lane, in "The Politics of Consensus in an Age of Affluence," discusses the relationship between economic developments and stable, effective consensus politics and projects some trends for future political party interaction. Gordon E. Baker deals with some of "The Implications of Reapportionment," and Royce Hanson addresses himself to the problems and trends of "Representation in Metropolitan America." And finally, James Q. Wilson presents a comprehensive analysis of "The Negro in Politics."

STABILITY AND CHANGE IN 1960:
A REINSTATING ELECTION *

Philip E. Converse, Angus Campbell,
Warren E. Miller, Donald E. Stokes

JOHN F. KENNEDY'S narrow popular vote margin in 1960 has already insured this presidential election a classic position in the roll call of close American elections. Whatever more substantial judgments historical perspective may bring, we can be sure that the 1960 election will do heavy duty in demonstrations to a reluctant public that after all is said and done, every vote does count. And the margin translated into "votes per precinct" will become standard fare in exhortations to party workers that no stone be left unturned.

The 1960 election is a classic as well in the license it allows for "explanations" of the final outcome. Any event or campaign strategem that might plausibly have changed the thinnest sprinkling of votes across the nation may, more

* From Philip E. Converse et al., "Stability and Change in 1960: A Reinstating Election," in The American Political Science Review, Vol. LV, No. 2, 1961, pp. 269–280. Reprinted by permission of the authors and the American Political Science Association.

persuasively than is usual, be called "critical." Viewed in this manner the 1960 presidential election hung on such a manifold of factors that reasonable men might despair of cataloguing them.

Nevertheless, it is possible to put together an account of the election in terms of the broadest currents influencing the American electorate in 1960. We speak of the gross lines of motivation which gave the election its unique shape, motivations involving millions rather than thousands of votes. Analysis of these broad currents is not intended to explain the hairline differences in popular vote, state by state, which edged the balance in favor of Kennedy rather than Nixon. But it can indicate quite clearly the broad forces which reduced the popular vote to a virtual stalemate, rather than any of the other reasonable outcomes between a 60–40 or a 40–60 vote division. And it can thereby help us to understand in parsimonious terms why a last feather thrown on the scales in November, 1960, could have spelled victory or defeat for either candidate.

I. SURFACE CHARACTERISTICS OF THE ELECTION

Any account of the election should not only be consistent with its obvious characteristics as they filtered clear from raw vote tallies in the days after the election, but should organize them into a coherent pattern of meaning as well. These characteristics are, of course, the ones that have nourished post-election speculation. In addition to the close partisan division of the popular vote, the following items deserve mention:

(1) *The remarkably high level of turnout.* About 62.7 percent of estimated adults over 21 voted in the 1952 election, a figure which had stood as the high-water mark of vote turnout in recent presidential elections. The comparable turnout proportion for the 1960 presidential election appears to have been 64.3 per cent.

(2) *Upswing in turnout in the South.* The South appears to have contributed disproportionately to the high level in turnout. Outside the South, the increase in total presidential votes cast in 1960 relative to the 1956 election was about 7 percent, a figure scarcely exceeding estimated population growth in this period. In the South, however, presidential ballots in 1960 increased by more than 25 per cent relative to 1956, an increase far outstripping population growth in this region.

(3) *Stronger Republican voting at the presidential level.* On balance across the nation Nixon led Republican tickets, while Kennedy trailed behind many other Democratic candidates, especially outside of the Northeast. These discrepancies in the partisanship of presidential voting and ballots at other levels were not, of course, as striking as those in 1956. . . .

(4) *The stamp of the religious factor in 1960 voting patterns.* While the Kennedy victory was initially taken as proof that religion had not been important in the election, all serious students of election statistics have since been impressed by the religious axis visible in the returns. Fenton, Scammon, Bean, Harris and others have commented upon the substantial correlation between aggregate voting patterns and the relative concentration of Catholics and Protestants from district to district.

Of these surface characteristics, probably the last has drawn most attention. Once it became clear that religion had not only played some part but, as these things go, a rather impressive part in presidential voting across the nation, discussions came to hinge on the nature of its role. It could safely be assumed that Kennedy as a Catholic had attracted some unusual Catholic votes, and had lost some normally Democratic Protestant votes. A clear question remained, however, as to the *net* effect. The *New York Times,* summarizing the discussion late in November, spoke of a "narrow consensus" among the experts that Kennedy had won more than he lost as a result of his Catholicism. These are questions, however, which aggregate vote statistics can but dimly illuminate, as the disputed history of Al Smith's 1928 defeat makes clear. Fortunately in 1960 the election was studied extensively by sample surveys, permitting more exact inferences to be drawn.

The national sample survey conducted by the Survey Research Center of The University of Michigan in the fall of 1960 had features which give an unparalleled opportunity to comment on the recent evolution of the American electorate. The fall surveys were part of a long-term "panel" study, in which respondents first interviewed at the time of the 1956 presidential election were reinterviewed. In the fall of 1956 a sample of 1763 adults, chosen by strict probability methods from all the adults living in private households in the United States, had been questioned just before and just after the presidential election. This initial sample was constituted as a panel of respondents and was interviewed again in 1958 and twice in connection with the 1960 presidential election. These materials permit the linking of 1960 and 1956 voting behavior with unusual reliability.

II. THE EVOLUTION OF THE
ELECTORATE, 1956–1960

The difference in presidential election outcome between 1956 and 1960 might depend upon either or both of two broad types of change in the electorate. The first includes shifts in the physical composition of the electorate over time due to non-political factors, *i.e.,* vital processes. Some adult citizens who voted in 1956 were no longer part of the eligible electorate in 1960, primarily because of death or institutionalization. On the other hand, a new cohort of voters who had been too young to vote in 1956 were eligible to participate in the 1960 election. Even in a four-year period, vital processes alone could account for shifts in the vote. In addition, changes in the electoral vote, though not in the nationwide popular vote margin, might result from voters changing their residences without changing their minds.

Secondly, there are obviously genuine changes in the political choice of individuals eligible to vote in both elections. Such citizens may enter or leave the active electorate by choice, or may decide to change the partisanship of their presidential vote.

The contribution of these two types of change to the shift in votes from a 1956 Eisenhower landslide to a narrow 1960 Kennedy margin—a net shift toward the Democrats of almost 8 percent—may be analyzed. Somewhat less than 10 percent of the eligible 1956 electorate had become effectively ineligible by 1960, with death as the principal cause. Older people naturally bulk large in this category. The felt party affiliation or "party identification" expressed in 1956 by these "departing" respondents was somewhat Republican relative to the remainder of the sample. Nonetheless, these people cast a vote for president which was about 48 percent Democratic, or 6 percent *more Democratic* than the vote of the 1956 electorate as a whole. Although this appears to be a contradiction, it is actually nothing more than a logical consequence of existing theory. The high Republican vote in 1956 depended on a massive defection to Eisenhower by many people identified with the Democratic party. Since the strength of party attachments increases as a function of age, and since defections are inversely related to strength of party identification, it follows that 1956 defection rates were much higher among younger citizens than among older. The data make it clear that the group of older people voting for the last time in 1956 had cast a much straighter "party vote" than their juniors. Only about 5 percent of these older Democrats had defected to Eisenhower, as opposed to about a quarter of all Democrats in the electorate as a whole. So both things are true: this departing cohort was more Republican than average in party identification but had voted more Democratic than average in 1956. If we remove them from the 1956 electorate, then, we arrive at a presidential vote of about 60 percent for Eisenhower among those voters who were to have the option of voting again in 1960. Hence the elimination of this older group from consideration increases the amount of partisan change to be accounted for between 1956 and 1960, rather than decreasing it.

Comparable isolation of the new cohort of young voters in 1960 does very little to change the picture. Little more than one half of this new group of voters normally votes in the first election of eligibility; furthermore, in 1960 its two-party vote division differed only negligibly from that of the nation as a whole. As a result, its analytic removal leaves the vote among the remainder of the electorate nearly unchanged. By way of summary, then, differences in the 1956 and 1960 electorates arising from vital processes do not explain the 1956–1960 vote change; if anything, they extend the amount of change to be otherwise explained.

We may further narrow our focus by considering those people eligible in both 1956 and 1960, who failed to join the active electorate in 1960. A very large majority of these 1960 non-voters had not voted in 1956, and represent Negroes in the South as well as persistent non-voters of other types. Among those who *had* voted in 1956, however, the vote had been rather evenly divided between Eisenhower and Stevenson. As with the older voters, removal of this group leaves an active 1956–1960 electorate whose vote for Eisenhower now surpasses 60 percent, broadening again the discrepancy between the two-party divisions in the 1956 and 1960 votes. The final fringe group which we may set aside analytically is constituted of those citizens eligible to have voted in 1956 who did not then participate, yet who joined the electorate in 1960. The fact that young voters often "sit out" their first presidential election or two indicates part of the composition of such a group. Once again, however, these newly active citizens divided their ballots in 1960 almost equally between the two major candidates, and the residual portion of the 1960 electorate changes little with their removal.

By this point we have eliminated all the fringe groupings whose entry or departure from the active electorate might have contributed to change in the national vote division between 1956 and 1960. We come to focus directly, then, on the individuals who cast a vote for Kennedy or Nixon in 1960 *and had voted for president in 1956* (Table I). As we see, paring away the fringe groupings has had the total effect of increasing the net shift in the vote division between the two years from 8 percent to 11 percent. If we can explain this shift it will be clear that we have dealt with those broad currents in the electorate which brought the 1960 election to a virtual stalemate.

Naturally, the most interesting features of Table I are the cells involving vote changers. In a sequence of elections such as the 1956–1960 series it is a temptation to assume that about 8 percent of the Eisenhower voters of 1956 shifted to Kennedy in 1960, since this was the net observable change between the two years. Much analysis of aggregate election statistics is forced to proceed on this

TABLE I.   1956–1960 VOTE CHANGE WITHIN THE ACTIVE CORE OF THE ELECTORATE

1960 VOTE FOR ↓	1956 VOTE FOR		TOTAL %
	STEVENSON %	EISENHOWER %	
Kennedy	33	17	50
Nixon	6	44	50
	39	61	100

Note: Since we usually think of vote shifts in terms of proportions of the total electorate, percentages in this table use the total vote as a base, rather than row or column totals.

assumption within any given voting unit. However, we see that the net shift of 11 percent in the vote of the active 1956–1960 electorate in fact derived from a gross shift of 23 percent, over half of which was rendered invisible in the national totals because counter-movements cancelled themselves out.

A traditional analysis of these vote changers would specify their membership in various population groupings such as age and occupation category, union membership, race and the like. However, results of this sort in 1960 are so uniform across most of these population groupings that they seem to reflect little more than national trends, and change seems at best loosely connected with location in various of these specific categories. If we took the fact in isolation, for example, we might be struck to note that union members voted almost 8 percent more Democratic in 1960 than in 1956. However, such a figure loses much of its interest when we remind ourselves that people who are not labor union members also shifted their votes in the same direction and in about the same degree between 1956 and 1960. Such uniform changes characterize most of the standard sociological categories.

There is, of course, one dramatic exception. Vote change between 1956 and 1960 follows religious lines very closely. Within the 6 percent of the active 1956–1960 electorate who followed a Stevenson-Nixon path (Table I), 90 percent are Protestant and only 8 percent are Catholic. Among the larger group of Eisenhower-Kennedy changers, however, only 40 percent are Protestant and close to 60 percent are Catholic. In the total vote in 1956 and 1960, Protestants show almost no net partisan change. Eisenhower had won 64 percent of the "Protestant vote" in 1956; Nixon won 63 percent. Meanwhile, the Democratic proportion of the two-party vote among Catholics across the nation skyrocketed from a rough 50 percent in the two Eisenhower elections to a vote of 80 percent for Kennedy. These gross totals appear to substantiate the early claims of Kennedy backers that a Catholic candidate would draw back to the Democratic party sufficient Catholics to carry the 1960 election. Furthermore, it appears that Kennedy must have gained more votes than he lost by virtue of his religious affiliation, for relative to Stevenson in 1956, he lost no Protestant votes and attracted a very substantial bloc of Catholic votes.

The question of net gains or losses as a result of the Catholic issue is not, however, so simply laid to rest. The data cited above make a very strong case, as have the aggregate national statistics, that religion played a powerful role in the 1960 outcome. The vote polarized along religious lines in a degree which we have not seen in the course of previous sample survey studies. Moreover, the few interesting deviations in the 1960 vote of other population groupings, to the degree that they are visible at all, seem with minor exceptions to reflect the central religious polarization. That is, where a group exceeded or fell below the magnitude of the national shift to the Democrats, it is usually true that the group is incidentally a more or less Catholic group. The central phenomenon therefore was religious; the question as to its net effect favoring or disfavoring Kennedy remains open.

In a strict sense, of course, the answers to this question can only be estimated. We know how the election came out, with Kennedy a Catholic. We cannot, without major additional assumptions, know what the election returns might have been if Kennedy were a Protestant and all other conditions remained unchanged. We can make an estimate, however, if we can assume some baseline, some vote that would have occurred under "normal" circumstances. A number of such baselines suggest themselves. We might work from the 1956 presidential vote, as we have done above (42 percent Democratic); or from the more recent Congressional vote in 1958 (56 percent Democratic); or from some general average of recent nation-wide votes. But it is obvious that the simple choice of baseline will go a long way toward determining the answer we propose to the question of net religious effect. If we choose the 1958 vote as a baseline, it is hard to argue that Kennedy could have made any net gains from his religion; if we choose the 1956 presidential vote, it is equally hard to argue that he lost ground on balance.

Indeed, the most cogent arguments documenting a net gain for Kennedy— those accounts which appear to express the majority opinion of election observers—use the 1956 presidential vote quite explicitly as a baseline. Yet the second Eisenhower vote seems the most bizarre choice for a baseline of any which might be suggested. The vote Eisenhower achieved in 1956 stands out as the most disproportionately Republican vote in the total series of nation-wide presidential and Congressional elections stretching back to 1928. In what sense, then, is this extreme Republican swing plausible as a "normal vote?" Its sole claim seems to lie in the fact that it is the most recent presidential election. Yet other recent elections attest dramatically to the extreme abnormality of the 1956 Eisenhower vote. In the 1954 Congressional elections the nation's Democrats, although they turned out less well than Republicans in minor elections, still fashioned a solid majority of votes cast. The fall of 1958 witnessed a Democratic landslide. Even in 1956, "underneath" Eisenhower's towering personal margin, a Democratic popular vote majority exceeding that which Kennedy won in 1960 appeared at other levels of the ticket. Finally, if 1956 is taken as a normal baseline and if it is true that Kennedy did score some relative personal success in 1960, how can we possibly explain the fact that other diverse Democrats on state tickets around the nation tended to win a greater proportion of popular votes than he attracted?

It seems more reasonable to suggest that Kennedy did not in any sense *exceed* the "normal" vote expectations of the generalized and anonymous Democratic candidate; rather, he fell visibly below these expectations, although nowhere nearly as far below them as Adlai Stevenson had fallen. This proposition is congruent not only with the general contours of election returns in the recent period, but with the great mass of sample survey data collected in the past decade as well. With this proposition we can draw into a coherent pattern the several surface characteristics which seemed intriguing from the simple 1960 vote totals. With it, we can locate the 1960 election more generally in the stream of American political history.

III. THE BASIC VOTING STRENGTH OF
THE TWO PARTIES

We have found it of great explanatory value to think of election results as reflecting the interplay of two sets of forces: stable, long-term partisan dispositions and short-term forces specific to the immediate election situation. The long-term partisan dispositions are very adequately represented by our measures of party identification. The stability of these dispositions over time is a matter of empirical record. Their partisan division over any period, as it may favor one party or the other, provides the point from which one must start to understand any specific election. This underlying division of loyalties lends itself admirably to the goal of indicating what a "normal" vote would be, aside from specific forces associated with the immediate election.

In these terms, the basic Democratic majority in the nation is scarcely subject to dispute. Year in and year out since 1952, national samples of the American electorate have indicated a preference for the Democratic party by a margin approaching 60–40. However, since no election in recent years has shown a Democratic margin of this magnitude, it would be as absurd to take a 60–40 Democratic majority for a baseline as it would be to work from the 1956 presidential vote. Actually there is little temptation to do so. Over the years large amounts of information have been accumulated on the behavior of people identifying with the two major parties, and it is clear that the realistic voting strength of the Democrats—and this is the sort of baseline which interests us— falls well short of a 60–40 majority. The fact that heavy Democratic majorities in the South are concealed by low voting turnout is but one factor which reduces realistic Democratic strength. Outside the South, as well, Democrats under the same conditions of short-term stimulation are less likely to vote than Republicans.

It is possible to manipulate the data in such a fashion as to take into account all of the significant discrepancies between nominal party identification and realistic voting strength. We thereby arrive at a picture of the vote division which could be expected in the normal presidential election, if short-term forces associated with the election favored neither party in particular, but stood at an equilibrium. In such circumstances, we would expect a Democratic proportion of the two-party popular vote to fall in the vicinity of 53–54 percent. Outside of the South, such a vote would fall short of a 50–50 split with the Republicans; within the South there would be a strong Democratic majority exceeding a 2-to-1 division.

Short-term forces associated with a specific election may, according to their net partisan strength, send the actual vote in that election deviating to one side or the other of the equilibrium point. In 1952 and 1956 the popularity of Eisenhower constituted one such force, and this force was strongly pro-Republican. The distortions produced in the behaviors of party identifiers of different types have now become familiar. If the net partisan force is strong, as in 1956, identifiers of the favored party vote almost *en bloc,* without defection. The small group of "independents" who do not commit themselves to either party divide very disproportionately in favor of the advantaged party, instead of dividing their vote equally as in the equilibrium case. And members of the disfavored party defect in relatively large numbers, as Democrats did in 1956. A useful description of any specific election, then is an account of the short-term forces which have introduced these strains across the distribution of party identification.

In such a description, the existing division of deeper party loyalties is taken for granted. Its current character is not to be explained by the immediate political situation. The point is made most clearly by the 1960 election. The fact that the Democrats enjoyed a standing majority was in no way a consequence of the personal duel between Kennedy and Nixon, for it was a majority created long before either candidate became salient as a national political figure, and long before most of the campaign "issues" of 1960 had taken shape. In this perspective, then, we can consider some of the forces which drew the 1960 vote away from its equilibrium state.

IV. SHORT-TERM FORCES IN THE 1960
ELECTION

Popular vote tallies show that Kennedy received 49.8 percent of the two-party vote outside of the South, and 51.2 percent of the popular vote cast in the South. The vote outside the South is almost 1 percent more Democratic than our equilibrium estimates for this part of the nation. In the South, however, the Democratic deficit relative to the same baseline approaches 17 percent. Naturally, some short-term forces may balance out so that no net advantage accrues to either party. But the comparisons between our baselines and the 1960 vote suggest that we should find some short-term forces which gave a very slight net advantage to Kennedy outside of the South, and yet which penalized him heavily within the South.

As in all elections that attract a wide degree of public attention, a number of short-term forces were certainly at work in 1960. A comprehensive assessment of these forces must await further analysis. However, there can be little doubt that the religious issue was the strongest single factor overlaid on basic partisan loyalties in the 1960 election, and we have focused most of our initial analyses in this area. Fortunately we know a great deal about the "normal" voting behavior within different religious categories, and can use this knowledge to provide baselines which aid in estimating the net effect of Kennedy's Catholicism upon his candidacy.

The Catholic Vote. As we have observed, the vote division among Catholics soared from a 50–50 split in the two Eisenhower contests to an 80–20 majority in the 1960 presidential vote. However, it is hard to attribute all of this increment simply to the Kennedy candidacy. In the 1958 election, when there were mild short-term economic forces favoring the Democratic party, the vote among Catholics went well over 70 percent in that direction. Ever since our measurements of party identification began in 1952, only a small minority—less than 20 percent—of Catholics in the nation have considered themselves as Republicans, although a fair portion have typically styled themselves as "Independents." Most of what attracted attention as a Republican trend among Catholics during the 1950's finds little support in our data, at least as a trend peculiar to Catholics. To be sure, many Democratic Catholics defected to vote for Eisenhower in 1952 and 1956. So did many Democratic Protestants. As a matter of fact, the defection rate among Democratic Catholics in 1952 was very slightly less than among Democratic Protestants, and in 1956 was very slightly more. In neither case do the differences exceed sampling error. There is some long-term evidence of a faint and slow erosion in the Catholic Democratic vote; but this has been proceeding at such a glacial pace that the 1956–1960 vote trends which we are treating here dwarf it completely. There is no reason to believe that the short-term personal "pull" exerted on Democrats generally by Eisenhower had a different strength for Catholics than for Protestants. The myths that have arisen to this effect seem to be primarily illusions stemming from the large proportion of Democrats who are Catholics. Their loss was painful in the two Eisenhower votes. But they were at the outset, and remained up to the first glimmer of the Kennedy candidacy, a strongly Democratic group.

We may specify this "normal" Democratic strength among Catholics by applying the same operations for Catholics alone that we have employed for the electorate as a whole. In the equilibrium case, it turns out that one would expect at least a 63 percent Democratic margin among Catholics. The difference between 63 percent and the 80 percent which Kennedy achieved can provisionally be taken as an estimate of the increment in Democratic votes among Catholics above that which the normal, Protestant Democratic presidential candidate could have expected.

We can readily translate this 17 percent vote gain into proportions of the total 1960 vote, taking into account levels of Catholic turnout and the like. On such grounds, it appears that Kennedy won a vote bonus from Catholics amounting to about 4 percent of the national two-party popular vote. This increment is, of course, very unequally divided between the South and the rest of the nation, owing simply to the sparse Catholic population in the South. Within the 1960 non-Southern electorate, Kennedy's net gain from the Catholic increment amounts to better than 5 percent of the two-party vote. The same rate of gain represents less than 1 percent of the Southern popular vote.

The Anti-Catholic Vote. Respondents talked to our interviewers with remarkable freedom about the Catholic factor during the fall of 1960. This is not to say that all respondents referred to it as a problem. There were even signs that some Protestant respondents were struggling to avoid mention of it although it was a matter of concern. Nonetheless, nearly 40 percent of the sample voluntarily introduced the subject before any direct probing on our part in the early stages of the pre-election questionnaire. Since this figure certainly understates the proportion of the population for whom religion was a salient concern in 1960, it testifies rather eloquently to the importance of the factor in conscious political motivations during the fall campaign.

These discussions of the Catholic question, volunteered by our respondents, will, in time, provide more incisive descriptions of the short-term anti-Catholic forces important in the election. Our interest here, however, is to estimate the magnitude of anti-Catholic voting in terms of otherwise Democratic votes which Kennedy lost. In such an enterprise, our material on the political backgrounds of our respondents is most useful.

We focus, therefore, upon the simple rates of defection to Nixon among Protestants who were identified in 1960 with the Democratic party. As Figure 1 shows, this defection rate is strongly correlated with regularity of attendance at a Protestant church. Protestant Democrats who, by self-description, never attend church, and hence are not likely to have much identification with it, defected to Nixon only at a rate of 6 percent. This rate, incidentally, is just about the "normal" defection rate which we would predict for both parties in the equilibrium case: it represents the scattered defections which occur for entirely idiosyncratic reasons in any election. Therefore, for Democrats who were nominal Protestants but outside the psychological orbit of their church, the short-term religious force set up by a Catholic candidacy had no visible impact. However, as soon as there is some evidence of identification with a Protestant church, the defection rate rises rapidly.

Although Protestant Independents are not included in Figure 1, they show the same gradient at a different level of the two-party vote division. The few Protestant Independents not attending church split close to the theoretically-expected 50–50 point. Then the Nixon vote rises to 61 percent in the "seldom" category; to 72 percent for the "often" category; and to 83 percent for the Protestant Independents attending church regularly. This increment of Republican votes above the "normal" 50–50 division for Independents matches remarkably the increment of Republican votes above the "normal" figure of 6 percent in the case of the Democrats.

We customarily find in our data certain substantial correlations between church attendance and political behavior. The correlation between church attendance and vote among Protestant Democrats and Independents is not, however, one of these. The strong associations seem linked in an obvious way to the 1960 election. We need not assume, of course, that each defection pictured here represents a sermon from the pulpit and an obedient member of the congregation. Social science theory assures us that whether through sermons, informal communication or a private sense of reserve toward Catholicism, the faithful Protestant would react more negatively to the presidential candidacy of a Catholic than would more indifferent Protestants. It remains notable, however, that Democrats who were at the same time regular Protestants defected to Nixon at rates far exceeding those which Eisenhower had attracted in 1952 or 1956.

We may use Figure 1, then, as a tool to estimate the magnitude of the anti-Catholic vote. It is easily argued that the area below the dotted line in Figure 1 represents "normal" defections within each category of church attendance, and that the votes represented by the triangle above the dotted line are votes which Kennedy lost on religious grounds. It is then a simple mechanical matter to convert this triangle into proportions of the popular vote for South and non-South.

On the surface, Figure 1 seems to say that the impact of the religious factor was very nearly the same, North and South, for the Southern gradient of defections is only slightly higher than the non-Southern gradient. If we think of the impact of short-term forces *on individuals* as a function of their party and religious loyalties, this conclusion is proper. Indeed, as we consider in later analyses the impact by different types of Protestantism, it may well be that the character of the impact will show no remaining regional difference whatever. However, to construe Figure 1 as suggesting that the *magnitude* of the anti-

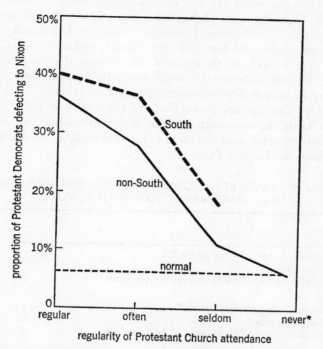

* The number of Protestant Democrats who "never" attend church in the South is too small for inclusion.

FIGURE I. Defections to Nixon among Protestant Democrats as a Function of Church Attendance.

Catholic effect was about the same in votes cast in North and South, is quite improper. The differences between the regions turn out to be substantial.

We must consider first that less than two-thirds of the active non-Southern electorate is Protestant, whereas within the South the electorate is almost completely (95 percent) Protestant. Secondly, Protestants are more faithful churchgoers in the South than outside it. Quite specifically, we find that over half of the Southern presidential vote is cast by Protestants who go to church regularly, whereas less than 20 percent of the vote outside the South comes from regular, church-going Protestants. Finally, of the minority outside the South who are Protestant and attend church regularly, only a small proportion are Democratic identifiers: Republicans clearly predominate in this category. In the South, the situation is reversed, with regular Protestants being far more often than not Democratic identifiers.

This conjunction of regional differences means that the defecting votes represented in Figure I are of vastly different sizes, South and non-South. It turns out that outside the South regular, church-going Protestants who are Democrats cast only about 5 percent of the total non-Southern vote. Within the South, however, regular, church-going Protestants who are Democrats contributed over 35 percent of the total Southern vote. Thus it is that the anti-Catholic impact in the South turns out to involve a much larger share of the votes than elsewhere. The anti-Catholic vote in the South fulfills our search for a short-term force of strong net Republican strength in that region.

Summing up these apparent anti-Catholic votes as proportions of the total vote in the South, the non-South, and the nation as a whole, we can compare them with our estimations of the bonuses received by Kennedy from Catholics. Table II shows the balance sheet.

TABLE II.   OFFSETTING EFFECTS OF THE CATHOLIC ISSUE,
1960 DEMOCRATIC PRESIDENTIAL VOTE

AREA	% OF 2-PARTY VOTE IN AREA
Outside the South, Kennedy's "unexpected" . . .	
Gains from Catholics	5.2%
Losses from Protestant Democrats and Independents	—3.6
NET	+1.6%
Inside the South, Kennedy's "unexpected" . . .	
Gains from Catholics	0.7%
Losses from Protestant Democrats and Independents	—17.2
NET	—16.5%
For the *nation as a whole*, Kennedy's "unexpected" . . .	
Gains from Catholics	4.3%
Losses from Protestant Democrats and Independents	—6.5
NET	—2.2%

There is every reason to believe that these preliminary estimates under-estimate the importance of religion in the 1960 vote and, in particular, underestimate the magnitude of the anti-Catholic vote. We have at no point taken account, for example, of the possibility that certain Republican identifiers, exposed to short-term forces which would normally have produced defections to the Democrats, may have been inhibited from such defection by Kennedy's Catholicism. In the midwest there were signs of a "farm revolt" favoring the Democrats which failed to materialize in the presidential balloting. At lower levels on farm belt tickets one finds that major Democratic candidates consistently surpassed "normal" Democratic expectations. Yet Kennedy seems to have been peculiarly insulated from any of this profit-taking: in these areas he lagged behind other major Democrats by a rather consistent 5 percent. It is difficult not to believe that at lower levels of office net short-term forces were favoring the Democrats, and Republican identifiers were defecting at unusual rates. Analyses may show that religion was a primary force inhibiting such defections at the presidential level.

Other early glimpses of our data also suggest the estimates of anti-Catholicism in Table II are conservative. It is likely that a number of non-religious short-term forces generated by the campaign itself were favorable to Kennedy on balance. As a number of other surveys reported, Nixon held a substantial lead over Kennedy in the early stages. At the outset, Kennedy was little known to the public: he stood primarily as the Democratic candidate and a Catholic. As the campaign went on, other and non-religious aspects of the Kennedy image filled in, and the public impression was usually positive. In this crucial shift in sentiment during the campaign, the television debates probably played an important role. Although there were Democrats who reacted warmly to Nixon's performance, our materials show quite strikingly that the net response to the debates favored Kennedy, as has been commonly supposed. In case studies, a reading of interviews has already turned up numerous Protestants of varying partisanship who were much more impressed by Kennedy as a candidate than by Nixon, yet who could not bring themselves to vote for a Catholic. In the measure that Kennedy's attractiveness as a candidate exceeded Nixon's and other short-term forces apart from religion were favoring the Democrats, the total popular vote should have been drawn to the Democratic side of the equilibrium point. The fact that it stayed instead on the Republican side may represent further damaging effects of religion for Kennedy.

Refined analyses at a later date will permit us to estimate more adequately the role which all the major motivational factors, including religion, played in the 1960 outcome. For the moment, however, it is impressive the degree to which the surface characteristics of the 1960 election become intelligible even when viewed simply as the result of an "ancient" and enduring division of partisan loyalties overlaid by a short-term cross-current of religious motivation.

Normally we would expect a national vote falling as close to its equilibrium point as the 1960 case to be a relatively low-turnout election. That is, a vote near the equilibrium point suggests either weak short-term forces or else a balance of stronger forces creating conflict in individuals and thereby lowering their motivation to vote. It is rare that forces strong enough to compel indifferent citizens to come out and vote do not also favor one party over the other quite categorically.

In 1960, however, the motivational picture underlying the vote was somewhat different, and can best be understood by separating the Protestant South from the rest of the nation. In the South, of course, a strong and unidirectional short-term force was reflected in a sharp departure from equilibrium and a surge in turnout, as fits normal expectations. What is abnormal is that this strong Republican short-term force raised motivation in a Democratic preserve, rather than diluting it through conflict. It is likely that conflict *was* created, especially where Democratic partisanship was strong. "Strong" Democrats in our sample made virtually no contribution to the 1960 rise in Southern turnout. The increase came from weaker Democrats, whose participation increased so radically over 1952 and 1956 that their turnout even surpassed that of strong Democrats in very exceptional fashion. For these voters, it seems likely that such forces as anti-Catholic feelings rapidly overcame relatively weak party loyalties and left strong motivation to turn out.

While turnout elsewhere did not show the same remarkable surge which appeared in the South, it remained at the fairly high level characteristic of the 1952 and 1956 elections, despite a partisan division of the vote near the regional equilibrium point. Strong balancing forces appear to have been in operation which did not create much conflict within individuals. The reason is clear: to the degree that religious motivations were engaged, forces were conflicting between groups rather than within individuals. Non-Southern Catholics, predominantly Democratic, were exposed to strong unidirectional short-term forces motivating them to get out and vote for Kennedy. Non-Southern Protestants, predominantly Republican, were exposed to contrary forces, at least where Protestant religious fidelity was strong. Thus the vote fell near the equilibrium point, but there was rather high turnout as well.

The other surface characteristics of the election are equally intelligible in these terms. Despite his position as majority candidate, Kennedy very nearly lost and tended to run behind his ticket. In the northeast, where concentrations of Catholics are greatest, his relation to the rest of the ticket was not generally unfavorable. The penalty he suffered becomes visible and consistent in the Midwest, where Catholics are fewer and Protestant church attendance is more regular. In the South, and for the same reasons, the differences between the Kennedy vote and that of other Democrats become large indeed. Everywhere, if one compares 1956 vote statistics with 1960 statistics, the course of political change is closely associated with the religious composition of voting units.

There was some relief even outside the more committed Democratic circles when the Kennedy victory, slight though it was, demonstrated that a Catholic was not in practice barred from the White House. Yet it would be naive to suppose that a Catholic candidate no longer suffers any initial disadvantage before the American electorate as a result of his creed. Not only did Kennedy possess a type of personal appeal which the television debates permitted him to exploit in unusual measure, but he was also the candidate of a party enjoying a fundamental majority in the land. Even the combination of these circumstances was barely sufficient to give him a popular vote victory. Lacking such a strong underlying majority, which Al Smith most certainly lacked in 1928, it is doubtful that the most attractive of Catholic presidential candidates in 1960 would have had much chance of success. It remains to be seen how far the experience of a Catholic president may diminish the disadvantage another time.

V. THE 1960 ELECTION IN HISTORICAL
PERSPECTIVE

In a publication which appeared a few months prior to the 1960 elections we posed the question of "how long a party can hope to hold the White House if it does not have a majority of the party-identified electorate." We had identified the two Eisenhower victories as "deviating elections," in which short-term forces had brought about the defeat of the majority party. We had not found any evidence in our 1952 or 1956 studies that these short-term forces were producing any significant realignment in the basic partisan commitments of the electorate. We felt that unless such a realignment did occur, "the minority party [could] not hope to continue its tenure in office over a very extended period."

We now know that the eight-year Eisenhower period ended with no basic change in the proportions of the public who identify themselves as Republican, Democrat, or Independent. If there had been an opportunity in 1952 for the Republican party to rewin the majority status it had held prior to 1932, it failed to capitalize on it. The Democratic party remained the majority party and the 1960 election returned it to the presidency. It was, to extend the nomenclature of our earlier publication, a "reinstating" election, one in which the party enjoying a majority of party identifiers returns to power. The 1960 election was remarkable not in the fact that the majority party was reinstated but that its return to power was accomplished by such a narrow margin. We had recognized the possibility that "the unfolding of national and international events and the appearance of new political figures" might swing the vote away from its natural equilibrium. We now see that such a deflection did occur and that it very nearly cost the majority party the election.

It may be argued that the deficit the Democratic presidential candidate suffered from his normal expectation did not derive from damaging circumstances which were specific to the 1960 election but from a progressive weakening in the willingness of some Democratic partisans to support their ticket at the presidential level. It has been suggested that some voters who consider themselves to be Democrats and customarily favor Democratic candidates at the lower levels of office may have come during the Eisenhower period to have a perverse interest in favoring Republican candidates for president, either because of notions of party balance in government, because of local considerations in their states, or simply out of admiration for Eisenhower.

Important differences no doubt exist between voting at the presidential level and voting for a congressman. Our studies have shown, for example, that the popular vote for lesser offices is a more party-determined vote than the vote for president and varies around the normal equilibrium vote figure within a much narrower range than does the presidential vote. However, the supposition that Kennedy failed to win a normal Democratic majority because of a cadre of Democrats who are covertly Republican in their presidential voting is not supported by our data.

Table I has already demonstrated that the overall shift in partisanship of the vote between 1956 and 1960 cannot be explained as a simple unilateral movement of erstwhile Eisenhower Democrats. The election did not depend, as was often supposed, upon the number of Eisenhower Democrats whom Nixon could retain as "covert Republicans." Our panel materials show that if Nixon had been forced to depend only upon the Eisenhower Democrats whom he retained, he would have suffered a convincing 54–46 defeat, assuming that other Democrats had continued to vote for Kennedy. He did not suffer such a defeat because he drew a new stream of Democratic defections nearly sufficient to put him in the White House.

The patterns of short-term forces in the 1960 election were independent of those shaping the 1956 election, then, in the sense that they affected a new set of people, on new grounds. There were Democrats susceptible to Eisenhower in 1956; there were Democrats sensitive to religion in 1960: the two sets of people do not intersect much more than one would expect by chance. In short, there is little evidence that the two Eisenhower elections had created a set of Democrats peculiarly disposed to vote for a Republican presidential candidate.

Analysis of our 1960 data is not sufficiently complete to enable us to describe the entire pattern of forces to which the electorate was reacting on Election Day. We do not know, for example, what the partisan impact of international affairs, which had favored the Republican candidate so strongly in the preceding two elections, was in the 1960 election. We do not know the effect of the Negro discrimination issues. We do not know in detail as yet how the personal attributes of the major candidates, other than their religious affiliations, were evaluated by the public. We feel confident, however, that we will not find any short-term force which moved as large a fraction of the 1960 electorate as did the issue of a Catholic president. This was the major cause of the net departure of the vote totals from the division which the comparative underlying strength of the two parties in 1960 would have led us to expect. After two consecutive "deviating" elections won at a presidential level by the minority party, the 1960 election reinstated the Democratic party. But short-term forces generated by the immediate 1960 situation once again favored the Republicans on balance, and the difference in votes which separated this "reinstating election" from a third "deviating election" was slight indeed.

ELECTORAL MYTH AND REALITY:
THE 1964 ELECTION *

Philip E. Converse, Aage R. Clausen, Warren E. Miller

ON Election Day, 1964, the aspirations of Senator Barry Goldwater and the conservative wing of the Republican Party were buried under an avalanche of votes cast for incumbent President Lyndon Johnson. The margin of victory, approaching 16 million votes, was unprecedented. Historical comparisons with other presidential landslides are left somewhat indeterminate by the intrusion of third parties. However, it is safe to observe that Johnson's 61.3 per-

* From Philip E. Converse et al., "Electoral Myth and Reality: The 1964 Election," in The American Political Science Review, Vol. LIX, No. 2, 1965, pp. 321–336. Reprinted by permission of the authors and the American Political Science Association.

cent of the two-party popular vote put him in the same general range as the striking victories of Franklin Delano Roosevelt in 1936, Harding in 1920, and Theodore Roosevelt in 1904.

Before the fact, the election was also expected to be the most intensely ideological campaign since 1936, in no small measure because of Goldwater's reputation as a "pure" conservative. After the fact, doubts existed as to whether this expectation had been fulfilled. Goldwater supporters, in particular, expressed disappointment that President Johnson had refused to join battle on any of the fundamental ideological alternatives that were motivating the Goldwater camp. However, as we shall see, the mass public had some sense that "important differences" between the two major parties were heightened in 1964 compared with parallel data from either 1960 or, as is more impressive, the relatively tense election of 1952. And certainly no one questioned the importance of ideological differences in the factional dispute that split the Republican Party along liberal-conservative lines with an enduring bitterness unmatched in decades.

Indeed, these three prime elements of the 1964 election—faction, ideology and the contest for votes—became intertwined after the manner of a classic script. That is, the "outer" ideological wing of a party captures its nomination, leaving a vacuum toward the center of gravity of national opinion. This vacuum is gleefully filled by the opposing party without any loss of votes from its own side of the spectrum. The outcome, logically and inexorably, is a landslide at the polls.

With a script so clearly written in advance, the outsider would naturally ask why any party controlled by rational strategists should choose a course likely to lead to such massive repudiation in its name. The answers to this question in the 1964 case are not particularly obscure, although they can be made at numerous levels. One answer, of course, is that Republican Party strategists were themselves in deep disagreement as to just what script was relevant: many recognized the classic script and predicted the eventual outcome, with all of its attendant losses for other Republican candidates, in deadly accuracy.

For the factional dispute within Republican ranks involved not only an ideological clash, but also major differences in the perception of that political reality which becomes important in winning votes and elections. The Goldwater faction was told by its Republican adversaries, as the conservative wing had been told for years, that a Goldwater could not conceivably defeat a Democratic President, and would instead greatly damage the party ticket at all levels. The Goldwater group countered that a victory for their man was entirely plausible despite the danger signals of the spring polls and the normal difficulties of challenging an incumbent. It is not clear how sincere or widespread this confidence was: some statements sounded as though the Goldwater candidacy had little chance of winning but would at least provide a forum for the conservative philosophy, along with control of the Republican Party. But even in their more pessimistic moments, the Goldwater people would argue that while victory might be difficult, they certainly saw no reason to believe that Goldwater would do worse than any other Republican challenger, or encounter the electoral disaster the liberals were predicting.

Similarly, at the San Francisco nominating convention, his opponents vehemently charged that Goldwater was a "minority candidate," even among Republicans in this country. In another direct clash of perceptions, Senator Goldwater is said to have remarked to a group of Midwestern delegates, "What the minority [the convention liberals] can't get through their heads is that this is a true representation of the Republican Party."

In this article we wish to examine the relationship between such conflicting perceptions and what is known of the relevant reality in the context of the 1964 election. Our information comes primarily from sample survey studies of the mass public that formed the electorate in 1964, and whose reactions represent one level of political reality about which so many conflicting opinions and predictions were made. While the most important aspect of that reality was unveiled by the election outcome, there remained some of the customary latitude of interpretation as to its full significance. And with respect to the interplay between the stratagems of party elites on one hand and the grass-roots American voters on the other, the chronology of the 1964 election does indeed provide a fascinating composite of sheer myth, genuine but discrepant reality worlds, and self-fulfilling prophecies.

I. THE MYTH OF THE STAY-AT-HOME
REPUBLICANS

The first theory of electoral reality on our agenda may be rapidly disposed of, for it lies more simply and unequivocally in the realm of myth than any of the others we shall treat. It should not be overlooked, however, both because of its historical persistence and because of its enshrinement in the battle cry of 1964 Goldwater supporters: "A choice, not an echo!"

In the quadrennial competition between liberal and conservative wings of the Republican Party for the presidential nomination throughout the 1940s and 1950s, the conservatives were consistently bested. One of the prime contentions of the liberals was that all of the entries of the conservative wing were so distant from the "middle-of-the-road" that they had no hope of attracting the independent votes necessary for victory over the Democrats. At an ideological level, the conservative wing coined the epithet "me-tooism" to ridicule the liberals for their refusal to reject Democratic innovations of the New and Fair Deal eras root and branch. The liberals, it was charged, were slowly selling out the fundamental principles on which earlier days of G.O.P. ascendancy had been based.

This accusation of ideological "flabbiness" was not, however, compelling of itself without some further comment on the problem of winning votes. As a consequence, a theory became widely current among conservative Republicans that G.O.P. difficulties in maintaining much contact with the White House were in fact directly tied to the "me-tooist" flavor of its presidential candidates. Republicans running for that office tended to lose not because there was any lack of potential Republican votes (as the superficial observer might have thought), but because many of the "real" Republicans were sufficiently offended by "me-tooism" that they simply didn't bother to vote at all. Nominate a true Republican rather than a Tweedledee, the theory went, and enough of these stay-at-homes would return to the polls to put him into the White House.

As such theories go, this contention was remarkably verifiable. That is, the critic need not argue that few Republicans were disappointed by the nominees of their party, for disappointment in itself is irrelevant for argument. The question is simply whether or not Republicans, however disappointed, did continue to turn out and vote even for "me-tooist" candidates through this period —a matter much easier to ascertain. Nor is there any point in arguing that there were *never* any stray Republicans who in the last analysis vented their frustrations by refusing to go to the polls. Undoubtedly there were. But the theory hinges less on the question as to whether such people existed, than on the contention that they existed in significant numbers: not merely several hundred or several thousand or even a few hundred thousand, but in the millions needed to overcome the persistent Democratic majorities.

Such a pool of potential voters would be large enough to be discriminated reliably in most sample surveys. And we know of no reputable sample surveys at any time in this period that gave any shred of reason to believe that this significant pool of stay-at-home Republicans existed. Indeed, such findings as were relevant pointed massively in the opposite direction. From 1944 on, for example, one can contrast turnout rates between Democrats and Republicans of comparable strengths of identification. And over election after election featuring "me-tooist" Republican nominees, one finds that turnout rates are consistently higher—and often much higher—on the Republican side. Indeed, each time we isolate that polar minority who not only have an intense commitment to the Republican Party, but whose commitment is of a highly sensitive ideological sort, turnout typically reaches proportions staggering for the American system: 96 percent, 98 percent—levels almost implausible in view of registration difficulties, travel, sickness and other accidents which can keep the most devoted American from the polls upon occasion. More impressive still, we find that in 1952 those Republicans who reported during the campaign that they would have preferred the "conservative" Taft over the "liberal" Eisenhower—exactly those Republicans to whom the theory refers—actually turned out at much *higher* rates to vote for Eisenhower in the November election (94 percent) than did the set of Republicans who indicated satisfaction with Eisenhower's nomination (84 percent).

These brief observations do not begin to exhaust the evidence, none of which lends any support whatever to the theory of a silent pool of frustrated conservative Republicans. Hence it is scarcely surprising that the Goldwater cause in 1964 was not buoyed up by some sudden surge of new support at the polls which other strategists had overlooked; for the hitherto silent people expected to provide such a surge existed principally in the imaginations of conservative strategists who in time of adversity needed desperately to believe that they were there. It is less of a wonder that this theory was generated, particularly before sample survey data took on much scope or stature in the 1940s, than that it persisted with greater or lesser vigor into the 1960s in the face of repetitive contradictory evidence readily available to any proponents with an edge of interest as to what the facts actually were.

II. THE MINORITY CANDIDATE OF
A MINORITY PARTY

On the eve of the Republican nominating convention, an irate Goldwater supporter wrote to the Paris edition of the *Herald Tribune,* upbraiding it for the doubts it had expressed as to the extent of Goldwater sentiment beyond the convention delegates themselves, and pointing out that a massive ground-swell of support had built up for Goldwater throughout the country "west of Madison Avenue."

The charge of the liberal wing of the G.O.P. that Goldwater not only was unattractive to Democrats and Independents but was not even the majority preference of Republicans was a particularly severe allegation in view of the constraints under which the Republican Party has been obliged to operate in recent years. It has been the consensus of observers for quite some time that the Republican Party is a minority party in the affections of the American public. Our relevant data collections at frequent intervals since 1952 have left little question in our minds both as to the minority status of the Republicans, and as to the stability of the status during this epoch. For most of this time, our estimates would suggest that in terms of underlying loyalties, the Democrats could expect to receive, all other things equal, something in the neighborhood of 54 percent of the national popular vote; and if any change has been occurring in this figure in the past 15 years, it is that this Democratic majority is slowly increasing. In practical terms, this means that a Democratic candidate need not have much attraction for grass-roots Republicans: he can win easily if he can but carry the votes of a reasonable share of independents, and has general appeal for Democrats. A Republican candidate, on the other hand, can only win at the national level by drawing nearly monolithic support from Republicans, attracting the votes of a lion's share of independents, and inducing unusual defection among the less committed Democratic identifiers as well. The latter was the Eisenhower formula, and one which Nixon had nearly succeeded in following in 1960. More generally, the liberal wing of the Republican Party had sought candidates with this kind of broad appeal throughout this period. In this light, the question of Goldwater's popularity was serious: for if a minority party nominates a figure enjoying only minority support within his own party, it is an obvious invitation to disaster.

In the spring and early summer of 1964, the opinion polls lent much weight to the contention that Goldwater enjoyed no broad support even among Republicans. The Goldwater supporters tended to counter this kind of evidence either (1) by ignoring the polls; or (2) by questioning the validity of the polls (some Goldwater placards were to read "Gallup didn't count us!"); or (3) by questioning the immutability of the early poll readings. Of these reactions, certainly the last-mentioned was entirely appropriate. That is, in the very early stages of a push toward the presidency, even a person who has been something of a "national" figure as Senator or major Governor for a considerable period may not be recognized by very large portions of the public. Until he has received much more intense national exposure in the limelight of presidential primaries and the nominating convention, "straw polls" as to his popularity can be highly misleading and unstable, particularly if the polling pits such a candidate against other figures with more long standing national prominence and "household" names.

However, survey data gathered over the course of 1964 can be put together with "hard" data from the presidential primaries to provide an illuminating picture of Goldwater's general popularity and, in particular, the reactions of grass-roots Republicans to him. In January, 1964, before the beginning of the spring primaries, we asked a national sample of the electorate:

Many people are wondering who will run for President on the Republican side this fall. . . . If you had to make a choice, which Republican leader do you think would be best for our country in 1964?
Who would be your second choice?
Are there any of the leading Republicans that you think would make very bad candidates?

Table I summarizes the responses to this sequence of questions. The open-ended nature of the questions meant that individuals only rated those Republicans whom they were aware of at the time, and thought of as plausible candidates. The table excludes a thin scattering of other mentions. Since the scoring used reflects both the breadth and the intensity of support, a Republican receiving relatively few mentions could not achieve any very high score. Thus, for example, another possible scoring could have shown Henry Cabot Lodge vastly outdistancing all other aspirants, as his references were almost unanimously positive, whereas the other Republicans suffered numerous descriptions as "very bad candidates." However, at this time he was not commonly regarded as an aspirant for the nomination, and the scoring deliberately puts this warm but limited positive feeling toward him in perspective.

The table speaks for itself as to Goldwater's attractiveness as a candidate. Clearly Goldwater's problem was not that he was still too little known: he received mentions from a wider proportion of the electorate than any of his competitors. But for much of the electorate he was an object of antagonism even in January, 1964. And among grass-roots Republicans, where his strength was concentrated, he remained fourth in a field of six.

The sequence of Republican primary elections in the succeeding months tended, with some local variation, to fit the lines suggested by these January reactions. The table presages the startling Lodge write-in victory over both Goldwater and Rockefeller among New Hampshire Republicans in March, as well as his numerous subsequent strong showings. It contains ample warning as well of the amazingly poor Goldwater record in the primaries throughout the spring, including the scattered victories in such seemingly congenial states as conservative Nebraska, where by standing alone on the ticket he managed to win about half of the votes cast over a flood of Nixon and Lodge write-ins. It even renders intelligible the crucial Goldwater victory in California, where write-ins were not permitted, where the sole opponent was Rockefeller, and where Democrats had a hotly fought primary of their own. Indeed, there is room to wonder whether any presidential aspirant has ever contested so many primaries with as disastrous a showing, and still captured the nomination of his party's convention.

No evidence from polls of the period, moreover, suggests that Goldwater's popularity showed any sudden increase, even among Republicans, in the short interval between the final primary and the San Francisco convention. In interviewing our sample of the national electorate in September and October, we asked respondents to recall their reactions to the decisions of the Republican convention, including the identity of the candidates they had preferred at the time the convention began, as well as their gratification, indifference or disappointment at the outcome. While these responses suffer the inevitable frailties of any retrospective accounts that go back over an evolving situation, the social and political lines of support and antagonism for the various major contestants in July as reported during the campaign bear so close a resemblance to the lines of support visible in the January, 1964 data, as to make it unlikely that they are badly distorted by selective recollection, *post hoc* rationalization, and the like.

It is most instructive, perhaps, to set these popular reactions to the 1964 Republican convention against a fairly comparable set of data collected in 1952 after the conservative wing had lost its bid to nominate Senator Taft for the presidency against the liberal wing's offering of General Eisenhower, for the bitterness engendered in the 1952 struggle came closer to matching that of 1964 than either of the intervening conventions. Our question in 1952 asked respondents irrespective of partisan allegiance whether they would have preferred to have seen any other candidate nominated in either of the major-party conventions held in Chicago. Thus Republican identifiers could focus their remarks on the Democratic convention in a way that the 1964 question did not permit. However, partisans tended to comment primarily on the outcomes of their own party's nominating conventions.

Among Republican identifiers in the fall of 1952, about one in five recalled having felt a preference for Taft at the time of the convention. Another eight percent had preferred some third candidate. The vast majority of the remaining 72 percent indicated that they had been indifferent to the choices at either convention, or expressed gratification in the selection of Eisenhower as the Republican candidate. Some other Republicans responded that they would have preferred a candidate other than Stevenson from the Democratic convention. Presumably, however, these citizens were satisfied with the Republican conven-

TABLE I. PREFERENCES FOR THE REPUBLICAN PRESIDENTIAL
NOMINATION AMONG SELECTED SEGMENTS OF
THE ELECTORATE, JANUARY, 1964

| | | SEGMENTS OF THE ELECTORATE | | |
	PER CENT MENTIONS[a]	SCORE ACROSS TOTAL ELECTORATE[b]	SCORE WITHIN "MINIMAL MAJORITY": ALL INDEPENDENTS AND REPUBLICANS[b]	SCORE AMONG ALL REPUBLICANS[b]
	(%)			
Nixon	42	+25	+32	+37
Lodge	10	+11	+13	+13
Romney	11	+ 9	+11	+10
Rockefeller	49	+19	+10	+ 1
Scranton	11	+ 7	+ 6	+ 5
Goldwater	54	— 8	— 5	+ 9

[a] The percentage entered represents the proportion of individuals in the total sample mentioning the Republican leader indicated, either as one of two best or one of two very bad candidates.
[b] Each mention of a leader as the "best" candidate received a score of +2. Each mention as second best received a score of +1. The first-mentioned "bad" candidate received a score of —2. Any negative second mentions were scored —1. The entries in the table represent the net balance of positive or negative scores for the leader, expressed as a proportion of the maximum possible positive score an individual would have received had he been awarded all of the "best" choices given by the indicated segment of the electorate.

tion, and it seems reasonable to conclude that a maximum of some 30 percent of all Republicans in 1952 had ground to recall any disappointment over their party's nomination.

The picture from 1964 is remarkably similar in one respect, and drastically different in another. Among Republican identifiers in this latter year, slightly less than 20 percent of all Republicans recalled having preferred Goldwater at the time of the convention. This figure is only one percent less than the proportion of Taft supporters among Republicans in 1952. What was different, of course, was that in 1952 Taft lost the nomination on the first ballot, whereas in 1964 Goldwater won it handily on the first ballot. Although in our 1964 data a large segment (30 percent) of Republican identifiers indicated that they had held no preference for a specific candidate at convention time, very nearly half of all of our Republicans did recall some preference other than Goldwater. Thus these grass-roots Republicans with non-Goldwater choices outnumbered the Goldwater supporters within Republican ranks by a margin of better than two and one-half to one. A clear majority (60 percent) of those with other preferences, when asked "Were you particularly unhappy that Goldwater got the nomination, or did you think that he was nearly as good as your man?," expressed their lingering unhappiness about the outcome.

In sum, then, it is hard to turn up any bit of evidence to challenge the conclusion that Goldwater was, in rather startling degree, a minority candidate within a minority party. If his camp actually believed that the San Francisco delegates represented a true cross-section of grass-roots Republican sentiment, then they had grossly misunderstood the situation. There was, however, at least one extenuating circumstance: the support among Republican citizens for other candidates than Goldwater was split badly among the four or five other leading candidates. Thus while any of several pairs of other candidates had grass-roots party support at convention time which would have outnumbered the Goldwater faction quite readily, the fact remains that the 20 percent Goldwater support represented a plurality for any single candidate.

However this may be, disappointment at the convention outcome in 1964 had radically different consequences in November than the comparable disappointments among Republicans in 1952. As we have seen above, the former Taft supporters in that year turned out at the polls in near-perfect proportions and cast a very faithful Republican vote for Eisenhower. In 1964, however, the widespread defections among Republicans necessary to account for the Johnson landslide tended to follow rather closely the lines of lingering discontent with the nomination.

These recollections of San Francisco varied according to the different camps in which rank-and-file Republicans had located themselves at the time. So, for example, about three Lodge supporters in four reported they were unhappy with the Goldwater nomination; for Rockefeller supporters, the figure was closer to two in three. Slightly over half of the Nixon supporters, however, indicated that they thought Goldwater was "nearly as good" as their man, Nixon. With minor departures, similar patterns marked the ultimate defections to Johnson among these varying Republicans. Since Nixon supporters were, like Goldwater's, more frequently "strong" Republicans than the adherents of some of the other camps, lower defection rates here were only to be expected. However, defections to Johnson among Republicans who had preferred Nixon at convention time remained about double what could be expected from past norms for Republicans of this particular mixture of strengths of identification. Over three times as many Republicans for Lodge and Scranton defected to Johnson as parallel "normal" expectations would suggest, and—perhaps surprisingly—defections among Republicans who expressed no pre-convention favorite at all were in this range as well. Most extreme were the Rockefeller and Romney supporters, with defection rates at the polls exceeding expectation by a factor of greater than four.

These differences across the several non-Goldwater camps are intriguing, in part because they appear related to reactions of the various G.O.P. leaders to the Goldwater candidacy. That is, of the set of major Republicans under discussion, Nixon took greatest pains to maintain relations with the Goldwater group before the convention, and undertook to help unify the party behind him after the nomination. Therefore it seems fitting that dismay at the nomination was least in his camp, and defections relatively limited. Neither Rockefeller nor Romney made any major show of reconciliation after the nomination, and subsequently went to some lengths to dissociate themselves from the Goldwater aspects of the Republican campaign.

Yet if it were true that nothing more than a "follow-the-leader" response is needed to account for these variations in defection rates among Republicans, the data would cast a somewhat different light on the question of conflicting perceptions between liberal and conservative wings of Goldwater's voting strength. For in such a case the Senator's problem would have been less one of gross overestimates of his strength, than of self-fulfilling prophecy on the part of the disgruntled liberal leaders. In other words, they first refused to support Goldwater on grounds that he could not win enough votes, and then proceeded to withhold in large quantities the votes of their "followers" to assure exactly this outcome.

No airtight way is available to determine whether or not Republican defections at the presidential level might have been reduced significantly had Rockefeller or some of the other liberals effected a more genuine reconciliation with Goldwater to unite the party for the campaign. Nevertheless, if we were to compare the issue positions and ideological persuasions of 1964 Nixon Republicans with those of Rockefeller or Romney Republicans and find no substantial differences, we might be tempted to judge that differences in leader behavior did play some independent role in minimizing or maximizing Republican defections in November. Preliminary analyses suggest rather clearly, however, that substantial ideological differences did exist across the range of Republican factions. Republicans enthusiastic about Goldwater showed a rather unique (or "extreme") pattern of ideological positions. Nixon supporters, while unmistakably different, looked more nearly like the Goldwater people than the adherents of any of the other camps. Next in order moving away from the Goldwater position were the Scranton and Lodge followers, and the Rockefeller and Romney adherents show slightly more liberal positions still. Ideological differences, therefore, plainly existed between grass-roots supporters of the various factions, and these differences were indeed correlated with defections from a Goldwater vote. This does not exclude the possibility that the defections might have been lessened by a genuine "unity" move on the part of more liberal Republican leaders. It indicates nevertheless that the desertions were rooted not only in leader-follower behavior, but in a more personal sense of ideological distance between many rank-and-file Republicans and the Goldwater faction—a distance that would have produced increased defections quite apart from examples set by the leadership.

However this may be, it was a significant feature of the election that the customary post-convention reconciliation between party factions was in the 1964 Republican case lack-lustre at best, and at many levels simply non-existent. Many of the liberals wished to avoid the Goldwater platform. At the same time, Goldwater seemed to do less than most candidates in making it easy for the dissident brethren to return to the fold. Among several possible reasons, one may have been that in the blueprint laid out by Goldwater strategists for a November victory, the support of most of these leaders did not appear to be critical.

III. CAMPAIGN STRATEGY:
THE SOUTH AS REPUBLICAN TARGET

The strategy of the Goldwater camp for a November victory was both simple and relatively selective. Goldwater felt, to begin with, that he could hold on to essentially the same states that Nixon had won in 1960. This meant a clean sweep of the populous states of the Pacific Coast, most of the Mountain and Plains states, and a scattering east of the Mississippi. To reap the additional electoral votes for victory, Goldwater believed that the way lay open, under proper circumstances, for the Republican Party to make further major inroads in the once solidly Democratic South. The plan implied that Goldwater could largely afford to write off the populous industrial states of the Northeast and some, if not all, of the Midwest—a matter which greatly reduced the importance of the dissident liberal Republican bloc. And it represented a dramatic departure from any past Republican strategy in making of the South a fulcrum for victory.

Such a strategy was not only unusual, but, against the long sweep of American electoral history, it might even be thought of as implausible. Yet it was no hastily devised scheme. For years Goldwater had participated in the Congressional coalition between conservative Republicans and Southern Democrats. The same drive for ideological neatness that led him to call for the reorganization of American politics into "Conservative" and "Liberal" parties impressed upon him the grotesque incongruity of a Democratic South. The South had no reason to be a Democratic bastion; by all of its affinities and traditions, it should long since have become Republican. Part of the problem lay with the national Republican Party, which, in the control of the Northeastern bloc, had failed to present national-level candidates making clear that Republicanism was the natural home of the Southern voter. This had been a frustrating fact since Goldwater's entry into national politics—a period during which political observers had frequently predicted an imminent partisan realignment of the South; but gains in the region, while very obvious, had remained rather modest. In discussions of Republican difficulty in recapturing majority status in the land, Goldwater had opined that the Party had to learn to "go hunting in the pond where the ducks are"—the South. As bitterness began to mount in that region toward the civil rights pressures of the Kennedy Administration, the time seemed more ripe than ever for the presentation of a purely conservative Republican candidate who could appeal to the Southern ethos in a most direct way, thereby breaking the Democratic hold on the region in one dramatic and decisive stroke.

This long-planned strategy had suffered two temporary but alarming setbacks. The assassination of President Kennedy suddenly placed a Southerner in the White House, and removed from power the most feared personal symbols of federal intrusion. The continuation of the Kennedy beginnings by the Johnson Administration, however—particularly in the 1964 Civil Rights bill—helped to reset the stage. So did the increased signs of Negro unrest, and the new element of "white backlash" in the North as well as the South that seemed apparent in the spring primaries. The capping touch was Goldwater's vote against the Civil Rights bill. This vote, to be sure, represented no condoning of segregationism *per se,* but rather a blow for states' rights against the encroachment of the federal government. Nevertheless, white supremacists in the South had so long paraded under the states' rights banner as to leave little room for fear lest the Goldwater gesture go unappreciated. The liberal wing of the Republican Party, having worked for years to prevent the Democrats from "gaining position" on the civil rights issue, was further horrified as it envisioned the G.O.P. suddenly transformed into "the party of the white man" at just the moment when the Negro vote was becoming effectively mobilized.

The second setback threatened when Governor Wallace of Alabama decided to enter the presidential race as a states' rights candidate. This was especially alarming, for Wallace would have competed for exactly the same votes that Goldwater had been wooing toward the Republican column. However, Wallace's subsequent withdrawal left the field open again for the original victory blueprint, and the implementation began in force. Mid-campaign accounts of the Goldwater organizational efforts spoke of a high-powered, modernistic campaign apparatus in the South stocked with volunteer labor in numbers that would have been unbelievable for the earlier Eisenhower and Nixon campaigns. While this machine had been humming efficiently from the start, the Goldwater organization in the West was described as effective but less advanced; in the Midwest it was chaotic, and in the Northeast next to nonexistent. At few if any points in recent political history have so many campaign resources—in both issue positions taken and organizational efforts made—been devoted to the cultivation of a single region. The first discordant note came when, during the campaign and apparently as the result of new poll data, Goldwater remarked to reporters that he was not as strong in the South as everybody seemed to think.

After the votes were counted, what was the success of this strategy? The verdict must come in two halves. From one point of view, the strategy was a brilliant success, and it left its imprint on the geographical voting returns with greater strength than any other of what we have called "short-term forces" in the 1964 election. One crude way of separating these immediate or new effects from those better attributable to long-term standing loyalties is to create a different kind of electoral map, entering state by state or region by region the departure of a particular presidential vote in a more Republican or more Democratic direction than the normal voting of the area involved. A map so constructed for 1964, with pro-Goldwater deviations regarded as "high ground" and pro-Johnson deviations as "low," would show one primary "tilt" or gradient across the nation. The very lowest ground would appear in the northern reaches of New England, and the gradient would move upward with fair regularity all the way west to the Pacific Coast. The same gradient would appear, but much more sharply tilted still, as one moved southward to the Gulf of Mexico. In other words, Goldwater's regional emphases were indeed profoundly reflected in the vote.

As soon as one leaves the relative question of the regional and the geographic, however, the strategy was a dismal failure. For while the whole continent tilted in the expected direction, the strong Democratic tide nationally left virtually all of the country submerged under what from a Goldwater point of view was "sea level"—the 50-50 mark in popular votes. In terms of electoral votes, Goldwater was stranded on a few islands which remained above the tide on the outer Southern and Southwestern fringe of the continent. These islands represented stunning "firsts" or dramatic historic reversals in states like Georgia, Alabama, Mississippi and South Carolina. But their historic interest did not bring Goldwater any closer to the presidency.

Indeed, while Goldwater scored sharp Republican gains through the "Black Belt" of the deepest South, his assault on the South as a whole produced rather pathetic results. All observers agree, for example, that the South has been drifting away from its old status as a one-party Democratic bastion for at least two decades, if not for five or more. Hence Goldwater could have hoped to profit from four years more of this drift than Nixon, and a decade more than Eisenhower. Secondly, all observers are equally agreed that not only in the Black Belt but well north into the Border States of the South, civil rights was the prime political issue, and there is no doubt where the mass white population stood on the matter. Our data from the late 1950s and the early 1960s have consistently made clear that the potential of this issue for dramatic partisan realignment in the South had been muffled because of lack of clarity in the eyes of the mass population, prior to 1964, that either of the two major national parties offered much hope to the Southern white. It was exactly this ambiguity that Goldwater set out to remove by providing a clear party differentiation on civil rights at the national level. Putting these two ingredients together, the actual 1964 election results from the South as a whole might seem astonishing. For Goldwater actually did less well in the region than either Nixon in 1960 or Eisenhower in 1952 and 1956. One has to return at least to 1948 to find a comparably poor showing for a Republican presidential candidate; and there are reasonable treatments of the 1948 Thurmond vote which would send one back to 1944 for a parallel. Given the fact that Goldwater wooed the South so straightforwardly, and injected the new and potent ingredient of clear party differentiation on civil rights into the 1964 picture, this retrogression of Republican popular voting strength for a presidential candidate back to levels of the 1940s may seem quite incomprehensible.

A possible explanation, although one that we can summarily reject, would be that the clear party differentiation on civil (or "states'") rights which Goldwater tried to communicate failed to come across to the mass voters. Perhaps to the dismay of the liberal wing of the Republicans, however, the communication was near-perfect. In our 1960 election study, a measure of association between the two parties and the policy extremes of the civil rights controversy showed values of .02 and .05 (the Democrats only very slightly associated with a pro-civil rights position) on two different civil rights policy items. In 1964, the perceived association in the same terms on the same two items had risen to values of .54 and .50. The change in *volunteered* identifications of the two parties with the issue, among the much smaller subset of people so concerned that they brought the matter up themselves, showed even more dramatic change. In 1960 these civil rights-concerned people had tended to associate Kennedy somewhat with a pro-civil rights position, and Nixon with more of a "go-slow" approach (an association of .30). For Johnson and Goldwater in 1964, the association had mounted to .84, approaching consensus. The same volunteered materials include images of the parties, as well as of the candidates, and it is a matter of some interest to know in what measure Goldwater's 1964 position "rubbed off" on the Republican Party as a whole. In 1960, the civil rights association appeared to lie more clearly with the Kennedy-Nixon pairing (.30) than with any differences between the two parties, for these volunteered references to the parties showed only an association of .08. The comparable figure for the two parties in 1964 was .86. In short, we cannot explain why Goldwater produced a retrogression of Republican presidential voting strength in the South by suggesting that his key civil rights position failed to get across.

The Southern vote for Goldwater becomes intelligible if we add three elements to the consideration. First, while civil rights lent an important new pro-Goldwater force to the situation, various strong short-term forces which had pushed the Southern electorate in a pro-Republican direction in 1952, 1956 and 1960 were no longer present. We have argued elsewhere that the popular vote for Eisenhower and Nixon in the South was a very misleading index of the degree of solid Republican advance there. While our data do show the Republican Party inching forward in the affections of mass Southern voters, the pace has been slow; the South remains a preponderantly Democratic region. In 1952 and 1956, the Southern presidential vote swung far to the Republican side of normal for the region, just as it did in all other parts of the United States. In 1960, with the Eisenhower appeal gone, most other regions moved back toward the Democrats as we expected. This return toward normal was almost invisible in the South, since a new and offsetting short-term force—Kennedy's Catholicism—had arisen which was peculiarly repugnant to the Southern population with its concentration (Louisiana excepted) of devout and fundamentalist Protestants. Thus if any other of the Republican aspirants had run in 1964, we might have expected a delayed return toward a much more normally Democratic vote in the South. From this point of view, the injection of a new civil rights differentiation by Goldwater did not occur in a void, but was something of a replacement for other forces which had kept the Southern vote extended in a remarkably pro-Republican direction for three consecutive presidential elections.

Once we take this into account, the Republican retrogression is less perplexing, although intuitively we would expect civil rights to have an impact on the Southern voter more potent than either Eisenhower's appeal or fear of a Catholic president. It is here that the second and third considerations enter.

While Goldwater's civil rights position drew Southern whites toward the Republicans, Negroes both South and North moved monolithically toward the Democrats. Although Southern Negro voting was still limited by registration difficulties, it increased over 1960 and was almost unanimously Democratic for the first time. If this sudden increment of Negroes votes could be removed from the Southern totals, the Goldwater vote proportion would undoubtedly appear to be a slight progression, rather than a retrogression, over the Eisenhower and Nixon votes.

Finally, it must be recognized that civil rights, while the primary issue in the South, was not the only one. Beyond civil rights, Southerners reacted negatively to the Goldwater positions much as their fellow citizens elsewhere. Many Southern white respondents said in effect: "Goldwater is right on the black man, and that is very important. But he is so wrong on everything else I can't bring myself to vote for him." From this point of view, the civil rights issue did indeed have a powerful impact in the South: without it, the 1964 Goldwater vote probably would not only have slipped to normal Republican levels, but would have veered as elsewhere to the pro-Democratic side. The more general ideological appeal to what Goldwater saw as Southern "conservatism" aside from the Negro question, did not have major impact.

Much the same comments hold for the failure of "white backlash" to develop in the way many expected outside the South. Our data show that civil rights feeling did not lack impact elsewhere. But for many non-Southern whites who resented the advance of the Negro cause and the summer of discontent, the election involved other important issues as well; and Goldwater's positions on them struck such voters very negatively. Thus "white blacklash" feelings were translated into Goldwater votes by Democrats only where fear of the Negro was so intense as to blot out virtually all other considerations. Voters fitting this description existed in fair number and geographic concentration in the deepest latitudes of the South. Elsewhere, they were thinly scattered.

IV. THE ELECTION "POST-MORTEM"

Up to this point we have referred only vaguely to the many negative reactions Goldwater occasioned in all sectors of the country, which tended to dim out isolated attractions he did present. The Goldwater "image" was indeed phenomenally unfavorable. We have measured such images in the past, among other ways, by tallying the simple number of favorable and unfavorable references made by respondents to broad questions inviting them to say what they like and dislike about each of the candidates. Typically, American voters have tended on balance to speak favorably, even about candidates they were about to send down to defeat. The least favorable image we have seen—in Adlai Stevenson's second try in 1956—involved only about 52 percent of all responses that were favorable. Less than 35 percent of the Goldwater references were favorable.

Just after the election, Goldwater observed that "more than 25 million people" voted "not necessarily for me, but for a philosophy that I represent. . . ."

At another time, in assessing the magnitude of his defeat, he chastised himself for having been a personally ineffective spokesman for that philosophy. This seemed particularly odd against the descriptions of Goldwater before his nomination, in which even opponents concurred that at long last the right wing had found an articulate spokesman with a magnetic personality.

The candidate references we collect are a mixture of observations concerning the personality and leadership qualities of the individuals themselves as well as reactions to policy positions they represent in the public eye. Ideally, we could take this image material and split it cleanly into references to personal attributes as opposed to policy positions, in order to judge the accuracy of the proposition that what the public repudiated was the spokesman, and not the philosophy. Practically speaking, such divisions present many difficult coding decisions.

Nevertheless, we have sifted Johnson and Goldwater references into categories more or less purely reflecting "policy" as opposed to "personality" significance. Among the most pure policy references, Johnson's were favorable by an 80–20 margin, visibly ahead of the 69–31 balance of his total image. Mentions of Goldwater policies ran less than 30–70 favorable, thereby trailing the rest of his image slightly. In general, the farther one moves from pure policy to pure personality, Johnson's advantage declines. His "wheeler-dealer" style and the aura of conflicts-of-interest which dogged him during the campaign came through to dilute his attractiveness. Against this backdrop, Goldwater's personal "integrity" and "sincerity" drew praise. Throughout, the data suggest that Johnson was carried along to an image nearly as positive as Eisenhower's best, less by his personal characteristics than by the policies with which he was associated (many of them identified by respondents as continuations from the Kennedy Administration). For Goldwater, if anything, the reverse was true.

Aside from civil rights and a faint flutter of approval brought by Goldwater's latter-day stand against immorality, none of his major positions was attractive to voters outside the most hard-core Republican ranks. In general, the mass of public opinion has been quite unsympathetic to traditional Republican thinking in areas of social welfare and other domestic problems for several decades. A major Goldwater theme involved attacks against the increasingly heavy hand of "big government," yet this struck little in the way of a responsive chord. Most Americans in the more numerous occupational strata do not appear to feel the governmental presence (save for local civil rights situations) in any oppressive or day-to-day manner, and as a consequence simply have no reactions to the area which have any motivational significance. Among those more aware of the practices and potentials of federal government, a slight majority feels that if anything, governmental services and protections are inadequate rather than overdone. Thus for better or for worse, such contentions on Goldwater's part had little popular resonance.

Goldwater's failure to make much capital of domestic policy was not uncharacteristic of a Republican presidential candidate. What was new for a Republican, however, was his performance in the area of foreign policy. In a degree often overlooked, the 1950s were a period during which, from the point of view of many Americans inattentive to the finer lines of politics and reacting to the parties in terms of gross associations and moods, something of an uneasy equilibrium prevailed between the two major parties. Much more often than not, for these Americans the Democratic Party was the party of prosperity and good-times, but also the party more likely to blunder into war. The Republican Party, conversely, was more skilled in maintaining peace, but brought with it depression and hard times.

The foreign policies proposed by Goldwater and refracted through the press and other commentators, shifted this image more dramatically than one might have thought possible (Table II). Setting aside the large mass of voters who throughout the period did not see any particular differences between the parties in foreign policy capability, the balance of expectations in the area favored the Republicans by better than a 5-1 margin in 1956. This margin deteriorated somewhat in the late stages of the Eisenhower Administration, but remained at an imposing 2-1 edge. During the Goldwater campaign it reversed itself to a 3-1 margin favoring the Democrats.

TABLE II.   PERCEPTIONS AS TO THE PARTY MOST LIKELY TO KEEP
THE UNITED STATES OUT OF WAR IN
THE ENSUING FOUR YEARS

	1956	1960	1964
	(%)	(%)	(%)
Democrats would handle better	7	15	38
No party difference	45	46	46
Republicans would handle better	40	29	12
Don't know, not ascertained	8	10	4
	100	100	100

Thus to the many ways of describing the public's repudiation of the Goldwater candidacy, another may be added: between a party of prosperity and peace, as against a party of depression and war, there is little room for hesitation.

V. LEVELS OF PUBLIC OPINION AND THE BASES FOR MISPERCEPTION

From at least one point of view, it is less interesting that Goldwater lost the 1964 election than that he thought he had a chance to win. What most of our descriptions of the election year have had in common is a sort of chronic miscalculation of electoral reality: miscalculations of standing strength, of new strength that might be won, and of what appeals were necessary to win that new strength. Since "electoral reality" is at many points a nest of uncertainties, and since we are told that in the face of uncertainty personal needs are likely to color perceptions the more strongly, there is little surprising in the fact that Goldwater overestimated his strength and drawing power. But as these misperceptions of Goldwater and his aides went grossly beyond what many observers felt were the margins of uncertainty, they deserve closer comment.

Rather than write off these perceptions as figments of imagination, let us suppose that to persist in the way many electoral misperceptions of the right wing have persisted, there must be some sustaining reality bases; and let us ask instead what such bases might be. For "public opinion" is a protean thing, and we shall discover that there are perfectly sound ways of measuring public opinion during the 1964 campaign which, instead of illustrating Johnson's towering lead in the opinion polls, would actually have shown Goldwater enjoying a slight margin.

As is well known, public opinion was spoken of and roughly gauged long before the operations of public opinion polling were developed. What was gauged was opinion from a variety of kinds of sources: informal reactions to events among ancillary elites around the centers of government; the writings of intellectuals and newspaper editors; representations from leaders of interest groups, and the like. While it was apparent that this conglomerate of opinion came disproportionately from relatively elite and informed sources and hence need not have coincided with what the "real public" thought, beyond mass elections themselves there were (and *are,* for those who totally distrust the polls) few further ways of understanding what the public below an elite level was thinking. One of those few ways of "digging down" into the real population was letters of opinion: letters sent from unassuming constituents to public officials, "letters to the editor" composed by non-professional writers reacting to daily events and even, in no few cases, to the opinions of the editor himself. This was one level of public opinion that seemed to be generated below the elite level and that, for the observer interested in opinion beyond the localisms of municipal government, could be monitored regularly on a wide geographic base.

In our 1964 interview schedule we spent some time investigating the behavior of our respondents with respect to the writing of politically relevant letters. We ascertained first whether or not they had ever written such a letter either to any kind of public official, or to the editor of a newspaper or magazine. Then, among the minority who could recall ever writing such a letter, we went on to ask about the frequency of such activity—whether any of the letters had been written in the past four years, and if so, roughly how many such letters the respondent would estimate he had written to each of the two types of targets over that recent period.

Many aspects of these data remain intriguing despite their general predictability. Thus, for example, the materials demonstrate handsomely that the large bulk of letters to public officials or the printed media come from a tiny fraction of the population, which tends to write very repetitively. Thus, in the data summarized in Figure 1, we find that only about 15 percent of the adult population reports ever having written a letter to a public official, and of the total stream of such letters from the grass-roots, two-thirds are composed by about 3 per cent of the population. Where letters to newspapers or magazines are concerned, the constituency is even more restrictive still: only about 3 percent of the population recalls ever having written such a letter, and two-thirds of such letters are turned out by not more than half of one percent of the population. Needless to say, there is fair overlap between those who write to the printed media and those writing to public officials, so that the observer monitoring both lines of communication would tend to count the same people twice.

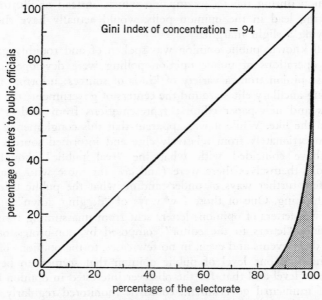

FIG. I. Letters to public officials and letter-writers within the electorate.

Furthermore, as these few people write more and more letters over time, they are counted again and again, and this of course is the phenomenon that interests us. What we have done is to reconstruct our data on various preferences relevant to the 1964 election *not* by a raw head-count, which is what a mass election measures, but rather with each individual's preference on an item weighted by the number of letters that he has reported writing to either target in the four preceding years. This provides a basis, within reasonable limits, for a fair replication of a different kind of "public opinion" as it might be assessed by a hypothetical observer.

Figure 2 contrasts "public opinion" in the head-count sense, with that form of public opinion as measured by letter-writing. We suggest that this figure may usher us into the reality world on which many of Goldwater's assessments and stratagems were based. This is not to say that Goldwater had no other bases from which to calculate public opinion. He had, among other things, public opinion as measured by the polls, and he did not entirely discredit this information. Yet as we have noted there was evidence that poll data perplexed him, not simply because they customarily brought bad news, but also because they failed to square with all of his other intuitive impressions as to what the public was thinking. In the measure that these impressions came from a variety of sources not very different from the letter-writers among the public (*i.e.,* from party activists, from campaign personnel and from informal associations), it is not hard to believe that they may have been displaced from the head-count of public opinion in much the same ways.

If we accept letter-writing for the moment then as a relevant indicator of public opinion, we see a rather marvelous change in the state of political affairs. In Figure 2(a), instead of trailing Johnson sadly in the anonymous crowd in mid-campaign, Goldwater holds a visible lead. Moving back to the time of the San Francisco convention (b), Goldwater is no longer the candidate of a small minority among Republicans and Independents, but rather is the toast of an absolute majority, even counting "no preferences" against him. In (c), we discover that not only is a vast majority of the public interested in the problem of the growing strength of the federal government, but those upset by this growing strength outnumber their opponents by a ratio approaching 3 to 1! In Figure 2(d), the displacement of "letter opinion" from public opinion is much less in part because the item wording brought a relatively consensual response. However, it is clear that Goldwater's "hard" inclinations in foreign policy are somewhat overrepresented as well in the letter-writing public.

In some ways, Figure 2(e) contains more grist than any of the others, however. First, the very form of the distributions of ideological preference differs rather dramatically. Where "public opinion" is concerned, nearly half the population falls in the "zero" category, making no affective distinction whatever between conservatives and liberals. In addition, the clustering around this zero-point is very tight: over three-quarters of the population is located within one category of the zero-point. The distribution of "letter opinion," however, is quite different. The central mode of indifference or ignorance shrinks dramatically, and voices from more extreme positions on the continuum gain in strength. Other analyses show that virtually all letter-writers rank very high on measures we have used of ideological sensitivity. Hence those who remain toward the middle of the continuum in the right half of Figure 2(e) are not there through indifference or ignorance: they understand the ideological alternatives and place themselves toward the middle of the road with forethought. And, as the bimodal shape of the distribution suggests, political discourse becomes most notably a dialogue between very mild liberals and ultra-conservatives.

It is to the world of letter opinion or one like it that the Goldwater campaign, in its original design, was addressed. At least until its late stages, it assumed an electorate with near-total ideological comprehension and sensitivity. The appeal to the Southern conservative tradition in any abstract vein was indeed joyfully received in the South, and created great ferment among a part of the Southern population. Except as this theme became concretized in day-to-day problems with Negroes, however, the part of the population affected was tiny, even though in the letter-writing and related senses it was so visible as

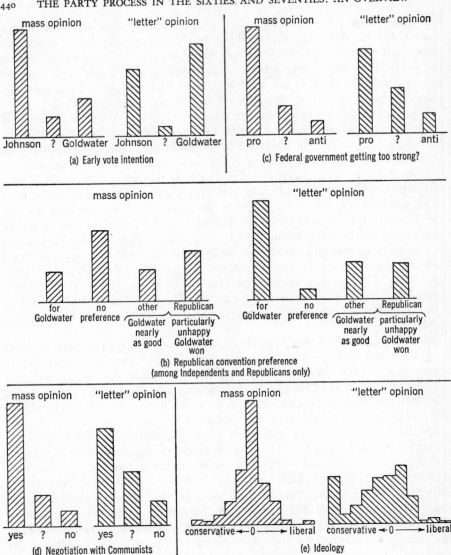

Fig. 2. Public opinion as measured by people or political letters.

to appear to be "most of the South," politically speaking.

Similarly, the distribution of the population in this world of letter opinion helped maintain persistent overestimations of strength. Empirically speaking, the center of Goldwater support lay roughly in the third bar of the figure on the conservative side. It weakened rapidly with any further steps toward the center, and was relatively solid in the outer two bars of the graph. If one looks at "letter opinion" with this zone in mind, it would appear that the base of standing Goldwater support was very substantial. Goldwater hoped to firm up the support on his side of the center sufficiently to create a majority, and in this figure it would have taken only a modest extension of influence to achieve this. In the world of public opinion relevant for mass elections, however, the distribution of actual and potential support was radically different. Rather than starting from a solid base of support on the conservative wing, the initial springboard was scarcely populated at all. To win a majority, a much deeper penetration into the center would have been required.

In the measure that we have delineated in Figure 2(e), the kind of political environment familiar to many practicing politicians, we can also better understand the first of our puzzles, the myth of the stay-at-home Republicans. For ultra-conservatives who found a wide measure of social support and resonance for their views in the world of public opinion which they understood, it must indeed have been perplexing that uniquely at election time, and uniquely in vote totals, this vigorous support had a habit of evaporating. How could one interpret this gross discrepancy between what one heard and read about public sentiments and what happened at the polls? The easiest explanation was that strong conservatives in large numbers simply refused to go to the polls, however vigorously they would express themselves otherwise. And as soon as a useful reason was worked out as to why this willful nonvoting should occur, a theory was born. It persisted in part because it was a handy tactical weapon, but it persisted in some part as well because the discrepant realities which helped to catalyze the theory also persisted. For its proponents, the election of 1964 was a sobering reality test.

VI. CONCLUSIONS

It should be apparent that the phenomena we have examined in this paper have a significance that stretches considerably beyond the 1964 election, or questions of the credibility of public opinion polls, or the playing of games with the epistemologies of practicing politicians, fascinating though each of these subjects may be.

But the more important implications flow from the reflection that while these opinion worlds may be discrepant from one another in many regards, and it behooves us not to confuse them, it is not a simple matter of fact *vs.* fantasy: both worlds are real, and have real effects on the political process. Save for the obvious fact that the reality of "one man, one vote," governs the mass election with greater or lesser modification, while other public-opinion realities like the letter-writing world tend to hold sway otherwise, we know all too little empirically about the counterpoint between the two in actual political systems, and the normative significance of motivation-weighted votes is largely unexamined.

However this may be, if the reality of one of these worlds was manifest on Election Day, 1964, then the reality of the other was equally apparent in the San Francisco convention. For it is obvious that the intense levels of political motivation which underlie the letter-writing of the ultra-conservative wing are part and parcel of the ingredients which led to a Republican convention delegation so markedly discrepant from either the rank-and-file of the Party or its customary leadership. What had been lacking around the country in bodies was made up for in dedication; but the outcome of the convention was in no sense the less real for it. And from this juxtaposition of two worlds, the oddities of the 1964 election grew.

THE GOLDWATER PHENOMENON: PURISTS, POLITICIANS, AND THE TWO-PARTY SYSTEM *

Aaron B. Wildavsky

THE Goldwater phenomenon is the great mystery of American politics. His nomination as presidential candidate by the Republican Party and his campaign for election have profoundly challenged accepted theories of American politics. Merely to enumerate some of the puzzling questions suggests how badly we need explanations.

How was it possible for a presidential nomination to go to a staunch conservative whose popularity among the electorate was known to be exceedingly low and who was far from being the preferred choice of most Republican voters? Why, in a competitive two-party system in which leaders normally seek essentially the same votes, did the parties seem to be hurtling further apart instead of coming closer together? Why, indeed, did not the minority party (the Republicans) imitate the majority party (the Democrats) in search of votes as had previously been the case? Why did the Goldwater Republicans not follow the traditional practice of "balancing the ticket" by choosing a more liberal person as their vice-presidential candidate? Why did Goldwater and his followers put such great stress on consistency and yet appear so inconsistent in their pronouncements? Since Goldwater said that the race question should not become an issue in the campaign, why did he refuse to take the steps which would have helped accomplish that end—voting for the Civil Rights Act of 1964, and making some conciliatory statement to Negroes? Why did Goldwater slant his appeal to working-class people and Johnson to middle- and upper-class voters in an apparent shift from the usual tendencies in electioneering? Since the candidates were further apart on issues than at any time in recent decades, why was there so little discussion of issues and so much talk about personalities in the campaign?

To put the questions in this way suggests that we are surprised; that our expectations concerning the behavior of parties and politicians have been violated. Ordinarily, we expect both major parties to choose popular candidates with a good chance of winning. The death wish is not supposed to be dominant among politicians. Party leaders are expected to conciliate groups of voters in

* From Aaron B. Wildavsky, "The Goldwater Phenomenon: Purists, Politicians, and the Two-Party System," in *The Review of Politics*, Vol. 27, No. 3 (July, 1965), pp. 386–413. Copyright, 1965, by the University of Notre Dame. Reprinted by permission of the editors.

order to get at least part of their vote. Abandoning a large number of citizens to the enemy is not usually done. The vice-presidential nominee is usually chosen, as were Lyndon Johnson and Henry Cabot Lodge in 1960, to broaden (not further to restrict) the appeal of the party. And the major parties often accommodate themselves to the most popular part of the opposition's policies in order to enhance their prospects of victory. Yet none of these things happened—at least on the Republican side—in 1964. Why? . . .

SPECIAL POLITICAL CONDITIONS

By far the most important special condition of 1964 was that for the first time in 30 years there was no moderate Republican candidate who was both popular with the voters and willing to contest the nomination actively. Whatever the reasons, Nelson Rockefeller simply did not appeal to voters in Republican primaries. Henry Cabot Lodge would not campaign and go on the ballot in California. Richard Nixon had ruled out an active public role for himself. And Governor Scranton could not or would not overcome his reluctance to seek the nomination until it was too late. It is difficult to stop something with nothing, as Goldwater's opponents learned to their sorrow.

Participation in presidential primaries is usually the preferred strategy of aspirants who cannot be chosen by compromise at the national conventions. Men like Kennedy and Humphrey in 1960 or Goldwater with Rockefeller in 1964 actively contest many primaries because they have to establish overwhelming support before the conventions meet in order to have a chance. Candidates like Nixon, Lodge, and Scranton, however, may reasonably hope to be the choice of the convention after the front-runners have demonstrated that they cannot win. So they stay out of primaries and wait to pick up the pieces. This strategy proved disastrous in 1964 because Nelson Rockefeller was unexpectedly unable to play the role allotted to him; he failed to defeat Goldwater in the California primary and the contest was over before it was supposed to have started.

Another significant condition involved the almost universal expectation that no Republican candidate had a chance of beating Lyndon Johnson. This belief vastly reduced the persuasiveness of the usual argument that the Republican Party should put up a popular candidate who might win. Goldwater's opponents had to content themselves with the much weaker argument that another candidate would lose by less.

A strong case might still have been made that the fortunes of Republicans running for state and congressional offices would be improved, or at least not seriously impaired, by running a more popular candidate for the presidency. But this argument was weak in some respects. Republicans from the South and portions of the West and Southwest contended that Goldwater would run as well as, if not better than, any other Republican. And some Republicans were so intensely committed to a conservative victory at the convention, and so frustrated at their previous inability to win the nomination, that they convinced themselves that a "hidden conservative vote" would emerge to help them at the state level.

There were state leaders who winced at the thought of a disastrous defeat in November. But there were fewer such leaders than there might have been precisely because the Republicans are a minority party. There were only 17 Republican state governors at the Republican Convention. These were the men who might have had sufficient hierarchial control over their delegations to keep them from precipitantly joining the Goldwater bandwagon. In the absence of such central leadership, the tendency of most delegates to favor a highly conservative candidate had greater scope to manifest itself.

One might suppose that when the goal of nominating a winner could not be met, some of the delegates would have put a premium on the goal of party unity. To be sure, there was less urgency in achieving unity because victory in the election was not expected anyhow. But if defeat seemed to be inevitable, delegates who cared about the Republican Party as an organization might have hoped at least to salvage unity. Goldwater had the advantage here because he could work to unify the party around him. Since he had the lead, his backers could claim that the great danger to party unity lay in stubborn refusal to accept him.

Again, the belief that the Republican Party was bound to lose the election not only reduced the need to nominate a popular candidate, but also opened up the possibility of using the conflict over the nomination as a means of gaining control of the various state parties. The leaders still cared about winning, but their notion of the relevant contest changed. Wherever Goldwater had strong support among Republican activists, opposing party factions could be beaten down in the name of support for him. Had there been a popular candidate to oppose Goldwater, the opposition might have elected to fight the battle around this champion. In the circumstances, however, they were faced in many states with the choice of going down to defeat or nominally accepting Goldwater. Some Republican leaders, as was apparently the case with Charles Percy in Illinois, decided to try to maintain their influence within the party by rolling with the Goldwater tide and thus living to fight another day. This is precisely what Governor DiSalle of Ohio did in 1960 when a hostile faction of the Democratic Party threatened to use John F. Kennedy's popularity as a club with which to beat him. By supporting Kennedy, he was able to defeat his opponents within the party.

Although its effects are difficult to determine, a third contemporary condition must also be mentioned. The impact of the civil rights issue had given rise to hopes that, for the first time since the unsuccessful presidential campaigns of William Jennings Byran (1896, 1900, 1908), a party might win by carrying a coalition of southern and western states. The attraction of such a coalition was that it made a conservative candidate more plausible by removing the necessity to appeal on the basis of welfare issues to the labor and minority groups in the populous industrial states. These carry so much weight in the electoral college that the Republican Party has had to appeal to them in the past through moderate candidates and platforms.

Yet even if Goldwater's supporters could convince themselves that his cause was not utterly hopeless, the very fact that they chose him suggests that winning the election was not uppermost in their minds. Politicians have been accused of many things; up till now no one has accused them of wishing to lose elections. Has the United States, then, given birth to a new kind of political activist for whom other things rank above winning office? Interviews held with Goldwater delegates to the Republican Convention may help to answer this question.

PURISTS VS. POLITICIANS

"The delegates are for Goldwater because they agree with his philosophy of government. That's what you people will never understand—we're committed to his whole approach." This Goldwater delegate was undoubtedly correct. There was a remarkable fit between Goldwater and a substantial majority (approximately 80 percent) of his followers. What they liked about Goldwater, however, was not merely or even primarily his policy positions but rather his "approach," his style of operation. When we asked Goldwater delegates to tell us what they most liked about their candidate only a few mentioned his position on the issues, and those who did were content with brief references to constitutional principles like states' rights.

By far the most frequent characterizations of Goldwater referred to his consistency, honesty, integrity, and willingness to stick by principles. It was not so much his principles (though these were undoubtedly important) but the belief that he stuck to them that counted most with his supporters. "He can be trusted." "He is straightforward." "He does not compromise." "He doesn't pander to the public; he's against expediency." "He is frank." "He has courage." "He stands up for what he believes." "He won't play footsie with the people." "He votes his convictions when he knows he's right." "He doesn't go along with the crowd." "He meets issues head-on." "Goldwater speaks about things others avoid. Most politicians like to avoid issues." "He keeps promises." "He doesn't change his mind." "He is not confused." As one of Goldwater's supporters perceptively observed, "He's different than most politicians." And so are most of Goldwater's followers "different than most politicians."

It thus becomes possible to divide delegates into "politicians" and "purists" according to their characteristic modes of approaching political life. While not all Goldwater supporters were purists (some 20 percent were politicians), all purists were Goldwater supporters.

In order to derive typologies of politicians and purists, let us observe the "pure" types as they were revealed through interviews at the Republican Convention. This Goldwater purist was a delegate from a rural area in Pennsylvania attending his first convention.

Interviewer: What qualities should a presidential candidate have?
Delegate: Moral integrity.
I.: Should he be able to win the election?

D.: No; principles are more important. I would rather be one against 20,000 and believe I was right. That's what I admire about Goldwater. He's like that.

I.: Are most politicians like that?

D.: No, unfortunately.

I.: What do you like about Goldwater?

D.: I am in sympathy with many of his philosophies of government, but I like him personally for his moral integrity. I always believed that a candidate should carry out his promises. Scranton didn't do that. But now, for the first time in my life, we have a candidate who acts as he believes. He doesn't change his position when it is expedient.

I.: Do you think that if the party loses badly in November it ought to change its principles?

D.: No. I'm willing to fight for these principles for ten years if we don't win.

I.: For 50 years?

D.: Even 50 years.

I.: Do you think it's better to compromise a little to win than to lose and not compromise?

D.: I had this problem in my district. After we fighters had won [the nomination for] the congressional seat the local [Republican] machine offered to make a deal: they wouldn't oppose our candidate if we didn't oppose theirs. I refused because I didn't see how I could make a deal with the men I'd been opposing two years ago for the things they did. So I lost and I could have won easily. I've thought about it many times, because if I had agreed I could have done some good at least. But I don't believe that I should compromise one inch from what I believe deep down inside.

Here we begin to see the distinguishing characteristics of the purists: their emphasis on internal criteria for decision, on what they believe "deep down inside"; their rejection of compromise; their lack of orientation toward winning; their stress on the style and purity of decision—integrity, consistency, adherence to internal norms.

The professionals look at politics quite differently. Here is a California delegate strongly for Goldwater, with more than 15 years in party work, attending his third Republican convention.

Interviewer: You seem different from many of the Goldwater supporters. How would you characterize your position in comparison with them?

Delegate: Yes, I'm more practical. I realize you have to live together. For example, I'm going up now to a meeting of the California Republican committee and we've got to handle a liberal candidate and an ultra-conservative. I'm going to urge them to accept the liberal because we've got to work together. We [the Republicans] are a minority party in California and we can't afford to squabble amongst ourselves. The art of politics is the art of compromise. If I can get a whole loaf, I'll take it. If not, I'll take half rather than lose it all.

I.: What would Goldwater do about the Cuban situation?

D.: Well, it's there now and we'll just have to live with it.

I.: The Berlin Wall?

D.: He won't tear it down; I know him very well.

I.: Social Security?

D.: We've had it for a long time, it's part of our system. That's something some of these Goldwater people don't realize. They're a new breed and sort of naive on things like this. They think you can suddenly shift the whole range of government to the right. What they don't realize is that you can only bend a little back away from the left.

I.: What if Goldwater loses by a landslide?

D.: Well, I don't think that will happen.

I.: Suppose it does?

D.: Well, then, maybe the people aren't ready for a change. . . . Yes, we'll have to try to change, maybe a little more toward the liberal side.

The belief in compromise and bargaining; the sense that public policy is made in small steps rather than big leaps; the concern with conciliating the opposition and broadening public appeal; and the willingness to bend a little to capture public support are all characteristics of the traditional politician in the United States.

Having sketched some of the esssential attributes of purists and politicians, we can proceed to a closer examination of these two types, with special emphasis on the purists.

WINNING ELECTIONS

"I've talked to some of the California delegates," a citizen who observed the convention informed us, "and I don't understand them at all; they talk like they don't care if we win." In a sense he was wrong, because the delegates desperately wanted Goldwater to win. But our informant was essentially correct in the sense that they cared more about maintaining their purity—"I would rather lose and be right"—than about winning. The essential element of this style was a devotion to principles especially the principle that they should have, maintain, and cherish their principles.

When asked why they entered politics, Goldwater delegates often answered, "For the same reason as any man: principles." When asked if the party should change some of its policies if Goldwater lost badly, the delegates responded by reiterating their devotion to principles. "God, no. These are American principles; these are what we stand for." "No, we want a clear party which will represent principles to the people." "I'd rather stick by the real principles this country was built on than win. Popularity isn't important; prestige isn't important; it's the principles that matter."

Although the politicians put a high premium on popularity with the electorate, there were things they would not do and ways they would not prefer to win. A Scranton delegate, in politics for many years in Philadelphia, pointed out that in his white, upper-class ward he and his party had benefited from a "white blacklash" issue in a local election. "But we don't want that; that divides the country. We don't want whites and blacks to fight: it's not good for the country." A New Jersey delegate with many years of political experience did not really like any of the candidates for the nomination and feared that the party would fare badly at the polls if Goldwater were nominated. Yet he felt that things could happen: "a white backlash building up if the Negroes have a lot of big demonstrations in the cities; or if Viet Nam blew up in our faces. But I'd rather lose than have those things happen. I'd rather lose than have race fights or war."

One great difference between the purists and the politicians lay in what they would consider grounds for preferring not to win. The politicians emphasized specific unfortunate consequences for people in the country such as race riots and war. The purists emphasized departures from internal principles held by their party leaders such as consistency, integrity and standing firm. The politicians were oriented toward what happens to other people, the purists toward their individual consciences.

EMPHASIZING DIFFERENCES

An important component of the Goldwater style was the guiding principle that the parties ought to be different. The maintenance of wide and sharp differences between the parties was seen as a fundamental purpose of engaging in politics. As an enthusiastic woman delegate from New Jersey put it "I think everything should be an issue, civil rights should be an issue, Cuba should be an issue. This is the first time a campaign will be on issues; I think it's wonderful. It's just terrible the way personality has been in politics, like Kennedy winning on his hair and teeth and Nixon losing because there was a shadow on his chin . . . it's ridiculous."

Hence when Goldwater supporters were asked whether they should balance the ticket with a liberal vice-presidential candidate, they replied: "We don't want a blurred image, we've been a me-too party for too long. We want to take a clear position." If, in order to provide clear differences between the parties, the Republicans lose, that is all right. For "even if the party loses at least we have presented a clear alternative to the people. At least we'll have a strong party." What is meant by strong? "Cohesive, united on principles." The chorus of Goldwater purists rose to a crescendo when they insisted, in almost identical words, "We don't want to become a me-too party, we don't want to be the same as the Democrats." The possibility arose, therefore, that if they were offered accommodations or compromises on issues they would reject them because they wanted to be different.

The ideal party of the purists is not merely a conservative party; it is also a distinct and separate community of co-believers who differ with the opposition party all down the line. To this extent their style merges with that of the liberal party reformers, described by James Wilson in *The Amateur Democrat,* who wish to see the parties represent clear and opposed alternatives and gain votes only through appeals on policy difference rather than on such "irrational" criteria as personality, party identification, or ethnic status. But the Goldwater purists went even further in their willingness to cast aside whole groups of voters who did not agree with them. "We won't get Negro votes anyway, so there's no point in trying." "They can vote for the other party for all I care." "We won't change our principles just to get a few votes from

Negroes." In the same spirit, Barry Goldwater suggested that people who favored the kind of government the United States has had since 1932 should vote not for him but for his opponents.

For the politicians, the desire to win is intimately connected with the belief that a political party should try to get as much support from as many diverse groups as possible. In describing the qualities a presidential candidate should have, a professional will say, "He should be diplomatic. He should be able to gather support from a lot of groups underneath him. That's what Eisenhower had, that's what Kennedy had, and that's what Johnson has. You know there's one thing about politics, there's no such thing as second place, you don't get anything for coming in second."

Hence the professionals were concerned with losing a substantial part of the small Negro vote they had received in the past. "You just can't go around throwing away votes. The object of a party is to draw voters together to the party, not to push them away." A delegate from Philadelphia was more specific. He had "nothing personal against Goldwater" but feared that if he were to run "we'll get the hell kicked out of us. We've been out of [state] power for ten or 12 years. Now we're getting some of the Polish vote and the Italians don't treat us too bad. The Jews and the Negroes go about 75 percent against us, but at least we get part of the Negro vote and that helps us hold the line in the state generally."

To their dichotomous view of political parties and their belief that issue preferences were the only moral way to choose between them, the purists added a strong desire to simplify political choice: a party for the growth of government and a party against; a party which believes in standing up to the enemy and one which believes in appeasement; a party which believes in private initiative and one which wishes to stifle it; the party of free enterprise versus the party of socialism.

The desire to dichotomize and simplify found expression in ways of locating political supporters and opponents. Perhaps the most charming example came from a California delegate who expressed the wish to see all liberals in the East and all conservatives in the West. Presumably, if one knew where a man came from, one could immediately discern his political tendency. Many delegates voiced the desire to divide friend from foe by simple criteria and then do joyous battle.

THE "PRIVATIZATION" OF POLITICS

We may sum up the Goldwater style by saying that it represented a virtually complete privatization of politics. The private conscience of the leader rather than his public responsibilities became the focal point of politics. Internal criteria—possession of, devotion to, standing up for private principles—became the standard of political judgment. This is far from Burke's principle that the representative be allowed to use his own judgment about what course of action will bring the greatest benefit to his constituents. Rather, the constituents disappear, and we are left with a political leader determining policy on the basis of compatibility with his private principles.

From this perspective we can better understand why Goldwater voted against the Civil Rights Act of 1964 despite his agreeing with the view that the race issue should not become a matter of political partisanship. Goldwater's conscience dictated that he vote against an act which contained two sections he felt violated the Constitution. Although he knew that the act would pass anyway, he was simply unwilling to sacrifice his private conscience in order to achieve what he agreed was the public good. Goldwater undoubtedly believed that adherence to the Constitution was also part of the public interest. The point is that when faced with competing conceptions of public good, he chose a remote abstraction over a direct and specific human value. Nor would he or his supporters agree to make rather innocuous concessions on the civil rights plank in order to placate Negroes because that would have suggested compromise; and compromise suggests that one has not stuck to one's principles.

Once the platform became identified as a Goldwater platform, presumably derived from careful scrutiny of conscience, it became a matter of principle not to permit any alteration whatsoever, even if this meant alienating other party factions on the extremism issue. The very idea that the Republican Party should try to balance its ticket with a less conservative vice-presidential candidate was uniformly regarded as immoral and despicable. Such thoughts reeked of inconsistency, me-tooism, expediency, and other political vices stemming from the lack of conscience in politics.

Conspicuously missing from purist thought was consideration of voters. Party was defined entirely without reference to the people who would have to vote for it. True, the purists believed that there was a "hidden Republican vote," and they fully expected a huge upsurge of support as most Americans discovered that a party embracing their most cherished principes had at last appeared on the scene. But the "real Republican Party," as they were fond of calling it, was far removed from vulgar pandering for votes. It stood on its principles. It did not change to attract votes. Voters were attracted to it when people changed.

One can see the privatization of politics at work when Goldwater delegates expressed their feelings about President Johnson and former President Eisenhower. Extremely hostile feelings were expressed about both men because they were seen as traditional politicians gifted in the arts of compromise. Goldwater's castigation of Johnson as a "faker," for example, was uniformly regarded as accurate and appropriate. "Originally and historically," a delegate told us, "Johnson was a conservative, but he's willing to do things, to change to stay in power. This shows weakness of character."

The purists did not think it appropriate that a Senator on becoming President should act differently. If a public official need consult only his private conscience, of course, there should be little change in his actions in different offices. If Johnson acted differently in the two offices this could only be because "he has no principles. L.B.J. is a consummate politician. He is inconsistent and immoral." Goldwater is different. "He doesn't talk from both sides of his mouth."

If the essence of politics is to be found in the relationship between leaders and their principles, one would ask quite different questions and give much different answers to queries about the positions taken by candidates. When we asked delegates about Goldwater's position on racial matters, the purists would always respond by saying that Goldwater himself was not bigoted. They knew the exact percentage of employees in the Goldwater department store in Phoenix who are non-Caucasians. They pointed with pride to this statistic as evidence of their candidate's favorable disposition toward Negroes. There was no mention of what Goldwater might do as President; there was no understanding that the public role of a Presidential aspirant might be of interest. Negro delegates to be sure, could not have cared less about Goldwater's personal predilections. They wanted to know what he would do for Negroes in his capacity as President of the United States. That Goldwater shared this perspective became evident during the campaign when he asked if Negroes would not rather have a President who dealt with race relations as a matter of conscience instead of as a political football. Since political action is a major method of redressing Negro grievances, it is not surprising that Goldwater failed to get his conscience accepted as a substitute for favorable presidential action.

The privatization of politics leads to an *a priori* approach to politics. Problems are met by stating one's first principles and assuming that they must be relevant to whatever is in hand. One gets no sense whatsoever that Goldwater purists approached problems by inquiring how special circumstances might be taken into account in order to achieve desirable results. The pragmatic spirit was completely lacking. Indeed, the purists manifested amazingly little interest in specific issues. In our interviews at the convention, we simply could not get them to talk about anything concrete, unless references to welfare-statism and too-much-government are considered specific replies. The purists did express strong belief in the importance of being interested in issues, but this is not equivalent to being interested in specific issues.

All this makes one wonder whether the Goldwater phenomenon did not represent a retreat from politics through politics. Purists are interested in being interested in politics. They care about people caring about politics. They are far more concerned about the need for substantial differences between the parties than they are about the differences themselves. If only one has principles and stands up for them, their position seems to suggest, the messy world of politics—compromise, bargaining, exceptions, modifications, inconsistencies—will disappear. Political style thus becomes a substitute for politics itself.

CAMPAIGN STYLE

The campaign speeches of Barry Goldwater are a testimonal to the extraordinary importance he assigned to political style. It would be difficult to find another candidate so insistent that people not vote for him if they did not share his views. Rarely has so much attention been given to stylistic reasons for supporting a candidate. This approach is epitomized in a Goldwater speech delivered to a rally at Madison Square Garden and its overwhelming stylistic emphasis is noteworthy.

Goldwater began by saying that although he knew what statements would get him the votes he was not going to make them.

> I can't help wondering sometimes, if you've asked yourselves why my campaign is what it is.
>
> I wonder, my fellow Americans, if you think I don't know what views would be most popular. Do you think I don't know what labor wants to hear, what management . . . what housewives and diplomats and white-collar workers want to hear?
>
> Do you honestly think, after all these years in politics, that I don't know the easy ways to get votes? The promises to make? The subjects to talk about—and the ones to avoid? Well, I do!

He then proceeded to tell his audience why he did not "take the easy way."

> First of all, if I just went around telling people what they want to hear, I'd sound like Lyndon Baines Johnson. And I still think the American people are entitled to a choice.
>
> But more important, if I had to cater to every special interest in the country to get elected, I wouldn't want the job.

Like his followers, Goldwater was a political purist who objected to telling people what they wanted to hear, catering to "special interests," or being like the other party in order to gain popularity.

As a political purist, Goldwater was careful about the kind of people who should and should not support him. The Nazi and Fascist types, the Communists and left-wing radicals, were clearly beyond the pale. But Goldwater included "The lazy, dole-happy people who want to feed on the fruits of somebody else's labor" and people who believed in promises and those "who are willing to believe that Communism can be 'accommodated.'" Most revealing, for our purposes, was his characterization of the people he believed would vote for him.

> People who take the trouble to reread, thoughtfully, the Declaration of Independence and the Constitution of the United States will vote for me. . . .
>
> People who have learned to be suspicious of never-ending promises of "something for nothing"—they will vote for me.
>
> People who have the courage and the intelligence to listen to the truth, and think about it. People whose votes can't be bought. They'll vote for me.

People who are sick to death of politicians coming out in favor of happiness and declaring war on misery. People who are fed up with so-called leaders of government promising to legislate worry out of existence. People who will listen for a little while to such transparent, vote-grabbing demagoguery and say—"Baloney." They'll vote for me.

But most of all, it will be the people who know that something must be done.

The types of people who Goldwater thought would vote for him were stylists. They were not merely people who agreed with Goldwater on specific issues. Rather, they were people who harked back to basic principles, such as may be found in the nation's venerable documents, people who were suspicious of promises, who had courage, who were "sick to death of politicians," and who knew that something must be done.

CAMPAIGN STRATEGIES

Fought between a political purist and a traditional politician, the 1964 election campaign was most peculiar by recent American standards. The parties appeared to slant their appeals somewhat differently from past emphases. The Democrats appealed much more to upper-income groups and the Republicans to lower-income groups than was usually the case. Despite (or perhaps because of the larger differences in positions on issues, questions of personality and morality—was Goldwater irresponsible or Johnson a crook?—seemed to dominate the campaign. For the first time in many years, the Republicans made more appeals based on party identification than did the Democrats. And the candidate who put so much weight on consistency appeared to his opponents at least to be a most inconsistent man. Beginning with a brief discussion of the usual pattern of campaign strategies, we shall use our analysis of the Goldwater style and the specific context of the time in an effort to provide a coherent explanation of these apparent anomalies.

Holding the allegiance of approximately three out of every five voters, the Democratic Party can expect to win any election which is determined on the basis of party preference. As a result, Democratic candidates typically stress their party identification, while Republican candidates play it down. In 1964, however, the fact that Senator Goldwater was so far to the right of most Republican voters gave President Johnson the opportunity to detach a significant portion of that party's traditional supporters. In search of this Republican vote, Johnson eschewed the usual partisan appeals. Instead, he went out of his way to praise the good old Republican Party of yesteryear and to ask the electorate to reject the unnamed extremists who had temporarily taken control of it. While maintaining his party's historic position on welfare issues, Johnson carefully toned down his comments so as not to give moderate Republicans an excuse for voting against him. If he could not positively attract Republicans, he would do nothing to repel them. So the President adopted the stance of national unity, calling insistently on Americans to get together against certain demagogues and hotheads who might get the United State into a nuclear war or foment racial strife.

So far as domestic welfare policies were concerned, there was overwhelming evidence that the vast majority of voters were far closer to the liberal Democrats than they were to the most conservative Republicans. Hence Democratic candidates traditionally hit hard on "bread and butter" issues, while Republicans were caught in a dilemma: they could not please their conservative party activists and the voters at the same time. Since there are many more voters than activists, Republican candidates have normally chosen to go along with most welfare policies, claiming that they could carry out these measures better and cheaper. But Goldwater's conservatism and his unwillingness to change course to get votes made it difficult for him to make any appeal on welfare matters. As a result, Lyndon Johnson was placed in the unique position of being able to make gains on two issues—prosperity and poverty—even while playing down an aggressive pro-welfare stand in order not to alienate Republicans. And Goldwater spent a good deal of time plaintively arguing that he would not really take social security checks from the pockets of workers when they were not looking.

In the realm of foreign policy, the Democrats were subject to attack as "the party of war" because they happened to be in power during the three major wars of this century. Given Goldwater's proclivity for an adventurous foreign policy, however, a product in part of the style of "stand up and be counted," he could hardly expect to gain votes by appearing to advocate extension of military conflict in South Viet Nam, Berlin, Cuba, and other places. After all, Eisenhower made political capital out of promising "to bring the boys back from Korea," not by promising to send more of them over there. Again, Goldwater was placed on the defensive. He had the extraordinary task of assuring voters that he would not launch a nuclear war immediately upon assuming office.

If voting behavior theory was correct, as the election returns would suggest, Goldwater could not pick up votes on either foreign policy or on the broad spectrum of domestic welfare policy. At the same time, he could not count on full support from normal Republican identifiers and thus had to make repeated calls for party unity. What kind of appeal, then, could he make and to whom?

The answer appeared to be that he could appeal to ordinarily Democratic working class as well as lower-middle-class voters on the racial issue. Hence the many references to safety in the streets and the scarcely veiled suggestions that women would know what he was talking about. Yet this approach also created problems for Goldwater. As a self-professed constitutional conservative, he could hardly call for a federal police force or for most forms of national action except, perhaps, for the appointment of tougher judges. His running mate, William Miller, could suggest that the jobs of workers would be taken by hordes of immigrants who would be let in by new immigration procedures proposed by the Johnson Administration. The trouble was that many of the workers who might have been influenced by this type of appeal came from ethnic groups sensitive to selective limitation of immigration.

A surface reading of the election returns suggests that outside the South the so-called "white backlash" could not have been very large. The workers whose "authoritarian tendencies" presumably left them responsive to a racial appeal, were among the most fervent supporters of the Democratic Party. Racial feelings would have had to be highly salient and intense for them to vote against their traditional party and the social welfare legislation which is so important to them. If a group had felt its jobs threatened, or if it was desperately trying to ward off Negro encroachment on its residential areas, it might be sufficiently moved to change the direction of its vote. But there simply were not enough people in this kind of position. Apparently, more Republicans were frightened by Goldwater than whites were frightened by Negroes.

On the basis of this analysis, derived from standard voting behavior theory, it was possible to predict long before the election that Goldwater would suffer a drastic defeat. Nor is there any reason to believe that the outcome will be different in 1968 or 1972 so long as the overwhelming purist component of the Goldwater conservatives prevents them from making more successful appeals to the voters. Indeed, immediately after the election Goldwater proposed that the parties be organized into pure conservative and liberal denominations. There cannot be much hope for the future when the first reaction of a leader who has suffered overwhelming defeat is to give away to the opposition a substantial percentage of his party's support—the Republican moderates and liberals.

CAMPAIGN MORALITY

The focus of the campaign upon problems of personal competence was directly connected with the existence of profound differences on public policy. No doubt it was naive to believe that the candidates could differ more and more over issues while saying better and better things about each other. Once Goldwater had moved rather far away from positions traditionally taken by Republican presidential candidates, Johnson seized the opportunity to gain Republican votes by denouncing Goldwater as an extremist. The charge of extremism was built into a situation in which any party moved far from where it had been, especially if it also moved far from the voters. It would be easy to say that Goldwater responded to being called an extremist by raising the morality issue or that, lacking appeal on other issues, he used the Bobby Baker episode or undermine Johnson's claim to being defender of the traditional political faith. There may be some truth in this. But I believe that we have more significant answers at our disposal if we turn again to Goldwater and his followers as political purists.

If politics should be concerned with the private conscience of the political leader and his stock of basic principles, as many Goldwater supporters believe, then the morality of the candidates necessarily assumes prime importance. The politician is immediately condemned as immoral by virtue of his usual practices. He is immoral because he alters his role orientations to suit different constituencies. He is immoral because, at times, he alters his position to gain votes. Even when the politician hangs on to his fundamental position but gives a little to assure a wider consensus he is immoral because of his inconsistency and vacillation. Because Lyndon Johnson epitomizes the practicing politician, famed for his love of votes, compromise, bargaining, maneuver, and conciliation, his immorality was beyond all dispute for the political purists.

There is still another way in which concentration on political style made morality a central focus of election campaigns. The Goldwater purists were patently unwilling to believe that difficulties facing America, particularly in foreign affairs, might have been due to forces beyond the control of any leader. On the contrary, they thought that if the United States just had the right approach, if it stood up for what it believed and enunciated its principles with sufficient force, its problems would be solved. This was presumably what Goldwater meant when he said that he had a "rational solution" to the cold war, without specifying what it was, or when he insisted that our foreign policy difficulties were not complex but simple. If the world situation was not exactly rosy, therefore, the blame lay with immoral leaders who behaved as politicians instead of as purists. They sold out their country because they either did not have the right American principles or did not stand up for them or both. From the Goldwater point of view, it was necessary only to look at the state of the world to see that American political leaders were immoral. Reasoning from effect to cause, the purists would be bound to place the simple moral test—does the candidate have the right political style?—at the heart of a campaign taking place when decay had set in from the remotest Asian principality to the nearest city street.

CAMPAIGN ISSUES

Although the candidates in 1964 were not subject to the kind of abuse characteristic of the early days of the American republic, there apparently was more personal vilification than in the past decade or two. Of greater importance for our purposes, however, is the undoubted fact that in a campaign in which the parties were further apart on issues than they have been in our time, at least since 1936 and possibly in this century, there was relatively little discussion of issues. Certainly, the existence of wide and deep policy differences did not, as has sometimes been thought, lead directly to a campaign focusing on specific issues. Why not?

It might be the case that when candidates are virtually identical in their views, there is little else for them to talk about except their respective personalities. When they are moderately far apart, separated by marginal but real differences, however, the possibility for fruitful debate may be at its highest point. For the parties are then far enough apart to make debates meaningful and yet close enough together so that a real dialogue is possible. Both the candidates and attentive publics can understand what a marginal change from one proposal to another might mean. Yet when the parties and candidates are separated by a huge gulf there may literally be nothing to talk about. The differences may be so severe as to appear to be beyond discussion.

The experience of the 1964 presidential campaign suggests that the old proposition, the greater the differences on issues, the greater the discussion of specific issues, might be replaced with a new hypothesis, discussion of issues varies directly with moderate, marginal disagreements on issues and inversely with the extremes of total agreement or total disagreement. Such has been the situation in France where election campaigns typically involved disagreements among the parties closest to each other and little or no direct confrontation among the parties which were furthest apart in ideology.

CAMPAIGN CONSISTENCY

In the light of Goldwater's professed devotion to consistency a major paradox of the campaign was his apparent inconsistency. The syndrome characteristically began with a Goldwater statement about atomic defoliation in South Viet Nam, or giving military commanders control of "conventional" nuclear weapons, or about extremism not being a vice if it is in defense of liberty. In the ensuing furor, Goldwater complained that he had been misquoted or misconstrued; he issued clarifications which puzzled newsmen, and the cycle began again. In other instances, Goldwater maintained consistency; comments that the Tennessee Valley Authority ought to be sold to private interests are not usually made in the heart of the Tennessee Valley. How can we account for this ambivalence?

Goldwater's campaign managers did their best to keep him away from the press; not a single news conference was held during the campaign. One clue may be found in the disparity beteen the Goldwater supporters and the vast majority of voters. They simply could not believe they were so different from the vast majority of people. Statements unquestioningly accepted by the Senator's most enthusiastic supporters, therefore, occasioned an uproar in the world outside—to the Senator's genuine surprise.

In the final analysis, however, Goldwater's inconsistency may have arisen directly out of his political style. He and his supporters were impatient with the practical substance of policy decisions. They believed that if the government only approached politics in the right way then everything would be all right. They could hardly be bothered about verbal niceties when they knew in their hearts that their style was fundamentally correct. Traditional politicians may say inconsistent things to gather votes from an electorate which holds inconsistent policy preferences. Goldwater may take inconsistent positions because he is not seriously interested in specific policies.

What, then, have been the major consequences of having a purist candidate on the ballot? Compared to other recent campaigns, 1964 was (1) more bitter; (2) less moral; (3) more concerned with personalities; (4) less concerned with issues; (5) more involved with consistency; (6) less consistent, and (7) for the first time since the Civil War era introduced the explosive question of race relations as a major issue dividing the parties. But these distinctive accomplishments were at least confined to 1964. What will be the future of the party system if purists continue to represent one of the major parties?

THE FUTURE

It has often been said that parties in democratic countries like Great Britain are much more ideological, more strongly divided by serious cleavages over issues, than is the case in the United States. The evidence suggests that this view must be seriously modified. In Great Britain, for example, the political elites of the Labour, Conservative, and Liberal parties are extraordinarily united on domestic policy. They are almost all Keynesians in their economics, pragmatists in their policies on state intervention in the economy, supporters of the welfare state, and fundamentally at peace with the general development of governmental policy in the postwar world. The United States offers a striking contrast: a conservative political elite, disproportionately located in the Republican Party, regards Keynesian economics as a dirty word, views governmental activity in the economy with ideological hostility, and is reconciled neither to the future growth of the welfare state nor to its steady development over the past 30 years. While not all political leaders in Great Britain are satisfied with its foreign policy, the impression is that most are agreed on essentials. There is no equivalent of the increasing frustration the Republican conservatives feel because the superior resources of the United States do not confer an automatic ability to control events beyond its borders. Of course, some Democrats share these feelings, but they cannot prevail within their national party.

This is not the place to argue about which views are correct or more nearly in tune with the realities of our time. But it is the place to say that the existence of a political elite, in a position to control a major national party, which holds views widely at variance both with the general voting population and its own followers, presents a major political problem in the United States. Goldwater's nomination and defeat are merely a sign of an old problem, but one hidden by the normal operation of the party system. What are some of the consequences for American political parties?

One possibility is that the Republican Party will return to its previous course and seek out popular candidates whose moderate views will give it a chance to win presidential elections. Once it is understood, however, that the Goldwater movement is not a temporary aberration, but represents a profound current within the Republican Party, it becomes impossible for me to join the wishful thinkers who believe that the moderates and liberals in the party will automatically gain control after Goldwater's severe defeat in the election. A majority of party activists now support the political tendency Goldwater represented. (It might be well to recall that an Associated Press poll of Republican county chairmen, taken in April, 1964, showed that 722 chose Goldwater as their personal preference compared to 301 for Nixon.) If these conservatives are to be defeated they will have to be challenged by a rival, moderate elite, willing to engage in the daily tasks of political organization over the next four years. No one has been able to tell where these people will come from, especially after the Republican Party has been swept out of office at all levels in a Johnson landslide.

The possibility cannot be ruled out that the Republican Party will continue to nominate conservatives like Goldwater and will continue to lose badly. I believe that those who see in this development the likelihood of a realignment of the major parties along conservative and liberal lines will be grievously disappointed. What incentive would there be for conservative Democrats from the South to join a lost cause? On the contrary, they would more than ever be impelled to cling to the Democratic affiliation which at least promises them continued influence in Congress and some chance to modify the policies of Democratic Presidents. Republican moderates and liberals, however, might find association with the prevailing centers of power in the Democratic Party more and more attractive.

In a study of state party systems, the late V. O. Key, Jr., has shown that as one party dominates the political scene by gaining continual electoral victories, nomination becomes tantamount to election; and there is a strong tendency for voters to move into the primaries of this party in order to gain some influence over its decisions. The minority party loses its moderates and becomes the preserve of the "diehards." Hence it becomes increasingly difficult for a candidate who might appeal to the electorate to win nomination in the minority party. Nor are the consequences for the majority party necessarily good. As it grows in relative size and importance it becomes more heterogeneous. At the same time the weakness of the opposition removes a powerful incentive to party cohesion.

Should this vision of the future materialize, we can expect an end to a competitive, two-party system. In its place we will have a modified one-party system with a dominant Democratic Party. As its leaders find that their potential for controlling policy decisions has enormously increased they will also discover that greatly intensified factionalism within the party has strikingly diminished their capacity for united action. The immediate policy goals of an accelerated welfare state—medical care for the aged, aid to education, antipoverty programs—may be achieved ahead of schedule as a result of extraordinary Democratic Party majorities in Congress. But these victories for liberal Democrats may be achieved at the price of inability to meet new problems. For the more overwhelming the dominance of the party, the less may be their importance within it. The success of liberal ideas will have been sacrificed to the triumph of their party. The Republican Party, which diminished in size, will find that its greater potential for unity is accomplished by a drastically reduced capacity to get its preferences translated into government policy. It will have gained cohesion in exchange for impotence. The 1964 election may turn out to be a disaster for conservative Republicans and a Pyrrhic victory for liberal Democrats.

There has been a great deal of loose talk in the past about the desirability of having an avowed conservative run for the presidency on the grounds that a severe defeat would put his backers "in their place" and demonstrate once and for all that they lack support in the country. The Goldwater candidacy, however, visibly increased the cost of losing the election to those who disagreed profoundly with him. As a result, there was a much more bitter campaign fraught with much greater anxiety than in the past. Will the comforts of a political system which is ordinarily kind to losers (because campaigns are fought between parties and candidates which differ somewhat but are not separated by too large a gulf) be more highly valued in the future? That depends on whether the rest of us learn the lessons which the Goldwater phenomenon has to teach us.

It is possible that the Goldwater phenomenon represents the beginnings of ideology in the United States. Although markedly different in their policy preferences, there are segments of the left as well as the right who are repelled by the usual patterns of democratic politics. There appears to be little difference in style between the Goldwater purists and the leftists who constantly complain about hypocrisy in public life and how the politicians sell out the people. Could it be that the United States is producing large numbers of half-educated people with college degrees who have learned that participation (passion and commitment) is good but who do not understand (or cannot stand) the normal practices of democratic politics? If this is true, we shall be hearing a great deal more from those who identify compromise with moral degeneracy. Political scientists might then wish to present their knowledge about the consequences of political purism. They might also wish to impart some wisdom on the relative desirability of flexible and inflexible political styles under varying conditions. For the Goldwater phenomenon, which once seemed so strange, may become a persistent feature of the American political scene, nonetheless disturbing because it reappears under different ideological guises.

THE POLITICS OF CONSENSUS
IN AN AGE OF AFFLUENCE *
Robert E. Lane

MARX is surely right when he says that the way men earn their living shapes their relations to each other and to the state; but this is, of course, only the beginning. Aside from all the other non-economic factors which also have these effects, there is the matter of the *source* of income, the *level* of income,

* From Robert E. Lane, "The Politics of Consensus in an Age of Affluence," in *The American Political Science Review*, Vol. LIX, No. 4, 1964, pp. 874–895. Reprinted by permission of the author and the American Political Science Association.

and especially, the *security* of income. Moreover, each of these factors has both an individual effect, a set of influences apparent in the study of individual enrichment or immiseration, and a social effect, the influences which appear when whole societies become richer or more secure economically. So I am led to inquire into what is happening to men's political interests, behavior, and attitudes toward politics and government in an Age of Affluence, a period when men's economic security and income have increased and when, for the first time in history, it appears likely that the business cycle can now be controlled. Like Marx's, my interest is in change over time.

Quite candidly, this is a descriptive account of attitudinal change in recent years, portrayed against a background of economic change. Only argument supports the inference that it is the economic change—implied in the term "Age of Affluence" shortly to be explicated—that is accountable for much of the attitudinal change. It would take another paper with closer attention to subsections of the population and specific economic conditions to establish this argument on a firmer footing. In the meantime, perhaps these findings can help illuminate the more general problem of the relationship between economic development and stable and effective politics, as well as to help us to see where American politics is heading.

The elements of the economy which are most relevant to such an investigation are five-fold, and the term "affluent society" or "Age of Affluence" refers here to more than higher per capita national income, though it includes that. The term embraces:

(1) a relatively high per capita national income;
(2) a relatively equalitarian distribution of income;
(3) a "favorable" rate of growth of per capita Gross National Product (GNP);
(4) provisions against the hazards of life—that is, against sickness, penury, unemployment, dependence in old age, squalor—the features now associated with the term "welfare state"; and
(5) a "managed economy" in the sense of conscious and more or less successful governmental use of fiscal and monetary powers to smooth out the business cycle and avoid depressions, as well as to provide for the economic growth mentioned in (3) above.

These five points include both economic conditions and governmental policies.

The appropriateness of the term "affluent society" or "Age of Affluence" rests upon intercultural and chronological comparisons; but in making these comparisons it is important to remember that an affluent society may still include a large number of very poor people: the average income of the poorest fifth of the families (consumer units) in the United States in 1962 was $1,662 and this had to provide for a little over three people, on the average. The term "affluence," however, is clearly relative both to other societies and previous periods. On the first point, comparison with other societies:

(1) The United States ranked second (out of 122 countries) in GNP per capita (Kuwait was the first) in 1957, with no other country even a close competitor.

(2) According to one measure of "inequality of income distribution before taxes," the United States ranks about 7th in equality of income distribution. (Four British Commonwealth countries and India, for different reasons, are somewhat more equalitarian).

(3) Although until the last few years the annual increase of GNP was lower in the United States than in most developed and many developing countries (in Russett's volume, the United States is about 45th out of 68 countries), recently this has changed and the rate in the United States 1962–65 is about the same as in the Common Market countries.

(4) Although relatively less extensive than in most European countries, the American welfare programs, now that medicare has been enacted, compare favorably in coverage and especially in absolute level of support with contemporary European programs.

(5) With the possible exception of Italy, no European or developed Commonwealth country has suffered a recession (after the postwar reconstruction period) with anything like the depth or duration of the depressions of the twenties and thirties. This is also true of the United States, as we shall see below.

But our main interest here lies, not in comparative economics and politics, but in changing patterns in the United States. Were we not always an *Affluent Society, a People of Plenty,* bothered by the question *"Abundance for What?"* Relative to other nations, perhaps! But the modern era is different from previous eras in several important and relevant ways. It will be convenient to designate four economic time periods in the United States, of which only the last three are of current interest to us (and only the latter part of the earliest of these). The periods are: Agricultural State of Nature (1789–1869), Industrial State of Nature (1870–1929), Period of Economic Crisis (1930–1941), and Age of Affluence (marked by a preliminary uncertain period, 1946–50, and beginning to take on its central characteristics in 1951 and then continuing through the present). Inevitably, since we are dealing with more or less continuous change, the margins of the periods blur into each other. Each leaves its historical "deposit" in the milieu of the next, so that—as with countries still struggling with the remnants of the feudal order in the modern period—we have with us today substantial economic characteristics of the Agricultural State of Nature (not to mention the political and cultural residues of that period).

But since periods must have boundaries, let us mention our reasons for selecting these. The Industrial State of Nature began in 1870 when the society became more than half industrial and commercial, as indicated by the decline below the fifty per cent mark in value added to the national product by agriculture. During this industrial period, and prior to the great economic crisis of the 1930s, we find a decelerating rate of development, as indicated by the number of years required for the GNP to double (in constant prices): 13 years, then 18 years, then 21 years—taking us up to the mid-twenties. But we are concerned with more than economic performances; we are interested in government policy as well. "Reform" during this period focused upon the regulation of "natural monopolies," such as railroads, grain elevators, and the like; pure food and drug laws; and policing certain trade practices. There was no concept of a welfare state, and the nearest thing to an argument over a "managed economy" was the chronic debate over "easy" *versus* "hard" money.

The period of Economic Crisis (1930–1941) was, of course, marked by economic depression, the most extended and severe in our history. In this period GNP (in constant dollars) remained below the 1929 figure until 1939; investment fell off drastically, and widespread unemployment and suffering ensued. The period defines itself by these facts of economic life *plus* two things: first, the advent of welfare state policies (especially social security, unemployment insurance, extended home and work relief, and a variety of agricultural policies designed to relieve the insecurities and penury of farm life); and second, the early beginnings of a fiscal and monetary policy (pump priming, inflationary monetary policies) designed to eliminate the troughs of the business cycle. These policies, of course, were extremely controversial, but—if we omit the war years—one might say that the passage of the Employment Act of 1946 represented a turning point in governmental (but not business) acceptance of responsibility for a "managed economy" in this special moderate sense. Specific policies to implement this concept remained controversial in many circles for a long time thereafter.

The 1940s represent an anomalous period, partly because of the war, and partly because per capita GNP (hovering around $2,000 in constant 1954 dollars) scarcely changed during the reconversion period, with its widespread shortages and rapidly rising prices, from 1946 into 1950. People were much better off than in the 1930s, but civilians generally were not much better off (economically) than had been in the first half of the decade. Although there were no recessions as serious as the 1920–21 recession, yet both 1947 and 1949 were difficult years. As a consequence the annual rate of growth of GNP was low (1.8 per cent from 1946 to 1950), and, moreover, this period, like all postwar periods, was marked by high industrial strife. Yet there was an important difference, compared to 1929, and also compared to 1935–36; the share of income going to the very rich, the top 5 per cent, declined substantially. . . . From 1950 on, this proportion going to the richest 5 per cent scarcely changed, drifting down a percentage point or two, for the next fifteen years. Aside from this last feature, however, the period of the forties seems to have been characterized by some of the economic elements of earlier periods; but at the same time, the basic welfare state measures provided assistance for the very poor, the economically insecure, and for the unemployed—rapidly increasing in 1949 and 1950.

The Age of Affluence, after its poor beginning in the 1940s, may be said (for analytical purposes) to commence in the 1950s, especially after the Korean fighting had stopped. From that time on although three recessions have occurred, only the one in 1957–58 involved any decline at all in per capita GNP in real terms. The rate of growth improved substantially: from 1950 to 1961 the annual rate of growth was 3.1 per cent in constant dollars. Industrial strife declined; prices were more stable, and in this decade available spending money rose dramatically (50 per cent increase in disposable income—current dollars) with goods to spend it on.

While the 1950s began to resemble a period appropriately termed an "Age of Affluence" (except for the unemployment), the 1960s look even better. From early 1961 into 1966 there have been *no* recessions, the longest continuous period of prosperity in our history. The annual rate of increase of GNP in constant dollars is about 4.2 per cent in real terms. Unemployment has declined somewhat, though it remains a "spot" on the affluent portrait. Equally important, the Kennedy and Johnson administrations make an explicit point of their use of fiscal policies, especially tax policies, to reduce or eliminate depressions and to encourage growth. Finally, in 1964 certain anti-poverty programs were instituted to attack unemployment, poverty and squalor with more precise instruments; and in 1965, for the first time in 20 years, major new advances were scored toward the realization of the welfare state, especially, medicare, extension of social security coverage; and a "break-through" was made on federal aid to education.

This long (but too brief) review of the economic and policy characteristics of recent times shows, then, a profile of increasing per capita income but decreasing economic effectiveness in the period of Industrial State of Nature (1870–1929); a period of Economic Crisis (1930–1941) with low income and no growth; an anomalous decade in the Forties; and then an accelerating economy in the Age of Affluence. No doubt the implications as drawn seem overly optimistic, but I see no reason to anticipate a reversal of any of the major trends (unless there is a war), though a slowing down of growth may take place. The question, then, is how these changes relate to political behavior and attitudes, especially in the contemporary period.

I. POLITICS AND CIVICS IN AN AGE OF AFFLUENCE

The relationships between individual affluence and political attitudes are comparatively well known, but the relationships between communal affluence and political behavior are somewhat obscure. Even more obscure are the relationships between *change* in affluence and *change* in politics. Consider the following plausible hypotheses:

One might expect an increased conservatism in the Age of Affluence, on the ground that as people become more prosperous they take on the known attitudes of prosperous individuals in an earlier period. Or, to the contrary, one might expect increasing support for the kinds of measures which have worked successfully in the past in helping to bring about the Age of Affluence, *i.e.*, support for an extension of the welfare state.

One might expect a declining urgency of political concern, on the ground that when men are more satisfied with their lot in life they become less desperate for political help. Or, one might expect increased political interest and concern because these attitudes are generally related to higher income and an improved capacity to take an interest in matters other than immediate day-to-day breadwinning problems.

One might expect a shift in political cleavage from social class to religious and ethnic bases on the ground that economic issues would become less important, thereby releasing men's attention for other submerged conflicts. Or, one might argue that because religious and ethnic cleavages are nourished by economic insecurity and poverty, growing affluence and security would weaken the intensity of these conflicts too.

Finally, one might expect a decline in political partisanship, *i.e.*, the extent and intensity of identification with a political party, on the ground that both parties are likely to accept the policies of the welfare state and the managed economy, thus depriving party differences of much of their meaning. Or, one might argue that since social class is likely to lose its cuing function in elections, parties will remain important, or even become stronger, as intellectual and emotional "props" in electoral decisions.

The fact is that, as usual, both "theory" and common sense lead in diverse incompatible directions, and only evidence will help. The evidence to be presented here suggests a lessening of hostility between parties and religious groups, and a *rapprochement* between men and their government—a combination of changes which I cover in the term "politics of consensus." This does not imply that there are no sharp, intensely felt, hostile cleavages in society, but rather that these have (1) lost most of their political and emotional impact for most people (but not for Civil Rights workers), and (2) changed from cleavages in which the public was more or less evenly divided, to cleavages where the division is between a main body of opinion and a small and dwindling group. Specifically, the thesis has six themes. In the Age of Affluence:

(a) people will come increasingly to trust each other, to feel less at the mercy of chance and more in control of their lives, and so to be more optimistic regarding the future. These changes, in turn will help to promote others.

(b) people will slowly lose their sense of high national, personal, and group stakes in elections; political partisanship, while not changing on the surface, will change its meaning.

(c) people will slowly change their class awareness and consciousness, so that the relationship between ideology and class status will change; but occupation and class will continue to influence electoral choice—even as the electoral "pivot" shifts.

(d) religious institutions and dogmas will slowly lose their influence over men's secular thought, inter-faith hostility will decline, but religious community identification may retain a constant political "cuing" function.

(e) the struggle for racial equality will be facilitated by affluence and its associated attitudes, but the sense of crisis and strife in this arena will continue or grow for an indefinite period.

(f) there will be a *rapprochement* between men and their government and a decline of political alienation.

We cannot explore (for want of time and survey data) these changes in the earlier periods, so we will focus upon recent changes. The reader will understand the difficulties of relying on survey materials, with their different questions, eclectic timing, and, hence, ambiguous inference. He will, I hope, further understand that the nature of the changes we are considering are glacial in their slow movements, interrupted by dramatic events abroad and influenced by changing leadership appeals at home. One can, moreover, write interpretative historical essays without data, or more closely controlled and specific studies well documented by data, and both seem equally immune from criticism. This paper lies in between; it is a speculative historical study making use of such data as come to hand.

II. TRUST, OPTIMISM AND ALIENATION

(a) *In an Age of Affluence, people will come increasingly to trust each other more, to feel more in control of their lives, and to be more hopeful regarding their future. Social alienation will decline.*

Greater economic security and protection against life's hazards should, one would imagine, increase people's sense of well-being or happiness, and occasion a decline in various kinds of anxiety. In some ways, this seems to be the case, while in other respects it is not. Over the years, both in the United States and abroad, survey organizations have asked people "In general, how happy would you say you are—very happy, fairly happy, or not very happy?" (AIPO). The question, in spite of its superficial naiveté, has been found to be related to many concrete symptoms of adjustment and happiness and thus to have a promise of some validity. Comparatively speaking, by this test, the United States was in 1949 the third happiest nation (this statement sometimes amuses one's friends), with Australia by far the happiest and France the unhappiest. But over time, it would be impossible to conclude that the evidence suggests that Americans have become "happier" in the Age of Affluence. In the three-year period 1946 to 1949 there seemed to be a drift in this direction (from 39 per cent "very happy" to 43 per cent), but, when in 1957 the Survey Research Center asked an almost identical question of a national sample ("Taking all things together, how would you say things are these days—would you say you're *very happy, pretty happy,* or *not too happy* these days?"), only 35 per cent reported themselves to be "very happy." Since happiness, as the reader might suspect, is strongly related to education and income and since both education and income have been increasing, the findings are puzzling and suggest further inquiry.

But there is other evidence to suggest the kind of basic changes in orientation predicted in the Age of Affluence. One of the fundamental attitudinal ingredients of successful democracies is a relatively widespread sense of interpersonal trust. It is a correlate of several important democratic attitudes and, I believe, an ingredient in economic development itself, since this requires cooperation, responsibility and integrity to facilitate the working out of informal agreements. Comparatively, the United States is a "trusting" nation, perhaps the most trusting; but we may not always have been that way. In Table I(a) there is some suggestion that inter-personal trust has increased since the war and the immediate postwar period. If this is true it would provide the strongest attitudinal foundation for some of the political changes we shall examine shortly.

While the sense of current happiness does not seem to have grown in the Age of Affluence, nevertheless an important change has occurred in attitudes about the past, present, and future chances for happiness or life satisfaction. In Table I(b) we see a very strong suggestion that, compared to people in the later phases of the Period of Economic Crisis, people today believe that their lives provide greater satisfaction than their parents or grandparents had. The nostalgia of the Thirties for an earlier, possibly "village" America, seems to have declined, in spite of the resurgence of these attitudes said to be characteristic of the Goldwater campaign. If this is a measure of an emotional traditionalism, this change, too, is important.

Looking toward the future as a period offering greater promise of a happier life, could imply some dissatisfaction with the current state of things; but, on the contrary, it seems to me to imply exactly the opposite view, namely, that the present is full of hope, carrying within it the seeds of fruitful change. In any event, the increase in the past ten years of faith in the future compared to a plateau of relatively lower hope during the previous 13 years (Table I(c)) seems to me to reflect exactly that sense of security in the future which one might expect from the protective arm of the welfare state and newly acquired control over the ravages of the business cycle.

This theme is further reflected and more directly stated in a question on the carrying out of plans, shown in Table I(d). Here, unfortunately, the time span between measures is short (1958 to 1964), and the change in attitudes relatively small. Moreover, the first measure is taken in a period of recovery from the only important recession in the Age of Affluence. Nevertheless it is suggestive that a growing sense of mastery over fate emerges—the very antithesis of the traditionalist orientation suggesting that one is the helpless object of forces beyond human control.

Finally, we must note in Table I(e) a somewhat larger increase in the belief

TABLE I. TRUST IN OTHERS; PERCEPTIONS OF LIFE NOW, EARLIER,
AND LATER; CONTROL OVER ONE'S OWN LIFE,
AND SHARE OF GOOD LUCK

(a) "Do you think most people can be trusted?" (OPOR, March 26, 1942; NORC, Aug. 1, 1948; Jan. 1964)[a]

	1942	1948	1964
	(%)	(%)	(%)
Yes	66	66	77
No	25	30	21
No opinion	9[*]	4	2

[Continued on next page]

* includes 5% qualified answers
[a] Erskine, POQ, pp. 517, 523, 525. AIPO refers to American Institute of Public Opinion; OPOR to Office of Public Opinion Research; and NORC to National Opinion Research Corp.

(b) "Do you think Americans were happier and more contented thirty years ago than they are now?" (AIPO, March 8, 1939).[a] "Do you think the average man gets more satisfaction out of life these days or do you think he got more out of life 50 years ago?" (SRC, Nov. 1964)[b]

	1939	1964
	(%)	(%)
In earlier period people were happier; got more satisfaction out of life	61	34
Not happier in earlier period; get more satisfaction out of life these days	23	59
Other, it depends, no opinion	16	7

(c) "Ten years from now, do you believe Americans will generally be happier than they are today?" (AIPO, May 18, 1939). "As you look to the future, do you think life for people generally will get better—or will it get worse?" (AIPO, March 15, 1952; Aug. 29, 1962)[a]

	1939	1952	1962
	(%)	(%)	(%)
Better (happier)	42	42	55
Worse (not happier)	35	34	23
No difference		13	12
No opinion	23	11	10

(d) "When you make plans ahead, do you usually get to carry out things the way you expected, or do things usually come up to make you change your plans?" (SRC, Nov. 1958; Nov. 1964)[b]

	1958	1964
	(%)	(%)
Things work out as expected	52	59
Depends, other	1	4
Have to change plans	42	36
Don't know and NA	4	1
No. of cases	(1822)	(1450)

(e) "Do you feel that you are the kind of person that gets his share of bad luck, or do you feel that you have mostly good luck?" (SRC, Nov. 1958, Nov. 1964).[b]

	1958	1964
	(%)	(%)
Mostly good luck	63	75
Pro-con; it depends	5	10
Bad luck	29	14
Don't know and NA	4	1
No. of cases	(1822)	(1450)

[b] Inter-university Consortium for Political Research, Codebook for 1964 Survey Research Center Election Study. These sources will hereafter be abbreviated as "Consortium Codebook" and the initials SRC will be used for the Survey Research Center (University of Michigan).

that one is, in some sense, the child of fortune, blessed with better than the average share of good luck. Again we are dealing with "late" (for us) changes in the Age of Affluence, but the halving of the proportion of those who think of themselves as dogged by bad luck is surely significant. The implication is twofold: men feel more in control of their lives, as we said before, and "nature" or "the fates" or even "society" is less malevolent—perhaps even benign.

In review, in spite of the findings on "happiness," one can only conclude that during this period the direction of changing personal orientation has been toward a sense that life is better than it was, and will get still better; that people are more trustworthy; that events are more under control and fate is kinder. There is a group of intellectuals who have, in one sense, inherited the place once held by the proponents of Marx's immiseration theory of capitalism. With tongue in cheek, we may refer to them as "alienists," for their apostle is a psychoanalyst, Erich Fromm, and their theme is the increasing alienation of men from work, society and government. I have long suspected that they reflected their own discontent with society rather more than any mass discontent—some, like C. Wright Mills, have said as much. Partly too, I think, their views reflect their own alienation from the field of endeavor where there is a true *elan*, the field of science. Whatever the reason, and somewhat apart from the main argument of this piece, I suggest that the above data cast doubt upon the principal themes of these alienist thinkers.

III. POLITICAL PARTISANSHIP

(b) *In an Age of Affluence, the sense of crisis and of high national, personal, and group stakes in national elections declines; political partisanship takes on a new meaning.*

This change in "sense of crisis" is, perhaps, the most important attitudinal change from the Period of Economic Crisis to the Age of Affluence, and it is the most difficult to substantiate with really good evidence. The argument, however, is straightforward.

In an Age of Affluence an increasing proportion of the working class achieve sufficient income and security to adopt middle class social and political patterns —but they nevertheless are likely to remain Democrats. At the same time, the middle class will associate its own increasing welfare and security with the policies of the welfare state, including flexible fiscal policies, and will be in no mood for change. Many will become Democrats; others will be liberal Republicans. Many industrialists and businessmen will come increasingly to perceive that the fight against a limited management of the economy is not in their interests because these "liberal" policies provide the basis for the prosperity and growth in which they share. It is certainly not true that the more prosperous a person becomes, the less likely he is to be alarmed about political events. But, generally, I think it is true that the more secure he is about his income, and the more it appears to him that the government will not jeopardize that income, the less intense he is likely to feel about political decisions in the realm of economic affairs.

Before turning to time comparisons in the United States, something may be learned from cross-cultural comparisons of attitudes toward victory by opposition parties. From the data in Table II, one learns that the sense of electoral crisis is lower in the United States than elsewhere. This is enormously significant for the smooth functioning of democratic institutions, not only because it makes transition easier from one administration to another, but also because it reduces antagonism and hostility in electoral campaigns. The data also show a sensitivity in these foreign nations to real dangers; but for our purposes, let us note only one other point. In every country except Mexico the more conservative party is in power, but only in the United States—and there only in a minor way—is a larger proportion fearful of the conservative party policies than of the more liberal party. So much has the welfare state been accepted here that its mild opponents, even when in power, were considered more threatening than its apostles. This was true in 1960—perhaps the 1964 election may be interpreted as further confirmation of this point.

Not infrequently the American experience is taken by (American) scholars to represent a kind of prototype for modernizing societies, a model of what is to become of them. If that interpretation is true, it implies that we have passed through some of the phases of economics and politics which these other nations are now experiencing—a hypothesis which runs counter to the notion of American uniqueness, and runs counter to much common sense as well. Nevertheless, the implication of Table II is in line with our major theme: the decline of a sense of high stakes involved in national electoral decisions.

These stakes might be national stakes, where the welfare of the *country* is somehow "risked," as implied by the question eliciting the Almond-Verba data; or the stakes might be more personal, turning on one's *own economic condition*; or they might refer to the welfare of the *group* to which one belongs. Changing attitudes toward these three kinds of stakes are reflected in Tables III and IV.

The argument for a declining sense of national urgency in electoral outcomes must rest on two comparisons over time, the only comparable ones I could find (Tables III(a) and (b). One of them compares the responses to two similar questions: how much difference it makes which party wins, in 1946, and how much difference it makes which party runs the country, nineteen years later in May 1965. Note that the latter time follows by only several months an election in which the candidates were thought to have sharply different views on domestic and foreign policy. The decline in those believing partisan victory or partisan government of one kind or another makes "a great deal of difference" is suggestive of the process of consensus revealed in Table II and anticipated in our argument. The other comparison is between attitudes directly mentioning "difference to the country" or "important to the country" in 1944 and in 1952—the beginning of the politics of consensus. Fortunately, in 1952 the question was asked twice, once before the election—mentioning only parties—and again after the election, mentioning the candidates' name. The lack of difference between these two times and wordings gives us a sense of the reliability of the attitudes involved. And the magnitude of the apparent change in attitude over this 8-year period suggests that chance or sampling error or minor differences in wording could not account for the change. But perhaps it is the difference between a war election and a peacetime election, rather than any between an election colored by the politics of the Period of Economic Crisis

TABLE II. SENSE OF ALARM OVER THE VICTORY OF AN OPPOSITION PARTY, IN FIVE NATIONS

"The Republican Party now controls the administration in Washington. Do you think that its policies and activities would ever seriously endanger the country's welfare? Do you think that this *probably* would happen, that it *might* happen, or that it *probably wouldn't* happen?" *

"If the Democratic Party were to take control of the government, how likely is it that it would seriously endanger the country's welfare? Do you think that this would *probably* happen, that it *might* happen, or that it *probably wouldn't* happen?*"

COUNTRY	RESPONSE	PER CENT "PROBABLY WOULD HAPPEN," OF TOTAL SAMPLE
United States		(%)
Republicans probably endanger welfare		5
Democrats probably endanger welfare		3
Great Britain		
Conservatives probably endanger welfare		7
Labour probably endangers welfare		17
Germany		
Christian Democrats probably endanger welfare		7
Socialists (SPD) probably endanger welfare		12
Right wing (DRP) probably endangers welfare		35
Italy		
Christian Democrats probably endanger welfare		10
Communists (PCI) probably endanger welfare		60
Socialists (PSI) probably endanger welfare		43
Socialists (PSDI) probably endanger welfare		23
Right Wing party like MSI probably endangers welfare		41
Mexico		
Party of Revolutionary Institutions (PRI) probably endangers welfare		13
PAN (minor party) probably endangers welfare		18
PP (minor party) probably endangers welfare		37

* Appropriate changes in wording, of course, for each nation.
Source: Almond-Verba five-nation study; *Consortium codebooks*. The major report on these surveys is made in Gabriel A. Almond and Sidney Verba, *The Civic Culture, op. cit.* The number of cases for each country is about a thousand; U.S. survey was made in March 1960, others in June and July 1959.

compared to the politics of consensus in the Age of Affluence? This would be a more plausible construct were it not for a previous (AIPO) poll in (August) 1942 asking people whether they thought the outcome of the election would "make *any* difference in the war effort"; only 30 per cent thought—correctly, as the election consequences for domestic mobilization programs showed—that it would make any difference in this particular respect, compared to 88 per cent seeing some unspecified difference in 1944. The implication is clear: people were carrying into the 1944 election—when postwar reconversion anxieties loomed—their sense of partisan alarm learned in the 1930s. In 1952, with a war in the Far East still unresolved, and the cold war in full swing, the sense that the country's welfare hinged on the election nevertheless dwindled drastically and the conditions were prepared for the very low sense of partisan alarmism seen in the 1960 Almond-Verba data presented above.

Part of the political style of the period of transition to the welfare state—and, we must add, its brief resurgence in 1964—is the hostile posture of each partisan toward his opponents, something which follows naturally from the view that a great deal is at stake in the political contest. Not infrequently, in such a strained atmosphere, the election seems more of an effort to keep the other man out, rather than to elect one's own candidate. The evidence (not presented here) suggests that the intensity of opposition—except on the extreme fringes —is greater among the *defenders* of the liberal established order; the threat of deprivation of the welfare state is apparently felt more intensely than the threat which the welfare state, once established, implies to its opponents. In any event,

TABLE III. DOES IT MAKE MUCH DIFFERENCE TO THE COUNTRY WHICH PARTY WINS?

(a) "Do you think it makes much difference or only a little difference which party wins the elections for Congress this fall?" (AIPO, Sept. 1946)[a]

"Do you think it makes a great deal of difference or just a little difference which political party runs the country?" (AIPO, May 1965)[b]

	1946	1965
	(%)	(%)
Great deal of difference	49	39
Little difference	31	40
No difference	11	14
Don't know	9	6

(b) "Which one of these ideas comes closest to the way you feel about this election: It is very important to the country that Roosevelt be elected; the country will be better off if Roosevelt is elected; the country will be better off if Dewey is elected; it is very important to the country that Dewey be elected?" (NORC, Oct. 2, 1944)[a]

"Do you think it will make a good deal of difference to the country whether the Democrats or the Republicans win the election this November or that it won't make much difference which side wins?" (SRC, Oct 1952)[e]

"Do you think it will make a good deal of difference to the country that Eisenhower won instead of Stevenson, or don't you think it will make much difference?" (SRC, Nov. 1952)[e]

	1944	1952	
		October	November
	(%)	(%)	(%)
Very important to the country; good deal of difference	54	21	20
Country will be better off; some difference; it depends	34	40	42
Won't make much difference; no difference	9	32	31

[a] Hadley Cantril and Mildred Strunk, *Public Opinion, 1936–1945* (Princeton University Press, 1951).

[b] AIPO release, May 1965.

[e] *Consortium Codebook.*

it is our thesis that the politics of consensus is also the politics of support, rather than the politics of opposition. There is some evidence for this in the responses of three national samples to questions almost identically worded asking "would you say you are voting mostly to get one man into office (for 'R's candidate'), or mostly to keep the other man out (against 'opposing candidate')?" In 1944 the oppositional vote was 25 per cent, and in 1964, with the return of anti-welfare state politics, it was 21 per cent. By contrast, in the 1960 election—marked by some anti-Catholic voting, but not by threats to the welfare state and a managed economy, and basically in the consensual style—oppositional voting was only 10 per cent, less than half as large.

These findings and arguments deal essentially with the question of national stakes and concerns, but one might well argue that political life more directly reflects a person's own perceived self interest—at least Campbell, Converse, Miller and Stokes do seem to take this position. This is a fundamental question, for the heart of my argument rests on the view that the Age of Affluence produces, with occasional regression, political contests which do not jeopardize a person's income or economic security. Unfortunately, here, the time series only

TABLE IV. DOES IT MAKE MUCH DIFFERENCE TO A PERSON'S
OR A GROUP'S WELFARE WHICH PARTY WINS?

(a) "Do you think it will make any important difference in how you and your family get along financially whether the Democrats or the Republicans win? How is that?" (SRC, Oct. or Nov. of years indicated)[a]

	PER CENT SAYING "NO DIFFERENCE" OR UNABLE TO THINK OF ANY DIFFERENCE (DON'T KNOW).					
	1952	1954	1956	1958	1960	1964
	(%)	(%)	(%)	(%)	(%)	(%)
Presidential elections	53		66		66	66
Congressional ("off year") elections		65		72		
No. of cases	(1799)	(1139)	(1762)	(1822)	(1954)	(1571)

(b) "As of today, which political party—the Democratic or the Republican—do you think serves the interests of the following groups best: Business and professional people? White collar workers? Farmers? Skilled workers? Unskilled workers?" (AIPO, months uncertain, years as indicated)[b]

	PER CENT SAYING "NO DIFFERENCE"		
	1952	1960	1964
Response referring to own group (business and professional people referring to the interests of business and professional people, etc.)	(%)	(%)	(%)
Middle groups (less class conscious)			
White collar	12	15	17
Skilled workers	13	14	16
Farmers	10	16	17
Extreme groups (more class conscious)			
Business and professional	11	15	12
Unskilled workers	11	13	12

[a] *Consortium Codebooks* for election studies of years indicated.
[b] AIPO release, Feb. 28, 1965.

goes back to 1952 and hence the comparison must rely upon trends within the later era. My thesis, as it turns out, is only partially supported by the evidence, as may be seen in Table IV(a). Where, according to the argument, a slowly growing number of persons should emerge who do not believe that their own income will be greatly affected by the outcome of an election, we find instead, for the presidential years, a marked increase in this sense of "indifference" only between 1952 and 1956—followed by no change at all, a plateau. For the congressional years, a crucial datum is missing for 1962, but the change from 1954 to 1958 is in the expected direction. There are, of course, natural limits to the rise of this "indifference curve" and a counter tendency in the increased level of education in the population, for the more educated are more likely to see the links between their economic well-being and governmental policy. Nevertheless, if one might project these figures backward into time, one would infer, albeit somewhat hesitantly, a lower sense of indifference in the politics of the Period of Economic Crisis to correspond to the greater sense of national stakes we discovered in the earlier data.

Finally, there is the question of perceived group or class stakes in a national election. As has often been said, politics is a group process, men often take their cue for party identification by some simple phrase such as "party of the business man" or "party of the working man." Where issues are obscure, categoric group tradition and alignment, mediated through primary groups, is central. The measure for this perception of group stakes in politics, as seen in Table IV(b), is the response to a question on the party which best serves the interests of each of five groups, classified by the group membership of the respondent. Here I have omitted some data on 1962 since congressional years are different in most series from presidential years (these data suggest an acceleration of the indifference effect prior to the 1964 election) and I have grouped the socioeconomic classes in two divisions: the more flexible middle group and the more extreme and usually more class conscious group. The evidence, again rather tenuous, suggests that within the middle groups whose class identifications are likely to be less clear, there is a slowly growing sense that neither party will jeopardize the interests of one's own particular class. Even among the unskilled workers who have been the most partisan of any of these groups, this sense of indifference seemed waxing in 1962 (when the "no difference" responses were 19 per cent, a gain of 6 points in two years), only to be sharply cut back in 1964. Since the 1964 election was, as I have mentioned, a return to welfare state issues, the fact that the sense of "no difference" continued to grow at all, compared to 1956, for these three middle groups is a tribute to the strength of this attitude.

The importance of this measure of sense of indifference is, I think, much greater than is indicated by the small size of the groups involved. For if, at this extreme, the group is slowly growing which claims that there are no important group stakes in an election, then, for a much larger group, there must be doubts, inarticulate mood changes, and declining intensity of conviction.

Before closing this section on the declining sense of crisis, declining perception of threatened policies that might endanger the country, and declining belief that personal or group welfare is involved in an electoral decision, let us note two implied consequences which do *not,* in fact, take place. One implication is that people are becoming less interested in politics. Two extensive series of questions have been asked over time, inquiring into people's interest in the elections, and neither of them shows any decline; indeed, the SRC series catching every national election from 1952 to 1964 (except 1954) shows with some variation over the years, a peak interest in 1964 (41 per cent "very much interested") and a marked increase from 1958 to 1962 (from 26 per cent to 36 per cent "very much interested")—suggesting, if anything, an increased interest in this time period.

Moreover, rather paradoxically, no decline has been reported in the strength of party identification. That is, the proportion reporting that they are "strong Democrats" and "strong Republicans" has remained remarkably constant (with a slight increase in "strong Democrats" in 1964). Furthermore, although the proportion of people reporting themselves "independent" has increased slightly—from around 20 per cent in the 1930s and 1940s, to between 21 and 24 per cent in the 1950s and 1960s—the change is very moderate indeed.

The consequent pattern emerging, therefore, is of the interested, party-identified citizen, following politics at least as closely as he did in the days of the great intense clashes when the welfare state was first launched and when men were harassed by insecurity and poverty; voting more regularly, and, indeed "personally caring" about the outcome as before; but believing that the national and personal stakes involved were not so great. People need their party identification as cues for voting decisions. For most voters, these identifications are the most significant means of orientation in politics. Hence, people wll not give them up easily, and if they did, they would have to find others, such as race, or class, or religion, or charismatic leadership. But people are changing the meanings assigned to their party membership, and increasingly believe that the opposition is not so dangerous after all.

We can apply one test to this theory of the politics of consensus. If partisanship has lost some of its "bite" and acrimony, one would expect the views of partisans of both parties on the way in which the president is conducting his business to vary more or less together. Approval of the way the president is "handling his job as president" has usually been higher than the partisan vote for the president, in any case. But if we could show that the difference between the approval of members of his own and of the opposition party (Republicans for Roosevelt, Truman, Kennedy and Johnson; Democrats for Eisenhower) was less in the Age of Affluence than in the Period of Economic Crisis (including the ambiguous 1940s), our case for historical change would be that much stronger. Since approval and disapproval fluctuate within presidential terms, an ideal measure would take each president at the beginning of his term; but we are forced here to employ the time periods in which the data are given by party breakdown as shown in Table V. By subtracting the per cent of the op-

position party approving the president's handling of his job from the per cent
of his own party so approving, we have a measure of partisanship.

TABLE V. POLITICAL PARTISANSHIP AND APPROVAL OF
THE PRESIDENT'S COURSE

"Do you approve or disapprove of the way (name of President) is handling his job as
President?" (AIPO)

TIME	PRESIDENT	% SUPPORT BY PRES.' OWN PARTY	% SUPPORT BY OPPOSITION PARTY	PARTISANSHIP OF SUPPORT: PRES. PARTY LESS OPP. PARTY	AVERAGE PARTISANSHIP DIFFERENCE
A. Presidents Associated with Conflict over Welfare State		(%)	(%)		
Feb. 1941	Roosevelt	90	40	50	
Feb. 1947	Truman	59	41	18	} 36.3
Oct. 1952	Truman	50	9	41	
B. Presidents in the Age of Affluence (post-transition)					
Jan. 1953	Eisenhower	90	70	20	
Jan. 1957	Eisenhower	95	66	29	
Feb. 1960	Kennedy	84	55	29	} 27.5
Jan. 1964	Johnson	85	74	11	
May 1965	Johnson	77	51	26	

As may be observed (Table V) from the average figures for the two periods,
a substantial decline occurred in the partisanship of judgment, the degree to
which the judgments reflect partisan divisions. Moreover, except for the special
tragic circumstances bringing Johnson into power—circumstances which produced a burst of sympathetic good will toward the new incumbent—the variation in partisanship in this period is rather slight. It seems to have stabilized
(to the extent that any set of attitudes at the mercy of historical events may be
so described) in a modest 20 to 29 per cent rage. In short, our expectations
of the consequences of a consensual politics are generally confirmed.

IV. SOCIAL CLASS

(c) *In an Age of Affluence, (1) people slowly lose (or relax) their class
awareness, (2) the link between social class and ideology changes; but, (3) in
spite of their security and prosperity, people do not increasingly think of themselves as middle class, and (4) social class does not (after a transition period)
lose its link to partisan political choice, although the changing political "pivot"
diminishes the importance of class voting in many electoral districts.*

The absence, in American history, of a feudal structure or a landed class—
and therefore of a peasant class—has given it a unique lack of class consciousness, as so many observers have noted. Yet American society has always been
stratified and important differences in life chances, honor, and distribution of
rewards inevitably enter into the experience of Americans, like others, and have

been historically associated with political choice as well as many other attitudes toward society. Different social strata have always been the vehicles or *milieux* for different social movements, social ideas, and political parties. In the Age of Affluence, we would expect a continuation of past behavior and opinion modified very slowly by new feelings of security, life styles, and perspectives. I stress the slowness because social class, unlike political party, refers to the basic pattern of life experiences, learned early, reinforced daily, and inevitably loaded with emotion.

First, one wants to know both the nature of objective social change and the nature of subjective responses. Briefly, the proportion of white-collar workers has increased by an average of a little less than five percentage points in every decade for fifty years, with a much smaller increase during the Period of Economic Crisis and a larger increase in subsequent years (1940 to 1960). In 1960 43.2 per cent of the employed persons were in white-collar occupations (professional, technical, managerial, clerical and sales).

But, of course, there is a great deal of slippage between objective and subjective class identifications (some estimates indicate that self-misclassification is as large as 25 per cent), and, hence the objective occupational change is not a very good immediate indication of how people will see themselves over time. Measures on this go back to 1945 and 1946 and, after 1952 continue in rather orderly fashion to 1964. Any expectation that the increasing proportion of workers engaged in white-collar jobs, and the general levelling up of economic security and income, would produce an increased middle class identification, would turn out to have been wrong; about 40 per cent thought of themselves as middle or upper in 1946, and about 40 per cent again in 1964. In between, the decline in middle class identification noted by Converse in his comparison of 1945 data with 1952 and 1956 data has subsequently been reversed and, without finer examination of special groups, one can only conclude in 1965 that this aspect of "bourgeoisification" of society has not taken place. Men appear to be as willing today as they were about twenty years ago to see themselves as members of "the working class." As a nation we are certainly not "putting on airs."

But, as with party identification, it may be that class identification is slowly assuming a new meaning, a lack of intensity, a different reference. Here the SRC series shown in Table VI(a) gives us some clues, though rather slight ones. We would not—particularly just before the 1964 election—have expected much change, in any event; but we would expect a drifting decline in class awareness or consciousness in the sense of "thinking of oneself as belonging to a social class," partly because of the erosion of the intense feelings evoked by the experience of the 1930s, and partly through a change in age cohorts (in 1956 people in their fifties were the most class conscious age group). The time period is short, one of the figures is anomalous and is omitted from the table (in 1960 the comparable figure was 25 per cent), but after grouping contiguous years and thus doubling the sample sizes, a slow increase does appear in the proportion of people for whom social class is not a conscious reference. And if this is overtly true of this third of the population or so, one suspects that the meaning of class is *changing* for the other two-thirds, as well.

TABLE VI. CHANGING PATTERNS OF CLASS CONSCIOUSNESS AND CLASS IDEOLOGY

(a) "There's quite a bit of talk these days about different social classes. Most people say they belong either to the middle class or to the working class. Do you ever think of yourself as being in one of these classes?" (SRC, Oct., Nov. years indicated)[a]

	THE LATE 1950S (AVERAGE FOR 1956 AND 1958)		THE EARLY 1960s (AVERAGE FOR 1962 AND 1964)	
	PER CENT	(N)	PER CENT	(N)
No, never thinks of self as being in a social class	34.6	(1241)	37.6	(1078)
Yes, thinks of self as being in a social class	64.2	(2302)	60.8	(1744)
Don't know and other	1.1	(41)	1.6	(46)
Total	99.1	(3584)	100.0	(2868)

(b) "Are you in favor of labor unions?" (AIPO, Oct. 26, 1941)."In general do you approve or disapprove of labor unions?" (AIPO, Feb. 19, 1949; Nov. 11, 1953; Feb. 8, May 1 1957; Feb 8, 1959; Feb. 15, May 26, 1961; Jan. 30, 1963)[b]

	PER CENT APPROVE			INDEX OF UNLIKENESS	
	MANUAL WORKERS	BUSINESS & PROFESSIONAL	WHITE COLLAR	MANUAL WKRS. MINUS BUS. & PROF.	MANUAL WKRS. MINUS WHITE COLLAR
	(%)	(%)	(%)		
1941 (October)	73	—	69		4
1949 (February)	67	65	63	2	4
1953 (November)	81	70	75	11	6
1957 (February)	83	73	77	10	6
1961 (February)	77	64	65	13	12
1963 (January	75	61	67	14	8

(c) "As things stand today, do you think the laws governing unions are too strict or not strict enough?" (AIPO, Jan. 15, 1960). "Do you think the laws regulating labor unions are too strict, or not strict enough?" (AIPO, Oct. 22, 1961)[b]

	PER CENT "NOT STRICT ENOUGH"	
	1950	1961
	(%)	(%)
Business and Professional	54	60
White collar	43	48
Manual workers	34	35

[a] *Consortium codebooks.*
[b] Erskine, *POQ*, Vol. 26 (1962), pp. 284, 288 (and AIPO release, Jan. 30, 1963).

Converse, in neat analysis, has already given a strong indication that this is probably the case. He relates, for each of the two periods, class identification and certain social opinions dealing with the government's responsibility for employment, medical care, and housing and electricity; and finds that the correlations between class and opinions decline markedly in each case. Moreover, this is true of both objective status and subjective class identification. This is strong evidence for a changed meaning of class identification so far as government policy is concerned. After all, government is increasingly seen as the agent for improving *everyone's* prosperity.

But would this also be true of attitudes toward unions, organizations which do not have this trans-class role and which, indeed, áre often seen as (and are) the agents of class conflict? From 1936 to 1963 the Gallup polls have asked national samples about their attitudes toward unions: "Are you in favor of labor unions?" and "In general do you approve or disapprove of labor unions?" (Responses in contiguous years to these different questions indicate no difference in response patterns.) Three things are most notable about these responses. First, in this 26-year period, some fluctuation has occurred (from 58 per cent approve in 1938 to 76 per cent in February, 1957), with increased disapproval following severe strikes or critical investigations (like McClellan's in 1957), but no long term decline or increase in public criticism or support. Second, at no time has a majority of any group, including the business and professional group, failed to approve of unions. And third, and most important for our purposes, the discrepancy between working class and middle class support of unions seems to be growing, as may be seen in Table VI(b). Moreover, in the eleven years between 1950 and 1961, a modest increase has occurred in the proportion of business and professional and of white collar workers—but *not* of manual workers—who believe that the laws regulating labor unions are "not strict enough" (Table VI(c)). Such evidence, running contrary to my main thesis (the weakening effect of socio-economic status upon "ideology") suggests that there may be two themes here instead of one. Social class (objective and subjective) may have a weakening relationship to opinions about welfare state policies but not to opinions about labor unions. Perhaps, in a period when attention turns to questions of productivity and growth, rather than social justice and equality, and when the government, rather than unions, is the main agent of economic protection—especially for the underdog—unions will seem somewhat different to middle class and working class people. If this were the case, it would give us a better understanding of why it is that just at the time when the relationship between class and opinion on the welfare state is (in Converse's measure) weakening, the relationship between class and attitudes toward unions is growing stronger.

But political choices, as we know, are only loosely related to ideology. The facts seem to be as follows: the relationship between social status or class membership and political choice ("status polarization" or "class voting") tended to become closer, as one might expect in presidential elections during the Period of Economic Crisis, at least from 1936 to 1940; then, after a depressed relationship in 1944 due to attention to war issues, the correlation reached a peak in 1948, whereupon it declined in 1952 and again in 1956. At this point it reached a plateau and remained at about the 1956 level in 1960 and, surprisingly, in 1964. By Alford's measure (a variation of Rice's "index of likeness") this 1956–64 plateau is at about the same level as the starting point of the series in 1936, suggesting that class voting has a kind of "natural level" for a given country in a given period, altered only occasionally by certain "critical elections."

But, while the measure of likeness (or, actually, "unlikeness") which Alford uses and which I have employed elsewhere in this paper, is useful in indicating some elements of similarity, it does not taken into account the *level* at which these similarities and discrepancies occur. For example, a situation where 60 per cent of the manual workers and 40 per cent of the non-manual workers vote Democratic (index=20), and another situation where 80 per cent of the manual workers and 60 per cent of the non-manual workers vote Democratic, (index=20) are scored alike. Yet in the first instance, a majority of the manual workers is on one side of the political division, and a majority of the white collar and business and professional workers is on the other, whereas in the second case, a majority of both groups is on the same side.

Let us suppose that the party responsible for innovative institution of welfare state measures, and fiscal and monetary measures designed to level out the business cycle and promote growth, gradually extends its following in the Age of Affluence so that it becomes overwhelmingly the dominant party. This is done partly by a gradual shift in the middle "white collar" groups so that they see the more liberal party as appropriately "their own," and by some defection of business and professional groups, especially among Catholic and Jewish communicants. Our measure of political likeness does not change, but the pivot changes and we have a situation where class voting differences, with their winner-take-all payoff, become less important.

The evidence that this is the case is strong. A majority of the skilled and unskilled workers have been Democrats at least since 1928 and probably before, with a variable minority occasionally voting outside the party (especially in 1952 and 1956). Even these defectors, however, tended to identify with the Democratic party throughout. On the other hand, historically the business and professional groups, the white collar groups, and usually the farmers, have identified with the Republican party, occasionally voting for Democratic candidates, but then returning to the fold—though returning in decreasing numbers. The consequence was that in terms of party identification at the end of the Period of Economic Crisis both parties started about even: in 1940 some 42 per cent of the population said they were Democrats, 38 per cent Republicans, and 20 per cent claimed to be Independents. By July 1964, just prior to the nomination of Barry Goldwater, the count was 53 per cent Democrats, 25 per cent Republicans, and 22 per cent Independents. And the shift seemed to be accelerating: between 1960 and 1964 all major groups became more Democratic, with the business and professional group moving a little faster than average (7 per cent shift compared to an average of 6 per cent) and thus becoming more Democratic than Republican for the first time. Thus, as far as party identification goes, all groups have Democratic pluralities, and although proportions differ between social classes, majorities tend to agree.

The difference between the kind of situation where majorities of all major social groups (business and professional, farmers, manual workers, etc.) agree, compared to a situation where the majority of one group is for one party and the majority of an opposing group is for another, is illustrated by the 1964 election. In such an election business and union spokesmen (like Henry Ford and Walter Reuther), support the same candidate; the candidate of the dominant coalition assumes a moderating "national unity" tone and his opponent sounds "shrill"; references to class-linked slogans such as "union bosses," and "economic royalists" are muted in the dominant party. In short, the shifting "pivot" of class allegiance implies a very different kind of "democratic class conflict"— even though the index of unlikeness or of "class voting" may remain constant. Within the dominant party, the politics of consensus takes over, while the minority party occasionally reverts to the older politics of economic crisis.

V. RELIGION

(d) *In the Age of Affluence, religious institutions* slowly *lose their influence over men's thought and behavior; religious prejudices and hostilities decline; but the influence of religious identification upon partisan political choice is among the slowest influences to change.*

It may be argued that class divisions in politics, and the influence of status upon social and political opinion, are "healthier" for a society than are religious divisions and influences. They are less likely to be "moralized," therefore less likely to be intransigent; conflicts are more easily solved by economic growth and economic change; compromise is easier because the stakes are often divisible and allocable by small units; the controversies are increasingly subject to empirical proof, referring, as they do, to cause and effect in *this* world. Therefore, whatever one's feelings about religion in its own sphere, a declining influence of dogmatic religion (as contrasted to some Judeo-Christian ethics) on social thought, and of religious affiliation on political choice, might be seen as a step toward a more healthy polity.

Since the space is brief, let us, for the record, summarize some evidence pointing generally, with some exceptions, in this direction. The basic facts on religious affiliation and church attendance are these: the proportion of the population with some kind of religious affiliation increased in the 1920s, remained constant in the 1930s, increased substantially in the 1940s, increased very moderately in the 1950s, and from 1959 to 1962 (the latest date on which I have figures) increased not at all. Church attendance (as contrasted to affiliation) increased in the late 1940s and early 1950s to a peak average attendance of 49 per cent in 1958, and from that time decreased slowly but steadily to 45 per cent in 1964, with Protestants and Catholics moving in the same direction. Since affiliation and church attendance have been higher among white collar than blue collar, and among better educated than less well educated groups, this levelling off and decline are, so to speak, "bucking" the educational and occupational trend. Some perception of this tendency seems to have entered the public consciousness. Asked whether religion is "increasing or losing its influence on American life," the proportion seeing religion losing its influence has recently grown: 1957: 14 per cent; 1962: 31 per cent; 1965: 45 per cent. These changes are late in the Age of Affluence; their political and ideological effects would not be expected to appear for some time.

Such observations refer to the theological or institutional aspects of religion, but the community effect, the identification with co-religionists, is something else. This can take a variety of forms, but, briefly, identification with co-religionists in recent years seems to include a declining element of suspicion and declining ideological component. The evidence for this is partly in the changes among Catholics (but not so much among Protestants) indicating greater hope for *rapprochement* of the Christian religions—ecumenicism. Among Protestants, on the other hand, there is increasing support for federal aid to religious schools, thus almost eliminating one of the major bones of contention between communicants of the two religions. National resistance to voting for "a well qualified man who happened to be a Catholic," decreasing over the years, collapsed with Kennedy's term in office (Table VII (a)). Attitudes toward Jews, as measured by the same question, willingness to vote for a "well qualified person who happens to be Jewish," have continuously been more accepting (Table VII (b)). And Jews themselves, a declining proportion of the population, indicate, in a brief series (1956, 1958, 1960) a modestly declining sense of greater "feelings of closeness" to other Jews, compared to closeness to non-Jews. The evidence is strong that ideological divisions, suspicion, prejudice, and sense of difference, especially as these relate to political matters, are declining.

But not, apparently, the influence of religious identification on political choice. Employing, once again, the "index of unlikeness" (per cent of Catholics voting Democratic, less the per cent of all Protestants so voting), the series is as follows: 1948: 19; 1952: 19; 1956: 14; 1960: 40; 1964: 21. The decline of the relationship between religion and vote, predicted by Berelson on the basis of age-group differences in 1948, has not materialized, at least at this gross level. But, as the above attitudinal evidence indicates, the meaning has changed; and as the above trends in affiliation and attendance portend, the institutional reinforcement is likely to decline.

VI. RACE

(e) *In an Age of Affluence, the struggle for equality by a deprived racial group will be facilitated by the expanding economy, the availability of governmental resources for special assistance, and the relative security of otherwise challenged and more hostile "opposition" groups. These conflicts will be expressed by the increased militance of the deprived minority group, and the vacillating, often reluctant, sometimes idealistic acceptance of these claims by the more affluent majority.*

Racial cleavage, strife and politics are different from class politics in the United States, and, indeed, everywhere. Mobility ("passing"), inter-marriage, ecological scattering, and inter-group communication are much more difficult across race (caste) lines than across class lines; the middle groups identifying now with one side, now with the other are smaller; the role of property and relations of the different groups to the means of production are different; visibility and, hence, treatment by the dominant group are different. Changing group proportions are not induced by technology and the demand for new and

TABLE VII. INDICATIONS OF DECLINING RELIGIOUS
HOSTILITY IN POLITICS

(a) "If your party nominated a generally well-qualified man for President, and he happened to be a Catholic, would you vote for him?" (AIPO, Oct. 4, 1963)

YEAR	YES	NO	UNDECIDED
	(%)	(%)	(%)
1940	62	31	7
1958	68	25	7
1959	69	20	11
1960	71	20	9
1961	82	13	5
1963	84	13	3

(b) "Would you vote for a Jew for President?" (AIPO, Feb. 8, 1937). "If your party nominated a generally well-qualified man for President, and he happened to be a Jew, would you vote for him?" (AIPO, Oct. 23, 1963)

YEAR	YES	NO	NO OPINION
	(%)	(%)	(%)
1937*	49	51	(excluded)
1958	62	28	10
1960	72	22	6
1963	77	17	6

* Data for this year are from Cantril and Strunk, *Public Opinion*.

different services; rather they are a matter of birth and mortality rates. And, most important, in the United States there are only 22 million Negroes, about half of them still in the South. As a consequence, there cannot be a Negro party and a white party, except in some Southern communities; but for a national or a state contest, current trends suggest a division between one party regarded as more friendly to the Negro, made up of Negroes *and whites* pitted against a predominantly all-white party. These trends rest in large measure on the wholesale northward migration of Negroes, stemming initially from wartime conditions of extreme manpower shortages and consequent job opportunities; and the repercussions of the migration in the South as well as the North. Under these circumstances, how have the Age of Affluence and the politics of consensus affected the situation?

In the first place, one needs to know whether or not the non-white population has shared in the affluent society. The answer, of course, is that they are still faring very badly, economically, educationally, and socially:

The median income of the non-white population is about the half median income of the white population (1962).

The median school years completed for non-whites is 8.2; for whites it is 10.9

(1960). This understates the difference, for the caliber of education in most non-white schools is notoriously poorer.

The proportion of non-whites in white collar jobs is 17.7 per cent; for whites it is 46.9 per cent (1963).

When, however, we turn to recent rates of change, the picture is a little better, for the Negro rate of increase in median income is about half again as high as for whites in recent years (1959–1962) and also in the war period. Similarly, in the past decade and a half, the proportion of workers in white collar jobs has increased about three and a half times as fast among Negroes as among whites. But in terms of education, there is little difference in rate of change; indeed, most recently it seems the white rate of increase has been greater than the Negro rate. On balance, the Negro has participated increasingly in some of the rewarding aspects of affluence, but for him the term "affluence," comparatively speaking, is anomalous: aspirations are running much beyond achievement, and the current *level* seems to belie the hopes for full equality.

I know of no available series of questions asked of Negroes over time to indicate whether or not they experience a greater or lesser sense of deprivation today compared to some previous time; whether their anger at the white community is greater or less; whether the frustration expressed in recent riots is greater or less than it was when anger and frustration may have been differently expressed; whether a sense of special community among Negroes is growing or declining and whether or not whites are more easily embraced in this community than they once were. But, perhaps these are straws in the wind:

(1) Electoral participation in the South has been increasing for the past 15 years and will now (1965 and 1966) increase dramatically in certain places with federal voting registrars. It has always been high (education and income held constant) in the Northern cities. Where non-voting indicates coercion, the lifting of this coercive force may remove some sources of hostility; where it indicates apathy and withdrawal, the change may mean a decline of these symptoms.

(2) In 1960 a set of extended interviews (by a Negro) of working class Negroes in New Haven revealed, in the midst of hostility and frustration, a kind of non-alienated faith in "Washington" as a reliable (indeed, almost omnipotent) source of help.

(3) Two AIPO surveys in August 1963 and May 1965 revealed in the South (but not in the North) an increase of about 20 percentage points in the Negro group believing that Negroes were treated "the same as whites."

I put little stock in these indicators. I suspect the fact that about the same proportion of Negroes in 1946 and 1965 (roughly 70 per cent) believed that the Negro was "unfairly treated" or "treated less well than whites" in his community is a better measure of resentment. At the same time, I would expect a substantial change in the quality of this resentment: fear, apathy, self-hatred, and latent hostility in the 1940s and earlier; disappointment, frustration, manifest hostility, ambivalence, and qualified hope, in the later period. One indication of this last quality, hope, lies in the growing support among Southern Negroes for integrated schools, and the high proportion (70 per cent in 1956) of Southern Negroes who believe that "the day will come in the South when whites and Negroes will be going to the same schools, eating in the same restaurants, and generally sharing the same public accommodations."

The survey evidence is substantial that for the white community, nationally, there is a growing sense that integration in schools (without bussing), residential neighborhoods, and in public accommodations is inevitable, socially desirable, and, with many reservations, personally acceptable. These data are presented in Table VIII. The rate of change is slow, and there are setbacks,

TABLE VIII. CHANGING ATTITUDES TOWARD INTEGRATION

(a) "Would you, yourself, have any objection to sending your children to a school where a few of the children are colored? Where half of the children are colored?" (AIPO)

	PER CENT "YES"			
	WHERE A FEW CHILDREN ARE COLORED		WHERE HALF OF CHILDREN ARE COLORED	
	OUTSIDE SOUTH	SOUTH	OUTSIDE SOUTH	SOUTH
	(%)	(%)	(%)	(%)
1958	13	72	39	81
1959	7	72	34	83
1963 (June)	10	61	33	78
1965 (May)	7	37	28	68

(b) "Do you think the day will ever come in the South when whites and Negroes will be going to the same schools, eating in the same restaurants, and generally sharing the same public accommodations?" (AIPO)

	SOUTH ONLY		
	YES	NO	UNCERTAIN
	(%)	(%)	(%)
1957 (August)	45	33	22
1958 (October)	53	31	16
1961 (January)	76	19	5
1963 (July)	83	13	4

Sources: Erskine, *POQ*, Vol. 26 (1962), pp. 138, 141; AIPO releases, July 19, 1963 and May 23, 1965.

now and then; but the series reveals a growing willingness to accommodate to the demands for change of a deprived group. At the same time, variable tensions emerge over the actual implementation of these demands by governmental action (or, probably, over any action by any agency). Thus, when asked "Do you think the Kennedy (Johnson) administration is pushing integration too fast, or not fast enough?" from 36 to 50 per cent have said "too fast." This is a measure of resistance to change, a measure of the lack of strength or salience of the ideal and of the discrepancy between verbal and behavioral support. Perhaps, too, it indicates a response to style or manner of "pushing"—consensual or argumentative and coercive; Johnson has fared better than Kennedy in this respect. In any event, this apparent ambivalence and reluctant acceptance indicates exactly those attitudes which, in an insecure, depression-ridden, stagnant society might easily become violent hostility and implacable opposition. The lower income and less well educated people are more resistant than others to integration. What would their responses be if they were fearful of unemployment, less hopeful of the future, more suspicious of people generally and feeling victimized by fate; if, in short, they had the attitudes which we saw had changed with growing affluence in recent years?

How then has the Age of Affluence, shaped for the Negro by a partially sympathetic dominant white majority, affected his politics? In one sense "consensus" describes two aspects of the situation. First, Negroes have, ever since the New Deal, become partisan advocates of welfare state policies. Ideologically, in this sense, they are in tune with the dominant political theme of the times. Second, their partisan party preference has gradually, and with some reversals of direction in the 1950s, shifted toward the Democratic camp so that they are now more partisan than any other major group. In 1964, only 6 per cent voted Republican; nine months later only 9 per cent identified with the Republican party. Since there are about twice as many Democrats as Republicans in the United States, again, it seems, the Negro community has adopted the "in" party; in this respect they are in agreement with majorities in almost all other major demographic groups.

On the other hand, this dramatic increase (and it might be viewed with caution since, in the past, the Negro vote has been more volatile than others—more volatile than the manual worker vote, for example), has meant, according to the index of unlikeness, an increase in racial voting and partisanship, at least in 1964 and 1965. In one sense, this *is* a measure of hostile cleavage, since it reflects the partisan politics and policies of recent years. Moreover, the Republican party, having lost almost all of its Negro following, may come to believe that it is in its interest to stress "states rights," "law and order in the streets," and "voluntarism in school assignments," and other themes with barely disguised white racial appeal; in which case there will be a re-sorting, not of the Negroes, but of some village traditionalists, many Southerners, and some alienated and marginal Northern and Western urban dwellers. The Goldwater trial run for these themes was not encouraging in the North, but feelings on such matters run deep for an uncertain number of people, and the search for a winning theme may lead the Republican leadership in this direction. Then, racial voting, unlike class voting, will take on a new intensity and move away from the politics of consensus.

But, probably, for most white people, neither the Negro's problem nor the "threat" of integration in their own communities (and certainly not elsewhere), is sufficiently important to determine partisan choice. The politics of consensus can go on around this "American dilemma," within sound of the battle but relatively undisturbed by it.

VII. POLITICAL ALIENATION

(f) *In the Age of Affluence, there will be a rapprochement between men and their government and a decline in political alienation.*

It is easier to make the argument that political alienation should decline than to find the evidence to support this view. The argument, again, is simple: the declining intensity of partisanship implies a decline in hostility toward government on the part of the "out" group—with, perhaps, a reverse effect and embitterment on the "far out" right. Politics, then, deals less with moral absolutes and becomes more a discussion of means than ends;—its ideological component declines. Since everyone is "doing better" year by year, though with different rates of improvement, the stakes are not so much in terms of gain or loss, but in terms of size of gain—giving government more clearly the image of a rewarding rather than a punishing instrument. Taxes, while primarily the instrument for financing government, now also may be seen as instruments for maintaining prosperity and financing benefits for all rather than for redistributing income.

The difficulty with the use of some evidence supporting this is that I seem to have adopted a "heads I win, tails you lose" strategy with respect to the main source of recent data, the 1964 surveys. If these data show a decline in symptoms of alienation, they seem to support the argument that historical trends are thus revealing themselves. If they show an increase in alienation symptoms, they support the argument that the 1964 election was a regression to the politics of crisis. If we had a long enough time series, this dilemma of ambivalence could be avoided by showing a decline in alienation symptoms up to 1964, with a rise at that time.

In one series we do have exactly this pattern. Figure 1 shows a decline from 1952 to 1960 and then a rise in the proportion of (1) people who feel that public officials are indifferent to what "people like me think," and (2) those who believe "people like me don't have any say about what the government does," and (3) those for whom politics and government are "too complicated" to understand. The trouble is that I can see no very plausible reason why the themes or personalities of the 1964 election should occasion these particular changes. That particular election might well have increased the crisis atmosphere; it might (and apparently did) increase the salience of "corruption in politics" themes; it might have created new cleavages in society and thus have disrupted the politics of consensus. But why this campaign, at least compared to 1956 and 1960, should encourage a sense of ineffectiveness and lack of responsiveness in government, is obscure. Therefore, in spite of the appearance of a confirming pattern, we must leave this evidence as anomalous.

Nevertheless, as may be seen in Table IX, some evidence exists for believing that in certain ways there has been a *rapprochement* between men and their government and a decline in political alienation. In the first place, the increase

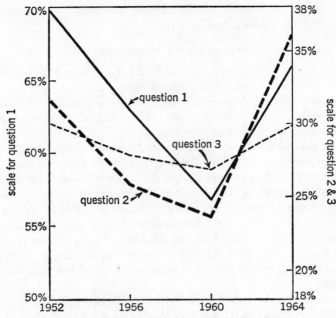

Fig. 1. Decline and Rise of Political Alienation

Q. 1. "Sometimes politics and government seem so complicated that a person like me can't really understand what's going on."
Q. 2. "I don't think public officials care what people like me think."
Q. 3. "People like me don't have any say about what the government does."
Source: SRC questions in election studies of years indicated, reported in *Consortium codebooks*.

in the proportion of the public who would like to see their sons (if they had any) enter politics as a career, is, I think symptomatic of a growing attitude that political life is both rewarding and honorable. One reason for interpreting this series in this way is the sharp decline in the proportion of arguments against such a career which refer to corruption: from 30 per cent in 1946 to 17 per cent in 1965.

On the other side of politics, the voter side, note the marked increase in the sense that one "ought" to vote under various more or less discouraging circumstances. These items, taken together, have been called a "citizen duty" scale and one may interpret these data as indicating a reinforced or growing belief that good citizenship means a politically more active citizen. From 1952 to 1960, in the eight possible comparisons over time in Table IX(b), each shows a growth of the sense of citizen duty.

In the argument set forth above, I suggested that attitudes toward taxation should change. The AIPO question, "Do you consider the amount of income tax which you (your husband) (had, have) to pay as too high, too low, or about right?" has been asked many times since 1947. The earlier years are non-comparable for several reasons, and show great variability, but we have data from 1952 to 1962 not only by national totals, but also by major occupational groups (Table IX(c)). The data reveal two things, especially: first,

TABLE IX. RAPPROCHEMENT BETWEEN MEN AND POLITICS: POLITICS AS A CAREER, ELECTIONS AS A DUTY, AND TAXES AS A BURDEN

(a) "If you had a son just getting out of school would you like to see him go into politics as a life-work?" (NORC, Nov. '43, Nov. '45). "If you had a son would you like to see him go into politics as a life's work when he gets out of school?" (AIPO, Dec. 28, 1944). "If you had a son, would you like to see him go into politics as a life's work?" (AIPO, July 20, 1953; March 5, 1955; March 3, 1965)[a]

	YES	NO	NO OPINION
	(%)	(%)	(%)
1943 (Nov.)	18	69	13
1944 (Dec.)	21	68	11
1945 (Nov.)	24	65	11
1953 (July)	20	70	10
1955 (March)	27	60	13
1965 (March)	36	54	10

(b) The duty to vote in elections: 1952, 1956, 1960.[b]

	PER CENT AGREE		
	1952	1956	1960
	(%)	(%)	(%)
"If a person doesn't care how an election comes out he shouldn't vote in it."	53	45	43
"A good many local elections aren't important enough to bother with."	17	13	12
"It isn't so important to vote when you know your party doesn't have any chance to win."	11	9	7
"So many other people vote in the national elections that it doesn't matter to me whether I vote or not."	12	10	8
No. of cases	(1799)	(1762)	(1954)

(c) "Do you consider the amount of income tax which you (your husband) (had, have) to pay as too high, too low, or about right?" (AIPO)[c]

YEAR	PER CENT SAYING "TOO HIGH"			
	PROF. & BUS.	WHITE COLLAR	FARMERS	MANUAL WORKERS
	(%)	(%)	(%)	(%)
1952 (March 12)	74	73	63	72
1953 (March 8)	61	61	55	59
1957 (April 24)	63	69	51	62*
1959 (April 15)	50	51	51	51*
1961 (March 8)	42	50	47	49
1962 (March 11)	50	49	36	51

* Skilled workers only; in 1957 unskilled workers were 65%, in 1959, 58% saying "too high."
[a] Cantril and Strunk, *Public Opinion*, p. 534; AIPO releases as indicated for 1953, 1955, 1965.
[b] *Consortium codebooks;* SRC election studies, October or November of years indicated. These questions were not asked in 1964.
[c] Erskine, *POQ*, Vol. 28 (1964), p. 161.

the lack of any substantial assocation between occupational status and attitudes toward taxation. We have known for some time that working class attitudes toward taxation did not fit into conventional concepts of "liberalism" (high taxes and high welfare payments); this is only further illumination of that point. And second—the point to be made here—is the general decline in a sense of taxation as too burdensome. (These findings, it will be observed, do not include the period of great discussion and final legislative action on tax reduction to improve the state of the economy.) Since opposition to "tax-eaters" and the burdens of taxation have traditionally been symptomatic of alienation from government, I think we may quite appropriately see this set of changing attitudes as a part of the *rapprochement* between men and their governments.

In spite of certain anomalies associated with 1964 data, including a constant state of "trust in government" from 1958 to 1964, I am persuaded that there has been a growing state of confidence between men and government, perhaps especially men and politics, during the Age of Affluence. This argument takes on weight when it is placed against the increased life satisfactions and self-confidence examined earlier, the decline in sense of crisis in elections, the changed meaning of class cleavages, the slow drift toward religious harmony, and even the reluctant yielding to the demands for racial equality. The headlines will not show this consensus, nor will the demonstrations at city hall or on the campus, but the ordinary man in the Age of Affluence is beginning to find some greater sense of hope and peace and self-assurance expressed in a less acrimonious political style.

THE IMPLICATIONS OF REAPPORTIONMENT:
CONSEQUENCES OF UNBALANCED
REPRESENTATION IN THE STATES *

Gordon E. Baker

ON THE TWO-PARTY SYSTEM

THE far-reaching effects of rural legislative advantage are not always sufficiently appreciated. Whenever "rotten borough" situations have aroused publicity the problem is often treated in isolation, as though the controversy concerned only cities versus farmers. Such a view obscures the widespread ramifications of urban-rural representation. One of the most important effects of a distorted legislative pattern concerns the political party balance. In a number of states the party split bears a high correlation to the extent of urbanism. As a general rule, the Democratic party in the industrialized states of the North and Midwest is stronger in city districts, while Republicans usually find most solid support in rural, small-town, and suburban regions. However, in some

* From *The Reapportionment Revolution* by Gordon E. Baker. © Copyright 1955, 1966, by Random House, Inc. Reprinted by permission of the publisher.

border states—Oklahoma, Kentucky, and Maryland are examples—Republican support is often weaker in rural than in urban and suburban areas. This is becoming increasingly true also in some parts of the South, where a sizable increase in Republican urban voting strength has long been minimized by the apportionment system. With the major electoral decisions in the South still made in the Democratic party primary, intraparty factionalism typically finds the more liberal Democratic elements stronger in urban areas. In fact, the hard core of Southern conservatism has traditionally been the rural "black belt," where a small white minority, grossly overrepresented in state legislatures as well as in other political institutions of the section, has exercised enormous power.

With this general situation in mind, it is obvious that a representative system allowing urban areas less legislative strength than their populations merit gave an immediate advantage to the political party or faction that is stronger in smaller towns and rural areas. This could result in legislative control by the actual minority party, even in states that vote heavily in the opposite direction. In other instances, even if the successful party represented a popular majority, its legislative strength was often greatly bloated due to a monopoly of rural seats. In New York, the two-party struggle is closely contested, and statewide offices might go to either party. But the state legislature was frequently termed "Republican by constitutional law." Since New York City is heavily Democratic and the upstate region largely Republican, the impact of city underrepresentation was apparent. The situation was reversed across the continent in Arizona, where Republicans (heavily concentrated in the two most urban counties) have managed to gain several major statewide offices, but comprised a distinct minority in the legislature, especially the rural-based senate. And in traditionally Democratic Oklahoma, Henry Bellmon became the first Republican governor in the state's history, with a comfortable margin in the 1962 election. But while Republican legislative candidates in Oklahoma also did much better than previously, they were hopelessly outnumbered in both houses (38 to 6 and 95 to 25), due in part to underrepresentation of urban centers.

One consequence of an apportionment system that favors less populous areas in either house is the increased likelihood of divided government. In some cases the party receiving a popular statewide majority controlled one house while the minority had an advantage in the other because it elected more legislators from overrepresented areas. In other states divided control took the form of a governor elected by a statewide majority that was still unable to control one or both houses of the legislature. The table illustrates some past examples of divided government in several states.

The figures in the table reveal sharp disparities in partisan success in each house of the legislature and in seeking the governorship. Since the state executive is chosen at large, his election is generally a more accurate index of popular feeling than the election of a legislature whose electoral districts are distorted for partisan or rural advantage. While many other factors—including weak local party organization, less well-known candidates, and "wasted" votes through

YEARS OF PARTY CONTROL IN SELECTED STATES
1947–1965

STATE	SENATE		HOUSE			GOVERNORSHIP	
	D	R	D	R	Tie	D	R
Illinois	0	18	4	14		8	10
New Jersey	0	18	6	12		10	8
Michigan	0	18	0	16	2	14	4
Connecticut	12	6	2	16		12	6
New Mexico	18	0	16	2		10	8
Maryland	18	0	18	0		10	8

SOURCE: Adapted from Malcolm E. Jewell, *The State Legislature: Politics and Practice* (New York: Random House, 1962), p. 11. Data for Maryland have been added to the figures drawn from portions of Jewell's table. Other figures have been updated to include sessions ending in early 1965.

heavy concentration of party strength in one or a few areas—can contribute to a discrepancy between a party's statewide and legislative strength, the examples in the table also suggest the importance of disproportionate representation. Illinois and New Jersey are states that had a close two-party struggle for the governorship during the years covered. Democrats were also able to control the more popularly based lower house on some occasions, but the area-based senates were invulnerable bulwarks for the Republicans regardless of statewide voting trends. Michigan Democrats suffered from both "wasted" votes concentrated in urban centers, and underrepresentation of these areas in both houses, but particularly the senate. Connecticut is a two-party state where the vote for governor and the population-based senate tend to coincide. But in the lower house, based on towns, the Republicans held solid majorities with one "freak" exception in the 1958 election, when a 62 percent landslide gave the Democrats a slim majority, their first since 1876. The situation returned to normal in 1960. Finally, New Mexico and Maryland are examples of Democratic advantage through rural-oriented apportionments. Statewide offices were closely contested, but the legislatures were overwhelmingly Democratic.

Even in states where one party is traditionally dominant, disproportionate representation has contributed to weakening the minority party still further, both in numbers elected and in the general discouraging effect on the zeal with which the party contests many constituencies. Florida furnished an excellent example of a growing minority party held severely in check by the legislative apportionment pattern. The state's rapid urbanization has greatly strengthened Republican opposition, with that party's candidate for governor in 1960 taking 40 percent of the statewide vote. But the northern influx of Republican voters to Florida's cities and suburbs had made little dent on the state's heavily rural legislature; in that same 1960 election only seven Republicans won election to the lower house of ninety-five members, a high point which receded to five two years later. During the same period only one senator out of thirty-eight was a Republican. The impact of reapportionment on a minority party's fortunes was clearly demonstrated when Florida, under judicial prodding after

Baker v. Carr, partially reapportioned its lower house in 1963. In a special election that year, Republicans contested twenty-seven of the twenty-eight new seats in metropolitan areas where the party had been making some effort, winning eleven, thus increasing their total house membership from five to sixteen.

The effect upon the two-party system within the states is surely one of the most telling indictments that can be brought against a condition of representative inequality. The whole rationale of the two-party system is that it should offer the electorate alternative choices of candidates and programs. In this way the parties give meaning and purpose to public sentiment and also serve to strengthen the element of responsibility among governing officials. Ideally, parties should contest for public support in such a way that votes can be translated into some sort of public policy. In a democracy there should be a reasonably direct relationship between predominant public opinion and the power to govern. With this in mind, the implications of a distorted pattern of representation are obvious. How meaningful is an election in which one party is guaranteed, in advance, control of the legislature (or of one of its houses) even if a substantial vote is cast against it? Yet such a result has occurred in several American states frequently enough to raise serious questions for a people that supposedly professes democracy as a value system.

While political parties in many states are not noted for having a high degree of internal cohesion or unity of purpose, there are often issues on which the party balance can make a decided difference. This is particularly true when the governorship is held by a popular leader who has dramatized certain matters of public policy. Yet a misrepresentative legislature (or even one house) can nullify whatever attempt is made to embody into law a program apparently endorsed by the electorate. Even a governor's choice of his own cabinet and other important appointive posts must often meet the approval of a hostile upper house.

To criticize divided government is not to rule out the role of compromise. Differences of opinions and approaches within and between parties and branches of government will inevitably demand conciliation, without the added handicaps of a structural framework that typically fosters irresponsibility or stalemate. After a close analysis of the problem, Malcolm E. Jewell concluded that "compromise in divided state governments is too often simply bargaining for favors, organized bilateral logrolling." And Jewell added perceptively: "The most valid criticism of an apportionment system that encourages divided government is that it breeds irresponsibility. Both parties can make promises that need not be kept because the other party can be blamed for inaction."

ON INTRAPARTY STRUCTURE

In addition to affecting the two-party balance, rural dominance has also played an important role *within* each party. Legislative districts or county units have commonly served as the basis for party organizations, with a consequent advantage for rural leaders. State central committees as well as state conventions of the major parties have usually reflected urban underrepresentation. The make-up of conventions is especially important in those few states where party nominees are selected by the convention method rather than the direct primary.

The apportionment pattern can have other consequences within a party. As we have seen, one of the parties in two-party states frequently had an artificial advantage in one or both houses because its actual electoral strength was magnified in the number of seats held. Yet, paradoxically, this was also a source of weakness. Gubernatorial candidates of the weaker party frequently found their campaigns handicapped by the kind of records established by their party's legislators. Examples are Kentucky and Rhode Island, where statewide Republican candidates had to appeal to the significant urban and suburban vote, but where the party's legislative delegations reflected a largely rural or small-town composition and a more conservative record on political issues.

It is in the one-party states, however, where the party's organization, rules, and practices are of particular importance. In most of the South the Democratic primary is the only effective election. Until 1963 the most noteworthy instance of rural-urban representative imbalance was the Georgia county unit system, under which there was no necessary relationship between the popular vote and the nominations for statewide and congressional offices. Instead, every county was granted twice as many unit votes as it had representatives in the legislature, with each county recorded as a unit for the leading candidate within its boundaries. The long-existing apportionment formula for Georgia's lower house meant that about 22 percent of the state's population, located in the smallest counties, could not only elect a majority of the house, but could also produce a majority of unit votes for the other offices. Georgia's most populous county, Fulton (Atlanta), with a 1960 population of 556,326, had no more strength in either the lower house or in statewide primary elections than the state's three least inhabited counties with a combined population of only 6,980. Under the county unit system, candidates for governor, United States Senator, and other offices could, and sometimes did, win the nomination (and hence the election) without even a plurality of the popular vote. In addition, such an electoral arrangement meant that candidates made little attempt to gain a popular majority, but instead directed their programs and appeals to the small, rural districts with the preponderant political weight.

One of the earliest and most promising consequences of the Supreme Court's 1962 decision in *Baker v. Carr* was the judicial invalidation of Georgia's county unit system, which had survived several previous legal challenges. On the basis of a Federal district court ruling after the Baker decision, the state Democratic Committee decided to hold the 1962 primary election for statewide offices on a popular vote basis. For the first time in half a century, Georgia's urban voters had a proportionate weight in choosing such officials. On March 18, 1963, the United States Supreme Court decided the case on appeal and ruled out the kind of unequal voting inherent in the county unit system as a violation of the Fourteenth Amendment's equal protection clause. While sidestepping any application of its decision to legislative districts, the high tribunal, speaking through Justice Douglas, declared: "Once the geographical unit for which a representative is to be chosen is designated, all who participate in the election are to have an equal vote—whatever their race, whatever their sex, whatever their occupation, whatever their income, and wherever their home may be in that geographical unit." The state of Maryland had long employed a county unit system for primaries similar to Georgia's, but the consequences were less severe, since voters did have a choice between two major parties in the final general election. While the Maryland legislature refused to abandon the system after the judicial decisions in the Georgia case, a three-judge Federal court soon invalidated the Maryland county unit practice on the basis of the precedent established in the Georgia case.

ON SOCIAL AND ECONOMIC POLICIES

While numerous factors, both formal and informal, determine the political product, the structural characteristics of government itself are important elements in the evolution of public policy. Thus a legislative system based upon an unequal allocation of popular strength yields special advantages to certain interest groups and makes the articulation of other groups more difficult. The long-standing overrepresentation of rural areas meant that organized agricultural interests were usually in a favorable position to influence state legislation. At the same time the system placed certain urban interest groups at a disadvantage. Those urban interests whose policies were compatible with the general outlook of rural representatives were, however, in a more favorable position. In their perceptive analysis of the legislative process in Florida, William Havard and Loren Beth pointed out in 1962 that the heavy rural bias in the apportionment of both houses "obviously gives some pressure groups privileged access to the legislature by providing them with a sure bloc of friendly legislators who hold a majority or close to it." These authors added that the strongest interest groups in rural Florida included the Farm Bureau and the phosphate and wood-pulp industries. In addition to these were a host of large and small business interests (banks, utilities, insurance companies) that were not particularly rural, but that were powerful in rural areas and thus were in a better position to influence a majority of legislators than were groups confined only to metropolitan areas.

Such facts help explain the behavior of some urban business interests that have staunchly defended inequitable representation for their own areas. These groups apparently found greater representation for their political outlook among rural delegates. The alliance is not surprising in view of the frequent similarity in attitudes held by both interests. In addition, representatives from rural constituencies are often not farmers, but small-town lawyers and businessmen. On many issues they share a natural community of interests with city groups representing a similar social and economic outlook. By contrast, other urban interests, notably labor groups, seldom find support for rural representatives.

An interesting example of certain urban attitudes on representation can be found in California, where the "Federal Plan," restricting each county to only one seat in the state senate, found its main support among such groups as the state Chamber of Commerce and most of the urban press. Opponents of the system periodically sought its modification, primarily through initiative campaigns in 1948, 1960, and 1962. While the less populous counties naturally opposed any change, the major battles took place within the large metropolitan counties that would have multiplied their legislative strength. Not until the 1962 campaign did a proposal attract the support of significant interests and the daily press in Los Angeles, while the northern urban bay area consistently fought any plan from which Los Angeles County would be the largest beneficiary. The 1962 initiative, which lost in a fairly close vote, was the most moderate of the ballot measures yet attempted. It would have retained the existing forty-district pattern, but would have added ten seats for the most populous counties. The list of major financial contributors to the campaign against the proposition hardly looks like a constellation of agrarian forces: the Pacific Gas and Electric Company, the Standard Oil Company of California, the Southern Pacific Railroad, the Richfield Oil Company, the Bank of America, plus several other oil companies, banks, and railroads.

Recognition of a heterogeneous framework of interests is helpful in understanding the difficulty long encountered by labor and consumer groups in influencing state legislative decisions on social and economic policy. A survey of restrictive labor legislation in a number of states revealed the leading role of rural lawmakers, often working with business approval or assistance. Other issues that have characterized distinct urban and rural (or small-town) conflicts include: regulation of wages and hours, protection of migrant workers, distribution of certain tax revenues (especially from gasoline), daylight-saving time, and state aid to roads and education.

It is difficult to pinpoint to what extent the representative pattern of state legislatures has affected the resolution of such issues. For one thing, influences on the legislative product are myriad, and variables differ in relative importance from state to state. It appears that the apportionment structure has been highly significant in affecting policy outcomes in some states, while in others it has had only a slight or negligible bearing, at least on *positive* enactments of public policy. To predict how a differently constituted legislature *would* act was even more difficult until the recent revolution in legislative patterns stimulated by judicial pressure. Now, comparative studies of policy questions within a state before and after a comprehensive reapportionment should be most informative. Judging from the amount of concern, money, time, and effort expended by differing interest groups in so many states over proposed reapportionments, it is clear that major segments of society and economic interests have at least assumed that the make-up of the legislature makes a difference in the real world of policy formation. In many cases the impact of legislative representation seems pervasive but not always easily measurable. As Professors Havard and Beth concluded in their detailed study of legislative politics in Florida: "The fact that no simple cause and effect sequence can be ascribed to the influence of the apportionment system does not bear out the claim that the system has no substantive effect on public affairs; instead it indicates that the influences are in most cases subtle and deeply embedded in the structure of government."

As this discussion of public policy has already indicated, inaction can be as important as positive legislative action. Some interest groups gain their objectives mainly through affirmative enactments, whereas others rely primarily on inaction and delay. The traditional American institutions of separation of powers and checks and balances, specifically devised to discourage positive government, give an immediate advantage to those groups benefiting mostly from inaction. In state legislatures a further check was frequently established by a pattern of representation that placed additional obstacles in the path of interest that otherwise might have influenced more directly the formulation of public policy.

REPRESENTATION IN METROPOLITAN AMERICA *

Royce Hanson

IT now is given that personal political equality is the only permissible basis for apportionment of legislative representatives. Majority rule, based on equal representation of equal voters, follows as an assumption of the new system. Given these assumptions, how shall the political system be structured to permit it to meet the problems of modern life through democratic processes and in the context of democratic values? In organizing the political system, the process of representation, as distinguished from the mere basis for it, plays a central role. The problem is to match the functions performed by a representative system with both political values and the conditions and needs of the polity.

Reapportionment merely reflected the fundamental transformation of American society into a highly urbanized, science-oriented, and technologically precocious civilization. With this transformation much disappeared which had provided the basis for traditional ideas of representation.

With the use of the metropolis as the dominant pattern of economic and social relationships, and with the technological revolutions in transportation and communications, the old community patterns have eroded. The metropolis, in many respects, is an antithesis of the "community." Its basic pattern of

* From Royce Hanson, *The Political Thicket: Reapportionment and Constitutional Democracy* (Englewood Cliffs, N.J.: Prentice-Hall, Inc., 1966), pp. 129–35. © 1966. Reprinted by permission of Prentice-Hall, Inc., Englewood Cliffs, N.J.

politics is conflict rather than consensus or common interest. Its economies are specialized and competitive, its society is by comparison with the old villages and towns, unstable. Mobility within the metropolis and among separate metropolitan areas is common. Social mobility is also increasing. Among the residents of any given neighborhood, there is rather extensive mobility of the working force commuting to work. Social relationships, especially among the middle and upper classes, are restricted neither to neighborhood nor even the metropolis itself.

In this new environment, some of the traditional worries of theorists of representative government are sterile. The new politics of technological complexity and urban pluralism is not well defined by the majority-minority dichotomy. There is, for all practical purpose, no MAJORITY; there are only coalitions of minorities. While a party might statistically dominate an urban area, there often is a considerable difference between an electoral majority and a stable governing majority.

With the weakening of the sense of community in the metropolis, the old familiar concepts of constituency also tend to deteriorate. Jurisdictional boundaries are no clue to communities in the metropolis. Legislative constituencies built on residential neighborhoods or political subdivisions in the metropolis are quite likely to fail to reflect either a community of interest or salient relationships or interests of metropolitan life. Such districts, so congenial to tradition and so convenient to established power systems, tend to accentuate class, ethnic, and interjurisdictional conflict, rather than make the legislature a place for the management and resolution of conflict.

But this is one purpose which a representative system ought to attempt. It is not necessary to have a community of interest in order to manage the conflicts of a plural society. It is, however, necessary to organize political power, largely through the official system of representation in such a way that a vested interest is created in resolving conflict rather than in maintaining it.

The organization of consent and the principle of accountability coincide to suggest that the character of the constituency greatly conditions the kind of consent the electorate will grant, and the range of action which the representative can afford to undertake. The mandate of a representative is to be found in the next election, not in the past one. Thus, a tendency for accommodation can be built into a constituency. A representative of a purely suburban district or of a crowded ghetto is more likely to campaign as a parochial spokesman and to serve as a delegate of his constituency than to perform as a broker among interests.

The institution of bicameralism offers some assistance in meeting the problems of constituency construction. While one house may indeed be built from constituencies with a parochial cast, the other can be fashioned from districts which reflect cross-currents of opinion and are heterogeneous in composition. The second house offers the opportunity to cut across jurisdictional boundaries and "neighborhoods" to require representatives to have built into their political strategies different views of the metropolis or the state. And consideration might be given to districts in one house, at least, which are not compact, in the traditional sense, but which radiate from the center of the metropolis or which are narrow columns or sectors of the metropolis encompassing elements from the business and residential core to the fringe areas. Under satisfactory administrative safeguards to prevent partisan or racial gerrymandering, such districts conceivably would produce representatives more sensitive to the realities of metropolitan life than more traditional approaches.

The representative system functions as the basis for the aggregation of interests and management of conflict, but it also functions as one means of socializing the electorate, of integrating people into the political system. These different objectives can be reconciled, although they are not necessarily complementary. A system which is designed for the optimum management of conflict may offer only minimal political socialization.

In the pre-metropolitan state, the single-member and jurisdiction-wide districts were useful in developing a sense of participation and membership in the political community. Before the revolutions in transportation, communications, and environmental sanitation made the modern metropolis possible, relationships tended to be more localized. Voters could meet candidates. Politics was an entertainment. The ward, the district, the town, or the county might actually have resembled a miniature republic. Personal participation in government through direct representation was more nearly possible than it is now. Mobility has created neighborhoods of strangers and jurisdictions without traditions. Mass communications, which can place an assassination in every living room, has become so costly a resource that local and state politics are virtually blacked out in comparison with national and international affairs. And the gossip structure of the commuting community, served by national chain stores and housed in jurisdictional enclaves separated from both employment and evening social contacts, has little to offer that is relevant to the political system in which representatives are chosen.

In this context, alienation from the political process, nonparticipation in the official system of politics, or support for mass movements as an anti-politics reaction appears to be increasing in metropolitan areas. Somehow the representative system must be made relevant to the conditions of the metropolis that call for attention and still accommodate the demands of groups for recognition and meaningful participation in their government. The "representativeness" problem reappears in modern dress.

The objective of constructing a district may be to give its representative an inter-group perspective; to broaden his outlook. Another is to assimilate the groups into the political system, giving them a broader perspective and an education in democratic politics also. But what are the chances of extensive and "responsible" political participation by Negroes in a district where no Negro has a chance to be elected? Such voters are quite likely to feel unrepresented, just as some rural voters accustomed to their "own" representative in the days before *Reynolds* will feel unrepresented under the new apportionments. This attitude is most likely to occur in multi-class and multi-racial districts from which no representative will really be "typical." Again bicameralism, with its larger capacity to incorporate alternate approaches to representation, may provide a workable framework for reconciling the need for representativeness and political socialization with the need for conflict reconciliation.

Another aspect of the problem of representativeness is also a problem in political communications: accessibility of the representative to his constituents. The Dirksen Amendment's backers made this one of their major issues, envisioning great physical distances separating the representative and the voters in the sparsely populated districts. The urban counterpart of the problem is social distance, the crush of business and the cost of communications as well as the competition for electoral attention. The state legislative candidate can rarely afford to use metropolitan television or newspaper advertising. He must depend more largely on direct mailings, organization support, or personal contact. If he has a populous city-wide or county-wide constituency, even if shared with other legislators, he cannot become known to most of his constituency. In a city of a half-million people, it is extremely unlikely that a legislator can personally contact or confront more than fifteen per cent of his electorate.

The result of such a districting situation is not only the production of voter alienation due to the inaccessibility of the politicians, but the frequent construction of tickets of legislative candidates loaded with plodding party regulars who can depend for their election on a dependable primary vote, which rarely needs to exceed twenty per cent of all voters registered. The dominant faction of the dominant party tends to win all seats. The election system filters out the conflicts needed to confront the state government with the basic problems of the metropolis. In the bargain, the quality of the legislators is also depressed. One of the cautions in constituency construction, then, is to create no more outsized constituencies than there are likely to be outsized legislators to represent them. The objective of attaining an at-large view of problems can be readily frustrated by the election of members whose crucial pluralities depend upon only a narrow segment of the electorate.

The test of systems of representation will be both in what they produce and how they produce it. The predictable growth of population and the innovations of technology will create functional pressures which government must meet. And it is useful to keep in mind that it is not necessary to have a democracy to make trains run on time or to provide an efficient police force.

Representation, therefore, must be structured to make the system respond to the salient relationships and problems of modern life. A way must be found to permit the people affected by government's acts to hold the government accountable for what it does, and to associate meaningfully with others in conditioning and controlling what government does. Grave functional pressures can be easily foreseen. The availability, accessibility, variety, and cost of housing will be a major problem for both state and federal governments, as will the problem of racial segregation in housing and other economic activity.

Racial assimilation can be greatly assisted through the structuring of the representative system. while racial frustrations can be allayed by the integration of politics, political integration can also lay foundations for meeting the legal, psychological, and social obstacles to racial equality.

Transportation, as a shaper of cities and regions, is a function upon which much controversy will center. Representative systems which allow expression of suburban interests in commutation and core city interests in the housing, market, and social impact of metropolitan transportation systems are more likely to find an acceptable resolution for transportation problems than systems which box the conflicting interests into segregated power cells.

And in other fields such as personal security and education the quality, type, and extent of programs will reflect the power transmitted through the representative process. The challenge of reapportionment will hardly be met by making only the *pro forma* adjustments necessary to reconcile the old systems of representation with the bare requirements of the Supreme Court's pronouncements.

The future of representative government begins with the constitutional mandate for political equality. The Supreme Court's action was a necessary prelude to rethinking the problem of representative government. It does not assure, however, that the old sterile patterns will be broken. Most of the problems discussed here do not seem susceptible to the development of an official philosophy through the same processes of constitutional politics which produced *Reynolds* and preserved its ruling. The Supreme Court decision institutionalized a value upon which there was extensive agreement. On these other matters, there is no consensus, not even wide agreement. Room for experimentation is needed.

There has been little updating of the political theory of representative government and inertia has ruled both thought and practice. Much advocacy of proportional representation and syndicalism has not met the kind of needs discussed here. The legislature needs to be more than a mere assembly of the ambassadors of interest groups. But now that the inertia has been broken, it is time to re-examine the role representative government should play in the American states. That opportunity presents itself, in all probability, in the series of constitutional conventions which seem likely to follow reapportionment.

The politicians of constitutional democracy devised the strategy which ultimately destroyed the Old Order. Have they the vision, the wit, the courage to fashion the New?

THE NEGRO IN POLITICS *

James Q. Wilson

PERHAPS the best way to understand the political position of the American Negro today is to compare what some Negroes are asking of politics with what politics seem capable of providing. I mean here politics in the narrower sense—the competitive struggle for elective office and deliberate attempts to influence the substance of government decisions—and not, in the broadest sense, as any activity by which conflict over goals is carried on. Although something is sacrificed by limiting the definition (rent strikes, boycotts, and sit-ins may have consequences for office-holders and legislation), the sacrifice is necessary if we are to understand what is meant by the statement that the civil rights movement, and Negro protest generally, ought to become a *political* movement. Bayard Rustin, in a recent issue of *Commentary*, has put the argument in its most succinct and lucid form in an article significantly entitled, "From Protest to Politics: The Future of the Civil Rights Movement." Briefly, Rustin argues that the problems of the Negro cannot be solved by granting him even the fullest civil rights, for it is his fundamental social and economic conditions, more than his legal privileges, which must be changed. Such changes, in the magnitudes necessary, require radical—indeed revolutionary—programs in education, housing, and income redistribution; these programs, in turn, will be attained only by an organized radical political coalition of Negroes, trade unions, church groups, and white liberals.

Those who remember the political currents of the 1930's may smile wanly at the call today for a Negro-labor alliance. When the call was issued thirty years ago, few responded. In the South, the Negro was almost entirely disfranchised; in the North, he was politically unorganized except by a few (largely Republican) big-city machines. Everywhere, Negroes—including the miniscule leadership class—were effectively excluded from almost all the institutions of American life. Negroes had nothing and attempted little. It was probably fortunate for A. Phillip Randolph that he was not required to deliver his threat of a massive march on Washington in 1941. In their most charitable mood, even the more radical trade union leaders saw Negroes as a group which could produce (perhaps worthy) demands but not votes or money or influence; less generously, they viewed Negroes as scabs and strike-breakers.

Apparently, enough has changed since to suggest that a reappraisal may be

* From James Q. Wilson, "The Negro in Politics," in *Daedalus*, Vol. 94, No. 4 (Fall, 1965), *The Negro American*, pp. 949–970. © 1965 by the American Academy of Arts and Sciences. Reprinted by permission of Professor Wilson and the editors of *Daedalus*.

in order. The Negro electorate has grown greatly in both North and South. It is estimated (no one knows) that as many as six million Negroes were registered in 1964, about a third of whom were in the South. In most of the large cities, where these voters are to be found, there is no political machine; in the typical case, leadership is competitive, uncontrolled, sometimes demagogic but just as often responsible, and to an increasing extent aggressive. A massive and impressive march on Washington has occurred. The proliferation and vigor of civil rights organizations suggest that expectations are rising more rapidly than achievements; the national leaders of these groups have become *the* spokesmen of the American Negro, virtually eclipsing elective officials. Among these men, all shades of radical (as well as moderate) opinion can be found, accompanied, as one might expect, by a passionate concern for distinguishing subtle (and sometimes vague) sectarian differences. And in 1964, the Negroes gave President Johnson an unprecedented 94 per cent of their vote (according to an estimate by the Gallup Poll). Perhaps these changes are sufficient to make the Negroes ready for an effective and liberal coalition.

While there is little doubt that Negro voters will continue to exert a liberalizing influence on American politics, the possibility of a stable, organized liberal—to say nothing of radical—coalition is, I believe, slight. Furthermore, attempts to fashion one may be dangerous unless it is a very loose and *ad hoc* arrangement. The Negro is already a partner in a set of tacit, though unorganized, coalitions; they are probably the only viable ones but they are certainly not radical ones. To break existing alliances, tenuous though they are, in favor of a new alliance which may be impossible of realization may be a costly experiment. This is particularly true in the South; it is to a lesser extent true in the North.

I. THE NEGRO VOTER IN THE SOUTH

A useful oversimplification is that, in the South, the enemy of the Negro is the lower- and lower-middle-class, particularly rural, white, and the ally of the Negro is the upper-middle-class, particularly urban, white. Since Reconstruction, the Bourbons and the Populists have engaged in intermittent political warfare; occasionally the Negro has been used—particularly in the last two decades of the nineteenth century—as an ally of one white class against the other, while at other times—particularly in the first half of the twentieth century—he has been disfranchised in order to prevent him from being allied with either class. The political suppression of the Negro did not, as C. Vann Woodward makes clear, occur immediately after the withdrawal of Union troops but only after the white community, divided along class lines, discovered that the competitive wooing of Negro votes created a politically unstable situation best resolved by eliminating the Negro vote—and thus the Republican party—and bringing the white majority into the dominant Democratic Party.

But the Negro is no longer disfranchised, except in Black Belt counties; probably one-third of the potential Negro vote has been registered, and more gains can be anticipated. Negroes of voting age constitute one-fifth of the adult population of the eleven Southern states but less than one-twelfth of the registered Southern voters. If another 570,000 Negroes can be added to registration rolls now estimated to contain nearly two million Negores, half the potential Negro voters will be eligible. In those areas where the Negro vote is already significant, the politics of a "Second Reconstruction" seem to be emerging—with the important difference that the Negro may no longer be disfranchised if competition for his vote proves unsettling.

Negroes, when they vote, can cause a startling change in the style, if not the substance, of Southern politics. Segregationists will have to choose between abandoning race-baiting as a political tactic or getting out of politics. (The prospect of large numbers of politicians quitting politics—especially in the South, where politicians are shrewd and politics is a way of life—seems, to say the least, remote.) And politicians who are by nature inclined to entertain sympathetically legitimate Negro demands will be encouraged to entertain them publicly. For example, Rep. Charles L. Weltner, Democratic of Georgia, voted against the 1964 Civil Rights Act when it first came before the House in February, 1964. By July, however, when the bill came back from the conference committee for final passage, he had changed his mind and voted in favor of it. It does not detract from the moral quality of Weltner's bold action to note that between the two crucial votes the governor of Georgia signed into law a bill to redistrict the state's congressional seats in a manner that substantially increased the proportion of enfranchised Negroes and decreased the proportion of lower-middle-class whites in Weltner's district.

In the past, at least, neither political party could take the Southern Negro vote for granted. A majority of their votes twice went to Dwight Eisenhower and frequently were cast for Republican candidates in such cities as Atlanta and Louisville. In 1960, many—though not all—Southern Negro precincts voted for President Kennedy; in 1964, almost all of them supported President Johnson!

The independence—which, to the politician, can mean only uncertainty—of the Southern Negro vote has various causes. One, of course, is that the Southern Democratic party has so conspicuously been the enemy, its candidates in all but a few cases outbidding each other in defending segregation. Another is that the issue confronting the Southern Negro in many elections is clear and dramatic: which white candidate scores lowest on the segregation scale, this being, for the Negro, the only important scale. Unstable politics is here the result of a single-issue politics. A third reason is that potential Negro political leaders, being largely excluded from an active role in both the majority party and the increasingly "lily-white" Republican minority party, have not been co-opted by the system. Negro politicians, without permanent organizational commitments to white leaders, have been free to deliver Negro votes to whichever candidate or party seemed most attractive in each election. Where the Negro leader was corrupt, he delivered the vote in exchange for tangible considerations; where honest, in exchange for intangible concessions. Negro politics in the South has yet to be professionalized, and thus the distinction—commonplace in the North—between the (usually moderate) party hierarchy and the (often militant) civic and "race" leadership has not become widespread.

To say that the Southern Negro political leadership is unprofessional does not mean that it is either unskillful or unsuccessful. In those cities or counties where the Negro voter is neither terrorized nor apathetic, he is capable of voting with almost incredible unanimity and precision, at least for the most visible offices. When Ivan Allen, Jr., ran against Lester Maddox in 1961 for mayor of Atlanta, Negro precinct 7-D gave Allen 2,003 votes, or 99.9 per cent of the total, and Maddox 4 votes. Since there were five white voters living in the precinct, it is quite likely that Allen got *all* of the Negro votes— an almost unbelievable feat of organization and communication, especially when one recalls that Allen was a wealthy white businessman who was scarcely an all-out integrationist. The single-issue politics of the South has produced a form of political behavior among Negroes and whites which is highly rationalistic and extraordinarily sophisticated. Voters become exceptionally sensitive to almost imperceptible differences in the positions candidates take, publicly or privately, on "The Issue" and go to considerable lengths to conceal group preferences lest premature revelation prove counterproductive.

In the South, more than anywhere else, a deliberate balance of power politics may be practiced in which viable coalitions may be formed. The most important and most successful example of this is what might be called the Atlanta Coalition. Formed in the 1950's by Mayor (now Mayor "Emeritus") William B. Hartsfield and continued by Mayor Ivan Allen, Jr., it is, stripped to its essentials, a tacit alliance between upper-middle-class whites and Negroes against lower-middle-class whites. In even blunter terms, the Bourbons and the Negroes have voted together to exclude the rednecks from power in the city. There are, of course, strains in the alliance. The more militant Negroes are restless with the leadership of the Atlanta Negro Voters' League and with what they regard as the insufficient progress in race relations under Hartsfield and Allen. White businessmen, in turn, often feel the mayor has gone too far, as when Allen testified before Congress in favor of the elimination of segregation in public accommodations. Furthermore, it is not clear that every Southern city could put together such a coalition even if it wanted to do so. Some cities have lost their Bourbons to the suburbs (Atlanta carefully annexes all upper-income suburbs and avoids annexing any working-class suburbs) while others have a business leadership that is composed of small shopkeepers rather than a commercial and industrial élite concerned with establishing the city as a great regional center. And in some cities, such as New Orleans, the Negroes themselves have been unable to create a stable and effective political organization representative of all elements of the community.

Whatever the limitations or difficulties, however, there can be little doubt that the natural ally of the Southern Negro, for the foreseeable future, is the cosmopolitan white bourgeoisie. In part, this reflects self-interest: race conflict is bad for business, destructive of property, and productive of unfavorable national publicity. In part, it reflects an enlarged conception of the common interest: Negroes have a moral right to vote, to be free from arbitrary arrest, and to be protected from official abuse, even if century-old prejudices require that the Negro not live next door to whites. The issues now being pressed by the Negro in the South make the most fundamental claims of elementary justice; when the claims of simple justice are reinforced by self-interest, the potential for effective action is great. But this white ally has little interest in a massive redistribution of income, the nationalization of political authority, or the reordering of society.

In the Black Belt, where Negroes outnumber whites, such alliances are hard to create. In Mississippi, there seem to be no allies whatsoever. It is precisely in such areas that a more radical Negro politics is emerging, though it is still so apocalyptic in its vision and unrealistic in its methods that it can point to little progress. The Freedom Democratic party won a great victory at the Democratic National Convention in Atlantic City, but the radical leadership which now appears to influence it not only rejected that convention's seating compromise but seems intent on rejecting all compromises with what, to it, is an essentially corrupt and hypocritical society. Given the massive, unyielding, and violent nature of white resistance to Negro demands in many Black Belt counties, it is not hard to understand some of the attitudes of the increasingly radical Negro political leadership. Early and measured accommodation to Negro political demands has, in many Southern cities, led to the emergence of relatively moderate Negro leaders and of a Negro strategy emphasizing limited objectives. But the Black Belt has not, except in a few cases, made concessions—in part because Negroes there are in the majority and in part because such largely rural or small-town areas lack a white upper class of sufficient size and strength to challenge white extremists.

There are some Black Belt counties where Negroes can and do vote, but ironically the gains that have accrued to them from politics in these areas are less than the gains from politics in areas where Negroes are a minority but where social and economic conditions are more favorable to political organization, articulation of demands, and bargaining over changes in the welfare or status of Negroes. Where Negro voting has occurred in the Black Belt, it has meant (in general) the cessation of police abuse and administrative discrimination, the appointment of Negroes to certain government positions, and higher expenditures on public facilities in Negro neighborhoods. It has rarely meant general integration of schools or public accommodations or new public works programs to improve Negro living conditions. The financial resources and community tolerance for such efforts simply do not exist. White voters do not even approve such projects for themselves. By contrast, in some of the highly urbanized areas where Negroes vote but are in a distinct minority, a combination of factors—the availability of tax resources, a well-organized white political structure with which bargains can be struck, and a large and self-sufficient Negro leadership class—makes it easier to translate votes into substantive gains.

All this suggests that the substantive, rather than psychological, consequences of Negro voting in Black Belt counties are not likely to be so great as the diehard white resistance might imply. The resistance itself, however, should it continue for long, may change this significantly. When the social, economic, and political demands for a group are linked with a protracted and bitter struggle for the franchise, the members of that group are more likely to acquire a permanent sense of political identity and a more intense commitment to the goals of the group than would be the case if substantive goals were asserted long after the franchise had been won. (One of the reasons—there are many— that no socialist or labor party developed among American workers may be that their major economic demands were made long after the franchise had been acquired without a struggle.) The campaign for the voter now developing among Southern Negroes is likely to have profound effects on subsequent Negro political organization and tactics, for the campaign can generate morale, a sense of unity (the vote is a wholly instrumental objective that permits otherwise competing leaders to submerge their differences), and an independence from traditional party loyalties.

Discussion, in such states as Mississippi, of the possibility of a Negro political party suggests one alternative—in my judgment, a disastrous one—to the pattern of coalition politics now being practiced outside the Black Belt. For the Negro vote to be (potentially) the marginal vote, it is not enough that it be an uncommitted vote. Since Negroes in every Southern state are a minority (although in some states a very large one), it is also necessary that the white vote be divided. In such states as Georgia and North Carolina, the Negro vote can be the marginal vote—both because white votes are divided along party or factional lines and because the Negro vote is not an automatic expression of traditional party loyalties. Within the Black Belt, not only must the franchise be won for the Negro, but some way must be found of dividing the white vote. This is not the case in Mississippi, where in a clear choice Barry Goldwater defeated Lyndon Johnson by winning an incredible 87 per cent of the vote. In the table below, the present and potential Negro vote is shown for

THE SOUTHERN NEGRO VOTE, PRESENT AND POTENTIAL

STATE	PERCENTAGE OF ALL REGISTERED VOTERS WHO ARE NEGRO (APRIL, 1964)	PERCENTAGE OF ALL VOTING-AGE PERSONS WHO ARE NEGRO (1960)
Alabama	5.7%	26.2%
Arkansas	7.7	18.5
Florida	7.8	15.2
Georgia	9.9	25.4
Louisiana	9.0	28.5
Mississippi	2.4	36.0
North Carolina	9.7	21.5
South Carolina	10.5	30.6
Tennessee	10.1	15.0
Texas	6.8	11.7
Virginia	5.2	18.9
THE SOUTH	7.7	20.0

each Southern state. In the first column is the percentage of registered voters who, in 1964, were estimated (by the Voter Education Project) to be Negro; in the second column is the percentage of all voting-age persons who in 1960 were Negro. If *all* adults, Negro and white, voted, this last figure would be the "Negro vote." If every Negro in Mississippi had voted, in 1964, Goldwater would still have won; in other states, the Negro's need for allies is even greater.

Dividing the white vote will not be easy under the best of circumstances, but it is not likely to be easier if Negro political strategists either elect to form a separate party or emphasize objectives which draw closer the white cosmopolitan élite and white lower-middle-class extremists. Continued Negro pressure, with federal assistance, for the franchise and for the observance of constitutional and legislative guarantees will ultimately divide the opposition; broadening Negro demands at this time to include more radical objectives may unite it. This may be an expression of the willingness on the part of the bourgeoisie to support demands for *liberty* (the franchise, legal justice, and equal access to public facilities) but to oppose demands for *equality* (the elimination of intergroup differences in income, occupation, and place of residence). Negro-white coalitions in the South, where they exist at all, are by and large libertarian rather than egalitarian in purpose.

The history of one such coalition—or rather sequence of coalitions—is illuminating. Described by Donald Matthews and James Prothro in their forthcoming book on Southern Negro politics, the events took place in a city which the authors call "Urbania." A thriving commercial center in the Piedmont region, the city has a cosmopolitan white business élite as well as a strong Negro middle-class and a unionized industrial labor force. As early as 1935, a Negro political organization was formed (at a meeting held at the Negro Tennis Club!); by the 1940's, a coalition of Negroes and white liberals and union leaders had been formed that was strong enough to capture the county Democratic organization. The alliance, never a firm one, was successful as long as it had limited political objectives. After the 1954 Supreme Court school desegregation decision, however, strains developed. Because of the defection of white workers, the coalition lost control of the party by 1958; nonetheless —and this may be suggestive of the emerging pattern of Southern politics—the mayor remained sympathetic to the Negro demands and he and other city officials worked openly, before and after the tense months of the 1963–1964 protest demonstrations, to integrate public facilities and private business. This policy of accommodations apparently was in part the result of the attitude of the white business élite, part (but not all) of which was sufficiently cosmopolitan to favor whatever degree of integration was necessary to avoid a "bad business climate" or unfavorable national repercussions. It was not, on the other hand, in favor of the liberal economic policies of the early labor-Negro coalition. In Urbania, the Negroes found unionized white workers the appropriate allies when political power was the object; when progress on certain libertarian issues (here, school desegregation) was at stake, the labor alliance collapsed and the support of white businessmen became important.

Coalition politics is important not only because of the need for allies, but also because of the problem of motivating Negro voters. As a result of their low socio-economic position, getting Negroes to register and vote even after all administrative barriers have collapsed can be very difficult. (In 1959, Southern urban Negroes had a median income less than *half* that of Southern urban whites.) Surprisingly high voter participation can be obtained, however, when the contest is important *and the Negro vote may decide the outcome*. In the Allen-Maddox election in Atlanta, for example, 80 per cent of the registered voters in nine predominantly Negro precincts turned out to vote; by comparison, only 69 per cent of the regstered voters in ten predominantly lower-income white precincts voted. (Negroes participate less than whites in elections for offices less visible than mayor; they also register in slightly smaller proportions.) Although there is no direct evidence on this, it seems likely that the remarkably high Negro voter turnout in cities like Atlanta might be much lower if the candidate supported by Negroes had no chance of winning —as would be the case if he did not have the backing of a substantial block of white voters.

II. THE NEGRO VOTER IN THE NORTH

It is in the North that politics as conventionally practiced seems less relevant to the needs of the Negro. This may appear paradoxical, given the great importance attached to the Northern urban Negro vote in influencing contests for President, governor, and senator. It is of course true that the Negro is concentrated in areas of high strategic significance for state-wide or national political candidates. The Negro vote for President Kennedy was, in several Northern industrial states, greater than the margin by which Kennedy carried those states. The same, however, can be said for the Jewish vote, the Catholic vote, and the labor vote. With so many apparently marginal votes cast, a President might be forgiven if he allowed himself to be paralyzed by the competing demands of their spokesmen. (For some time it appeared that President Kennedy was in exactly this position, but he responded to Negro protests which began in the spring of 1963 with a vigorous affirmation of the moral rights of Negroes—becoming not only the first President to have said this, but perhaps the first to have believed it.) In Congress, the Negro vote is likely to have a much greater long-run effect in the South than in the North. Over *half* of all Southern congressional districts in 1963 had a population that was one-fifth or more Negro. In the North and West, by contrast, fewer than one-twelfth of the districts had so high a proportion of Negroes.

Furthermore, the civil rights legislation so far enacted has been directed primarily at remedying discrimination against the Negro in the South—in voting, public accommodations, and the like. To the extent that Negro political influence in the North contributed to the passage of these bills, it was influence wielded on behalf of Southern Negroes and as part of a much larger liberal coalition in which religious organizations played an exceptionally important role. Further legislative progress on behalf of Southern Negroes is still possible; the question, however, is what prgress can be made on behalf of Northern Negroes and what political tactics should be used.

The utility of politics to the Northern Negro is limited for a variety of reasons. First, his traditional party loyalties are strong and thus his vote, particularly in general elections, is less likely to be uncertain. There are some obvious exceptions to this pattern, of course. In cities such as Boston, where party organization is almost nonexistent and where an attractive Negro candidate can be found in the Republican party, Negroes will cross party lines in very large numbers. (Edward Brooke, the Negro Republican Attorney General of Massachusetts, carried Negro precincts by margins of ten to one at the same time that Democrat Lyndon Johnson was carrying these precincts by margins of fifty to one.) In most of the largest Northern cities, however, the only question surrounding the Negro vote in partisan elections is its size rather than its direction.

Second, the major issues confronting the mass of Northern Negroes are economic and cultural rather than political or legal. Rustin is entirely correct in saying that "at issue, after all, is not *civil rights,* strictly speaking, but social and economic conditions." The paradox is two-fold. On the one hand, American political institutions provide no way for the organized political pressure of a particular disadvantaged group to reshape in any fundamental sense social and economic conditions. Whereas the identity and political obligations of a sheriff or a governor can profoundly affect the lives of Negroes in the South by determining whether or how they will be intimidated or harassed, the election of a public official in the North rarely has any direct or obvious consequences for the average Negro voter. (It is *because* it makes so little difference, of course, that Northern party leaders have found it relatively easy to instill traditional party commitments in Negroes. A simple decision rule—such as "vote Democratic"—is more economical, for both the party and the voter, than the kind of elaborate and subtle group interest calculations that occur where, as in the South, the outcome *is* important.)

That is not to say that it makes no difference which party or faction controls the White House or Congress. The probability of there being certain kinds of redistributionist and welfare programs enacted does depend on election outcomes, but not in a way that makes it possible for any particular voting bloc to hold any particular public official responsible for such programs. Such considerations ought to be borne in mind when one evaluates assertions about the "alienation" of the urban voter, particularly the low-income Negro. That politics seems irrelevant to their preoccupations is not necessarily an expression of neurotic withdrawal or separateness but may well be the rational conclusion of a reasonably well-informed citizen.

The other paradoxical element is that, when major programs *are* launched to deal with basic social and economic conditions, they are likely to be the product of a political coalition in which the persons whose lives are to be changed play a relatively small role. The recent federal programs to deal with delinquency, poverty, and housing were assembled by bureaucrats, professors, and White House politicians. The most dramatic of these—the "war on poverty"—did not come about, as Daniel Patrick Moynihan makes clear, as the result of any great upsurge of popular demand. Nor were these programs aimed explicitly at the "Negro problem." Indeed, it might have been much harder to get them adopted if they had been defined as "Negro programs." (In fact, some of these programs—particularly the antipoverty program— were in part intended by many of their supporters, probably including the President, to dampen the civil rights "revolution" by improving the material condition of Negroes.) At the local level, public expenditures for the benefit of the poor are often authorized in local referenda elections in which the civic leadership as well as a substantial portion of the votes comes from upper-class whites who join with lower-class Negroes to secure the adoption of measures which, if they were national rather than local matters, these whites would oppose. Rich suburbanites will favor free medical care for the indigent if the issue is stated in terms of building a new county hospital and is voted on locally but not if the issue is called "socialized medicine" and is voted on in Washington.

All this suggests that the Negro is in need not of a single grand alliance, but of many different and often conflicting alliances which take into account the different bases of support available for different kinds of issues. Nationally, organized labor may support civil rights and income-transfer measures but locally it is often likely to support (at least tacitly) segregated housing and economy in government. Religious groups are very effective when the issue is voting rights; they are much less effective in dealing with economic questions where simple morality is not at issue. Upper-class businessmen may support Negro voting claims in Southern cities and Negro oriented public works programs in Northern cities, but nationally they will oppose large-scale income redistribution. A grand Negro-liberal coalition, if achieved, may so rationalize these inconsistent positions as to deliver the leadership of would-be allies into the hands of those elements who are least in favor of (or least effective on behalf of) Negro causes. Nowhere are these problems better seen than in the relationship between Negro and white workers in our major industrial cities.

While it may be true that Negroes and whites have a common interest in ending unemployment, improving housing and education, and resisting technological displacement, a stable and enduring alliance to attain these objectives will not be easily achieved. The only major political mechanism by which poor whites and Negroes have in the past been brought into alliance—the big-city machine—is collapsing; except for a few large industrial unions, no substitute has yet appeared.

Only Philadelphia and Chicago, of the larger Northern cities, have strong city-wide machines (that is, political parties based on the distribution of material rewards). In these areas, Negro and white political leaders are paid to work together, albeit for very limited objectives; Negro and white voters, in turn, are induced by door-to-door persuasion to vote together, particularly in primaries. Such organizations cannot endure much longer, for the resources at their command are diminishing. When they collapse, Negro political leadership will fall into the hands of men who can find effective substitutes for organization: personal charisma and bellicose militancy (such as that of Adam Clayton Powell in New York or Cecil Moore in Philadelphia), expertise in factional manipulation and strategic alliances (such as that of J. Raymond Jones in New York), or successful appeals to middle-class white voters and white political leaders (such as that of Edward Brooke in Massachusetts or Augustus Hawkins in Los Angeles). Yet to emerge, but certain to come, are Negro political leaders who will obtain their major support from the more militant civil rights organizations. In only a very few cases does there seem to be much likelihood of organized political coalition between white and Negro workers similar to that found from time to time in Detroit. The United Auto Workers, and to a lesser extent the United Steel Workers, have, through the political action of integrated locals, elected carefully balanced tickets of Negro and white politicians.

Even under UAW leadership, the Negro-white workers' coalition has been subject to tensions. The most important of these has been the necessity of emphasizing economic objectives that do not require social reorganization (such as integrated housing) close to home. The UAW cannot deliver votes of white workers for liberal mayors or those of Negro workers for conservative mayors without great difficulty. Furthermore, the coalition was created in a period of rising demand for workers; how it will function when Negroes and whites are competing for a decreasing number of jobs remains to be seen. (The fact that the locals are integrated and that an elaborate code of seniority rules has been devised may help reduce what might otherwise be a starkly racial conflict over jobs.) Finally, no one should allow himself the comfort of believing that President Johnson's massive victory over Barry Goldwater disproves the existence of strong anti-Negro sentiments among many white Northern Democratic voters. At most it suggests that, faced with a complex political decision involving issues of foreign relations, economic policy, and welfare programs as well as civil rights, the white worker decided that peace and security were, under the circumstances, more important than registering a protest against Negro claims.

The area in which this latent conflict between Negro claims and white resistance is most likely to erupt is that of public safety and administration of criminal justice. It is one of the few issues (schools are another) in the North over which a clear political contest can be waged. The police are highly sensitive to the explicit and implicit directives of local elective officials; unlike economic issues, a political victory here can have direct and immediate—although perhaps not drastic—consequences for Negroes. The white concern over "violence in the streets" and unchecked criminality is not (as critics of Goldwater charged) simply a rhetorical mask of opposition to civil rights demonstrations or even for anti-Negro sentiment (though it involves a significant element of this). Polls taken by both parties during the campaign suggest that Johnson was never able to meet this issue effectively; perhaps a majority of voters thought Goldwater was best able to handle this problem. For the Negroes, the issue of "police brutality" and police corruption is probably the single most effective appeal for the mobilization of mass Negro protest activity, particularly among rank-and-file lower-income Negroes. Many middle-class Negroes will, of course, admit privately that they, too, would like to see the police check criminal behavior among lower-class Negroes, but it is becoming increasingly difficult for them to say this publicly.

What is remarkable is that so few candidates for mayor or governor are openly exploiting white fears of crime, particularly Negro crime. In part this is because too many of them must face Negro voters who would immediately interpret such views as anti-Negro prejudice even if, in fact, prejudice had nothing to do with it. And in part this is because there is a deep and general distrust of the police among upper-middle-class whites, particularly white liberals, such that it is often better politics to be "anti-cop" than "anti-Negro." On this issue, even more than on the issue of income redistribution, the natural Northern ally of the Negro is the white liberal.

It is, of course, fashionable today to attack the "white liberal" as hypocritical on civil rights issues. After all, he is likely to live in a "lily-white" suburb, attend a "lily-white" church, and perhaps teach in a university with no Negroes on its faculty. And the white liberal, in the eyes of Negro radicals, makes the fatal error of believing that meaningful change can be accomplished within the present political, social, and economic system. By accepting the system, he accepts the necessity of compromise, and compromise is seen as both morally wrong and practically unworkable.

All this misses the point, which is that the white liberal is, in the North, one of the Negro's *only* significant allies in a situation in which allies are essential. He is not and cannot be an all-purpose ally, however. The upper-class business or professional man is a more useful ally in the South where, by halting and nervous steps, his support is being mobilized to achieve voting rights and end police abuse; he is also a more useful ally in the North when the issue is legitimating the local public welfare program. The principal value of the white liberal, on the other hand, is to supply the votes and the political pressures (increasingly mobilized through religious organizations) that make it almost suicidal for an important Northern politician openly to court anti-Negro sentiment.

The alliance, however, is as much tacit as explicit. If Negroes increasingly distrust liberals (because they are both ideologically suspect and rivals for power), liberals have had difficulty finding Negroes who have both a genuine mass following and a commitment to what the liberals regard as appropriate means and ends. The hoped-for alliance in Manhattan between liberal Democratic reform clubs and Harlem political leaders has not materialized to any degree. The most popular Negro leader in Philadelphia, Cecil Moore, is regarded with incredulous disdain by white liberals. Negro machine politicians, such as William Dawson of Chicago, are rejected by both those middle-class Negroes and those middle-class whites whose commitment to social change exceeds their faith in the Democratic party leadership. Negroes, such as Edward Brooke, whom white liberals find attractive are usually prevented by their position (that is, being responsible to a largely white constituency) from being in the visible forefront of civil rights campaigns. The cause of most of this unrequited love is that the Negro has come of age politically at a time when not only machines are collapsing, but the whole lower-class style of politics—the politics of friendships, trades, patronage, and neighborhood localism—is falling into disrepute. Negroes are expected to climb a political ladder which, as a result of several decades of successful reform efforts, is now missing most of its rungs. For whites, vaulting to the top is easy—television is one way; converting an established business or civic reputation into appointive and elective office is another. But the Negro community lacks the business and civic infrastructure which is necessary to convert private success into public office. Enough money has yet to be earned by enough Negroes to produce a significant precipitate of Negro civic statesmen.

Negroes know this and therefore are demanding that economic differences between Negroes and whites be eliminated. If the white liberal reformer is to be allowed to abolish the system by which political and economic progress was once made, then he must (many Negroes argue) replace it with something better. The Negro demand for economic quality is no longer, as Nathan Glazer points out, simply a demand for equal opportunity; it is a demand for equality of economic *results*. American politics has long been accustomed to dealing with ethnic demands for recognition, power, and opportunity; it has never had to face a serious demand for equal economic shares. Thus, in the North as well as the South the principal race issue may become a conflict between liberty and equality. This may be the issue which will distinguish the white liberal from the white radical: the former will work for liberty and equal opportunity, the latter for equal shares. This distinction adds yet another complication to the uneasy liberal-Negro alliance.

If the alliance is hard to sustain today, it will be subject to even greater strains in the future. The Northern Negro community, lacking a single clear objective and a well-organized and unified leadership, will continue to be volatile. Protest demonstrations will reveal less discipline than those in the South, and the likelihood of violence will be greater. The church simply does not have the importance to the Northern Negro that it does to the Southern, nor are the targets in the North so visible as those in the South. The Negro riots of the summers of 1964 and 1965 in Harlem, Rochester, Chicago, Brooklyn, Los Angeles, and elsewhere were not in any obvious sense "race" riots (that is, riots of Negroes against whites in protest against claimed injustices) or the outgrowth of civil rights demonstrations. But whatever their cause (simple hooliganism was an important element), their lesson for genuine civil rights demonstrations is clear: there is always a potential for violence, particularly when the demonstration is as much against indifference as against injustice.

That the movement is badly organized, understaffed, and threatened by violence does not mean it is ineffective. As other sources of power decline in strength, the power of the civil rights organizations increases. It is not yet possible for them to *elect* candidates, even in all-Negro districts, to many significant offices, but it is entirely possible for them to *prevent* someone else from being elected, even in heavily white districts. In most Northern cities, there are now a small number of Negro civil rights leaders whose reputation is such that their concerted opposition to a Negro candidate would prevent his election. They are often strong enough to hurt the chances of white candidates by casting on them (rightly or wrongly) an "anti-civil-rights" label which will be the kiss of death for white liberal (and even not-so-liberal) voters. As one Negro leader in Boston, a hopelessly unorganized city, told me recently, "We are entering a new political era of guerrilla warfare in which the lack of organization and discipline will not be nearly so important as the possibility of well-placed sniping at the enemy."

Competition to get the pro-civil-rights label (or, more accurately, to avoid getting the anti-civil-rights label) will become more intense. The 1964 presidential campaign may well have facilitated this process by involving Negroes in unprecedented numbers both as voters and as campaigners. The intense opposition to Goldwater resulted in Negroes registering as Democrats in overwhelming proportions in both North and South. The Democratic National Committee mobilized ministers, barbers, beauticians, and other strategically placed Negroes as volunteer campaigners. Nationally known civil rights leaders, particularly Martin Luther King, toured the country giving ostensibly "nonpartisan" speeches, urging Negroes to vote but not telling them whom to vote for (that was hardly necessary). Only time will tell what effect Goldwater will have on Negro political loyalties (particularly in the South, where they have been in doubt) and on the number and style of Negro political activists. It is possible, though far from certain, that 1964 will have fixed Negro political loyalties in the same way that Al Smith in 1928 and Franklin D. Roosevelt in 1936 fixed white loyalties and will bring into politics a new cadre of Negro leaders just as 1952 and 1956 brought in new white cadres. Regardless of whom the Republicans nominate, the Democrats will be running against Goldwater for the next twenty years.

Apart from building fires under politicians, there remains the question of what Negro (or Negro-white liberal) politics can accomplish. Simply electing more Negroes to public office will make some difference, for politics depends as much as anything on communication. Groups not in a position to know in time cannot act in time; protest as a strategy is better suited to *blocking* change than to initiating it, and this requires a good intelligence network. There are already an estimated 280 Negroes holding elective office, including 6 congressmen and 90 state legislators. And as Negroes rise in seniority in various legislative systems, they will acquire power with which to bargain. (For better or worse, Representative Adam Clayton Powell, as chairman of the House Committee on Education and Labor, is an astute bargainer perfectly prepared to trade a concession on a bill favoring organized labor for a consession by labor on a matter of interest to Negroes.) Furthermore, the greater and more direct involvement of the federal government in the affairs of cities and metropolitan areas under circumstances which require that federal authorities not visibly deny the precept of equal justice for all means that Negroes, through injunctive procedures as well as political pressure, will be able to compel changes in the administration of local programs in schools, housing, and the like as a precondition to receiving the growing volume of federal aid.

In those areas where elective officials administer and are directly responsible for programs affecting the lives of Negroes, Negro voting strength will, of course, be important. One such area is the administration of justice. In the South, the impact of Negro enfranchisement on these practices could be revolutionary; even in the North, Negro political power can significantly constrain mayors and police chiefs. (The mayor of Detroit, Jerome Cavanaugh, attracted widespread—and possibly decisive—Negro electoral support because of Negro discontent with Detroit police practices under the previous administration; immediately upon assuming office, Cavanaugh replaced the police commissioner and supported efforts to alter police behavior in Negro neighborhoods.) Education is another area where elected officials can sometimes be held accountable to the voters. But here the Negro voter faces a paradox: in cities (such as New York) where Negroes are sufficiently numerous to be taken seriously by politicians, they are also so numerous as to make a solution to the problems of racial imbalance or low standards in the public schools very hard to find. Where (as in Boston) Negroes are sufficiently few in number to make solutions possible (at least in principle), they are also so few as to be a relatively inconsequential political force.

Negroes, in short, will increasingly be able to play marginalist politics. But this approach rarely produces wholesale or fundamental changes in the life chances of large numbers of people. Some Negro (and white) leaders, recognizing the limitations of conventional politics, are suggesting new forms of organization. One of these is the power-oriented neighborhood association, exemplified by The Woodlawn Organization (TWO) in Chicago. Such groups mobilize Negroes (or lower-income voters generally) by defining and dramatizing adverse local conditions which are the result of the indifference or hostility of outside forces, such as the city administration or nonresident white businessman. Relying on indigenous leadership, the organization mounts a neighborhood protest against the outside "enemies"; by blocking proposed changes or by effectively challenging current programs, the group acquires the power to bargain with outsiders, especially city politicians and administrators. Demands are made and enforced concerning the appropriate kinds and levels of city services to be provided in the area.

The key to this strategy is the effort to build an indigenous political organization which is not part of the city-wide poltical apparatus and thus is not subject to its constraints. The plan is to fill the vacuum created by the decay of the ward organization of city-wide machines by substituting a nonpartisan but power-oriented civic association which seeks to provide collective rather than divisible benefits (such as patronage) for its members and follow-ers. Since it trades in general rather than individual benefits, the civic associa-tion must find new ways to motivate its members; it does so by relying on a combative ideology. There are at least two major problems with this strat-egy, however. First, the resources with which to sustain such an organization are very scarce. It obviously cannot rely on government or business support (although the recent history of New York's mobilization for Youth, pat-terned in many ways on the TWO model, suggests that at least in the imme-diate future it may be possible to use government funds—such as federal antipoverty or antidelinquency money—to launch organizations aimed at challenging government policies). Foundation and philanthropic support is available (TWO was begun in this way), but such support depends on the programs of the action groups being consistent with what middle-class white liberals who operate foundations will tolerate. In short, it depends on a Negro-liberal white alliance.

The second problem is that it may prove difficult to generalize such a strategy. Building a coalition of several neighborhood combat organizations necessitates finding the terms on which groups with essentially local interests can work together. This is difficult even for a traditional political party which can control patronage and nominations for office. A nonpartisan neigh-borhood association, on the other hand, which attempts to maximize benefits for its area often must do so at the expense of other areas; this potentially competitive situation may make collaboration difficult. A coalition might, of course, be formed out of a common allegiance to a candidate for major political office, but this means accepting the constraints (principally, moder-ation) that inevitably accompany electoral contest.

III. THE NEGRO VOTER IN THE FUTURE

In short, the possibility for an effective radical Negro political strategy seems remote and the effort to achieve it costly. In the South, the potential supporters of at least current Negro objectives are the members of the commer-cial and industrial élite. Although they are everywhere slow to emerge and in some places wholly absent, there is at present no reasonable alternative. Atlanta is an example of both the strengths and weaknesses of such an alliance; even there, of course, it rests on a delicate population equilibrium which could be upset should either the Negroes become too numerous or the upper-class whites too few. What will happen after federal intervention has opened the ballot box to Negroes in the Black Belt counties remains to be seen. There are very few precedents from which one might infer predictions about political behavior when Negroes are in the majority in a city or county and vote. (In Washington, D. C., Negroes are the voting majority, but there are few issues of substance to decide.) There are some Southern communities which are over 50 per cent Negro and in which many (though not all) Negroes vote. Little is known about them except that, while the franchise has ended harassment by public officials and law enforcement officers, it has not revolutionized the living conditions of the Negroes. Perhaps the safest prediction is that the vote will have very different effects in different places. In some communities, patronage-based Negro political machines will emerge; in others, non-ideological Negro-white alliances will develop; in still others, militant and even radical Negro movements will appear (particularly, perhaps, in parts of Mississippi where the young cadres of SNCC and the Freedom Democratic party have begun to instill a radical ideology though not yet to build a serious organization). In general, the type of Negro political organization which emerges will depend crucially on the type of white political organization already in existence.

In the North, the Negro, facing goals more complex and less clearly moral than those faced in the South, will continue to require white liberal, business, and union support for slow progress toward programs productive of income, education, and wider opportunities. The urban vote already greatly influences the presidential election; how much more it will influence state and congressional elections now that reapportionment is upon us is uncertain. It will clearly be on state legislatures that the Supreme Court's edict will fall most heavily. Congress is not likely to be revolutionized; indeed, there is some evidence that an absolutely equal apportionment system might *strengthen* the "conservative" vote. In any case, the role of Congress is more the product of our localistic political structure than of the apportionment system, and this is not likely to change significantly for a very long time.

Negro-labor alliances will still be possible, but like all such alliances in American politics they will be *ad hoc,* imperfectly organized, and difficult to sustain. From the point of view of the Negro, one of the chief advantages of the American political system is surely that the "undemocratic" convention and caucus system by which political parties are governed makes possible *leadership* coalitions that, while not based on a perfect fusion of interests and aims, are not without influence in the choice of candidates and even the outcome of elections. Indeed, to the extent political parties are made internally more "democratic"—by abolishing conventions in favor of primaries, by reforming the governance of local political organizations, and by flooding the deliberations of party leaders with the merciless light of publicity—these coalitions may become more difficult to assemble and sustain, for an informed rank and file requires leaders who emphasize rather than compromise the very great differences which now separate, for example, white and Negro working-class voters.

The fact that many different alliances must be maintained will not only call for a high degree of tactical flexibility; it will probably also mean that the civil rights movement will remain divided and even at war with itself. The divisions among Negro leaders are the result not simply of personal rivalry or organized ideology, but of the effort to adapt a movement to the necessity of simultaneously occupying incompatible positions in order to draw strength from others.

The various white partners in these alliances will themselves be changed by civil rights activity. The nonpolitical strategies developed by the Negro for gaining bargaining power—the sit-in, the protest march, the passive resistance—have already been adopted by whites concerned with everything from American foreign policy to university administration. Physically obstructing the operation of an organization—often illegally—has, in the 1960's, become a commonplace method for attempting to change the behavior of that organization. This "spill-over" of civil rights tactics into other areas of social conflict has probably been one of the most important consequences of increased Negro militancy.

Because of the structure of American politics as well as the nature of the Negro community, Negro politics will accomplish only limited objectives. This does not mean that Negroes will be content with those accomplishments or resigned to that political style. If Negroes do not make radical gains, radical sentiments may grow. How these sentiments will find expression is perhaps the most perplexing and troubling question of all.

PRINCIPAL CONTRIBUTORS

RICHARD C. BAIN. Author of *Convention Decisions and Voting Records* (1960).

GORDON E. BAKER. Department of Political Science, University of California, Santa Barbara. Author of *The Reapportionment Revolution: Representation, Political Power, and the Supreme Court* (1955, 1965); *State Constitutions: Reapportionment* (1960); *The Politics of Reapportionment in Washington State* (1960).

EDWARD C. BANFIELD. Faculty of Public Administration, Harvard University. Author of *Government Project* (1951); *The Moral Basis of a Backward Society* (1958); *Political Influence* (1961); *Big City Politics* (1965); co-author of *Politics, Planning and the Public Interest* (1955); *City Politics* (1963); *Boston: The Job Ahead* (1966); editor of *Urban Government* (1961).

HUGH A. BONE. Department of Political Science, University of Washington. Author of *"Smear" Politics: Analysis of 1940 Campaign Literature* (1941); *Grass Roots Party Leadership* (1952); *American Politics and the Party System* (3rd edition, 1965); *Party Committees and National Politics* (1958); co-author of *Politics and Voters* (1963, 1967).

JAMES MACGREGOR BURNS. Department of Political Science, Williams College. Author of *Congress on Trial* (1949); *Roosevelt: The Lion and the Fox* (1956); *John Kennedy: A Political Profile* (1960); *The Deadlock of Democracy: Four Party Politics in America* (1963); co-author of *Government By The People* (6th edition, 1966).

ANGUS CAMPBELL. Department of Psychology and Department of Sociology and Director of The Survey Research Center, The University of Michigan. Co-author of *Public Use of the Library and Other Sources of Information* (1950); *The Voter Decides* (1954); *Group Differences in Attitudes and Votes* (1956); *The American Voter* (1960); *Elections and the Political Order* (1966).

AAGE R. CLAUSEN. Department of Political Science, University of Wisconsin. Author of articles in professional journals.

HUGH McDOWALL CLOKIE. Department of Political Science, University of California, Berkeley. Author of *Origin and Nature of Constitutional Government* (1936); *Canadian Government and Politics* (1944); co-author of *Royal Commissions of Inquiry* (1937).

PHILIP E. CONVERSE. Department of Sociology and Department of Political Science and Program Director of The Survey Research Center, The University of Michigan. Co-author of *The American Voter* (1960); *Social Psychology: The Study of Human Interaction* (1965); *Elections and the Political Order* (1966).

PAUL T. DAVID. Department of Political Science, University of Virginia. Author of *The Economics of Air Mail Transportation* (1934); co-author of *Presidential Nominating Politician 1952* (1954); *Executives for Government* (1957); *The Politics of National Party Conventions* (1960).

JOHN H. FENTON. Department of Government, University of Massachusetts. Author

521

of *Politics in the Border States* (1957); *The Catholic Vote* (1960); *Midwest Politics* (1966); *People and Parties in Politics* (1966).

RALPH M. GOLDMAN. Department of Political Science, San Francisco State College. Co-author of *The Politics of National Party Conventions* (1960); co-editor of *Presidential Nominating Politics in 1952* (1954).

FRED I. GREENSTEIN. Department of Government, Wesleyan University. Author of *The American Party System and the American People* (1963); *Children and Politics* (1965); co-author of *An Introduction to Political Analysis* (4th edition, 1967).

MORTON GRODZINS (1917–64). Late Professor of Political Science, University of Chicago. Author of *Americans Betrayed* (1949); *The Loyal and the Disloyal* (1956); *The Metropolitan Area as a Racial Problem* (1958); co-author of *Government and Housing in Metropolitan Areas* (1958); co-editor of *The Atomic Age* (1963); *A Nation of States* (1963).

ROYCE HANSON. Department of Government, The American University. Author of *The Political Thicket: Reapportionment and Constitutional Democracy* (1966).

ALEXANDER HEARD. Chancellor of Vanderbilt University. Author of *A Two Party South?* (1952); *The Costs of Democracy* (1960); editor of *State Legislatures in American Politics* (1966); co-editor of *Southern Primaries and Elections* (1950).

ESTES KEFAUVER (1903–63). Member of U.S. House of Representatives 1939–49, U.S. Senate 1949–63. Democratic candidate for Vice-President in 1956. Author of *Crime in America* (1951); co-author of *A Twentieth Century Congress* (1947).

STANLEY KELLEY, JR. Department of Politics, Princeton University. Author of *Professional Public Relations and Political Power* (1956); *Political Campaigning* (1960).

ROBERT E. LANE. Department of Political Science, Yale University. Author of *The Regulation of Businessmen* (1954); *Political Life: Why People Get Involved in Politics* (1959); *The Liberties of Wit: Humanism, Criticism, and the Civic Mind* (1961); *Political Ideology: Why the American Common Man Believes What He Does* (1962); co-author of *Public Opinion* (1964); *An Introduction to Political Analysis* (4th edition, 1967).

MURRAY B. LEVIN. Department of Government, Boston University. Author of *The Alienated Voter* (1960); *Kennedy Campaigning: The System and Style as Practiced by Senator Edward Kennedy* (1966); co-author of *The Compleat Politician: Political Strategy in Massachusetts* (1962).

HERBERT MCCLOSKY. Department of Political Science and Research Psychologist, University of California, Berkeley. Co-author of *The Soviet Dictatorship* (1960); author of numerous articles.

WARREN E. MILLER. Department of Political Science and Program Director, The Survey Research Center, The University of Michigan. Co-author of *The Voter Decides* (1954); *The American Voter* (1960); *Elections and the Political Order* (1966).

PETER H. ODEGARD (1901–67). Late Professor of Political Science, University of California, Berkeley. Author of *Pressure Politics: The Story of The Anti-Saloon League* (1928); *The American Public Mind* (1930); *Prologue to 1940* (1940); *The Power to Govern* (1957); co-author of *American Politics* (1938, 1947); editor of *Religion in Politics* (1960); *American Government: Readings and Documents* (1964, 1966).

NELSON W. POLSBY. Department of Political Science, University of California, Berkeley. *Community Power and Political Theory* (1963); co-author of *Presidential*

Elections: Strategies of American Electoral Politics (1964); co-editor of *Politics and Social Life: An Introduction to Political Behavior* (1963); *New Perspectives on The House of Representatives* (1963).

GERALD POMPER. Department of Political Science, Rutgers University. Author of *Nominating the President: The Politics of Convention Choice* (1963); co-editor of *American Party Politics: Essays and Readings* (1966).

ALEX ROSE. Union leader and labor spokesman, Vice-Chairman of the New York Liberal Party.

BERNARD ROSENBERG. Department of Sociology, City College of the City University of New York. Author of numerous articles.

FRANCIS E. ROURKE. Department of Political Science, Johns Hopkins University. Author of *Intergovernmental Relations in Employment Security* (1952); *The Campus and the State* (1959); *Secrecy & Publicity: Dilemmas of Democracy* (1961); *Bureaucratic Power in National Politics* (1967).

E. E. SCHATTSCHNEIDER. Emeritus Professor of Government, Wesleyan University. Author of *Politics, Pressures and the Tariff* (1935); *Party Government* (1940); *Struggle for Party Government* (1948); *Guide to the Study of Public Affairs* (1952); *The Semi-sovereign People* (1960).

ALLEN SCHICK. Department of Government, Tufts University. Co-author of *American Government* (1965); author of articles in professional journals.

GORDON SMITH. Political scientist. Author of articles.

HERBERT SONTHOFF. Consultant. Author of numerous articles.

FRANK J. SORAUF. Department of Political Science, University of Minnesota. Author of *Party and Representation* (1963); *Political Parties in the American System* (1964).

MURRAY S. STEDMAN, JR. Department of Government, Trinity College. Author of *Exporting Arms* (1947); *Discontent at the Polls* (1950); *Religion and Politics in America* (1964); co-author of *The Dynamics of Democratic Government* (1954).

DONALD E. STOKES. Department of Political Science and Program Director, The Survey Research Center, University of Michigan. Author of *Voting Research and the Businessman in Politics* (1960); co-author of *The American Voter* (1960); *Elections and the Political Order* (1966).

DAVID B. TRUMAN. Vice-President and Provost, Columbia University. Author of *Administrative Decentralization* (1940); *The Governmental Process: Political Interests and Public Opinion* (1951); *The Congressional Party: A Case Study* (1959); editor of *The Congress and America's Future* (1965).

O. DOUGLAS WEEKS. Department of Government, University of Texas. Author of *Two Legislative Houses or One* (1938); *Research in the American State Legislative Process* (1947); *Texas Presidential Politics in 1952* (1953); *Texas One-Party Politics in 1956* (1957).

AARON B. WILDAVSKY. Department of Political Science, The University of California, Berkeley. Author of *Studies in Australian Politics, The 1926 Referendum* (1958); *Leadership in a Small Town* (1964); *The Politics of the Budgetary Process* (1964); co-author of *Presidential Elections: Strategies of American Electoral Politics* (1964); editor of *American Federalism in Perspective* (1967).

JAMES Q. WILSON. Department of Government, Harvard University. Author of *Negro Politics* (1960); *The Amateur Democrat* (1962); co-author of *City Politics* (1963).